Teacher's Manual

ELEMENTS OF LITERATURE

FIFTH COURSE

Teacher's Manual

ELEMENTS OF LITERATURE

FIFTH COURSE

Barbara Freiberg
English Department
Louisiana State University Laboratory School
Baton Rouge, Louisiana

Patricia Brundage-Rude
English Department
North High School
Bakersfield, California

Richard Zahner
English Department
Bunnell High School
Stratford, Connecticut

Andyce Orde
English Department
North High School
Bakersfield, California

HOLT, RINEHART AND WINSTON, INC.
Austin New York San Diego Chicago Toronto Montreal

A teacher's manual is not automatically included with each shipment of a classroom set of textbooks. However, a manual will be forwarded when requested by a teacher, an administrator, or a representative of Holt, Rinehart and Winston, Inc. A teacher's manual is available for every level of *Elements of Literature*. For information, please contact your sales representative.

Copyright © 1989 by Holt, Rinehart and Winston, Inc.

All rights reserved. No part of this publication may be reproduced or transmitted in any form or by any means, electronic or mechanical, including photocopy, recording, or any information storage and retrieval system, without permission in writing from the publisher.

Requests for permission to make copies of any part of the work should be mailed to: Permissions, Holt, Rinehart and Winston, Inc., 1627 Woodland Avenue, Austin, Texas 78741.

Printed in the United States of America

ISBN 0-15-717541-3

90123456   125   98765432

Acknowledgments

For permisison to reprint copyrighted material, grateful acknowledgment is made to the following sources:

American Heritage Publishing Co., Inc.: From "Puritans and Pilgrims" by A. L. Rowse in *American Heritage*, v. X, no. 6, October 1959. Copyright © 1959 by American Heritage Publishing Co., Inc.

The Atlantic Monthly: From "Farewell to Europe" by Richard Aldington in *The Atlantic Monthly*, CLXVI (1940).

Elizabeth Barnett, as Executor of the Literary Estate of Norma Millay Ellis: From "Dirge Without Music" and from "Recuerdo" in *Collected Poems* by Edna St. Vincent Millay. Copyright © 1922, 1928, 1950, 1955 by Edna St. Vincent Millay and Norma Millay Ellis. Published by Harper & Row Publishers, Inc.

Gwendolyn Brooks: From "Of De Witt Williams on his way to Lincoln Cemetery" in *Blacks* by Gwendolyn Brooks. Copyright © 1987 by Gwendolyn Brooks. Published by The David Company, Chicago.

Delacorte Press / Seymour Lawrence: From "Tamar" in *Ellis Island & Other Stories* by Mark Helprin. Copyright © 1976, 1977, 1979, 1980, 1981 by Mark Helprin. Originally published in *The New Yorker*.

Dodd, Mead & Company, Inc.: From "The Haunted Oak" in *The Complete Poems of Paul Laurence Dunbar* by Paul Laurence Dunbar. Published by Dodd, Mead & Company, Inc.

Doubleday, a division of Bantam, Doubleday, Dell Publishing Group, Inc.: From "Elegy for Jane" in *The Collected Poems of Theodore Roethke* by Theodore Roethke. Copyright © 1941, 1950 by Theodore Roethke.

Farrar, Straus & Giroux, Inc.: From "Homage to Mistress Bradstreet" in *Homage to Mistress Bradstreet* by John Berryman. Copyright 1956, renewed © 1984 by John Berryman. From "Winter Landscape" in *Short Poems* by John Berryman. Copyright 1940, renewed © 1968 by John Berryman. From "Little Exercise" and from "First Death in Nova Scotia" in *The Complete Poems 1927–1979* by Elizabeth Bishop. Copyright © 1946, 1955, 1962 by Elizabeth Bishop; copyright renewed © 1973 by Elizabeth Bishop; copyright © 1983 by Alice Helen Methfessel. From *Babel to Byzantium* by James Dickey. Copyright © 1956, 1957, 1958, 1959, 1960, 1961, 1962, 1963, 1964, 1965, 1966, 1967, 1968 by James Dickey. From "The Death of the Ball Turret Gunner" in *The Complete Poems* by Randall Jarrell. Copyright © 1945, 1969 by Mrs. Randall Jarrell; copyright renewed © 1973 by Mrs. Randall Jarrell. From "For the Union Dead" in *For the Union Dead* by Robert Lowell. Copyright © 1960, 1964 by Robert Lowell. From "The Magic Barrel" in *The Magic Barrel* by Bernard Malamud. Copyright © 1954, 1958 by Bernard Malamud. From "The Key" in *A Friend of Kafka and Other Stories* by Isaac Bashevis Singer. Copyright © 1962, 1966, 1967, 1968, 1969, 1970 by Isaac Bashevis Singer. Originally published in *The New Yorker*.

Grove Press, Inc.: From "How I Learned to Sweep" in *Homecoming* by Julia Alvarez. Copyright © 1984 by Julia Alvarez.

G. K. Hall & Company: From *Amy Lowell* by Richard Benvenuto. Copyright © 1985 by G. K. Hall & Company. Published by Twayne Publishers, a division of G. K. Hall & Company. From *Donald Barthleme* by Lois Gordon. Copyright © 1981 by G. K. Hall & Company. Published by Twayne Publishers, a division of G. K. Hall & Company.

Harcourt Brace Jovanovich, Inc.: From "what if a much of a which of a wind" in *Complete Poems 1913–1962* by E. E. Cummings. Copyright 1944 by E. E. Cummings; copyright renewed 1972 by Nancy T. Andrews. From "The Love Song of J. Alfred Prufrock" and from "Preludes" in *Collected Poems 1909–1962* by T. S. Eliot. Copyright 1936 by Harcourt Brace Jovanovich, Inc.; copyright © 1963, 1964 by T. S. Eliot. From *Babbitt* by Sinclair Lewis. Copyright 1922 by Harcourt Brace Jovanovich, Inc.; copyright renewed 1950 by Sinclair Lewis. From "The Life You Save May Be Your Own" in *A Good Man Is Hard To Find* by Flannery O'Connor. Copyright 1953 by Flannery O'Connor; renewed 1981 by Mrs. Regina O'Connor. "Fog" and from "Chicago" in *Chicago Poems* by Carl Sandburg. Copyright 1916 by Holt, Rinehart and Winston, Inc.; copyright renewed 1944 by Carl Sandburg. From "Notes for a Preface" in *The Complete Poems of Carl Sandburg* by Carl Sandburg. Copyright 1916 by Holt, Rinehart and Winston, Inc., renewed 1944 by Carl Sandburg. From "The Beautiful Changes" in *The Beautiful Changes and Other Peoms* by Richard Wilbur. Copyright 1947, 1975 by Richard Wilbur. From "Year's End" in *Ceremony and Other Poems* by Richard Wilbur. Copyright 1959 by The New Yorker, Inc.; copyright renewed 1977 by Richard Wilbur.

Harper & Row, Publishers, Inc.: From "Tableau" in *On These I Stand* by Countee Cullen. Copyright 1925 by Harper & Row, Publishers, Inc.; copyright 1953 by Ida M. Cullen. From "Homework" in *Collected Poems 1947–1980* by Allen Ginsberg. Copyright © 1980 by Allen Ginsberg. From *Huckleberry Finn* by Mark Twain. From

Black Boy by Richard Wright. Copyright 1937, 1942, 1944, 1945 by Richard Wright.

Harper's Magazine: From the review of Emily Dickinson's *Poems* by William Dean Howells in *Harper's New Monthly*.

Harvard University Press and the Trustees of Amherst College: From "A Bird came down the Walk-," from "I never saw a Moor-," from "Tell all the Truth but tell it slant-," from "If you were coming in the Fall," from "I heard a Fly buzz—when I died-," from "The Soul selects her own Society-," and from "Apparently with no surprise" by Emily Dickinson in *The Poems of Emily Dickinson*, edited by Thomas H. Johnson, Cambridge, Mass.: The Belknap Press of Harvard University Press. Copyright 1951, © 1955, 1979, 1983 by The President and Fellows of Harvard College.

Henry Holt and Company, Inc.: From "Neither Out Far Nor In Deep," from "Design," from "Birches," from "Mending Wall," from "Once by the Pacific," from "The Death of the Hired Man," and from "Nothing Gold Can Stay" in *The Poetry of Robert Frost*, edited by Edward Connery Lathem. Copyright 1916, 1923, 1928, 1930, 1939, © 1969 by Holt, Rinehart and Winston; copyright 1936, 1944, 1951, 1956, 1958 by Robert Frost; copyright © 1964, 1967 by Lesley Frost Ballantine. From "Puritan Poetry" by Michael L. Lasser in *Major American Authors*, edited by D. Bruce Lockerbie. Copyright © 1970 by Holt, Rinehart and Winston, Inc.

Houghton Mifflin Company: From *James Russell Lowell* by Martin Duberman. Copyright © 1966 by Martin Duberman.

Houghton Mifflin Company/Sterling Lord Agency, Inc.: From "Her Kind" in *To Bedlam and Part Way Back* by Anne Sexton. Copyright © 1980 by Anne Sexton.

Alfred A. Knopf, Inc.: From *Dispatches* (Retitled: "The Highlands," "Tell my Folks . . . ," "The Wounded," "The Correspondent," "Back Home," "Remembering the Dead," and "The War Ends") by Michael Herr. Copyright © 1977 by Michael Herr. From "A Noiseless Flash" in *Hiroshima* by John Hersey. Copyright 1946 and renewed 1974 by John Hersey. Originally published in *The New Yorker*. "The Negro Speaks of Rivers" and from "The Weary Blues" in *Selected Poems of Langston Hughes*. Copyright 1926, 1948 by Alfred A. Knopf, Inc.; renewed 1954 by Langston Hughes. From *The Woman Warrior: Memoirs of a Girlhood Among Ghosts* by Maxine Hong Kingston. Copyright © 1975, 1976 by Maxine Hong Kingston. From "Spinster" in *The Colossus and Other Poems* by Sylvia Plath. Copyright © 1961 by Sylvia Plath. From "Parting, Without a Sequel" and from "Bells for John Whiteside's Daughter" in *Selected Poems, Third Edition, Revised and Enlarged* by John Crowe Ransom. Copyright 1924, 1927 by Alfred A. Knopf, Inc.; renewed 1952, 1955 by John Crowe Ransom. From "Anecdote of the Jar" in *The Collected Poems of Wallace Stevens*. Copyright 1923 and renewed 1951 by Wallace Stevens.

Little, Brown & Company, in association with The Atlantic Monthly Press: From *Yankee from Olympus* by Catherine Drinker Bowen. Copyright 1943, 1944 by Catherine Drinker Bowen. School version published by Houghton Mifflin Company for Little, Brown and Company, Inc., in association with the Atlantic Monthly Press. From *Blue Highways* by William Least Heat Moon. Copyright © 1982 by William Least Heat Moon.

Liveright Publishing Corporation: From "nobody loses all the time" in *IS 5, poems* by E. E. Cummings. Copyright 1926 by Horace Liveright; copyright renewed 1954 by E. E. Cummings. From "Summertime and the Living" in *Angle of Ascent, New and Selected Poems* by Robert Hayden. Copyright © 1966, 1970, 1972, 1975 by Robert Hayden.

Macmillan Publishing Company: From "The Steeple-Jack" in *Collected Poems* by Marianne Moore. Copyright 1951 by Marianne Moore; copyright renewed 1979 by Lawrence E. Brinn and Louise Crane. From *Literary History of the United States*, edited by Robert E. Spiller, Willard Thorp, Thomas H. Johnson, and Henry Seidel Canby. Copyright 1946, 1947, 1948, 1953 by The Macmillan Company.

Ellen C. Masters: From "Richard Bone" in *Spoon River Anthology* by Edgar Lee Masters. Published by Macmillan Publishing Company.

James Merrill: From "Kite Poem" in *First Poems* by James Merrill. Copyright 1950 by Alfred A. Knopf, Inc.; copyright renewed © 1978 by James Merrill.

New Directions Publishing Corporation: From "Dulce et Decorum Est" in *Collected Poems of Wilfred Owen*. Copyright © 1963 by Chatto & Windus. From "A Pact," from "The Garden," and from "The River Merchant's Wife" in *Personae* by Ezra Pound. Copyright 1926 by Ezra Pound. "December at Yase" from *The Back Country* by Gary Snyder. Copyright © 1957, 1958, 1959, 1960, 1961, 1962, 1963, 1964, 1965, 1966, 1967, 1968 by Gary Snyder. From "The Red Wheelbarrow," from "Tract," and from "Spring and All" by William Carlos Williams. Copyright 1938 by New Directions.

The New York Times Company: From "Little Red Riding Hood Revisited" by Russell Baker in *The New York Times*, January 13, 1980. Copyright © 1980 by The New York Times Company. From "School vs. Education" by Russell Baker in *The New York Times*, September 9, 1975. Copyright © 1975 by The New York Times Company.

W. W. Norton & Company, Inc.: From *Blood, Bread, and Poetry: Selected Prose 1979–1985* by Adrienne Rich. Copyright © 1986 by Adrienne Rich. From "Power" in *The Fact of a Doorframe, Poems Selected and New, 1950–1984* by Adrienne Rich. Copyright © 1975, 1978 by W. W. Norton & Company, Inc., copyright © 1981, 1984 by Adrienne Rich.

Harold Ober Associates Incorporated: From "The Egg" by Sherwood Anderson. Copyright © 1921 by B. W. Huebsch, Inc.; copyright renewed 1948 by Eleanor C. Anderson.

Random House, Inc.: From "Spotted Horses" by William Faulkner in *Uncollected Stories of William Faulkner*. Copyright 1931 and renewed 1959 by William Faulkner; copyright 1940 and renewed 1968 by Estelle Faulkner and Jill Faulkner Summers. From "Love the Wild Swan" in *The Selected Poetry of Robinson Jeffers*. Copyright 1935 and renewed 1963 by Donnan Jeffers and Garth Jeffers. From "Shine, Perishing Republic" in *The Selected Poetry of Robinson Jeffers* by Robinson Jeffers. Copyright 1925 and renewed 1953 by Robinson Jeffers. From *The Glass Menagerie* by Tennessee Williams. Copyright 1945 by Tennessee Williams and Edwina D. Williams; copyright renewed 1973 by Tennessee Williams.

Charles Scribner's Sons: From *The Great Gatsby* by F. Scott Fitzgerald. Copyright 1925 by Charles Scribner's Sons; copyright renewed 1953 by Frances Scott Fitzgerald Lanahan. From "In Another Country" by Ernest Hemingway in *The Short Stories of Ernest Hemingway*. Copyright 1927 by Charles Scribner's Sons; copyright renewed © 1955 by Ernest Hemingway. From *Look Homeward, Angel* by Thomas Wolfe. Copyright 1929 by Charles Scribner's Sons; copyright renewed © 1957 by Edward C. Aswell, administrator, C.T.A. and/or Fred W. Wolfe. An imprint of Macmillan Publishing Company.

The Sewanee Review and the estate of Hi Simons: From "The Genre of Wallace Stevens" by Hi Simons in *The Sewanee Review*, v. LIII, no. 4, Autumn 1945. Copyright 1945 by The University of the South.

Simon and Schuster Inc.: Adapted from *T. S. Eliot: A Life* by Peter Ackroyd. Copyright © 1984 by Peter Ackroyd.

Southern Illinois University Press: Adapted from *E. E. Cummings: The Growth of a Writer* by Norman Friedman, Preface by Harry T. Moore. Copyright © 1964 by Southern Illinois University Press.

Twayne Publishers, a division of G. K. Hall & Company, Boston, MA: From "America" in *Selected Poems of Claude McKay* by Claude McKay. Copyright 1981 by Twayne Publishers, a division of G. K. Hall & Co. From *Henry Wadsworth Longfellow* by Cecil B. Williams. Copyright © 1964 by Twayne Publishers, Inc.

The Ungar Publishing Co. Inc.: From *The Literary History of the American Revolution, 1763–1783; Volume I, 1763–1776* by Moses Coit Tyler. Published by Frederick Ungar Publishing Co., NY, 1957.

University of Chicago: From "The Uses and Abuses of Commitment" by F. W. Dupee in *"The King of Cats" and Other Remarks on Writers and Writing*, edited by F. W. Dupee. Copyright © 1984 by The University of Chicago.

University of New Mexico Press: From *The Way to Rainy Mountain* by N. Scott Momaday. Copyright © 1969 by The University of New Mexico Press. Originally published in *The Reporter*, January 26, 1967.

Viking Penguin, Inc.: From "Go Down Death" in *God's Trombones* by James Weldon Johnson. Copyright 1927; renewed 1955 by Grace Nail Johnson. From *The Grapes of Wrath* by John Steinbeck. Copyright 1939 by John Steinbeck, renewed © 1967 by John Steinbeck. From "Ceti" by Lewis Thomas in *The Lives of a Cell: Notes of a Biology Watcher*.

Wesleyan University Press: From "Sled Burial, Dream Ceremony" in *Poems 1957–1967* by James Dickey. Copyright © 1965 by James Dickey. From "A Blessing" in *The Branch Will Not Break* by James Wright. Copyright © 1961 by James Wright.

Contents

Using the Teacher's Manual — xv
Scope and Sequence of the Program in *Elements of Literature: Fifth Course* — xvi

Unit 1: The Colonial Period: The Age of Faith — 1

William Bradford — 2
From *Of Plymouth Plantation* — 2

Mary Rowlandson — 5
From *A Narrative of Her Captivity* — 5

Sarah Kemble Knight — 8
From *The Journal of Madam Knight* — 8

Jonathan Edwards — 10
"Sinners in the Hands of an Angry God" — 10

Anne Bradstreet — 12
"Upon the Burning of Our House" — 12

Edward Taylor — 14
"Upon a Spider Catching a Fly" — 14
From "God's Determinations" — 14

William Byrd — 18
From *The History of the Dividing Line* — 18

The American Language: Native American Languages — 20
Exercises in Critical Thinking and Writing: Determining the Precise Meanings of Words — 21

Unit 2: The Revolutionary Period: The Age of Reason — 23

Benjamin Franklin — 24
From *The Autobiography* — 24
Remarks Concerning the Savages of North America — 27
Sayings of Poor Richard — 29

Patrick Henry — 31
Speech to the Virginia Convention — 31

Thomas Paine — 34
The Crisis, No. 1 — 34

Thomas Jefferson — 36
From *The Autobiography* — 36

The American Language: "Revolutionary" English — 39
Exercises in Critical Thinking and Writing: Analyzing and Evaluating Persuasion: Logic — 40

Unit 3: American Romanticism — 41

Washington Irving — 42
"Rip Van Winkle" — 42

William Cullen Bryant — 45
"To a Waterfowl" — 45
"Thanatopsis" — 47

Henry Wadsworth Longfellow — 50
"The Cross of Snow" — 50
"The Ropewalk" — 52
"The Tide Rises, the Tide Falls" — 53

John Greenleaf Whittier — 55
From "Snow Bound: A Winter Idyll" — 55

Oliver Wendell Holmes — 57
"Old Ironsides" — 57
"The Chambered Nautilus" — 60

James Russell Lowell — 62
"She Came and Went" — 62
From "A Fable for Critics" — 64

The American Language: "Noah's Ark": Webster's Dictionary — 66
Exercises in Critical Thinking and Writing: Responding to Literature — 66

Unit 4: The American Renaissance: Five Major Writers — 67

Ralph Waldo Emerson — 68
From *Nature* — 68
From *Self-Reliance* — 70
"Concord Hymn" — 73
"The Rhodora" — 74
"The Snow-Storm" — 76

Henry David Thoreau — 78
From *Walden* — 78
From *Resistance to Civil Government* — 82

Edgar Allan Poe   85
"The Masque of the Red Death"   85
"The Fall of the House of Usher"   88
"Eldorado"   91
"Annabel Lee"   92
"To Helen"   94
"The Raven"   95

Nathaniel Hawthorne   98
"The Minister's Black Veil"   98
"Rappaccini's Daughter"   102

Herman Melville   106
From *Moby-Dick*   106
"Shiloh"   113
"Art"   113

Exercises in Critical Thinking and Writing: Analyzing and Evaluating Persuasive Writing: Rhetoric   114

Unit 5: A New American Poetry: Whitman and Dickinson   117

Walt Whitman   118
"I Hear America Singing"   119
"Song #1," from "Song of Myself"   120
"Song #10"   122
"Song #26"   123
From "Song #33"   124
"Song #52"   126
"On the Beach At Night"   127
"On the Beach At Night Alone"   128
"When I Heard the Learned Astronomer"   130
"A Sight in Camp in the Daybreak Gray and Dim"   131

Emily Dickinson   133
"Heart! We will forget him!"   134
"Success is counted sweetest"   135
"The Soul selects her own Society"   136
"A Bird came down the Walk"   138
"I died for Beauty—but was scarce"   139
"I Heard a Fly buzz—when I died—"   140
"If you were coming in the Fall"   141
"Because I could not stop for Death"   142
"I never saw a Moor—"   144
"Tell all the Truth"   145
"Apparently with no surprise"   146
"To make a prairie it takes a clover and one bee"   147

Unit 6: The Rise of Realism: The Civil War and Post-War Period   149

Frederick Douglass   150
"The Battle With Mr. Covey"   150
Spirituals and "Code" Songs   152

Bret Harte   154
"The Outcasts of Poker Flat"   154

Mark Twain   157
From *Life on the Mississippi*   157
From *The Adventures of Huckleberry Finn*   159

Ambrose Bierce   163
"An Occurrence at Owl Creek Bridge"   163

Stephen Crane   166
From *The Red Badge of Courage*   166

Exercises in Critical Thinking and Writing: Making Inferences and Analyzing Point of View   175

Unit 7: The Moderns: The American Voice in Fiction   177

Sherwood Anderson   178
"The Egg"   178

Sinclair Lewis   181
From *Babbitt*   181

Willa Cather   184
"A Wagner Matinée"   184

Thomas Wolfe   187
From *Look Homeward, Angel*   187

F. Scott Fitzgerald   189
"Gatsby's Party"   189

Ernest Hemingway   192
From *A Farewell to Arms*   192
"In Another Country"   193
"The End of Something"   196

John Steinbeck   198
"The Leader of the People"   198
"The Migrant Way to the West"   201

James Thurber   203
"The Secret Life of Walter Mitty"   203

Katherine Anne Porter   206
"The Grave"   206

William Faulkner	208
"Spotted Horses"	208
Flannery O'Connor	212
"The Life You Save May Be Your Own"	212
Eudora Welty	215
"A Worn Path"	215
The American Language: American Slang	217
Exercises in Critical Thinking and Writing: Making Generalizations	218

Unit 8: Poetry: Voices of American Character — 219

Edwin Arlington Robinson	220
"Richard Cory"	220
"Miniver Cheevy"	222
Edgar Lee Masters	224
"Richard Bone"	224
"Lucinda Matlock"	225
"'Butch' Weldy"	227
Paul Laurence Dunbar	228
"The Haunted Oak"	228
Edna St. Vincent Millay	230
"Recuerdo"	231
"Dirge Without Music"	232
Robert Frost	234
"Design"	234
"Neither Out Far Nor In Deep"	236
"Birches"	238
"Mending Wall"	239
"Once by the Pacific"	241
"The Death of the Hired Man"	242
"Nothing Gold Can Stay"	245
John Crowe Ransom	246
"Bells for John Whiteside's Daughter"	247
"Parting, Without a Sequel"	248
Robinson Jeffers	250
"Shine, Perishing Republic"	250
"Love the Wild Swan"	252
James Weldon Johnson	253
"Go Down Death"	253
Claude McKay	255
"America"	255

Langston Hughes	257
"Harlem"	257
"I, Too"	258
"The Weary Blues"	259
Countee Cullen	261
"Tableau"	261
"Incident"	262
The American Language: American Dialects	263
Exercises in Critical Thinking and Writing: Interpreting and Responding to a Poem	264

Unit 9: Imagism and Symbolism — 265

Ezra Pound	266
"The River-Merchant's Wife: A Letter"	266
"The Garden"	266
William Carlos Williams	269
"The Red Wheelbarrow"	269
"The Great Figure"	269
"Tract"	269
"Spring and All"	269
Marianne Moore	273
"The Steeple-Jack"	273
Carl Sandburg	276
"Chicago"	276
"Limited"	276
E. E. Cummings	279
"nobody loses all the time"	279
"what if a much of a which of a wind"	279
T. S. Eliot	282
"The Love Song of J. Alfred Prufrock"	282
Wallace Stevens	287
"The Death of a Soldier"	287
"Anecdote of the Jar"	287
Exercises in Critical Thinking and Writing: Analyzing a Poem	290

Unit 10: American Drama — 291

Tennessee Williams	292
The Glass Menagerie	292
Lorraine Hansberry	301
A Raisin in the Sun	301

Exercises in Critical Thinking and Writing:
   Evaluating a Play … 307

Unit 11: Fiction 1945 To The Present … 309

Isaac Bashevis Singer … 310
"The Key" … 310

Bernard Malamud … 314
"The Magic Barrel" … 314

John Updike … 317
"Son" … 317

Mario Suarez … 320
"Maestria" … 320

Donald Barthelme … 322
"Game" … 322

Mark Helprin … 325
"Tamar" … 325

Tim O'Brien … 329
"Speaking of Courage" … 329

James Alan McPherson … 331
"Why I Like Country Music" … 331

Anne Tyler … 334
"Your Place is Empty" … 334

Andrea Lee … 338
"New African" … 338

The American Language: Euphemisms … 341
Exercises in Critical Thinking and Writing:
   Evaluating a Story's Ending … 341

Unit 12: Modern Nonfiction … 343

E. B. White … 344
"Death of a Pig" … 344

Lewis Thomas … 347
"Ceti" … 347

Russell Baker … 349
"Little Red Riding Hood Revisited" … 349
"School vs. Education" … 351

Richard Wright … 353
From *Black Boy* … 353

N. Scott Momaday … 356
From *The Way to Rainy Mountain* … 356

James Baldwin … 358
"Autobiographical Notes" … 358

Maxine Hong Kingston … 360
"The Girl Who Wouldn't Talk" … 360

Susan Allen Toth … 363
"Out East" … 363

Sandra Cisneros … 365
"Straw Into Gold" … 365

John Hersey … 367
"A Noiseless Flash" … 367

Michael Herr … 370
From *Dispatches* … 370

William Least Heat Moon … 373
From *Blue Highways* … 373

The American Language: High Tech's Influence … 375
Exercises in Critical Thinking and Writing:
   Evaluating Nonfiction: Fact and Opinion … 376

Unit 13: Poetry in a Time of Diversity … 377

Theodore Roethke … 378
"Elegy for Jane" … 378

Robert Hayden … 379
"'Summertime and the Living...'" … 379

Elizabeth Bishop … 381
"First Death in Nova Scotia" … 381
"Little Exercise" … 383

Randall Jarrell … 385
"The Death of the Ball Turret Gunner" … 385

Gwendolyn Brooks … 386
"Of De Witt Williams on His Way to Lincoln
   Cemetery" … 386

Robert Lowell … 388
"For the Union Dead" … 388

Richard Wilbur … 390
"The Beautiful Changes" … 390
"Year's End" … 390

James Dickey … 392
"Sled Burial, Dream Ceremony" … 392

James Merrill … 394
"Kite Poem" … 394

Adrienne Rich 396
"Power" 396

Sylvia Plath 397
"Spinster" 397

Anne Sexton 399
"Her Kind" 399

John Berryman 400
"Winter Landscape" 400

James Wright 402
"A Blessing" 402

Julia Alvarez 404
"How I Learned to Sweep" 404

Allen Ginsberg 405
"Homework" 405

Exercises in Critical Thinking and Writing:
  Evaluating a Poem 407

Bibliography 409

Writing About Literature 419

Assessing Students' Mastery of Subject Matter
  and Concepts 426
Reading Development in the *Elements of
  Literature Program*
  Nancy E. Wiseman Seminoff 434
Using Literature to Teach Higher-Level
  Thinking Skills 438
Teaching Students to Vary Reading Rates 442
Promoting the Growth of Students' Vocabulary 445
Varying Teaching Techniques 449
Obtaining Audio-Visual Aids 452
Index of Authors and Titles 454

Using the Teacher's Manual

This manual contains student objectives and teaching strategies for each unit and selection in the anthology. It provides complete coverage of the text's instructional features, as well as sample student essays, extension activities, and a bibliography. Following the teaching guides you will find special sections on assessment, reading development, critical thinking, reading rates, vocabulary growth, and classroom techniques.

For each selection, the manual's introductory material includes, as appropriate, an **outline of major elements**, suggestions for **introducing the selection**, helpful **background information**, and a **plot summary**. The teaching strategies focus on discussions of **cultural differences** pertinent to the selection; teaching approaches for students of **different ability levels**; **vocabulary study**, including Glossary words and teaching suggestions; considerations in **reading the selection**, including prereading activities, oral reading, method of assignment, and audio-visual presentation; and **reteaching alternatives**.

The manual also reprints the literary analysis questions in the student text and suggests answers, which are to be considered guidelines, not absolutes. Answers are also provided for each of the language and style exercises in the text, as well as ideas for presenting the writing assignments. A notable feature is **evaluation criteria** for every writing assignment, which suggest the major points you will want to look for in assessing students' writing.

The Scope and Sequence chart beginning on the next page shows the literary elements, writing assignments, and "Primary Sources" and "Elements of Literature" features in each unit of the student text.

The *Elements of Literature* program includes several additional supplemental teaching resources at each grade level. The *Annotated Teacher's Edition* contains systematic suggestions for teaching all selections as well as a wealth of background material on the literature, the authors, and the illustrations. Other components of the program are *Elements of the Novel* booklets, which are study guides to commonly taught novels; a *Test Book*, with tests covering all selections, units as a whole, critical thinking and writing, and word analogies; *Reading Check Test* blackline masters for all selections (except some poems); *Test Generators; Vocabulary Activity Worksheets; Workbooks,* featuring lessons to accompany all selections; *Study and Reinforcement Worksheets; Connections Between Reading and Writing,* providing self-directed work on key selections; *Instructional Overhead Transparencies,* including a set, with overlays, for teaching and interpreting poetry; *Reader's Response Journals* (First and Second Courses only); *Audiocassettes,* with professional readings of selections; *Posters;* and a *Video Series* of five videos on literary topics.

SCOPE AND SEQUENCE OF THE PROGRAM IN *ELEMENTS OF LITERATURE: Fifth Course*

Level 11: Unit 1 The Colonial Period: The Age of Faith	Elements Taught in Questions, Introduction, or Exercises	Writing	Analyzing Language and Style	Primary Sources	Elements of Literature
Introduction: The Europeans Visit the New World					
The Puritans in New England: A Spiritual Journey	Who Were These Puritans? Puritan Beliefs The Puritans' Model: The Pilgrim The Bible in the American Wilderness Puritan Writings Plain Style				
Of Plymouth Plantation, William Bradford		*Creative:* Using Another Point of View *Critical:* Contrasting Two Historical Accounts		The First Thanksgiving	The Plain Style
A Narrative of Her Captivity, Mary Rowlandson	Subjective Reporting Attitude Allegory	*Creative:* Using Another Point of View *Critical:* Explaining an Allusion			
The Journal of Madame Knight, Sarah Kemble Knight	Metaphor Tone	*Creative:* Writing a Journal Entry *Critical:* Analyzing Character			
Sinners In The Hands of an Angry God, Jonathan Edwards	Purpose Figures of Speech	*Creative:* Adapting the Sermon Using Another Point of View			Journals

Scope and Sequence

SCOPE AND SEQUENCE OF THE PROGRAM IN ELEMENTS OF LITERATURE: *Fifth Course*

Level 11: Unit 1 **The Colonial Period:** **The Age of Faith**	**Elements Taught in Questions, Introduction, or Exercises**	**Writing**	**Analyzing Language and Style**	**Primary Sources**	**Elements of Literature**
Here Follow Some Verses upon the Burning of Our House, July 10, 1666, Anne Bradstreet	Extended Metaphor	*Critical:* Analyzing the Writer's Attitude	The "Poetic" Style Meter Iambic Tetrameter Iamb		
Upon a Spider Catching a Fly, Edward Taylor	Parable Rhymes	*Creative:* Rewriting the Poem *Critical:* Comparing Spiders			The Conceit
God's Determinations Touching His Elect, Edward Taylor	Imagery Puns Paradoxes	*Critical:* Comparing the Poem with Job	Imagery Sights Sounds Textures		
The Southern Planters					
The History of the Dividing Line, William Byrd	Satire Diction	*Critical:* Contrasting Two Histories Analyzing the History			
The American Language: Native American Languages					
Exercises in Critical Thinking and Writing: Determining the Precise Meanings of Words	Archaic	Discussing the Precise Meanings of Words			

Scope and Sequence   xvii

SCOPE AND SEQUENCE OF THE PROGRAM IN ELEMENTS OF LITERATURE: Fifth Course

Level 11: Unit 2 The Revolutionary Period: The Age of Reason	Elements Taught in Questions, Introduction, or Exercises	Writing	Analyzing Language and Style	Primary Sources	Elements of Literature
Science in the New World					
An American Pattern: Thought in Action	The Age of Reason in America Deism and the Rationalist Mind American Literature in the Age of Reason				
The Autobiography, Benjamin Franklin	Characterization	*Critical:* Comparing and Contrasting Two Writers Responding to Critical Comments	American English		
Remarks Concerning the Savages of North America, Benjamin Franklin	Satire		Loaded Words Connotations		
Sayings of Poor Richard, Benjamin Franklin	Irony	*Creative:* Analyzing Contemporary Maxims		A Letter to Samuel Mather	
Speech to the Virginia Convention, Patrick Henry	Main Idea Metaphor Rhetorical Question Allusions	*Creative:* Reporting on the Speech *Critical:* Comparing and Contrasting Speeches			Persuasion

xviii   Scope and Sequence

SCOPE AND SEQUENCE OF THE PROGRAM IN ELEMENTS OF LITERATURE: *Fifth Course*

Level 11: Unit 2 The Revolutionary Period: The Age of Reason	Elements Taught in Questions, Introduction, or Exercises	Writing	Analyzing Language and Style	Primary Sources	Elements of Literature
The Crisis No. 1, Thomas Paine	Arguments Main Idea Imagery Metaphor Analogy	*Creative:* Writing a Firsthand Account *Critical:* Evaluating a Generalization			
The Autobiography, Thomas Jefferson	Parallelism	*Critical:* Analyzing Its Reasoning Responding to a Point of View Responding to Changes in the Document	Precise Meanings	A Letter from Jefferson to His Daughter	
The American Language: "Revolutionary" English	Americanisms and Their Critics "What language should Americans speak?" American English and American Democracy				
Exercises in Critical Thinking and Writing: Analyzing and Evaluating Persuasion: Logic	Fallacy Paraphrase Purpose Assumption Reasons Opinions Facts Evidence Logic Thesis statement				

Scope and Sequence xix

SCOPE AND SEQUENCE OF THE PROGRAM IN *ELEMENTS OF LITERATURE*: *Fifth Course*

Level 11: Unit 3 American Romanticism	Elements Taught in Questions, Introduction, or Exercises	Writing	Analyzing Language and Style	Primary Sources	Elements of Literature
Introduction: The Pattern of the "Journey"					
The Romantic Escape					
The Romantic Sensibility					
The American Hero in Romantic Fiction					
Rip Van Winkle, Washington Irving	Characterization Theme Tone Setting Satire Stereotyped Characters	*Creative:* Writing an Epilogue *Critical:* Modernizing the Story Explaining a Parallel Analyzing a Conflict	Inflated Language	Domestic Manners of the Americans, Frances Tollope	
To a Waterfowl, William Cullen Bryant	Onomatopoeia Symbol Theme	*Critical:* Analyzing the Poem			
Thanatopsis, William Cullen Bryant	Personification Tone Imagery Metaphors Iambic Pentameters	*Creative:* Writing a Letter *Critical:* Comparing and Contrasting Poems Analyzing Imagery and Meaning	Inversions and Archaic Language		

xx Scope and Sequence

SCOPE AND SEQUENCE OF THE PROGRAM IN *ELEMENTS OF LITERATURE: Fifth Course*

Level 11: Unit 3 American Romanticism	Elements Taught in Questions, Introduction, or Exercises	Writing	Analyzing Language and Style	Primary Sources	Elements of Literature
The Cross of Snow, Henry Wadsworth Longfellow	Figurative Language	*Critical:* Responding to the Poem			The Sonnet Petrarchan Italian Elizabethan Shakespearean
The Ropewalk, Henry Wadsworth Longfellow	Simile Imagery Metaphor Tone	*Creative:* Describing an Idyllic Scene	Trochaic Meter		
The Tide Rises, the Tide Falls, Henry Wadsworth Longfellow	Onomatopoeia Personification	*Critical:* Comparing and Contrasting Poems		Longfellow: His Life and Work, Newton Arvin	
Snow-Bound: A Winter Idyll, John Greenleaf Whittier	Imagery	*Critical:* Analyzing the Poem's Appeal	Allusions		
Old Ironsides, Oliver Wendell Holmes	Metaphors Irony Symbolism	*Creative:* Applying the Poem to Other Situations *Critical:* Finding Contemporary Parallels	Connotations		
The Chambered Nautilus, Oliver Wendell Holmes	Metaphor Imagery Paraphrase	*Creative:* Taking Another Point of View *Critical:* Responding to a "Message" Analyzing the Poem's Appeal	Poetic and Archaic Language Inverted Syntax		

Scope and Sequence   xxi

SCOPE AND SEQUENCE OF THE PROGRAM IN *ELEMENTS OF LITERATURE*: *Fifth Course*

Level 11: Unit 3 American Romanticism	Elements Taught in Questions, Introduction, or Exercises	Writing	Analyzing Language and Style	Primary Sources	Elements of Literature
She Came and Went, James Russell Lowell	Similes Imagery Paraphrase Refrain	*Critical:* Comparing Two Poems on the Same Theme			
A Fable for Critics, James Russell Lowell	Incongruity Paradox	*Critical:* Summarizing a Verse			
The American Language: "Noah's Ark": Webster's Dictionary	An American Spelling Book Webster's Dictionary "Noah's Ark"				
Exercises in Critical Thinking and Writing: Responding to Literature	Enjoyment Emotions Style Meanings Topic Statement	Analyzing and Evaluating a Speech			

xxii Scope and Sequence

SCOPE AND SEQUENCE OF THE PROGRAM IN ELEMENTS OF LITERATURE: *Fifth Course*

Level 11: Unit 4 The American Renaissance: Five Major Writers	Elements Taught in Questions, Introduction, or Exercises	Writing	Analyzing Language and Style	Primary Sources	Elements of Literature
Introduction: Five Famous Writers	Melville and Hawthorne: An Unlikely Friendship A Declaration of Literary Independence The Intellectual and Social Life of New England The Transcendentalists Emerson and Transcendentalism: The American Roots Melville, Hawthorne, and Poe: The Power of Darkness Symbolism				
Nature, Ralph Waldo Emerson	Imagery	*Critical:* Comparing Two Descriptions	Paradoxes		
Self-Reliance, Ralph Waldo Emerson		*Creative:* Writing an Essay *Critical:* Writing a Response	Figurative Language Figure of Speech Metaphor		
Concord Hymn, Ralph Waldo Emerson	Apostrophe Hyperbole Figurative Language	*Creative:* Writing a Letter *Critical:* Paraphrasing the Poem			
The Rhodora, Ralph Waldo Emerson	Personification Apostrophe	*Critical:* Analyzing the Poem Comparing Philosophies	Inversions		
The Snow-Storm, Ralph Waldo Emerson	Personification	*Critical:* Comparing Poems			

Scope and Sequence xxiii

SCOPE AND SEQUENCE OF THE PROGRAM IN ELEMENTS OF LITERATURE: Fifth Course

Level 11: Unit 4 The American Renaissance: Five Major Writers	Elements Taught in Questions, Introduction, or Exercises	Writing	Analyzing Language and Style	Primary Sources	Elements of Literature
Emerson's Aphorisms, Ralph Waldo Emerson				Hawthorne Talks About Emerson	
Walden, or Life in the Woods, Henry David Thoreau		*Creative:* Writing a Journal Entry Writing From Another Point of View *Critical:* Developing a Topic Comparing a Poem with Walden	A Metaphorical Style Metaphor Simile		
Resistance to Civil Government, Henry David Thoreau	Paradox	*Creative:* Taking Another Point of View *Critical:* Supporting a Statement Comparing or Contrasting Two Political Statements	Precise Meanings	Two Journals	
The Masque of the Red Death, Edgar Allan Poe	Imagery Climax Symbolism Allegory Allusion Theme Psychological Effect	*Creative:* Staging the Story Writing an Opening Sentence *Critical:* Commenting on a Criticism	Emotional Effects	A Visit to the Poes	

xxiv   Scope and Sequence

SCOPE AND SEQUENCE OF THE PROGRAM IN ELEMENTS OF LITERATURE: *Fifth Course*

Level 11: Unit 4 The American Renaissance: Five Major Writers	Elements Taught in Questions, Introduction, or Exercises	Writing	Analyzing Language and Style	Primary Sources	Elements of Literature
The Fall of the House of Usher, Edgar Allan Poe	Imagery Setting Point of View Allegory	*Creative:* Using Another Point of View *Critical:* Analyzing the Story's Effect Comparing the Two Stories Analyzing the Story's Meaning	Suggestive Words Personification		Symbols
Eldorado, Edgar Allan Poe	Meter Connotations Tone Symbolism				
Annabel Lee, Edgar Allan Poe	End Rhymes Internal Rhymes Meter Repetition	*Creative:* Imitating the Poem *Critical:* Comparing Poems			
To Helen, Edgar Allan Poe	Simile Alliteration Rhyme Allusion	*Critical:* Analyzing the Poem			
The Raven, Edgar Allan Poe	Imagery Tone Symbolism	*Creative:* Describing an Alternate Setting Imitating Poe's Techniques *Critical:* Comparing Poems Analyzing the Poem		Poe's Essay on the Writing Process	Sound Effects

SCOPE AND SEQUENCE OF THE PROGRAM IN ELEMENTS OF LITERATURE: *Fifth Course*

Level 11: Unit 4 The American Renaissance: Five Major Writers	Elements Taught in Questions, Introduction, or Exercises	Writing	Analyzing Language and Style	Primary Sources	Elements of Literature
The Minister's Black Veil, Nathaniel Hawthorne	Characterization Symbolism Tone Theme Parable	*Creative:* Using Another Point of View *Critical:* Comparing the Story to a Sermon Comparing the Story to an Essay	Archaic and Old Fashioned Words		
Rappaccini's Daughter, Nathaniel Hawthorne	Characterization Climax Setting Irony Moral Foils Symbolism	*Creative:* Ending the Story *Critical:* Analyzing the Story's Romantic Elements Comparing Stories Describing Biblical Parallels	Connotations Figures of Speech	Hawthorne and the Monument at Concord	
Moby Dick, Herman Melville	Foreshadowing Characterization Figurative Language Figure of Speech Point of View Omniscient Point of View Metaphor Parody Personification Imagery Attitude Symbolism	*Creative:* Describing an Event from Another Point of View *Critical:* Comparing Ahab's Speech with Transcendental Ideas Analyzing a Character Explaining a Symbol	Names and Their Significance	A Letter and a Journal Entry	

xxvi   Scope and Sequence

SCOPE AND SEQUENCE OF THE PROGRAM IN *ELEMENTS OF LITERATURE: Fifth Course*

Level 11: Unit 4 The American Renaissance: Five Major Writers	Elements Taught in Questions, Introduction, or Exercises	Writing	Analyzing Language and Style	Primary Sources	Elements of Literature
Shiloh, Herman Melville	Paraphrase Irony				
Art, Herman Melville		*Critical:* Comparing Poems			
Exercises in Critical Thinking and Writing: Analyzing and Evaluating Persuasive Writing: Rhetoric	Rhetorical Question Hyperbole Ridicule Connotations Rhythm Repetition Parallel Structure Purpose Paraphrase Thesis Statement	Analyzing and Evaluating Rhetoric			

Scope and Sequence xxvii

SCOPE AND SEQUENCE OF THE PROGRAM IN ELEMENTS OF LITERATURE: Fifth Course

Level 11: Unit 5 A New American Poetry: Whitman and Dickinson	Elements Taught in Questions, Introduction, or Exercises	Writing	Analyzing Language and Style	Primary Sources	Elements of Literature
Introduction	Cadence Free Verse				
I Hear America Singing, Walt Whitman					
Song of Myself, 1., Walt Whitman					Free Verse
Song of Myself, 10., Walt Whitman	Imagery Cadence Tone Attitude				
Song of Myself, 26., Walt Whitman	Catalogue Parallel Sentence Construction Onomatopoeia				
Song of Myself, 33., Walt Whitman	Sentence Structures Rhythm Imagery Tone				
Song of Myself, 52., Walt Whitman	Purpose	*Creative*: Writing an Essay as a Poem *Critical*: Comparing Whitman to Emerson Comparing a Poem to a Psalm			

xxviii   Scope and Sequence

SCOPE AND SEQUENCE OF THE PROGRAM IN ELEMENTS OF LITERATURE: Fifth Course

Level 11: Unit 5 — A New American Poetry: Whitman and Dickinson

	Elements Taught in Questions, Introduction, or Exercises	Writing	Analyzing Language and Style	Primary Sources	Elements of Literature
On the Beach at Night, Walt Whitman	Symbolism Imagery				
On the Beach at Night Alone, Walt Whitman	Catalogue	*Critical:* Comparing the Poem to "Thanatopsis"			
When I Heard the Learned Astronomer, Walt Whitman		*Critical:* Comparing Poems			
A Sight in Camp in the Daybreak Gray and Dim, Walt Whitman	Setting Message Cadences Catalogues Tone Rhythms Diction Subject Matter Imagery	*Creative:* Writing a Free-Verse Poem *Critical:* Analyzing the Ideas in the Poems Explaining the Poet's Statement Contrasting Whitman with a Fireside Poet Comparing Whitman to Taylor and Emerson Analyzing the Prose		"Specimen Days"	
Heart! We will forget him!, Emily Dickinson	Paraphrase Tone				
Success is Counted Sweetest, Emily Dickinson	Imagery				
The Soul selects her own Society, Emily Dickinson	Imagery Metaphor Meter	*Critical:* Evaluating a Title			Slant Rhyme

Scope and Sequence xxix

SCOPE AND SEQUENCE OF THE PROGRAM IN ELEMENTS OF LITERATURE: Fifth Course

Level 11: Unit 5 A New American Poetry: Whitman and Dickinson	Elements Taught in Questions, Introduction, or Exercises	Writing	Analyzing Language and Style	Primary Sources	Elements of Literature
A Bird came down the Walk, Emily Dickinson	Simile Figures of Speech Imagery				
I Died for Beauty—but was scarce, Emily Dickinson	Meter Slant Rhymes Metaphor Message				
I heard a Fly buzz—when I died—, Emily Dickinson	Irony Paraphrase Tone				
If you were coming in the Fall, Emily Dickinson	Simile Paraphrase Tone				
Because I could not stop for Death—, Emily Dickinson	Personification Irony Tone	*Critical:* Commenting on a Critic			
I never Saw a Moor—, Emily Dickinson					
Tell all the Truth, Emily Dickinson	Paraphrase Metaphor				

xxx Scope and Sequence

SCOPE AND SEQUENCE OF THE PROGRAM IN ELEMENTS OF LITERATURE: Fifth Course

Level 11: Unit 5 A New American Poetry: Whitman and Dickinson	Elements Taught in Questions, Introduction, or Exercises	Writing	Analyzing Language and Style	Primary Sources	Elements of Literature
Apparently with no surprise, Emily Dickinson	Personification Theme Pun				
To make a prairie it takes a clover and one bee, Emily Dickinson	Metaphors Imagery Themes	*Creative:* Writing Quatrains *Critical:* Analyzing a Poem Analyzing an Edited Edition Comparing Poems	Diction and Syntax	Higginson's Account of Dickinson	
Exercises in Critical Thinking and Writing: Comparing and Contrasting Poems	Subject Figurative Language Imagery Sound Effects Form Theme Meter Rhyme Tone	Comparing and Contrasting Two Poems			

Scope and Sequence   xxxi

SCOPE AND SEQUENCE OF THE PROGRAM IN *ELEMENTS OF LITERATURE*: *Fifth Course*

Level 11: Unit 6 The Rise of Realism: The Civil War and Post War Period	Elements Taught in Questions, Introduction, or Exercises	Writing	Analyzing Language and Style	Primary Sources	Elements of Literature
The Civil War	Responses to the War: Idealism . . . and Disillusionment The War and Literature				
The Rise of Realism	Romantic Novel The European Roots of Realism American Regional Writing				
Representative American Realists	William Dean Howells Frank Norris and Naturalism Henry James and Psychological Realism Stephen Crane and the Uses of Irony				
Introduction	Romantic Novel Realists Regionalism Naturalist Ironist				
The Battle with Mr. Covey, Frederick Douglass	Characteristics Characterization	*Creative*: Applying Meanings *Critical*: Responding to an Idea	Metaphors		

SCOPE AND SEQUENCE OF THE PROGRAM IN ELEMENTS OF LITERATURE: *Fifth Course*

Level 11: Unit 6 The Rise of Realism: The Civil War and Post War Period	Elements Taught in Questions, Introduction, or Exercises	Writing	Analyzing Language and Style	Primary Sources	Elements of Literature
Spirituals and "Code" Songs Go Down, Moses, Frederick Douglass Follow the Drinking Gourd, Frederick Douglass		*Creative:* Writing a Stanza *Critical:* Analyzing Allusions Reporting on Other Spirituals Comparing the Spirituals to the Puritans' Writing Analyzing a Code Song			
The Outcasts of Poker Flat, Bret Harte	Complications Foreshadowing Theme	*Creative:* Casting a Film *Critical:* Comparing Depictions of the Frontier	Euphemism and Comic Irony		
Life on the Mississippi, Mark Twain	Catalogue Imagery Characterization	*Creative:* Writing an Exaggerated Boast Rewriting Dialect	Dialect and Frontier Humor Hyperbole Metaphors Incongruity Boasts Digressions		
The Adventures of Huckleberry Finn, Mark Twain	Imagery Figures of Speech Characterization Symbolism Comic Tone	*Creative:* Imitating a Writer's Technique Writing a Journal Entry *Critical:* Responding to a Critic Analyzing the Selection Evaluating "Voice"	Descriptive Language Imagery	The "Original" Huckleberry Finn	

Scope and Sequence   xxxiii

SCOPE AND SEQUENCE OF THE PROGRAM IN ELEMENTS OF LITERATURE: *Fifth Course*

Level 11: Unit 6 The Rise of Realism: The Civil War and Post War Period	Elements Taught in Questions, Introduction, or Exercises	Writing	Analyzing Language and Style	Primary Sources	Elements of Literature
An Occurrence at Owl Creek Bridge, Ambrose Bierce	Setting Flashback Point of View Theme	*Creative:* Imitating a Technique *Critical:* Analyzing Suspense Responding to a Critical Comment			
The Red Badge of Courage, Stephen Crane					
Chapters 1–6	Ironic Reversal Style Impressionistic Metaphors Dialogue Dialect				
Chapters 7–12	Title Irony Turning Point				
Chapters 13–18	Personification Imagery Irony Antithesis Metaphor Simile Point of View				

xxxiv   Scope and Sequence

SCOPE AND SEQUENCE OF THE PROGRAM IN ELEMENTS OF LITERATURE: *Fifth Course*

Level 11: Unit 6 The Rise of Realism: The Civil War and Post War Period	Elements Taught in Questions, Introduction, or Exercises	Writing	Analyzing Language and Style	Primary Sources	Elements of Literature
Chapters 19–24	Turning Point Symbolism Imagery Synaesthesia Irony Theme Hero Setting	*Creative:* Imitating the Writer's Style Extending the Novel *Critical:* Analyzing Theme Comparing Crane's Poetry and Fiction Responding to a Critique Analyzing Character	Impressionism Imagery Fragmented Quotations Ambiguity Syntax		
The American Language: A Period of Vocabulary Growth					
Exercises in Critical Thinking and Writing: Making Inferences and Analyzing Point of View	Motivation Character Traits Theme Point of View	Analyzing a Story's Point of View			

Scope and Sequence   xxxv

SCOPE AND SEQUENCE OF THE PROGRAM IN ELEMENTS OF LITERATURE: *Fifth Course*

Level 11: Unit 7 The Moderns: The American Voice in Fiction	Elements Taught in Questions, Introduction, or Exercises	Writing	Analyzing Language and Style	Primary Sources	Elements of Literature
War, Depression, and a Rejection of Tradition	Modernist The American Dream The Breakdown of Beliefs and Traditions Stream of Consciousness A New American Style and "Hero" in Fiction				
The Egg, Sherwood Anderson	Symbol Theme	*Creative:* Using Another Point of View *Critical:* Analyzing Conflict		A Letter from Sherwood Anderson	
Babbitt, Sinclair Lewis	Satire Irony	*Creative:* Answering Babbitt Updating Babbitt *Critical:* Comparing and Contrasting the Speech with "Self-Reliance"	Clichés		
A Wagner Matinée, Willa Cather	Flashbacks Omniscient Narrator Theme Setting Imagery	*Creative:* Describing a Character *Critical:* Analyzing Imagery Comparing Responses to Nature	Figures of Speech		
Look Homeward, Angel, Thomas Wolfe	Title Paraphrase	*Critical:* Comparing Two Descriptions	Poetic Prose Alliteration Figures of Speech Onomatopoeia		

xxxvi   Scope and Sequence

SCOPE AND SEQUENCE OF THE PROGRAM IN ELEMENTS OF LITERATURE: Fifth Course

Level 11: Unit 7 The Moderns: The American Voice in Fiction	Elements Taught in Questions, Introduction, or Exercises	Writing	Analyzing Language and Style	Primary Sources	Elements of Literature
Gatsby's Party, F. Scott Fitzgerald	Foreshadowing Irony Characterization Theme	*Creative:* Describing a Party *Critical:* Responding to the Story	Imagery	A Letter to His Daughter from F. Scott Fitzgerald	
A Farewell to Arms, Ernest Hemingway	Incongruity Imagery Setting Understatement				
In Another Country, Ernest Hemingway	Characters Setting Attitude Theme	*Creative:* Describing a Setting *Critical:* Responding to Theme Comparing Stories			
The End of Something, Ernest Hemingway	Imagery Metaphor Theme	*Creative:* Imitating Hemingway's Style *Critical:* Responding to a Critic	The Plain Style	Nobel Prize Acceptance Speech, 1954, Ernest Hemingway	
The Leader of the People, John Steinbeck	Characterization Irony Conflicts Theme	*Creative:* Using Another Point of View *Critical:* Comparing and Contrasting Characters Comparing Themes	Figures of Speech Simile Metaphor Personification Oxymoron Hyperbole		

Scope and Sequence xxxvii

SCOPE AND SEQUENCE OF THE PROGRAM IN ELEMENTS OF LITERATURE: *Fifth Course*

Level 11: Unit 7 The Moderns: The American Voice in Fiction	Elements Taught in Questions, Introduction, or Exercises	Writing	Analyzing Language and Style	Primary Sources	Elements of Literature
The Migrant Way to the West, John Steinbeck		*Critical:* Comparing Imagery		Nobel Prize Acceptance Speech, 1962, John Steinbeck	
The Secret Life of Walter Mitty, James Thurber	Setting Free Association Irony Parody Jargon	*Critical:* Analyzing Characters Comparing Stories		*The New Yorker's Farewell,* E.B. White	
The Grave, Katherine Anne Porter	Setting Theme	*Critical:* Responding to a Critical Comment	Imagery and Symbolism		
The Spotted Horses, William Faulkner	Characterization Comparisons	*Creative:* Writing a Tall Tale *Critical:* Responding to a Critic Comparing Two Writers	Dialect Context	Nobel Prize Acceptance Speech, 1950, William Faulkner	
The Life You Save May Be Your Own, Flannery O'Connor	Setting Characterization Dialogue Theme Effect Irony Tone	*Creative:* Extending the Story *Critical:* Expressing an Opinion Analyzing the Story	Connotations Figures of Speech	The Adventures of Mr. Shiftlet, Flannery O'Connor	The Four "Modes" of Fiction

SCOPE AND SEQUENCE OF THE PROGRAM IN *ELEMENTS OF LITERATURE: Fifth Course*

Level 11: Unit 7 The Moderns: The American Voice in Fiction	Elements Taught in Questions, Introduction, or Exercises	Writing	Analyzing Language and Style	Primary Sources	Elements of Literature
A Worm Path, Eudora Welty	Appearance Speech Behavior Characterization Irony Setting Theme	*Creative:* Extending the Story *Critical:* Analyzing the Journey Responding to a Comment Analyzing Character		"Is Phoenix Jackson's Grandson Really Dead?" Eudora Welty	
The American Language: American Slang					
Exercises in Critical Thinking and Writing: Making Generalizations	Generalization Theme Subject Plot Summary Character Key Passages	Stating the theme of a story in the form of a generalization			

Scope and Sequence xxxix

SCOPE AND SEQUENCE OF THE PROGRAM IN ELEMENTS OF LITERATURE: *Fifth Course*

Level 11: Unit 8 Voices of American Character	Elements Taught in Questions, Introduction, or Exercises	Writing	Analyzing Language and Style	Primary Sources	Elements of Literature
American Poetry: 1890–1910	Voices of New England Voices of the Middle West Voices of the Black Experience Voices of the West Voices of the South				
Richard Cory, Edward Arlington Robinson	Irony Tone Moral		Connotations	Robinson on "Richard Cory"	
Miniver Cheevy, Edward Arlington Robinson	Personification Tone	*Creative:* Using Another Point of View *Critical:* Answering a Speaker Responding to the Poems Comparing Characters			
Richard Bone, Edgar Lee Masters	Analogy	*Creative:* Inventing Names for Characters			
Lucinda Matlock, Edgar Lee Masters	Theme				
"Butch" Weldy, Edgar Lee Masters	Simile Irony Tone	*Critical:* Comparing and Contrasting Poems		The Genesis of Spoon River	
The Haunted Oak, Paul Laurence Dunbar	Symbolism Meter Rhyme Repetition Tone	*Creative:* Setting the Poem to Music *Critical:* Analyzing Imagery	Archaic Diction	Dunbar and Dialect Poetry	

xl Scope and Sequence

SCOPE AND SEQUENCE OF THE PROGRAM IN ELEMENTS OF LITERATURE: *Fifth Course*

Level 11: Unit 8 Voices of American Character	Elements Taught in Questions, Introduction, or Exercises	Writing	Analyzing Language and Style	Primary Sources	Elements of Literature
Recuerdo, Edna St. Vincent Millay	Metaphor Meter Rhyme Scheme Mood		Imagery and Feelings Connotations		
Dirge Without Music, Edna St. Vincent Millay	Tone Rhythm Rhyme	*Creative:* Writing a Conversation *Critical:* Responding to the Poem Comparing and Contrasting Poems		"The brawny male sends his picture"	
Design, Robert Frost	Similes Octave Sestet Tone Rhyme Scheme	*Critical:* Responding to a Critic Contrasting Three Selections Comparing Poems			
Neither Out Far Nor in Deep, Robert Frost	Simile Irony Symbolism Tone	*Creative:* Revising the Poem *Critical:* Comparing Literary Works Comparing Poems			
Birches, Robert Frost	Metaphor Onomatopoeia Similes Symbolism Parable	*Creative:* Reading Nature *Critical:* Comparing Writings Comparing Attitudes Responding to the Poem			

Scope and Sequence xli

SCOPE AND SEQUENCE OF THE PROGRAM IN ELEMENTS OF LITERATURE: Fifth Course

Level 11: Unit 8 Voices of American Character	Elements Taught in Questions, Introduction, or Exercises	Writing	Analyzing Language and Style	Primary Sources	Elements of Literature
Mending Wall, Robert Frost	Simile Symbolism	*Creative:* Changing the Poem's Voice *Critical:* Comparing Poems			
Once by the Pacific, Robert Frost	Personification Title Symbolism	*Critical:* Comparing Poems			
The Death of the Hired Man, Robert Frost	Imagery Setting Characterization Irony Message	*Creative:* Extending the Poem *Critical:* Analyzing Characters	Blank Verse		
Nothing Gold Can Stay, Robert Frost	Allusions Symbolism Rhymes Rhythm Alliteration Slant Rhyme Sound Echoes Tone	*Creative:* Paraphrasing *Critical:* Comparing Poems		"I must have the pulse beat of rhythm...."	
Bells for John Whiteside's Daughter, John Crowe Ransom	Simile Tone				

SCOPE AND SEQUENCE OF THE PROGRAM IN ELEMENTS OF LITERATURE: *Fifth Course*

Level 11: Unit 8 Voices of American Character	Elements Taught in Questions, Introduction, or Exercises	Writing	Analyzing Language and Style	Primary Sources	Elements of Literature
Parting, Without a Sequel, John Crowe Ransom	Conflict Symbolism Rhyme	*Critical:* Comparing Poems Filling in Meanings Comparing Poems Responding to a Critic	Multiple Meanings of Words		
Shine, Perishing Republic, Robinson Jeffers	Implied Metaphor Tone				
Love the Wild Swan, Robinson Jeffers	Symbolism Sestet Extended Metaphor	*Creative:* Rephrasing a Poem *Critical:* Responding to the Poem	Rhymes Exact Rhymes Slant Rhymes Approximate/Imperfect Rhymes		
Go Down Death, A Funeral Sermon, James Weldon Johnson	Similes Symbolism	*Creative:* Extending the Poem *Critical:* Comparing Sermons Comparing and Contrasting Poems	Free Verse and the Orator's Style	The Preface to God's Trombones	
America, Claude McKay	Personification Imagery Paradox	*Creative:* Capturing the Poet's Feelings *Critical:* Comparing and Contrasting Poems			
Harlem, Langston Hughes		*Creative:* Writing a News Report *Critical:* Comparing Poems			

Scope and Sequence xliii

SCOPE AND SEQUENCE OF THE PROGRAM IN *ELEMENTS OF LITERATURE*: *Fifth Course*

Level 11: Unit 8 Voices of American Character	Elements Taught in Questions, Introduction, or Exercises	Writing	Analyzing Language and Style	Primary Sources	Elements of Literature
I, Too, Langston Hughes	Tone				
The Weary Blues, Langston Hughes	Mood Alliteration Onomatopoeia Imagery Similes	*Creative:* Creating Music for a Poem *Critical:* Comparing the Voices in Two Poems Comparing Poems			
Tableau, (for Donald Duff) Countee Cullen	Metaphors				
Incident, Countee Cullen	Ironic Overtones	*Creative:* Writing Dialogue Planning a Screenplay Setting the Poem to Music *Critical:* Comparing Poems			
The American Language American Dialects					
Exercises in Critical Thinking and Writing: Interpreting and Responding to a Poem	Analyzing Paraphrasing Tone Imagery Figures of Speech Symbolism Feeling Rhyme Meter Sound Effects				

xliv   Scope and Sequence

SCOPE AND SEQUENCE OF THE PROGRAM IN *ELEMENTS OF LITERATURE*: *Fifth Course*

Level 11: Unit 9 Imagism and Symbolism

Level 11: Unit 9 Imagism and Symbolism	Elements Taught in Questions, Introduction, or Exercises	Writing	Analyzing Language and Style	Primary Sources	Elements of Literature
Introduction: The Influence of Poe					
Symbolism: The Search for a New Reality	Symbolism vs. Romanticism Americans and Symbolism				
Imagism: "The Exact Word"	Haiku Free Verse				
The River Merchant's Wife: A Letter Lit'ai Po, Ezra Pound	Imagery Mood			"A Few Don'ts by an Imagist"	The Objective Correlative
The Garden, Ezra Pound	Punning	*Creative:* Creating an Image *Critical:* Explaining Images			
The Red Wheelbarrow, William Carlos Williams					
The Great Figure, William Carlos Williams	Metaphor Imagery				

Scope and Sequence xlv

SCOPE AND SEQUENCE OF THE PROGRAM IN *ELEMENTS OF LITERATURE*: *Fifth Course*

Level 11: Unit 9 Imagism and Symbolism	Elements Taught in Questions, Introduction, or Exercises	Writing	Analyzing Language and Style	Primary Sources	Elements of Literature
Tract, William Carlos Williams	Main Idea				
Spring and All, William Carlos Williams	Imagery Paradox	*Creative:* Retitling the Poems *Critical:* Analyzing a Poem		William talks about Poetry	
The Steeple-Jack, Marianne Moore	Syllables Rhyme Scheme Imagery Tone	*Creative:* Imitating the Poet's Technique *Critical:* Comparing the Poem to a Prose Text	Precise Meanings	Animals and Athletes	
Chicago, Carl Sandburg	Epithets Imagery Parallelism	*Creative:* Writing an Apostrophe *Critical:* Comparing and Contrasting Poems			
Limited, Carl Sandburg	Paradox Main Idea Irony			"Rhymes are iron fetters"	
nobody loses all the time, E. E. Cummings	Irony	*Creative:* Writing in Cumming's Style *Critical:* Comparing and Contrasting Poems			

xlvi   Scope and Sequence

SCOPE AND SEQUENCE OF THE PROGRAM IN *ELEMENTS OF LITERATURE*: *Fifth Course*

Level 11: Unit 9 Imagism and Symbolism	Elements Taught in Questions, Introduction, or Exercises	Writing	Analyzing Language and Style	Primary Sources	Elements of Literature
what if a much of a which of a wind, E. E. Cummings	Imagery Rhyme Scheme Slant Scheme	*Critical:* Comparing Poems Comparing the Poems to a Statement	Diction	"Miracles are to come"	
The Love Song of J. Alfred Prufrock, T. S. Eliot	Simile Imagery Extended Metaphors Setting Metaphor Irony Paraphrasing	*Creative:* Writing a Dialogue Imitating Eliot's Style *Critical:* Evaluating a Character Comparing Characters Responding to a Critic	Rhythms, Rhymes, Metaphors, and Allusions		
The Death of a Soldier, Wallace Stevens	Symbolism Elegy				
Anecdote of the Jar, Wallace Stevens	Symbolism	*Critical:* Comparing Poems Analyzing the Poem's Message	Precise Meanings	Poetry and Meaning	
Exercises in Critical Thinking and Writing: Analyzing a Poem	Analyzing Subject Paraphrasing Tone Imagery Figures of Speech Symbolism Feelings Rhyme Meter Sound Effects	Analyzing a Poem			

Scope and Sequence xlvii

SCOPE AND SEQUENCE OF THE PROGRAM IN *ELEMENTS OF LITERATURE: Fifth Course*

Level 11: Unit 10 American Drama	Elements Taught in Questions, Introduction, or Exercises	Writing	Analyzing Language and Style	Primary Sources	Elements of Literature
The Elements of Drama	The Basic Principles of Drama Conflict Protagonist Exposition				
How a Play is Produced	Producers Agent				
The History of American Drama	Theater as a Social Art The Influence of Ibsen, Strindberg, and Chekhov American Realism and Eugene O'Neill Arthur Miller and Tennessee Williams The Revolt Against Realism Expressionist Drama				
The Glass Menagerie, Tennessee Williams				The Model for Laura	
Scenes 1 and 2					
Scenes 3 and 4	Conflict				

xlviii   Scope and Sequence

SCOPE AND SEQUENCE OF THE PROGRAM IN ELEMENTS OF LITERATURE: *Fifth Course*

Level 11: Unit 10 American Drama	Elements Taught in Questions, Introduction, or Exercises	Writing	Analyzing Language and Style	Primary Sources	Elements of Literature
Scenes 5 and 6	Dramatic Situation Surprise Suspense Characterization				
Scene 7	Basic Dramatic Elements Progression				
The Play as a Whole	Symbolism Climax	*Creative:* Extending the Play *Critical:* Responding to the Play Commenting on "Biographical Criticism" Evaluating Different Versions of the Play Describing the Use of Lights Comparing the Play to Memoirs			
A Raisin in the Sun, Lorraine Hansberry				A Letter from the Playwright	
Act One	Conflict Characterization				

Scope and Sequence xlix

SCOPE AND SEQUENCE OF THE PROGRAM IN *ELEMENTS OF LITERATURE: Fifth Course*

Level 11: Unit 10 American Drama	Elements Taught in Questions, Introduction, or Exercises	Writing	Analyzing Language and Style	Primary Sources	Elements of Literature
Act Two	Characterization Reversal				
Act Three	Climax Symbol Dynamic Character Static Character Theme Suspense Reversal	*Creative:* Extending the Play *Critical:* Responding to the Characters Evaluating the Play			
Exercises in Critical Thinking and Writing: Making Judgments	Analyzing Evaluating Subjective Responses Characterization Motivation Plot Conflict Suspense Theme Setting Mood Thesis Statement	Evaluating a Play			

1 Scope and Sequence

SCOPE AND SEQUENCE OF THE PROGRAM IN *ELEMENTS OF LITERATURE*: *Fifth Course*

Level 11: Unit 11 Fiction: 1945 to Present

	Elements Taught in Questions, Introduction, or Exercises	Writing	Analyzing Language and Style	Primary Sources	Elements of Literature
Introduction: Literature in the Atomic Age	The New Voices in Fiction The Search for Trancendence				
The Key, Isaac Bashevis Singer	Setting Conflicts Foreshadowing Figuratively Comedy	*Creative*: Adopting Another Point of View *Critical*: Analyzing the Theme Relating the Speech to the Story Comparing Stories	Imagery	Nobel Prize Acceptance Speech, 1978	
The Magic Barrel, Bernard Malamud	Paradox Theme Plot	*Creative*: Extending the Story *Critical*: Comparing Two Stories Responding to a Critic			
Son, John Updike	Theme Tone	*Creative*: Imitating the Story's Structure *Critical*: Analyzing the Writer's Method	A "Pictorial" Style Simile Personify		

Scope and Sequence li

SCOPE AND SEQUENCE OF THE PROGRAM IN *ELEMENTS OF LITERATURE*: *Fifth Course*

Level 11: Unit 11 Fiction: 1945 to Present

	Elements Taught in Questions, Introduction, or Exercises	Writing	Analyzing Language and Style	Primary Sources	Elements of Literature
Maestria, Mario Suarez	Tone Irony	*Creative:* Describing a Character *Critical:* Analyzing the Story			
Game, Donald Barthelme	Narrator Setting Conflict Resolution Repetition Theme Title	*Creative:* Writing the Beginning Extending the Story *Critical:* Comparing the Story to a Poem			Satire
Tamar, Mark Helprin	Paradoxes	*Creative:* Writing a Journal Entry *Critical:* Explaining a Statement Responding to a Title	Figurative Language Simile Personification Metaphor Irony		
Speaking of Courage, Tim O'Brien	Setting Symbolism Irony Internal Conflict	*Creative:* Comparing Stories Inventing an Interview *Critical:* Comparing and Contrasting Stories			
Why I Like Country Music, James Alan McPherson	Conflict Comedy Tone	*Creative:* Writing a Characterization *Critical:* Analyzing a Character Analyzing Humor			

Scope and Sequence

SCOPE AND SEQUENCE OF THE PROGRAM IN ELEMENTS OF LITERATURE: *Fifth Course*

Level 11: Unit 11 Fiction: 1945 to Present	Elements Taught in Questions, Introduction, or Exercises	Writing	Analyzing Language and Style	Primary Sources	Elements of Literature
Your Place is Empty, Anne Tyler	Flashbacks Conflict Tone Theme	*Creative:* Taking Another Point of View *Critical:* Comparing Two Stories Responding to the Story		"Still Just Writing"	
New African, Andrea Lee	Setting Resolution Conflict Characterize Title Theme	*Creative:* Imitating the Writer's Style *Critical:* Analyzing Character Making Generalizations About the Stories			
The American Language: Euphemisms	Euphemism				
Exercises in Critical Thinking and Writing: Evaluating a Story's Ending	Predicting Outcomes	Analyzing an Ending			

Scope and Sequence liii

SCOPE AND SEQUENCE OF THE PROGRAM IN ELEMENTS OF LITERATURE: Fifth Course

Level 11: Unit 12 Modern Nonfiction

	Elements Taught in Questions, Introduction, or Exercises	Writing	Analyzing Language and Style	Primary Sources	Elements of Literature
Introduction: Nonfiction's Coming of Age	Nonfiction's Critical Terminology The "New Journalism" Nonfiction: A Popular Form				
Death of a Pig, E.B. White	Hyperbole Purpose Theme	*Creative:* Imitating White's Technique *Critical:* Analyzing Style Describing Character Explaining Allusion			
CETI, Lewis Thomas	Tone	*Creative:* Expressing Your Point of View *Critical:* Evaluating the Essay			
Little Red Riding Hood Revisited, Russell Baker	Ironic Slang Jargon Pleonasm Euphemism Satire	*Creative:* Imitating Baker's Technique	Jargon Cliches		
School vs. Education, Russell Baker	Satire Hyperbole Theme	*Creative:* Answering the Writer *Critical:* Supporting an Assertion with Examples	Irony		

liv   Scope and Sequence

SCOPE AND SEQUENCE OF THE PROGRAM IN *ELEMENTS OF LITERATURE*: *Fifth Course*

Level 11: Unit 12 Modern Nonfiction	Elements Taught in Questions, Introduction, or Exercises	Writing	Analyzing Language and Style	Primary Sources	Elements of Literature
Black Boy, Richard Wright	Imagery Characterization	*Creative:* Experimenting with Point of View *Critical:* Comparing and Contrasting Two Writers	Dialogue		
The Way to Rainy Mountain, N. Scott Momaday	Symbolism Imagery Mood Elegy	*Creative:* Writing a Description *Critical:* Analyzing Atmosphere Responding to a Statement	Poetic Prose Figure of Speech Imagery Comparison Metaphor Simile Personification		
Autobiographical Notes, James Baldwin	Tone	*Creative:* Writing a Response			
The Girl Who Wouldn't Talk, Maxine Hong Kingston		*Critical:* Analyzing a Character	Imagery and Feelings		
Out East, Susan Allen Toth	Characterization Stereotyping	*Creative:* Imitating Toth's Technique Changing the Point of View *Critical:* Developing a Statement Evaluating Objectivity		"The Importance of Being Remembered"	
A Noiseless Flash, John Hersey	Imagery Human Interest Characterization Irony Attitude	*Critical:* Analyzing Suspense Classifying a Literary Work Evaluating the Report	Foreign Terms		

Scope and Sequence lv

SCOPE AND SEQUENCE OF THE PROGRAM IN ELEMENTS OF LITERATURE: Fifth Course

Level 11: Unit 12 Modern Nonfiction	Elements Taught in Questions, Introduction, or Exercises	Writing	Analyzing Language and Style	Primary Sources	Elements of Literature
Dispatches, Michael Herr	Imagery Why?	*Creative:* Assessing the Impact of an Essay *Critical:* Comparing and Contrasting Two Writers Analyzing a Writer's Personality Analyzing Women's Roles			
Blue Highways, William Least Heat Moon	Complete Detailing Imagery Expressions Proverbs Grammar	*Creative:* Writing an Essay *Critical:* Describing the Writer's Character Comparing and Contrasting Literary Journals	Metaphors		
The American Language: High Tech's Influence					
Exercises in Critical Thinking and Writing: Evaluating Nonfiction: Fact and Opinion	Fact Opinion Objective Criteria Subjective Responses Personal Experiences Research Purpose Tone Interest	Evaluating Nonfiction			

SCOPE AND SEQUENCE OF THE PROGRAM IN ELEMENTS OF LITERATURE: *Fifth Course*

Level 11: Unit 13 Poetry in a Time of Diversity	Elements Taught in Questions, Introduction, or Exercises	Writing	Analyzing Language and Style	Primary Sources	Elements of Literature
Introduction: A Time of Diversity	The Decline of Modernism Modernist Poetry The Beat Poets Poetry and Personal Experience Confessional Poems				
Elegy for Jane, My Student, Thrown by a Horse, Theodore Roethke		*Critical:* Comparing Poems			
"Summertime and the Living . . .", Robert Hayden	Imagery Irony Tone	*Creative:* Giving an Oral Reading *Critical:* Analyzing the Poem			
First Death in Nova Scotia, Elizabeth Bishop	Imagery Rhetorical Questioning Tone				
Little Exercise, Elizabeth Bishop	Similes Personification	*Creative:* Imitating the Writer's Technique *Critical:* Comparing Poems	Multiple Meanings		
The Death of the Ball Turret Gunner, Randall Jarrell	Turret	*Creative:* Writing from Another Point of View		The Ball Turret	
Of De Witt Williams on His Way to Lincoln Cemetery, Gwendolyn Brooks	Irony Tone	*Creative:* Preparing a Choral Reading			

Scope and Sequence   lvii

SCOPE AND SEQUENCE OF THE PROGRAM IN ELEMENTS OF LITERATURE: *Fifth Course*

Level 11: Unit 13 Poetry in a Time of Diversity	Elements Taught in Questions, Introduction, or Exercises	Writing	Analyzing Language and Style	Primary Sources	Elements of Literature
For the Union Dead, Robert Lowell	Metaphor Imagery Tone	*Creative:* Writing a Description Comparing and Contrasting Poems			
The Beautiful Changes, Richard Wilbur	Paraphrasing				
Year's End, Richard Wilbur	Problem Imagery	*Critical:* Analyzing the Poems	Sound Effects Rhyme Scheme Internal Rhymes Meter Alliteration Assonance		
Sled Burial, Dream Ceremony, James Dickey	Metaphor Simile				
Kite Poem, James Merrill	Internal Rhymes Alliteration	*Creative:* Taking Another Point of View			
Power, Adrienne Rich	Irony	*Critical:* Analyzing the Poem			
Spinster, Sylvia Plath	Symbolism Metaphors		Multiple Meanings		

SCOPE AND SEQUENCE OF THE PROGRAM IN *ELEMENTS OF LITERATURE*: *Fifth Course*

Level 11: Unit 13 Poetry in a Time of Diversity	Elements Taught in Questions, Introduction, or Exercises	Writing	Analyzing Language and Style	Primary Sources	Elements of Literature
Her Kind, Anne Sexton	Paradox				
Winter Landscape, John Berryman		*Creative:* Imitating the Poet's Technique			
A Blessing, James Wright	Anthropomorphism Metamorphoses Subject	*Critical:* Comparing Two Writers			
Homework, Allen Ginsberg	Metaphor Tone Title Main Idea	*Creative:* Imitating the Writer's Technique Evaluating the Poem			
How I Learned to Sweep, Julia Alvarez	Rhymes Meter	*Critical:* Analyzing an Image Comparing Poems			
Exercises in Critical Thinking and Writing: Evaluating a Poem	Idea Word Imagery Figures of Speech	Evaluating a Poem			

Scope and Sequence lix

Unit One: *The Colonial Period: The Age of Faith*

Teaching the Colonial Period Unit

A nation's literature is most often studied in the order in which it was written. A key word in that sentence is *written*. Although many American Indian tribes had outstanding public speakers and long oral traditions, they lacked a method of writing down their speeches, poems, stories, and legends. Colonial explorers and settlers were therefore the first people in what is now the United States to create written records of what they observed, thought, and experienced.

Teaching American literature chronologically—beginning at the beginning—presents an obvious challenge. The nation's earliest literature is not the fast-paced prose or engaging poetry of later years. Instead, it consists mainly of serious-minded journals, sermons, personal narratives, religious poetry and histories, written in a language that may seem archaic and rather difficult. In spite of these obstacles, the literature of the Colonial period is important to students, for it introduces them to a way of thinking and living—the Puritan ethic—that has shaped many of our values and that continues to affect our lives. With this unit, it is especially important to provide a historical context for the literature students will read. The unit introduction in the student text (pages 2–10) and the background information on the authors and the selections provide students with a much needed overview of Puritan history and beliefs.

This unit concentrates on the Puritans of New England, because the Puritans, inward-looking and industrious, were America's principal writers of the pre-Revolutionary period. Their religion encouraged written self-examination as a manifestation of the workings of God. Even their poetry had a devout purpose, as critic Michael L. Lasser explains:

> Most important and most rewarding to the Puritans was poetry's moral significance: beyond its capacity to delight, poetry must offer its readers profound spiritual insights. To the Puritans, then, the subject matter of poetry was primary, regardless of the didacticism of the presentation. While they readily accepted poetic expression, it would nonetheless be incorrect to say that the Puritans cared particularly about literary theory, about matters of style, about the development of cultivated literary judgment. Like scientific investigation, political maneuvering, and all other secular activities of Puritan New England, poetry was a means to an end. And that end was spiritual.

Of the seven writers featured in this unit, six are New Englanders, five of whom are deeply religious Puritans. Well-educated Southern planters, sophisticated though they were, produced little writing of permanent interest. A notable exception was the Virginia planter William Byrd, whose witty and graceful journals were published after his death.

Objectives of the Colonial Period Unit

1. To improve reading proficiency and expand vocabulary
2. To gain exposure to notable writers of the American Colonial period
3. To define and identify significant literary techniques: allusion, allegory, metaphor, conceit, pun, paradox, and tone
4. To interpret and respond to historical accounts, a journal, a sermon, and poetry, orally and in writing, through analysis of their elements
5. To write an essay discussing the precise meanings of words or phrases
6. To trace the origins of American Indian words
7. To practice the following critical thinking and writing skills:
   a. Analyzing a writer's attitude
   b. Comparing and contrasting historical accounts
   c. Interpreting an allusion
   d. Analyzing character
   e. Comparing and contrasting the use of metaphors
   f. Analyzing the use of imagery
   g. Interpreting metaphor
   h. Analyzing a conceit

Introducing the Colonial Period Unit. Your students will already have some knowledge about the early exploration and colonialization of America. Be sure they understand the meaning of "Colonial period"—the years (1607–1776) during which England governed the American colonies. After the Revolutionary War, the colonies became the thirteen original states. Although students are unlikely to have studied Puritan life and thought in any detail, most will know the stories of the *Mayflower*, Myles Standish, and the first Thanksgiving. To get an indication of what else they know about the Puritans, you may want to begin with a series of questions: 1. Who are the Puritans? 2. Why are some of them called Pilgrims? 3. Where did the *Mayflower* Pilgrims come from? 4. Where did they settle? 5. How many were there? 6. What were they seeking? 7. Why was the first winter so hard? 8. Who were the two or three most prominent leaders? 9. What were the Puritans fundamental beliefs about God and the Bible? These questions are answered in the unit introduction, pages 2–10.

William Bradford

Text page 11

From *Of Plymouth Plantation*

Text page 13

Objectives

1. To interpret the writer's attitude
2. To write narration from a different point of view
3. To write an essay comparing and contrasting two historical accounts

Introducing the History

Of Bradford's history, the British critic and author A. L. Rowse observed, "It is indeed the qualities that give enduring life to a book: absolute fidelity, lifelikeness, and trustworthiness; its moral purity—the selflessness, submission, and control—shines through. Its tones are russet and gray and white.... Perhaps there is a sober, subdued poetry in Bradford...."

Background on the History. Never intended for publication, Bradford's history was probably written to remain in his family as a tribute to the founders of this colony. Coming to rest in the library of the Old South Church in Boston, the manuscript was lost after the church was plundered by British troops in the Revolutionary War. Thought to have been destroyed, it was found a century later in England and was first published in 1856.

Summary. In Chapter 9 of his history, Bradford tells of the death of a profane sailor who earlier condemned the sick Pilgrims. Bradford explains the repair of the main mast and the landing at what is now Provincetown. He gives his own thoughts on the Pilgrims' situation. In Chapter 10 Bradford relates the incidents that occurred during the search for a harbor and a permanent place to settle. At the end of the chapter, he notes the landing at Plymouth Rock. In Chapter 11 he narrates the events of the "Starving Time" and discusses Indian relations, including the treaty with Massasoit. The chapter concludes with a paragraph about the first Thanksgiving.

Teaching Strategies

Providing for Cultural Differences. American Indian students may be especially interested in the tribes that met the new settlers. In Virginia, Captain John Smith was met by the Powhatans, the tribe to which Pocahontas belonged. In Massachusetts, the Pilgrims were met by the Wampanoags, Massasoit's tribe. Squanto, a Pawtuxet, was not a native of the Plymouth region.

Since the great majority of Americans are immigrants, many students potentially have stories to tell of their families' arrival in this country. You may want to try to elicit some of these stories.

Providing for Different Levels of Ability. Less advanced readers may need help in understanding Bradford's rather difficult sentence structure and archaic wording. Capable volunteers might explain orally each of the main incidents that Bradford describes. Also, knowledgeable students can expand on some of the Biblical allusions that are briefly identified in the footnotes; there is usually more to be said about them.

Introducing Vocabulary Study. Knowing the meanings of the following words is important to understanding the selection. (Starred words appear in the Glossary. Italicized words either are archaic or have special meanings in context.)

profane*	13	*aught*	15
execrations*	13	manifest	17
buckling	13	*barricado*	17
halyards	14	grampus	17
sundry*	14	lee	18
tacked	14	manifold	18
multitudes*	14	lamentable	18
soever	14	inaccommodate	18
habitation	15	calamity*	18
importunity*	15	recompense	18
tendered	15	jollity	19
espied	15	skulking*	19

Students may use prior knowledge about the Pilgrims' voyage to guess at meanings of unfamiliar words. Point out that many of the words have to do with the *Mayflower* and with the Pilgrims' experience on it. Ask students which two words in the list exemplify the hardships and dangers faced by the Pilgrims. (*lamentable*, *calamity*)

Since many of the words used by the writers in this unit are archaic, the vocabulary can be a stumbling block even for advanced students. As students locate each word in the selection, have them use their dictionaries or the Glossary to find the definition that fits the word as it appears in context. Working with the archaic words in the unit selections should give students an idea of how the English language has changed since the Colonial period.

Reading the History. Before students read, ask them to discuss what they already know about the reasons the

2   The Colonial Period

Pilgrims were willing to leave the security of Europe and travel 3,000 miles across turbulent seas and about the dangers and hardships they endured during the voyage and as they settled in their new home. Help students to understand that these first settlers were arriving in what to them was a totally new world, a vast, unexplored continent thinly populated with unknown people of whom they had heard sometimes frightening reports. At the same time, the settlers had broken free from the political and religious bonds of Europe. They were truly on their own.

Reading Check. You might want to use the following exercises as a reading check. Have students choose the letter of the word or phrase that best completes each of the following sentences.

1. The sailor who condemns the sick Pilgrims (a) has been drinking too much (b) falls overboard during a fight (c) becomes ill and dies (d) is converted to Puritanism _(c)_
2. Expeditions are sent out in a shallop to search for (a) food and water (b) friendly natives (c) a suitable place to make a settlement (d) other English settlers to the south _(c)_
3. In an encounter with the Indians, (a) several Pilgrims receive arrow wounds (b) Squanto is taken captive (c) the Pilgrims offer to sign a treaty (d) the Pilgrims follow the "savages" for some distance _(d)_
4. During the first winter, (a) half of the settlers die (b) the *Mayflower* sinks in Plymouth Harbor (c) gifts of corn from the Indians help to avert disaster (d) the Pilgrims build a church _(a)_
5. The Native American most responsible for teaching the Pilgrims how to the survive in the wilderness was (a) Samoset (b) Massasoit (c) Squanto (d) Gorges _(c)_

Reteaching Alternatives. Ask students to compile on the chalkboard a chronology of the incidents in Bradford's history, beginning with the account of the profane seaman and ending with the first Thanksgiving. Have a different student add the next item to the chronology each time.

Responding to the History Text page 21
Analyzing the History
Identifying Facts

1. Historian Samuel Eliot Morison has said that "Bradford...had a constant sense of an unseen hand...that seemed to be guiding Puritan policy." What events on the voyage to the New World does Bradford credit to the direct intervention of God? Bradford says that death from God's "just hand" punished the profane young seaman for his curses. Bradford also seems to credit God with the repair of the main beam. He believes that divine intervention saves John Howland's life when the young man catches hold of a halyard upon being swept overboard. Bradford sees God's hand, too, in the decision to return to Cape Cod when the ship encounters dangerous shoals on the way to Manhattan.

2. According to the end of Chapter 9, what hardships and dangers still face the settlers after the voyage is over? They have no friends and no towns or other places of refuge. The season is winter, and travel is dangerous because of fierce storms. They face a desolate wilderness, which they believe to be full of wild men and wild beasts. The ocean bars their escape back to civilization. They can expect no help or supplies from their brethren in Holland or elsewhere.

According to Bradford, what is the one thing that can sustain the group during these trials? Bradford says that the Pilgrims need the Spirit of God and His grace.

3. The famous entry in Chapter 10 reports in detail on the Pilgrims' first landing in the New World. What events during those first explorations does Bradford credit to God's Providence? He credits the finding of seed corn to God's Providence. Without the seed, planted the following spring, the Pilgrims might not have survived the second winter. Bradford also credits Providence with preserving the company in their small boat after the mast and rudder break.

4. Bradford wrote his history of the "Old Comers" in part for the newcomers, the young people who, he hoped, would carry on the Pilgrims' ideals. What acts of charity and kindness during the "Starving Time" (Chapter 11) would remind later Puritans of their uniqueness and their obligations to the community? About fifty of the original hundred settlers die during the first winter. Six or seven healthy settlers faithfully attend the sick, who include Bradford himself. The ship's company share their beer with the settlers, even though this means none for them on the return journey. When a proud young boatswain who had earlier cursed the Pilgrims falls ill, they care for him.

Interpreting Meanings

5. Consider the treaty drawn up with Massasoit (page 19), and explain whether or not you feel its terms were equally favorable to both parties. What seems to be Bradford's attitude toward the Indians? In general, the terms seem favorable to both parties, although students may note that the first three provisions appear to assume that the Indians, not the settlers, are the potential aggressors. Likewise, the last provision requires the Indians to leave their weapons behind when visiting settlers, but contains no such requirement for the settlers visiting Indians. Bradford is very favorable to Squanto, "a special instrument sent of God."

6. There is a certain timelessness in the Pilgrims' story. What practical and ethical problems common to many societies are reflected in their experience? Answers will vary. Practical problems among the Pilgrims involve the necessity for mutual confidence, loyalty, hard work, and the ability to endure setbacks. Ethical problems are raised by the behavior of the crew and by the settlers' dealings with the Indians, as when the Pilgrims borrow corn.

In what ways might this wilderness experience be relevant to contemporary pilgrims or pioneers? Answers will vary. Current events or reading can provide appropriate examples. The Pilgrims' endurance under pressure would be helpful in any pioneering venture, such as space exploration or medical research. Students may want to analyze the Puritans' mixture of faith and practicality. Do they find the mixture paradoxical? Or do they think that bold efforts require such a combination?

7. One event that Bradford does not describe is the death of his wife, who either fell or jumped overboard in Provincetown Harbor. How would his history have been different if he had included this tragedy? Students will probably agree that the inclusion of this event would have made Bradford's history more moving and deeply personal.

What reasons can you propose for his having omitted it? Answers will vary. Puritanical acceptance of God's will may have played a part. Or Bradford may have felt that mention of the event would be depressing to his readers, whom he hoped to encourage to emigrate. Some students may suggest that, if his wife did commit suicide, her despair was very possibly linked to the journey, and Bradford might have suppressed mention of the event from feelings of shame, guilt, or regret.

8. Using what you have read, comment on the famous painting on page 20. Do you think it is realistic? Or does it idealize the First Thanksgiving? Answers will vary. Encourage students to discuss the painting in specific detail and to exchange freely their reactions to it.

Writing About the History
A Creative Response

1. Using Another Point of View. Have students list the events in Chapter 10, and then determine which ones the Native Americans could have observed. Next have them discuss what the Native American observers might have found strange about the English scouts' appearance and behavior. Discuss especially how they might have interpreted the scouts' following them and later taking some of their corn and beans.

Criteria for Evaluating the Assignment. The point of view is that of a Native American of that time. Events are ones the narrator would have been able to observe. Feelings attributed to the narrator are appropriate. Any additional creative details fit both the narrator and the situation.

A Critical Response

2. Contrasting Two Historical Accounts. Read aloud the excerpt from Smith's pamphlet, checking for literal comprehension, and the prompt. Call students' attention to the fact that the prompt outlines the expected content and organization of their essays.

Criteria for Evaluating the Assignment. The essay contrasts the purposes and the intended audiences of the two writers. It mentions three promises made by Smith and the relevant, real experiences narrated by Bradford. It cites elements of New World experience omitted by Smith. It names the writer more likely to attract settlers and offers at least one reason why this writer would ''sell'' better.

Extending the History

Bradford did not write his history to attract new settlers, nor was most of it even published until long after his death. Yet prospective settlers did need honest information on what to expect if they came to the New World. Have students put themselves in the position of a young person living in London several years after the settlement of Plymouth Plantation. He or she would like to move permanently to New England, but does not know what to expect. Have this person write a letter to William Bradford, asking him for advice: How dangerous is the voyage? How friendly are the Indians? What kind of work is available in Plymouth? What skills are needed? What should a settler bring from England? You might choose the best of these letters and have volunteers respond to it in William Bradford's name.

Primary Sources: The First Thanksgiving   Text page 22

Explain to students that a primary source is an original, or firsthand, source. Since Edward Winslow was present at the first Thanksgiving, his letter about the event is a primary source. You might mention that a primary source may leave out something the reader wishes to know, such as the date of the first Thanksgiving. It may also be inaccurate, although historians generally regard a primary source as sometimes more trustworthy than a secondary source—an account that is not original, but rather is based on other, earlier sources. Ask students whether Bradford's *History* is a primary source. (It is.)

Elements of Literature: The Plain Style   Text page 22

Students may find it hard to see why a style as difficult as Bradford's is called ''plain.'' Remind them that its plainness is in contrast to the style then popular in England, a style

The Colonial Period

ated with figurative language and classical allusions. Bradford uses allusions, but they are Biblical. When students recast the beginning of Chapter 10 into simple modern prose, they are almost sure to find that the sound of older Biblical translations (such as the King James version) is indeed lost.

Mary Rowlandson
Text page 23

From *A Narrative of Her Captivity*
Text page 24

Objectives

1. To identify examples of subjective reporting
2. To interpret allegorical meanings
3. To write a journal entry from a different point of view
4. To write an essay explaining an allusion

Introducing the Journal

At the start of King Philip's War—55 years after the Pilgrims had landed—there were about 40,000 whites in New England and about 20,000 Indians. According to an English friend of his, King Philip (Metacomet) said, "... little remains of my ancestor's domain. I am resolved not to see the day when I have no country." King Philip was killed a few months after the events in Rowlandson's narrative.

Summary. Rowlandson and her six-year-old daughter Sarah, both of them wounded, accompany their Indian captors into the wilderness. Although Rowlandson's faith is strong, she realizes that her life and Sarah's are in deadly peril. They travel from place to place, under constant threat, in bitter weather, and with little food. On the ninth day of captivity, Sarah dies and is buried by the Indians. Rowlandson's son, also a captive, visits her. One Indian gives her a Bible taken in a raid. The traveling continues, still with virtually no food, but Rowlandson discovers she can eat the "filthy trash" that the Indians have also been forced to eat. Rowlandson meets King Philip (Metacomet), who asks her to make his son a shirt, which she does and for which he gives her a shilling. After that, other Indians ask her to make shirts, one in exchange for some bear meat, another for a knife. The Indians' travel never ceases, nor does the quest for food. A friendly squaw gives her a piece of bear and some groundnuts. Throughout the ordeal, Rowlandson is sustained by her faith in God, to which she refers frequently.

Teaching Strategies

Providing for Different Levels of Ability. For less advanced classes grouped homogeneously, divide students into six groups before assigning the entire selection. (With mixed classes do the same, distributing more advanced students among all groups.) Have each group read, discuss, and summarize on paper a separate section of the Rowlandson narrative. One student can then present each group's summary orally, with the rest of the class taking notes. Finally, assign the entire selection as homework. This prereading is especially helpful to less advanced students, and it also gives critical reading opportunities to more advanced students.

Introducing Vocabulary Study. Knowing the meanings of the following words is important to understanding the selection. (Starred words appear in the Glossary. Italicized words either are archaic or have special meanings in context.)

furniture	24	lamenting*	27
affliction*	24	plunder (n.)*	27
tedious*	24	bier*	27
wigwam	26	groundnuts	28
garrison	26	parched	28
Praying Ind.	27	pagans*	28
bereaved	27	papoose	29
entreated	27	*fain*	29

A concept-formation exercise with words such as *affliction, plunder, lamenting,* and *bier* should help students to predict that this second selection in the unit will reveal even more of the dangers and hardships of life in colonial America.

Students will note, from the words *wigwam, papoose,* and *pagans,* that American Indians have a part in Rowlandson's journal. As a prereading vocabulary exercise, ask students to describe what they think Rowlandson's experience with the Indians has been. Encourage students to use as many of the vocabulary words as possible in their descriptions.

R*eading the Journal.* You may want to ask students what modern experiences might compare to a seventeenth-century capture by Indians? (Capture by terrorists? Capture by enemy forces in a war?)

R*eading Check.* You may want to use the following questions as a reading check. Have students respond *True* or *False.*

1. After her capture, Rowlandson is not allowed to see any of her children except Sarah.   False
2. An Indian who has plundered a Bible gives it to Rowlandson.   True
3. Despite the constant traveling and the cold weather, the Indians have enough dried fruit and meat with them so that food is not a problem.   False
4. Rowlandson agrees to smoke a pipe with King Philip (Metacomet) because it is an Indian custom and she hopes not to offend him.   False
5. Mary Rowlandson interprets her captivity as God's test of her faith.   True

R*eteaching Alternatives.* Have one student take the part of Mary Rowlandson and another the part of King Philip. Ask the person playing Rowlandson to compile a list of grievances against her captors, arranging them in the order in which the events occurred. She then presents them, one by one, to the Indian chief. He responds to each one as fully as he can, making his answers conform, as nearly as possible, to Indian customs and beliefs.

Responding to the Journal   Text page 30
Analyzing the Journal
Identifying Facts

1. In the first extract, what does Rowlandson tell us about how she was treated? One of the Indians carries her wounded child on a horse, while Rowlandson walks. Later, after carrying Sarah and becoming exhausted, both of them are put on a horse. At nightfall, the Indians stop. Throughout the night Rowlandson shivers in the snow by a fire with her child in her arms.

What details in the narrative reveal how her religious faith helped her survive? Rowlandson refers several times to God's presence and to His renewal of her faith. She says that the Lord upheld her during the night, enabling both her and Sarah to survive until morning.

2. Find the details in Rowlandson's later diary entries that reveal that her captors themselves are desperate to find food. The Indians at one point refuse her a spoonful of meal. Later, they boil an old horse's leg they have found.

3. What jobs does Rowlandson do, to earn her food? She makes a shirt and a cap for King Philip's son. She later knits a pair of stockings and makes a shirt for one of the Indians.

How does her attitude toward food change while she is a captive? By the third week, she is so hungry she is ready to eat food she would once have considered inedible.

4. Identify at least three occasions during her captivity in which Rowlandson is able to see Divine Providence at work. Students will find many examples. Early in her account, Rowlandson praises the Lord for having saved a number of members of her family from death. God, she believes, preserves her sanity and prevents her from committing suicide after the death of her daughter. She credits Providence with bringing her son, who is held captive by a different group of Indians, to meet her. Providence impels her to read the verses in Deuteronomy that promise mercy in return for repentance. On the move to Ashuelot Valley, she praises the Lord for preserving her as she travels alone over hills and through swamps to meet with her son.

Interpreting Meanings

5. Despite her efforts to be accurate, Rowlandson's journal is full of *subjective reporting*. Select any extract from the journal and find the words that reveal her *attitude* toward her captors—words that a detached historian would not use. Answers will vary. Rowlandson, quoting Job 16:2, calls the Indians "miserable comforters" (page 26) and describes their food as "filthy trash" (page 28). She refers to some of King Philip's men as "a numerous crew of pagans" and regrets that there is "no Christian soul" near her.

6. What instances of kindness does Rowlandson mention in her later entries? The Indians permit her to ride on a horse with her wounded child on her lap. An Indian gives her a Bible to read. At Coasset, she is reassured that no one will harm her, and she is comforted with two spoonfuls of meal. King Philip offers her tobacco, which she refuses. The Indians permit her to visit her son when they reach New Hampshire, and a kind squaw offers her a piece of bear meat. Several other Indians invite her to share the warmth of their fire on a bitter cold day.

Does she reveal any conflicting attitudes toward her captors? Do you think her attitude changes? Explain. Throughout the narrative, Rowlandson mentions instances of kindness toward her, for which she is deeply grateful. For instance, she marvels at not being harmed during her trip alone to see her son. She points out the kindness of the Indians who invite her to sit at the fire in their wigwam on a cold day. Early in the narrative, however, Rowlandson makes a few barbed comments about the Indians. They will not, she says, "be troubled with such spectacles" as seeing her daughter die. They will not let her attend the burial of her daughter. Yet despite her sufferings, she is not vindictive. Her attitude seems to become more favorable toward the Indians in the later extracts of the journal. Students may feel that Rowlandson displays some inconsistency. Remind them that her deep faith leads her to regard her captivity as a heaven-sent affliction, which may account in part for her mixed feelings.

7. The Puritans' habit of seeing specific allegorical meaning in their experiences helped them find significance in even very minor events. In an *allegory***, events, characters, and setting possess both a literal and a symbolic meaning. Describe at least two events in Rowlandson's captivity that she sees as allegories of Biblical stories.** Answers will vary. Rowlandson's "miserable comforters" quotation from the Book of Job suggests that the Indian attack on her house is an affliction similar to the one visited on Job—a severe testing by God. Job, like Rowlandson, loses his family, his health, and his possessions. Later in her journal, Rowlandson refers to Jacob's lament for his absent children (see Genesis 42:36).

Identify the specific ways in which each of these Biblical stories resembles Rowlandson's. Answers will vary. In each Biblical story, severe afflictions threaten to destroy people's faith in God. But that faith, even in the most dire circumstances, is maintained and rewarded.

8. What personal characteristics do you think helped Rowlandson survive her experience? Answers will vary. Students may mention her religious faith, her concern for her family, her courage, and her ability to do useful work.

Do you think personal courage or religious faith was more significant? Explain. Answers will vary. Some students may point out that an either-or answer ignores the apparent connection between Rowlandson's courage and her faith.

9. This captivity account was enormously popular in England. What reasons can you propose for its popularity? Students may mention the suspenseful plot (albeit a true story), the setting (which to the English would have been remote and exotic), and the religious motif (in an era of religious fervor).

What aspects of Rowlandson's journal would promote stereotyped (and hostile) views toward Native Americans? Many aspects of the journal might promote such views: for example, the fact that Rowlandson is held in slavery as the consequence of an Indian raid; her depiction of the Indians as savages, eating bear meat, obtaining broth from a horse's leg, and the like; her references to them as pagans. Remind students, however, that it was not so much Mrs. Rowlandson's factual journal as it was later, hair-raising, fictional accounts that promoted hostile and stereotypical views.

10. Are "captivity stories" still popular today? In what ways are contemporary captivity stories different from Rowlandson's? The captivity motif appears in modern novels and short stories, but seldom with so strong a religious component as in Rowlandson's journal. Few stories today deal with captivity on the American frontier. They are more likely to deal with the seizing of hostages by terrorists, the kidnapping of a wealthy industrialist, or the abduction of a victim in some other kind of crime.

In what ways are they similar to her account? Answers will vary. All captivity stories are likely to contain elements of fear, hardship, and suspense.

Writing About the Journal
A Critical Response

1. Using Another Point of View. Research should lead students to a greater understanding of the difficulty of determining responsibility for the war and to a grasp of how the expansion of settlements contributed to depletion of Wampanoag food sources.

Criteria for Evaluating the Assignment. The point of view is that of a member of the Wampanoag tribe. The entry accounts for the desperate conditions of the Wampanoag people and gives believable reasons for the attack on the English settlement. Feelings and creative details are appropriate to the journal writer and the situation.

2. Explaining an Allusion. Read aloud Psalm 137, checking for literal comprehension, and the prompt. Before students begin their essays, have them identify the verses Rowlandson quotes (page 28) and the events that brought them to mind.

Criteria for Evaluating the Assignment. The essay cites several parallels Rowlandson would have seen between her own and the psalmist's experiences, such as destruction of her town ("Jerusalem"), homesickness, the sheer fact of being a captive, strange villages as a kind of "Babylon," and finally, being unable to cope with unexpected—potentially hostile—laughter.

Extending the Journal

When students think of the frontier, they are likely to think of the American West. They may realize, but probably have not thought about it, that when European settlers arrived in the New World, the frontier began at Plymouth, Massachusetts, and Jamestown, Virginia. Mary Rowlandson was a true frontierswoman, living in the outpost settlement of Lancaster, about thirty miles west of Boston. Have students discuss the meaning of the word *frontier*. When did the traditional frontier disappear? (Most historians say 1890.) What is today's frontier, if there is one? (The usual answer is space, although metaphorically the word is often applied to science, technology, medicine, and other fields in which advances continue to be made.) This discussion could lead to the writing of an essay comparing and contrasting Mrs. Rowlandson's frontier with what students view as the frontiers of today.

Sarah Kemble Knight

Text page 31

From *The Journal of Madam Knight*

Text page 32

Objectives

1. To recognize style and wit in early eighteenth-century prose
2. To contrast the use of metaphor in two writers
3. To analyze differences in tone among three writers
4. To write a journal entry narrating a trip
5. To write an essay analyzing two characters

Introducing the Journal

Mrs. Knight was thirty-eight years old when she made her famous trip. Her journal, although delightfully written, was not intended for publication. It first appeared in print in 1825, published by Theodore Dwight in New York, and has been reprinted many times since then. The original handwritten journal has been lost.

Summary. On October 3, Kemble, on horseback, pauses first at a post stop, where she finds the meal very unappealing. At a river, her guide (a mail carrier) gets a boy with a canoe to take her across. After dark, her horse carries her across a second, hazardous river. They stop at a public house. After drinking some chocolate milk, she tries to sleep, but two "town topers" keep her awake with their arguing. She composes a verse, imploring the rum to "still their tongues." On October 6, she gets a new guide to accompany her to New Haven. They proceed along bad roads to Saybrook ferry, cross the river, and stop at an inn. Once again the food is inedible.

Teaching Strategies

Providing for Cultural Differences. Students for whom English is a second language may have difficulty with Knight's journal. The language is unusual, the sentence structure complex, the vocabulary somewhat archaic. Before assigning the entire selection, you may wish to assign each of the seven paragraphs to a student. The seven students can read and study their paragraphs, and then paraphrase them orally in class. In this way, all students will have some understanding of the events in the narrative before attempting to read it on their own.

Providing for Different Levels of Ability. To provide groundwork for slower students, assign the selection to everyone—but ask a capable student (female, if possible) to read it with special care. On the day you discuss it in class, have this student, pretending to be the feisty Mrs. Knight, relate her series of adventures orally in class. She (or he) should use note cards to keep the sequence of events in order. This oral paraphrasing will help slower students and should also provide a springboard for discussion.

Introducing Vocabulary Study. Knowing the meanings of the following words is important to understanding the selection. (Starred words appear in the Glossary. Italicized words either are archaic or have special meanings in context.)

cud	32	signification	34
circumspect*	32	prodigious	34
sculler	32	impertinences*	34
travail	32	dram	34
luminary	33	perplexity	34
formidable*	33	encumbered	34
discern*	33	*sixpence*	35

Have students define the words as homework. Then discuss with students which of the words might be applied to travel today. Why, for example, is driving through a large city such as Los Angeles or Chicago a *formidable* undertaking? Are travelers at airports *encumbered* with suitcases, boxes, coats, radios, and tennis rackets?

Reading the Journal. Be sure students read the brief biography of Sarah Kemble Knight on text page 31 before reading the narrative itself. In introducing this selection, ask students to try to visualize what travel must have been like in the early 1700's. Were there roads? (Yes, but not paved roads) Was there any motorized transportation? (No) Were there road signs? (Perhaps, but not many) Were there bridges? (Only over smaller streams) Were there inns and public houses? (Yes, quite a few because of the short distances that could be covered) Were there hostile Indians? (Yes, but not along the Boston to New York route)

You may wish to ask student volunteers to tell the class about any travel experiences, including camping or hiking, they have had in wilderness locations. How do such experiences resemble Colonial travel, and how do they differ from it?

Reading Check. You might want to use the following questions as a reading check. Have the students respond *True* or *False*.

8   The Colonial Period

1. Despite her guide's suggestion that she hire a canoe to take her across the first river, Mrs. Knight insists on riding through it on her horse.   **False**
2. Although the beds are often uncomfortable, the post stations on Knight's journey usually provide excellent food.   **False**
3. Knight writes her journal entries at night before going to bed.   **True**
4. On the night of October 3, two town drunks keep Knight awake until late at night.   **True**
5. While crossing a bridge over a swift river, the wheel of a carriage in which she is riding gets caught on a loose board, almost tipping the carriage into the river.   **False**

Reteaching Alternatives.   Have students trace the general route that Sarah Kemble Knight followed from Boston to New York. They should be able to find one specific place that Mrs. Knight mentions for October 3 (Providence, Rhode Island) and two that she mentions for October 6 (New Haven and [Old] Saybrook, Connecticut).

Responding to the Journal   Text page 35
Analyzing the Journal
Identifying Facts

1. Name at least five facts that you learned from Knight's diary about daily life in eighteenth-century America—facts about food, inns, and travel. We learn that traveling conditions in the eighteenth century were uncomfortable. The food was bad, often consisting of boiled leftovers. The beds in the inns were hard. Other patrons or guests might keep travelers awake with loud conversation. Travel on horseback was difficult because of rocky terrain and dangerous river crossings. Travelers had to be sure they could make the journey from one inn to the next before nightfall.

2. Identify the "twisted thing like a cable" that is spread on the table before lunch (page 32). The "twisted thing" seems to be a tablecloth. (Some students may have more imaginative guesses.)

3. Find at last three details in the journal that indicate that Knight's grammar and syntax were different from today's standard English. Answers will vary. Students may mention the placement of the prepositional phrase ("with the post") in the first sentence on the October 3 entry; the word order of the last sentence of this entry: "And I know not but my wishes took effect"; and the idiom in the first sentence of the second paragraph of the October 6 entry: ". . . arrived at Saybrook ferry about two of the clock afternoon."

Interpreting Meanings

4. Find at least three details in the entry for October 3 that show Knight's talent for wry humor and comic comparisons. Answers will vary. Wry humor comes through in her remark that the cabbage she swallowed served for a cud, implying that the cabbage was suitable for animals, not people. Kemble makes a comic comparison between herself and Lot's wife—daring not even to *think* of turning her head for fear of upsetting the canoe. Another comic comparison is that between the *Narragansett* topers and the two drunks trying to square a triangle.

5. Explain the comparison implied in the *metaphor* describing the sunset on October 3. Is this stylistic device different from what you might have found in William Bradford's or Mary Rowlandson's writings? Explain. Knight's metaphor compares the trees in the darkened forest to armed enemies, waiting like "ravenous devourers." This stylistic device, together with the mythological allusion to the sun god and his "swift coursers," would not be typical of the writing of Bradford or Rowlandson.

6. How does Knight's journal differ in *tone* from the writings of William Bradford and Mary Rowlandson? Answers will vary, but most students will agree that Knight's sprightly humor gives her writing a light tone that is quite different from the serious, pious tones of Bradford's history and Rowlandson's journal.

7. What did you like or dislike about Sarah Knight's journal? How does it compare with travel literature written today? Answers will vary. Travel literature today has great variety. When its purpose is to interest travelers in visiting a place, it is more positive than Knight's, sometimes even effusive. Knight was simply reporting her experiences on a difficult and rather primitive journey.

Writing About the Journal
A Creative Response

1. Writing a Journal Entry. Read the prompt aloud and, with the students, list on the chalkboard several kinds of trips which would lend themselves to the purposes of this assignment. Discuss how the same event could be treated humorously, as in Knight's journal, or seriously, as in Rowlandson's, by changing one's style.

Criteria for Evaluating the Assignment. The tone—whether satiric or serious—is consistent throughout the paper. The account comments on methods of travel, length of the trip, discomforts or dangers encountered, and the types and quality of food and accommodations.

A Critical Response

2. Analyzing Character. Have students first brainstorm events or situations they recall which show, for both Rowlandson and Knight, the facets of character listed in the prompt. Have them check their accuracy by locating suitable journal passages before they write their essays.

Criteria for Evaluating the Assignment. The essay describes both Rowlandson's and Knight's ways of responding to danger, their ways of surmounting hardship or suffering, their views on food, and the degree to which religious convictions affect their lives. The essay quotes from the journals to support its major points.

Extending the Journal

Knight's journal is not filled with religious references as Bradford's history and Rowlandson's journal are. Ask students to play the part of context detectives and see if they can find one statement that suggests each of the following traits: (a) Knight's familiarity with at least one Bible story (b) Knight's acceptance and probable tolerance of a different religion (c) Knight's faith in God, expressed in a way that sounds rather like Rowlandson. *Suggested answers*: (a) page 32: "not so much as think of Lot's wife" (b) page 33: "at the best, like a holy sister just come out of a spiritual bath in dripping garments" (c) page 34: "through God's goodness I met with no harm."

Jonathan Edwards

Text page 36

"Sinners in the Hands of an Angry God"

Text page 37

Objectives

1. To analyze the writer's use of figures of speech
2. To analyze the use of imagery and emotional appeals
3. To rewrite two paragraphs in modern English
4. To rewrite a paragraph from another point of view

Introducing the Sermon

The series of religious revivals known as the Great Awakening aroused tremendous enthusiasm, although it could not restore Puritanism to its former status. It did have other important effects, however. It led to increased missionary work among the Indians, early antislavery activity, and the founding of a number of colleges, including Princeton, Brown, Rutgers, and Dartmouth.

Summary. "Natural men"—those who have not accepted Christ as their Savior—deserve hellfire and will get it. The purpose of this sermon is to awaken such unconverted people by letting them see the horror of their fate should the wrath of God be let loose upon them. Only the pleasure of God prevents His vengeance from being wreaked at this very moment. God's pure eyes are angered by wickedness; He abhors the unconverted. Their punishment will be frightful and infinite. Some members of the congregation will no doubt meet this fate, and perhaps soon. The time to obtain salvation is now.

Teaching Strategies

Providing for Cultural Differences. Students who are familiar with modern evangelism, either from television or personal experience, might share their insights with the class. Have them discuss the intense emotionalism that can accompany evangelical sermons. If your class has no experience with Biblical evangelism, you may wish to have students do some library research on the Great Awakening and give oral reports on the subject prior to reading "Sinners in the Hands of an Angry God."

Providing for Different Levels of Ability. Students of all ability levels can experience the intensity of Edwards's sermon through the audiocassette recording that accompanies this selection.

Introducing Vocabulary Study. Knowing the meanings of the following words is important to understanding the selection. (Starred words appear in the Glossary. Italicized words either are archaic or have special meanings in context.)

provoked*	37	inconceivable*	38
abate*	37	omnipotent	38
uncovenanted	37	loathsome	39
forbearance*	37	abhors*	39
brimstone	37	abominable*	39
sensible	38	venomous	39
contrivance	38	asunder	39
*waxing**	38	mitigation	39

10   The Colonial Period

wresting*   39   vexation   40
heretofore*   40

A concept-formation exercise with words such as *loathsome, abhors, brimstone, abominable*, and *venomous* should help students to predict Jonathan Edwards's attitude toward sinners.

Reading the Sermon. Today's charismatic religious leaders are the successors to Jonathan Edwards and other revivalist preachers of the Great Awakening. You may want to introduce this selection with a discussion of what tendencies in society make today's evangelical movement popular. What do evangelists offer the people who see and hear them? What influence do they have on the rest of society?

Reading Check. You might want to use the following questions as a reading check. Have students respond *True* or *False*.

1. In his sermon, Edwards concentrates on God's mercy and love.   False
2. Edwards says that God's anger is like dammed waters.   True
3. Only the good works of certain people, says Edwards, keep the rest of mankind from being dropped into the fiery pit.   False
4. Edwards says that an unrepentant person will spend eternity in hell.   True
5. According to Edwards, some of his congregation may be in hell by the next day.   True

Reteaching Alternatives. Since Edwards's fire-and-brimstone sermon is based on the Bible—on people being "out of Christ"—you may find it worthwhile to read one or more passages on wrath and hellfire from the New Testament. See Luke 3:1–9 (John's preaching) and Revelation 6:8–17 (breaking of the fifth through seven seals) in particular. Have students compare the content and style of these passages with Edwards's sermon.

Responding to the Sermon   Text page 40
Analyzing the Sermon
Identifying Facts

1. Where does Edwards declare his *purpose*? At the beginning of the second paragraph of the selection, Edwards says that "the use of this awful subject" (namely, the terrible danger of being condemned to the torments of hell) "may be for awakening unconverted persons" in the congregation.

2. There are three famous *figures of speech* in Edwards's sermon: the images of the dam, the bow and arrow, and the spider. To what does Edwards compare these familiar, ordinary things? All three images relate to the wrath of God. Like waters temporarily blocked by a dam, God's anger is ready to burst forth. His wrath will bend like a bow to send the arrow of retribution into a sinner's heart. His wrath holds humanity like a spider over the fire of the pit of hell.

In each case, how does Edwards extend the figure of speech? Edwards extends all three metaphors with powerful rhetoric. He speaks of rising waters and of God's hand on the floodgate. He tells of the mounting tension on the bow, which will inevitably lead to God's letting loose the arrow of vengeance on sinful man. He extends the figure of the spider when he says to the congregation, "You are ten thousand times more abominable in his eyes, than the most hateful, venomous serpent is in ours."

3. In the sixth paragraph, where does Edwards remind his audience of what action they must take to escape God's wrath? Edwards tells his listeners that they must "pass under a great change of heart" and be "born again."

What behavior does he say is useless to prevent their everlasting destruction? He warns the congregation that it is useless to reform their lives privately, taking refuge in illusions of "peace and safety." He implies that they must publicly profess a lasting conversion to the ways of God.

Interpreting Meanings

4. What does Edwards mean when he says at the end of his sermon that the "door of mercy" is wide open? He means that sinners may return to God with sincere repentance at any time.

Does he talk of God's mercy elsewhere in the sermon? His references to the "hand of God" holding his listeners up and keeping them out of hell, at least for the moment, might be interpreted as allusions to divine mercy. However, he does not use the word *mercy* until the end of the sermon.

5. Edwards is directing his sermon to what he called "natural men," those members of the congregation who have not been "reborn." He wants to make these people *feel* the truth of his statements, as direct experience. He does not want them simply to understand his sermon abstractly. What images in the first four paragraphs do you think helped his listeners to feel the peril of their unregenerate condition? Edwards refers to the "fiery pit of hell" in the first paragraph and mentions its "gaping mouth" in the second. In the third paragraph, he speaks of man's falling through thin air if the sustaining hand of God should be withdrawn. In the fourth paragraph, he compares man's weakness to the heaviness of lead, which will draw him down to hell just as surely as a heavy rock will smash a spider's web.

6. Why does Edwards want his listeners to feel or experience what eternity is? Answers will vary. Probably he wants his listeners to comprehend the nature of eternity so that they will understand what they must go through if they fail to repent.

What does he say to help them experience this difficult concept? He refers to the "millions and millions of ages" that they will spend suffering "this almighty merciless vengeance." He says it is entirely possible that within a very short time some of his listeners will face the everlasting torment of damnation. In other words, hell is not far off and abstract—it is, or may be, imminent and real.

Did you find his description effective? Answers will vary.

7. During Edwards's sermon, some members of the congregation were said to have cried out and fainted in terror. Identify the parts of the sermon you think would have called forth such emotional responses. Answers will vary. One likely part is near the end where Edwards states that some in the congregation may die soon and suddenly, unrepentant, and have to face eternal damnation.

8. Literature offers several examples of "hellfire" sermons. (Another famous one is found in James Joyce's *Portrait of the Artist as a Young Man*.) Think of orations you might hear today. Do they exhibit the imagery and emotional appeals of Edwards's sermon? Answers will vary.

9. Compare Edwards's idea of God in the sermon with the ideas expressed in his autobiography (page 41). Answers will vary. Encourage students to express and defend their views.

Writing About the Sermon
A Creative Response

1. Adapting the Sermon. As a replacement for Edwards's "O sinner!," ask students to suggest some forms of address a television evangelist might use today. Discuss the differences between Edwards's audience and the mass-media audience of today.

Criteria for Evaluating the Assignment. The paper adapts two paragraphs of Edwards's sermon so that the parallels with Edwards's sermon are clear, but does so in language appropriate for a contemporary American audience.

2. Using Another Point of View. The assignment implies a first-person reaction. Students might think of the paragraph as a journal entry or segment of a conversation or letter. Remind students that the sermon so affected the original congregation that the minister had to ask for quiet several times.

Criteria for Evaluating the Assignment. The paragraph reveals *either* the effect of the sermon personally on the member of the congregation *or* the effect the writer saw revealed by the faces, words, and behavior of others present.

Extending the Sermon

In *The Minister's Wooing*, an all but forgotten novel published in 1859, Harriet Beecher Stowe, daughter of the famous minister Lyman Beecher, describes a mother lamenting the death of her unreligious son. Have students comment on the mother's reaction:

> I cannot, will not be resigned. It is all so unjust, cruel! To all eternity I will say so. To me there is no goodness, no justice, no mercy. . . . Think of all those awful ages of eternity! And then think of all God's power and knowledge used on the lost to make them suffer! . . . Frightful, unspeakable . . . !

Primary Sources: Journals — Text page 41

Students may be asked to read these journal entries aloud. Point out that journals, as highly personal primary sources, often reveal the character of the writer. Ask students how they would characterize Jonathan Edwards based on these three journal entries. Have them note that the character of a person (Jonathan Edwards) can also be revealed by the observations of another person (Esther).

Anne Bradstreet — Text page 42

"Here Follow Some Verses upon the Burning of Our House, July 10, 1666" — Text page 43

Objectives

1. To identify and explain an extended metaphor
2. To analyze word choice
3. To write a paragraph analyzing the writer's attitude
4. To analyze the use of inversions to accommodate meter

12   The Colonial Period

Introducing the Poem

Background on the Poem. Even though Anne Bradstreet was recognized in her own time as a significant poet, the Puritans did not celebrate earthly glory. There is no portrait of Anne Bradstreet, no grave marker for her, and no Bradstreet house still standing. Her poetry is her monument. It reveals her as a talented poet and a charming woman.

The Literal Meaning. Awakened by shouts of "Fire!," Bradstreet escapes from her house, then watches the flames consume it. When she passes the ruins, she thinks about her lost possessions, her memories, and the events that will never occur there. She chides herself for contemplating "wealth on earth," knowing that it is God who laid her worldly goods "in the dust." She realizes that her true house, hope, and treasure lie in heaven.

Teaching Strategies

Providing for Cultural Differences. Students from different backgrounds will be able to identify more easily with Bradstreet's sorrow than with many other Puritan sentiments. Discuss how cultures differ in the emphasis they place on material things. For instance, would the Wampanoags have been equally disturbed by the destruction of one of their lodges?

Providing for Different Levels of Ability. With less able readers, you may want to go through the poem line by line, "translating" each one—especially those with inversions—into language that all students can understand.

Introducing Vocabulary Study. Knowing the meanings of the following words is important to understanding the selection. (Starred words appear in the Glossary. Italicized words either are archaic or have special meanings in context.)

piteous	l. 4	vanity	l. 36
*spy**	l. 7	chide	l. 37
repine	l. 18	mold'ring	l. 39
recounted	l. 32	dunghill	l. 42

In considering the vocabulary for this selection, students should be aware of the connotations of the words. Discuss with students, for example, the effect achieved by the poet through the use of the words *piteous, mold'ring,* and *dunghill.*

Reading the Poem. Remind students that although the Puritans were industrious and often acquired material goods (the Bradstreets lost 800 books in this fire), they were not supposed to desire possessions. Bradstreet's emotional conflict between the loss of a comfortable, memory-filled house and her Puritanical belief that such a loss does not matter is what gives Anne Bradstreet's poem its poignancy. It is what prompts the extended metaphor at the end.

Reading Check. You might want to use the following questions as a reading check. Have students choose the letter of the word or phrase that best completes each of the sentences.

1. Anne Bradstreet's first thought on hearing "Fire!" was (a) to rescue her books (b) to ask God for strength (c) to try to find whoever was shrieking (d) to save her jewels   (b)
2. When she can no longer watch the flames, she (a) lays down the goods she had saved (b) cries (c) walks sadly away (d) praises God   (d)
3. Later on, one thing she does *not* think about is (a) her former guests (b) her trunk and chest (c) her lost clothing (d) her memories of stories told in the destroyed house   (c)
4. Bradstreet begins to chide herself because (a) she made no fire-prevention plans (b) she is glad the house burned down (c) she has been thinking about material goods (d) there is no insurance on the property   (c)
5. The house she feels she should be thinking about is (a) a house in heaven (b) a house far more richly furnished than the one that burned (c) her home in England (d) a house being planned by an architect   (a)

Reteaching Alternatives. The last verse of the 23rd Psalm is one of many Biblical references to a home in heaven: "Surely goodness and mercy shall follow me all the days of my life: and I will dwell in the house of the Lord for ever." You may wish to read that verse in class and have students discuss how it applies to Bradstreet's poem.

Responding to the Poem   Text page 44
Analyzing the Poem
Identifying Details

1. What are some of the specific losses that Bradstreet dwells on in the first half of the poem? She mentions the loss of her dwelling place in line 12 and of her goods in line 15. In lines 23–26 she nostalgically recalls the places where she used to sit and lie in the house, and she mentions a trunk and a chest. In lines 27–34 she laments the loss of future pleasant hours in the house.

2. Bradstreet speaks of another "house" in an extended metaphor at the end of the poem. What is this house, who is its architect, and how is it more perfect than the house she has lost? The house is heaven, whose architect is God ("framed by that mighty Architect," line 44). It is more perfect than the poet's earthly home because it is richly furnished with glory. It has also been paid for with a price "so vast as is unknown" (line 49), probably a reference to the suffering, death, and resurrection of Christ.

Anne Bradstreet   13

Interpreting Meanings

3. *Pelf*—a word designating riches or worldly goods—is usually used only when the riches or goods are considered to be slightly tainted, ill-gotten, or stolen. Why do you suppose Bradstreet uses such a bitter word in line 52 to describe her own cherished treasures? Bradstreet uses this surprisingly negative word because she has come to regard her earthly treasures as insignificant—even bad—compared with the treasure of immortal life.

4. At the very end of the poem, are you convinced that the speaker means what she says? Some readers have felt that, by so lovingly enumerating her losses, Bradstreet is "crying to heaven" in a way that, unconciously, reveals more attachment to her earthly possessions than she would admit to. Do you think these readers have a point? Explain. Answers will vary. Encourage students to express their opinions. Stress that there is no single right way to react to or interpret a poem. It is a bit difficult, however, to argue for a meaning that the author seems not to have had in mind (note the word *unconsciously* in the question). Within the context of the poem there is little reason to doubt Bradstreet's sincerity or religious beliefs. Her human impulse to lament misfortune seems, on the textual evidence, to have been conquered by her faith.

Writing About the Poem
A Critical Response

Analyzing the Writer's Attitude. Review the information on Puritan thought ("A Comment on the Poem," page 44) before students do the assignment.

Criteria for Evaluating the Assignment. Paraphrased, lines 14–20 should read something like this:

> I blessed God, who gave and took away,
> Who reduced everything I owned to dust.
> That's the way it was, and it was fair:
> My property was His anyway, not mine,
> So it's not my place to complain.
> It would have been fair for Him to take everything,
> 20 But He left us with enough.

The paragraph interprets the lines as revealing a belief that God has a purpose for everything, and states that this belief could be especially comforting to an immigrant, who would face many hard times.

Analyzing Language and Style
The "Poetic Style"

Students should note that the iambic beat disappears when lines are written in normal order, even if they are not paraphrased. For example, lines 27–30 would scan as follows:

> My pleasant things lie in ashes,
> And I shall behold them no more.
> No guest shall sit under thy roof,
> Nor eat a bit at thy table.

Extending the Poem

In his 1956 poem "Homage to Mistress Bradstreet," John Berryman pictures the struggle that this intelligent Puritan woman had in her life and with her beliefs. Students may be asked to interpret the following lines from the poem:

> John Cotton shines on Boston's sin—
>
> I am drawn, in pieties that seem
>
> The weary drizzle of an unremembered dream.
>
> Women have gone mad
>
> at twenty-one
>
> I must be disciplined,
>
> in arms, against that one, and our
>
>   dissidents, and myself.

Edward Taylor   Text page 45

"Upon a Spider Catching a Fly"   Text page 46

From "God's Determinations Touching His Elect"   Text page 49

Objectives

1. To interpret a complex metaphor
2. To identify and analyze poetic elements
3. To rewrite a poem as prose

14 The Colonial Period

Background on the Poems. The editors of W. W. Norton's *The American Tradition in Literature* sum up Taylor's poetry in this way:

> Taylor's work was uneven; yet at his best he produced lines and passages of startling vitality, fusing lofty concept and homely detail in the memorable fashion of great poetry. He was a true mystic, whose experience still convinces us, and one of four or five American Puritans whose writings retain the liveliness of genuine literature.

The Literal Meaning. "Upon a Spider Catching a Fly": In the first five stanzas, a spider weaves a web to catch a fly. Instead it catches a wasp. Because the wasp can match the spider's powers and ruin the web, the spider treats the wasp gently. A trapped fly is less fortunate; the spider bites its head, killing it. The last five stanzas explain the meaning of this parable. The spider represents Satan; the wasp represents a person with grace, one who therefore has the power to destroy Satan's web; the fly is a sinful person, destined to be destroyed by the power of Satan.

From "God's Determinations—the Preface": In a series of metaphorical questions, the speaker asks who created the world and "hung the twinkling lanthorns [lanterns/stars] in the sky." His answer is God—the "Might Almighty." God's power is infinite. He created "nothing man" and gave him "all." But "nothing man" threw it all away by sinning and now, burdened with evil, is darker than coal.

Teaching Strategies

Providing for Cultural Differences. All the writers discussed so far, including Taylor, came from English backgrounds. Some were born in England. All lived in what is now the state of Massachusetts. This narrow focus should not blind students to the fact that many nations had a hand in the exploration and building of America. By the early 1700's all the following nations had played a role in our colonial history: Iroquois, Algonquin, and other eastern groups or tribes; Spain; Holland; France; Italy. You may want to ask students to specify some of these nations' contributions. Why are their writers not represented in American literature? [Indians—lack of written language; others—writing not in English; most of it utilitarian, not literary]

Providing for Different Levels of Ability. "Upon a Spider Catching a Fly" is a delightful poem that looks easier to read than it is. With slower students, you may want to explain the meaning of each stanza, then have one student read the poem aloud. Advise all students to read the accompanying explanatory material carefully. It helps clarify both this poem and the next one. Better students will find the Creative Response assignment challenging.

Introducing Vocabulary Study. Knowing the meanings of the following words is important to understanding the selection. (Starred words appear in the Glossary. Italicized words either are archaic or have special meanings in context.)

"*Upon a Spider Catching a Fly*"

| *fret* | l. 19 | stratagems | l. 37 |

From "*God's Determinations Touching His Elect*"

trim	l. 4	*span*	l. 26
lanthorns	l. 18	*imbossed*	l. 39
mete*	l. 26	lightsome	l. 42

Reading the Poems. For both poems, students may find it helpful to go over the questions at the end before reading the poems. Most students probably know how and why a spider spins a web, but before reading the first poem, it may be a good idea to reinforce that knowledge. Before reading the second poem, students might try to name five kinds of seventeenth-century crafts. In reading the poem, they can see whether Taylor includes these crafts when marveling at God's creation of the world. An audiocassette recording of the excerpt from "God's Determinations Touching His Elect" is available.

Reading Check. You might want to use the following questions as a reading check. Have students respond *True* or *False*.

1. The fly in the poem "Upon a Spider Catching a Fly" represents the "elect" or saved Puritan.   False
2. The spider treats the wasp with gentleness and careful attention.   True
3. In the "Preface" from "God's Determinations," the poet asks a number of metaphorical questions about how the world was created.   True
4. The poet believes that God's power, although great, is limited by events beyond even His control.   False
5. God's gift of "all" to "nothing man" was stolen by Satan and cast into a coalpit.   False

Reteaching Alternatives. Have all students write a one-sentence statement of the theme of each of the Taylor poems. Read five of the statements aloud for each poem and have students select the one they think best. Put the two statements on the chalkboard. See if further improvements or refinements can be made in either of them.

"Upon a Spider Catching a Fly"

Responding to the Poem   Text page 47
Analyzing the Poem
Identifying Details

1. The poem begins with a parable, a brief story drawn from everyday life that is used to teach a lesson. This parable has three characters: the spider, the wasp, and the fly. How does the spider treat the wasp that has fallen into its net, and how does it treat the fly? The spider stays apart from the wasp and gently taps its back. When the fly is caught in the net, the spider catches it and kills it.

Why does the spider treat its two victims differently? The spider is afraid of the wasp's sting, but the fly is defenseless and poses no threat.

2. Like the fly, who has no defenses against the spider, people have no strength of their own to fight sin. What warning does Taylor give in lines 28–30? Taylor urges us not to overestimate our own strength by struggling against nature and God, or by struggling against temptation without God's grace. We are likely to be destroyed, just as the fly is destroyed by the spider.

3. In line 31, the poet begins to talk about connections he notices between this natural scene and something in our own existence. What is "Hell's spider," and what does it do to "Adam's race"? Hell's spider is the devil, or Satan, who seeks to trap humanity ("Adam's race") in a web of temptation and evil.

Who alone can break the cords spun by Hell's spider? God alone is powerful enough to break these cords.

4. Taylor uses rhymes to create an intricate network or "web" of repeated sounds. Describe the pattern of end rhymes in the poem. What examples can you find of internal rhymes, that is, rhyming words that occur within the lines? The end rhyme scheme is generally abacc, although this is sometimes varied to ababb (in the sixth stanza, for example), and the rhymes are often slant rhymes (or half rhymes), as in *tap* and *back* in lines 14 and 15. Examples of internal rhyme occur in line 26, "this goes to pot, that not," and line 43, "Thy grace to break the cord, afford."

Interpreting Meanings

5. Summarize the lesson Taylor is teaching in his parable of the spider, the wasp, and the fly. Taylor's parable teaches the lesson that to prevail against evil, we must have a strong defense (God's grace), similar to the wasp's defense (its sting) against the spider. If we try to prevail against evil on our own, without the help of God, we will be defenseless and doomed, like the fly.

What kinds of people do you think the wasp and the fly represent? The wasp represents the faithful person who strives against evil, using God's grace as a weapon to defeat Satan. The fly represents the foolish person who believes he or she can prevail without the help of God. Taylor probably intends the wasp as a figure for the good Puritan.

6. Explain how you feel about poems like this one that teach lessons. Answers will vary.

Writing About the Poem
A Creative Response

1. Rewriting the Poem. Before students begin to write, review the concepts of word inversion and paraphrasing. Suggest that students read "Elements of Literature: The Conceit" (page 48) in order to be able to paraphrase "glory's cage" (line 48). Paraphrases should resemble the following:

You sad, poisonous thing. Is this your game—spinning webs out of yourself to catch a fly? Why do you do it? Once I saw an agitated wasp fall into your web. Fearing its sting, you didn't grab it. You stroked it gently so that it wouldn't get angry and wreck your web. But when a stupid fly got caught by one leg, you quickly bit it to death. Just as that fly was doomed, so are people who don't follow natural reason. Reader, don't try to go beyond your own strength or you too will lose the fight. The battle looks like this to me. The devil spins out tough cords, weaving tricky nets to entangle us descendants of Adam and lead us into sin. Please Lord, send your grace to break the cords and lead us through your heavenly gates. When we sit on high in glorious sanctuary with you, we will sing your praise as joyfully and gratefully as nightingales.

A Critical Response

2. Comparing Spiders. Have students reread the paragraph in which Edwards uses a spider image (page 39). Elicit from students that his spider stands not for the devil, as in Taylor's poem, but for the loathsome (human) sinner.

Criteria for Evaluating the Assignment. The paragraph notes a resemblance in that both Edwards and Taylor connect the spider with sin; but also a difference, in that Edwards uses the spider to represent a sinful human being fit only to be cast into hell, while Taylor uses the spider to represent the cruel, clever devil who traps human beings into sinning.

Elements of Literature: The Conceit
Text page 48

You might tell students to think of a conceit as a "far-out" metaphor. Because it *is* "far-out", the associations the writer is making often require careful thought on the part of the reader. Students are asked how Taylor can compare salvation to being caged. The text goes on to explain the paradox and complexity involved in the answer. When students write their own conceit, remind them of the "far-out" requirement. An original metaphor, even a good one, is not enough—the metaphor must be unusual or fanciful. Ask students to be prepared to explain their conceits.

From "God's Determinations Touching His Elect"

Responding to the Poem *Text page 51*
Analyzing the Poem
Identifying Details

1. According to the first two lines, what was the whole world "built" from? It was built from nothing.

2. The poet draws images from human life—specifically, from life in a Puritan village—to talk about the act of creation, something that is impossible for human beings to imagine. Identify the various crafts and practical occupations that the poet refers to. Taylor refers to pottery (lines 3–4), blowing the bellows of a furnace (line 5), casting an object in a mold (line 6), building (lines 7–8), embroidery (lines 9–12), and decorating the rooms of a house (lines 13–17).

3. Find the lines in which the poet conveys to us the terrifying power of God, a power far greater than that of any human artisan. In lines 25–26, Taylor says that God's "little finger at his pleasure can/Out mete ten thousand worlds with half a span." The whole passage from line 19 to line 30 stresses God's terrifying power.

4. According to lines 37–38, what is the purpose of human existence in God's world? The purpose of human existence is to glorify God.

Interpreting Meanings

5. What is the "gem" that God sets in "nothing" (line 39)? The gem is the immortal soul of every human being.

   In the last image of the poem, what has become of this gem? The gem is like a diamond that has grown darker than a piece of coal.

   What Biblical event might the poet be referring to here? The poet is probably referring to Adam's disobedience in the Garden of Eden.

6. The first part of the poem is a series of questions. How does Taylor answer his own questions? He begins his answer at the end of line 19 ("Why, know..."). The answer stresses God's omnipotence and humanity's ingratitude and sinfulness.

   What feelings about God is this series of questions designed to create? The questions are intended to produce awe in man at God's great power in creating the universe. God is infinitely powerful, and man is puny and insignificant—even "nothing"—in comparison.

7. Taylor often uses puns, or plays on words, and paradoxes, or expressions that seem to be contradictory. What paradox do you find in line 36? The paradox is that God has created "all" out of "nothing" (the void).

   What pun does the poet use in line 28? The poet puns on the noun *rocks*, meaning "stones," and the verb *rock*, meaning "to shake."

8. It is possible that Taylor used this poem in one of his sermons. What effect do you think it would have had on a congregation? Answers will vary. You may suggest that students compare its likely effects on an audience with the effects mentioned for Jonathan Edwards's "Sinners in the Hands of an Angry God" (page 36).

Writing About the Poem
A Critical Response

Comparing the Poem with Job. Read aloud the excerpt from the Book of Job and provide the students with reference copies of Chapters 38–41. Call to their attention the organizational outline given in the final paragraph of the writing assignment.

Criteria for Evaluating the Assignment. The essay cites the question-answer format as a structural similarity; cites, as the answer used by both writers, "See what God can

Edward Taylor 17

do!"; lists "homely" images and metaphors from both Taylor and Job, such as "foundations," "doors," "quilts," and "bowling alley"; and concludes that each passage suggests that, compared with God, man is nothing.

Analyzing Langauge and Style
Imagery

A few of the sights are a marked globe, a vast furnace, a mold for making the world, pillars, rivers like green ribbons, a silver box, a bowling alley, and twinkling lanterns. Some sounds include God's voice, rocking of the hills, and quaking aspen leaves. Textures are implied by the "laced and filleted" earth, the touch of a little finger, "spun" curtains, "imbossed" gems.

Students will vary in selection of the images they find most fantastic and most successful in describing the world and its creation. Crafts and occupations Taylor might use today could range from the microchip industry to laser surgery or the piloting of space ships.

Extending the Poems

Students may be asked to interpret the following two stanzas from Edward Taylor's "Sacramental Meditations, XXXVIII."

I JOHN II: 1: And if any man sin, we have an
   advocate with the Father.

God's Judge himselfe, and Christ Atturny is;
   The Holy Ghost Regesterer is founde.
Angells the sergeants are, all Creatures kiss
   The booke, and doe as Evidence abounde,
   All Cases pass according to pure Law,
   And in the sentence is no Fret nor flaw.

My Case is Bad, Lord, be my Advocate.
   My sin is red: I'me under Gods Arrest.
Thou hast the Hit of Pleading; plead my state.
   Although it's bad, thy Plea will make it best.
   If thou wilt plead my Case before the King,
   I'le Waggon Loads of Love and Glory bring.

William Byrd
Text page 53

From *The History of the Dividing Line*
Text page 54

Objectives

1. To analyze the writer's point of view
2. To interpret elements of satire
3. To analyze the writer's diction
4. To write an essay contrasting purpose, tone, and style in two selections
5. To write a paragraph analyzing the position of women

Introducing the History

Although Byrd's journal reads as if it were written for publication, it was not. The manuscript was found among Byrd's papers at Westover and was first published in 1841, nearly a hundred years after his death.

Summary. Byrd discusses the aims and character of the early settlers, calling Jamestown's founders "about a hundred...reprobates of good families." He praises John Smith's bravery and leadership. He argues that English settlers should have intermarried with the Native Americans, comments somewhat sarcastically on the Puritans of New England, and describes in detail the religion of the expedition's Indian guide, Bearskin.

Teaching Strategies

Providing for Cultural Differences. Byrd's liberal views on marriage between the Indians and settlers can provide background for discussion. Students might discuss reasons Byrd favors intermarriage and whether they feel Byrd's position to be a reasonable one.

Providing for Different Levels of Ability. This is a much

18 The Colonial Period

easier selection to read than preceding ones. If you discuss with students the biographical material on page 53 and then have students work with the vocabulary before beginning to read the selection, students should have few problems. More advanced students can be asked to point out examples of satire in the history.

Introducing Vocabulary Study. Knowing the meanings of the following words is important to understanding the selection. (Starred words appear in the Glossary. Italicized words either are archaic or have special meanings in context.)

maritime*	54	blanched	56
modish	54	*livres*	56
massy	54	propagated	56
frugality*	54	idolatry	57
distemper	54	innumerable	57
eminent*	54	venerable*	57
vigilance*	54	insupportably	58
gentiles	55	tresses	58
enfeebled*	56	tribunal	58
heathens	56	bliss*	58
affinities	56		

Reading the History. Before students read the selection, you might ask them to assume the identity of a Puritan and write a journal entry expressing a Puritan viewpoint toward the worldly and sophisticated Southern plantation life in Virginia, as it has been described in published accounts and rumors. After students have read the selection, have them compare their journal accounts with the views Byrd expresses.

Reading Check. You might want to use the following questions as a reading check. Have students choose the letter of the word or phrase that best completes each of the sentences.

1. Byrd pictures the earliest Virginia settlers as (a) pious (b) lazy (c) timid (d) enterprising   (b)
2. Intermarriage with the Indians, according to Byrd, would have served to (a) ensure peace (b) disgrace Captain Smith (c) promote trade (d) enrage the Puritans   (a)
3. Byrd writes that, despite mistakes, the Plymouth Colony (a) was more prosperous than Virginia (b) encouraged intermarriage with the natives (c) revolted (d) succeeded   (d)
4. Bearskin believes in (a) one supreme God (b) an angry god (c) many equal gods (d) predestination   (a)
5. In hell, as Bearskin pictures it, the weather is always (a) warm (b) wintry (c) blazingly hot (d) rainy   (b)

Reteaching Alternatives. Ask four volunteers to play the part of William Byrd. Have each of them take one of the four excerpts—"Early Virginia Colonies," "Intermarriage," "The New England Colonies," "The Native Religion"—and present Byrd's ideas orally, putting them entirely in modern conversational English. The class might be asked to judge the four Byrds on the basis of each one's accuracy, thoroughness, and persuasiveness.

Responding to the History   Text page 58
Analyzing the History
Identifying Facts

1. What reasons does Byrd suggest for the failure of the first Virginia settlement? Byrd says that the entire idea of settling America was a "modish frenzy." Furthermore, he suggests that the company sponsoring the first expedition was too frugal. Finally, he notes that the first settlers were "starved or cut to pieces by the Indians," and he comments on the colonists' disagreements and laziness.

2. According to Byrd, did the first colonists have realistic expectations of life in the New World? Explain his point of view. Byrd thinks the expectations of the first colonists were unrealistic. He believes that many settlers were encouraged to travel to Virginia by false accounts of explorers and adventurers that proclaimed the New World to be a paradise.

3. For what reasons is Byrd in favor of intermarriage with Native Americans? Byrd thinks that lasting peace could have been achieved if the English had been willing to marry Native Americans, who were tall, healthy, strong, and generally moral. He believes that the French benefited from intermarriage and thinks that the English would have, too.

Are his interests here primarily moral or primarily practical? Explain. Byrd's interests seem decidedly practical, although he "cannot think that the Indians were much greater heathens than the first adventurers, who, had they been good Christians, would have had the charity to take this only method of converting the natives to Christianity."

Interpreting Meanings

4. Like many English writers of the time, Byrd excels at satire, the use of ridicule to expose the faults or weaknesses of people or institutions. From his scathing portrait of the early settlers of Virginia in the first passage of this selection, what personal qualities do you think Byrd admired? Byrd evidently admired a realistic outlook, practicality, industriousness, cooperation, and—as shown by his remarks on Captain John Smith—bravery and vigilance.

5. What is Byrd's attitude toward the Puritans of New England? Tell how his diction, or choice of words, reveals this attitude. Byrd does not seem to be an admirer of the New England Puritans. He speaks of a "swarm of dissenters" fleeing there. A "false delicacy" made them "disgusted" with the Indians. A hint of jealousy appears in Byrd's assertion that they triumphed over difficulties, "being well supported from home." Finally, Byrd says they "thought themselves persecuted at home," implying that he tends to doubt the reality of the persecution.

6. According to his description of the native religion, what "articles," or elements, of religion does Byrd consider most important? In his discussion of Bearskin, Byrd reveals that he considers "three great articles of natural religion" important: belief in God, the moral distinction between good and evil, and the expectation of rewards and punishments in another world.

Consider Byrd's attitudes toward religion as revealed in his remarks on intermarriage, on the New England colonists, and on Native American theology. How closely do his views accord with those of Mary Rowlandson (page 24)? Whereas Mary Rowlandson shows the Puritan tendency to regard even the most mundane event as evidence of God's will, William Byrd is more worldly and practical. Students may agree, however, that Byrd's essential religious beliefs do not differ greatly from those of Rowlandson. It is Byrd's *style* that contrasts with Rowlandson's. Breezy, down-to-earth, and witty, his history differs from the scrupulously serious Puritan journals.

7. Did you find Byrd a more or less interesting writer than the other Colonials? Answers will vary.

Writing About the History
A Critical Response

1. Contrasting Two Histories. Briefly review the content, tone, purpose, and style of Bradford's account of the Puritan landing before students begin to write.

Criteria for Evaluating the Assignment. The essay contrasts the sober historical purposes of Bradford with the entertaining, informative purposes of Byrd. The essay contrasts the serious, religious tone of Bradford with the light, mocking tone of Byrd. The essay contrasts the Biblical allusions of Bradford with the literary allusions of Byrd.

2. Analyzing the History. Having students list passages that explicitly mention women should lead them to conclude that women are simply not important in Byrd's world view except as marriage partners or as fierce goddesses. They are not even explicitly mentioned in the section on "Intermarriage"; they are mentioned only in paragraph 2 of "Early Virginia Colonies," page 54, and passages from "The Native Religion," page 58.

Criteria for Evaluating the Assignment. The paragraph comments on the scarcity of mention and the negative images conveyed in those passages. The writer concludes that in Byrd's world, men must have dominated, and women simply did not count, except as beings to be wooed or placated by men.

Extending the History

William Byrd's Westover, one of the first large plantation houses on the James River, is a notable example of Georgian architecture. Built in the 1730's, it still stands and is privately owned, as are a number of the elegant plantation houses of Tidewater Virginia. For a research project, you may want to have students report on one or more of the prominent families or great estates of colonial Virginia.

Family	*Estate*
Byrd	Westover
Mason	Gunston Hall
Harrison	Berkeley *and* Brandon
Carter	Carter's Grove *and* Shirley
Lee	Stratford
Tyler	Sherwood Forest

The American Language   Text page 62

1. Students are to choose any five of the following state names. They should use a dictionary to find out what language each name comes from, and what the name means.

Alabama: probably after the Alibamu Indian tribe and river
Arizona: < Papago, "place of the small spring"
Arkansas: French derivation for the name of the Quapaw Indians
Connecticut: < Algonquian, "long-tidal-river-at"
Idaho: < Kiowa-Apache name for the Comanche
Illinois: French derivation from Iliniwek, "tribe of superior men"
Iowa: named for Iowa Indians of the Siouan family
Kansas: named for the Kansa Indians, "people of the south wind"
Kentucky: < Wyandot, "land of tomorrow," or < Iroquois, "meadow land"
Massachusetts: < Algonquian, "at the Great Hill"

Michigan: < Algonquian, "big lake"
Minnesota: < Sioux, "sky-tinted water"
Mississippi: < Ojibwa, "great river"
Missouri: < Iliniwek, "owners of big canoes"
Nebraska: < Sioux, "flat water"
North Dakota: < Sioux, "allies"
Ohio: < Iroquois, "beautiful"
Oklahoma: < Choctaw, "land of the red people"
South Dakota: < Sioux, "allies"
Tennessee: from the proper name for a Cherokee town
Texas: < Caddo, "friends"
Utah: named for the Ute Indians
Wisconsin: < Ojibwa, "place of the beaver"
Wyoming: < Delaware, "large plains"

2. Students are to use a dictionary to trace the origins of the following words. They should tell what each word means in contemporary American usage.

bayou: a marshy arm, inlet, or outlet of a lake or river; from Choctaw *bayuk*, a river forming a part of a delta
caucus: meeting of party leaders or a faction within a party; perhaps from Algonquin
mackinaw: a short, double-breasted coat; origin uncertain
podunk: any small or insignificant town or village; from the name of a village near Hartford, Connecticut
poke: pokeweed; perhaps a variant of *puccoon*, from Virginia Algonquin
toboggan: a long, flat-bottomed, narrow sled; from Maliseet-Passamaquoddy
totem: a natural object or animate being assumed as an emblem of a clan, family, or group; from Ojibwa

3. Students are to locate the original meanings of the following words.

opossum: white dog
moose: moose

chipmunk: red squirrel; headfirst
caribou: snow-shoveler
tobacco: a pipe for smoking; a roll of leaves smoked
squash: squash
pecan: nut
hominy grits: something ground or beaten

4. Students are to tell what language each of the following geographical names comes from and what it translates to. They should then use their answers to explain why Cooper called Indian languages "figurative."

Chattahoochee River: < Muskogean (Creek), "rocks-marked"
Cheyenne: from an Indian tribal name
Erie: from an Indian tribal name
Lake Mohawk: from an Indian tribal name
Nantucket: < Algonquian, "narrow-river-at"
Okefenokee Swamp: < Muskogean (Hichiti), "water-shaking"
Omaha: from an Indian tribal name
Minneapolis: < Sioux, "water-falls," combined with Greek *polis*, "city"
Missouri: < Iliniwek, "owners of big canoes"
Potomac River: possibly < Algonquian, "something brought"
Spokane: < Siwash, "sun"
Tacoma: possibly means "mountain" or "snow-peak" in language of Washington Indians
Winnebago: from an Indian tribal name
Yosemite: from an Indian tribal name, possibly meaning "grizzly bear"

5. Students should identify the figures of speech in the Tewa song of "the sky loom." Possibilities include the following metaphors: "warp" in line 1, "weft" in line 2, "fringes" in line 3, "border" in line 4, and "mother" and "Father" in line 8.

Exercises in Critical Thinking and Writing Text page 63

Determining the Precise Meanings of Words

For this exercise, it is important that students use an unabridged dictionary, such as the ones mentioned in the student text, since abridged dictionaries do not give complete etymologies, nor do they indicate archaic meanings. If students need help in reading etymologies, refer them to the explanatory material in the front matter of the dictionary. Students will also need to refer to the key to abbreviations and symbols used in etymologies, also found in the front matter.

As a prewriting exercise, you might select one word from the excerpts on text page 64 and complete the chart during a class discussion.

Criteria for Evaluating the Assignment. Student essays should include the etymology of the word and its meaning in the context of the excerpt. If the word implies a value judgment, adequate evidence should be cited to support that judgment.

Exercises in Critical Thinking and Writing 21

Unit Two: *The Revolutionary Period: The Age of Reason*

Text page 28

Teaching The Revolutionary Period Unit

This unit focuses on the founding of the American nation and the development of a distinct American character and philosophy. The literary style of this period swings from the plain prose and sly wit of Benjamin Franklin's *Remarks Concerning the Savages of North America* to the impassioned oratory of Patrick Henry's speech to the Virginia Convention. Despite the varieties of style, students will recognize two themes that link each selection: the moral progress both of the individual and of the state. The selections emphasize self-examination and self-improvement, most notably in Franklin's autobiography, in Jefferson's letter to his daughter that appears in the student text as a primary source, and in Thomas Paine's and Patrick Henry's exhortations to fellow citizens to search themselves for the strength and spirit to support the Revolution. You may want to emphasize the similarities among the selections, for students may not always recognize the thematic relationship of an essay to a letter or autobiography.

As the unit introduction in the student text notes, some of these early American writings have equivalents in such contemporary forms as the popular autobiography and the self-help book. The popularity of these genres, then and now, makes for some interesting literary and social comparisons. Then, as now, America has been, in the words of the art critic Harold Rosenberg, "the civilization of people engaged in attempting to transform themselves." You might ask students whether this perception of the American spirit matches their own perception and experiences. This unit introduces literary devices and forms such as persuasion, propaganda, allusion, imagery, metaphor, first-person point of view, and the aphorism, or maxim. Discussions of rhetorical devices are particularly suited to this unit because eighteenth-century prose was often propagandistic in nature and marked by fluency and balance derived from classical models.

The writings in this unit are by the men most closely associated with the American Enlightenment. They lived in a time of turbulence and change that America did not experience again until the Civil War. They used the written word almost as a weapon, to rail against Great Britain and to gain support for the Revolution. These men gave shape to our country. They did not have the social, political, or cultural establishment of Great Britain or Europe to rest upon. They had to make a society and culture, build towns and banks and schools, wring a government from the conflicting needs of the great variety of peoples who emigrated to America. They sought to create and define an American character that could encompass the manifold religions and cultures that made up the colonies. A hundred years later Walt Whitman addressed this idea in "Song of Myself," when he wrote, "Very well then, I contradict myself, I contain multitudes." From the first, American thought was as divergent as the many nationalties that today make up the country.

It might be useful for students to look ahead to the Enlightenment's influence on the philosophies, attitudes, and writing styles in nineteenth- and twentieth-century American literature. In this regard, you could cite the wit of Mark Twain, the democratic embrace of Whitman, and the vitalization of the "American idiom" by William Carlos Williams. It would be interesting to test later American literature against the deism and humanistic ideas that are the foundation of this country. Encourage your students to keep in mind such a comparison of theme and style as they progress through the text.

The Enlightenment of the Age of Reason as an international movement was spread throughout the western world, most noticeably in England, France, and Germany. It was an age that believed that there was virtually no limit to what well-intentioned people could accomplish when guided by reason. Reason could alter a corrupt environment and even—as in Adam Smith's version of a free marketplace, guided by an "Invisible Hand"—harmonize competing self-interests. Ignorance, prejudice, and unchecked power were considered primary factors in the corruption and sinfulness of human beings. Such concepts of the Enlightenment, many derived from the British philosopher John Locke, were put directly into the Declaration of Independence and are reflected in much of the other literature in this unit.

Objectives of the Revolutionary Period Unit

1. To improve reading proficiency and expand vocabulary
2. To gain exposure to notable writers of the American Revolutionary period
3. To define and identify significant literary techniques: tone, irony, rhetorical question, allusion, imagery, metaphor, analogy, parallelism, and point of view
4. To interpret and respond to autobiography, an essay, maxims, a speech, and a pamphlet, orally and in writing, through analysis of their elements
5. To identify examples of "heightened style"
6. To recognize the growth of American English
7. To write an essay evaluating a logical argument

8. To practice the following critical thinking and writing skills:
   a. Comparing and contrasting writers
   b. Responding to critical comments
   c. Evaluating word connotations
   d. Comparing and contrasting speeches
   e. Evaluating a generalization
   f. Analyzing reasoning
   g. Responding to a point of view

Introducing the Age of Reason Unit

Before beginning the unit, you might want to discuss how Americans before the Revolution generally felt about Great Britain, how their attitudes changed over time, and how that change was reflected in the writings of the period. This excerpt from Moses Coit Tyler's great literary history of the Revolutionary period gives some of the flavor of that change:

> The deep, true love of Americans for the mother country, their pride in the British empire, their sincerity in the belief that all their political demands were compatible with their own loyalty and with the honor of England, their desire that the solution of every vexing problem should be reached in peace,—all these were realities, realities as genuine as they were pathetic. In the transactions of the nineteenth of April, 1775, at the hands of official representatives of the mother country, all these sacred realities were foully dealt with,—they were stamped upon, were spit upon, they were stabbed and shot at and covered with blood and cast into the mire. Accordingly, reaching this fatal point in his journey across the period of the Revolution, the student of its literature becomes then and there conscious of crossing a great spiritual chasm—of moving from one world of ideas and sentiments to a world of ideas and sentiments quite other and very different.

You might want to discuss briefly with your students how they imagine they would have felt if they had lived in these times. Would they have wanted to remain within the protection of a great empire whose language, culture, and values they shared, or rebelliously declare their independence and face the task of building a new kind of nation? The best reasons for doing the latter can be found in the writings of the authors in this unit, who combined fiery spirit with towering nationality.

Benjamin Franklin

Text page 72

From *The Autobiography*

Text page 74

Objectives

1. To write an essay comparing and contrasting two writers
2. To write an essay evaluating a critical commentary
3. To recognize varieties of English

Introducing the Autobiography

As the text indicates, Benjamin Franklin's life story is a great and various one. Yet for all he accomplished and all that is known about him, he reamins difficult to define. He is for some readers the ideal American. He achieved material success at a young age. He took risks, tried his hand, and succeeded, at many endeavors, and constantly strove to better himself. Other readers find Franklin's emphasis on moralism and materialism restrictive. He has passed on a brilliant and fascinating autobiography, but many critics believe Franklin has removed his personal self from the work and given us instead an idealized life, or, at least, a self-created one. According to these critics, Franklin has created in his *Autobiography* a Benjamin persona, just as he created the persona of Silence Dogwood for his first essay, and later Richard Saunders of *Poor Richard's Almanack*, Father Abraham of *The Way to Wealth*, the Busy Body in the *American Weekly Mercury*, and many others. On the other hand, Frederick Tolles, in an essay on Franklin, writes, "Not only his final *Autobiography* but also a large part of his written work... followed the steps of his life, recording it." Tolles believes the personae Franklin created were mere masks for autobiographical writing.

Background on the Autobiography. Franklin wrote his autobiography with an eye towards reporting his life for the benefit of those who wished to learn from it. Just as he strove to improve his writing style by imitating Addison and others, so the readers of his book might improve themselves by imitating or studying his life. Franklin says just this on the first page of *The Autobiography*:

Having emerg'd from the Poverty & Obscurity in which I was born & bred, to a State of Affluence & some Degree of Reputation in the World, and having gone so far thro' Life with a considerable Share of Felicity, the conducing Means I made use of, which, with the Blessing of God, so well succeeded, my Posterity may like to know, as they may find some of them suitable to their own Situations, & therefore fit to be imitated.

You might use this ideal of Franklin's to discuss the concept of learning by imitation. Do students think they learn this way?

Summary. In "Leaving Boston," young Franklin decides to leave his brother's service. He goes to New York seeking work as a printer, and finds nothing. He next ventures to Philadelphia and has quite an adventure getting there. He gets caught in a storm, saves a drunken man who had fallen overboard, and becomes ill. He walks fifty miles to Burlington, Pennsylvania, stopping at an inn where he is befriended by a retired doctor. He is given shelter by a woman who would have him set up a print shop in Burlington, but instead he finds a boat that will give him passage for Philadephia.

In "Arrival in Philadelphia," Franklin describes his first day in the city. He has trouble communicating with a baker, he passes his future wife. He follows a group of Quakers to their meeting house, where he falls asleep.

"Arriving at Moral Perfection" describes Franklin's plan for achieving moral perfection. He includes his list and definitions of the important virtues, the most important of which is temperance because it is the first step towards self-discipline. This section concludes with a description of his plan for mastering each virtue.

Teaching Strategies

Providing for Cultural Differences. Explain to students that although Franklin and others were committed to developing an American identity, many Colonists thought of themselves as British rather than American.

Providing for Different Levels of Ability. Because of the difficult language and sentence structure, you might find it helpful to list for less advanced students the events that Franklin describes. More advanced students might evaluate the slightly ironic tone of the autobiography and consider whether Franklin is directing it towards himself. All students will be interested in discussing Franklin's plan for moral perfection.

Introducing Vocabulary Study. Knowing the meanings of the following words is important to understanding the selection. (Starred words appear in the Glossary.)

indiscreet*	74	itinerant*	76
obnoxious*	74	arduous*	78
avarice	78	precept*	78
facilitate*	78	rectitude	78
habitude	78	temperance	78
prattle	78		

Point out to the class the abundance of words having to do with bahavior or states of being: *indiscrete, itinerant, temperance, rectitude, avarice, obnoxious.* Have students use as many of the words as possible to write a character description of an imaginary person they would like to know or an imaginary person they would not like to know.

Reading the Autobiography. To prepare students for reading the selection, you might first explain that Franklin's first intent was to teach or edify. Students should be encouraged to read first for the story and then for insight into Franklin's character. You might also ask students to imagine themselves in Franklin's position at age sixteen or seventeen.

Reteaching Alternatives. To ensure that students understand Franklin's method of attaining moral perfection, you might have them paraphrase the paragraph directly following the list of virtues. You might also have students write their own definitions of Franklin's virtues.

Responding to the Autobiography   Text page 80
Analyzing the Autobiography
Identifying Facts

1. Why did Franklin decide to leave Boston secretly? He felt that his brother and father would prevent him from departing if he tried to leave openly.

  How did he raise some money for the journey from Boston to New York? He sold some of his books.

2. What method of writing in John Bunyan's *Pilgrim's Progress* does Franklin single out for praise? He says that John Bunyan was the first to mix narration and dialogue, a method which Franklin considers "very engaging to the reader."

3. Franklin's arrival in Philadelphia has become a favorite American anecdote. At the time he wrote this part of his life story, Franklin was living in England and was already one of the most famous Americans of his century. In contrast, what was Franklin's condition in life when he arrived in Philadelphia? Franklin provides vivid details of his shabby state: he is wearing dirty work clothes, their pockets bulging with shirts and stockings; he is tired and hungry and has only a few coins in his pocket.

4. What virtue does Franklin place first on his list for achieving moral perfection? Why? He places temperance at the head of his list, since it "tends to procure that coolness and clearness of head, which is so necessary where

Benjamin Franklin   25

constant vigilance was to be kept up, and guard maintained, against the unremitting attraction of ancient habits, and the force of perpetual temptations."

Interpreting Meanings

5. Though Franklin discusses his own character at length in his autobiography, many of his personality traits are revealed not through direct statements but through his actions. Explain what the events of the difficult journey from Boston to Philadelphia disclose about the character of the young Franklin. Franklin's saving the Dutchman during the storm reveals that he is quick-thinking; his curing himself of a fever with a remembered "prescription" reveals that he is practical and self-reliant; his speed in locating lodgings when he misses the boat to Philadelphia reveals that he is resourceful and personable.

Do you feel Franklin is being honest, or is he trying to make himself look good? Student answers will vary. Many students may suggest that Franklin may be writing from both motives!

6. What does Franklin's scheme for achieving moral perfection reveal about his views of human nature? Franklin's scheme suggests that he believes that human beings are capable of improving themselves.

What does it suggest about his attitudes toward education? The scheme suggests that Franklin believes education should be methodically organized and planned.

What is your opinion of these views? Student answers will vary.

7. Franklin ends his list of virtues with humility. Did you find evidence of pride—the opposite of humility—in his history, and if so, where? Student answers will vary. Most students will agree that Franklin is disarmingly direct, and that he does not hesitate to criticize his own feelings when he feels he deserves such criticism.

8. Which virtue on his list do you consider most important? Which is least important? Why? Student answers will vary.

9. How does Franklin's scheme for arriving at moral perfection compare with the self-help books available today? Again, student answers will vary. Try to encourage students to name some specific "self-help" titles on subjects such as health, finance, diet, exercise, vocabulary development, etc. Most of the students will agree that these books have material accomplishments, rather than moral perfection, as their goal. Students may point out, however, that Franklin was certainly not immune to the appeal of material accomplishments and worldly success.

Writing About the Autobiography
A Critical Response

1. Comparing and Contrasting Two Writers. The students' writing prompt contains helpful suggestions on how students should prepare to write, but clarify how you want them to organize their papers. You might suggest that they first state how Edwards and Franklin are alike, and then how they differ, citing examples from Edwards's sermon and from Franklin's *Autobiography* to support all major points.

Criteria for Evaluating the Assignment. The essay states one way in which Franklin and Edwards are alike, and three or more ways in which they differ. The essay supports its major points with details from Edwards and Franklin.

2. Responding to Critical Comments. Read aloud the excerpt from Mark Twain, checking students' literal comprehension. Call students' attention to the fact that the prompt outlines the content and organization of their essays.

Criteria for Evaluating the Assignment. The essay consists of three paragraphs. The first paragraph states in the student's own words how Twain felt about Franklin and why he felt that way. The second paragraph correctly describes Twain's tone as satiric (or humorous). The third paragraph gives the student's own reaction to Twain's comments.

Analyzing Language and Style
American English

1. Answers will vary by region of the United States.
2. An English "biscuit" is an American "cookie."
3. Answers will vary by region of the United States.

Extending the Autobiography

Have interested students read *Ben Franklin Laughing,* an entertaining book that also provides a good picture of life in the eighteenth century, or the entire *Autobiography.* Students can discuss whether or not these books changed the image of Franklin they formed from the selections in the text.

Remarks Concerning the Savages of North America

Text page 81

Objectives

1. To analyze satirical devices
2. To evaluate word connotations

Introducing the Essay

Historically, there are two types of satire: Horation satire, which lightly laughs or pokes fun at people or institutions, and Juvenalian satire, which is biting, harsh, and angry. Although this essay is an example of Horation satire, students should know that Franklin did not always write such gentle satire. In other writings, his expression was biting and sarcastic. In one such piece, *An Edict by the King of Prussia,* written in response to England's Stamp Act, Franklin assumes the identity of Frederick III, King of Prussia. He claims that historically England is still a territory of Prussia and therefore is subject to taxation. Franklin was so convincing that many English people believed the "edict" to be real.

Summary. The essay opens with a general assessment of manners. It then describes the social order and responsibilities of the Indian peoples. The Indian life is seen as leisurely compared with the laborious European life. Franklin then describes two incidents between Indians and white men. The first concerns the offer by Virginians to educate Iroquois youths. The Iroquois politely refuse and offer instead, seriously yet sardonically, to educate Virginia youths. Franklin compares the extreme politeness of Indian council meetings and conversation to the argumentative and impolite Europeans. Finally he relates the story of a Swedish minister addressing the Susquehanna Indians. The minister tells the story of Christianity. The Indians respond respectfully and tell their own story, at which the minister scoffs.

Teaching Strategies

Providing for Cultural Differences. Students should be aware that the prevailing attitude of the eighteenth century was that Indians were savages, an attitude that grew out of the vast cultural differences between the European Americans and the nomadic American Indians.

Providing for Different Levels of Ability. The style of the essay is fairly straightforward, and most students will have little trouble understanding the scene. Some, however, may need a bit of help grasping the irony of the piece.

Introducing Vocabulary Study. Knowing the meanings of the following words is important to understanding the selection. (Starred words appear in the Glossary.)

laborious*	81	stipulations	82
posterity	81	maize	83
loquacity*	82		

You might have students collaborate on writing sentences with these words in a style similar to Franklin's. Have students included "loaded words" in their sentences. (See "Analyzing Language and Style," page 83 in the student text.)

Reading the Essay. Refer students to the section of selection headnote that asks them to consider the word "savages." You might want students to pay particular attention to the exchange of European and Indian beliefs on page 83 of the student text, as this section is the crux of Franklin's judgment of the Colonists' attitude to the Indians.

Reading Check. You may want to use the following questions as a reading check. Have students respond with short answers.

1. Why did the Indians refuse the offer to send their youths to white universities? *Their young men returned ignorant of their own people's ways.*

2. How do the Indians record family and tribal histories? *The memory of their women*

3. Why does Franklin say the politeness of Indians was excessive? *Because it left no room for disagreement*

4. How does the Indian orator react to the missionary's story of the beginnings of Christianity? *He misunderstands the import of the story of the forbidden apple, and takes it to mean that it's better to make cider of apples than to eat them as they come off the tree.*

5. How does the missionary react to the Indians' story of their origins and gods? *With disgust*

Reteaching Alternatives. Have students look for techniques Franklin uses that might bring reluctant readers into agreement with him. You might point out his criticism of Indian civility as one means, because it appears to put Franklin in the position of impartial observer.

Benjamin Franklin 27

Responding to the Essay

Text page 83

Analyzing the Essay

Identifying Facts

1. Like many of Franklin's writings, this essay is satirical; it holds certain attitudes up to ridicule. In his opening paragraph, how does Franklin immediately mock the settlers for the name they have given the native inhabitants of North America? Franklin states that the settlers call the American natives "savages" simply because "their manners differ from ours" and points out that the "savages" consider their own manners to be "the perfection of civility," just as the settlers do theirs.

2. Explain how the "savages" differ from the English and the Europeans in their government, education, courtesy, division of labor, and values. The "savages" are ruled by wise, experienced elders. They study oratory as well as hunting and other survival skills, but consider European-style learning to be a waste of time. They consider it rude to give an answer to an official proposal on the day it is made, to interrupt someone who is speaking, or to contradict or disagree with anyone. The women cultivate the land and preserve history through oral tradition as well as bring up the children, while the men hunt and fight. The natives live simply and thus have ample time for "improvement by conversation."

3. Franklin uses a common satirical device in this essay when he reverses certain traditional roles. Such reversals occur when a country bumpkin turns out to be smarter than a city slicker, or when a child turns out to be wiser than a professor. In what ways do the so-called "savages" turn the tables on the "civilized" settlers? When the Virginian settlers offer to educate six Indian youths at college, the Indians refuse—believing a college education would be useless—but politely offer in turn to educate six Virginian youths in hunting and other Indian skills. Again, when a missionary preaches Biblical stories to the Indians, they reciprocate by telling some of their own legends.

Interpreting Meanings

4. How effective do you think this role-reversal is? Most students will agree that the pointed role-reversal in the essay effectively serves Franklin's aims.

5. According to Franklin, who might be the real savages of North America? Why? The real savages of North America might be the European settlers, who cannot appreciate cultures different from their own, and whose manners in some respects appear rude and insensitive in contrast with those of the Indians, as is illustrated in the anecdote of the Swedish minister.

6. What relevance, if any, might this essay have to the world today? The relevance is that people should not think of others as savages before they examine themselves.

Analyzing Language and Style

Loaded Words

Although it is clear that Franklin respects the manners and myths of the American Indians and finds fault with some of the ways of white people, he makes his points mostly through word choice and descriptions of the behavior of Indians and white men. He reports, for example, how politely the Susquehanna chiefs listen to a sermon and how rudely the minister then derides Susquehanna beliefs.

1. "Restricted" is somewhat neutral in connotation; "slavish" and "base" convey far more strongly a life of bondage to inferior values.

2. The statement suggests that the Indians see no practical applications of white men's education in daily life.

3. Words that reveal Franklin's respect for the Indians include "great order and decency," "memories" that are "exact," and "profound silence." Words mocking the English include satiric use of "polite," "makes the speaker hoarse in calling to order," and "impatient loquacity."

Extending the Essay

Have students read other satires by Franklin, including *Rules by Which to Lose a Kingdom* and *King of the Hessians.* The former piece contains a list of "rules" that an empire should follow if it wishes to lose its territories or colonies. The irony is that England had already committed every rule listed.

Sayings of Poor Richard

Text page 84

Objectives

1. To analyze irony
2. To analyze contemporary maxims

Introducing the Maxims

The sayings have affected the lives of countless young Americans, among them Mark Twain, who once wrote, "It has taken me many years and countless smarts to get out of that barbed wire moral enclosure that Poor Richard rigged up." What Twain and others object to is the moral strictures that Franklin imposed (seemingly) on himself, and, through the force of his writing, on his readers. In response to such criticism, Theodore Hornberger, in a pamphlet titled *Benjamin Franklin,* argues that "Franklin often acted upon rasher impulses and nobler principles than those which he publicly avowed." This seems a fair assessment when considering the hundreds of projects in which Franklin involved himself. It often seems he immersed himself in every passing societal need or idea.

Background on the Maxims. To give students an idea of the personality Franklin originally created for Richard Saunders, you might read part of the preface to the first *Poor Richard's Almanack* in 1733.

COURTEOUS READER,

> I might, in this place attempt to gain thy Favour, by declaring that I write Almanacks with no other View than that of the publick Good; but in this I should not be sincere; and Men are now adays too wise to be deceived by Pretences how specious soever. The plain Truth of the Matter is, I am excessive poor, and my Wife, good Woman, is, I tell her, excessive proud; she cannot bear, she says, to sit spinning her Shift of Tow, while I do nothing but gaze at the Stars; and has threatned more than once to burn all my Books and Rattling-Traps (as she calls my Instruments) if I do not make some profitable Use of them for the Good of my Family. The Printer has offer'd me some considerable share of the Profits, and I have thus begun to comply with Dame's Desire.

Critics are divided in how to take the persona of Poor Richard. Some see him as an autobiographical mask, some as a playful and useful creation. Students will want to judge for themselves whether the sayings reflect the character of the Franklin they have studied in the other selections. The Richard Saunders in the 1733 passage quoted above appears cynical and oppressed at home. Many of the maxims certainly convey a similar message. You might lead students to consider whether Poor Richard is more a pragmatist or opportunist. Do they see evidence of either quality in other writings?

Teaching Strategies

Providing for Cultural Differences. Students may be unfamiliar with ideas expressed in proverb form. Explain to them that proverbs, or maxims, take generally known truths or stories and condense them into concise and often terse language. Proverbs, which were very common in Franklin's time, were passed on from one person to another as jokes and gossip are today.

The second maxim uses the image of a man emptying his purse into his head as a metaphor for pursuing knowledge. Students should know that men carried small purses rather than wallets in the eighteenth century.

Providing for Different Levels of Ability. The parallel form of many maxims might confuse some students. To clear up any confusion, you might explain the structure of one or two of the maxims. For instance, maxim number 12 uses the word "composes" in its two clauses. To some students the parallel senses of composing oneself and composing or writing a book will be clear. Other students may need help in understanding that the use of "composing" is a metaphor for developing one's life as carefully as one would write a book.

Reading the Maxims. Before students read the maxims, you might explore the ideas of cynicism and practicality. You can suggest that what appears to be a cynicism initially can prove to be a piece of practical wisdom on subsequent readings. Just as often a reader might mistake for wisdom what is actually cynicism. More often a maxim is open to various interpretation. Suggest that students consider carefully maxims whose meanings seem obvious on first reading.

Reteaching Alternatives. You might bring to class a facsimile of *Poor Richard's Almanack* or another almanac from the period to give students a clearer picture of the uses of the almanac and to provide insight into the daily life of the times.

Also, you might read to the class Robert Frost's poem "The Mending Wall," which addresses more fully the idea expressed in the first maxim in the text.

Responding to the Maxims
Text page 85
Analyzing the Maxims
Interpreting Meanings

1. The sharpness of these sayings is partly due to Franklin's ironic view of human nature and human relationships. People, he implies, are not always what they would like to be (or what they think they are). Which of these sayings reflect this attitude? The first, third, sixth, twelfth, fifteenth, sixteenth, twenty-second, twenty-third, twenty-fourth, and twenty-fifth sayings may be said to reflect this attitude.

2. Franklin is sometimes criticized for equating virtue with wealth and success. Which of these sayings support that criticism? The eighth, tenth, eleventh, and twentieth might be said to support that criticism.

Which do not? The second saying points out that knowledge is more valuable and enduring than wealth, and the fourteenth cautions against placing too much importance on money.

3. A character in a story by Nathaniel Hawthorne says that he does not like Franklin's proverbs because "they are all about getting money or saving it." Hawthorne thought that the proverbs taught people only a very small proportion of their duties. What sorts of duties do you think Hawthorne felt were omitted from Poor Richard's sayings? Do you agree? Answers might suggest that Hawthorne may have felt that duties such as piety, charity, and kindness were omitted from Poor Richard's sayings.

4. Take at least five of these maxims and apply each to a situation in contemporary life—to politics, society, family life, social and private morality, or business. Student answers will vary. Encourage the students to apply the maxims they select to as many diverse situations as they can.

Writing About the Maxims
A Creative Response

Analyzing Contemporary Maxims. To prompt students' recall of contemporary maxims and their creation of new ones, read a few selections from Paul Dickson's *The Official Rules* (Delacorte Press, 1978), or these modern sayings or bumper stickers:

1. If anything can go wrong, it will. (Murphy's Law)
2. There's no such thing as a free lunch.
3. In the fight between you and the world, back the world. (Franz Kafka)
4. Nice guys finish last. (Leo Durocher)
5. It works better if you plug it in.

Criteria for Evaluating the Assignment. The student has listed ten popular sayings or slogans and has made up three new maxims. Each is a complete sentence and rings true in its literal or ironic comment on contemporary life.

Extending the Maxims

Share a modern almanac, such as *The Farmer's Almanac*, and then have students create their own almanac for one month. In addition to astrological forecasts and weather, tides, sunrise, sunset, and so on, suggest to students that the almanac include special school and community events and their own sayings, or maxims. Newspapers and calendars will provide much of the forecasting information that students will need.

Primary Souces: A Letter to Samuel Mather
Text page 86

In this letter Franklin tells a personal anecdote of his learning humility. He also expresses homesickness for Boston, which he has not seen for twenty-two years. The letter is tender and even sentimental, showing a side to Franklin not seen in other selections.

Patrick Henry

Text page 87

Speech to the Virginia Convention

Text page 88

Objectives

1. To identify counter-arguments
2. To analyze the use of metaphor as a tool of persuasion
3. To identify rhetorical questions and explain their uses
4. To interpret allusions
5. To write a newspaper article

Introducing the Speech

The introductory material on Patrick Henry in the student text (page 87) discusses Henry's personal background as well as the historical setting in which the speech was delivered. Although the speech that Henry delivered to the Virginia House of Burgesses in reaction to the Stamp Act did secure Henry's political future (he was later elected to five successive terms as governor of Virginia), he was at the time declared an outlaw by the Virginia governor. Students will also be interested to know that in 1787 Henry was one of many distinguished dissenters (James Monroe was another) to the Constitution who claimed that it did not protect the rights of large numbers of the community, including the poor. Henry became instrumental in the fight to add the amendments to the Constitution that became known as the Bill of Rights.

Background on the Speech. To understand why Henry's speech had to be powerful and convincing, it is important for students to understand the American hesistance to bear arms against Great Britain. As the following excerpt from a Congressional declaration on July 6, 1775, makes clear, even after fighting broke out leaders in America still hoped for reconciliation with the "mother country."

"Lest this declaration should disquiet the minds of our friends and fellow-subjects in any part of the empire, we assure them that we mean not to dissolve that union which has so long and so happily subsisted between us, and which we sincerely wish to see restored.... We have not raised armies with ambitious designs of separating from Great Britain, and establishing Independent States."

Moses Coit Tyler puts the conflict and Henry's crucial role into the clearest perspective when he writes, "After ten years of words, the disputants come at last to blows. Prior to this day, the Revolutionary controversy was a political debate: after that it was a civil war. [And an] immense transformation then and there [was] made in the very character and atmosphere of the struggle—in its ideas, its purposes, its spirit, its tone...." Patrick Henry was at the apex of this transformation. Through the power of words and ideas he helped move the controversy away from ideas into armed resistance.

Summary. Henry opens the speech by paying respect to previous speakers. He then begs to differ with desire to compromise, and states the decision to arm or not arm is a matter of slavery or freedom. He understands the desire to reconcile, but the facts do not warrant such a hope. He asks members of the House to judge from experience, not words, and experience demonstrates that the king means to subjugate. Henry begins the third paragraph with a series of rhetorical questions regarding British military forces and American attempts at reconciliation. The next paragraph, beginning with another series of questions, defends the strength and unity of the Colonies and states that war is inevitable. Henry concludes with a statement that war has already begun and that it is time to rise and fight for liberty.

Teaching Strategies

Providing for Cultural Differences. There will probably be few culturally bound difficulties with this selection; however, the concept of "patriotism" could bear review. In the period just before the Revolutionary War, "patriotism" could refer to patriotism to Great Britain as well as to America. In fact, one Tory argument was that the only thing the Colonies had in common was their relationship to Great Britain, a statement that reveals the enormous cultural and political heritage the Colonies shared with Great Britain.

Providing for Different Levels of Ability. With less-advanced students, you may want to concentrate on having them understand Henry's political ideas rather than his use of language. For these students, you may want to examine the speech paragraph by paragraph, summarizing as you go.

More advanced students will profit from studying the structure of the speech and the literary devices Henry employs so profusely. Guide students through the speech by referring them to specific allusions, metaphors, and rhetorical questions. They can deduce for themselves the intended purpose (such as emotional hook, appeal to common sense, appeal to safety) and determine the effectiveness of Henry's language.

Introducing Vocabulary Study. Knowing the meanings of these words is important to understanding the selection. (Starred words appear in the Glossary.)

anguish*	88	irresolution	90
magnitude*	88	prostrate*	90
solace*	88	remonstrated	90
temporal	88	rivet	90
comports*	89	spurned	90
basely	90	subjugation	90
extenuate	90	supinely*	90
inestimable	90	supplication	90
insidious*	90	vigilant	90
inviolate	90		

The words *anguish, irresolute, prostrate, remonstrated, supplication,* refer to the varying attitudes of Americans to Great Britain. Have students use the context of the speech to determine the meaning of each of these words. Then have them write a sentence using each word, describing America's *anguish, irresolution,* and so on at the time that the speech was delivered.

Reading the Speech. The speech warrants a number of readings. You might first reemphasize to the class the suggestion in the textbook headnote to envision the surroundings in which the speech was delivered. Students will want to imagine a 26-year-old man, delivering an impassioned, urgent, yet controlled speech before a distinguished group of men. Then play the accompanying audiocassette recording of the speech. This professional reading gives students an indication of the tone, rhythm, and passion with which the speech was likely delivered. Students should attempt to put themselves in the position of listener in 1775.

Responding to the Speech Text page 91
Analyzing the Speech
Identifying Facts

1. According to the first two paragraphs of this speech, why is Henry speaking out? He is speaking out because, however painful the truth may be, he considers it vital that the truth be known and spoken at this critical point for the country.

2. Countering the arguments of opponents is essential to any persuasive speech or essay. How does Henry deal with the fact that the British have yielded somewhat to the Continental Congress's petition? Henry compares the threat of subjugation to Britain to the threat of slavery and chains, saying that the British soliders are "sent over to bind and rivet upon us those chains which the British ministry has been so long forging," and later warning, "Our chains are forged! Their clanking may be heard on the plains of Boston!"

3. According to Henry, why do the Colonists have no choice but to go to war? They have no choice because their petitions have failed; if they wish to be free, they must fight.

Interpreting Meanings

4. State in your own words the *main idea* of Henry's impassioned speech. The main idea is that, if the Colonists don't act immediately to protect their freedoms, they will lose them completely.

5. Throughout his speech, Henry uses *metaphors* to seize his listeners' feelings and at the same time to advance his arguments. In paragraph four, what metaphor does he use to describe the coming war? Warlike preparations "cover our waters and darken our land," like clouds. The British army intends to "bind and rivet" the Americans on the chains which the British have been long forging. Finally, Henry compares the British threat to a storm.

6. Perhaps like the preachers whose sermons he heard as a child, Patrick Henry makes use of a time-honored device in this speech: the rhetorical question. This is a question for which no answer is provided because the answer is obvious. Find a series of rhetorical questions in the fifth paragraph of this speech. What is the answer to each question? The series of questions occurs near the beginning of the paragraph. The answer to each question implies that Henry believes that the Americans can no longer postpone their resistance to the British threat. "Irresolution and inaction" will be fatal to the American cause.

Why do you think the speaker makes these points in the form of rhetorical questions rather than in the form of straightforward statements? It is rhetorically more effective to let the audience draw its own conclusions, rather than for the speaker to assert his opinion directly. Provided that Henry is sure that the audience will answer the questions for themselves in a certain way, he will be able to count on their forceful support, since they will be convinced that their answers are their *own* opinion, rather than merely the speaker's view.

7. Because Henry's audience knew classical mythology and, especially, the Bible, the orator knew he could count on certain allusions to have emotional effects. Look up the classical and Biblical passages alluded to in each of the following statements. How would each one relate to the conflict in Virginia in 1775? Could any of them relate to life today?

a. "We are apt to... listen to the song of that siren, till she transforms us into beasts." (*Odyssey,* Books 10 and 12) Henry's point is that illusory hopes are like the sirens and the beautiful maiden Circe in Homer's *Odyssey,* who were attractive on the surface but destructive in reality. Henry urges his listeners not to surrender their freedom in exchange for false hopes of peace. Students will probably agree that the statement might have equal relevance to some situations today.

b. **"Are we disposed to be of the number of those who, having eyes, see not, and having ears, hear not, the things which so nearly concern their temporal salvation?" (Ezekiel 12:2)** The allusion to the Old Testament is a graceful, but pointed, way for Henry to remind his listeners that they must not be like the heedless people whom the prophet upbraided in ancient Israel.

c. **"Suffer not yourselves to be betrayed with a kiss." (Luke 22:47–48)** The allusion is to the disloyal apostle Judas, who betrayed Jesus to the authorities with a kiss the night before Jesus was crucified. Henry warns his listeners not to heed the apparently mild British reaction to their latest petition against the new taxation laws.

8. What contemporary people—individuals or groups—can you name who might use Henry's closing sentence as a slogan? Student answers will vary.

Writing About the Speech
A Creative Response

1. Reporting on the Speech. Review the fact that a *news* story presents information but does not offer the reporter's opinions. Review also the news story's "inverted pyramid" format: The first or *lead* sentence catches the reader's attention and succinctly covers as many as possible of the W's—Who, What, When, Where, and Why. Remaining information is given in the order of descending importance so that cuts (from bottom up) will not destroy the story. Elicit one or two sample leads to alert students to the need to draw information from text introductory pages 87–88.

Criteria for Evaluating the Assignment. The paper reports; it does not editorialize. The lead includes all or most of the W's. Subsequent sentences state the assembly's response to the speech, summarize Henry's major points, and describe how Henry made his points. Additional sentences may quote others present.

A Critical Response

2. Comparing and Contrasting Speeches. Urge students to make a chart on the two episodes, like the one suggested in the writing prompt, before they write their essays.

Criteria for Evaluating the Assignment. The essay notes specific similarities and specific differences in the speeches of Edwards and Henry. The essay is organized in a coherent manner such as all similarities first, then all the differences, or the reverse.

Extending the Speech

Have students compare the rhetorical devices of noted twentieth-century speeches to Patrick Henry's speech. As examples of orators whose speeches stirred the nation, you might refer the class to John F. Kennedy, Martin Luther King, Jr., or Franklin Delano Roosevelt.

Elements of Literature: Persuasion   Text page 92

Students will be able to find a great many examples of "heightened style," including the following ones:

"of awful moment to this country" (text page 88)

"nothing less than a question of freedom or slavery" (text page 88)

"the implements of war and subjugation" (text page 90)

"preserve inviolate those inestimable privileges" (text page 90)

"the glorious object of our contest" (text page 90)

"the delusive phantom of hope" (text page 90)

Thomas Paine

The Crisis, No. 1

Text page 93

Text page 94

Objectives

1. To identify persuasive arguments
2. To analyze the use of analogy, metaphor, and imagery
3. To write a firsthand account
4. To write an essay evaluating a generalization

Introducing the Pamphlet

The introduction to Paine in the student text notes his condemnation and exile from England after the publication of *The Rights of Man*. He fled to France where he was at first lionized but then imprisoned. The direct cause of his imprisonment was that Paine spoke against the executions of the French Revolution, and, more specifically, he advocated the exile rather than execution of King Louis XVII. When Paine returned to the United States he was ostracized because his great work *The Age of Reason* was misinterpreted as an attack on Christianity. Students should be led to see that Paine was never able to find a place for himself in the world.

Background on the Pamphlet. After finishing work on the selection you may want to read the excerpt below from *The Crisis, No. 13*. It can be interpreted as a companion piece to *Crisis, No. 1*, and is very moving. It will take students full swing, from the call to arms of *The Crisis, No. 1* to the winding down of the war. Paine calls on his countrymen to exert reason over an exuberant release of emotion. Note the grace and poetry of the prose. Note also his reference to *Crisis, No. 1* in the first sentence.

"The times that tried men's souls" are over—and the greatest and completest Revolution the world ever knew, gloriously and happily accomplished.

"But to pass from the extremes of danger to safety—from the tumult of war to the tranquility of peace—though sweet in contemplation, requires gradual composure of the senses to receive it. Even calmness has the power of stunning, when it opens too instantly upon us. . . .

"In the present case, the mighty magnitude of the object, the various uncertainties of fate which it has undergone, the numerous and complicated dangers we have suffered or escaped, the eminence we now stand on, and the vast prospect before us, must all conspire to impress us with contemplation.

"To see it in our power to make a world happy, to teach mankind the art of being so, to exhibit on the theatre of the universe a character hitherto unknown, and to have, as it were, a new creation entrusted in our hands, are honors that command reflection, and can neither be too highly estimated, nor too gratefully received.

"In this pause, then, of reflection, while the storm is ceasing, and the long-agitated mind vibrating to a rest, let us look back on the scenes we have passed, and learn from experience what is to be done."

Summary. Paine begins by exhorting Americans to fight the tyranny of Great Britain. Fighting should have begun earlier, but victory can still be attained. He argues that God is on the side of the just and compares George III with a thief. To counter the American panic after numerous battle defeats, Paine relates a story of the weakness of Britain. He describes the courageous retreat of militiamen from Fort Lee to the Delaware and provides a character study of Washington. He berates the behavior of the Tories and tells an anecdote of the selfishness of a Tory tavern owner. He again describes the strengths and courage of American forces and the harm Tories will bring on themselves from both Americans and British. He persuades the uncommitted and fearful sympathizers to commit themselves. He argues that a victorious Britain will be brutal and pictures a ravaged country if the people do not join the fight for liberty.

Teaching Strategies

Providing for Cultural Differences. Some students may have emigrated from a country whose government was more restrictive than that of England, perhaps even repressive. Thomas Paine's ideas may seem as revolutionary or radical to them as they did for many of Paine's contemporaries in England—and America. Discuss with students the fact that Paine and others fought for the freedom of the individual at a time when the king of England had absolute power over an individual's life.

Providing for Different Levels of Ability. Although Paine's language is reasonably clear, some students may become confused by the string of aphorisms that run through the essay, particularly in the first paragraph. You might want to spend some time discussing these aphorisms. If students become lost in Paine's strategy, you might want to break the pamphlet into four parts: a. Setting the emotional tone for the appeal to Tories and uncommitted supporters b. Describing the soundness of the military retreat, mostly to encourage militiamen c. Haranguing Tories and appealing to the consciences of sympathizers d. Exhibiting faith in the cause and conviction that the Revolution will succeed.

Reading the Pamphlet. You might clarify further to the class the dire conditions under which the pamphlet was written. The writing is plain, strong, and clear, and yet the essay was written while on retreat from a battle. The fate of America was at stake, and Paine rose to the occasion. The pamphlet was an inspiration to thousands, many of whom joined the Continental Army after reading or hearing it.

Have a student read *The Crisis, No. 1* aloud, as it was read to the troops and later to the general populace. Then you might read aloud Patrick Henry's speech. Ask students to consider why Paine's essay might be more appealing to the general and less learned population than Henry's speech.

Introducing Vocabulary Study. Knowing the meanings of these words is important to understanding the selection. (Starred words appear in the Glossary.)

dearness*	94	apparition*	95
impious*	94	inevitable*	96
infidel*	94	remote*	96
hypocrisy*	95	appropriate*	97
petrified	95		

Reading Check. You might wish to use the following questions as a reading check. Have students respond *True* or *False*.

1. Paine believes that the colonies should have acted against Britain eight months before they did. _True_
2. Paine compares the king of Britain to a murderer and a thief. _True_
3. Paine describes the retreat to the Delaware as disorganized but courageous. _False_
4. Paine believed American isolation from Europe would create necessary hardship after gaining independence. _False_
5. Paine believed only those should fight who had nothing or no one to lose. _False_

Reteaching Alternatives. You might point out specific ideas and sentences that reflect Enlightenment beliefs. One such idea is that a king does not have the right to impose unjust laws on the people. The appeal to the general population, Tory and Whig alike, suggests that the people's fate is in their own hands.

You could also explore further the use of analogies and examples in the essay. Have students look for all analogies to hell and devils, and then note whether they apply to the British or Americans. Ask students how the story example of the tavern owner and his child demonstrates the immortality of the Tory position, and whether the example was likely to win over Tories.

Responding to the Pamphlet   Text page 99
Analyzing the Pamphlet
Identifying Facts

1. **What reasons does Paine give for his confidence that Divine help will be given to the Americans and not to the British?** Paine says that the Americans have tried "every decent method" to avoid war; he also claims that the British king is evil and unjust.

2. **Washington's march across New Jersey to the Delaware was actually a retreat from General Howe's British forces. Explain how Paine makes the event seem positive, even heroic.** Paine points out the military logic of the retreat, commends the fortitude of the fatigued retreating soldiers, and remarks that hardship brings out people's best qualities.

   How does he link the results of the retreat to Divine Providence? He suggests that only God could have prevented the British from attacking the troops at Perth Amboy and halting the march.

3. **Find details in the middle of the essay that identify at least part of Paine's audience.** Paine is addressing "these middle provinces"—primarily those Colonists who are Tory sympathizers.

   What arguments does he use to persuade these listeners of their errors? Paine tries to persuade the Tories of their errors by asserting that self-interested fear is the foundation of Toryism, and by warning them that their conduct is an invitation to the enemy.

4. **Explain Paine's point in telling the anecdote about the Tory tavern keeper and his child.** The point of the anecdote is to emphasize that allegiance to the king is based on selfish fear, and is merely deferring a conflict that is inevitable.

5. **What powerful emotional appeal does Paine make in the conclusion of his essay to sum up the choice facing the Colonists?** Paine states that the Colonists' choice is between a "glorious issue"—that is, triumph and independence—and enslavement by the British.

   List the descriptive details that make this appeal especially vivid. To make it vivid, Paine draws a picture of enslavement that includes such details as ravaged country, depopulated cities, unsafe houses, and "our homes turned into barracks and bawdy houses for the Hessians."

Interpreting Meanings

6. **What is Paine's *main idea*? What are his chief supporting ideas?** Paine's main idea is that the Colonies must

Thomas Paine   35

stand together against Britain. He supports this by saying that even the Tories will be crushed after their usefulness to the British is over. Also, that even if one colony is conquered by the British, all of the others will still be fighting.

7. The pamphlet opens with an emotional statement that is now famous, and it continues with two equally famous images. What kinds of people does Paine identify with summer and sunshine? Why are these images appropriate? Paine is suggesting that such people are willing to stand by their country only when it is as easy and pleasant as sunny summer weather to do so. The images are appropriate because they conjure up universal, easily understandable mental pictures.

8. Explain the meaning of Paine's metaphor, "Mutual fear is the principal link in the chain of mutual love." Do you agree or disagree with this idea, and why? In this metaphor, Paine suggests that self-interest—mutual protection—may be the most compelling reason for standing united. Students should clearly explain whether they agree or disagree with this idea, and should give reasons for their opinions.

9. An analogy is a comparison between two things that are alike in certain respects. Analogies are often used in argument and persuasion to demonstrate the logic of one idea by showing how it is similar to another, accepted idea. Analogies can be tricky, because few ideas or situations are completely alike in all aspects. What analogy does Paine draw when he talks about the thief (page 97)? Paine is arguing that it is as fair to rebel against England, which has trespassed on the Colonists' rights, as it is to turn on a thief who trespasses on one's own property.

What point is he making, and how might an opponent answer? Student answers will vary, but may suggest that this argument is effective because it appeals both to logic— in the analogy comparing the king to a lawbreaker—and to emotion, by rousing indignation through the suggestion that the Colonists' rights are being violated just as if they were being robbed.

10. How do you think people today would respond to Paine's pamphlet? Are any of his arguments applicable to contemporary political situations? Explain. Student answers will vary.

Writing About the Pamphlet
A Creative Response

1. Writing a Firsthand Account. Read the writing prompt aloud and discuss probable reactions of the volunteer soldiers who heard this pamphlet read aloud. Clarify directions as necessary.

Criteria for Evaluating the Assignment. The paragraph is written in first person. As it explains the feelings of the speaker and describes the responses of the people around him, it reveals the speaker's own attitude toward the war.

A Critical Response

2. Evaluating a Generalization. Define "generalization" as a principle that is true for the most part, but to which there may be exceptions. Read the quote from Paine and ask students to explain what makes it a generalization. When they begin to move into arguing about whether or not Paine is right, they are ready to write their essays.

Criteria for Evaluating the Assignment. The essay, while brief, consists of at least one paragraph. It clearly states either agreement or disagreement with Paine's words, and offers a response that reflects in a reasonable manner the realities of today.

Thomas Jefferson
Text page 100

From *The Autobiography*
Text page 101

Objectives

1. To identify examples of parallelism
2. To write an essay analyzing persuasive arguments
3. To write an opinion in favor of or against omitting certain passages
4. To explain particular words and phrases

36   The Revolutionary Period

Introducing the Autobiography

Critic Adrienne Koch calls Jefferson the greatest of the "philosopher-statesmen," the others being Hamilton, James Madison, and John Adams. She assesses that these four men "taken together almost define the range of our national ideology—our objectives, our character as a people, our economic and social patterns, our 'Americanism.'" She states that Jefferson's prime contribution was his promotion of "the fullest participation in political control, . . . [and his great] confidence in the educability of the common people." Contrary to Alexander Hamilton, he saw that the people could govern themselves, or, at least, choose responsible representation.

Background on the Autobiography. The Declaration of Independence has been criticized on many fronts for lack of originality. John Adams said it was an amalgamation of ideas and statements considered for two years in the Continental Congress. Jefferson himself was acutely aware that the work was not original in idea, but it was not his intent or duty to be original. He was "rather to regard himself as . . . the mouthpiece and prophet of the people he represented." The originality of the Declaration is in the quality of its expression: its moral strength, its phrasing, the inspirational tone of the aphorisms, and in its timeless and passionate appeal to the "rights of man." You might advance this idea of originality, by asking students to define the term themselves. You can suggest that although ideas can be, and often are, original, it is far more common for originality in literature to come in the aspect of style and form. You might turn to the first paragraph of the Declaration to support this statement. The power and profundity of the ideas stem not from the ideas themselves but rather from the nobility of the expression.

The Declaration of Independence was a source of strength and inspiration to the French Revolution and continues to be inspirational to peoples seeking liberty and justice from oppressive governments. Be sure to point out that the Declaration makes clear that revolution is not a frivolous act, but must only be enacted under the extreme threat of loss of liberty.

Teaching Strategies

Providing for Different Levels of Ability. The long sentences and sometimes elaborate phrasing may cause difficulty for some students; however, hearing parts of the Declaration read aloud may be helpful. The significance of the passages struck out and/or replaced will be particularly difficult to understand. You may want to clarify the reasons for the deletions and insertions. Question 3 in "Identifying Facts," and question 3 in "A Critical Response," text page 107, deal with this issue.

Introducing Vocabulary Study. Knowing the meanings of the following words is important to understanding the selection. (Starred words appear in the Glossary.)

censures*	101	sufferance	102
reprobating*	101	dissolution	104
assent*	102	inestimable*	104
envinces	102	execrable*	105
expunge*	102	obtrude*	105
impel*	102	opprobrium	105
inalienable*	102	amity	106
prudence*	102	consanguinity	106

After students have determined the definitions of these words, you might divide the class into four groups, giving each group four words from the list. Then have each group write out a declaration, or resolution, about an issue of their choice, using their four words. Students can then debate these declarations among themselves.

Reading the Autobiography. Have students read aloud the opening two paragraphs of the Declaration. The first of these paragraphs establishes the intention of the document and states why independence is being declared. The second establishes the relationship between a people and their government. Call attention to the radical, yet seemingly reasonable, words, "whenever any form of government becomes destructive of these ends [the rights of man], it is the right of the people to alter or abolish it." This idea will seem revolutionary to many students and so it still is. The remainder of the paragraph defines specifically the situation in which revolt is justified. Explain that the rights of man were most crucial to Jefferson and that he was later instrumental in having the Bill of Rights added to the Constitution. The rest of the Declaration works as a support of the first and second paragraphs.

Reading Check. You may want to use the following questions as a reading check. Have students respond *True* or *False*.

1. The Declaration of Independence explains the necessity and right of the Colonies to declare independence. ___True___
2. Jefferson was unconcerned that Congress struck out passages of his draft. ___False___
3. The Declaration blames the king of England, rather than the British people, for the state of war. ___True___
4. Jefferson's draft of the Declaration states the king has waged war on human nature. ___True___
5. The Declaration states that the Colonies had declared allegiance to the king, not to the jurisprudence of British parliament. ___True___

Reteaching Alternatives. Have students pay particular attention to the omissions and additions to the Declaration. Have them note on a paper while rereading, places where omissions were made for the sake of clarity and where they were made for political reasons, such as in the passage on

Thomas Jefferson 37

slavery. Point out, also, the delegates' concern for meaning and precision. For example, the Congress made several substitutions of *colonies* for *states*, because the colonies were not yet states. Ask students to consider while reading if most of the changes clarify and strengthen sentences and passages, or whether, as Jefferson felt, the changes were detrimental to the document. Students are asked to write an opinion on the changes in "A Critical Response," page 107 in the student text.

Responding to the Declaration
Text page 107

Analyzing the Declaration

Identifying Facts

1. The Declaration opens with a rational statement defending an act that was to have violent consequences. Explain why the Continental Congress wanted to publish its reasons for separating itself from Britain. The Congress felt that a "decent respect" for the opinions of others required them to explain the reasons for such a drastic and violent action.

2. The word *self-evident* (added by Franklin) refers to the truths that are accessible to our common sense. List the truths that Jefferson cites in particular. Jefferson cites as truths that "all men are created equal," and that all have "certain inalienable rights" that include "life, liberty, and the pursuit of happiness."

3. List the offenses charged to the King of England. Among these offenses are: the refusal to assent to necessary laws; the harassment of legislative bodies; the capricious dissolution of the "representative houses"; the attempt to prevent the states from being settled and populated; the coercion of judges; the maintenance of hostile standing armies and warships in the colonies without the colonists' consent; the plunder of the seas and coasts and the destruction of the towns; the coercion of citizens taken prisoner on the high seas; the inciting of the Indians to war and of fellow citizens to insurrection.

4. The omissions made by Congress are instructive. In the first paragraph of this passage from his *Autobiography*, Jefferson explains why one clause in particular was struck out. Which clause is it, and what precisely did it accuse the King of doing? Jefferson refers to the deletion of the clause accusing the King of perpetuating the slave trade.

5. Jefferson frequently employs parallelism, which is the repeated use of sentences, clauses, or phrases with identical or similar structures. For example, when he cites the truths that are "self-evident," he begins each clause with *that*. The parallelism emphasizes Jefferson's view that all these truths are of equal importance. The parallel structure also creates a stately rhythm or cadence in the Declaration that you will hear if you listen to the words read aloud. Find at least two other sections of the Declaration in which parallel structures are repeated. As one example students may point to the sentences listing grievances against the King. These sentences all begin with "He has...." Parallelism also makes statements grand, formal, and memorable, as in the last line, where Jefferson speaks of "*our* lives, *our* fortunes, and *our* sacred honor."

Interpreting Meanings

6. What changes indicate a desire on the part of the Congress not to make one last break—that is, with the English people themselves? Changes reflecting the colonists' desire to maintain ties to the English people include: the omission of the passage objecting to submission to the English Parliament; the change suggesting that the King's outrages "would inevitably" (rather than "were likely to") destroy the colonists' connection with the English people; the deletion of the passage swearing to "renounce forever these unfeeling brethren;" and the omission of mention of the *people* of Great Britain in the vow to "dissolve all political connection" with the English government.

Why do you think it would be important that the new country maintain its "consanguinity," or close kinship, with the English people? Most of the citizens of the new country still felt close personal ties to England—many had near relatives there.

7. The intent of the Congress is clarified when we examine the words that were changed in Jefferson's original draft. Which of the changes seem to have been adopted primarily for stylistic reasons (for clarity, or to avoid repetition, or to make greater impact)? Changes that seem to have been made for stylistic reasons include: the change of "inherent and" to "certain"; the deletion of "begun at a distinguished period"; the change of "among which appears...have" to "all having"; the deletion of "and continually."

Which seem to have been made for political reasons? Changes that seem to have been made for political reasons include: the change from "expunge" to "alter"; the insertion of "in many cases"; the deletion of the reference to slavery; the change from "a people who mean to be free" to "a free people."

Writing About the Declaration

A Critical Response

1. Analyzing Its Reasoning. Call to students' attention the three questions in the writing prompt which outline a structure for the organization of their essays.

Criteria for Evaluating the Assignment. The essay lists Jefferson's major arguments, cites examples of the evidence Jefferson uses to support his points, and explains which elements of Jefferson's conclusion summarize and justify his arguments.

2. Responding to a Point of View. Read the excerpt from Abigail Adams's letter aloud, and elicit from students their first reactions. Have them respond to her in a letter as personal and informal as her own.

Criteria for Evaluating the Assignment. The letter is clearly a response to Abigail Adams's letter. It offers the writer's own opinion on "remember[ing] the ladies." It is informal in tone and style.

3. Responding to Changes in the Document. Clarify with students how deleted passages are identified in the text, and discuss which deleted passages may have seemed "manly," but wiser to remove, to Abigail Adams. Note, however, that this assignment calls for an *essay*—not a letter response.

Criteria for Evaluating the Assignment. The essay selects two deleted passages suited to Abigail Adams's comments. It offers the student's own opinion as to whether deletion of the passages made the document stronger or weaker, and explains why the student has that opinion.

Analyzing Language and Style
Precise Meanings

While answers will vary, these are examples of suitable responses:

1. *Equal:* alike in nature or status
2. *Pursuit of happiness:*
   a. efforts to achieve a comfortable standard of living
   b. efforts to achieve political freedom
   c. efforts to achieve satisfying relationships with other people.
3. *Equal* does not mean alike in talent or ability.
4. *Pursuit of happiness* does not imply a right to ignore the rights of everyone else in order to please oneself.

Primary Sources: A Letter from Jefferson to His Daughter   Text page 108

The letter can be approached in various ways. It is a fountain of Enlightenment ideals—fortitude, industry, self-improvement, and self-reliance. You might ask students what they would know of the American Age of Reason if the letter were the only piece of writing left from the period. Another approach would be to compare the virtues described in the letter with Franklin's list of virtues for achieving moral perfection.

The American Language   Text page 112

1. Students are to use a dictionary to find the English meaning of the italicized words. They should then propose reasons why these meanings were lost in America.

chase: private game preserve

bog: lavatory, bathroom

common: tract of land owned jointly by the residents of a community

shire: a British county

Reasons for the disappearance of these meanings will vary.

2. Students should find out what each of the following words means and when it came into usage in American English. They should then comment on what the words reveal about features and customs that were peculiar to American life.

cold snap: sudden onset of cold weather (1770–1780)

dude: fellow, chap (1880–1885)

everglade: tract of low, swampy land (1815–1825)

Indian summer: period of mild, dry weather in late October or early November (1770–1780)

pot pie: deep-dish pie with a pastry crust, containing meat or chicken (1785–1795)

ranch: large farm (1800–1810)

salt lick: place to which animals go to lick natural salt deposits (1735–1745)

snowshoe: shoe for walking in snow (1655–1665)

Comments on the words will vary. Possible areas of comment may include distinctively American elements of climate, diet, geography, topography, agriculture, and development of the economy.

3. **Students should comment on the histories of the following words in the context of the eighteenth-century purists' insistence that words should develop historically from their roots.**

clue: variant of *clew,* < Middle English *clewe:* "a ball of thread"; "a hint leading to the solution of a mystery"

companion: < Middle English, Old French, Late Latin, "messmate"; "associate"

daughter: < Middle English, German

expedite: < Latin, "set the feet free"; "hasten"

precocious: < Latin, "early ripening"; "unusually advanced or mature"

steward: < Old English, "house" or "hall"; "manager of a household"

town: < Old English, "walled or fenced place"; "populated area"

4. **Students should determine how each of the following words is pronounced in England and in America.**

been: bĕn in England, bin in America

clerk: klark in England, klerk in America

lieutenant: lef te′ nənt in England, lyoo ten′ ant in America

schedule: shed′ yool in England, sked′ yool in America

Exercises in Critical Thinking and Writing

Text page 113

Analyzing and Evaluating Persuasion: Logic

To help students evaluate the underlying logic of Patrick Henry's "Speech to the Virginia Convention," it may be necessary to discuss the highly charged emotional language that permeates the speech and that may obfuscate Henry's use of logical appeals. Students should understand, for example, that Henry carefully chooses his language to make an "either-or" choice seem logical. On the British side, there are the "chains which the British ministry have so long been forging" and the "tyrannical hands of the ministry and Parliament." On the Colonists' side, however, there are the "appeal to arms and to the God of Hosts" and the "holy cause of liberty."

Criteria for Evaluating the Assignment. While students' essays do not necessarily have to follow the plan for writing outlined on text page 114, a thesis statement should be included. Students should also be aware that in evaluating Henry's argument, they are developing an argument of their own. Students' opinions about Henry's logic should be supported with specific evidence from the speech.

Unit Three: *American Romanticism*

Teaching the American Romanticism Unit

The literature of Romanticism differs decisively from earlier American literature, as the editors of *The American Mind* point out:

"... the publication of Washington Irving's *Sketch Book* in 1819 marked the end of an epoch. Before that time American writing had for the most part been bound to religion, economics, or politics. It had been an instrument for the accomplishment of specific objectives. With the *Sketch Book,* writing in America became an end in itself. The ideal of literature as a fine art began to take form in the American mind. In Irving and in Cooper, whose writing quickly followed, American civilization produced two men of letters who achieved international recognition."

This observation that before *The Sketch Book* American letters were an instrument for the accomplishment of specific objectives may help students understand why, as the text points out, "Romanticism came relatively late to America." Writers like Franklin and Jefferson were only secondarily men of letters, primarily builders of a nation. The entire nation's attention, in fact, was on practical accomplishment—the opposite of Romanticism.

As the text suggests, Romanticism, a movement that began in Europe, developed distinct American characteristics out of our Colonial past and the development of the new nation. As students read the works in this and the following units, ask them to keep in mind the two principal ways in which the text stresses that the Romantic sensibility sought to rise above "dull realities": by exploring exotic settings, whether past or present; and by contemplating the natural world. Both activities were well suited to the luxuriant new land that faced Americans. It was perhaps inevitable that the first celebrated American novelist, James Fenimore Cooper, would be a Romantic celebrator of wilderness virtues.

Even while Cooper was taking Natty Bumppo into the frontier and celebrating American skill and initiative, the Fireside Poets, as the text points out, "looked backward ... at established European models." The first two poems in the unit, "To a Waterfowl" and "Thanatopsis," lend themselves to a discussion of this question of whether poets such as Bryant were distinctively American. Students might agree that "Thanatopsis" could more easily be mistaken for a British poem, whereas they may see the barrenness of the setting of "To A Waterfowl" as more suggestive of early New England.

The Romantic period fostered the beginning of what we consider today to be distinctively American literature. Pathfinders such as Irving, Cooper, and Bryant were to make way for such giants as Hawthorne, Melville, and Poe. But, more significantly, as time went on, it was not only the writers but also their themes that attracted readers in Europe as well as in America.

*O*bjectives of the American Romanticism Unit

1. To improve reading proficiency and expand vocabulary
2. To gain exposure to notable authors and their works
3. To define and identify the elements of the short story and poem
4. To define and identify significant literary techniques: figures of speech, sound effects, imagery, satire, tone, and paradox
5. To respond, orally and in writing, to short stories and poetry
6. To analyze the language and style of notable authors
7. To write original works
8. To practice the following critical thinking and writing skills:
    a. Analyzing conflict, style, imagery, and meter
    b. Interpreting tone
    c. Comparing and contrasting poems
    d. Analyzing a poem
    e. Analyzing the appeal of a literary work
    f. Responding to a poem's message
    g. Paraphrasing a poem

*I*ntroducing the American Romanticism Unit

The names of some of the Romantics will be familiar to students: Longfellow, Cooper, Irving. But students may have an inexact idea about when they lived and wrote, and what was happening in America in their lifetimes. The time line on text pages 120–121 should help students visually to get a sense of the period of Romanticism, usually thought of as flourishing in the half century before the Civil War; and it will also help students see themselves in relation to American history.

Among other things, the time line will remind students of how short a time America has been a nation. Some will recall the 200th anniversary of the Constitution in 1987. While two centuries in the past seems like ancient history to forward-looking teenagers, if you suggest that their great-grandparents might conceivably have known someone who saw George Washington, the relative youthfulness of our nation will be more striking.

Remind students as they look at the time line that when the Romantics were at the height of their careers, America had been a nation for only as few years. You might ask them to imagine that they were aspiring American writers living in 1815, when Bryant wrote "To a Waterfowl." If they had been embarking upon literary careers at that time, what would they have chosen to write about? Where would they have sought their material? In the western frontier? In the established civilization of Europe? Or in their own imaginations? The American Romantics, you can inform students, took all these routes to inspiration.

Washington Irving

Text page 122

"Rip Van Winkle"

Text page 125

Objectives

1. To analyze characters
2. To state the theme
3. To identify tone
4. To define Romantic aspects of setting
5. To write an epilogue to the story
6. To write an essay explaining parallels between the story and the awakening of the American nation
7. To write an essay analyzing conflict

Introducing the Story

In outline form, for your reference, here are the major elements of the story:

- **Characters:** Rip; Dame Van Winkle, his wife; their children, young Rip and Judith; Nicholas Vedder, the "self-important man in the cocked hat"; the villagers; Rip's dog Wolf
- **Setting:** a remote village in the Catskills before and after the American Revolution
- **Point of view:** third-person, with intrusions by Irving's narrator, Diedrich Knickerbocker
- **Conflict:** husband vs. wife; individual vs. environment; youth vs. age; past vs. present

Background on the Story. Even to its first readers, the story was set in the past (the story was first published in 1819, thirty years after Washington's first inaugural). The antiquity of Rip's village is evoked by placing its origin "just about the beginning of the government of the good Peter Stuyvesant" (1646). Students may appreciate that readers of that time would have had a natural interest in the early history and legend of their new nation, and they may see that Irving's interest in the past suggests that he was an early American Romantic.

The remoteness of the village in the Catskill Mountains also helps us see the story as folklore, not intended to be realistic.

The Plot. When Rip's wife scolds him for not helping around the house, Rip leaves home and takes an afternoon ramble in the mountains with his dog Wolf. He is beguiled into a mystical ravine, where several little people dressed in "the antique Dutch fashion" are playing at ninepins. Rip is given some drink, and falls asleep. When he wakes up, twenty years have gone by. He returns to his village and is surprised to find no faces he recognizes. He discovers his son and daughter, now grown, and enters into the life of the village in its new era.

Teaching Strategies

Providing for Cultural Differences. Not until after the Romantic era did Americans become conscious of the possibilities for women in society; but at least two of the early Romantics, Longfellow and Lowell, wrote sensitively of women in their families.

Providing for Different Levels of Ability. It is a good idea to read the first three paragraphs of the story aloud in class (or have a good student reader do it) so that students will get used to Irving's style and have a chance to ask questions about meaning. You might also point out that Irving is establishing a tone of legend through his use of such words as "noble," "lording," "magical," "fairy," and "chivalrous." Particularly you can help students through the last three sentences of the third paragraph, which for many will be a stumbling block.

42 American Romanticism

Introducing Vocabulary Study. Students will benefit from knowing the meanings of the following words before they read the selection. Starred words appear in the Glossary.

descried*	125	daunted	128
scrupulous*	125	patriarch	128
chivalrous	126	clamor*	129
martial*	126	alacrity	129
obsequious*	126	amphitheater	129
shrew	126	reiterate	129
squabble*	125	connubial*	131
impunity	126	disputatious	131
insuperable*	126	phlegm	131
aversion	126	akimbo*	133
patrimonial	126	austere	133
sages	128	despotism	135
rubicund	128		

The vocabulary at the beginning of the story will be somewhat more difficult for students. Adequate attention at that point will accustom them to Irving's style.

Reading the Story. Some students will be familiar with the plot of Irving's tale from other sources, such as television cartoons, without having it read in the original version. You might ask whether any of your students can recount the story line before the class reads the story. This will ease some of the burden of comprehension for less advanced students, and help the more advanced students plunge deeper into the subtleties of the work.

Reading Check. You might want to use the following questions as a check for literal compehension of the story. Have students respond *True* or *False*.

1. Rip was usually one of the first to volunteer to help a neighbor build a stone wall. ___True___
2. When Rip woke up, he found the amphitheater again, but everyone had gone. ___False___
3. When Rip returned to the village, Dame Van Winkle took up scolding him where she had left off. ___False___
4. When Rip returned to the village after his sleep, the villagers were talking about whether America should remain subject to King George. ___False___
5. At the end of the story, Rip was one of the patriarchs of the village. ___True___

Reteaching Alternatives. You might concentrate on a limited part of the story—for example, Rip's experience in the mountains (page 129–130). Ask students to note the natural setting, described in the second paragraph on page 129, and the imagined setting of the amphitheater in the next column. Students might ask if the amphitheater itself was a dream, since Rip couldn't find it when he woke up. But they should realize that one does not ask a question like this of a folktale, any more than one asks how Jack could climb up a beanstalk.

Responding to the Story   Text page 136
Analyzing the Story
Identifying Facts

1. Name Rip's positive *character* traits. What are his negative traits? Rip is kind, helpful, and good-natured; however, he is also lazy and irresponsible.

Describe Rip's relationship with his wife. Rip is nagged and harassed by his wife, who complains continually about his laziness.

2. What does the narrator himself say about the character of Dame Van Winkle? The narrator says that Dame Van Winkle is a shrew and a termagant.

3. Describe the appearance and behavior of the group that Rip meets on the mountain. The group are dressed in old-fashioned Dutch garb; they are silently and expressionlessly bowling at ninepins.

What causes him to fall asleep? Drinking the group's liquor causes Rip to fall asleep.

4. When Rip awakens, what clues tell us that a great deal of time has passed? Rip's gun has rusted; his dog Wolf has disappeared; his joints are stiff; and a new mountain stream has formed.

5. Compare the appearance and activities of the inn before and after Rip's sleep. The village inn has become the "Union Hotel"; a liberty pole has been raised by it and the face of King George III on the inn sign has been altered and relabeled "George Washington"; the crowd at the inn is livelier and more argumentative, and much political discussion is heard; an election is going on.

How does the inn reflect the political and social changes that have taken place in the country as a whole? These changes reflect America's break with England, its gaining of independence, its becoming a democracy, and the vital importance politics have assumed to all citizens.

6. As Rip begins to understand what has happened to him, how does he react? Rip is bewildered, but seems slightly relieved at the news of his wife's death!

Once he has adjusted to his situation, how does his new life compare to his old one? His new life is more peaceful than his old, although just as "do-nothing." He is happy with a number of his former cronies, and delights in telling his story to anyone who will listen.

Interpreting Meanings

7. In what ways is this a classic story of wish fulfillment? Student answers may vary. Most students will agree, however, that the idea of "escape"—from the world, from responsibilities, and from decisions—is at the heart of the

Washington Irving 43

plot of "Rip Van Winkle." Since Rip succeeds in that escape, the story is a classic example of wish fulfillment.

Do you think the *theme* of the story is still relevant to readers in the late twentieth century? Explain. Student answers will vary.

8. In his introductory note, the narrator (who is Geoffrey Crayon) explains that the manuscript of "Rip Van Winkle" was written by Diedrich Knickerbocker, the narrator of Irving's earlier *History of New York*. How does Irving use his two narrators—Geoffrey Crayon and Diedrich Knickerbocker—to defend the tale's credibility? Knickerbocker's literary merit is "not a whit better than it should be," but his accuracy has been "completely established," according to Crayon. In the "Note" at the end of the tale, Irving indulges in some more playful humor, "supporting" the tale's veracity.

What is Irving's *tone* in these introductory passages? The tone of the comments is lightly ironic, or mock-serious.

9. What details in "Rip Van Winkle" do you think reveal Irving's fascination with the past? In his descriptions of the group Rip meets on the mountain and in references to New York's Dutch past in the seventeenth century, Irving clothes history with an air of mystery and romance.

Find some of Irving's descriptions of the *setting* which you think reflect a Romantic's view of nature. Irving presents the Kaatskill mountains as beautiful and as harboring mysteries and secrets. Significantly, the natural landscape in Irving's story is the place where Rip can escape the conventions and limitations of the town; through his sojourn in the mountains come Rip's freedom and "re-birth."

10. Irving was a Romantic, but he was also a satirist. What elements of this story—including the narrator's commentaries—are *satirical*? Who or what are Irving's targets? Irving satirizes the Van Winkles's way of life with his overblown, exaggerated language. He also pokes fun at some of the local "characters" in the town, especially the "patriarch" Nicholas Vedder and the schoolmaster Derrick Van Bummel.

11. Dame Van Winkle and Rip are stereotyped characters that have been found in literature throughout the ages—the nagging wife and the henpecked husband. Can you identify these character types in current literature and in popular movies and TV shows? Students should be able to suggest many examples of these popular character types.

What is your response to Irving's characterization of Dame Van Winkle? Student answers will vary.

Was Irving (who remained a bachelor) biased in favor of the ne'er-do-well, Rip? The story certainly seems to support such a conclusion; but allow the students to present and defend their own opinions.

Writing About the Story
A Creative Response

1. Writing an Epilogue. An *epilogue* is an addition to a literary work that rounds out the story. Discuss with students the point at which the Dame Van Winkle epilogue would fit into the story as a whole, and the advantages and disadvantages of choosing her or Knickerbocker as narrator.

Criteria for Evaluating the Assignment. The story provides insight into Mrs. Van Winkle's character and makes imaginative use of the peddler incident which is said to have led to her death.

A Critical Response

2. Modernizing the Story. Make sure students understand that their task is to explain *how* to modernize the story—not actually to do so.

Criteria for Evaluating the Assignment. The paragraph comments on changes necessary in setting, characters, and conflict to reset the story in the late twentieth century.

3. Explaining a Parallel. Before students write their essays, read with them "A Comment on the Story," page 136; and point out the organizational pattern implicit in the writing prompt.

Criteria for Evaluating the Assignment. The essay cites several parallels between Rip's emancipation and that of the United States. The essay uses details from the story to support points made about parallels in independence, peace, and maturity.

4. Analyzing a Conflict. Discuss other comedies, such as Shakespeare's *The Taming of the Shrew* and the still-shown TV series *I Love Lucy*, that focus on "the battle of the sexes." Call to students' attention the fact that the writing prompt asks for a three-part essay.

Criteria for Evaluating the Assignment. The essay briefly summarizes the conflict between Rip Van Winkle and his wife, names at least two other comedies that use the "battle of the sexes" conflict, and gives the student's personal reaction to the theme's continued use.

Analyzing Language and Style
Inflated Language

1. Two of the possible answers: Rip's farm "was the most pestilent little piece of ground in the whole country... weeds were sure to grow quicker in his fields than anywhere else..."; Rip's dog Wolf "sneaked about with a gallows air, casting many a sidelong glance at Dame Van Winkle, and at the least flourish of a broomstick or ladle he would fly to the door with yelping precipitation."

2. "Rip's farm was a terrible piece of ground where weeds grew easily." "Rip's dog watched Mrs. Van Winkle carefully, and yelped and ran every time she used a broom or a ladle."

3. Most students will have enjoyed the hyperbole.

Extending the Story

Students who enjoyed the story should be encouraged to read "The Legend of Sleepy Hollow" if they have not already done so. Or they might find other works of Irving in the library. Further reading of the author would be an excellent way to start the study of this unit, since he was such a major figure of his time. You might suggest that students who read further present oral reports so others may share their experience.

Primary Sources: A Traveler Comments on American Manners   Text page 137

Students may be amused by Mrs. Trollope's comments on American manners. Be sure that they understand that more than politeness is meant by the term: Mrs. Trollope was commenting on the impressions Americans made on her through their attitudes and everyday behavior.

It is of course impossible to judge how good a reporter Mrs. Trollope was from this brief account. You might ask students to trust her reporting and to suggest some specific ways in which Americans might have seemed to lack enthusiasm or to have been, like Rip Van Winkle, in a long sleep.

William Cullen Bryant   Text page 138

"To a Waterfowl"   Text page 139

Objectives

1. To recognize onomatopoeia
2. To interpret symbols
3. To analyze theme
4. To write a paragraph analyzing the poem

Introducing the Poem

In outline form for your reference, here are the major elements of the poem:

- **Rhyme:** abab
- **Rhythm:** iambic
- **Significant techniques:** alliteration, onomatopoeia, imagery, varied line length

Background on the Poem. Bryant's status as a child prodigy did not immunize him from the same youthful doubts that your own students may have experienced. He was inspired to write "To a Waterfowl" after taking a seven-mile walk one December twilight in 1817, "forlorn and desolate, not knowing what was to become of him in the big world," according to his biographer Parke Godwin. While communing with his own soul, he watched a solitary bird flying along the sunset horizon and asked himself where it had come from and where it was going.

The Literal Meaning. The narrator observes a waterfowl flying far off in the "rosy depths" of the sunset. He imagines that it will soon find its destination, having flown all day in "the cold, thin atmosphere." The narrator reflects that the "Power" that has guided the bird will also guide him "in the long way" ahead of him.

Teaching Strategies

Providing for Cultural Differences. The poem is more accessible to students who have lived in the country than to city dwellers, if only because of its setting. However, everyone at one time or another has been alone, and much of the poem's appeal derives from our ability to share with the narrator the sense of being along with nature. You may want to ask students to write or tell of experiences when they have been alone for a time and have let their eyes and their thoughts roam.

Providing for Different Levels of Ability. Less advanced students may be helped to understand the poem if they can reduce it to its simplest terms. A little help with the stylized diction would be appropriate ("Seek'st thou..." could be translated, "Are you looking for..."), and students will need to notice that stanzas one and three are questions. The first stanza can be reduced to, "Where are you going?" and the second to "The hunter won't be able to shoot you." To accustom students to the idea of apostrophe, encourage them to think of times when they have talked to their pets or even to an inanimate object like a bicycle; they may understand better how the narrator feels as he addresses the bird.

Reading the Poem. Before discussing the poem, students may need help in understanding the vocabulary and diction. It is useful to speak of a narrator, a persona that the poet assumes and that need not be the poet's own voice. Thus, in the background statement we learn that Bryant wrote the poem in December, but his persona in the poem speaks of the bird's soon finding a "summer home." Students need to recognize the apostrophe starting with the first line and extending through the poem. The effect is to establish a bond between the narrator and the bird.

Reteaching Alternatives. You might have students create a sequence of eight drawings, one for each stanza, in comic-strip format. Artistic ability should not be a prerequisite: stick figures would do well; it is the expression of the idea that is important. When the drawings have been completed, let students share them and learn from their own and others' comments how close they have come to agreeing on the story line implied in the poem and on the feeling it evokes.

Responding to the Poem Text page 141
Analyzing the Poem
Identifying Details

1. What danger to the bird is mentioned in the second stanza? In lines 5–8, the speaker mentions the hunter, or fowler, who might seek to do the bird some harm.

2. According to the speaker, what guides the waterfowl in its flight? A "Power" teaches the waterfowl its way (lines 13–14).

Describe how the speaker envisions the end of the bird's "toil" in the sixth stanza. The speaker says that the bird will find a summer house in which to rest and be with its fellows; it will build a nest, sheltered by reeds.

3. The third stanza contains examples of *onomatopoeia*, or words that actually imitate the sounds of the things they refer to. Name these words. Examples are "plashy" (line 9) and "billows" (line 11).

Interpreting Meanings

4. In line 27, the point toward which the poem is building becomes explicit with the word *lesson*. In your own words, what is that lesson? The lesson is that God will guide and protect us in our journey through life.

Who is "He" in line 29? "He" refers to God, or to some supernatural power.

What are the "zones"? The "zones" refer to parts of the sky, or perhaps to different regions of the earth marked by differences of climate.

5. The phrase "to do thee wrong" (line 6) is a curious way of describing what the fowler, or hunter, wants to do to the bird. What do you think Bryant intends the fowler to *symbolize*, other than just someone who is hunting birds? Answers will vary, but may suggest that the fowler represents misfortunes or evil forces in general, or the devil in particular.

6. Throughout the poem, certain words and phrases emphasize that the waterfowl is a migratory bird. What are some of these? Some examples are: "pursue" (line 3), "distant flight" (line 6), "seek'st" (line 9), "summer home" (line 22), "certain flight" (line 30).

What does the idea of a *lonely* migration contribute to the *theme* of the poem? The lonely migration of the waterfowl becomes a metaphor for each individual's solitary pilgrimage through life. The happiness of the bird in the "summer home" it finally attains may thus suggest the bliss of heaven for the individual after the journey of life.

7. In the eighteenth century, rationalist thinkers had perceived the operations of nature as a "clockwork universe." They saw the universe as governed by "natural law," under which the stars and the seasons moved and rotated with mechanical precision. In their view, the creator of this mechanism did not control its workings but remained merely an indifferent spectator. In what way is this Romantic poem a rejection of that rationalist view? This poem suggests that God actually intervenes in the universe to provide guidance for humanity.

8. Do you believe the lesson the speaker learns is a useful one? Explain. Student answers will vary.

9. Can Nature still present "lessons" to people today? Most students will agree that this is possible.

How would you describe the way most people today view the natural world? Student answers will vary.

46 American Romanticism

Writing About the Poem
A Critical Response

Analyzing the Poem. Discuss the questions raised in the writing prompt, until students are able to formulate and defend their own interpretations of Bryant's intent in "To a Waterfowl."

Criteria for Evaluating the Assignment. The paragraph states the writer's interpretation of Bryant's intention, explains why Bryant took so long to get to the lesson, and states what the poem does for the reader that a simple statement of Bryant's belief in Divine guidance would not have done.

"Thanatopsis"   Text page 141

Objectives

1. To recognize the use of personification
2. To analyze the use of imagery to create tone
3. To identify metaphors and imagery
4. To recognize iambic pentameter
5. To write a letter from the point of view of a Puritan reading the poem
6. To write an essay comparing and contrasting two poems
7. To write an essay analyzing imagery and meaning
8. To recognize inverted syntax and archaic diction

Introducing the Poem

In outline form for your reference, here are the major elements of the poem:

- **Rhythm:** blank verse
- **Theme:** the identification of death with sleep
- **Significant techniques:** variation of meter, inversion of word order, shifts of tone, personification, metaphor, imagery

Background on the Poem. Bryant left Williams College in his sophomore year in 1811. He had been reading eighteenth-century British poems, including Robert Blair's "The Grave." In this and other poems of the period, blank verse had replaced the heroic couplet and for the first time since Milton was a widely used verse form.

Of the genesis of "Thanatopsis" Bryant himself later wrote: "I cannot give you any information of the occasion which suggested to my mind the idea of my poem Thanatopsis. It was written when I was seventeen or eighteen years old... and I believe it was composed in my solitary rambles in the woods."

The Literal Meaning. The narrator reflects on what nature means to a person who "holds communion" with her: she confirms his glad hours and heals his "darker musings." When death comes, we will "mix forever with the elements"; but we will be lying down with kings and others and have the entire world of nature as our sepulchre. The dead are everywhere. The narrator draws this lesson from his "musings": Live in such a way that when your time comes to die, you will go trustfully, looking forward to pleasant dreams.

Teaching Strategies

Providing for Cultural Differences. Students may be aware that ideas of death vary among cultures. You might have students research ideas of death among different peoples: ancient Greeks, Hindus, Moslems, American Indians, and others. Ask them to compare their findings with the implied ideas of death in "Thanatopsis," and to volunteer to tell of the ideas they have learned through their own family/cultural experience.

Providing for Different Levels of Ability. For less advanced readers the language of the poem may need paraphrasing. Lines 17–30 are among those that may cause difficulty. You might want to help the class through the syntax and diction.

Introducing Vocabulary Study. Students will benefit from knowing the meanings of the following words. (Starred words appear in the Glossary. Italicized words either are archaic or have special meaning in context.)

communion	l. 2	clod	l. 28
eloquence*	l. 5	patriarchs	l. 34
musings	l. 6	*vales*	l. 38
blight	l. 9	pensive	l. 39
shroud	l. 11	venerable	l. 40
insensible	l. 27	abodes	l. 47

lapse	l. 48	quarry	l. 77
phantom	l. 64	scourged	l. 78
innumerable	l. 74	unfaltering	l. 79
caravan	l. 77		

This is a long list, but it can be made more manageable if you divide it into clusters: words describing earthly features (clod, vales, quarry), words related to death (shroud, blight, phantom), words indicating the speaker's frame of mind (musings, communion, pensive, unfaltering).

Reading the Poem. Ask students to write freely for ten minutes about some experience they have had that is associated with death. It might be visiting a cemetery, taking part in a Memorial Day ceremony, attending a funeral, or simply reading a novel or play in which a funeral occurs. They should be encouraged to write their recollection of the experience in some detail and to examine their feelings about it. You may wish to suggest that they will not have to share their writing unless they wish to. A brief discussion and some voluntary sharing of the writing should develop the sense that death is a common subject about which everyone has done some thinking, and that there are a number of ways of thinking about it.

Tell students that "Thanatopsis" expresses one of these ways, and that Bryant wrote it when he was about their age or perhaps a year or two older.

Reteaching Alternatives. You might select a group of students to give a dramatic reading of the poem, with students taking various parts. One student could play Nature and one the person spoken to in the poem. Others could represent, through movement and sound, other people and some of the inanimate objects or abstract terms of the poem: the "all-beholding sun," the "rude swain," the "venerable woods," the "Oregon," and so on. When the poem becomes visual and spatial as well as aural, its meaning should become clearer—even if, in the process, a little comedy creeps into it. The correct tone can be established after the performance by one final serious reading of the poem.

Responding to the Poem Text page 145
Analyzing the Poem
Identifying Details

1. As the poem opens, Nature is *personified* as someone who speaks to us in various languages. What kind of language does Nature use to speak to us in our "gayer hours"? She speaks with gladness, a smile, and "eloquence of beauty" (lines 4–5).

How does Nature respond to our "darker musings"? She responds with a "mild and healing sympathy" (lines 6–7).

2. In line 8, the poet's *tone* grows more somber. The speaker refers to "sad *images*" that make us "shudder and grow sick at heart." What are these images? The images include the "stern agony" of the ill, the "shroud" and "pall" in which a dead person and coffins are wrapped, the "breathless darkness," and a "narrow house."

What does each image refer to? The images all refer to death. The "stern agony" suggests the throes of the dying; the "shroud and pall" are the coverings for a corpse; the "breathless darkness" may be death itself; and the "narrow house" suggests the coffin.

What does the speaker advise us to do when we have these thoughts? He advises us to go outdoors and listen to Nature's teachings.

3. A "still voice" is a phrase often used to refer to intuition, a perception of something not clearly defined—like the "still, small voice" of conscience. In this poem, the still voice is that of Nature. What does this still voice (lines 17–72) say will happen to our individuality at death? The voice says that our individuality will be lost as we become mingled with the elements.

4. In line 31, what shift in the *tone* of the poem occurs? The poem shifts from a tone of stern finality to a tone of consolation.

What comfort is offered in this section of the poem? The voice says that we will not be alone in death; that our resting place will be magnificent; that we will lie down with the great of past generations; and that everyone alive will share this fate.

5. Find at least two *metaphors* in lines 31–54 that are used to describe the earth as a whole. Examples include: "Couch... magnificent" (line 33), "mighty sepulcher" (line 37), "the great tomb of man" (line 45).

What are some other *images* in these lines that reinforce the impression of the earth's vastness and greatness? Other images include: "hills/Rock-ribbed and ancient as the sun" (lines 37–38); "vales/Stretching..." (lines 38–39); "the venerable woods" (line 40); "rivers that move/In majesty" (lines 40–41); "Old Ocean's gray and melancholy waste" (line 43).

6. Beginning with line 51, what is death compared with to make it seem less threatening? In this passage, the dead are compared to the inhabitants of the vast, majestic wilderness. Death itself is a "last sleep" (line 57).

7. Read the first thirty lines of the poem aloud, noting the *iambic pentameter* meter. Find at least three places in these lines where Bryant varies his meter to avoid a singsong rhythm. Examples of variation are furnished by the many enjambements in these lines; for example, lines 1, 2, 3, 4, 8, 10, 14, 17, 22, 27, and 29. Note also that many sentences end in the middle of a line.

48 American Romanticism

Interpreting Meanings

8. How does this poem reveal the Romantic conviction that the universe, far from being mechanical in nature, is really organic and undergoes constant cyclical changes? Perhaps the most important passage embodying this idea occurs at lines 60–72.

Why do you think this organic view of creation is a comfort to the speaker? This view of creation is a comfort because it emphasizes the organic unity of all the living and the dead; such a view holds out the hope that existence after death can be dignified and meaningful.

What would the opposite view suggest about the speaker's ultimate fate? The opposite view would suggest that death is utterly final, and that after death there is no meaning for the human soul.

9. At the conclusion of the speech of the "still voice" (line 73), the speaker's voice resumes for the concluding section, or summing up. What is the main thrust of his advice? The poet advises readers to face the sleep of death with peaceful acceptance, rather than with fear and reluctance.

What is your response to this advice? Do you find it wise and consoling? Do you find it disturbing? Or do you have some other reaction? Explain. Answers should express and support students' opinions.

10. Bryant wrote "Thanatopsis" when he was sixteen years old. Does the poem seem to you to be the work of a teen-ager? Why or why not? Most students will respond that the poem's philosophical depth would indicate that it was the work of a far more mature writer. You may want to remind them, however, that works of genius have been created by some astonishingly young people: Mozart would be a good example.

11. What do you think is the most important word or phrase in the poem? Student answers will vary.

Writing About the Poem
A Creative Response

1. Writing a Letter. Before students begin to write, review the Puritans' world view (text pages 5–10) and elicit from students some possible reactions a Puritan might have.

Criteria for Evaluating the Assignment. The paper is in formal letter form and accurately reflects reactions to "Thanatopsis" appropriate to a Puritan reader.

A Critical Response

2. Comparing and Contrasting Poems. Have students rephrase the prompt to show that they grasp the assignment. Discuss patterns they can use to structure their essays, noting that they must include both similarities and differences in terms of how Nature speaks and the lessons Nature delivers.

Criteria for Evaluating the Assignment. The essay explains similarities and differences in the two Bryant poems in terms of how Nature speaks and the messages delivered.

3. Analyzing Imagery and Meaning. Have students work together to list all phrases referring to death as sleep (for example, "thine eternal resting place," line 31; "couch," line 33; "last sleep," line 57), thus freeing them to move on to focus on the poem as a whole and form opinions as to whether or not Bryant suggests an afterlife.

Criteria for Evaluating the Assignment. The essay traces the sleep images in "Thanatopsis" and uses specific details from the poem to support the opinion that Bryant does or does not suggest an awakening into an afterlife.

Analyzing Language and Style
Inversions and Archaic Language

1. These are five of the many examples of inversion:
    a. "To him who in the love of Nature holds / Communion with her visible forms, she speaks / A various language. . . ."
    b. ". . . while from all around . . . / Comes a still voice . . . ."
    c. "Yet not to thine eternal resting place / Shalt thou retire alone. . . ."
    d. "Are but the solemn decorations all. . . ."
    e. "Where rolls the Oregon. . . ."

Altering the syntax destroys the regular iambic rhythm, despite the many iambic stresses natural to English speech:

"Nature speaks a various language to him
Who, in love of Nature, holds communion
With her visible forms."

2. Some of the archaic words (and their modern equivalents) are "holds communion" (communicates), "visible forms" (appearances), "shroud and pall" (burial clothes), "rude swain" (hick, country bumpkin), "hoary seers" (old prophets), "the drapery of his couch" (bedclothes), etc.

3. Archaic diction in "To a Waterfowl" (pages 139, 141) includes "Whither" (where to), "dost" (does), "thou" and "thy" (you, your), "fowler" (hunter), "seek'st" (seek), "plashy" (splashing), "marge" (edge), "stoop" (descend), "toil" (work, labor), "shalt" (shall or will), "o'er" (over), "thou'rt" (you are), "hath" and "hast" (has), "tread" (walk), and "aright" (correctly). Substituting the modern words destroys the tone of the poem.

Henry Wadsworth Longfellow

Text page 146

"The Cross of Snow"

Text page 147

Objectives

1. To recognize the sonnet form
2. To identify tone
3. To interpret symbolism
4. To write a paragraph responding to the poem

Introducing the Poem

In outline form for your reference, here are the major elements of the poem:

- **Form:** Petrarchan sonnet
- **Rhythm:** iambic pentameter
- **Rhyme:** abba abba cde cde
- **Significant techniques:** figurative language

Background on the Poem. This poem is as close as one can get to being able to say that the poet and the narrator are the same person. "Eighteen years" (line 13) did in fact pass between the death of Frances Appleton (Fanny) Longfellow and the writing of this sonnet. The biographer Edward Wagenknecht calls the death of Fanny Longfellow "the great crisis of his life."

The Literal Meaning. The narrator, unable to sleep, contemplates the picture of his wife, who died from burns in the same room eighteen years before. He remembers what an exceptional person his wife was. He then tells of a mountain which, because of its sheltered ravines, keeps a "cross of snow" all year long: and he likens this "changeless" cross to the cross he wears in memory of his wife.

Teaching Strategies

Providing for Cultural Differences. The cross of snow is clearly a symbol—students may decide exactly what it is they believe it symbolizes. Ask them to describe a picture or some artifact that symbolizes for them something important in their lives. Compare these symbols, and discuss how they help to reveal and interpret the cultural backgrounds of individual students.

Providing for Different Levels of Ability. Students should be able to analyze the rhyme of the sonnet in a minimal way at least, by assigning letters to each end rhyme and discovering the abba abba cde cde pattern.

Some students will be able to state how the thought or focus shifts after each quatrain or tercet: the sleepless narrator contemplating his wife's picture; his remembering her death and recalling what an excellent woman she was; the narrator shifting his thought to the mountain in the West; and finally, his bringing the two thoughts together—the cross on the mountain suggesting to him the grief he still bears.

Reading the Poem. After having a student read the poem aloud, you might have them examine each quatrain and tercet more closely.

In the first line, the two stressed syllables *long sleep*less slow the reading to accentuate their meaning. The contrast between the night and the halo created by the night lamp gives a remarkable visual image. The second quatrain emphasizes the exceptional qualities of the dead woman. The word "legend" reminds us of the Romantic's interest in the past. In the first tercet, "sun-defying" provides a visual contrast of the white snow with the darker surroundings. Having evoked feelings of darkness broken by shifting patterns of light, the narrator in the final tercet introduces the symbol of the cross to make us understand why his tone is so unsettling and his night sleepless. (An audiocassette recording accompanies this poem.)

Reteaching Alternatives. Divide the poem up into its quatrains and tercets and have students paraphrase each group of lines. Next, ask students to suggest a word or two that describes the feeling that the poem produces in each section. Students with artistic talent may wish to draw a sketch for each group of lines.

Responding to the Poem

Text page 148

Analyzing the Poem

Identifying Details

1. What precisely is Longfellow looking at when he refers to the "gentle face" in line 2? He is speaking of his dead wife, who is pictured in a portrait on the wall.

2. What is a halo usually associated with? A halo is usually associated with saints or angels.

In line 4, what is the literal halo that the poet sees? The literal halo that the poet sees is the circular glow cast by

50 American Romanticism

the lamp on his wife's portrait. The lamplight makes it look as if she wears an angel's halo.

3. What does the poet tell us about his wife's character? He tells us that his wife was gentle, pure, and kindly.

Interpreting Meanings

4. The words "martyrdom of fire" in line 6 might confuse readers who did not know that the poet's wife actually died in a fire. What is Longfellow suggesting about his wife's character when he uses such a powerful word to describe her death? In the Christian tradition, martyrdom is usually associated with saints who have died for the faith. The poet is emphasizing his wife's purity and spirituality.

5. The phrase "watches of the night" usually refers to the rounds made by a watchman as he guards a house or a neighborhood. At certain hours, the watch would call, "All is well." What are Longfellow's *figurative* "watches of the night" (line 1)? These are the times when, unable to sleep, the poet broods on the past and mourns his wife.

6. In line 10, explain how the phrase "sun-defying" suggests conditions of weather and geology that might actually produce a permanent cross of snow on the side of a mountain. The literal sense is untouched, or impenetrable, by sunlight. High altitudes and deep crags might result in a permanent cross of snow on a mountainside.

How does the poet relate the idea of a "sun-defying" formation of snow to his own feelings? The poet's grief is too deep to be melted by any ray of happiness, just as the cross of snow in the deep crags cannot be melted by the rays of the sun.

7. What specific event does the common expression "a cross to bear" refer to? The expression refers to Christ's carrying the cross on the way to the crucifixion.

In everyday speech, a cross, in the sense of a burden, is something to *bear* or *shoulder*. But Longfellow says that his is "the cross I wear upon my breast" (line 12). **Why does he use that phrase instead of referring to it as a cross he bears?** Longfellow wears his "cross"—his grief—upon his breast because it is in his heart.

8. Imagine that a contemporary celebrity had written a similar poem (or song) about a sad personal event. Would you think publication of the work appropriate? Why or why not? Student answers will vary.

Writing About the Poem
A Critical Response

Responding to the Poem. Although these papers may be very personal, remind students they should include specific details from the poem that aroused their responses.

Criteria for Evaluating the Assignment. The paragraph states the writer's general response to "The Cross of Snow" and cites specific examples of message, language, rhyme, rhythm, and tone that aroused that response.

Elements of Literature   Text page 148
The Sonnet

The subject (in the octave) is that Longfellow's wife is dead and he still misses her. The comment (in the sestet) is that the pain of his loss is as enduring as the cross of snow in a certain mountain ravine which is never touched by sunlight. The rhyme scheme is abba cddc efg efg.

Extending the Poem

Writing an Italian sonnet may seem more difficult than it really is. Suggest that students find a picture or some symbol that has special meaning for them, and write about it in the form of a sonnet, possibly taking clues from the Longfellow sonnet on how they might structure their work.

"The Ropewalk"

Text page 149

Objectives

1. To recognize trochaic meter
2. To respond to images and metaphors

Introducing the Poem

The poem has a precise structure. The stanzas are six lines of trochaic tetrameter, with the rhyme scheme aabccb. In the first three and last stanzas the narrator observes the ropewalk. In the middle stanzas he describes a sort of daydream.

Background on the Poem. Longfellow's journal entry for May 20, 1854, was very brief: "A lovely morning. Wrote a poem—'The Ropewalk.'" Longfellow's broad sympathies are hinted at in the poem: his love for children, his associations with Europe, where bellringing was more common than in this country (though Cambridge would have had its bellringers in his time); his interest in the farm and the sea—both typical of the Romantics.

The Literal Meaning. The narrator describes a ropewalk and presents different pictures of the uses that he imagines the rope being manufactured will be put to: stanza four, "two fair maidens" swinging; stanza five, a girl on a tightrope; stanza six, a woman drawing water from a well; stanza seven, a ringer in a bell tower; stanza eight, a gallows; stanza nine, multiple pictures: a boy flying a kite, a roundup, trappers with their snares, and a fisherman; and stanza ten, ships at sea with ropes being used not only for anchors and rigging, but for sounding the depths.

Teaching Strategies

Providing for Cultural Differences. Students whose backgrounds include manufacturing, factory work, or sailing, may identify with the subject of the poem, and may also be interested in telling about the changes these activities that have occurred since Longfellow's day.

Providing for Different Levels of Ability. If some students who do not find the connections that the poem makes between the manufacture and the uses of the rope, you might ask them to concentrate on the central metaphor. What does mention of a spider make them think of? What words do they associate with "thread" and "cobweb"? What does a spider look like while it is spinning a web? How would you describe the way a spider works? Their answers will help students to see the similarity between a rope walker and a spider.

Reading the Poem. For the first three poems of this unit the focus has been on nature and death; now we have a poem that seems to have as its focus manufacturing. Poetry, like stories and drama, can be written about anything in the human experience. Students will become aware, however, that though this poem starts as a description of the manufacture of rope, it soon shifts, through the dream, to descriptions of other scenes that are more typical of the Romantics. Once students have understood the structure of the poem, call their attention to such poetic elements as alliteration, repetition, metaphor, and imagery. Through judicious questioning you may be able to have students say how the tone and feeling change from one stanza to the next.

Reteaching Alternatives. Stanzas four to ten are self-contained descriptions. Is there some rational explanation for their order, or does it simply represent the random wandering of the narrator's mind? Ask students to explain the order of these stanzas. They might try shifting the order and reading the poem with the stanzas rearranged, to see if this makes any difference to the tone or feeling. They will note that such rearranging cannot be done with the last stanza.

Even if they do not notice much difference between the original and their new version of the poem, students will better understand the poem's structure and how it contributes to the total effect.

Responding to the Poem

Text page 151

Analyzing the Poem

Identifying Details

1. In the first stanza, Longfellow uses a *simile*. What is the factory compared to? The building is compared to a "hulk," or large ship, with windows in a row like portholes.

2. By the end of stanza 3, the poet has presented a series of *images* of the factory and of the spinners at work. Describe what the workers are doing. The spinners climb up and down as they operate the machines that spin out the lengths of rope.

What are the "cobwebs" mentioned at the end of this stanza? The "cobwebs" are the images spun in the poet's own imagination.

3. Beginning with stanza 4, Longfellow takes an imaginary "ropewalk" and gives us a succession of pictures in which some kind of rope or cord plays a part. Briefly describe each of these scenes. The scenes are as follows: two young girls in a rope swing; a girl on a circus tightrope;

52 American Romanticism

a farm woman drawing water from a well; an old man ringing bells in a tower as the bell ropes almost drag him from the ground; prisoners in front of a gallows in a prison yard; a schoolboy flying a kite, with hunters and people fishing; ships sailing, wrecks aimlessly floating, anchors losing their grip in "faithless sand," and sailors "feeling for the land" by means of their slackening ropes.

Interpreting Meanings

4. New England factories of the nineteenth century often were unpleasant places with working conditions that would be regarded as intolerable today. What is the implication of the *metaphor* comparing the factory workers to spiders? The metaphor implies that the work has turned these people into mere, unthinking insects. It has dehumanized them.

5. Describe the changes of *tone* as the poet imagines scene after scene. What opposing aspects of human life is the poet holding "in balance"? The shifts in tone may be described as follows: playful and gay in stanza 4; hectic and tense in stanza 5; homely and peaceful in stanza 6; dramatic and tense in stanza 7; dark and bitter in stanza 8; a sudden shift to a lighthearted tone in stanza 9; rapid shifts in tone from light to dark to hopeful in stanza 10. Stanza 10 opens with a lighthearted scene of ships "rejoicing" in the breeze, then shifts to a grim picture of aimlessly floating wrecks, and of anchors losing their grip in the sand; the stanza closes with a hopeful tone, with sailors using rope leads to determine that they are approaching land. The shifts in tone in these stanzas suggest that the human condition is varied; great joy and great misery either exist at the same time or follow each other swiftly in succession.

  How do you think he feels about the "human spiders"? The speaker seems to sympathize with their plight.

6. Can you think of any occupations today in which the workers could be compared to insects or animals? Student answers will vary.

Writing About the Poem
A Creative Response

Describing an Idyllic Scene. Question 3 ("Analyzing the Poem") will have given students a list of scenes from which to choose, but clarify the meaning of "idyllic." Use the final question of the writing prompt—which are definitely *not* Currier & Ives subjects—for this discussion, not as part of the writing assignment.

Criteria for Evaluating the Assignment. The paragraph cites a scene from "The Ropewalk" that would make an apt Currier & Ives subject, and describes the scene and its mood.

Analyzing Language and Style
Trochaic Meter

Longfellow does repeat his count faithfully. The only exception is one use of two unaccented syllables—the last two syllables of "lessening" in line 59. The carrying power of the rhythm would, however, induce one to pronounce even this word as a trochee: "less'ning."

Extending the Poem

You might suggest that students describe a process that they are familiar with and that affects the lives of other people, as rope manufacture does. For example, a boy who works as a cashier might imagine how the goods he sells will be used; or a girl who pumps gas could imagine where the cars she services are going. Encourage students to write about these, using the same short descriptive technique that Longfellow does. Maintaining Longfellow's rhythm is not necessary.

"The Tide Rises, the Tide Falls"   Text page 152

Objectives

1. To identify theme
2. To recognize personification and onomatopoeia
3. To write an essay comparing two poems

Introducing the Poem

This short poem is generally considered one of Longfellow's finest lyrics. The "traveler" of line four may be taken as one traveling through life. The facts that Longfellow wrote the poem near the end of his own life, and that the

Henry Wadsworth Longfellow   53

traveler returns to the shore "nevermore," may suggest that the poem is about the end of the journey.

The restrained diction, the concrete images, and the absence of moralizing keep the tone from becoming sentimental.

Background on the Poem. Critic Cecil Williams says of this poem:

> In 1879, when he was seventy-two and only three years from death, [Longfellow] wrote the lovely "The Tide Rises, The Tide Falls," a poem reminiscent of "My Lost Youth." He returns again to his boyhood in Portland, where he had loved to listen to the sough of the waves and to the gentle rush of the tide coming in. As he visualized in old age the phenomena of water behavior, it became symbolic of life. Once again, as in the early "Psalm of Life," he uses the figure, "footprints in the sands." By now he seems not very certain that he has made lasting footprints in the sands of life, but the tone implies that it does not greatly matter.

The Literal Meaning. The narrator stands at the shore near evening. He notices a traveler hastening "toward the town," darkness settling on the town, and the "little waves" effacing the footprints, the last signs of the traveler. The next morning the horses are ready, but the traveler does not return to the shore. Through it all, the tide rises and falls.

Teaching Strategies

Providing for Cultural Differences. The rising and falling of the tide is of course universal, crossing cultures and generations. Some students, however, will have experienced the tides more than others. Students who have lived at the shore can describe what the shore is like as the tide rises and falls, and can perhaps relate the feeling of having something they have created on the beach disappear with the tide.

Providing for Different Levels of Ability. Less advanced readers may have trouble understanding the repetition in the poem. After all, there are only fifteen lines, and four of them are the same. If the question comes up, ask students to tell you the lyrics of their favorite songs. They may discover that the repetition in this poem serves somewhat the same purpose as it does in song lyrics. More advanced readers should be able to note other musical devices such as the alliteration and assonance.

Reading the Poem. A good reading of this poem will reveal the alliteration, the softness of the sounds, and the steady and regular movement of the rhythm. (An audiocassette recording accompanies the poem.) You may want to introduce the poem by giving students a little background, pointing out that Longfellow wrote it near the end of his life. This would prepare them for at least thinking about the journey the traveler is making as life's journey.

Reteaching Alternatives. You might have the class decide on a thematic statement they would like to make about school, and follow the pattern of "The tide rises..." to create a class poem developing the theme. It will be most meaningful if they think of something that, like the tide, keeps coming and going, like the bell, school books, or lunch period. The purpose of this exercise is to help students understand, by means of the composing process, how the elements of a poem come together to develop a theme and create a feeling. Having tried it themselves, they may appreciate more fully what Longfellow has achieved.

Responding to the Poem   Text page 154
Analyzing the Poem
Identifying Details

1. How does the division into stanzas reflect the passage of time in the poem? Stanza 1 presents twilight darkening into night; stanza 2 presents the passage of night; in stanza 3 morning is breaking.

Interpreting Meanings

2. "Footsteps on the sands of time" is a common expression referring to mortality and the passing of time. What do you think is implied about the fate of the traveler when his footprints are washed away in the second stanza? It is implied that the traveler disappears or dies.

3. What feeling is suggested by the stamping and neighing of the horses the next morning? With this detail the poet suggests a feeling of renewed life.

What contrasting feeling is suggested by what we are told about the traveler in this stanza? With the information that the traveler never returns to the shore, the poet suggests a contrasting, somber hint of death.

4. *Onomatopoeia* **is a poetic technique in which the sounds of words are used to echo their sense. If you have ever heard the call of a shore bird, you know that the words "curlew calls" in line 2 echo the sound the bird itself makes (its cry is particularly mournful when heard at dusk). What sound do you think dominates this poem?** Most students will agree that the sound "alls" dominates the poem.

What atmosphere or feeling does it suggest? It suggests a melancholy, mournful atmosphere, perhaps suggesting the sound of wailing or of the tolling of a bell, or the mournful cry of a sea bird.

How does the rhythm of the poem reflect the movement of the tides? The rising and falling of the tide is

54   American Romanticism

suggested by the rising and falling effect of the meter in the first and last halves of the refrain.

5. The waves are *personified* in stanza 2 as having "soft, white hands." This is an example of Longfellow's poetic style that some readers think is too cute, or too sentimental, to be effective. Do you think the personification is justified here? Why or why not? Answers will vary, but students should clearly express an opinion as to whether the personification is effective, and give reasons.

6. Do you think this is a poem about one specific traveler? Or could it be seen as a "drama" about everyone's life? Most students will agree that the poem could be both.

What do you think is suggested by the tide's continuing to rise and fall, despite the fact that the human traveler is gone? Student answers will vary. Students may suggest that this detail implies a contrast between the permanence of nature, symbolized by the sea and its tides, and the transitoriness of human existence.

Writing About the Poem
A Critical Response

Comparing and Contrasting Poems. Read both "The Tide Rises, the Tide Falls" and "Break, Break, Break," aloud. As a prewriting activity, help students chart the poems' similarities and differences as suggested in the writing prompt.

***C**riteria for Evaluating the Assignment.* The essay cites differences between the poems in mood (Longfellow's has a trace of sadness, while Tennyson's is filled with grief), meter (Longfellow uses iambic / anapestic tetrameter; Tennyson, a mix of iambic / anapestic trimeter and tetrameter, with the opening line consisting of three spondees), rhyme patterns (Longfellow's is aabba; Tennyson's, abcb), and what the sea represents (for Longfellow, time; for Tennyson, heartless nature). But the paper notes the similarity of message—the sea washes away the past: "The day returns, but nevermore / Returns the traveler to the shore" (Longfellow); "the tender grace of a day that is dead / Will never come back to me" (Tennyson).

Extending the Poem

This is a good poem to ask students to memorize. For further reading and thinking, you might ask students to compare the poem with Robert Frost's "Neither Far Out Nor In Deep" (text page 676), another deceptively simple poem about watching the sea.

Primary Sources: Visiting Mr. Longfellow   Text page 155

This brief extract, from a biography by a prominent contemporary critic, will be useful in lending a note of humor to your class's study of the Romantics, and in leading them to see early nineteenth-century people as being lively and irreverent. You might, if time permits, ask students if they can compare the "bloopers" uttered by Longfellow's visitors with ones they have heard about present-day celebrities.

John Greenleaf Whittier   Text page 156

From "Snow-Bound: A Winter Idyll"   Text page 157

Objectives

1. To identify allusions
2. To write a paragraph analyzing the poem's appeal
3. To analyze imagery

Introducing the Poem

This poem is autobiographical, written when the poet was nearing sixty and inclined to reminisce about his youth. Whittier lived in northern Massachusetts, where in those days a snowstorm could completely isolate a family for days. Whittier describes the storm and its aftermath in realistic but imaginative terms. There is humor in the descriptions, but the details of the cold and darkness create a tone of loneliness, almost of horror. Thus, while the poem has the quality of an idyll and evokes a warm and for some a nostalgic response, it does have its dark side.

Background on the Poem. The first part of the poem, which appears in the text, sets the stage for the nearly six hundred lines that follow. There we learn of the family and guests: father, mother, two sisters, aunt, uncle, the schoolmaster, another guest, and the two boys themselves. The descriptions of these people and the accounts of the stories they told when the family was snowbound touched a responsive chord in American readers, who needed just such a romantic and nostalgic idyll to help them recover from the Civil War. The poem sold thousands of copies and gave Whittier financial security for the first time in his life.

The Literal Meaning. The poet recalls a December day in his youth when all the signs pointed to an approaching snowstorm. The family lived on a farm, removed from the nearest neighbors, so a heavy storm meant isolation. After bringing in wood and bedding down the animals, the two boys went to bed early, when it was already snowing. After the storm, the boys dug a path to the barn—tunneling where the drifts were deepest—and were welcomed by the animals. That evening the family gathered at the hearth, and sitting around the roaring fire, enjoyed warm cider, apples, and "nuts from brown October's wood."

Teaching Strategies

Providing for Cultural Differences. Very few people in our industrial and electronic world have had an experience comparable to the one described in the poem, regardless of their cultural background. However, students may relate "Snow-Bound" to their own experiences if they are led to think of and to write or tell about a time when the family had to fall back on its own resources: a car breakdown on a trip, perhaps, of a power outage, a storm during a camping trip, or some other unusual and unexpected occurrence. What did the family do on such an occasion?

Providing for Different Levels of Ability. There should not be much difficulty for any readers in following the narrative line of the poem. Less advanced students, however, may benefit from help with allusions and imagery. You might encourage them to sketch their interpretations of a few objects or scenes: for example, the "clothesline posts" (lines 39–40); the tunnel (line 75); or the fire being laid (lines 120–126).

Introducing Vocabulary Study. Knowing the meanings of the following words will help students understand the poem. (Starred words appear in the Glossary. Italicized words either are archaic or have special meaning in context.)

waning	l. 4	harem	l. 86
mute (adj.)	l. 6	reproach	l. 88
ominous*	l. 6	patriarch	l. 89
portent	l. 7	sage (adj.)	l. 91
scaffold	l. 28	*rude-furnished*	l. 130
querulous*	l. 30	pendent	l. 136
aloof	l. 63	transfigured	l. 136
supernal	l. 80	baffled	l. 158
speckled*	l. 86		

The clustering of these words may help you pinpoint some potential trouble spots for student comprehension of the poem: the opening descriptive passage, for instance, and the description of the tunnels through the snow and of the barnyard, lines 73–92.

Reading the Poem. After you have introduced the poem, you might want to play the audiocassette recording, or read the poem aloud having students listen for the details that make the storm vivid. You might want to check for understanding by giving some line numbers and asking students to tell in their own words what picture is being presented in those lines. The sentence in lines 9–14 may be especially troublesome, for the main verb is the last word of the sentence, "told"; the direct object is the gerund "coming" just before it; and the subject is the first noun of the sentence, "chill." Written in the normal prose fashion, the sentence would read: "A chill which no coat could shut out . . . (fore)told the coming of the snowstorm."

Reteaching Alternatives. You might give students a group of words or phrases and ask them to state whether they describe something pleasant or something unpleasant. They might then be asked to find a word with comparable meaning that would have the opposite value. Substituting the new word for the old word should change the tone of the poem. For example, on line 54, "the old, familiar sight" could be changed to "the decrepit, boring sight."

Responding to the Poem Text page 160
Analyzing the Poem
Identifying Details

1. The first eighteen lines of the poem create a mood of foreboding and expectation. List the *images* that help build this suspenseful mood. Answers include the following: "the sun . . . Rose cheerless over hills of gray" (lines 1–2); "darkly circled, gave at noon / A sadder light . . ." (lines 3–4); "the roar / Of Ocean on his wintry shore" (lines 15–16); "the strong pulse" of the "inland air" (lines 17–18).

56 American Romanticism

2. Cite the *images* of sound in lines 100–105 that help you imagine the storm outside the house. Images include: "dreary-voiced elements," "shrieking of the mindless wind," "moaning tree boughs," "on the glass the unmeaning beat / Of ghostly fingertips of sleet."

In lines 110–115, what details help you imagine the isolated quality of farm life in the nineteenth century? The poet points out that the sound of the brook, now stilled, had provided companionship in their lonely life, and had come to have "an almost human tone."

3. In lines 155–174, what *images* show how the threatening situation outside is turned into a cozy and pleasant situation inside? The group sits contentedly before a cleanswept hearth; the logs give off a "tropic heat"; the wind roars in "baffled rage" outside, unable to get in; the dog and cat lie peacefully; mugs of cider are heating and apples roasting; a basket of nuts sits nearby.

Interpreting Meanings

4. The poet emphasizes the fabulous nature of the snowbound world. What *images* help us to see his farmyard as if it's an exotic sight from another world? Answers might include the following: the reference to a Chinese roof (line 62), and the allusion to the leaning tower of Pisa (lines 63–65).

5. Another reference to folklore and to the fabulous occurs in the lines describing the crystal cave. In line 80, what do the boys wish they could do? They wish they could use Aladdin's lamp to grant wishes.

What other details in the poem connect the fabulous or the imaginary with the snowbound farmhouse? The other details include: the rhyme mentioning witches in lines 140–142; the cat's shadow appearing to be a tiger's in line 168; the chimney seeming to laugh in line 164.

6. How might a realistic writer describe this storm? Student answers will vary.

Writing About the Poem
A Critical Response

Analyzing the Poem's Appeal. Before students begin to write, discuss the appeal of the clean, wholesome, simple, "romantic past" presented in "Snow-Bound."

Criteria for Evaluating the Assignment. The paper is a coherent paragraph with topic sentence and details explaining why the poem has appeal for readers even today.

Analyzing Language and Style
Allusions

(1) Allusions to architecture appear in lines 62 and 65 ("a Chinese roof," "Pisa's leaning miracle"); (2) to literature in lines 75–80 ("Aladdin's wondrous cave"); (3) to history in line 90 ("Egypt's Amun"). Such allusions suggest a broad acquaintance with world history and literature.

Extending the Poem

Students who enjoy the poem should be encouraged to read the complete version. They might report to the class, each student giving a summary of a reading of one of the characters at the hearthside.

Oliver Wendell Holmes

Text page 161

"Old Ironsides"

Text page 162

Objectives

1. To analyze symbolism
2. To write a paragraph applying the poem to a human situation
3. To write an essay finding contemporary parallels
4. To recognize connotations

Introducing the Poem

This poem was written for the specific purpose of arousing readers to persuade the government to preserve the frigate *Constitution*. Thus the tone is important; the poem catches the reader's attention immediately and builds to the end, without letting up. The many strong accents in the poem create a tone of strong emotion, possibly even anger. The vowel sounds and the alliteration of "beneath," "battle," and "burst" sustain the intensity of the sound.

The emotional pitch is kept high through to the end, where the poem verges on the melodramatic with its "shattered hulk" (the *Constitution* was not shattered but basically sound), its "nail to the mast her holy flag" (at the time the ship had no masts), and its calling on the "god of storms."

Background on the Poem. In August 1830, the *Constitution* was thirty years old—more than twice the lifespan of the average wooden warship. A Navy report indicated it had a sound frame but needed "very extensive repairs." However, the Boston *Advertiser* on September 14, erroneously reported that the Navy had condemned the ship. What happened in the Holmes household on that day or the next is dramatically recreated by Catherine Drinker Bowen in *Yankee from Olympus*:

> ...Oliver, bursting in the door one afternoon, found [Abiel Holmes, his father] sitting moodily at his desk, trying to compose a letter to the *Boston Daily Advertiser*....
>
> Oliver went upstairs and, sitting down by the western window, got out pen and paper. The lines poured from him, swept from him in a tide. It was as though he were writing someone else's poem, dictated carefully by its author and transcribed by Oliver Holmes....
>
> It was late when he took the poem downstairs.... His father was still at his desk.... Silently Oliver laid the poem on the desk and left the room.
>
> A moment later his father called him. When Oliver came in, Abiel Holmes was standing by the desk, the poem in his hand. He began to speak, and his voice choked. With enormous surprise and a great lift of the heart, Oliver, looking up, saw tears in his father's eyes, saw that the hand holding his verses was trembling.

The Literal Meaning. In lines 1–12 the narrator reviews in generalized but heroic terms the noble history of the frigate. In the next four lines he acknowledges that the ship will have no further victories. In the final stanza he says that it is better that she should be given "to the god of storms" and have an ending befitting her victorious career, rather than be broken up.

Teaching Strategies

Providing for Cultural Differences. Students of early American heritage, or from military, especially Navy, families, will respond most immediately to the emotional pull of the poem. Students from other cultures may be able to find in their own background, or in present-day America, something comparable to "Old Ironsides" for which they would want to fight, were it threatened. Ask them to suggest something that means as much to them as the frigate meant to the people of Boston, and to explain why it does.

Providing for Different Levels of Ability. Less advanced students may have difficulty understanding that the diction of the poem is deliberately elevated for purposes of arousing the reader's emotions and keeping them at a high pitch. You might have these students replace some of the phrases with others less emotionally loaded. "Tattered ensign" might be replaced with "ragged flag." The second line might be changed to "It's been up there for a while." Reading a stanza or two in the new version will help to convince students that the diction in the original does, in fact, contribute greatly to the success of the poem.

More advanced readers may want to examine the history of Old Ironsides and try to connect some of the imagery, such as "the vanquished foe," with actual events. They may discover that some suggestion of myth or legend had already crept into the consciousness of Holmes's readers, or that he was in fact putting it there.

Reading the Poem. Students may be interested to know that this poem was written rapidly, in a burst of emotion. Understanding the circumstances, they will be prepared to find examples of hyperbole, and diction that arouses a high pitch of emotion.

After reading the poem aloud, start off the discussion by asking students how the famous first line gets its impact. They may point to the alliteration, the strongly stressed first two syllables, the image of the "tattered ensign" (not just any old flag!), and above all to the verbal irony.

Keep the students' attention focused on the flag through discussion of the first stanza; it becomes a "banner in the sky." Finally, it becomes a "meteor of the ocean air" sweeping the clouds—or, if you interpret "meteor" to mean the ship itself, the flag is the topmost part of her.

Reteaching Alternatives. Some students may respond emotionally to the poem and enjoy it without wanting to analyze its structure or its technique. You might point out that at the time Holmes wrote the poem, Old Ironsides lay in Boston Harbor with no masts or rigging, and presumably no ensign, and in need of a great deal of new planking as well as new sails and anchor cable. Have them look once more at the specific descriptions that Holmes gives of the ship, and compare them with the reality of the ship's appearance. Perhaps they will see more clearly that such people as the Secretary of the Navy, whom Holmes may have had in mind with his line "The harpies of the shore...." had to make a decision about quite a different ship than the one Holmes's poem leads the reader to visualize.

Responding to the Poem
Text page 163
Analyzing the Poem
Identifying Details

1. What *metaphors* does Holmes use to describe the ship in stanzas 1 and 2? In stanza 1, Holmes uses the metaphor of "the meteor of the ocean air" for the ship, and in stanza 2, he calls it the "eagle of the sea."

2. What proposal concludes the poem? Holmes proposes that it would be better to sink the ship and give her back to the sea and the "god of storms" than ignobly to rip her apart for scrap.

Interpreting Meanings

3. In simple terms, what message does the first stanza present? Old Ironsides has too noble a history, and too much patriotic meaning, to be scrapped.

What is *ironic* about the way Holmes states his message? Rather than begging that the ship not be destroyed, Holmes first urges the opposite of what he really means: "Ay, tear her tattered ensign down!" He then emphasizes the irony of his statement by evoking the ship's former glory.

4. When a ship is broken up in the dockyards, she is said to be scrapped—that is, stripped of everything valuable or reusable. Is Holmes comparing the directors of the scrapping business to harpies in stanza 2, or is his scorn directed at someone else? Explain. Holmes is suggesting that those who are responsible for arranging that the ship be scrapped, and who will profit from it, are the vulture-like harpies.

5. What do you think the poet wants the ship to *symbolize*? Students may suggest that the ship symbolizes the nation's heroic past, threatened by "progress" and "modern ways."

6. In many circumstances where poets have seen things they love threatened by "progress," they have composed prayers or made petitions. How does Holmes's response differ from a prayer or a petition? Holmes uses irony and fiery rhetoric to make an angry statement appealing to readers' emotions, rather than offering a humbler prayer or a reasoned petition.

7. If, next year, Old Ironsides should be found to be in danger of sinking at her dock, do you think most Americans would let her go? Student answers will vary.

8. Do you think other historical relics like this old ship should be preserved? Or do you think they should be destroyed? Why? Encourage a lively discussion among the students, and urge them to support their opinions with convincing arguments.

Writing About the Poem
A Creative Response

1. Applying the Poem to Other Situations. Read and briefly discuss the writing prompt with students before they begin to write. Clarify parts of the ship as necessary.

Criteria for Evaluating the Assignment. The paragraph makes logical use of a ship's parts in human terms; for example, flag for hair/a hat, thunders for a voice, sails for garments, and so on.

A Critical Response

2. Finding Contemporary Parallels. Thinking of the poem as a call to honor the past, you might discuss restoration of the Statue of Liberty or appeals of the 1980's related to paying belated honor to Vietnam War soldiers.

Criteria for Evaluating the Assignment. The essay is at least one paragraph long. It names at least two issues (local or national) that have inspired appeals to honor the past, and describes the methods of communication used rather than poetry to make the appeals.

Analyzing Language and Style
Connotations

The original phrases, and some possible responses:

1. *meteor of the ocean air:* shrapnel of the ocean air
2. *red with heroes' blood:* red with children's blood
3. *harpies of the shore:* realists of the shore
4. *eagle of the sea:* old hulk of the sea
5. *shattered hulk:* worthless hulk
6. *holy flag:* meaningless flag
7. *threadbare sail:* ragged sail

Extending the Poem

Old Ironsides lies today in Boston Harbor. Some of your students may have visited Boston and had a tour of the ship and a look at the museum on the grounds. Ask them to share their impressions and any literature they may have brought back with them. Students who enjoyed the poem will be interested in knowing more about the history and present status of the frigate. You might recommend they read *A Most Fortunate Ship, A Narrative History of "Old Ironsides"* by Tyrone G. Martin, who was captain of the frigate from 1974–1978 (The Globe Pequot Press, Chester, CT 06412, 1982).

Oliver Wendell Holmes

"The Chambered Nautilus"

Text page 164

Objectives

1. To interpret metaphor
2. To understand imagery
3. To write an essay responding to the poem's message
4. To write a paragraph analyzing the poem's appeal
5. To identify archaic language and inverted syntax and recast them into contemporary English

Introducing the Poem

Here, in outline form for your reference, are the major elements of the poem:

- **Rhythm:** iambic
- **Rhyme:** aabbbcc
- **Figures of speech:** allusion (sirens, Triton); metaphor (the nautilus for growth of the human spirit)
- **Significant techniques:** alliteration, apostrophe

Background on the Poem. The poem first appeared at the close of a section of the *Autocrat of the Breakfast Table* in 1858. Holmes seemed to have been proud of the poem.

The Literal Meaning. The narrator reminds the reader of the legendary quality of the nautilus, which is now "wrecked" and "rent." He tells in the third stanza how the animal passed each year from one chamber to a larger one. In the fourth stanza, he thanks the now dead nautilus for bringing him a lesson. In the final stanza he draws the lesson: that his soul should leave its "low-vaulted past" and "build . . . more stately mansions" until it casts off its "outgrown shell" and becomes free.

Teaching Strategies

Providing for Cultural Differences. In this poem an American scientist and poet has focused on a sea creature respected by the ancient Greeks as he himself respects it, and has made it a metaphor for spiritual growth. You might ask students to tell or write about animals or other creatures that have been meaningful to them.

Providing for Different Levels of Ability. For less advanced readers, you might provide a description of the nautilus from an encyclopedia; or perhaps a student can provide one from a science text. You might also ask students to describe, in terms of their own experience, what they think Holmes may have had in mind in the last stanza. Can they make the analogy between the nautilus's leaving its "low-vaulted past" and some progress they have made in the last year—something they have learned or achieved, perhaps? More advanced readers will enjoy analyzing the rhythm and rhyme scheme of the poem and discussing how it supports the sense and tone of the poem.

Reading the Poem. Before you read the poem to the class, it would be a good idea to explain to them the nautilus and tell them briefly what to listen for in the structure of the poem and in its imagery.

In discussing the poem, ask students how its sounds and imagery affect the reader. Alliteration and assonance give the first two stanzas a soft musical quality in keeping with the imagery from myth and folklore.

The movement from long to short lines and back again surprises and pleases the listener by introducing a rhyme sooner than anticipated at first and then prolonging the wait for a rhyme while introducing alliteration (dim-dreaming; was-wont; irised-ceiling-sunless).

In this poem students may object to the moralizing of the last two stanzas, and be reminded of the Bryant poetry they have read earlier; or they may like it. You might pooint out that the best modern poets often imply a moral without making it explicit, suggesting that good writing today is more apt to show than to tell.

Reteaching Alternatives. You might have students in groups or individually "translate" the language of the poem, keeping the meaning the same, but getting rid of archaic language, dropping some of the modifiers that may complicate the sentences, and reducing the statements of the poem to simplified contemporary English. Then have the entire new version of the poem read aloud. Students will see that it has lost its poetry; but they may more easily understand what is literal and what is metaphor, what is observed scientific description and what is imagined. The poetic value of the original version may then be more apparent to them.

Responding to the Poem

Text page 166

Analyzing the Poem

Identifying Details

1. What *metaphor* describes the nautilus in line 1? The nautilus is compared to a "ship of pearl," sailing on the

60 American Romanticism

ocean. The metaphor suggests the nature of the nautilus as a marine creature and also the appearance of its pearly shell.

2. The poet says that the "main," or open sea, over which the nautilus sailed is "unshadowed" (line 2). What other *images* in the first stanza help you picture where the nautilus once sailed? Images include "gulfs enchanted" (line 5) and "coral reefs" (line 6).

3. What are the "webs of living gauze" referred to in line 8? These are the membranes of the animal inside the nautilus shell.

   According to the second stanza, what has happened to the nautilus? The nautilus has been "wrecked" (line 9)—taken from the sea and split open.

4. Who is the "frail tenant" of the shell? The "frail tenant" is the snail who lived inside the nautilus.

5. Stanza 3 describes the way the nautilus grows. The poet speaks of the nautilus *metaphorically,* as a person who changes homes. What details describe how this happens year after year? Details include: "silent toil/That spread his lustrous coil" (lines 15–16); "the spiral grew" (line 17); "left the past year's dwelling for the new" (line 18); moved through its "shining archway" (line 19); "built up its idle door" (line 20).

6. Why does the speaker thank the nautilus in the fourth stanza? The poet is grateful to the nautilus for its lesson or message to humankind: do not be afraid to move on from the old to the new.

Interpreting Meanings

7. In what part of the poem is the "heavenly message" of the shell revealed? This is revealed in the last stanza.

   Paraphrase this message—that is, state in your own words what the "voice that sings" says to the poet. The soul is told to reach higher and higher as time passes until it finally leaves its body behind and becomes free.

8. The central extended *metaphor* of the poem is revealed in the last stanza. What is that *metaphor*? Step by step, how is it extended—that is, what are the "stately mansions," the "low-vaulted past," "each new temple," the "outgrown shell," and the "unresting sea"? The creature building its nautilus shell is a metaphor for the human soul striving toward heaven. The "stately mansions," or nautilus chambers, represent the spiritual achievements of the soul; the "low-vaulted past," or previous chamber, represents the earlier, less spiritual state of the soul; "each new temple," or chamber, represents each step of the soul toward heaven; the "outgrown shell" is a suggestion of the body discarded by the soul in death; the "unresting sea" represents life.

9. Did you find this poem more optimistic than "Thanatopsis"? Student answers will vary. Encourage the students to compare the tone and specific motifs of the two poems in some detail.

10. Of all the nature poems you've read in this unit, which did you like best? Least? Student answers will vary. Have the students support their candidates by comparing them in detail with some of the other poems in the unit.

Writing About the Poem
A Creative Response

1. Considering the Shell Scientifically. Have students look up "chambered nautilus" in a dictionary or science text before they write the paragraph.

Criteria for Evaluating the Assignment. The paragraph makes use of the scientific description of the shell in answering the three questions contained in the prompt.

A Critical Response

2. Responding to a "Message." In discussion, lead students to see how carefully Holmes builds toward his moral, but do not force your view upon them.

Criteria for Evaluating the Assignment. The paragraph states a clear opinion as to whether the poem has a tacked-on moral or is "all of a piece," and uses specific details from the poem to support this opinion.

3. Analyzing the Poem's Appeal. Before students begin to write, discuss what students find attractive about the poem "The Chambered Nautilus," in terms of both its message and its sounds—for example, its frequent use of alliteration, as in the *s* sounds of line 7.

Criteria for Evaluating the Assignment. The paper is a coherent paragraph with topic sentence and supportive details explaining why the poem still appeals to readers.

Analyzing Language and Style
Poetic and Archaic Language

What plain, everyday English words could be substituted for the following "poetic" or archaic words from "The Chambered Nautilus"? Put your substitutes in the poem: does it sound more "modern"?

feign: imagine	thine: yours
main: sea	thou: you
bark: boat	beheld: saw
wont: accustomed	art: are
thee: you	

Oliver Wendell Holmes 61

Putting the substitutions into the poem makes it sound more modern, but the poem loses some of its appeal.

Now find lines that use *inverted syntax* in the poem, and put these passages in normal English sentence order. Does the poem now seem less inflated, less archaic?

Normal English sentence order for sample lines:

"Its webs of living gauze unfurl no more" (line 8)

"The ship of pearl is wrecked" (line 9)

"Lies revealed before thee" (line 13)

"Stole through its shining archway with soft step" (line 19)

Rephrasing to normal sentence order reduces the archaic effect; the rhyme pattern of the poem is, however, lost.

Which of the archaic words in the list above are used today in other senses?

feign: pretend
main: principal
bark: tree covering, dog's vocalization

Extending the Poem

Have students compare the last twelve lines of Robert Frost's "Birches" (text page 678) with this poem. In both poems the poets use natural objects as metaphors for aspects of life. Students may decide that the message each poet gives is different: that in the Holmes poem the end is freedom from being earthbound, whereas in "Birches," Frost says "Earth's the right place for love." Allow students to explore differences and similarities in theme and technique. Would they agree, for example, that the moral is more explicit in "The Chambered Nautilus," or do they feel that both poets are making their morals quite clear?

James Russell Lowell
Text page 167

"She Came and Went"
Text page 168

Objectives

1. To identify similes and images
2. To write a paraphrase of the refrain
3. To write an essay comparing and contrasting two poems

Introducing the Poem

Here, in outline form for your reference, are the major elements of the poem:

- **Rhythm:** four-line stanzas, iambic tetrameter
- **Rhyme:** abab cbcb dbdb ebeb fbfb
- **Figures of speech:** similes, metaphor (life's last oil), symbolism (angel, tent)
- **Significant techniques:** use of repeated line as a refrain in the first four stanzas, slightly varied in the final stanza

Background on the Poem. Blanche, born on the last day of 1845, was the Lowells's first child. Biographer Martin Duberman says, "Lowell vowed to bring Blanche up as independent as possible of all *man*kind . . . a great, strong, vulgar, mud-pudding-baking, tree-climbing, little wench."

Fifteen months later, Blanche died, according to Mrs. Longfellow of "rapid teething." Duberman says,

> Earlier, when [his friend Charles] Briggs had lost a child, Lowell had offered the comfort that death, however cold in touch, was God's angel in disguise. He now tried to embrace the same reasoning, especially for [his wife] Maria's sake. He talked of . . . knowing [Blanche] had gone to God, of the need for gratitude that they had been allowed to enjoy her for even a short time. . . .

Soon after the child's death, Lowell wrote this poem.

The Literal Meaning. The speaker tells, through simile, of his grief at the brief life of his daughter. In the final stanza he declares that even when death approaches and his eyes grow dim, he will be brightened by her memory.

Teaching Strategies

Providing for Cultural Differences. Students from different cultures may have different views on how much emotional display is suitable for mourning the death of a child, and therefore on whether the degree of sentimentality in this poem is excessive or appropriate.

Providing for Different Levels of Ability. You might ask less advanced students to find substitutes for "came" and "went" in the middle three stanzas. While this may disrupt the rhythm and destroy the rhyme, it should help them to understand the force of the simple diction and of the repetition, if they read their new version aloud. Examples, "was born and died," "arrived and departed," "appeared and disappeared," etc.

Reading the Poem. You might want to examine the similes in the first three stanzas with the students, since these can be difficult to follow. They may not all understand, for example, that "then leaves unbent" (line 2) means "when the bird leaves, the twig no longer bends." Ask students why Lowell uses "twig" instead of "branch," and why he has the bird "sing." How good a simile is this to explain his memory? In the second stanza students may not understand that the syntax reverses subject and verb, so that in simplified prose the lines would read: "As some lake, unruffled by the breeze, mirrors the peacefulness of the sky."

Reteaching Alternatives. Students who continue to have difficulty with the poem are probably confused by the vocabulary or the syntax. You might have them work together to put the poem into a prose form with vocabulary simplified so that they can understand it.

Responding to the Poem   Text page 168
Analyzing the Poem
Identifying Details

1. **Each of the first three stanzas maks a comparison that describes the effect Lowell's daughter has had on his life. Restate these three *similes* in your own words.** In the first stanza, the poet's memory is "thrilled and stirred" by thoughts of his daughter just as a twig is made to tremble, yet is unshaken, by a bird alighting on it to sing. In the second stanza, the poet's soul clasped his daughter's presence just as a still lake clasps the sky. In the third stanza, the daughter's presence revived the poet's life as spring awakens the world and fills it with fragrance after winter.

2. **What time of life does the last stanza refer to?** It refers to the end of life, when one is near death.

   What does the poet say will happen when this time of his life arrives? The memory of his daughter will be a final "gush of light" or life that will cause the poet's eyes to brim with tears as he nears death.

Interpreting Meanings

3. **What words and *images* in the poem emphasize the brevity of the daughter's life?** Such words and images include: the repeated line "she came and went"; the image of a twig unbent by the brief perch of a bird; the word "moment's" in line 7.

   What words and images express the joy she gave her father? Words and images expressing joy include: the image of a bird singing; the words "thrilled and stirred" (line 3); "measureless content" (line 6); "bloom and scent" (line 10); the images of spring and May; the image of the angel; the image of a gush of light (line 19).

4. **How would you *paraphrase* the *refrain*?** One possibility might be: "My grief is so great that I only remember two moments in my daughter's life: her birth and her death."

5. **This is a very personal poem. Do you think the ideas Lowell expresses apply only to his own personal tragedy?** Answers will vary, but most students should be able to see the poem as having broader meaning.

   Or does the poem's meaning transcend the limits of this one personal experience—and, if so, what other experiences might the poem speak for? Answers will vary, but might mention any type of brief but important experience that strongly affects a person.

Writing About the Poem
A Critical Response

Comparing Two Poems on the Same Theme. As preparation for writing, review the central image in Longfellow's "The Cross of Snow" and the images students listed for Lowell's poem in question 3 ("Interpreting Meanings"); and note Longfellow's use of sonnet form while Lowell chose four-line stanzas.

Criteria for Evaluating the Assignment. The paragraph cites the images used by Longfellow and Lowell to evoke the emotion of grief, comments on structural differences in the two poems, and states which lyric the student finds to evoke a more vivid image of the loved one who was lost.

James Russell Lowell 63

Extending the Poem

This poem naturally evokes comparison with John Crowe Ransome's "Bells for John Whiteside's Daughter," text page 693. Ask students to consider the differences in tone of the poems, as well as other differences.

From "A Fable for Critics"   Text page 170

Objectives

1. To identify paradoxes
2. To understand allusions
3. To summarize the poet's self-criticism

Introducing the Poem

Here, in outline form for your reference, are the major elements of the poem:

- **Rhyme:** rhymed couplets with an occasional extra rhymed line
- **Rhythm:** anapestic tetrameter
- **Significant techniques:** paradox (in lines 1–18 dealing with Hawthorne, the paradox is presented by the image of the rough oak blooming with "a single anemone," or by the image of Nature fashioning him with clay but also using "finer-grained stuff"); allusion, humor

Background on the Poem. Once published, the "Fable" was widely read and admired and became immensely popular. Even today it is thought to be one of Lowell's finest works. The section on Hawthorne was particularly praised. Predictably, Poe was not so enthusiastic.

The Literal Meaning. Lowell aims well-meaning satire at Hawthorne and Poe, and chides Poe and Cornelius Mathews for their harshness toward Longfellow.

Teaching Strategies

Providing for Cultural Differences. It is sometimes difficult for adolescents to see shades of gray. Often they see their peers, their parents, and other adults in extreme ways, either all good or all bad. It may be hard for some to understand how Lowell could criticize his peers, saying good and bad things about them, and expecting them to like it. You might suggest that students write a criticism of an anonymous person, even of themselves, or of a public figure, trying to blend the favorable with the unfavorable. Suggest that like Lowell, they be lighthearted and humorous.

Providing for Different Levels of Ability. Less advanced students should enjoy line 38, since many of them, like readers "of common sense" in the nineteenth century, would be likely to "damn meters." When you read Poe in Unit Four, you might ask your students to decide whether there is any truth in Lowell's criticism. You might also call attention to Lowell's own meter in this poem. Anapestic tetrameter tends to be singsongy. Do students think that while Lowell was ridiculing Poe for his use of rhythm, he might have had his tongue in his cheek because of his own? More advanced readers might wish to read more of the "Fable" and report to the class.

Reading the Poem. You might want to start by having students observe that Lowell deals first in his criticism with Hawthorne, then with Poe, and finally, briefly, with Longfellow. Discuss the metaphor in lines 6–9, and have them note that the rhythm and diction lend themselves to a tone that is not altogether serious. But be sure they observe the paradoxes, especially in the Hawthorne section, and that they note the marked contrast in the Poe section between lines 39 and 40, where the tone changes from modest approval to criticism a good deal more serious than "two-fifths sheer fudge."

Reteaching Alternatives. Since the poem moves quite rapidly from one idea to another, with adequate but not strong transition, students who have had a difficult time understanding it might be encouraged to paraphrase it. You might have them work by sections: lines 1–5, lines 6–9 (or lines 6–12), lines 10–12, lines 13–18, lines 35–40, and lines 41–46, or 41 to the end. In their paraphrasing, help students determine whether their section is mainly serious or humorous, figurative or literal, or a combination. This exercise will help you discover and address any problems the students have with vocabulary, syntax, or allusions.

Also, it should help students understand the shifting tone of the poem.

Responding to the Poem   Text page 171
Analyzing the Poem
Identifying Details

1. Hawthorne is described as having qualities that seem *incongruous*, or not matched. What is contradictory about the image of the oak and the anemone (lines 6–9)? Lowell compares Hawthorne to something rough and powerful—the oak—and to something delicate and fragile—the anemone.

What details in line 10 emphasize that *paradox*, or apparent contradiction, in Hawthorne's character? Line 10 emphasizes the contradiction with oxymorons, or statements connecting opposite terms: Hawthorne is described as having "tender strength" and "meek wildness."

2. What other details in Lowell's discussion of Hawthorne present *paradoxes*? Lowell calls Hawthorne a "John Bunyan Fouqué," combining the names of Puritan and Romantic authors, and a "Puritan Tieck," which presents the same contradiction. He concludes the passage by saying that Hawthorne was made "fully and perfectly man" by the addition of a little "finer-grained stuff for a woman prepared," another paradox.

3. What is Lowell's chief criticism of Poe's work, given in line 40? In Poe the "heart," or feeling, is overcome by the "mind," or intellectualization.

4. How does Lowell defend Longfellow's character? He says that Longfellow is generous to his fellow bards and even to his critics.

How does he defend Longfellow's work? Lowell reminds Longfellow's critics that "elegance also is force." In other words, even though some readers regard Longfellow's poetry as too smooth or facile, it is Lowell's opinion that Longfellow combines elegance with power.

Interpreting Meanings

5. How would you explain what Lowell means by saying that Poe is "two-fifths sheer fudge"? Lowell suggests that Poe's work contains much that is meaningless or mere embellishment.

6. Longfellow has endured a great deal of criticism, then and now. What passages from Longfellow (pages 147–152) support Lowell's point that "elegance also is force"? Answers will vary.

7. Of these writers, which do you think Lowell most admires, for both his character and his work? Student answers will vary. Most will agree that Lowell's choice would be Longfellow, although Lowell is also quite generous in his praise of Hawthorne.

Writing About the Poem
A Critical Response

Summarizing a Verse. Read Lowell's self-assessment aloud, checking for literal understanding. Discuss any other writers the students feel have not learned the distinction between singing and preaching, but make the assignment simply the summarizing of Lowell's self-criticism.

Criteria for Evaluating the Assignment. The summary notes that Lowell attempts to use classical meter and rhyme, which sometimes weighs down his work, and that he must learn to make his work sound less forced (to "sing" instead of "preach").

Extending the Poem

Lowell acknowledged that he wrote the poem rapidly. You might suggest that students try their hand at anapestic tetrameter couplets, perhaps criticizing in a humorous way a book they have had to read in English class or a speaker they have heard at an assembly, or perhaps just telling a story.

Warn students who have not tried to write rhyming couplets that it is important to end the first line of the couplet with a word which can easily be rhymed. Those students who are serious about the effort might want to purchase an inexpensive rhyming dictionary at the local bookstore.

The American Language

Text page 176

1. **Students are to identify spelling inconsistencies in the selection written by Webster with his reformed spelling.** Answers will vary. Possibilities include: "writers," "introduced," "preference," "force," "influence," "ancestors," "essays," "spelling," "possible," "reezon," "offered," and "full."

2. **Students are to make a list of words in which the sounds represented by the letters *a*, *e*, and *i* are very different.** Lists will vary. Possibilities for *a* include *late*, *hat*, and *ball;* possibilities for *e* include *let* and *equal;* possibilities for *i* include *if* and *ice*.

3. **Students are to list pairs of words that are still spelled in similar ways but are pronounced differently. They should then list pairs of words that are still spelled differently but are pronounced the same.** Student lists will vary. Possibilities for the first list include: *kite* and *night*, *rough* and *slough*, *read* and *lead*. Possibilities for the second list include *higher* and *fire*, *soul* and *mole*.

4. **Students are to make a list of five nonstandard, simplified spellings that they have noticed in product names, advertising signs, and road signs.** Answers will vary.

5. **Students are to make a list of school subjects or jobs that they think could be spelled more simply. Next to each word they should write its simpler spelling. They should then use the words in a paragraph and exchange paragraphs in class.** Answers will vary.

Exercises in Critical Thinking and Writing

Text page 177

Responding to Literature

After students have read the prewriting instructions and have written thesis statements, you might want to have them share their comments and questions with each other in class discussion. You may also want to have some students read their thesis statements aloud before they go on to write the body of the essay.

Criteria for Evaluating the Assignment. Students' essays should express their own personal responses to the poem, but should be supported by the language and tone of the poem itself.

66   American Romanticism

Unit Four: *The American Renaissance: Five Major Writers* — Text page 179

Teaching the American Renaissance Unit

The range of the five writers represented in this unit is considerable, yet each is essentially Romantic, developed within the cultural climate of the bold, new, wilderness-exploring American nation. None of them deals very much with ordinary life. Hawthorne, of the five, dwells most upon male/female relationships, but almost always in an historical or supernatural setting, highly charged with symbolism. Poe employs the emotion of love—usually lost love—primarily as a catalyst to terror. Women scarcely figure in Melville's work at all. And while Thoreau writes about the most humdrum daily occupations—hoeing beans, counting pennies—he is decidedly not writing about the life of the average Concord citizen; he is elevating the humdrum to the level of meditative bliss.

The similarities and differences among these writers can be seen in their different relationships to Transcendentalism. Transcendentalism was, according to the scholar Perry Miller, primarily a religious rather than a literary movement, but two of its prominent adherents were among the greatest of American prose stylists, and the documents of the movement have survived in literary form. Essentially, Transcendentalists sought to create a new religious consciousness that would exhibit the freedom and democracy of the new nation, as opposed to conventional religion, which they felt to be an ossified European product, or to science, which they distrusted as dehumanizing. Emerson and the others felt that the way to God led through the self: contemplation of one's own thoughts would lead one to a perception of the Infinite. Donald N. Koster, in *Transcendentalism in America,* finds four major historical influences contributing to this philosophy: Platonism, which held that there exists a universal Good, of which the things of the material world are a mere shadow, and which can be reached through intellectual contemplation; Romanticism, which glorified the self and the emotions rather than society and reason; Asian religious works such as the *Vedas* and the *Upanishads,* which teach that the individual self contains a piece of the universal Self; and the Puritan heritage, which made Transcendentalists into ethical idealists deeply concerned with questions of good and evil.

Emerson is the central Transcendentalist, perpetually seeking the God within himself. Thoreau, his protégé, shares Emerson's main beliefs and his aphoristic quality, but takes to its furthest point the search for an ecstatic experience in the outer world of nature, while Emerson mostly contemplates his own mind. Of the three fiction writers in the unit, none embraced Transcendentalism (perhaps because good fiction requires intellectual flexibility), yet all show its influence, since it was a major element of the intellectual climate of the times. Hawthorne, who was closest to the movement, was ambivalent about it: he lived for a while at the Utopian community Brook Farm, but soured on it, and satirized it in *The Blithedale Romance*. Melville outwardly mocked Transcendentalism, yet nothing is more Transcendentalist than Ahab's great line, "Strike through the mask!" The difference was that what Emerson and Thoreau found behind the mask of the external world was benign, while what Melville found was malign or, at best, indifferent and unfathomable. Melville, the ex-sailor, quested outward for the truth, while the Transcendentalists quested inward. Poe, more removed from the New England scene, expressed scorn for the movement, but a late philosophical essay of his, *Eureka*, comes to the rather Transcendentalist conclusion that everything is part of God and that God is reflected in the human mind.

The contrast between Hawthorne and Poe is striking. Both wrote symbolic, often supernatural, tales filled with atmosphere, but Hawthorne was burdened by a sense of sin that was a bequest from a specific time and place in history. Poe was burdened not by history or morality but by the sheer terror of the lonely human soul facing the fact of death: by the sheer power of his own imagination. Poe's settings are often vague, more like mere window-dressing, while the background of Puritan New England is central to Hawthorne. Alfred Kazin, in *An American Procession*, identifies Hawthorne with the sense of guilt and Poe with the sense of anxiety; he considers Poe a supremely skillful professional, a virtuoso audience-manipulator, while Hawthorne, who probably possessed less verbal and imaginative talent, went deeper. In *The Scarlet Letter,* Kazin says, Hawthorne achieved the "unity of effect" that Poe preached.

*O*bjectives of the American Renaissance Unit

1. To improve reading proficiency and expand vocabulary
2. To gain exposure to notable authors and their works
3. To define and identify the elements of the essay, poem, story, and novel
4. To define and identify significant literary techniques: imagery, paradox, figures of speech, apostrophe, hyperbole, personification, symbolism, allegory, allusion, point of view, meter, rhythm, rhyme, alliteration, and tone
5. To interpret and respond to nonfiction, fiction, and poetry, orally and in writing, through analysis of their elements

6. To analyze the language and style of notable authors
7. To practice the following critical thinking and writing skills:
   a. Comparing and contrasting descriptions, philosophies, moods, literary forms, and political statements
   b. Responding to a writer's views
   c. Paraphrasing a poem
   d. Analyzing metrical structure and rhyme scheme
   e. Analyzing metaphors and similes
   f. Interpreting paradoxes
   g. Determining precise meanings of words
   h. Analyzing emotional effects of language
   i. Analyzing a poem
   j. Analyzing word connotations and figures of speech
   k. Interpreting a symbol
   l. Analyzing and evaluating persuasive writing

*I*ntroducing the American Renaissance Unit

It will be useful to devote some attention to the philosophy of Transcendentalism before reading the selections from Emerson and Thoreau, since students are quite receptive to the ideas of the movement when they are couched in simple twentieth-century English. Thoreau's individualism and "back to nature" creed are traditional favorites with young people, and while Emerson can seem a bit musty nowadays, his rebellion against old institutions places him on the side of youth.

Since Emerson, Thoreau, and Hawthorne were great believers in the value of journal-keeping, this unit provides ample opportunities for students to write in journals of their own. You might suggest, as a journal entry in keeping with the spirit of this unit, that students write down their thoughts as to what material goods in the lives of Americans today seem truly essential, and what goods seem nonessential or dispensable. Or you might ask them, as a quick-write to imagine that they have the power to change their own lives completely, with no pre-existing social conditions. How would they choose to live? Some of their answers may reflect values similar to those of the Transcendentalists; others may be at the opposite end of the spectrum. The important thing, the Transcendentalists believed, is that each individual should think about the deepest questions of how to live, and should choose his or her own way of life through an act of individual freedom.

Ralph Waldo Emerson
Text page 187

From *Nature*
Text page 191

Objectives

1. To identify and analyze images
2. To write an essay comparing two descriptions
3. To discuss the use of paradoxes

Introducing the Essay

The basic assumptions underlying Emerson's view of nature are described in this essay. These include Emerson's belief that God is always near to us and reveals Himself everywhere and at all times and that nature is the revelation of God. Within the individual lies a divinity that allows human intuition to behold God's spirit in nature. Also, there is a correspondence between natural law and moral law; by use of intuition, humans can see in nature God's laws revealed.

***B**ackground on the Essay.* The year 1836 was memorable in Emerson's life; it saw the birth of his first son, the initial meetings of the Transcendentalist Club, and the publication of his book *Nature,* which would become the "bible of American Transcendentalists." Emerson completed the first draft of the book in the same room in which Hawthorne would later write *Mosses from an Old Manse.*

***S**ummary.* Emerson says that in nature, we are able to feel "the perpetual presence of the sublime." In the presence of nature, we can feel real delight in spite of sorrow. Nature gives us better, "higher" thoughts and emotions.

Teaching Strategies

***P**roviding for Cultural Differences.* Students' feelings about nature may vary depending on their backgrounds. Students from large urban centers may be unfamiliar with nature except in parks or resorts; they may feel that nature is glamorous but frightening. In contrast, students from rural areas may be so familiar with nature that they are inured to

68   The American Renaissance

its charms. Even the students' perceptions of what constitutes nature may vary. The same community, seen by people from three different backgrounds, could be called "the city," "the suburbs," or "the country." Point out that Emerson's view of nature, too, was a product of his background as a member of a highly cultured, leisured, landed gentry.

Providing for Different Levels of Ability. Even advanced students will have some difficulty with Emerson's mystical concepts and rather antiquated diction. You might want to guide the class in composing paraphrases of those passages that prove troublesome. For the thornier sentences and vocabulary words (such as *maugre*), paraphrases or definitions could be written on the board. You may want to divide the essay into smaller passages, each of which can be analyzed by a group of students. (The opening paragraph itself can be divided between two groups.)

Introducing Vocabulary Study. Knowing the meanings of the following words is important to understanding the selection. (Starred words appear in the Glossary.)

envoys	181	maugre	182
admonishing	181	impertinent*	182
manifold*	182	cordial	182
indubitably*	182	blithe*	182

Reading the Essay. The sermon-like quality of Emerson's style lends itself to oral reading, but the subtleties of his ideas are more suited to silent reading and re-reading than to auditory comprehension. You might want to read aloud only certain key passages, such as the one about the "transparent eyeball," in conjunction with paraphrase and explication.

Reading Check. You might want to use the following questions as a reading check. Have students respond *True* or *False*.

1. Emerson says that people marvel at the stars each night with the same wonder they would if they only appeared once in a thousand years. False
2. Emerson implies that adults do not delight in nature as much as children do. True
3. Emerson suggests that people only superficially see nature. True
4. In nature Emerson says there is perpetual age and wisdom. False
5. Emerson states that if we use our intuition, we will perceive that there is a very real, although mysterious and hidden, relationship between ourselves and the plant world. True

Reteaching Alternatives. A review session, in the form of class discussion, can help those students who have grasped Emerson's ideas transmit their understanding to those who have not.

Students who have difficulty with Emerson's philosophical metaphors might gain in understanding if you ask them, as a quick-write, to state, as simply as possible, what they think Emerson felt when he stood on a hill and looked at the sky.

Responding to the Essay Text page 193
Analyzing the Essay
Identifying Facts

1. Emerson wants his audience to look at some of the commonest elements of their lives—the natural environment that they see every day—in a new way. How would our attitude toward the stars change if they appeared only once every thousand years? Emerson says that people would surely believe in and adore God, and they would preserve for many generations the memory of the stars as showing the "city of God."

2. The second paragraph makes clear that Emerson is using the stars as an attention-getting example for a point about nature. What point is he making? Emerson says that all nature deserves our attention and reverence. The stars are an especially dramatic example because they are inaccessible.

3. "To speak truly," Emerson says, "few adult persons can see nature." He says that children somehow have the advantage over adults in this matter. Read carefully the paragraph that begins with that sentence. What do adults seem to lose as they grow older? According to Emerson, children have the "inward and outward senses still truly adjusted to each other." He urges adults to become like children in their pure and unfettered joy in nature.

Interpreting Meanings

4. What do you think Emerson means by a "poetical sense" of looking at nature? He says that he means the "integrity of impression made by manifold natural objects." He probably refers to an imaginative sense of looking at nature directly, in all its beauty and wholeness.

What *images* illustrate the distinction between nature used for practical benefits and nature viewed in this poetic way? Emerson says that, while a wood-cutter will see a stack of timber, a poet will see a tree; while an ordinary person will see a collection of farms, the poet will see them as an entire landscape, bounded by the horizon.

5. The most famous passage in *Nature,* and perhaps in all of Emerson's work, begins, "Standing on the bare ground..." and ends, "I am part or parcel of God." In what way is the *image* of a "transparent eyeball" a description of a visionary experience of God? Student

Ralph Waldo Emerson 69

answers will vary. In general, however, Emerson seems to be suggesting through this image a reciprocal channeling of human sight and the divine images of nature—both passing through the "transparent eyeball." This reciprocal relationship results in a perfect harmony of man and his natural surroundings; such a harmony, in turn, suggests to Emerson a visionary experience of God.

Describe the relation presented here between people, nature, and God. According to Emerson, is God to be found only in nature, only in people, or in some common element that they both share? The relation, as indicated above, is a perfect harmony of people and nature, which permits people to experience God. Emerson would presumably say that God is to be found both in people and in nature, but He can be fully experienced only when such a harmony exists.

6. Describe your response to Emerson's essay. Cite the passages you found yourself agreeing with and those you are doubtful about. Student answers will vary. Encourage the students to reread the essay carefully before they begin to answer each part of the question.

Writing About the Essay
A Critical Response

Comparing Two Descriptions. Students may wish to make a chart of similarities (e.g., feelings of exhilaration) and differences (e.g., Emerson's focus on nature as a whole vs. Edwards's focus on a thunderstorm) before they write their essays.

Criteria for Evaluating the Assignment. The essay is arranged in a logical, coherent manner. It uses specific details from the essays of Edwards and Emerson to support points made about similarities and differences between the two writers' views of God, nature, and human beings.

Analyzing Language and Style
Paradoxes

Answers will vary. The following statements are representative responses.

1. I'm not alone when I read and write because I am sharing ideas with people who aren't in the room.
2. Every night the beauty and light of the stars remind us really to see the universe.
3. Most people take the sun for granted.
4. I'm so happy that the intensity almost makes me afraid.

Extending the Essay

Socrates said, "Flowers and trees teach me nothing, but people in a city do." This quotation could spark discussion of this opposite, but probably equally valid, philosophical viewpoint from that in this essay.

From "Self-Reliance"   Text page 194

Objectives

1. To write an essay on a limited topic
2. To write an essay responding to the writer's views
3. To analyze figures of speech

Introducing the Essay

In outline form, for your reference, here are the main themes of the essay:

- Imitation of others is ignorance; we must take ourselves "for better, or for worse."
- Only as individuals do we know what is best for us or what we are capable of doing.
- People only "half express" themselves, in fear that what they have to say is not great.
- We must put our hearts into our work if we are to feel relieved and satisfied with it.
- We must trust ourselves and trust the divinity within each of us, for we are all made of "noble clay."
- Society is "in conspiracy" against the individual and demands that we conform to its "names" and "customs."
- To be fully human, one must be a nonconformist.
- The person who is always consistent has nothing to do in life but follow others.
- To be great is to be misunderstood.

Background on the Essay. It will help students appreciate Emerson's philosophy if they know that it arose, to some extent, out of his experiences in his own life. His father's death, when Emerson was eight, forced him to look to himself as a spiritual guide, and to seek role models in more remote sources, such as the Hindu sages who wrote the *Upanishads*. (Emerson's theory is to some extent a

70   The American Renaissance

transplanting, into individualistic America, of Hindu ideas about the relationship between the individual soul, or "atman," the world-soul.) Emerson practiced what he preached, in that he resigned his ministry at the Second Church of Boston over a matter of conscience.

Summary. Emerson speaks of an individualism and goodness that have always been part of the American character. He espouses nonconformity and self-reliance, finds sanctity in the individual mind, and calls upon us to express ourselves strongly rather than diffidently.

Teaching Strategies

Providing for Cultural Differences. While self-reliance exists potentially in all human beings, different cultures place different values on nonconformity versus conformity, individuality versus community. Anglo-American cultures may indeed possess the most individualistic ideology of any widespread culture on earth. Students from other ethnic backgrounds may have grown up with strong pressures to fulfill the expectations of their communities. On the other hand, the decision to emigrate to a new country is, in itself, usually one that demands a high degree of self-reliance. It might be fruitful to discuss the various forms of conformity and nonconformity that students' backgrounds have supplied to them, and the examples of self-reliance they find in the lives of their forebears.

Providing for Different Levels of Ability. After the complexities of *Nature*, "Self-Reliance" is relatively clear and straightforward in style. Discussion of concepts is more germane here than clarification of language. Students who have trouble with the abstract plane of the essay may find it more comprehensible if the discussion is shifted to a more concrete level. Draw students into a discussion of specific examples of self-reliant behavior that they know from life. You might also play the audiocassette recording that is available for this selection.

Introducing Vocabulary Study. Knowing the meanings of the following words is important to understanding the selection. (The starred word appears in the Glossary.)

| transcendent | 184 | conspiracy | 184 |
| aspirants | 184 | hobgoblin* | 185 |

Reading the Essay. Have students define the word *self*, writing suggested definitions on the board. Then have students think of words that begin with *self* and list these on the board under two columns—words with positive meanings or connotations and words with negative ones. You might conclude the discussion with a more in-depth look at the word *self-reliance*. What are the meanings of this word? When are people called upon to exhibit self-reliance? Have students been self-reliant? If so, when and why? What was the result of their self-reliance? Was it a positive or a negative experience? Do we tend too much to "follow the crowd," and what happens when we do (or don't)?

Reading Check. You might use the following questions as a reading check. Have students respond *True* or *False*.

1. Emerson says that imitation of others is "ignorance" and suicide. <u>True</u>
2. Emerson says that we must trust ourselves for within each of us is a divine being. <u>True</u>
3. Emerson says that to be great is to be understood by those around you. <u>False</u>
4. Emerson believes that consistency for its own sake is foolish and that we should speak in "strong words" what we think at any given time, even if this contradicts what we previously said. <u>True</u>
5. From this essay one may conclude that Emerson would say that we should listen to our own selves, our intuition, before listening to the wisdom of sages from the past. <u>True</u>

Reteaching Alternatives. Students who still have trouble understanding Emerson's view of self-reliance might benefit from a quick-write, in which they write, in their own words and without reference to Emerson's essays, their own views on nonconformity and on the importance of being true to oneself. Since Emerson's vision of self-reliance has helped shape the values of contemporary America, there are likely to be significant points of agreement between his vision and the students' own.

Responding to the Essay   Text page 195
Analyzing the Essay
Identifying Facts

1. According to the first sentence, what does every person realize at some moment in his or her education? Emerson says that every person must come to terms with his or her own individual self, or identity.

2. According to the second paragraph, what is the destiny of every human being? This paragraph asserts that every human being must accept the place that Providence has accorded; he or she must trust to what fate has in store for him or her.

3. Explain what Emerson thinks of society as a whole, according to the third paragraph. Emerson believes that society conspires to suppress the individuality of many of its members. Society pressures us to conform, rather than to fulfill ourselves as unique individuals. It "loves not realities and creators, but names and customs."

4. What is the opposite of "self-reliance," according to the third paragraph? The opposite of self-reliance is conformity—bowing to the pressures of society.

5. In the fourth paragraph, what does Emerson see as the most sacred aspect of a person? The most sacred aspect of a person, according to Emerson, is the integrity of one's own mind.

6. What does Emerson think of people who call for consistency in thought and action and who fear being misunderstood? He compares them with "aged ladies," and he urges us to ignore their advice, saying, "To be great is to be misunderstood," and reminding us that "a foolish consistency is the hobgoblin of little minds."

Interpreting Meanings

7. What do you think Emerson means by "the divine idea which each of us represents" (paragraph 1)? The "divine idea" is the potential in each of us for expression and fulfillment.

8. How do you think self-reliance differs from selfishness or self-centeredness? Student answers will vary. But most will agree that Emerson's concept of "self-reliance" had more to do with integrity and truth to one's own self than with egoism or selfishness.

9. Suppose this essay were to be delivered as a major political address during a Presidential campaign today. How do you think people would respond? Student answers will vary.

Writing About the Essay
A Creative Response

1. Writing an Essay. Help students choose the topic on which they have the strongest views by discussing the meaning of Emerson's five statements and eliciting examples that illustrate each.

Criteria for Evaluating the Assignment. The essay reflects the writer's personal views on the selected topic. The essay uses examples or reasons to support its theme. It does not stray to other topics.

A Critical Response

2. Writing a Response. Read through the writing prompt with the students, noting that its three basic questions offer a way to organize the three-paragraph essay assigned.

Criteria for Evaluating the Assignment. The essay responds to "Self-Reliance" by discussing which of Emerson's ideas are most significant today, which ideas are dated, and whether or not Emerson is condescending toward women. The essay consist of three paragraphs. Each paragraph develops its own topic.

Analyzing Language and Style
Figurative Language

1. a. making the best of one's own self
   b. the heart
   c. human beings in the hands of the Almighty
   d. society
   e. hard, clear words

2. It is a string made for strength rather than beauty. "Silken," "golden," or "silver" suggest beauty or value, but not the strength for daily life that "iron" suggests.

3. The metaphor suggests that fear or embarrassment at changing one's mind is like a mental hobgoblin. A hobgoblin is a sort of "bogeyman," a mischievous spirit or elf. A "little" mind is one too limited to see a new point of view. An example of a "wise" consistency is for a teacher to use consistent, announced grading practices. An example of a "foolish" consistency is to stick to one's first position on a ballot issue when new information shows that the opposite position fits the facts better.

Extending the Essay

The decade of the 1970's was properly called the "Me Decade," after the title of an essay by Tom Wolfe. Some social critics feel that unbridled self-interest has been largely responsible for insider-trading scandals and other manifestations of a decline in social cohesion in America today. What would Emerson say to these critics? How would he react to the modern social environment? For purposes of debate, you might divide the class into two groups, one supporting Emersonian self-reliance in light of modern developments, and one opposing it. Or you might have each student write a newspaper editorial about an aspect of modern life that calls for either more self-reliance or less selfishness.

"Concord Hymn"

Text page 196

Objectives

1. To identify and analyze apostrophe, hyperbole, and personification
2. To write a letter responding to the poem
3. To paraphrase the poem
4. To write an essay analyzing metrical structure and rhyme scheme
5. To write an essay comparing and contrasting two philosophies
6. To compare and contrast the moods of two poems
7. To rewrite an inverted sentence

Introducing the Poem

This occasional poem was written to commemorate the bravery of the Minutemen who fought the British troops at Concord in April 1775.

The Literal Meaning. The first stanza recalls the events of April 1775 and praises the heroic spirit of the "embattled farmers." The second stanza says that both foe and conqueror are dead and the bridge that once stood there is now gone. The third stanza states the occasion for the poem, the dedication of a "votive stone" to the memory of these men of Concord.

Teaching Strategies

Providing for Cultural Differences. Students from New England may feel more personally involved in the subject of the poem than other students and may wish to share their appreciation of their heritage with their classmates. Students whose forebears arrived in America recently, or whose ancestors were slaves, may wish to discuss what their peoples' struggles for freedom have in common with the struggles of the American Colonists.

Providing for Different Levels of Ability. Some students will need careful explanations of such phrases as "embattled farmers," "votive stone," and "spare the shaft," as well as of Emerson's rhetorical devices. You might also need to emphasize that the poem describes two separate historical events: the battle at Concord and the later commemoration of the memorial stone.

Reading the Poem. Most students will have already heard the fourth line of this poem. After this line you may want to stop to discuss the meaning of the phrase, "the shot heard round the world." This is a good poem to have a student read aloud; alternatively, you might ask a different student to read each stanza.

Reteaching Alternatives. Students who still have trouble visualizing the setting of the poem, or understanding Emerson's plea to "Time and Nature," may gain understanding if you ask them to paraphrase, either orally or in a quickwrite, the scene of the poem and the speaker's relationship to that scene.

Responding to the Poem

Text page 196

Analyzing the Poem
Identifying Details

1. Identify the "foe" and the "conqueror" mentioned in the second stanza. The foe is the British; the conqueror is the American force of Minutemen that repelled the British at Concord.

What has happened to them and to the bridge? Both foe and conqueror lie silent in their graves, and the bridge has collapsed with time.

2. According to Stanza 3, why are they putting up a monument here? The purpose of the monument is to ensure that people throughout the ages will remember the heroism of the first small band of Revolutionaries, the Minutemen.

3. According to Stanza 4, why did the heroes die? They died to "leave their children free."

4. What does the speaker ask of the Spirit in Stanza 4? He asks the Spirit to plead with "Time and Nature" to "gently spare the shaft" the people raise: in other words, he asks that the monument be allowed to endure through the ages.

Interpreting Meanings

5. The poem ends in an *apostrophe*—words spoken to a person or object who cannot or does not answer. How would you define the Spirit addressed in line 13? Emerson might mean God, or he may be addressing the spirit of courage.

Ralph Waldo Emerson 73

6. To say that the shot of the Minutemen was "heard round the world" is, on a literal level, to indulge in *hyperbole*, or exaggeration for effect. On a *figurative* level, how is this statement true? On a figurative level the statement is true because the American struggle for independence has served, over the course of two hundred years, as an example for many other nations fighting oppression and injustice.

What other "shots" can you think of that might be said to have been heard around the world? Student answers will vary. Encourage them to think about events from history with far-reaching consequences.

7. What other monuments have been erected to the dead so that "memory may their deed redeem"? Students will mention local war memorial monuments, and national monuments they have visited.

Do you believe that memory *can* "redeem" or recover the dead? Explain. Student answers will vary.

8. Could any stanzas of this hymn be sung at other war memorials erected in the years since 1837? Student answers will vary.

Writing About the Poem
A Creative Response

1. Writing a Letter. Discuss with the class the words and phrases from the poem that would be especially evocative for a veteran of Concord, and the added effect created by hearing the poem sung to a solemn melody.

Criteria for Evaluating the Assignment. The paper is written in first-person, letter form. It reveals the writer's emotions and memories.

A Critical Response

2. Paraphrasing the Poem. As a prewriting activity, have students list the *old-fashioned words* to replace, *missing words* to supply, *inverted words* to rearrange, and *figurative expressions* to rephrase literally.

Criteria for Evaluating the Assignment. The paraphrase reads something like this:

Stanza 1: The fighting farmers once stood beside the crude bridge across this river, and fired shots reported worldwide.

Stanza 2: Since then the river has swept the bridge toward the sea, and fighters on both sides have died.

Stanza 3: Today we are placing a plaque on the riverbank so the fighters' memory will last even when our children are dead, like our ancestors.

Stanza 4: God, you gave these men the courage to die for our freedom. Please see that time and weather spare this monument we erect in honor of them and you.

"The Rhodora"   Text page 198

Objectives

1. To identify and explain personification and apostrophe
2. To analyze metrical structure and rhyme scheme
3. To write an essay comparing and contrasting philosophies of nature
4. To rewrite inverted lines in normal word order

Introducing the Poem

Emerson says that beauty needs no excuse for being. He uses the rhodora, a New England forest flower, to exemplify beauty.

The Literal Meaning. The speaker of the poem says that in May, while walking in the woods, he found the fresh rhodora in a secluded spot. He notes its purple color and its beauty, which is greater than the red bird's. He says that if people ask the flower why its beauty seems wasted in this hidden area, it should reply that beauty is its own excuse for being and that the selfsame power that brought the man to this spot also placed the flower.

Teaching Strategies

Providing for Cultural Differences. Note that "Beauty is its own excuse for being" is an idea that can be applied to any geographic location. You might ask your students to describe, in a quick-write, some object connected to their backgrounds that exemplifies universal beauty to them.

Providing for Different Levels of Ability. The use of apostrophe may be the single largest point of difficulty in this poem. Be sure the students understand that the speaker is speaking to the flower.

Reading the Poem. Before students read the poem, define for them the word *apostrophe*. Be sure to distinguish it from its much more familiar homonym, the punctuation mark.

Responding to the Poem   Text page 198
Analyzing the Poem
Identifying Details

1. Describe where the poet comes upon the rhodora. He finds the rhodora in a damp nook in the woods, by the side of a brook.

Until then, whom or what had the flower been pleasing with its beauty? The flower was pleasing the "desert and the sluggish brook."

2. In line 9, who might the "sages" be? The sages are probably philosophers.

What is their question, and how does the poet answer it? The sages question why the charming flower has been "wasted"—that is, placed where no one, or few people, will appreciate it. The poet answers this question by claiming that beauty is its own justification, or its own "excuse for being."

3. There are several instances of *personification* in the poem. Identify and explain at least three of these. In line 4 the rhodora is personified when the poet says that it spreads its blossoms "to please" the desert and the brook. In line 8, the redbird is said to pay "court" to the flower whose blooms are more beautiful than its plumage.

4. Part of this poem is an *apostrophe*—a direct address to something that cannot answer. Where is the apostrophe? The apostrophe occurs in lines 9–16, where the poet directly addresses the flower.

Interpreting Meanings

5. How does Emerson say he is like the rhodora? Emerson is like the rhodora in that he, too, was created by God—the "selfsame Power" of line 16.

6. Line 12 is the key to the poem's meaning and one of Emerson's most famous sayings. How would you rephrase the line in your own words? Beauty needs no practical justification for its existence; it is an end in itself.

Do you agree with its statement? Student answers will vary.

7. Do you think everything in the world, including beauty, has to have a utilitarian purpose? Do many people behave as if they believe that usefulness is more important than beauty? Explain. Again, students may be divided in their opinions. Encourage them to defend their views with reasoned arguments and concrete examples.

8. The poet indicates in his subtitle that someone has asked him where the rhodora came from. What is the poet's answer? The poet implies in the last line that the rhodora comes from a creative "Power"—that is, the rhodora is one of God's creations.

If you were the questioner, would this answer satisfy you? Student answers will vary.

How would you have answered the question? Students' suggestions will vary.

9. What do you think the poet means by "Power" in the last line? Students will probably agree that the poet refers either to God or—possibly—to a less specific, divine, creative force.

10. How might a rationalist writer like Benjamin Franklin have answered the question "Whence is the flower?" A rationalist writer might have discussed the flower's origins in a seed or its botanical relationship to other plants. Or such a writer might have simply presented the flower as part of the variety of the universe.

Writing About the Poem
A Critical Response

1. Analyzing the Poem. Chart the rhyme scheme of "The Rhodora" (aa, bb, cdcd, ee, ff, ghgh), noting that the first two lines employ "slant rhyme" (slightly off); and scan the entire poem (using the chalkboard). Students should note that lines 3, 6, 7, and 11 begin with trochees rather than iambs (DUMda, not daDUM): *Spréading, Máde the, Hére might, Téll them*. Note also that in other places the iambic meter requires stress on such minor words as *in* (lines 2, 5, 15), *a* (line 3), and *on* (line 10). Students' personal response (at the end of the essay) means their opinion as to whether Emerson's variations enhanced the poem, prevented a singsong quality, detracted from the poem, or had some other effect on the student.

Criteria for Evaluating the Assignment. The essay notes where Emerson alters the iambic pattern and how he uses rhyme, and gives the student's response to these choices.

2. Comparing Philosophies. Read aloud and clarify the meaning of the quotation from *As You Like It*. Call students' attention to the fact that in their papers they should comment specifically on how Emerson and Shakespeare deal with the idea that nature contains signs of divinity.

Criteria for Evaluating the Assignment. The essay summarizes the philosophies of Emerson and of Shakespeare that can be deduced from the sources, and states whether or not the philosophies are similar.

Analyzing Language and Style
Inversions

Line 6: "Gay" is moved to the end instead of following "water." Line 7: "Here" is moved from mid-sentence to the beginning, "might" and "come" are separated, and "to cool" follows instead of preceding "his plumes." Lines 5 and 8 are in normal word order.

The sentence written in normal word order appears as follows:

5 The purple petals, fallen in the pool,
6 Made the black water gay with their beauty;
7 The redbird might come here to cool his plumes,
8 And court the flower that cheapens his array.

Extending the Poem

If beautiful things need no excuse for being, do ugly things, or merely ordinary things, need an excuse? Ask your students to discuss Emerson's possible reactions to a number of objects that are not so conventionally pretty as a flower: for example, a fast-food restaurant, an auto junkyard, an anthill, a homeless person. Is Emerson proposing an esthetic test for deservingness to exist?

"The Snow-Storm" Text page 200

Objectives

1. To explain personification
2. To compare and contrast the moods of two poems

Introducing the Poem

Emerson expresses his awe at the power and beauty of nature and says that human art merely mimics nature.

Background on the Poem. This was one of Emerson's earliest successful poems. In it he praises the turbulent, creative efforts of nature as the "fierce artificer" who creates a "frolic architecture." Subject matter is once again transcendentalized.

The Literal Meaning. "Announced by all the trumpets of the sky," the snow covers the farmhouse and garden and keeps "all friends shut out" and the family within the house huddled around the fireplace. The poet speaks of the north wind as a skilled craftsman whose hours of labor have left an astonishing art object.

Teaching Strategies

Providing for Cultural Differences. Depending on your area of the country and the composition of your class, students may have different experiences of, and attitudes toward, snow. Discuss these with them, and ask them how they feel about Emerson's awed pleasure at seeing snow.

Providing for Different Levels of Ability. Emerson's vocabulary and rhetoric may need to be gone over carefully for some students. You might want to use class discussion as a means of developing a line-by-line paraphrase of the poem.

Reading the Poem. For purposes of oral reading, it might be best to divide the poem among three students. While the subject is powerful, the oral interpretation should be calm and straightforward, rather than oratorical.

Responding to the Poem Text page 201
Analyzing the Poem
Identifying Details

1. What precedes the snow, according to line 1? The "trumpets of the sky" announce the storm.

2. Name some of the things and people that the snow affects in lines 1–9. Among them are the following: the fields, the hills and the woods, the river, the farmhouse, the sled and the traveler, and the courier.

76 The American Renaissance

Where do the people inside the house sit? They sit by the fireplace.

3. The second part of the poem (lines 10–28) is a lengthy *personification*. What type of person is the north wind personified as? The north wind is compared with an architect.

Point out at least three details that extend the personification. Details that extend the personification include the following: "masonry" (line 10), "quarry" (line 11), "artificer" (line 12), the mention of "bastions" and a "projected roof" (line 13), "Parian wreaths" (line 18), "tapering turret" (line 22), and "frolic architecture" (line 28).

4. The final adjective applied to the north wind is "mad" in line 27. How has that "madness" been demonstrated? The madness is demonstrated in the overwhelming speed and wildness with which the wind has piled up the snow in "architectural" forms. Emerson calls the wind's work "wild" and "savage" (lines 15–16); the wind cares not for "number and proportion," and is "mocking" (line 17).

What details in the poem suggest that this madness is also imaginative and joyful? Some details suggesting imagination and joy are "fanciful" (line 16), the mention of a "swan-like form" (line 19), and the adjective "frolic" in the last line.

Interpreting Meanings

5. Explain how the meanings of the words "tumultuous privacy" (line 9) make this a startling and vivid phrase. The adjective "tumultuous" suggests violence, noise, and anxiety; the noun "privacy" suggests quiet and peace. The phrase is virtually an oxymoron, or yoking together of opposites. It vividly conveys the contrast between the indoor scene and what is happening outdoors.

6. According to the last four lines, human art only mimics the work of nature. Why do you think Art's structures are described as "slow" (line 26)? They are described as slow because it takes many years, or centuries, to build in stone on a comparable scale to what nature builds in snow in a few hours.

7. Art is *personified* in this poem as "astonished." What is Art, or human work and creation, astonished at? Art is astonished at the beauty of the snow's "frolic architecture."

What overall idea about nature and human work is suggested by the poem? The poem suggests the awesome power, and equally awesome beauty, of the forces of nature. Nature mingles creation and destruction, or mad wildness and playfulness; before its power, people can only sit quietly by in wonder, just as the housemates sit in front of the radiant fireplace in the poem.

8. Could artists, writers, and composers also be called "fierce artificers"? Explain. Most students will agree that the phrase might be an apt description for some artists.

9. Can you think of other instances where art "mimics" nature? Student answers will vary.

Writing About the Poem
A Critical Response

Comparing Poems. Note that the assignment is to *compare* poems; that is, to state how they are alike and different in mood and in their pictures of the transformed outdoor and indoor worlds. Questions 1–4 ("Analyzing the Poem") will have called students' attention to **figurative language** in Emerson's "The Snow-Storm"; students should reread Whittier's "Snow-Bound" with special attention to **figurative** and **sensory language.**

Criteria for Evaluating the Assignment. The essay cites specific examples from Emerson's and Whittier's poems to show similarities and differences in mood and in the picture of how a snowstorm transforms both the outdoor and the indoor world.

Extending the Poem

Another poet studied in this text, T.S. Elliot, provides a very different description of a winter storm in the first of his four "Preludes":

> The winter evening settles down
> With smell of steaks in passageways.
> Six o'clock.
> The burnt-out ends of smoky days.
> And now a gusty shower wraps
> The grimy scraps
> Of withered leaves about your feet
> And newspapers from vacant lots;
> The showers beat
> On broken blinds and chimney-pots,
> And at the corner of the street
> A lonely cab-horse steams and stamps.
>
> And then the lighting of the lamps.

You might guide student discussion with the following questions: Which poem is about a prettier subject? Which poem is more beautiful? Would Emerson agree that Eliot's "Prelude," being beautiful, "needs no excuse for being"? If so, do the broken blinds and scraps of newspaper need excuses for being?

Emerson's Aphorisms

Text page 202

Discuss the meaning of the aphorisms with the class before students attempt to write paraphrases. Or you might read one or two of these paraphrases to give students the idea:

Maybe I'm a little cynical, but I question it when everybody's yelling about their patriotism. It seems to me that, as a rule, really serious citizens don't shout about their patriotism. Instead they quietly act like citizens, by doing things like voting.—*Journals,* 1824

We say, "Don't give children sharp objects." Please, God, don't trust us with more power until we've learned to use what we have. What a wreck we'd make of the world if we could do whatever we wanted! Put safeguards on our knowledge until we've learned not to hurt each other with it.—*Journals,* 1832

Just as God used words to create a universe out of chaos and darkness, so the writer of a well-made sentence creates something delightful.—*Journals,* 1834

Poetry should use both fresh, new words and solid old ones.—*Journals,* 1844

It's true wisdom to recognize everyday wonders.—*Nature*

A human being is a god with faults.—*Nature*

Peace can come only from living according to the principles that are inside you.—"Self-Reliance"

These *are* "the good old days" if we use them right.—"Self-Reliance"

Knowledge in itself is wonderful, but it becomes terrible if it is used wrongly.—"The American Scholar"

The greed of individuals and whole societies corrupts the very atmosphere.—"The American Scholar"

Primary Sources: Hawthorne Talks About Emerson

Text page 203

In this excerpt from "The Old Manse," Hawthorne describes Emerson as a "poet of deep beauty and austere tenderness" and as a philosopher with a "pure intellectual gleam." Using the selections by Emerson in the text as evidence, students might disucss how Hawthorne arrived at this evaluation of Emerson.

Henry David Thoreau

Text page 204

Walden, or Life in the Woods

Text page 207

Objectives

1. To analyze the essays
2. To write a journal entry
3. To write an entry from another point of view
4. To write an essay on "the miraculous"
5. To write an essay comparing and contrasting the essays with a poem
6. To analyze metaphors and similes

Introducing the Essays

In outline form, for your reference, here are the basic themes of the material from *Walden* included in the text:

- **From "Economy":** Thoreau describes the construction of his house at Walden Pond and his garden work there, in order to show the importance and feasibility of living a "stripped-down" lifestyle.
- **From "Where I Lived and What I Lived For":** Thoreau wants to live "deliberately" and "front the essential facts of life."
- **From "Solitude":** He describes his pleasure at being alone in nature and says that it is not space, but minds, that separate people.
- **From "The Bean Field":** He describes his planting and hoeing of beans and his battles against weeds, using metaphors from Greek mythology.
- **From "Brute Neighbors":** He describes a battle between black ants and red ants, drawing parallels with human warfare and describes loons and hunters trying to outwit each other on Walden Pond.

- From "Conclusion": He summarizes and universalizes the experiences of his two years at Walden Pond.

Background on the Essays

The privacy at Walden Pond gave Thoreau an opportunity to put his theories of plain, simple living to the test. He was not trying to be a hermit, however, and spent much time visiting with others. The Transcendalist philosopher Bronson Alcott spent every Sunday evening at Walden during Thoreau's second year there.

Teaching Strategies

Providing for Cultural Differences. Students' responses to Thoreau's attitudes may be affected by their socioeconomic backgrounds. Students from working class backgrounds, seeking upward mobility, may feel that Thoreau's antagonism to the work ethic is a luxury they could not afford. Students from low-income families may resent Thoreau's voluntary poverty and could justifiably claim that his family and friends cushioned him from real want. These responses are to be welcomed as valid critiques, stimulating discussion of such topics as the nature of independence, the necessity of money-making labor, and the socioeconomic role of philosophers—discussion Thoreau himself would doubtless welcome. In addition, you should be sensitive to the fact that Thoreau's remarks about the Irish were not always complimentary and were unfortunately typical of the prejudices of his era.

Providing for Different Levels of Ability. You might want to divide the class into small groups, making each group responsible for summarizing and reporting to the class about one section of *Walden*. "Economy" and "Brute Neighbors" can each be divided between two groups. "Brute Neighbors" is more suitable for less advanced students, "Conclusion" for more advanced ones.

Introducing Vocabulary Study. Knowing the meanings of the following words is important to understanding the selection. (Starred words appear in the Glossary. Italicized words either are archaic or have special meanings in context.)

obtrude*	208	superfluous	212
posterity	209	supernumerary	212
impervious*	209	iteration*	213
encumbrance*	209	invidious	213
temporal*	209	sedulously	213
improve	209	pertinacity	214
dearth	209	divested*	214
equable*	209	internecine*	214
transient	211	adversary*	214
*mean**	211	airs*	214
assiduously	215	*impressible*	217
omnipresent	215	*license*	217
reconnoiter*	216	perchance	218
tumultuous*	217		

Reading the Essays. You might begin by asking where students go when they want to be alone with their thoughts. Why have they selected this particular place? Did it help them to "escape" for a time? Why is this sort of "escape" necessary? How much solitude is good for people? At what point does solitude become harmful? What sorts of material comforts are absolutely necessary? If students were to live for two years in a cabin in the woods, what items would they feel they had to bring—TVs? Stereos? What do they feel they could live without?

Reading Check. You might want to use the following questions as a reading check. Have students respond *True* or *False*.

1. Thoreau gathers the material and builds the house on Walden Pond without help from neighbors. __False__
2. Thoreau had hoped to earn some money from his crops; however, woodchucks, worms and poor weather cause him to just barely break even after deducting planting and seed costs. __False__
3. A laughing loon easily outwits the naturalist as he chases the bird around Walden Pond in a small boat. __True__
4. Thoreau says he left Walden Pond because he had other lives to live and did not want to fall into a worn routine. __True__
5. Thoreau tells his readers that they should *all* live life as he did, for only by living away from society and with nature is man able to know his possibilities. __False__

Reteaching Alternatives. As with Emerson, Thoreau's aphoristic style and nineteenth-century diction many get in the way of some students who would otherwise grasp his ideas quite readily. Indeed, some of his most profound passages, such as the concluding paragraphs of the essays, are also his most metaphorical and elliptical. Thus, by having the class paraphrase those difficult passages, you will simultaneously be zeroing in on the heart of Thoreau's philosophy.

Responding to the Essays   Text page 218
Analyzing the Essays
Identifying Facts

1. **According to the second paragraph in "Economy," why has Thoreau decided to write about his life?** He has decided to write about his life because so many of his neighbors have asked him questions about his experiment in living at Walden.

How does he justify talking primarily about himself? Thoreau says that he does not know anybody else as well as he knows himself, and that—when *he* reads a book—he requires of every writer "a simple and sincere account of his own life." He says that his readers may accept such portions of his book as apply to them, and that for some of them the book may be like a coat, doing "good service to him whom it fits."

2. What does Thoreau think would happen if we made our houses with our own hands? He says that people building their own houses might resemble birds, who build their own nests; perhaps "the poetic faculty" would be "universally developed" in people, just as it is in the birds who sing.

3. How does Thoreau answer the questions implied in the title "Where I Lived and What I Lived For"? He says he went to the woods to live because he wanted to live simply enough to confront the essential facts of life.

4. What arguments does Thoreau present in "Solitude" to demonstrate that he is not lonely in his isolated situation? Thoreau says that since the earth is but a point in space, it is nonsense to assume that he would be lonely while at Walden. Besides, he is surrounded by the creatures and objects of nature, which furnish fine companionship.

What kind of space does he suggest *really* isolates human beings? That which really isolates them, Thoreau argues, is their removal from nature, the "perennial source of our life."

5. What satisfactions does Thoreau find in the labor of raising beans (in "The Bean-Field")? Thoreau cherishes the act of creation; he rejoices in looking at the fine plants; he takes pleasure in battling the beans' enemies, namely worms, cool days, and woodchucks; he likes getting to know the various kinds of weeds as he works in his garden.

How does he find humor and whimsy even in the task of weeding? He compares his weeding to an epic battle against the Trojans, and his hoe to a weapon that fells "many a lusty crest-waving Hector."

6. In his "Conclusion," what does Thoreau say he learned from his experiment? Thoreau says that he learned that if we advance confidently in the direction of our dreams, we will meet with a success we never imagined. If we simplify our life, we will be able to live in harmony with higher laws and at peace with ourselves.

Interpreting Meanings

7. Why do you think Thoreau goes to the trouble of itemizing the exact cost of his house? Students may have differing opinions. But most students will agree that, by providing a detailed accounting, Thoreau adds credibility to his account.

What might he have wanted to prove to his Concord neighbors? He might have wanted to prove that very few things are really essential for life, and that it is possible for human beings to shelter themselves for a very small outlay of worldly goods.

8. What does Thoreau mean when he says "Simplify, simplify" (page 212)? He means that we should always strive to cut through the nonessential aspects of our lives so that we can concentrate on the most important things.

Do you think he has a valid point here? Explain. Student answers will differ, but many students will agree that Thoreau's maxim is even more relevant today, now that we are living in a highly complex civilization.

9. How would you summarize Thoreau's ideas on progress, as exemplified by what he says about the railroad and other forms of new technology? Thoreau is skeptical about progress, as is revealed by his description of the miserable conditions in which the railroad laborers live. He asserts that the complexity of progress has only succeeded in fragmenting our lives, and that technology threatens to control and oppress us.

Do you agree with him? Why or why not? Student answers will vary.

10. Thoreau was a great observer of nature, though he was not a scientist. Compare Thoreau's description of the war between the ants and his game with the loon in "Brute Neighbors." In each case, what does he find in the natural occurrence that is remarkable or valuable? In the war between the ants, Thoreau marvels at the tenacity with which the two warring parties carry on their fierce struggle to the end. The battle suggests to Thoreau various human battles and wars. At the end of the description, he remarks that he never learned which party was victorious, nor the cause of the war; instead, Thoreau focuses on the carnage and waste. Perhaps he implies that all wars are futile.

In his game with the loon, Thoreau is struck by the wild laughter and the cunning maneuvers of the bird. Thoreau wonders why the bird announces its whereabouts; but he then concludes that the loon's laughter mocks his efforts to come closer to it. At length the air is filled with misty rain, and Thoreau gives up the game, thinking that perhaps the loon's "god" is angry with him for interfering with the bird's natural play.

11. What do you think is the lesson of the fable of the apple-wood table at the conclusion of *Walden*? The fable is of a beautiful bug which was hatched from an egg in the wood, years after the egg was laid in the tree from which the table was made. Thoreau's lesson concerns resurrection and immortality: He says that beauty may come forth from even the most trivial things in life, "to enjoy its perfect summer life at last."

12. Do you see evidences of the Romantic point of view

in *Walden*—the emphasis on intuition, on the power in nature, and on human emotions? Explain. Students should be able to identify numerous instances of a Romantic point of view in *Walden*.

13. What do you think Thoreau means in his final paragraph by the words, "Only that day dawns to which we are awake"? Thoreau probably means that, in order to enjoy the role of nature in our lives, we must take the trouble to observe nature carefully—or, in his metaphor, to actually "awake" to the "dawn" of each day.

14. Find at least two passages from these essays that you think pertain to life today. Describe the situations or the people each quotation might apply to or appeal to. Student answers will vary.

15. Suppose a Puritan, like William Bradford (page 11), Mary Rowlandson (page 23), Jonathan Edwards (page 36), or Anne Bradstreet (page 42) had spent time in Walden and were recording these same experiences. How might their journal entries differ from Thoreau's? Student answers will vary. Encourage the students to review the relevant selections from Colonial literature; perhaps they should examine Mary Rowlandson's first, since it is actually taken from a journal. In general, the students may suggest that a Puritan living at Walden would probably have recorded more explicit illustrations or examples of God's providence, together with moral lessons, than appear in Thoreau's account.

Writing About the Essays
A Creative Response

1. Writing a Journal Entry. The key point in the prompt is "Try to think like Thoreau for a day." Discuss with students how Thoreau's mind worked—the connections he saw between events and literary works, and the messages or lessons he drew from what he saw.

Criteria for Evaluating the Assignment. The journal entry records what the writer saw, heard, and thought, in a manner reminiscent of Thoreau in its use of allusions and its attention to lessons to be learned.

2. Writing from Another Point of View. Review especially the final column on page 73, on Benjamin Franklin's mind set. Discuss how Franklin's thinking differed from Thoreau's.

Criteria for Evaluating the Assignment. The journal entry records what the writer saw, heard, and thought, in a manner reminiscent of Franklin in its emphasis on the scientific and the rational.

A Critical Response

3. Developing a Topic. The writing prompt establishes the organization and content for the essay. Discuss with students the scenes from *Walden* best suited to the assignment—e.g., baking bread in the rain, weeding the beans, the battle of the ants, Thoreau and the loon, or other scenes.

Criteria for Evaluating the Assignment. The essay uses Emerson's statement as its topic sentence, and supports this sentence with details from a scene in which Thoreau sees "the miraculous in the common."

4. Comparing a Poem with *Walden*. Read aloud Yeats's "The Lake Isle of Innisfree," and with no discussion, have students immediately jot down similarities to *Walden* in terms of **imagery, tone,** and **subject matter.** Then discuss students' lists until a body of similarities has grown.

Criteria for Evaluating the Assignment. The essay explains clearly how Yeats's poem is like Thoreau's writings in terms of **imagery, tone,** and **subject matter.**

Analyzing Language and Style
A Metaphorical Style

1. Ideas are compared with a coat. Student expression of the same idea might read something like this: Readers should take only the ideas that fit them, and not try to "put on" ideas that fit others well, but don't fit them.

2. Life is compared with a bone. Rephrased: I wanted to live deeply and get everything I could out of life.

3. A person's life is compared with the unsettled German Confederacy. Rephrased: Our life is like the map of Africa, with new nations popping up every day.

4. Life is compared with a journey by ship. Rephrased: I didn't want to be carried along by others, but rather to get a first-hand view of everything. I don't want to change my ways now, either.

5. Ideas are compared with a drumbeat. Rephrased: If people don't go along with the crowd, maybe it's because they are being faithful to their personal vision.

6. One's life is compared with a river that sometimes floods. Rephrased: Our inner life has its ups and downs. Maybe this will be the year we are full of ideas that enrich the barren places in our lives and clear out the problems.

Extending the Essays

Many contemporary American nature essayists owe a deep debt to Thoreau. Among the best examples of this genre are Annie Dillard's *Pilgrim at Tinker Creek*, Edward Hoagland's *Walking the Dead Diamond Desert*, Peter Matthiessen's *The Snow Leopard*, and Ivan Doig's *This House of Sky*. Students interested in the outdoors, or in fine writing, might want to read those or similar books and report on them to the class.

From "Resistance to Civil Government"

Text page 220

Objectives

1. To interpret paradoxes
2. To write a short speech
3. To write an essay responding to a political statement
4. To write an essay comparing and contrasting two political statements
5. To determine precise meanings of words

Introducing the Essay

In outline form, for your reference, here are the major points Thoreau makes in the essay:

- Government is an expedient, a means to an end.
- The majority will inevitably, in some instances, harm the minority.
- People must do what they feel is right; they have an obligation not to support what they feel is wrong.
- The "free and enlightened state" is one that will "recognize the individual as a higher power."

Background on the Essay. Thoreau's influnce on the development of the theory and practice of civil disobedience—and thus on a great deal of twentieth-century history—can perhaps best be seen in this quotation from Martin Luther King, Jr.'s essay, "A Legacy of Creative Protest": "No other person has been more eloquent or passionate in getting his idea across than Henry David Thoreau. As a result of his writings and personal witness we are heirs of a legacy of creative protest. It goes without saying that the teachings of Thoreau are alive today, indeed they are more alive today than ever before." Students should be informed that the Mexican War was unpopular in New England in its day, sparking more than one protest. Thoreau's protest against the poll tax was perhaps inspired by Bronson Alcott's refusal, three years earlier, to pay taxes to a government that tolerated slavery.

Summary. Thoreau expounds his ideas about government and the dangers of majority rule, and then relates his experiences in being taken to Concord jail for nonpayment of poll taxes.

Teaching Strategies

Providing for Cultural Differences. Students' attitudes toward civil disobedience will vary with their backgrounds and experiences. Ask your students whether their lives, their families' lives, or their ethnic or racial groups have been affected by acts of political protest.

Providing for Different Levels of Ability. "Resistance to Civil Government" is more important as a "position paper" than as a stylistic achievement; therefore, the historical examples of Gandhi, King, and others can be used as valid points of entry to Thoreau's text. Real historical events can serve as "paraphrases," so to speak, of Thoreau's ideas. Once students have become familiar with the practical application of the ideas, their literary presentation will be easier to understand.

Introducing Vocabulary Study. Knowing the meanings of the following words is important to understanding the selection. (Starred words appear in the Glossary. Italicized words either are archaic or have special meanings in context.)

expedient (n.)*	221	effectual	222
alacrity	221	auditor	223
inherent	221	*circular*	223
prevail*	221	sanction	224
insurrection	222		

Reading the Essay. Before reading this essay, you might discuss the following questions: Why do we have laws? Do we really need them? What would happen if there were no laws? What options do Americans have when they believe a law is unjust? How, in the course of our history, did these options arise? Point out that Thoreau, among many others, helped create our ability as Americans to change laws we feel are unjust.

Reading Check. You might want to use the following questions as a reading check. Have students respond *True* or *False*.

1. Thoreau feels that we would live better lives if there were stronger state governments. _____False_____
2. Thoreau says that we need government for directing the tasks of educating, settling territories, and keeping the country free. _____False_____
3. Thoreau claims that jail is a ridiculous institution that locks up his body, but not his mind. _____True_____
4. Thoreau feels he gets a closer view of his town and understands its people better because of his night in jail. _____True_____
5. The ideal state, to Thoreau, is one in which individuals are free to be themselves even if they wish to live away from the society of others. _____True_____

82   The American Renaissance

Reteaching Alternatives. While civil disobedience is a familiar idea in the modern world, some students may have trouble seeing it in the context of the issues of the 1840's. You might ask the class to do a quick-write in which they discuss some rule that they have encountered and that they consider unjust; ask them to describe how they might go about protesting it. Since Thoreau's ideas have largely shaped the nature of protest in American culture as a whole, it is likely that the student's response will spontaneously incorporate them.

Responding to the Essay Text page 224
Analyzing the Essay
Identifying Facts

1. Explain what Thoreau thinks is wrong with majority rule. He says that a government based on majority rule in all cases cannot be based on justice, since the majority will, sooner or later, inevitably harm the minority.

 What does he say is the only obligation he has a right to assume? Thoreau says that his only obligation is to do what he thinks right.

2. What does Thoreau predict about slavery in America? He predicts that if even only one honest man were to fight against slavery by going to jail in protest, it would lead to the abolition of slavery in America.

3. Explain why Thoreau was put in jail. He refused to pay his poll-tax.

 What were his feelings about the government when he was in jail? Thoreau felt that the state was foolish in jailing him, since it punished his body and not his spirit. He lost his respect for the state, and pitied it.

4. How does Thoreau describe his sensations and thoughts as he lies in jail during the night? He says that the night was "novel and interesting." He describes his fellow prisoners and his conversation with his roommate. When his roommate retired to bed, Thoreau listened to the town clock and the evening sounds of the village, which became transformed in his mind to a medieval town.

5. At the end of the essay, what qualities does Thoreau envision in an ideal "perfect and glorious State"? Thoreau says that an ideal state will recognize the individual as a "higher and independent power," from which all the state's authority is derived. The perfect state will be just to all men, and will even allow some individuals to withdraw and live aloof from it.

Interpreting Meanings

6. *Paradox* **is a statement or expression that presents an apparent contradiction which actually contains a truth.** **What is the truth behind these two paradoxes?**
 a. **"I saw that, if there was a wall of stone between me and my townsmen, there was a still more difficult one to climb or break through, before they could get to be as free as I was." (Page 222)**
Thoreau means that his fellow townsmen are imprisoned by walls of conformity.

 b. **"I felt as if I alone of all my townsmen had paid my tax." (Page 222)**
Thoreau means that, by following his own conscience, he has figuratively paid his tax—that is, he had rendered a service to the state and to his fellow townsmen.

7. How are Thoreau's perceptions of his fellow citizens changed by his night in jail? Thoreau comes to feel that the friendship of his fellow townsmen is "for summer weather only"—perhaps he is consciously echoing Thomas Paine's phrase about "the summer soldier and the sunshine patriot" from *The American Crisis.* He says that he now feels that his neighbors are narrow-minded and hypocritical.

 What idea do you think he is stressing in telling us about getting his shoe fixed and leading the huckleberry party on the day he was released? Thoreau stresses that he is not allowing the experience of being jailed to disrupt his normal life or his enjoyment of nature.

8. From what you know about American Romanticism, would you say that Thoreau's assumptions and points in this essay are fundamentally Romantic? Explain. Student answers will vary, but most of them will see Thoreau's assumptions and points as Romantic. Note particularly the stress on the integrity of the individual, the emphasis on conscience as a higher imperative than the rules of the state, his vision of Concord at night as a medieval town on the Rhine, and the visionary conclusion describing an ideal government.

9. What influences of Emerson can you find in Thoreau's "Resistance to Civil Government"? In general, Emerson's faith in the power of the individual to shape his or her own destiny seems to be reflected in Thoreau's essay. Students will probably also point to echoes of Emerson's emphasis on the values of integrity and self-reliance.

10. Which of Thoreau's arguments did you find convincing, and which did you disagree with? Student answers will vary.

 Are you convinced that there would be civil order if each person followed his or her own conscience? Explain. Again, student answers will vary. Urge the students to discuss a variety of concrete situations in historical and contemporary contexts. You may want to point out that many celebrated works of literature have dealt with the conflict of individual conscience with the demands of the state or of civil order: for example, Sophocles's tragedy

Antigone, T.S. Eliot's *Murder in the Cathedral,* and Henrik Ibsen's *An Enemy of the People.*

11. Comment on how Thoreau's main points in this essay relate to contemporary life. What would happen to a Thoreau-type protest today? Student answers will vary.

Writing About the Essay
A Creative Response

1. Taking Another Point of View. Have students write the speech as if they were speaking either to Thoreau himself, or to their and Thoreau's neighbors.

Criteria for Evaluating the Assignment. The paper is in first-person language suitable for speaking aloud. The speaker defends the action of arresting Thoreau and reveals how he or she feels about Thoreau's beliefs and acts.

A Critical Response

2. Supporting a Statement. The writing prompt quotes a statement of Thoreau's. Students should support or oppose it on the basis of their own reasoning.

Criteria for Evaluating the Assignment. The paper is logical and forceful in making points that support or attack Thoreau's concept, "That government is best which governs not at all."

3. Comparing or Contrasting Two Political Statements. The assignment requires students to seek both similarities and differences between Thoreau's essay and ideas on rebellion found in the Declaration of Independence. In class, ask students to volunteer a few statements from the Declaration that might serve as a starting point.

Criteria for Evaluating the Assignment. The essay examines what both documents say about civil resistance, citing both differences and similarities, or explaining what makes them entirely alike or entirely different in stance.

Analyzing Language and Style
Precise Meanings

"After the first blush of sin," writes Thoreau on page 222, "comes its indifference; and from immoral it becomes, as it were, *unmoral.*..."

1. "Neutrality" means taking no stand. "Apathy" means simply not caring. In Thoreau, *indifference* means apathy.
2. *Unmoral* means having nothing at all to do with ethics. *Immoral* means ethically wrong.
3. The final sentence, quoted in part above, could be paraphrased as follows:
   Once you get used to sinning you quit caring about sin; and instead of seeming wrong, it just seems irrelevant, unconnected with life in general.

Thoreau was arrested because he did not pay "poll tax."

1. The text (page 222, note 5) has already defined "poll tax." Students who missed the note might guess that it is a special "head of household" tax or something similar.
2. *Poll:* An opinion survey. *Pollster:* Compiler of data. *Poll booth:* A place to register or take part in a poll. All three deal with "heads" in the sense of counting "heads" or individuals.

Extending the Essay

In Plato's dialogue, "Phaedo," Socrates, who has been unjustly condemned to death by an Athenian court, refuses to try to escape his punishment, saying that he has no right to rebel against the decisions of a state that has nurtured him and whose laws, by living there, he has implicitly agreed to obey. Socrates's view is diametrically opposed to Thoreau's. Have your students write a dialogue in which Socrates and Thoreau debate the individual's right to disobey the law for reasons of conscience. You might want to have the best examples from the class read aloud or distributed.

Primary Sources: Two Journals   Text page 225

In his journal entry, Nathaniel Hawthorne describes "Mr. Thorow," who dined at Hawthorne's home. Among his comments, Hawthorne says that Thoreau is a "keen and delicate observer of nature" and that he has "more than a tincture of literature." You might have students discuss, based on what they have read of Thoreau, how accurate an assessment of the young man Hawthorne has made.

84   The American Renaissance

Edgar Allan Poe

Text page 226

"The Masque of the Red Death"

Text page 228

Objectives

1. To analyze the story
2. To interpret symbolism, allegory, and allusion
3. To state the theme
4. To describe a movie or stage adaptation
5. To write opening sentences for stories
6. To write an essay commenting on a criticism
7. To analyze the emotional effects of language

Introducing the Story

In outline form, for your reference, here are the major elements in the story:

- **Protagonist:** Prince Prospero and his guests
- **Antagonist:** the Red Death
- **Conflict:** person vs. the supernatural (death)
- **Point of view:** third-person, partially omniscient
- **Significant techniques:** unity of effect, tone, allegory
- **Setting:** Prince Prospero's palace, probably in southern Europe in the sixteenth or seventeenth century
- **Theme:** Death is inescapable regardless of human vanity.

Background on the Story. Poe completed this story in 1842, just three months after Virginia Clemm, his young wife, had suffered one of her particulary bad attacks, which had caused a blood vessel in her throat to rupture. (This may explain Poe's preoccupation with blood in this story.) The effect of his wife's illness was devastating to Poe, whose nervous disposition left him unable to continue with his work as an editor. Although he had increased the sale of *Graham's Magazine* from 8,000 to 40,000—making it the most popular periodical in America—Poe's job came to end during this time, only thirteen months after he had begun work with the magazine. Having stayed out of work to attend his ill wife, Poe returned in late spring of 1842 to find someone else sitting at his desk; although he had actually not been replaced, Poe felt that he had been, and resigned.

The Plot. Prince Prospero invites a thousand of his friends to his palace to escape the plague that is ravaging the land. They hold a ball to celebrate, but the Red Death enters the palace in costume and kills all the people.

Teaching Strategies

Providing for Cultural Differences. Different cultures have different typical reactions to death, ranging from extremely histrionic to extremely stoical. You might ask your students to share their feelings on the subject and to discuss how they feel about Prince Prospero's particular mixture of unrealism and terror in the face of death.

Providing for Different Levels of Ability. Because of the story's ornate vocabulary, careful review of the vocabulary list will be helpful.

Introducing Vocabulary Study. Knowing the meanings of the following words is important to understanding the story. (Starred words appear in the Glossary. Italicized words either are archaic or have special meanings in context.)

sagacious	228	piquancy	230
eccentric*	228	arabesque	230
august (adj.)	228	*evolutions*	230
ingress*	228	disapprobation	230
egress*	228	vesture	231
voluptuous	228	spectral	231
dauntless*	228	gaunt*	231
impeded	228	aloft*	231
profusion	229	unimpeded	231
emanating*	229	impetuosity	231
precinct	229	illimitable	231
disconcert (n.)	230		

Reading the Story. The ending of the story—from the first entrance of the Red Death at midnight—is the most effective portion for reading aloud, and contains all of Poe's verbal and atmospheric effects in full measure. If your students have already read the story at home, you might want to have them read aloud from that point for heightened appreciation of Poe's language. Alternatively, you might play for your students the accompanying audiocassette recording for this selection.

Reading Check. You might want to use the following questions for a reading check. Have students fill in the blanks with the correct word or words.

1. Prince <u>(Prospero)</u> and one thousand of his friends lock themselves in his abbey in an effort to escape the Red Death.
2. In all but one of the seven rooms of the Prince's imperial

suite, there is a (stained glass window) that is the same color as the furnishings of the room.

3. During the masked ball, the revelers enjoy themselves except when the (ebony clock) sounds.

4. At midnight the Prince become infuriated when he notices a reveler in the costume of (the Red Death).

Reteaching Alternatives. The symbolic aspect of the story is the one most likely to elude students, but you may wish to reassure them that there is nothing wrong with simply enjoying the story as a well-written tale of the supernatural.

Responding to the Story   Text page 232
Analyzing the Story
Identifying Facts

1. **According to the first paragraph, what characteristics of the "Red Death" make it a horrifying disease?** Poe says that the symptoms of the disease are sharp pains, sudden dizziness, profuse bleeding at the pores, and then death. The disease runs its course in half an hour. The blood upon the faces and bodies of the victims appalls other people and prevents them from offering aid or sympathy to the afflicted.

2. **Describe Prospero's plan for surviving the epidemic.** Prince Prospero summons a thousand of his subjects; they retire together to an old abbey, which resembles a fortress in its seclusion from the outside world. The Prince and his subjects hope to defy the plague of the Red Death by sealing themselves off.

3. **Poe gives a great deal of space in the story to the palace plans and decorations, providing us with textures and colors in profusion. What are some of the sensory *images* that create a vivid, concrete impression of Prince Prospero's ball?** Poe describes the suite of seven rooms in which the ball is held. They are decorated in various colors, and Poe details the nature of the tapestries, stained-glass windows, ornaments, and carpets. The seventh chamber, decorated in black, is particularly striking; the window panes here are of scarlet.

4. **What happens at the *climax* of the story?** The Red Death confronts Prince Prospero and the revelers. The Prince pursues the specter with a dagger. Finally, the Red Death turns on the nobleman in the velvet apartment, and the Prince falls dead.

5. **The story concludes, "And Darkness and Decay and the Red Death held illimitable dominion over all." List the specific *images* of darkness, decay, and death in the final paragraph.** The Red Death is compared to a thief in the night; the halls are described as "blood-bedewed"; the revelers drop in "despairing postures"; the clock ceases to run; and the flames of the tripods are extinguished.

Interpreting Meanings

6. **What do the ebony clock and its arresting chimes add to the plot?** The clock and its chimes contribute elements of mystery and suspense. We wonder what the significance of the revelers' sudden confusion may be when they hear the chimes.

Can you think of any *symbolic* value the clock might have? The clock may represent the inevitable passage of time for the revelers. They have tried to seal themselves off from the world, but Poe implies that this is impossible. Within the story, the black clock perhaps suggests that it is only a matter of time until the Prince and the revelers are trapped by the Red Death.

7. **What *symbolic* significance can you find in Poe's use of numbers?** Note that Prospero's mansion has seven apartments; the number seven has often been regarded as symbolic or magical (as in the seven ages of man or the seven deadly sins). The Red Death makes his first appearance when the clock chimes midnight—again, perhaps, a symbol of the "witching hour."

In his use of colors, especially the black and the scarlet in the seventh room? The scarlet and black of the seventh chamber might be held to symbolize blood and death.

In the movement from east to west in the sequence of rooms? Perhaps this movement should be associated with the regions of the rising and setting sun, and hence, by extension, with birth and death.

8. **Poe's story is clearly not meant to be realistic; instead, it is a masterpiece of imaginative atmosphere that may be read as an *allegory*—a story in which characters, objects, and events symbolize various ideas and qualities. The mysterious guest, for example, turns out not to be a real person, but the embodiment of the Red Death. What, in a still larger sense, might this figure symbolize?** In a larger sense, the figure may represent the fact of mortality itself—that is, the death which awaits every human being.

What attitudes toward life and death do you think the Prince and his party-goers might symbolize? The Prince and the revelers perhaps symbolize the universal temptation to deny the fact of death and to devote our lives to carefree pleasures, with no thought that death must sooner or later overtake us. Encourage students to express and support their own opinions on Poe's symbolism.

9. **In the last paragraph, Poe *alludes* to a prophecy from the Bible: "For yourselves know perfectly that the Day of the Lord so cometh as a thief in the night." (1 Thessalonians 5:2). "The Day of the Lord" is a way of referring to the last day of the world, or Judgment Day. Explain how the allusion adds a layer of meaning to Poe's story.** Just as the prophecy implies that the end of the

86   The American Renaissance

world may come when we least expect it, so the Prince and his revelers are surprised by the Red Death, although they believed themselves immune to it.

10. How would you state the *theme* of this story—the main idea about human behavior that is revealed by the fictional events? Students will suggest various answers. In general, the theme seems to be that those who try to insulate themselves against such universal ills as disease and death are only cherishing an illusion.

How do you feel about this theme—is it a valid one, in your experience? Student answers will vary.

11. Poe felt strongly that the main concern of any story was its *psychological effect*. He believed that neither narrative nor characterization was as important as the reader's emotional response. What emotional effect did the first paragraph of this story have on you? Student answers will vary. In general, however, Poe's description of the devastating symptoms and effects of the Red Death is intended to evoke a response of horror in the reader.

How does Poe produce this effect? He produces this effect through carefully chosen words: devastated, fatal, hideous, dissolution, and pest ban are some examples.

Writing About the Story
A Creative Response

1. Staging the Story. Brainstorm a number of possible "first things" the audience would see and hear—a dying, shrieking plague victim; a violent thunderstorm; the "castellated abbey" with a clock tolling in the background; etc. Note which are best for stage and which for screen.

***C**riteria for Evaluating the Assignment.* The paragraph vividly describes the first thing the audience would see and hear. The scene and the sounds are suitable for setting the mood of terror.

2. Writing an Opening Sentence. Clarify the intent of the assignment: students are not imitating Poe, but writing sentences aimed at effects of their choice. To convey the possible range, read aloud the opening sentence from several different stories in the text.

***C**riteria for Evaluating the Assignment.* There are three sentences, each of which could open a story. Each sentence sets an identifiable mood.

A Critical Response

3. Commenting on a Criticism. Read and discuss Wilbur's comment on the dream world in Poe, clarifying Wilbur's meaning as necessary. When students begin to argue for or against Wilbur's theory, they are ready to write.

***C**riteria for Evaluating the Assignment.* The essay clearly supports or opposes Wilbur's interpretation of Prince Prospero's costume ball as a dream sequence, and explains fully why the writer agrees or disagrees with Wilbur.

Analyzing Language and Style
Emotional Effects

1. Blood is used to describe the color red in "the panes here were scarlet—a deep blood color" (p. 229); "... the blood-tinted panes..." (p.229); "... light through the blood-colored panes..." (p. 230). Alternative choices that would create a different effect: "a deep neon red color"; "scarlet-tinted panes"; "strawberry-colored panes."

2. The plague called "the Red Death" caused profuse bleeding.

3. Some possible choices include "... the duke's love of the *exotic*..." and "there was much of the ... *intricate*...."

4. Words adding to the emotional tone of repulsiveness and irrationality are *delirious, madman, wanton, terrible,* and *disgust*. Poe aims to provoke a sense of horror.

5. The sentence conveys despair and devastation. *Decay* is associated with death, rottenness, and foulness. Opposites are grow, bloom, increase.

Extending the Story

Plagues have long stimulated the literary imagination, the greatest examples in modern fiction being Defoe's *A Journal of the Plague Year,* Camus's *The Plague,* and Manzoni's *The Betrothed*. You might suggest that students write stories describing the possible reactions of contemporary Americans, in their own community, to a plague. Alternatively, you might suggest writing a story describing Prince Prospero's ball from the point of view of one of the other revelers, or of one of the Prince's subjects outside the palace—or of the Red Death himself.

Primary Sources: A Visit to the Poes   Text page 233

In this excerpt from a work on Edgar Allan Poe, Mrs. Gove Nichols describes a visit to Poe's cottage. Mrs. Nichols's account of the unfurnished cottage and of the distress caused by Poe's bursting his gaiters during a leaping game illustrates the grinding poverty that Poe faced throughout his life. The anecdote about the leaping game gives students the opportunity to see the human side of a man regarded in many circles as a literary giant.

"The Fall of the House of Usher"

Text page 234

Objectives

1. To analyze imagery, point of view, and allegory
2. To retell an incident from another point of view
3. To evaluate the use of detail to heighten mood
4. To write an essay comparing and contrasting the themes of two stories
5. To write an essay analyzing the story's meaning
6. To analyze the use of words for emotional effect
7. To identify and explain symbols

Introducing the Story

In outline form, for your reference, here are the major elements in the story:

- **Main characters:** Roderick Usher; Madeline Usher, twin sister of Roderick
- **Conflict:** person vs. fear
- **Point of view:** first-person (the narrator, a friend of Usher's)
- **Setting:** the House of Usher, whose location is never given or even hinted at
- **Theme:** the vulnerability of the human mind

Background on the Story. While serving as the editor of *Burton's Gentleman's Magazine* in Philadelphia, Poe published "The Fall of the House of Usher" in the September 18, 1839, edition of the magazine. Here, as in previous positions, he was extremely successful; however, his often unconventional methods and his unacceptable habits of drink and absenteeism lost him his job in the summer of 1840.

"The Haunted Palace," a poem that the narrator and Roderick read together in the story, was a poem that was published in the *Baltimore Museum* just five months before it appeared as part of his story. About the poem, Poe wrote to the editor, "By 'The Haunted Palace' I mean to imply a mind haunted by phantoms—a disordered brain."

The Plot. The narrator visits the home of his boyhood friend Roderick Usher, after receiving a desperate letter from him, and finds both Roderick and his sister Madeline in a state of depression and physical decline. The narrator tries to relieve Roderick's melancholy, to no avail. Madeline apparently dies, and the two men bury her, but it is a premature burial. On her reappearance, days later, Roderick dies of shock, and Madeline dies. As the narrator flees, the house itself collapses from the fungus whose "exhalations" had infected the Usher family.

Teaching Strategies

Providing for Cultural Differences. Few, if any, American students today would be able to identify with the frailties of a decaying landed aristocracy. Students from minority or low-income backgrounds could well be impatient with the problems of such people. Point out that the setting of the story, while important to the establishment of mood, is not really indispensable to Poe's theme of emotional collapse. As a thought exercise or as a written exercise, you might ask the class to imagine the same theme of emotional collapse set in the present day, or in some other cultural setting with which they are more familiar.

Providing for Different Levels of Ability. Careful attention to vocabulary study can make the descriptions, in particular, more comprehensible to students. Students who might be baffled by the idea of a "tarn" may be relieved to learn that it is simply a lake, and that a "valet of stealthy step" is simply a servant walking quietly or sneakily. For specific passages that give students trouble, encourage paraphrasing in the course of discussion.

Introducing Vocabulary Study. Knowing the meanings of the following words is important to understanding the story. (Starred words appear in the Glossary. Italicized words either are archaic or have special meanings in context.)

pervaded (v.)	234	tenanted	240
unredeemed	234	seraph	240
insoluble*	234	pinion	240
precipitous	234	pertinacity	241
lurid	234	sentience*	241
sojourn (n.)	236	collocation	241
importunate	236	importunate	241
sensibility	236	incubus	243
munificent	236	cadaverous	243
patrimony	236	impetuous	243
pallid	237	prolixity	243
abeyance	237	clangorous	244
irreclaimable	238	reverberation	244
affection	238	gibbering	244
anomalous	238	*without*	245
fervid	240		

Reading Check. You might want to use the following questions as a reading check. Have students respond *True* or *False*.

1. Roderick's nervous affliction causes him to be able to

88   The American Renaissance

eat only the most bland foods and to wear only certain types of clothing. ___True___

2. After Roderick introduces Madeline to the narrator, the narrator comments on her charming beauty and her frail physical appearance. ___False___

3. While burying Madeline, the narrator becomes aware of the fact that Roderick and his sister are twins. ___True___

4. Roderick changes after her sister's death and seems less depressed because he no longer has to worry about her illness. ___False___

5. After Roderick's death, the narrator flees the Usher mansion just before it collapses and sinks into the tarn. ___True___

Reteaching Alternatives. If students have trouble following the narrative in Poe's style, you might ask them to write, in small groups, brief descriptions of the Usher family's problem and the narrator's experiences in attempting to aid the Ushers. If your students have trouble grasping the mood and theme rather than the narrative itself, and if there is time, you might ask them to write and perform dramatic versions of the story. If there is less time, you might concentrate on oral reading and discussion of the poem-within-the-story, "The Haunted Palace," that contains in compressed form, the psychological themes of the story that surrounds it.

Responding to the Story   Text page 246
Analyzing the Story
Identifying Facts

1. As the story opens, how does the narrator respond to his first sight of the House of Usher? The narrator says that he feels "a sense of insufferable gloom." He is depressed and sick at heart, and he shudders as he looks at the reflection of the house in the tarn.

What *images* help you to see and hear this *setting*? The images are largely conveyed through carefully chosen descriptive words. Evocative adjectives in the first paragraph include: dull, dark, alone, dreary, melancholy, insufferable, bleak, rank, decayed, bitter, hideous, unredeemed, shadowy, sorrowful, precipitous, black, lurid, gray, ghastly.

2. Explain why the narrator has come to this house. He has come because his old childhood friend, Roderick Usher, has written him an urgent letter, saying that he is ill and begging the narrator to visit him.

3. Describe the symptoms of Roderick Usher's illness. The symptoms include paleness, nervous agitation, sudden shifts of mood, and a morbid acuteness of the senses.

What are his sister Madeline's symptoms? Madeline is apathetic; her body is gradually wasting away; and she has occasional cataleptic seizures, in which the body grows rigid like a corpse.

4. Summarize what happens during the narrator's visit to the House of Usher. At first, the narrator tries to comfort Roderick, his friend, by joining him in his pursuits and trying to understand his malady. Little by little, however, the narrator succumbs to melancholy and a vague feeling of apprehension. The news that Madeline has died from her illness depresses both characters still more. The narrator helps Roderick with his arrangements to preserve the corpse of Madeline for a period of two weeks in one of the vaults of the castle. Finally, during a stormy night, the narrator is seized by a feeling of horror. Roderick joins him, and they seek distraction in the reading of a medieval romance. But at the height of the storm, an apparition of Madeline confronts them. Roderick collapses dead in the arms of his sister. The narrator flees the house as it collapses into the tarn.

Interpreting Meanings

5. What do you think Roderick's artistic efforts—his guitar solo, his painting, and his poem "The Haunted Palace"—reveal about his state of mind? All of Roderick Usher's artistic efforts display a tortured sensibility and a disordered mind. The guitar solo is wildly emotional; the painting of the vault with no entrance or exit may symbolize that its creator feels himself trapped; and the poem reveals an obsession with death, melancholy, and the triumph of evil.

6. Why do you think Poe had Roderick and Madeline be *twins* instead of merely brother and sister? Students may have several interesting theories here; encourage them to express and defend their suggestions. Some critics have proposed that Poe intended the reader to conclude that Roderick and Madeline were two, closely related sides of the same personality.

7. The story is presented from the *point of view* of a typical Poe narrator—a character who claims to provide an objective, rational view of events, but whose rationality becomes suspect during the course of the tale. What evidence can you find suggesting that the narrator's state of mind may be approaching that of his friend Roderick? The narrator seems more and more drawn to Usher, as he tries to understand and sympathize with his old friend's malady. He repeatedly emphasizes the reliability of his report, as when he professes to record "The Haunted Palace" "very nearly, if not accurately." He emphasizes that he takes part with Roderick in his artistic pursuits, saying that they both painted together and pored over books of magic. The experience of conveying the body of Madeline to the vault seems to unnerve him profoundly. Finally, the narrator admits, "I felt creeping upon me, by slow yet certain degrees, the wild influences of his own fantastic yet impressive superstitions." On the final night of the tale, he is sleepless and begins to tremble, as if from some terrible nightmare. Despite his efforts to cling to sanity, he is addressed twice by Usher in the concluding scene as "Madman!"

How does this uncertainty about the narrator's objectivity affect your response to the events of the plot? Student answers will vary, but many of them may suggest that this uncertainty introduces another note of suspense and terror into the story.

8. **What do you think is happening at the end of the story, when Madeline Usher appears? Is she a hallucination of the narrator? Is she a ghost? Or is she a real, living person who has been buried alive?** Student answers will vary. Some students will agree that the very ambiguity of the situation serves to increase our response of awe and horror.

How do you interpret Madeline's appearance? Again, student answers will vary.

9. **Poe wrote of the poem within the story, "... by the Haunted Palace I mean to imply a mind haunted by phantoms—a disordered brain." How might the whole story be seen as an *allegory* of a journey into the human mind in its conscious and unconscious states?** Encourage students to express and defend their own opinions. Some will point to Usher's symptoms as symbolic of the chaotic, unordered impulses of the unconscious mind, and to the narrator's growing terror as a movement from the conscious to the unconscious state. But different interpretations are possible.

In this light, what, for example, would the final *fall* of the house represent? The fall of the house might be held to symbolize the final collapse of Usher (and by extension, of his family) into a maelstrom of chaos and death. Just as the house is flawed by the fissure and the family may have been flawed by its failure to produce abundant descendants, so Usher's mind is flawed by phantoms of terror and undisciplined, over-refined aesthetic impulses. In a more general sense, Poe's symbolism may suggest that if such impulses are given free rein in the human mind, the result may be that the mind will crack and disintegrate in insanity or death.

10. **Do you think a filmed version of Poe's story would be popular today? Why?** Student answers will vary. Remind the students that several film versions have been made and have proved enormously popular at the box office and on television.

Writing About the Story
A Creative Response

1. **Using Another Point of View.** Have the class list incidents which could be retold from Madeline's point of view (e.g., arrival of the narrator).

Criteria for Evaluating the Assignment. The story is done in first person and reveals the character of Madeline as she narrates an event or comments on other characters.

A Critical Response

Since the three critical writing assignments achieve different objectives, you may wish to discuss all three, but allow students to choose *one* for writing a critical essay.

2. **Analyzing the Story's Effect.** Read the quotation from Poe and make clear to students that this assignment requires cataloging of word choices that build the mood of terror.

Criteria for Evaluating the Assignment. The essay demonstrates, through a large number of examples, how Poe uses word choice to build the mood of terror.

3. **Comparing Two Stories.** Refer back to Richard Wilbur's comment, given in the third writing assignment on page 232, on imagination and reality in the stories of Poe. Students should proceed as if they agree with Wilbur if they choose to write on this topic.

Criteria for Evaluating the Assignment. The essay uses examples from "The Masque of the Red Death" and "The Fall of the House of Usher" to support the thesis that it is impossible to achieve the Romantic ideal of imagination transcending reality.

4. **Analyzing the Story's Meaning.** Discuss the three statements about the theme of the story, clarifying the meaning of each as necessary, before students begin to write.

Criteria for Evaluating the Assignment. The essay adopts one of the three statements as its topic sentence and uses cogent examples and quotations from "The Fall of the House of Usher" to support it.

Analyzing Language and Style   Text page 247
Suggestive Words

1. dull, dark, soundless, oppressively, dreary, shades of the evening, melancholy, insufferable gloom, sternest, desolate, terrible, bleak, vacant, rank, decayed, depression, hideous, iciness, sinking, sickening, unredeemed dreariness, unnerved, insoluble, shadowy fancies, annihilate, sorrowful, precipitous brink, black and lurid tarn, unruffled luster, gray sedge, ghastly tree stems, vacant and eyelike windows

2. The first sentence and several others repeat the *d* sound: "*D*uring the whole of a *d*ull, *d*ark, and soun*d*less *d*ay. ..." The *s* sound is also used often: "an ic*iness*, a *s*inking, a *s*ickening of the heart...." The sounds could be those of a dull, repeated thud or a hissing snake.

3. Adverbs and adjectives characterizing the mind of the narrator and revealing his feelings include: oppressively, melancholy, insufferable, desolate, terrible, bleak, sickening, sorrowful.

4. The main detail that personifies the house is "vacant eyelike windows," used twice.

5. The entire mood and atmosphere of the story would be different. You would expect a more light-hearted story.

6. Such changes alter the sentence's emotional effect entirely: "During the morning of a bright, sunshiny day filled with birdsong in the spring of the year, when white clouds floated benignly, high in the heavens, I had been passing alone, on horseback, through an unusually picturesque tract of country; and at length found myself, as noon approached, within view of the intriguing House of Usher."

Elements of Literature
Symbols   Text page 247

Reading and discussion of this section may lead to an additional critical writing topic for students to explore.

Extending the Story

"The Fall of the House of Usher" is a model of descriptive prose, particularly through the subtle—though overelaborate by today's standards—use of adjectives. You might want to have students list all the adjectives in the renowned first paragraph. Then have students read the passage, first with the adjectives, and then without them. For further exercise, have students rewrite the paragraph to express a happier mood, merely by substituting different adjectives.

"Eldorado"   Text page 248

Objectives

1. To analyze meter, word connotations, and tone
2. To interpret symbolic meaning

Introducing the Poem

In outline form, for your reference, here are the main elements in "Eldorado":

- **Conflict:** person vs. fate
- **Significant techniques:** rhyme, meter, symbolism, and tone
- **Theme:** the quest for the unreachable

Background on the Poem. This poem was written in 1849, just shortly before Poe's own death. In October of that year, Poe was found lying in the rain outside Ryan's Public House and was taken to Washington College Hospital in a coma. He remained delirious for three and a half days, and on Sunday, October 7, at only forty years of age, died, crying out, "Lord help my poor soul."

The Literal Meaning. A gaily clad knight journeys in search of Eldorado. As the quest continues, he is saddened and grows old, and his strength begins to fail him. Meeting a pilgrim traveler—a shadow—he asks the way to Eldorado. The pilgrim tells him that he must "ride, boldly ride" over the Mountains of the Moon and through the Valley of the Shadow if he wishes to find Eldorado.

Providing for Cultural Differences. This poem was written at a time when the search for gold was current news and when the American frontier was still being explored. Students from more recent immigrant backgrounds may vary in their ability to identify with the character of a questing knight. You might want to ask your students to discuss what their forebears' lives were like in 1849. You might lead them to understand that, despite differences in outward circumstances, the hopeful quest for a better life unites people from all backgrounds, and especially unites all Americans.

Providing for Different Levels of Ability. Because of its lively action, colorful setting, bouncy rhythm, and strong rhymes, this is a good poem for the less advanced students in your class. The more advanced students will probably want to concentrate on the symbolic implications.

Reading the Poem. The entire poem can be read aloud. (An audiocassette recording accompanies the selection.) You might want to have a different student recite each of the three stanzas. Alternatively, you might play for students the audiocassette recording that accompanies the selection.

Edgar Allan Poe   91

Reteaching Alternatives. If your students have trouble with the symbolic meanings of the story, you might focus on key words such as "Eldorado," "pilgrim," and, especially, because of its shifting meanings, "shadow." Have students write lists of the connotations of these words, and gather together the most helpful meanings through class discussion.

Responding to the Poem Text page 249
Analyzing the Poem
Identifying Details

1. Describe what happens to the knight in the course of the first two stanzas. The knight grows old in his search for Eldorado.

2. What directions does the shadow give him? The shadow tells him to ride boldly "over the Mountains of the moon and down the Valley of the Shadow."

Interpreting Meanings

3. What adjective does Poe use to describe the shadow the knight meets? He uses the adjective "pilgrim."

What do you think this word suggests about the nature of the shadow? The word suggests that the shadow, too, is on a journey or quest, but that this quest is perhaps of a spiritual, rather than a material, nature.

4. Describe the *meter* of the poem. Do you think the poem's beat is appropriate to its subject? Explain. The meter of the poem alternates between trochees and anapests (with the stress on the first syllable of a foot) and iambs (with the stress on the second syllable). The alternating rhythms perhaps suggest the movement of the knight on his quest and the ambiguous nature of its end.

5. The words *Eldorado* and *shadow* are rhymed in each stanza, creating a pleasant echo throughout the poem. How do the meaning and the *connotations* of the word *shadow* change from stanza to stanza? In the first stanza, "shadow" is used literally, as in "shade." In the second stanza, it acquires a figurative meaning: a shadow over the heart (line 9). In the third stanza, the word designates the mysterious pilgrim figure who speaks to the knight. Finally, in the last stanza Poe is perhaps echoing the phrase of Psalm 23, the "valley of the shadow of death."

How do these changes reflect a gradual change in the poem's *tone*? Just as the uses of the word "shadow" gradually suggest ominous and mysterious connotations, so the poem's tone gradually shifts from bright gaiety to somber melancholy.

6. The characters of the knight and the shadow have a *symbolic* meaning. What types of people, attitudes, or concepts might these two characters represent? Student answers may vary. In general, the character of the knight seems to represent active optimism; the shadow, on the other hand, is more ambiguous—students may suggest he is a symbolic representation of death, of philosophical wisdom, or of a number of other concepts. Their answers will depend to some degree on how they interpret the shadow's advice to the knight.

7. The response the shadow makes to the knight's question is open to interpretation. Explain what *you* think the shadow's answer means. Student answers will vary. Some may view the shadow's response as an indication to the knight that his perseverance will be rewarded; others may suggest that the shadow is cryptically telling the knight that Eldorado exists only in people's dreams. Urge students to express their own opinions.

8. Name some "Eldorados" that contemporary people might search for. Would the shadow's advice pertain to these quests? Student answers will vary.

"Annabel Lee" Text page 250

Objectives

1. To describe the pattern of end rhymes and internal rhymes
2. To evaluate the use of meter
3. To write a stanza imitating the poem
4. To write a paragraph comparing and contrasting two poems

Introducing the Poem

Background on the Poem. Poe suffered greatly, descending into alcoholism and mental illness, during the repeated, nearly fatal crises of his tubercular young wife, Virginia. For weeks after her death, he would wander off to her tomb and spend hours there, weeping hysterically. The remaining two years of his life were his most melancholy. "Annabel Lee" first appeared in the New York *Tribune* of October 9, 1849, just two days after Poe's death.

92 The American Renaissance

The Literal Meaning. The narrator says that many years ago, in a kingdom by the sea, he loved a girl by the name of Annabel Lee. Their love was so great that even the angels were jealous of the relationship. After her death, her "highborn kinsman" buried her by the sea. Each night the speaker lies by her side in the tomb where, though physically separated, their souls are united, for love is stronger than death.

Teaching Strategies

Providing for Cultural Differences. Idealized romantic love is particularly a Western notion and was at its most fashionable in Poe's day. To modern American teenagers, highly romantic ideals and anti-sentimental ones often coexist. This poem provides a good opportunity to discuss changing ideas of love over time and in different cultures.

Providing for Different Levels of Ability. Be sure that your students read the introduction to the poem on text page 250 and "A Comment on the Poem," text page 252. This simple love poem is as straightforward as a popular song. There is perhaps more risk of disdain by the more advanced students than of noncomprehension by less advanced ones. Point out, then, the emotional intricacies underlying the poem's surface simplicity: Poe seems to be infatuated with his own romantic pose, at least as much as with the woman, and yet, given the agonies of his life, it would be facile to dismiss his grief as insincere.

Introducing Vocabulary Study. Knowing the meanings of the following words is important to understanding the poem. (The italicized word is archaic.)

| sepulcher | l. 19 | *nighttide* | l. 38 |
| dissever | l. 32 | | |

Reading the Poem. This is an excellent poem for students to read aloud. A certain amount of lightheartedness will not hurt.

Reteaching Alternatives. Have students paraphrase the poem orally.

Responding to the Poem   Text page 252
Analyzing the Poem
Identifying Details

1. What explanation does the narrator give for Annabel Lee's death? The narrator says that a wind came from a cloud and gave the girl a fatal chill.

2. In Stanza 5, how does the speaker defy both the angels and the demons who succeed in separating him from his beloved? The speaker says that their love was stronger by far than the love of those who were older and wiser, and that neither angels nor demons can separate his soul from that of his beloved.

In Stanza 6, how does he attempt to show that loving memory can defeat death and absence? He says that the moon and the stars remind him of the eyes of his beloved every night, and that he lies nightly by her grave.

3. Describe the pattern of *end rhymes* in the poem. How many *internal rhymes*—rhymes within lines—can you find? The pattern of end rhymes varies from stanza to stanza. In the first stanza it is: a b a b c b. The long "e" sound of rhyme b is repeated at regular intervals in each succeeding stanza. Some internal rhymes are: "chilling" and "killing" (line 26), "beams" and "dreams" (line 34), "rise" and "eyes" (line 36), "night-tide" and "side" (line 38).

Interpreting Meanings

4. The poem's singsong *meter*, together with its *rhymes* and *repetition*, give it the effect of an old ballad. Some critics have felt that Poe was more concerned with the music of his composition than with the story it tells or the emotion it expresses. Do you feel that the poem is primarily memorable as "word music," or that it is primarily a haunting story of lost love? Give reasons for your opinion. Student answers will vary. Some students may suggest that the two elements—musical language and a haunting story—are effectively combined.

5. Grief is one kind of emotion; sadness is another. Which emotion do you think this poem more effectively expresses? Student answers will vary.

Writing About the Poem
A Creative Response

1. Imitating the Poem. Suggest word-for-word substitution that exactly matches Poe's accented and unaccented syllables as a way to begin.

Criteria for Evaluating the Assignment. The stanza, on a topic of the student's choosing, begins with the line, "It was many and many a year ago," and exactly imitates Poe's meter and rhyme in "Annabel Lee" for the rest of the stanza.

Edgar Allan Poe   93

A Critical Response

2. Comparing Poems. Read and discuss the lines from Wordsworth ("A Comment on the Poem," page 252), eliciting similarities to and differences from "Annabel Lee."

Criteria for Evaluating the Assignment. Paragraph 1 cites similarities between the two poems. Paragraph 2 cites differences: what Poe goes on to imagine that Wordsworth does not.

"To Helen" Text page 253

Objectives

1. To identify alliteration and rhyme
2. To evaluate the use of allusion
3. To write an analysis of the poem

Introducing the Poem

In outline form, for your reference, here are the major elements in the poem:

- **Speaker:** a "weary, way-worn wanderer"
- **Significant techniques:** rhyme, alliteration, literary allusion
- **Theme:** idealized, classical beauty as a timeless source of comfort

Background to the Poem. The initial inspiration for the poem, which was published in 1831, may have been Jane Stith Stanard, the mother of one of Poe's boyhood friends in Richmond. A revised version was printed in 1845; some critics believe that the Helen of this version was Sarah Helen Whitman, a widow Poe planned to marry.

The Literal Meaning. The narrator begins with a simile, that Helen's beauty is like that of the ships of ancient Greece that took the "way-worn wanderer" home, around which the entire poem is built. Helen's beauty has brought the narrator home to the grandeur of Greece and Rome, to a renewed awareness of beauty.

Teaching Strategies

Providing for Cultural Differences. Students today are not nearly so familiar with classical Greece as students of previous generations. In addition, ideals of beauty have changed over time. Discuss with your students their various ideals of beauty, and bear in mind that the image of ancient Greece as the home of harmony and restraint was largely a fabrication of Renaissance Europe.

Providing for Different Levels of Ability. Less advanced students may have trouble with the classical allusions, and particularly with the third stanza. Point-by-point memorization of each classical reference, however, is much less important than an overall appreciation of Poe's feelings about ancient Greece, and of why a woman's beauty brings it to mind.

Reading the Poem. It will be helpful to review briefly the story of Helen of Troy, the most beautiful woman of the ancient world, who ran off with Paris, a prince of Troy. When her husband, King Menelaus of Sparta, went to get her, the ten-year-long Trojan War began. "A Comment on the Poem," text page 254, is an excellent source of information on the allusions in the poem. An audiocassette recording accompanies this selection.

Reteaching Alternatives. If the weight of classical allusion is too heavy for your students, ask them to restate, in their own words, the speaker's feelings about Helen, stripped of their classical decorations.

Responding to the Poem Text page 254
Analyzing the Poem
Identifying Facts

1. **In Stanza 1, find the extended *simile* the speaker uses to describe Helen's beauty.** The speaker compares Helen's beauty to the "Nicéan barks of yore" (ancient Greek ships), which carried wanderers home over the "perfumed sea."

2. **In Stanza 2, where does the speaker say Helen's "Naiad," or nymphlike, airs have brought him?** He says they have brought him "home" to the glory and grandeur of Greek and Roman culture.

3. **In Stanza 2, who was "wont to roam on desperate seas"?** The speaker had roamed on these seas.

4. **Where does the speaker picture Helen in Stanza 3?** He pictures her as a statue, holding a lamp in a window-niche.

5. Subtle musical effects are created in the poem by *alliteration* and *rhyme*. List all the uses of alliteration you can find. Alliteration occurs in line 4 ("weary, way-worn wanderer"), line 7 ("hyacinth hair"), lines 9–10 ("glory that was Greece, / And the grandeur..."), line 12 ("statue-like I see thee stand").

What is the end-rhyme scheme, and where do you hear internal rhyming sounds? The end-rhyme scheme is different in all three stanzas. Stanza 1: a b a b b. Stanza 2: a b a b a. Stanza 3: a b b a a. Among the internal rhyming sounds are "beauty" and "me" in line 1, "gently" and "sea" in line 3, "way-worn" and "bore" in line 4, "brilliant" and "window-niche" in line 11, "lamp" and "hand" in line 13. (Some of these are slant rhymes.)

Interpreting Meanings

6. How would you explain what the speaker means when he says that Helen's beauty has brought him "home" to Greece and Rome? Poe presumably means that the classic beauty of the woman reminds him of the harmonious balance of Greek and Roman culture, and specifically of the beauty of classical art. He may mean "brought home" in the sense of "brought back to one's roots," since classical culture profoundly influenced the development of Western civilization.

What general ideas about beauty and classical civilization do you think the poem expresses? The poem expresses the general idea that classical culture is to be revered for its harmonious expression of beauty.

How do you feel about these ideas? Student answers will vary. You may want to provoke discussion by asking the students to define the term "classical." Also, you might point out some "classical" examples in architecture, music, sculpture, etc.

7. In Stanza 3, by what name does the speaker address Helen? Reread the Comment on the Poem, and explain why you think the speaker chose this *allusion*. The speaker addresses Helen by the name Psyche. The allusion emphasizes the woman's beauty, both in herself and in her role as the chosen lover of Cupid, god of love.

8. Critics often claim that Poe turns his women characters into statues. They say he is more concerned with idealized and unresponsive beauty than with beauty as it appears in the faces of real human beings. Do you feel that this poem is really a love poem addressed to an individual woman? Or does it seem to be the expression of an ideal? Explain. Student answers will vary. Encourage the students to present and defend their opinions. The students may note that in the third stanza of this poem, Helen is explicitly envisioned as a statue.

Writing About the Poem
A Critical Response

Analyzing the Poem. Read the writing prompt with the class, clarifying directions and discussing its content as needed. Refer students also to "A Comment on the Poem" (page 254).

***C*riteria for Evaluating the Assignment.** The essay on Poe's "To Helen" consists of at least three paragraphs. It analyzes the extended simile in Stanza 1, the word "desperate" in Stanza 2, and the vision in Stanza 3.

"The Raven"   Text page 255

Objectives

1. To analyze imagery, tone, and symbols
2. To describe an alternate setting
3. To write two verses imitating the poet's rhyme scheme and meter
4. To write an essay comparing and contrasting two poems
5. To write a paragraph analyzing the poem

Introducing the Poem

In outline form, for your reference, here are the major elements of "The Raven":

- **Narrator:** a scholar and bereaved lover of Lenore
- **Significant techniques:** alliteration, rhyme, repetition, tone, symbolism, narrative verse
- **Theme:** Death is irrevocable, but memory and grief linger.

Background on the Poem. In early versions of the poem, the bird was an owl, Athena's traditional bird of wisdom. Perhaps the idea to use the raven came from Poe's reading of Dickens's *Barnaby Rudge*. In reviewing the novel, Poe was critical of Dickens's failure to make more use of the bird: "Its croakings might have been *prophetically* heard in the course of the drama." The "lost Lenore" of the poem has variously been identified as Elmyra Royster, a sweetheart from Poe's youth, and as Virginia Clemm, Poe's wife. "The Raven" brought Poe immediate fame, but its printing in the January 29, 1845, New York *Evening Post*, earned him only ten dollars. In 1929 a manuscript of the poem was sold for $100,000.

The Literal Meaning. Reading old books at midnight, the speaker in the poem is sorrowing over his lost love Lenore. Hearing a tapping at his chamber door, he flings it open but sees nothing. Flinging open the shutter, he is greeted by a stately raven that enters the room and settles on the bust of Pallas Athena, the goddess of wisdom. When the speaker asks the bird its name, the raven's only reply is, "Nevermore." The gloomy, grave, and ungainly bird causes the speaker to experience momentary amusement, but the bird's repetition of "nevermore," especially when it is the answer to the speaker's desire to know about being reunited with Lenore, drives him into a state of frenzy.

Teaching Strategies

Providing for Cultural Differences. Cultural differences should provide no barrier to understanding this poem.

Providing for Different Levels of Ability. The rhythm and rhyme of this poem are so strong and so jaunty that for some students they may obstruct the meaning of the poem. The poem is also so familiar that students who have encountered it before may be more taken with its jingle-like aspect than with its depiction of frenzied despair. Try to break through this incrustation by clear, direct paraphrase, and by discussing the poem's sound as a symptom of its narrator's (and author's) state of mind.

Introducing Vocabulary Study. Knowing the meanings of the following words is important to understanding the poem. (Italicized words either are archaic or have special meaning in context.)

wrought	l. 8	obeisance	l. 39
surcease	l. 10	*mein*	l. 40
entreating*	l. 16	nevermore	

Reading the Poem. This dramatic narrative poem can be divided not only into stanzas, but also into roles. A separate student can be assigned the task of saying, "Nevermore"—perhaps even a different student for each repetition of the word—with informal evaluations by the peer group afterward.

Reteaching Alternatives. If the antique trappings deter some of your students from enjoying this extremely vivid poem, you might ask the class to offer possible updated paraphrases of key words such as "nevermore." A class vote could determine the winner among competing synonyms. Reassure your students that even in Poe's day, the classical lore the narrator studied was "quaint and curious" and "forgotten."

Responding to the Poem Text page 260
Analyzing the Poem
Identifying Facts

1. What experience has made the speaker seek "surcease of sorrow" in his old books? He seeks a remedy for, or a distraction from, his sorrow at the death of his beloved, the radiant maiden Lenore.

2. What does the speaker say in Stanza 5? He says that he peers into the darkness outside the door. His imagination is prey to wild fancies, and he whispers the name "Lenore." But nothing except an echo of this name resounds.

What do you think he may have expected to find at his door? In his wild, distracted state, the narrator may have expected that the spirit or soul of his beloved had come to visit him.

3. What is the first hint, in Stanza 10, that the Raven is here to stay? The Raven is immobile, sitting on the bust of Pallas. When the narrator mutters that the bird will doubtless leave on the morrow, the bird responds, "Nevermore."

Interpreting Meanings

4. Which *images* describing the setting in Stanzas 2 and 3 create an atmosphere of mystery or fear? The narrator describes the time of the events as "bleak December." The dying embers in the fireplace produce "ghosts" on the floor. The curtains rustle sadly, and the narrator is "thrilled . . . with fantastic terrors." He repeats to himself the statement that the noise at the door is merely being caused by a visitor—as if to reassure himself that the sound is not supernatural. Thus, many of the images in these stanzas contribute to a mysterious, ominous atmosphere.

5. In Stanza 14, the speaker talks to himself. What does he suggest is happening, and what is the nature of the "nepenthe" he is tempted to indulge in? The narrator suggests that this supernatural visitation is meant to comfort and console him for the loss of Lenore. Just as nepenthe provides oblivion from sorrow, he will forget the maiden.

What does the Raven's inevitable answer tell him about the possibility of this kind of oblivion? The Raven's repetition of "Nevermore" tells the narrator that his hope for oblivion is illusory.

96 The American Renaissance

6. In Stanza 17, what could the speaker mean by begging the bird, "Take thy beak from out my heart"? The bird has become a demonic force for the narrator; its prophecy that he may never forget his sorrow makes it seem to the narrator as if the raven wounds his heart with its beak.

7. The speaker's *tone* changes as the Raven gradually turns from a comic figure into a demonic figure. Trace these changes in tone. Although the poem starts somberly, the first appearance of the Raven evokes a kind of bemusement in the narrator (Stanzas 7–9); he even jokes that the Raven seems like a prodigy. The narrator's mood becomes more reflective in Stanzas 10–13; he wonders what misfortune can have befallen the Raven's master. It is only in Stanza 14 that the narrator realizes that the visit of the Raven may be specifically intended for him. In Stanzas 15 and 16, he tries desperately to wring some shred of hope or consolation from the bird, but in vain. In the final two stanzas, he gives full vent to his fury and despair.

Is there evidence in Stanza 18 that the speaker goes mad? Explain. The narrator tells us that the Raven has remained on the bust of Pallas to this day, his eyes resembling those of a demon. He also tells us that his own soul is in the shadow of the Raven, and will never be lifted up again. The exaggerated nature of both claims perhaps suggests that the speaker has gone mad.

8. The Raven in this poem is a *symbol*—it functions as a real raven in the story, but it also has a broader, figurative meaning. What, in your opinion, does the Raven symbolize? Student answers will vary. Some may suggest that the Raven symbolizes death, or the pain of loss. Others may suggest that the bird is a figure for despair. Let students present and defend their opinions. You may want to direct students' attention to Poe's own comment in the Primary Sources (see pages 260–261 of the student anthology), in which he says that the raven is "emblematical of Mournful and Never-Ending Remembrance."

Why do you suppose Poe chose a raven to carry this meaning, rather than—for example—a dove, a nightingale, or a chicken? Again, students may express different opinions. In general, the raven's color and demeanor make it the most suitable symbol in this somber situation. Students may point out that the other birds are associated with different concepts and moods (the dove with peace, the nightingale with sweet singing, the chicken with squawking, etc.).

Writing About the Poem
A Creative Response

1. Describing an Alternate Setting. Clarify for students that they are to write a descriptive paragraph, not a poem. Brainstorm settings that would work for the assignment.

Criteria for Evaluating the Assignment. The scene is one that would allow the events in "The Raven" to remain as disturbing as they are. It is vividly described.

2. Imitating Poe's Techniques. Brainstorm a list of names (to replace Lenore) for which there are many rhymes. Then analyze Poe's **rhyme scheme** (abcddb, with an internal rhyme in the third line) and **meter** (see "Sound Effects," page 262). Suggest that students try word-for-word substitution until they feel the meter.

Criteria for Evaluating the Assignment. The opening line is "Once upon a midnight dreary, while I pondered, weak and weary." Another name is substituted for Lenore. The two stanzas exactly imitate Poe's meter and rhyme scheme.

A Critical Response

3. Comparing Poems. Note that, despite the heading, the assignment is both to *compare* (state similarities), *and* to *contrast* (state differences) some aspects of the poems; and that the prompt tells students how to organize their essays.

Criteria for Evaluating the Assignment. The essay describes similarities in the overall **message** of "The Raven" and "Annabel Lee"; then cites how the poems are alike *and* how they differ in terms of **speaker**, **tone**, and **sound effects**.

4. Analyzing the Poem. Read Poe's essay (Primary Sources, text pages 260–261) and discuss the concept of "the human thirst for self-torture." To be sure that students understand Poe's phrase, ask them for examples they have observed.

Criteria for Evaluating the Assignment. The essay explains the meaning of Poe's phrase and uses examples from "The Raven" to support the idea that the speaker in the poem does or does not exhibit a compulsion for self-torture.

Elements of Literature:
Sound Effects   Text page 262

This section analyzes the **meter**, **internal rhyme**, and **alliteration** Poe uses in "The Raven." Read and discuss it before students attempt their imitations of Poe for creative writing assignment 2.

Extending the Poem

A present-day poet, Gary Snyder, wrote the following poem about the teenage love he parted from. You might have students compare the two views on love represented in these poems.

From "Four Poems for Robin"

December at Yase

You said, that October,
In the tall dry grass by the orchard
When you chose to be free,
"Again someday, maybe ten years."

After college I saw you
One time. You were strange.
And I was obsessed with a plan.

Now ten years and more have
Gone by: I've always known
      where you were—
I might have gone to you
Hoping to win your love back.
You still are single.

I didn't.
I thought I must make it alone. I
Have done that.

Only in dream, like this dawn,
Does the grave, awed intensity
Of our young love
Return to my mind, to my flesh.

We had what the others
All crave and seek for;
We left it behind at nineteen.

I feel ancient, as though I had
Lived many lives.

And may never now know
If I am a fool
Or have done what my
      Karma demands.

   Note that Snyder uses the word "never" in his final stanza, in a context similar to Poe's, with less dramatic effect but greater emotional reality.

Primary Sources: Poe's Essay on the Writing Process   Text page 260

According to the text, Poe describes the writing process in reverse, deciding on the effect he wants to achieve first, and then on the subject. In a class discussion, you might have students describe their own writing process and discuss how it compares with Poe's. Also, students might consider the point made by *The New Yorker* cartoon on text page 261. What is it about "The Raven" that has inspired so many parodies and so much humorous commentary?

Nathaniel Hawthorne   Text page 263

"The Minister's Black Veil"   Text page 265

Objectives

1. To describe a character
2. To analyze symbol, tone, and theme
3. To rewrite a paragraph of the story from another point of view
4. To write an essay comparing and contrasting the story with a sermon
5. To write an essay comparing and contrasting the story with an essay
6. To analyze the use of archaic and old-fashioned words

Introducing the Story

In outline form, for your reference, here are the major elements in the story:

98   The American Renaissance

- **Main characters:** Mr. Hooper, a "gentlemanly" bachelor and minister; Elizabeth, Mr. Hooper's fiancée; parishioners of the Milford church
- **Conflicts:** the individual psyche vs. guilt; the outspoken individual vs. the majority
- **Point of view:** limited third-person
- **Significant techniques:** allegory and symbolism, parable, and characterization
- **Setting:** Milford, Massachusetts, the early 1700's
- **Theme:** the pervasiveness of secret sin and the unwillingness of people to see it brought out into the open

Background on the Story. Hawthorne's use of allegory, where characters embody abstract qualities, is complex. Poe, among others, advised him to give up allegory in his otherwise favorable review of *Twice-Told Tales,* but moral symbolism and allegory were unalterable parts of Hawthorne's view of life. Of his own style, Hawthorne wrote the following comment in a letter to a friend in 1858:

> My own individual taste is for quite another class of works than those which I myself am able to write. If I were to meet with such books as mine, by another writer, I don't believe I should be able to get through them.

The Plot. The Reverend Mr. Hooper astonishes his congregation in the village of Milford by preaching to them one Sunday wearing a black veil. He explains, to his parishioners and later to his fiancée Elizabeth, that it is a symbol of universal secret sin, and that he will wear it for the rest of his life. The veil alienates his congregation and causes the breaking of his engagement. Hooper grows old and dies, isolated and unloved, but a respected, powerful minister.

Teaching Strategies

Providing for Cultural Differences. The definition of sin varies from one cultural group to another and Hawthorne's Puritan background was particularly sin-conscious. Explore with your students the similarities and differences among the concepts of sin in their various cultural groups—or between their groups's and that of "mainstream" America as seen in the media.

Providing for Different Levels of Ability. Somber and doleful on the surface, Hawthorne's stories are vividly dramatic at the core; the difficulty for many modern students is to cut through to that core. Paraphrasing of Hawthorne's old-fashioned, musty diction will help. It may also be helpful to highlight the dramatic qualities of the story by having students take the roles of the various characters, and read aloud their lines of dialogue. Also, allow the class to speculate aloud as to reasons for the minister's actions. Remind them that Hawthorne calls this story a parable; what lesson he is attempting to teach should be a consideration while reading the story.

Introducing Vocabulary Study. Knowing the meanings of the following words is important to understanding the selection. (Starred words appear in the Glossary. Italicized words either are archaic or have special meaning in context.)

gait*	266	*prodigy*	268
meditative*	266	protend	268
perturbation*	266	waggery	269
semblance	266	censure	269
abstracted (adj.)	266	*embassy*	269
venerable	267	*plighted*	269
iniquity*	267	remonstrance*	269
unwonted	267	obstinacy*	270
visage	267	zealous*	270
sagacious	267	consort (v.)	271
hoary	267	figuratively	271
intimate (v.)*	267	pensively*	271
vagary	267	*sway*	272
scrupled	268	solicitude	272

Reading Check. You might use the following questions as a reading check. Have students respond *True* or *False*.

1. Although the congregation is frightened by it, the veil actually has the effect of making Hooper a more effective minister.   True
2. Hooper is himself repelled by the way he looks and avoids looking at himself in mirrors and refuses to drink from a fountain in which he might see his own reflection.   True
3. Governor Belcher, who had asked that Hooper give the election day sermon, withdraws the offer when Hooper refuses to remove the veil for the delivery of the sermon.   False
4. Elizabeth, who after all these years still loves Hooper, is the only person with him at the time of his death.   False
5. At Elizabeth's insistence, Hooper momentarily withdraws the veil for her just before he dies.   False

Reteaching Alternatives. If some of your students have trouble grasping the themes of the story, you might ask them to write in their own words, or deliver orally, a brief character description of Reverend Hooper. Ask them why such a mild, law-abiding man would be so obsessed with sin. Guide them toward understanding that Hooper is concerned with both his own, unspecified, sinfulness, and with the universality of secret guilt.

Responding to the Story   Text page 274
Analyzing the Story
Identifying Facts

1. Describe the congregation's response to their first sight of Mr. Hooper's black veil. They are shocked. An

Nathaniel Hawthorne   99

old woman mutters that Mr. Hooper has changed himself into "something awful," while Goodman Gray declares that he has gone mad. Several women of "delicate nerves" leave the meetinghouse before the service is finished.

2. Briefly describe Hooper's *character*, based on the picture of him offered in the story's opening paragraphs. What does the congregation's attitude toward him seem to have been up to this point? Hooper is neat, gentle, and kind. He seems to have been an effective preacher, and the congregation seems to have been well disposed toward him, as evidenced by the periodic invitations of Squire Saunders to Mr. Hooper to dine with him and his family.

3. In a single afternoon, Hooper presides at both a funeral and a wedding. Explain how the veil is responsible for a shudder and a general heightening of mood at each event. At the funeral, Hooper bends over the body of the dead girl to take his last farewell. The veil shifts momentarily to reveal his face; an old woman later affirms that the corpse gave a shudder at that moment. But Mr. Hooper's funeral prayer deeply moves those of his congregation who are present. At the wedding, the guests regard the veil as an ominous portent that spreads a shadow over such a happy occasion. The bride's fingers are cold, and the bridegroom's hand trembles. The mood is heightened when Mr. Hooper, just as he raises a glass to toast the couple, catches sight of his veiled face in a looking glass. Terrified, he spills the wine on the carpet and rushes out into the night.

4. Elizabeth, Hooper's fiancée, demands to know why he must wear the veil. Locate the passage that gives Hooper's explanation. Hooper tells her that the veil is a "type and a symbol" which he is bound to wear so long as he is on earth. His remarks about sorrow, secret sin, and the Last Judgment indicate that he conceives of the veil as a symbol of his own sins—and perhaps of the sins of others. (The passage is on page 269.)

What arguments against the veil does Elizabeth make? Elizabeth says that the world may not believe that the veil is the sign of an innocent sorrow. She warns Hooper that people will gossip about him, whispering that he has been involved in some scandal. She then appeals to their love, and asks him to cast aside the veil once for her sake.

5. Does the black veil have any positive effects throughout Hooper's long ministry? Explain. Although the veil continually inspired fear, Hawthorne emphasizes that its one desirable effect was to make Hooper an even better clergyman than before. He was especially effective with sinners and with the dying. He was even invited to preach an election sermon before Jonathan Belcher, governor of the colony. His long life was irreproachable, and although he was unloved, he was highly respected.

Interpreting Meanings

6. Why do you think the villagers bury Hooper without removing the veil? The reason they do not remove the veil is probably that they are still so frightened. Hooper has also said that he would never remove the veil while he was on earth.

7. Poe said that Hooper wore the veil because: "... a crime of dark dye (having reference to the young lady) had been committed...." What do you think Poe refers to? Poe implies that Hooper and Elizabeth had been guilty of some indiscretion or sin together, while they were still unmarried.

What is your response to this explanation for the veil? Student answers will vary. However, students may point out that there is very little support in the story for such a theory. Ask the students if they do not believe that the conversations between Hooper and Elizabeth would have been somewhat different if they were conscious of having "sinned" together.

8. Describe Elizabeth's first response to the sight of her fiancé's veil, and tell how her reaction changes. How would you explain her sudden change of attitude? Elizabeth is the one person in the village who is not appalled by Hooper's veil. She dares what all the villagers had been afraid to do: she asks Hooper with a direct simplicity why he wears the veil. Up to this point, Elizabeth seems loving, caring, and full of common sense: as Hawthorne describes her thoughts, the veil "was but a double fold of crape." But in the course of her interview with Hooper, Elizabeth's attitude changes. When Hooper obstinately resists her entreaties and tells her that not even she can ever come behind the veil, Elizabeth becomes sorrowful, and then terrified. The power of the veil to frighten those who see it seems to have finally affected her. Hawthorne never directly explains her change of attitude, and students may have various opinions for its cause. But it seems reasonable that Hooper's references to universal sin have unnerved Elizabeth.

9. From his deathbed, Hooper makes it clear that he is not the only wearer of the veil, but that he sees similar veils all around him. Explain what you think the minister means by his deathbed statement. What does the veil *symbolize*, in your opinion? Hooper seems to assert that all those around him are secret sinners, who deny to themselves and to God the fact of their evil. Students will have different opinions on the symbolism of the veil. But Hooper's last speech appears to stress that the veil is a symbol, or "type," for human beings' habitual dishonesty—with their fellow beings, with themselves, and with God. Note especially Hooper's statement: "When the friend shows his inmost heart to his friend; the lover to his best beloved; when man does not vainly shrink from the eye of his Creator, loathsomely treasuring up the secret of his

100 The American Renaissance

sin; then deem me a monster, for the symbol beneath which I have lived, and die!" Students may also suggest that the veil acquires various subsidiary symbolic meanings throughout the story; for example, it becomes a symbol of the melancholy separation between Hooper and other human beings (including Elizabeth, who might have been closest to him), and also a symbol of the distinction between mortal life and eternity (note the phrase of Reverend Clark in the death scene, when he refers to death as lifting "the veil of eternity").

10. Would you describe the narrator's *tone* as neutral or emotional? Explain how the words the narrator chooses in referring to the veil affect the story's tone. Students will have various opinions, but in general it can be said that Hawthorne injects emotional language into the story to darken the atmosphere and the tone. The following adjectives are among those associated with the veil: black, darkened, gloomy, awful, mysterious, dismal, mortal, and material.

11. On page 272, the narrator remarks that the "saddest of all prisons" is a person's "own heart." What does this mean? Hawthorne probably means that the torment of a guilty conscience, or simply the acute awareness of one's own sinfulness, is like a "prison," confining a person in his or her own melancholy.

Do you agree? Explain your response. Student answers will vary.

12. What do you think is this story's *theme*, or main idea? In your answer, consider that Hawthorne subtitled the story "A Parable" and that a *parable* is a short, usually simple story from which a moral or religious lesson can be drawn. Encourage the students to exchange their own opinions. One statement of Hawthorne's theme might be that we are all secret sinners, although it is the rare person who will openly acknowledge and come to terms with this fact. The courage of such a person paradoxically inspires both respect and horror in others.

Writing About the Story
A Creative Response

1. Using Another Point of View. Discuss passages from "The Minister's Black Veil" (e.g., on pages 270 and 273) which hint at Reverend Hooper's intent. Students might see their paragraph as an entry in Reverend Hooper's diary or journal.

Criteria for Evaluating the Assignment. Building on remarks of Reverend Hooper, the paragraph believably explains what the veil means to Hooper, how he first thought of wearing it, and how wearing it all the time makes him feel.

A Critical Response

2. Comparing the Story to a Sermon. Have students chart the ideas in Edwards's sermon and Hawthorne's story on sin, hypocrisy, and conditions for salvation; and base their essays on the similarities or differences they find.

Criteria for Evaluating the Assignment. The essay compares or contrasts what Edwards's sermon and Hawthorne's story say about sin, hypocrisy, and conditions needed for salvation. Examples support all major points.

3. Comparing the Story to an Essay. A chart or a sheet of paper divided into columns headed "Emerson" and "Hawthorne" may be a helpful organizing tool for this assignment.

Criteria for Evaluating the Assignment. The essay explains the similarities or differences between Emerson's and Hawthorne's views of human nature. It cites examples from both writers to support points made. It states whether the student agrees with either writer, or has a third opinion.

Analyzing Language and Style
Archaic and Old-Fashioned Words

Rare today: crape, prodigy, well-nigh, waggery, wrought

Modern idiom:

1. *crape:* a light, crinkled fabric
2. *prodigy:* extraordinary phenomenon
3. *well-nigh, waggery:* nearly, mischief
4. *wrought:* worked

Different senses today:

Crape: Spelled *crepe*, a light, crinkled paper

Prodigy: Most often, to mean a highly talented child

Wrought: Only in set phrases—"wrought iron," "all wrought up over nothing"

Extending the Story

Ask your students to imagine what this story might have been like if Poe had written it. What might have been gained? What lost? Would they have enjoyed it more? Would they have gotten as much of a glimpse into human nature?

"Rappaccini's Daughter"

Text page 275

Objectives

1. To analyze character, climax, and setting
2. To explain irony and the moral
3. To analyze the use of character foils
4. To write a new ending for the story
5. To analyze romantic elements
6. To write an essay comparing and contrasting two stories
7. To write an essay describing Biblical parallels
8. To analyze word connotations and figures of speech

Introducing the Story

In outline form, for your reference, here are the major elements in "Rappaccini's Daughter":

- **Protagonist:** Giovanni, a young student at the University of Padua; Beatrice Rappaccini, beautiful daughter of Dr. Rappaccini and victim of his scientific experimentation
- **Antagonists:** Signor Pietro Baglioni, an elderly professor of eminent repute and a professional rival of Dr. Rappaccini; Dr. Rappaccini, a "tall, emaciated, sallow, and sickly looking scholar" who believes every disease can be cured by the use of the appropriate poison
- **Conflicts:** parent vs. child, science vs. nature; love vs. rationalism
- **Point of view:** third-person, partially omniscient
- **Significant techniques:** symbolism and allegory, setting, character foils
- **Setting:** long ago in Padua, Italy
- **Theme:** the overdevelopment of the intellect at the expense of the heart

Background on the Story. The major literary product of Hawthorne's stay in Concord was the 1846 publication of *Mosses from an Old Manse,* a book whose stories had been written in the same room in which Emerson had written "Nature." In this collection of tales is "Rappaccini's Daughter," a story first published in *Democratic Review,* December, 1844. The same year *Mosses from an Old Manse* was published, Hawthorne took a job at the Salem Custom House and would leave Concord for good. While preparing the second edition of *Mosses from an Old Manse* in 1854, Hawthorne wrote to his publisher this comment on his work:

I am not quite sure that I entirely comprehend my own meanings in some of these blasted allegories; but I remember that [when I wrote them] I always had a meaning, or at least thought I had.

The Plot. Staying in a room overlooking Rappaccini's garden of poisonous plants, Giovanni becomes infatuated with Beatrice Rappaccini, but is warned against her by Baglioni, for Rappaccini has infused a poisonous nature into his own daughter by rearing her among his plants. Giovanni then sees that he himself was acquired the same poisonous touch. He tries to free Beatrice with the aid of Baglioni's antidote, but it kills her, and she dies reproaching the men around her.

Teaching Strategies

Providing for Cultural Differences. Male and female students are likely to have different reactions to the characters in this story. Females may identify with Beatrice and see her primarily as the victim of the egotistical manipulations of the three men. Male readers may see her primarily as a "femme fatale"—a beauty with a poisonous nature. Hawthorne, a true artist, allows us to see both sides. Thus the story presents a good opportunity to explore your students' feelings on the eternally touchy subject of the gender power struggle, and to make the point that the most enlightened view of any complex interpersonal issue is that which respects all sides.

Providing for Different Levels of Ability. The Italian Renaissance setting, which gives the story a fashionably antique atmosphere in its own day, may now be a barrier for some students. All they need really know about it is that (as in Shakespeare) Renaissance Italy represented a vague, glowing atmosphere of bygone romance; the setting of "Rappaccini's Daughter" is not functionally indispensible.

The length of the story may also make it a challenge for your less advanced students. Class discussion can be used to elicit paraphrases. Students who may not be very interested in a story about a desiccated Paduan apothecary may become more interested upon realizing that the story is about an overprotective father, his beautiful, sheltered daughter, and a meddling neighbor.

Introducing Vocabulary Study. Knowing the meanings of the following words is important to understanding the story. (Starred words appear in the Glossary. Italicized words either are archaic or have special meaning in context.)

102 The American Renaissance

immortal	275	deign	283
opulent*	275	fain	283
vicissitudes	276	evanescent	283
assiduous	276	*wrought*	285
malignant	276	emaciated	285
exhalations	278	imbued	285
rectify*	278	sophistry	285
hap	279	manifestations	285
verdue	280	infringing	286
proximity	281	alembic	287
arrested	281	surmise (n.)	288
arcane	282	substantiated	288
ebullition	282	torpid	289
in fine	283	quelled	289
privity	283	quaff	290

Reading the Story. Because this is a rather long story, you may want to assign it as homework, and, afterward, read only the beginning in class. If you read at least through the Baglioni-Giovanni scene on text pages 272–274, you will have introduced the four major characters and foreshadowed the major conflict. An audiocassette recording of Hawthorne's exposition in this story is available, running from the beginning of the story through Giovanni's dream after his first sight of Beatrice in the garden.

Reading Check. You might want to use the following questions as a reading check. Have students respond *True* or *False*.

1. A large, magnificent plant with purple, gem-like flowers is a "breath of life" to Beatrice, who refers to the plant as her sister. __True__
2. Professor Pietro Baglioni, a friend of Giovanni's father, admires Rappaccini and is pleased to notice Giovanni's interest in Beatrice. __False__
3. Professor Baglioni believes that Giovanni is certainly part of one of Rappaccini's experiments. __True__
4. Although they never kiss or hold hands, the love grows between Giovanni and Beatrice. __True__
5. In her dying words, Beatrice claims that there is more poison in Giovanni's nature than in hers. __True__

Reteaching Alternatives. The mad-scientist aspect of this story will probably be easier for your students to grasp than the interpersonal-relations aspect, which is stronger here than in any of the other works in this unit. Using the board, and class discussion, you might want to list the characters' traits and the ways they manipulate each other. You might also divide the class into four groups, each taking the side of one of the characters against the other three.

Responding to the Story Text page 292
Analyzing the Story
Identifying Facts

1. Describe Dr. Rappaccini's behavior toward the plants in his garden. How does his daughter's behavior toward the plants differ from his own? Dr. Rappaccini intently examines the plants and shrubs, but with cold, scientific detachment: Giovanni notes that he avoids any contact with the flowers, and is even cautious not to breathe their odors. By contrast, Beatrice (who herself resembles a flower in Giovanni's eyes) handles and inhales the odor of several plants which her father avoids.

In particular, how does each treat the large plant by the fountain? When he comes to the magnificent plant, Dr. Rappaccini supplements the thick gloves he wears on his hands with a mask, which he ties about his mouth and nostrils. But when he summons his daughter, Beatrice tenderly attends to the plant, calling it her "sister" and her "splendor."

2. Name three of the early hints in the story that Beatrice may have deadly powers. A small lizard dies in the garden when struck by a tiny drop of liquid that falls from one of the purple flowers of the plant by the fountain. Likewise, a butterfly falls dead when it comes in contact with Beatrice's breath. And the fresh flowers which Giovanni throws to Beatrice at their first meeting begin to wither a few moments later, as Beatrice withdraws from the garden into the house.

3. Explain what we learn from Baglioni about the *character* of Dr. Rappaccini. Baglioni says that Dr. Rappaccini is a brilliant physician but is gravely flawed. He tells Giovanni that Rappaccini considers his patients merely as subjects for experimental science. Rappaccini is not to be trusted.

4. Cite the passages in the story that reveal Beatrice's relationship with the large flower. Among other passages, students may cite the opening scene, where Rappaccini commits the flower to his daughter's care; the scene in the garden between Giovanni and Beatrice, where Beatrice tenderly addresses the flower and then warns Giovanni not to touch it; and the final scene in the garden.

5. As a result of his first talk with Beatrice in the garden, how does Giovanni begin to feel about her? He begins to experience emotions of both love and horror.

6. Describe Baglioni's plan to save both Beatrice and Giovanni. Baglioni tells Giovanni to persuade Beatrice to drink some of the liquid he keeps in a silver vial. He claims that the liquid is an antidote to Rappaccini's poisons.

**7. After Baglioni's visit, what physical change does

Giovanni recognize in himself? Giovanni believes that he has contracted Beatrice's deadly powers. He breathes on some flowers and on a spider, and observes the effects: both the flowers and the insect die.

What change in attitude toward Beatrice begins to grow in his mind? Giovanni becomes deeply distrustful and angry. He believes that Beatrice has cursed him.

What does he accuse her of? He accuses her of trying to poison him.

8. Explain what Dr. Rappaccini wanted to do for Giovanni and Beatrice with his science. Rappaccini wanted to endow both of them with "marvelous gifts" that would set them apart from ordinary people. These gifts appear to be the power to destroy their enemies.

9. In Beatrice's last words, at the story's *climax*, what does she imply is the real poison that has spread through Giovanni's nature? She implies that the real poison is mental and emotional, rather than physical. She says that his words of hatred are "like lead" in her heart, and she reproaches him at the end: "Oh, was there not, from the first, more poison in thy nature than in mine?"

Interpreting Meanings

10. Giovanni's lodgings are in the house of an old Paduan family, "long extinct," one of whose members had been assigned by Dante to a place in Hell. What mood is established by the *setting*? These details of setting suggest a mood of decay, torture, corruption, and death.

How does the first paragraph set the mood for the whole story? The first paragraph, by emphasizing the gloominess of Giovanni's lodgings, the link with Dante's Inferno, and the extinction of the noble Paduan family, evokes a mood of decay and corruption.

11. What do you think actually killed Beatrice? Most students will agree that Beatrice dies from a lack of love. She is smothered by her father's obsessions and by Giovanni's suspicious distrust.

12. How are the circumstances of Beatrice's death *ironic*? The circumstances of Beatrice's death are ironic in at least two ways. First, Baglioni had promised an antidote when he gave the drink to Giovanni. When Beatrice falls dead, we realize that the liquid was an antidote only in an ironic, figurative sense: the death which it causes is a release from the evil that Dr. Rappaccini had inflicted upon her. Secondly, Beatrice's death is ironic because she is the only figure of love in the story. As she says just before she dies: "I would fain have been loved, not feared." Rappaccini is perverted; Giovanni is weak and distrustful; and Baglioni, while professing to honor humane science, is consumed with jealousy. It seems especially ironic, given the other characters' faults, that Beatrice should die.

In your opinion, which character or characters bear most responsibility for her fate, and why? Student answers will vary. Rappaccini, Giovanni, and Baglioni all must bear a measure of responsibility, despite the obvious fact that it is Baglioni's "antidote" that literally kills Beatrice.

13. During Giovanni's first meeting with Beatrice, what warning does she issue about truth and appearance? She tells him to believe only the words from her lips, not what he has heard or what he may have fancied about her.

Consider Beatrice's appearance, her physical nature, and her soul, and explain the *moral* about beauty and appearances the story might be teaching. Student answers will vary. Hawthorne's complex story exploits extensively the technique of ambiguity in literature—the deliberate suggestion of two or more conflicting meanings. Bearing this in mind, encourage students to present and support their own opinions. Some will say that Hawthorne's moral is that physical beauty is deceptive. They will argue that Beatrice has deadly powers, and that Giovanni is portrayed as weak in being unable to resist the charm of her outward loveliness. But other students may point to the fact that Beatrice's "powers" have been inflicted upon her by her father. Her last speech makes clear that she was capable (in her soul, at any rate) of sincere love. In this interpretation, Giovanni is not weak because he succumbs to her beauty, but rather because he allows distrust and hatred to overwhelm him. On this reading, Beatrice is, ironically, all she appears to be: a sweet, loving human being who is manipulated by her father and distrusted by her lover. As a footnote, you may want to point out to students the irony and special appropriateness of the name that Hawthorne selected for his heroine. Beatrice was the beloved of Dante, the epic poet referred to in the story's first paragraph. Dante pictured her as his guide in the journey to Paradise in the last major section of the *Divine Comedy*.

14. How are Rappaccini and Baglioni *foils*—or contrasting characters—both in personality and in the uses they make of science? On a *symbolic* level, what contrasting uses of science might these two characters represent? Rappaccini might represent the heartless, detached use of science for the sole pupose of increasing knowledge, irrespective of the human consequences. In contrast, Baglioni represents a more humane use of science, although his warnings and actions prove ineffective in the story. The picture of Baglioni gloating over Beatrice's death at the end of the story is disconcerting: we realize that he has been the direct cause of that death, and perhaps we suspect that he is more moved by his professional rivalry with Rappaccini at this moment than by the death of the girl.

15. What warning about our relation to science and nature might Hawthorne be implying in this story? Student answers will vary. But in general, Hawthorne seems to say that humanity trifles with nature at its peril.

Rappaccini has perverted beauty into poisons in his experiments, and he has changed regenerative symbols of life (the plants in the garden) into agents of death.

Is the warning any more or less relevant today than it was in the mid-nineteenth century? Explain. Many students will agree that Hawthorne's implied warning is even more relevant today than when the story was first published.

Writing About the Story
A Creative Response

1. Ending the Story. Brainstorm some possibilities for Giovanni, Dr. Rappaccini, and the garden that flow from characterization and events of Hawthorne's story.

Criteria for Evaluating the Assignment. The paper is at least one paragraph long. It proposes an ending—in terms of what happens to Giovanni, Rappaccini, and the garden—that reasonably flows from the story.

A Critical Response

2. Analyzing the Story's Romantic Elements. The writing prompt defines the hallmarks of the Romantic outlook, and, in doing so, suggests a plan of organization for the essay.

Criteria for Evaluating the Assignment. The essay briefly explains how "Rappaccini's Daughter" displays (1) a belief that nature is a source of moral lessons, (2) a fascination with the exotic past, (3) an interest in the supernatural, and (4) an interest in human psychology.

3. Comparing Stories. Briefly discuss what isolates Reverend Hooper ("The Minister's Black Veil") and Beatrice ("Rappaccini's Daughter") from others, and why.

Criteria for Evaluating the Assignment. The paragraph explains what isolates Reverend Hooper and what isolates Beatrice, and the purpose in each case.

4. Comparing Stories. Students may leap to the conclusion that it is the minister's veil and Beatrice's beauty which conceal evil. Discuss the concept until they probe the facade of the people around Hooper, and the scientific facade of Rappaccini and the beauty of his plants.

Criteria for Evaluating the Assignment. The paper explains the different ways in which "The Minister's Black Veil" and "Rappaccini's Daughter" reveal that evil can exist behind a facade of normalcy or beauty.

5. Describing Biblical Parallels. Read Genesis 1–3 aloud from a current translation. Have students jot down parallels as you read, and then discuss them. Note that the assignment also asks them to cite allusions to Genesis in Hawthorne's story.

Criteria for Evaluating the Assignment. The paper explains the six points requested: How the gardens are (1) similar and (2) different; and what or whom Hawthorne presents as equivalent to (3) the forbidden tree, (4) Adam, (5) Eve, and (6) the serpent. The paper also cites passages from the story that allude to elements of the Biblical account.

Analyzing Language and Style
Connotations

1. Students' answers may vary; these are possibilities:
   a. *emaciated:* feeble, skeletal, bones almost visible
   b. *sallow:* sickly, yellowish
   c. *sickly looking:* thin, pale, bent over
   d. *scholar's garb of black:* ceremonial gown, funeral gown
2. Rappaccini approaches the shrubs and flowers as if they were "savage beasts, or deadly snakes, or evil spirits." The figure of speech makes the reader want to recoil, and suggests that the doctor deals in evil, deadly matters.
3. *Deadlier malice, inward disease*
4. The words *rich and youthful voice*; figures of speech about a tropical sunset and delectable perfumes.
5. The words *beautiful*, *life*, *energy*, *health*, *fair*; figures of speech comparing her with a flower.
6. The fact that Beatrice freely handles deadly things her father must avoid suggests evil within her. The emotional effect is to make one back off from Beatrice in fear or awe.
7. The description of Beatrice on pages 279–280 reinforces the impression of beauty that conceals something deadly. The description of Dr. Rappaccini on page 281 suggests that inner energy is more powerful than the wasted appearance. See also pages 283, 285, and 288 (Beatrice) and 290 (Dr. Rappaccini). Only at its end (pages 290–291) does the story restore one's original impression that Beatrice is good; and her father, evil.

Extending the Story

Gothic horror tales, including mad-scientist tales such as Mary Shelley's *Frankenstein*, were at their height of popularity in the early nineteenth century, and have remained popular ever since: from turn-of-the-century science fiction like Wells's *The Invisible Man*, to classic horror movies like *Bride of Frankenstein*, to updated remakes like *The Fly*. Your students will probably have enjoyed some examples of the genre on their own. They might also enjoy discussing the reasons for the perennial appeal of the genre, the similarities and differences among earlier and later works, and the particular relevance of the subject matter to our highly technological age.

Primary Sources: Hawthorne and the Monument at Concord Text page 293

In this excerpt from "The Old Manse," Hawthorne relates a story about the Revolutionary War in which one wounded solider attacks with an ax another, already dead, solider. Hawthorne says that "this one circumstance has borne more fruit for me than all that history tells of the fight." In class discussion, have students use what they know about Hawthorne to consider why the author was so attracted to this story and what he felt that he learned from it.

Herman Melville Text page 294

From *Moby-Dick* Text page 297

Objectives

1. To analyze significant elements of the novel: point of view, foreshadowing, characterization, personification, imagery, and symbolism
2. To identify figurative language
3. To explain similes and metaphors
4. To describe an event from another point of view
5. To write an essay comparing and contrasting a speech with Transcendentalist ideas
6. To write a paragraph analyzing a character
7. To write an essay interpreting a symbol
8. To discuss the significance of names

Introducing the Novel

In outline form, for your reference, here are the major elements in the novel:

- **Protagonist:** Ishmael, the narrator, a young man who ships out on the *Pequod*
- **Antagonist:** Ahab, the one-legged, monomaniacal captain of the *Pequod*
- **Conflicts:** human obsession vs. nonhuman mystery, rational society vs. heroic madness
- **Point of view:** first-person, Ishmael
- **Significant techniques:** symbolism, allegory, allusion, metaphor, foreshadowing, parody, and characterization
- **Setting:** a whaling ship, out of Nantucket, sailing the south Atlantic, Pacific, and Indian oceans in the 1800's
- **Themes:** human self-destructiveness in the quest for the unrealizeable; the ability of an idealistic, self-reliant leader to gain absolute power; the cruelty and unfathomability of surrounding forces

Background on the Novel. Melville is the classic example of an author whose career suffered when his work deepened. He began *Moby-Dick* as a factual account of life in the whaling industry, and by late summer of 1850 was finished with the book. In September, however, he moved to a farm near Pittsfield, Massachusetts. This place, which he called "Arrowhead," was to be his home for the next twelve years. It was during this time, when *Moby-Dick* was being "broiled in the hell-fire" of his brain, that Melville became friends with his Lenox neighbor, Hawthorne. The two novelists shared an interest in the darker side of human nature and destiny, and both took an intellectually skeptical view of doctrines of human progress that were popular at the time. Both men were fascinated by the complexities of human psychology, especially the effects of alienation and distortions of the ego. Association with Hawthorne and other writers and critics during this time helped Melville express, in his sea story, his own quest for the ultimate truth of human existence.

Background on the Main Characters. In the Bible, Ishmael was the son of Abraham and Hagar, a serving maid of Abraham's wife, Sarah. Since Sarah did not have a son, the custom of the time made Ishmael the heir to Abraham's estate. When Isaac was born to Sarah, the two mothers became rivals, and Abraham was compelled to send Ishmael and his mother away. Although Ishmael grew up to be an archer and married an Egyptian woman, who bore him many sons, he was an outcast whose name has come to be symbolic of a displaced person or wanderer. In *Moby-Dick,* Ishmael is not only a wanderer in the physical world of the sea, but also a spiritual wanderer of the real meaning in life.

Ahab was the king of Israel from 869 to 850 B.C. He knew right, but failed to do it. Encouraged by his wicked wife Jezebel, he built temples to false gods, introducing pagan worship into his country. Although an excellent soldier, he was killed in battle; when he was buried, dogs drank his blood. His evil reign affected succeeding generations for evil.

The Plot of "Loomings." (Chapter 21 in the novel) *Moby-Dick* begins with the three words, "Call me Ishmael." Ishmael says that some years ago, "never mind how long precisely," having no money in his purse and nothing on shore to interest him, when life seemed to cause "a damp, drizzly November in my soul," he sought escape at sea. He went as an ordinary seaman, having no desire for the responsibilities of an officer. He claims that people in all times and places have been drawn to the magic of the sea. What he is unable to understand or explain is why he chose a whaling ship. Directed by "the stage managers, the Fates," he assumes that he has been selected for some role in a grand performance they are staging.

The Plot of "Ahab." (Chapter 18 in the novel) For several days after leaving Nantucket, nothing is seen of the ship's captain, who remains in seclusion in his cabin. One grey, gloomy morning as he goes to take his watch at noon, Ishmael glances toward the ship's stern, and shivers run over him as he realizes he is looking at Ahab. Ishmael is so shocked by Ahab's appearance that he initially fails to realize that part of the reason the captain appears so grim is "owing to the barbaric white leg upon which he stood." Ahab stands erect, his leg anchored in one of two small holes drilled into either side of the deck. Neither Ahab nor the officers speak as the captain looks forward over the prow of the boat. His look is one of "firmest fortitude" and "unsurrenderable willfulness." Before long, Ahab retreats to his cabin, but is seen every day thereafter seated, walking unsteadily on the deck, or standing with his leg anchored in the deck.

The Plot of "The Quarter-Deck." (Chapter 36 of the novel) Ahab intensely paces the deck, lost in thought. Even after he returns to his cabin, the sound of Ahab's ferocious pacing continues. Just before sunset, Ahab appears again on the deck and orders Starbuck to assemble the entire crew. When the crew stands before him, Ahab uses oratory to excite their passion for whale-killing. Then he nails a doubloon, a Spanish ounce of gold, to the main mast, and offers it to the first man who spots "that white-headed whale, with three holes punctured in his starboard fluke." He reveals that the quest for Moby-Dick is the true purpose of this voyage. The men are enthusiastic, except for the level-headed first mate, Starbuck. At the end of the chapter, the crew drinks to their quest, and Ahab pours grog into the inverted heads of the harpooners' shafts, in a blasphemous mock-communion.

The Plot of "Moby-Dick." (Chapter 41 in the novel) In this chapter the reader learns more of the character of the whale, and also comes to realize that Ahab is insane.

Teaching Strategies

Providing for Cultural Differences. Students with strong religious beliefs may be troubled by the mock-communion and by Melville's emphasis on the destructive or indifferent, rather than creative and loving, aspect of cosmic forces. Point out that in portraying evil, Melville is not endorsing it, and that in challenging God on the question of evil, he is directly in line with—and doubtless modeling himself on—Job and the prophets.

Providing for Different Levels of Ability. Your more advanced students will quickly devour these four tidbits from an immense feast, and should be encouraged to consume the entire novel on their own. Less advanced students may be intimidated by Melville's windy rhetoric and use of archaic allusions (Seneca, Cato, Cellini). Discuss problems of vocabulary and syntax as they arise; paraphrase freely. You may want to give your students a very brief synopsis of each chapter before they read it; this will be of considerable help in overcoming puzzlement at the outset.

Reading the Novel. "Loomings" is accompanied by a thirteen-minute audiocassette recording. Few, if any, passages in American literature are worthier of being spoken aloud than this prologue in the voice of Ishmael. The other chapters can be read aloud by students. In the scenes featuring the crew, a different student can be assigned to speak each sailor's lines.

Introducing Vocabulary Study. Knowing the meanings of these words is important to understanding the novel. (Starred words appear in the Glossary. Italicized words either are archaic or have special meaning in context.)

spleen	298	preternatural	303
reveries*	298	determinate	304
hypos	298	misanthropic	304
insular*	298	*anon*	305
circumambulate	298	imprecations	306
infallibly*	298	inscrutable	307
cataract	299	sinew (v.)	307
metaphysical	300	*unrecking*	307
consign*	300	presaging*	307
commonality	300	tacit	307
aught	302	acquiescence	307
allay*	302	admonitions	307
presentment	302	*ague*	308
vindictive*	302	axis	308
immemorial	303	volition	308
credulities	303	indissoluble	309

Herman Melville 107

maledictions	309	unsullied	312
malignity	310	exulting	312
unexempt	310	*fell* (adj.)	314
leviathan	311	intangible	314
preeminent	311	monomania	314
ubiquitous	311	dismemberment	314
credulous*	311	dissemble	315
erudite	311	unrelenting	315
gainsaid	311	corporeally	315

Reading Check. You might want to use the following questions as a reading check. Have students respond *True* or *False*.

1. Ishmael says that even though passengers tend to get seasick and grow quarrelsome, going to sea as a passenger is better than being abused as a common sailor. ____False____

2. Ishmael is one of the only sailors who has misgivings about the pursuit of Moby-Dick; he does not get swept up in Ahab's enthusiasm for killing the whale. ____False____

3. Stories about Moby-Dick claim that he has been seen at two different latitudes at the same time; it is also said that he is immortal. ____True____

4. Although it is known that Moby-Dick has injured and even maimed many sailors, nobody has been killed. ____False____

5. When he lost his leg, Ahab was a raving lunatic and had to be put in a straitjacket. ____True____

Reteaching Alternatives. Divide the class into four groups, one for each of the four chapters, and have each group present a report or a creative presentation to the class. "The Quarter-Deck" is ideal for dramatization. For "Moby-Dick," the students might actually want to present the whale's point of view. Alternatively, divide the class by characters rather than by chapters. (You might include some of the minor but revealing characters such as Starbuck and Queequeg.) This will allow students to arrive at insights they might not have reached through Ishmael's first-person narration alone.

"Loomings"

Responding to the Novel   Text page 301
Analyzing the Novel
Identifying Facts

1. What *point of view* will the novel be told from? The first paragraph makes it clear that the novel will be told from the first-person point of view.

What does the narrator tell us about himself and the mood that moves him to go to sea? Ishmael is morbidly depressed. Furthermore, he has no money, and nothing to interest him on shore.

2. **What details does the narrator offer to prove that waters and oceans hold a mysterious allure for humanity?** He mentions the crowd of water-gazers at the Battery in Manhattan, the paths in the countryside that lead to pools and streams, the streams in painted landscapes, the allure of Niagara Falls, and the reverence of the ancients for water.

3. **What details in the final paragraph *foreshadow* the fact that Ishmael's quest will be for the white whale?** The writer mentions "one grand hooded phantom," which he compares to a snow hill in the air. These details foreshadow the appearance of Moby-Dick, the great white whale.

Interpreting Meanings

4. **Ishmael prefers the lowliest of shipboard roles. What reasons does he give for this choice?** He says that he has enough trouble taking care of himself, without having to worry about the welfare of a ship. He says that he does not mind being ordered around by the officers, since every human being is—in a metaphysical sense—a slave to destiny.

What does this choice suggest about his *character*? The choice suggests that Ishmael is modest about his own abilities; perhaps it also suggests that he has a metaphysical, or philosophical, strain of resignation.

5. **What role does the idea of the whale play in Ishmael's decisions?** Ishmael says that the idea of the whale aroused all of his curiosity.

What does this information contribute to our knowledge of Ishmael's *character*? Ishmael is insatiably curious, especially about remote settings. He also has an itch to see the horrible and the forbidden.

6. **Ishmael wonders whether leaving the comparative safety of the merchant fleet for a whaling voyage was decided by fate or by his own free will. Why would this be a matter of importance to him? Or to us as readers?** Ishmael's speculations introduce the theme of fate and free will, which will be prominent throughout the novel. His remarks show us that the voyage he is about to undertake turned out to be highly unusual; the passage prepares us to pay close attention to the narrative.

7. **What does Ishmael mean by the whale's "island bulk" (page 301)?** He means that the great size of the whale in the ocean makes it look like an island.

8. **Ishmael calls us all "water-gazers"; he says we are fixed in "ocean reveries." Do you agree? What reasons**

108   The American Renaissance

can you suggest for our fascination with the ocean? Student answers will vary.

Why do you think the sea and the large creatures that inhabit it are so often used to symbolize evil or destructiveness? Student answers will vary.

"Ahab"

Responding to the Novel   Text page 304
Analyzing the Novel
Identifying Facts

1. **Even before Ahab makes his first appearance on deck, what evidence of his presence does Ishmael observe?** Ishmael observes the mates suddenly emerging from the captain's cabin with peremptory orders; this is for him a sign of the presence of Ahab, the "supreme lord and dictator."

2. **Apprehensions regarding the mysterious captain make Ishmael uneasy. By contrast, why does he find the presence of the rest of the ship's company reassuring?** Ishmael says that the harpooneers, although savage-looking, are appropriate crewmen for such a wild voyage. As for the mates, he says that one could hardly wish for better officers.

3. **Describe Ahab's "brand," or scar. What superstitions surround the scar?** The scar extends from his skull all the way down the side of Ahab's face. It is "lividly whitish" in color. The old Gay-Head Indian asserts that Ahab acquired the brand, or scar, when the captain was forty years old, "in an elemental strife at sea." The Manxman contends that the scar is a birthmark running the length of Ahab's entire body "from crown to sole."

4. **Describe the "position" Ahab maintains on the quarter-deck.** Ahab steadies his bone leg in one of two holes on either side of the quarter-deck.

5. **In the final paragraph, what hint is offered that Ahab's personality may have a gentler side?** Ishmael says that as the weather grew warmer, Ahab's personality seemed to unbend slightly.

Find the examples of *figurative language* **in this paragraph that help make this point about Ahab's character.** Melville uses an extended metaphor for the coming of spring, referring to the "red-cheeked, dancing girls, April and May," and he closes with a corresponding reference to Ahab's "faint blossom of a look, which, in any other man, would have soon flowered out in a smile."

Interpreting Meanings

6. **Find the three imaginative** *similes* **that describe Ahab's appearance on the quarter-deck.** Ishmael compares Ahab to a man who is released from the stake where the fire has wasted all his limbs without consuming them. Secondly, he compares the captain to a form of solid bronze, like Cellini's statue of Perseus. Finally, he likens the scar on Ahab's body to the mark made by lightning on the trunk of a great tree.

What do you think each simile implies about Ahab's *character*? The comparisons suggest the qualities of grimness, impermeable strength, and heroism; perhaps the mention of the tree and the lightning hint at human pride and divine retribution. The allusion to the Greek hero Perseus also carries a subtle hint. Perseus's most heroic deed in mythology was to slay the gorgon Medusa, a grotesque, supernatural monster. Melville implies that Ahab's quest is of similar, heroic proportions.

7. **Ishmael's first impression of Ahab is of terrifying grimness, in part because of Ahab's "barbaric white leg," crafted from the jawbone of a sperm whale. What additional feelings about Ahab are suggested by Ishmael's description of the captain at his post?** The story about the scar's origin prompts a feeling of awe and the supposition that "wild Ahab" has been involved in an "elemental strife at sea." Ishmael also mentions Ahab's immobility and silence, associating these qualities with "unsurrendering wilfulness" and "the nameless regal overbearing dignity of some mighty woe." The use of the word "crucifixion" suggests a hint of suffering and martyrdom.

8. **The old Gay-Head Indian says that Ahab "was dismasted off Japan" (see page 303). What** *figure of speech* **is implied in the word** *dismasted*? **(What is the Indian comparing to a mast?)** The Indian uses an implied metaphor to suggest that Ahab's leg is like the mast of a ship.

What other figures of speech does the Indian use in this speech to describe Ahab's affliction? The Indian uses a simile to compare Ahab to a craft, or ship. He then uses a figure of speech to compare Ahab's ivory leg to an arrow in a "quiver."

Why are his figures of speech particularly suitable? Student answers will vary. But the figures of speech imply an aura of mystery and violence; both qualities seem appropriate for the menacing sea captain.

Herman Melville   109

"The Quarter-Deck"

Responding to the Novel   Text page 309
Analyzing the Novel
Identifying Facts

1. After his endless, obsessive pacing of the deck, what unprecedented command does Ahab issue to the crew? Ahab commands the entire ship's company to assemble so that he can address them. The mate is astonished at this order, since it is seldom issued on shipboard "except in some extraordinary case."

2. What do you learn from Ahab's dialogue with his crew about Moby-Dick's appearance? According to Ahab, Moby-Dick has a white head, a wrinkled brow, and a crooked jaw. He also has three holes punctured in his starboard (right) fluke. He fantails curiously, and many harpoons are twisted in him.

3. Explain Ahab's pupose in meeting with the crew. Ahab's purpose seems to be to sharpen the crew's eagerness to chase and kill the great white whale.

4. Toward the end of the chapter, what does Ahab order the mates to do with their lances? He orders them to tilt their harpoons upwards, so that liquor can be poured into the sockets. He then orders them to drink and swear to the death of Moby-Dick.

5. After the story is underway, Melville shifts his *point of view*. Though Ishmael is still the narrator, some passages seem to be told from an *omniscient point of view*. What details in this chapter seem to be those that only an omniscient narrator would know? Among the details students may mention are the premonitions of the low laugh in the hold and the vibrations of the winds in the cordage, and the comparison of the Leyden jar.

Interpreting Meanings

6. Only Starbuck has misgivings about Ahab's pursuit of the great white whale. What are these misgivings? Starbuck says that Ahab's thirst for vengeance on a dumb brute seems blasphemous.

What do they tell us about Starbuck's *character*? Starbuck's misgivings suggest that he alone has a balanced sense of the order of the universe, and that he forsees that Ahab's unnatural quest for vengeance will lead to disaster. In voicing his misgivings to the grim captain, Starbuck also reveals that he is a man of considerable courage.

7. Why do you think Starbuck gives in to Ahab? Starbuck is probably afraid of the captain.

8. In your own words, explain the idea Ahab expresses in his famous *metaphor* comparing visible objects to "pasteboard masks" (page 307). One paraphrase might be: People, objects, and events are lifeless, irrational, and static until the energy of an action or deed gives them meaning.

In what way does Ahab see human beings as prisoners, and how does he hope to break out of his own "prison"? Ahab says that men are imprisoned by a wall until they "strike through the mask"; presumably, he means that men achieve freedom only through actions or deeds. For Ahab, the white whale represents (among other things) a wall of imprisonment; by killing the whale, Ahab will break down the walls of his prison and achieve freedom.

9. Describe the qualities and mysteries that the white whale represents for Ahab. As stated above, Ahab conceives of the whale as the wall imprisoning him. He says he sees in the whale "outrageous strength" and "inscrutable malice." He hates above all the inscrutable quality of the whale, and he vows that he will bring the beast and its hatred under control.

What do you think Ahab means when he says the white whale "is that wall...Sometimes I think there's naught beyond"? (See page 307.) Students may have various answers. Ahab probably means that the whale represents for him the limit of human experience. He implies in his second statement that he does not believe in any reality beyond this limit.

10. What details in the drinking scene suggest a *parody* or mockery of a religious ritual? Note especially Ahab's comparison of himself to the Pope and of the mates to his "cardinals." Melville's allusion to washing "the feet of beggars" refers to a traditional ceremony on Maundy Thursday when the Pope, as a sign of humility, washes the feet of twelve poor men.

What do you think the scene signifies about Ahab's quest? Many students may suggest that the details of the scene signify that Ahab's quest is somehow blasphemous.

11. What has the drinking scene revealed about Ahab's *character*? Do you have the impression that he is a clear-headed, if impassioned, crusader? Or that he is an unstable madman? Do you pity him or fear him? Cite specific details that contribute to your impression of Ahab. Students' answers will differ, although for most of them the drinking scene will probably create an impression of Ahab as a madman.

12. What is suggested about Ahab's *character* when he says "Talk not to me of blasphemy, man; I'd strike the sun if it insulted me"? (See page 307.) What did he say prior to this that sounded like blasphemy—that is, mockery of God? The statement suggests Ahab's qualities of pride, determination, and ferocity. In his prior statement,

110   The American Renaissance

he said that he would "wreak...hate" upon the "inscrutable thing"—perhaps this statement suggests that he regards the power of the whale (and maybe the inscrutable power of God?) as hateful and worthy of attack.

13. What details in this chapter do you think *foreshadow* disaster and destruction for the *Pequod* and her crew? Students may again point to the premonitions on page 307 (the "low laugh from the hold" and the "presaging vibrations of the winds in the cordage"), as well as to Melville's apostrophe beginning "Ah, ye admonitions and warnings!"

"Moby-Dick"

Responding to the Novel   Text page 316
Analyzing the Novel
Identifying Facts

1. Describe how Ahab's talk on the quarter-deck has affected Ishmael. Ishmael has been caught up in the crew's excitement, even though he feels a "dread" in his soul. He appears to identify with Ahab's cause, and he says that "Ahab's quenchless feud seemed mine."

2. Why has the spread of news about Moby-Dick through the world's whaling fleet been slow? News has spread slowly because of the great length of individual whaling voyages and the wide diffusion of whaling vessels around the globe.

3. According to Ishmael, why is superstition more powerful among whalers than among ordinary people? Ishmael says that superstition is more powerful among whalers because of whalers' direct contact with the most terrifying creatures of the sea, and because of their long periods of isolation, which tend to increase the power of fancy.

4. Describe the actual, observable characteristics of the white whale. He is uncommonly large, with an odd, snow-white wrinkled forehead and a high white hump. The rest of his body is streaked and marbled, and his lower jaw is deformed. He deceives his pursuers by pretending to swim before them in alarm, and then rounding on them to destroy their boats. He tore off Ahab's leg "as a mower a blade of grass in the field."

5. According to the passage beginning "His three boats" on page 314, what did Ahab "transfer" to the white whale? He transferred to the whale all his bodily woes, as well as his "intellectual and spiritual exasperations."

What did the whale *personify* to Ahab? The whale personified all evil for Ahab.

6. What is monomania? Monomania is a mental disorder characterized by a consuming obsession with one idea or action.

According to Ishmael, how did Ahab become monomaniacal? According to Ishmael, Ahab became monomaniacal sometime after his encounter with Moby-Dick, during the long months of his recuperation.

7. After Ahab recovers from the delirium brought on by Moby-Dick's attack, he seems to regain his sanity. In what way is his rational demeanor deceptive? Ahab only pretends to have recovered from his madness; in fact, he secretly cherishes his rage and hopes for vengeance.

How does it help him toward his goal? Ahab's rational demeanor persuades the people of Nantucket that he is fit to be trusted as the captain of another whaling voyage. They have no idea that his purpose is not commercial profit, but rather vengeance on Moby-Dick.

Interpreting Meanings

8. What supernatural qualities are attributed to Moby-Dick by the sailors? They suggest that he is ubiquitous, or present everywhere, and that he is immortal.

What is the effect of turning Moby-Dick into a mythical monster? The effect is to build up suspense and horror.

9. What *images* used to describe Moby-Dick in this chapter suggest beauty as well as horror? One such image occurs in the physical description of Moby-Dick, where Melville pictures the whale "seen gliding at high noon through a dark blue sea, leaving a milky-way wake of creamy foam, all spangled with golden gleamings."

Can you think of any other instances (from life or literature) where these two qualities are combined in one person or event or thing? Student answers will vary.

10. The final paragraph draws a picture of the *Pequod*'s crew as they travel the world's oceans on Ahab's quest. What is the narrator's *attitude* here toward the ship's captain, her crew, and her quest? The narrator's attitude seems ambiguous. On the one hand, he says he is "all a-rush to encounter the whale." On the other hand, he calls Ahab an "ungodly old man," and refers to the crew as a collection of "mongrel renegades, and castaways, and cannibals." He feels that the whale itself represents the "deadliest ill." Ishmael repeatedly underlines the idea of fate in this paragraph, referring to the "infernal fatality" of this particular crew turning up to help the captain in his "monomaniac revenge." Ishmael compares himself to a small boat being towed by a larger one, and asks rhetorically how he could have resisted the forces that bore him along, willy-nilly, despite his misgivings.

Herman Melville 111

11. Explain how the ship and her company can be seen as a *microcosm*—a world in miniature—and as a *symbol* for the "ship" of humanity. Melville refers several times to the diversity of races, outlooks, and backgrounds among the members of the ship's crew, and several references in the last paragraph of this chapter convey a generalized picture of the "Pequod's" voyage, so that it may be regarded as symbolic of the voyage of humanity as a whole. Ishmael refers to Ahab chasing a Job's whale "round the world." And in wondering about his mixed feelings, he uses the arresting image of "the subterranean miner that works in us all"—doubt and fear are compared to the sounds of a miner's pick deep below the surface of our conscious minds. On a more general level, the portrait of Ahab's struggle against fate and natural forces and of his mysterious power over the crew suggest a battle on a universal scale: humans vs. nature, humans vs. God, or humans vs. fate.

Writing About the Novel
A Creative Response

1. Describing an Event from Another Point of View. Discuss the questions at the end of the prompt to lead students into the content of their journal or log entry as Ahab. Have them choose between the events suggested in the writing prompt.

Criteria for Evaluating the Assignment. Through comments on an event, the log entry reflects the fears, desires, and feelings about the crew that seem true of Captain Ahab. The log entry is two or three paragraphs long.

A Critical Response

2. Comparing Ahab's Speech with Transcendental Ideas. Direct students to "The Transcendentalists," text pages 183–184; "Emerson and Transcendentalism: The American Roots," pages 184–185; and especially page 186, which comments specifically on Melville and Transcendentalism.

Criteria for Evaluating the Assignment. The essay presents in an orderly manner the ways in which Captain Ahab's speech agrees with Transcendentalist thought and the ways in which it rejects Transcendentalism.

3. Analyzing a Character. Have students work together to complete the suggested chart before they begin writing.

Criteria for Evaluating the Assignment. The paragraph offers several conclusions about Captain Ahab that can logically be deduced from his speech, actions, appearance, and thoughts.

4. Explaining a Symbol. Read D. H. Lawrence's prose about *Moby-Dick*, and discuss both the prose and the symbolism students see in the great white whale.

Criteria for Evaluating the Assignment. The essay briefly explains what the whale Moby-Dick symbolizes and cites supportive passages from the text.

Analyzing Language and Style
Names and Their Significance

The Biblical Ahab is a king of Israel whose name became a byword for evil when he married Jezebel and began to offer sacrificial worship to her foreign gods. Melville's Ahab is similarly willing to sacrifice everything to his "god," the pursuit of Moby-Dick.

In the Bible, Ishmael is the son of Abraham and the slave woman Hagar. Ishmael and Hagar are driven out to become wanderers after Abraham's wife Sarah bears him a legitimate son. Melville's Ishmael, too, is a wanderer; he goes to sea whenever he gets restless.

Extending the Novel

1. Melville and Poe might seem to be opposites in many ways: the former, an artist on the broadest canvas, grandiloquent and somewhat heedless of form, the latter a craftsman of exquisite miniatures on rather claustrophobic subjects. Your students may be surprised to learn that Poe's only book-length work of fiction, *The Narrative of Arthur Gordon Pym,* is about a bizarre sea voyage is which the color white has symbolic meaning. Many critics feel that it influenced Melville. Students might enjoy reading this work and comparing it with *Moby-Dick.*

2. Your students have now encountered the fiction of Hawthorne, Melville, and Poe, and have some ideas of the similarities and differences among the three. This may be a good time to place these writers in a larger context, and to get an idea of the extent of their particular range, which resulted from the mind-set of their cultures. You might initiate discussion by asking, "What kinds of things *didn't* Hawthorne, Poe, and Melville write about?"

Primary Sources: A Letter and a Journal Entry Text page 317

Melville's letter to Hawthorne and Hawthorne's more revealing, intimate journal entry about Melville that includes such details as Melville's being a "little heterodox in the matter of clean linen" illustrate the differences in these two literary forms. You might want students to rewrite Hawthorne's journal entry as a letter to Melville from Hawthorne, making the content changes necessitated by the change in form.

112 The American Renaissance

"Shiloh"   Text page 318

"Art"   Text page 319

Objectives

1. To analyze the poems
2. To paraphrase a statement
3. To write an essay comparing and contrasting the ideas

Introducing the Poems

Melville's style anticipated twentieth-century versification techniques. However, his poems are often flawed by archaic words, forced rhymes, and awkward, inverted word order.

The Literal Meaning of "Shiloh." This song-like poem reminds readers that the waste of life in battle can never be undone. The poet describes the swallows that fly over the field at Shiloh, where the log-built church had served as a hospital for the dying men of both sides. In death, fame and country were of little concern to the soldiers, who now lie buried in deep graves in the hushed fields of Shiloh.

The Literal Meaning of "Art." The main idea of this poem is that the creation of a work of art requires wrestling with unknown forces. Patience and energy, humility and pride, love and hate, and instinct and study, are some of the dissimilar qualities that must be fused together if one is to be able to "wrestle with the angel—Art."

Providing for Cultural Differences. The Civil War in "Shiloh" will seem more remote to students in some sections of the country than in others. You may want to draw an analogy with more recent wars, and point out that Melville's requiem could be spoken over the victims of any war. Melville's view of art, in "Art," arises from a highly individualistic culture. Much great art, in various cultures, has been produced as part of an informal process, or a group religious effort, or an individual fusion with—rather than wrestling with—spiritual forces. Additionally, Melville's reference to Jacob may be unfamiliar to students who are not from religious Judeo-Christian backgrounds. It may be clarified by reading the introductory paragraph to "Art" on text page 319.

Providing for Different Levels of Ability. It may be best to paraphrase "Shiloh" before students read it, so that they can have in mind a picture of the aftermath of a battle, with swallows flying over the field on which twenty thousand dead soldiers lie—enough to fill an arena. Because of its highly compressed syntax and mystical imagery, paraphrase of "Art" is essential for all students. More advanced students can work toward such a paraphrase on their own.

Reading the Poems. "Shiloh," a tranquil, descriptive piece, can be read aloud by a single student. Because it is more difficult, you might want to read "Art" aloud yourself, stopping where necessary to paraphrase and clarify.

Reteaching Alternatives. After students have read and discussed each poem, you might ask them to write in their own words, in a sentence or two, the poem's literal meaning.

"Shiloh"

Responding to the Poem   Text page 318

Analyzing the Poem

Identifying Facts

1. According to the poem, what natural element comforted the dying soldiers? The poet says that the "April rain" solaced the wounded (lines 5–6).

2. What are the only moving things in the poem? The swallows are the only moving things.

Interpreting Meanings

3. Explain how "foemen at morn" (line 14) could become "friends at eve." The soldiers on both sides meet death, a common fate, in the course of the day; the poet thus calls them "friends at eve."

4. The most forthright statement in the poem occurs in line 16. How would you *paraphrase* this statement? One paraphrase might be: there is nothing so concrete as a bullet to show us the brutal reality of war.

5. Shiloh Church is named after the place where the Israelites worshiped after they reached the Promised Land. What is *ironic* about a battle occurring at a

Herman Melville   113

church and on a Sunday? The battle is ironic because the religious teachings of the church stress peace, not war; according to the Bible, Sunday is the "Lord's day," and should be observed as a day of rest, not of battle.

6. Find the sounds in the poem's first two lines that suggest the movement of birds. The repetitions of "l" and "w" sounds suggest the movement of birds.

What sounds in the poem suggest moaning and hushed silence? The repetition of the long "o" sounds.

7. What is the effect of ending the poem as it begins, with the flight of swallows? The circular effect stresses that the natural world goes on, despite the tragic deaths of so many men.

"Art"

Responding to the Poem Text page 320
Analyzing the Poem
Identifying Facts

1. Define the word *unbodied* as it is used in line 2 to describe a daydream. The meaning is "formless" or "abstract."

2. The core of the poem is Melville's listing of opposites—most of them feelings that, at first glance, would seem to be contrary to one another. Find six of these sets of opposites in the poem. Six sets of opposites are: melting and freezing, sadness and joy, humility and pride, instinct (or intuition) and study, love and hate, audacity and reverence.

Interpreting Meanings

3. For the purposes of artistic creation, how might these opposites be reconciled—that is, how might they become equal, rather than divisive, contributions to the same end? Students' answers will vary. Urge them to express their own opinions, and to support their views with appropriate examples from literature and the other arts.

4. Reread Melville's poem, "Shiloh." Can you name some opposite feelings, conditions, or qualities that are brought together in this requiem? Some possibilities might include: a groan and a prayer (lines 11–12) and foemen and friends (line 14).

Writing About the Poem
A Critical Response

Comparing Poems. Have students first attempt to summarize the advice Melville and Emerson offer to the artist in their poems; then take each question of the prompt in turn, and seek an answer in each poem.

Criteria for Evaluating the Assignment. The essay cites the similarities and differences between Melville's and Emerson's poems, "Art," in terms of return to an ideal past, seeking of new transformations, advice to the artist, and the type of artist who would respond to each poet's advice.

Extending the Poem

Several poems in this textbook are natural candidates for comparison with "Shiloh": Whitman's "A Sight in Camp," Stephen Crane's "War Is Kind," and Stevens's "The Death of a Soldier." You might have students compare and contrast Whitman's, Crane's, and Stevens's war poems with those of Melville.

Exercises in Critical Thinking and Writing Text page 321

Analyzing and Evaluating Persuasive Writing: Rhetoric

Although student answers may vary somewhat, the following responses to the questions on the Emerson excerpt are representative:

1. Emerson's purpose is to convince his audience that they should learn to recognize their spontaneous thoughts and speak what they think.

2. I read some verses by a painter the other day that represented his original thought. This speaking your own thought is genius. The greatness of Moses, Plato, and

114   The American Renaissance

Milton, in fact, is that they spoke what they truly thought. We should learn to recognize our spontaneous thoughts, lest they come back to us later when someone else speaks them. Every person learns, at some time, that he or she has something new in the universe and that only he or she can make something of it. Each of us represents a divine idea that can be trusted, so we must speak our own thoughts.

3. Emerson develops his argument with several reasons, including the fact that our rejected thoughts may show up in works of genius and that each of us represents the divine idea.

4. Examples of rhetorical devices:
   a. hyperbole: "Speak your latent conviction, and it shall be the universal sense."
   b. connotations: "that is genius"; "trumpets of the Last Judgment"; "gleam of light"; "suicide"
   c. parallelism and repetition: "To believe is your own thought, to believe that what is true for you in your private heart"; "that envy is ignorance; that imitation is suicide..."

Criteria for Evaluating the Assignment. The essay should define Emerson's purpose and briefly state his argument. In a thesis statement, students should summarize their evaluation of Emerson's use of rhetorical devices. The evaluation should be supported with specific examples and quotations.

Unit Five: *A New American Poetry:*
Whitman and Dickinson

Text page 323

Teaching A New American Poetry Unit

Text page 323

You will find that Unit Five breaks naturally into three sections: Walt Whitman, Emily Dickinson, and review. Throughout, assignments in the text help students relate poems to their historical context and connect them with earlier American literature. Your challenge is simultaneously to present Whitman and Dickinson as unique individuals and to "place" them within the on-going flow of American literature.

The unit introduction (text pages 324–325) can help students focus both on the poets' uniqueness and on their places in American literature. The first part of the introduction presents Whitman and Dickinson as representing "two distinct seams in the fabric of American poetry." Help students note the contrasts between the two poets by having them prepare a chart summary such as the following one:

	WHITMAN	DICKINSON
Personality	sociable, gregarious	private, shy
Expectations	this message to be carried to the future	her message to die in oblivion
When Famous	during his lifetime	after her death
Poetic Style	sweeping catalogs and the cadences of free verse	meticulous word choice, rhyme, and hymnbook meters

The seventh paragraph of the unit introduction ("As the history of our poetry shows...") makes generalizations on American poetry subsequent to Whitman and Dickinson. Alert students to the fact that understanding Whitman and Dickinson will prepare them for Units Eight, Nine, and Thirteen, where they will encounter poets representing every facet of American life from the 1890's to recent times—poets who owe to Whitman and Dickinson their freedom and range of subjects and style. Have students preview the table of contents for a list of later poets and skim the unit introductions for a preview of their subjects and styles. They will note several poets who follow Whitman's free verse path and others who emulate Dickinson's traditional forms while adopting Whitman's range of subject matter.

Finally, the concluding paragraph of the unit introduction and the poem by Ezra Pound stress the "co-equal importance" of free verse and traditional forms. You may need to stress "co-equal" as you check students' understanding of the paragraph—some may be biased for or against one of the verse forms. (If some students have no idea what *free verse* is, Miller Williams' definition can serve for now: "Poetry in which line length and rhyme (if any) to come [are] not predictable from what has gone before nor prescribed by tradition.") You might end by reading aloud Pound's poem and asking students silently to jot down in their journals or notebooks their immediate interpretation of Pound's meaning—a "best guess." After a few minutes, ask two or three students to share what they have written. Make no judgments at this time, but ask students to leave space to write a second response to Pound's poem after they have completed the unit.

*O*jectives of A New American Poetry Unit

1. To improve reading proficiency and expand vocabulary
2. To gain exposure to two notable poets and their work
3. To define and identify elements of poetry: figures of speech (simile, extended metaphor, personification), symbol, imagery, sound effects (rhythm, meter, rhyme, free verse, onomatopoeia, incremental repetition), tone, irony, and theme
4. To respond to poetry orally and in writing
5. To practice the following critical thinking and writing skills:
    a. Comparing and contrasting a poem with another form
    b. Rewriting a paragraph as a poem
    c. Comparing and contrasting two poems
    d. Analyzing response to poetry
    e. Evaluating a title
    f. Commenting on a criticism
    g. Interpreting metaphors
    h. Analyzing and interpreting a poem

Walt Whitman

Text page 326

The text biography of Whitman (pages 326–329) refers repeatedly to Whitman's personality and poetic innovations—references with little meaning unless students have in mind both some of Whitman's poems and some of his contemporaries. You may therefore wish first to assign two Whitman poems ("I Hear America Singing" and "Song of Myself," text pages 331–332), and a quick review of two poems by his contemporary, Herman Melville ("Shiloh" and "Art," text pages 318–319). Have students list both what the poems reveal about their authors' lives and personalities and differences they notice in the style of the two poems. (Text questions on Whitman's poems can wait until later.) Students should find that Whitman's poems speak of his age, parentage, and so on, while Melville's poems reveal no directly biographical data; and that Whitman's style is loose and difficult to define in comparison with Melville's more predictable rhymes and meters. You may then wish to assign the biography of Whitman (text pages 326–329), asking students to keep in mind the fact that Whitman and Melville, born the same year, were writing for approximately the same audience.

After students have read the biographical material, you may wish to organize discussion around four questions:

1. How would Whitman's unexpectedly deep American roots have contributed to self-confidence? (Some of your own students may be able to speak from experience as only first- or second-generation Americans.) 2. What would it have been like to have Whitman as a friend—exciting? boring? frustrating? 3. How would Whitman's background have helped or hindered him in applying for a (hypothetical) "Poet in Residence" job at a university of his time? 4. How do today's critics and readers evaluate Whitman's contributions to literature?

During or after this discussion you may wish to expand upon Whitman's teen-age years and the fact that "for a time he taught school" (page 326). As a boy he was enthralled by the novels of Sir Walter Scott, and in his mid-teens was already contributing "pieces" (most likely correct, conventional poems) to a Manhattan paper, crossing the ferry from Brooklyn to attend debating societies, and using his journalist's pass to hear singers at Manhattan theaters. At fifteen he had reached physical maturity, and at sixteen was a journeyman printer in Manhattan. When two great fires disrupted the printing industry as he turned seventeen, he rejoined his family (irritating his father by refusal to do farmwork) and began five years of intermittent teaching at country and small-town schools. (He interrupted teaching to start a newspaper of his own in 1838 and to work briefly on another Long Island newspaper.) He was an innovative teacher, but the farm families he boarded with considered him lazy: instead of helping with chores, he preferred taking part in debates, writing poems, writing articles about teaching, or continuing his studies of Shakespeare, Scott, Dante, Homer, other Greek poets, and Hindu and German poetry. His teaching ended just before he turned twenty-one, when he began the life in New York described in the text.

You may wish to establish a historical context for Whitman's work by listing other events of the half-decade of 1850–1855. American literature saw the appearance of Hawthorne's *The Scarlet Letter,* Melville's *Moby-Dick,* Thoreau's *Walden,* and Whitman's *Leaves of Grass.* During the same five years, the Sioux ceded their lands in Iowa and most of Minnesota to the United States government, Senator Charle Sumner emerged as a leader in the fight against slavery, Florence Nightingale departed for Turkey to treat British soldiers fighting in the Crimean War, and Commodore Matthew C. Perry opened trade with Japan. Stephen Foster published "Old Folks at Home," Verdi was producing popular operas in Italy, and two Dickens novels appeared in England. In science and technology during the same years, Bunsen introduced use of the Bunsen burner (he didn't invent it), Isaac Singer of New York patented a continuous-stitch sewing machine, Elisha Otis of Vermont designed a passenger elevator, and Kier built America's first oil refinery in Pittsburgh.

Finally, include for students some reactions from Whitman's contemporaries. Early readers either hated *Leaves of Grass* or were fascinated by it—often simultaneously. It was bad enough that the first edition carried a "shocking" engraving of Whitman—a young man with a short beard, dressed in an open-collared shirt that revealed the top of his colored underwear, with one hand resting on a hip and the other thrust into a pocket of his work jeans. (Recall that this was a time when the stovepipe hat and formal, long-tailed coat we identify with Lincoln were a more expected standard of dress.) Even more provocative were the poems themselves. Edward Everett Hale, writing in a leading literary magazine, *Putnam's Monthly,* spoke of Whitman's "scorn for the wonted usages of good writing," use of "words usually banished from polite society," and a style "which may briefly be described as a compound of the New England transcendentalism and New York rowdy."

Many readers assumed that Whitman's eccentricities resulted from ignorance—that he was barely literate. In fact he *was* self-taught, but fully aware of conventional forms. Another myth, Whitman as con-man, arose at least in part because he (anonymously) wrote some of his own reviews.

118 A New American Poetry

In fact, he believed strongly enough in himself to advertise his message. A third myth was that Whitman's American emphasis was equivalent to paranoid suspicion of foreigners. In reality he was challenging the class-conscious resentment of recent immigrants who then crowded the New York slums and surrounding areas.

Mixed feelings blend with an ultimately favorable judgment in a *New York Times* review of the second (1856) edition of *Leaves of Grass:*

As we read it again and again, . . . a singular order seems to arise out of its chaotic verses. Out of the mire and slough[,] . . . keen philosophy starts suddenly. . . . A lofty purpose still dominates the ridiculous self-conceit in which the author, led astray by ignorance[,] indulges.

As you turn next to the poems of Whitman, you might give students the on-going challenge of responding to these early critics with their own interpretations.

"I Hear America Singing" Text page 338

Objectives

1. To recognize the use of the *catalogue*
2. To explain and support a response

Introducing the Poem

Like traditional forms of verse, free verse may be lyric or narrative. Whitman's poem is a lyric poem, one evoking an emotional response. Read it aloud, after reminding students to note how a natural cadence (rhythmic fall of words) dictates where lines break.

Background on the Poem. The poem is a prime example of *cataloging*, use of a list. In this case the list ultimately shows the equality of people whatever their occupation. The word "intermission" means "break." The word "carol" is evocative in two senses: its original meaning of a round dance accompanied by singing, and the meaning (as with Christmas carols) of joyous praise *as if* in song.

Teaching Strategies

Providing for Cultural Differences. Although some of the occupations are now rare (e.g., hatter), the poem poses no problems to understanding.

Providing for Different Levels of Ability. Elicit from the class a brief description of the precise work performed by a person of each occupation.

Introducing Vocabulary Study. Knowing the meanings of the following words is important to understanding the selection. (Starred words appear in the Glossary. Italicized words either are archaic or have special meaning in context.)

| carol | l. 1 | intermission | l. 7 |
| blithe* | l. 2 | robust* | l. 10 |

Reading the Poem. Have a student who reads well prepare in advance to read the poem in class, or read it aloud yourself. Since poetry is meant to be heard, you may wish to assign responses to poems, rather than leading them, as homework during this unit. Lead a class discussion of the five "Responding to the Poem" questions (on text page 331) yourself. (Later in the unit, when students are more familiar with Whitman, you may wish to have students work individually or in small groups.)

Reteaching Alternatives. While you move on with the class, assign a student who shows a good grasp of the poem to tutor those who missed or misunderstood the full-class discussion.

Responding to the Poem Text page 331
Analyzing the Poem
Identifying Details

1. Name the people whom the poet hears in lines 2–8. The people whom Whitman hears include: mechanics, the carpenter, the mason, the boatman, the deck-hand, the shoemaker, the hatter, the wood-cutter, the ploughboy, the mother, the young wife, and the girl sewing or washing.

What does each person sing, according to line 9? Each person sings "what belongs to him or her and to none else." That is, the song of each person is unique.

2. Most of the poem describes the songs of the day. What is the setting for the songs of the night in the

Walt Whitman 119

concluding lines? The setting is a party of young fellows, singing "strong melodious songs."

Interpreting Meanings

3. What Whitman has in mind here are not the actual work songs once associated with various trades and kinds of physical labor, but something more subtle. What would you say this poem is really about? Student answers will vary. Most students will suggest that the poem is really about the vast diversity of the American people. The "songs" Whitman hears are really symbolic—standing for an immense collection of individuals, each of whom is involved in his or her own unique work or occupation.

4. A feeling of acceptance, even of contentment, runs through the sounds of these many voices. Remembering the long hours and small pay of tradespeople and manual laborers in the nineteenth century, would you say that the poet is romanticizing or idealizing their lot? Or would you say that the songs he hears are expressions of independence and joy in life? Explain your response, and support it with specific references to the poem. Student answers will vary. But none of the songs mentioned by Whitman includes any complaint about low wages or long hours; on the contrary, by singing about their work, the singers seem to express independence and joy. The tone of the poem is decidedly optimistic.

5. If the poet of *Leaves of Grass* were alive today, what kinds of singing do you think he would hear? In what ways would these "songs" be different from those he heard in his own time? In what ways would they be the same as what Whitman heard? Does anything in the poem suggest that his America is different from ours? Explain your answer. Student answers will vary. Some students may suggest that many of the songs Whitman would hear would be produced by machines (such as radio, television, stereo), rather than by people. Others may suggest that the songs would be more clashing and discordant, expressing as much pessimism and protest as optimism. Let students feel free to advance their own opinions.

"Song #1," from "Song of Myself"

Text page 332

Objectives

1. To recognize the technique of incremental repetition
2. To recognize the poet's use of autobiographical data
3. To analyze word connotations

Introducing the Poem

You might ask, when is "loafing" not laziness? Throughout his life Whitman ignored schedules set by other people and baffled his friends and relatives by appearing to loaf away his time in purposeless strolls, random reading, and aimless writing. We, however, realize that he was absorbing sights, sounds, and details which later emerged in his poetry.

This selection also uses the phrase "a spear of summer grass," making this a good time to examine the book title, *Leaves of Grass*. Lead students to see that *leaves* may pun both upon "leaves," "blades," or "spears" of grass, and upon the "leaves" or "pages" of books.

Background on the Poem. The poem presents the philosophical notion that everyone is part of the whole of nature and that poet and reader are somehow one—a concept not specifically addressed in the response questions, but one that you may wish to explore. The opening lines also suggest that Whitman sees his book as an archetypal journey—a voyage of discovery he invites the reader to share with him. Throughout the poem the repetition is *incremental:* that is, more is added in the repetition, as in how line 5 repeats, then expands upon line 4.

Teaching Strategies

Providing for Cultural Differences. Strongly religious students may find Whitman's hedonistic joy and setting aside of "creeds and schools" offensive. Invite them to study his views as representing a type of American optimism about the goodness of human nature that they need to recognize to understand many pieces of American literature. They don't have to agree with Whitman to see his point.

Providing for Different Levels of Ability. After studying the vocabulary for this lesson, have students paraphrase the difficult last four lines. Suggest that they begin by inserting "with" ahead of "Creeds and schools," and "Nature" after "harbor" and "permit."

120 A New American Poetry

Introducing Vocabulary Study. Knowing the meanings of the following words is important to understanding the selection. (Starred words appear in the Glossary.)

abeyance* l. 10
sufficed l. 11
harbor (v.) l. 12

Reading the Poem. The complexity of thought in "Song #1" requires a sensitive reading such as that on the accompanying audiocassette, where "Song #1" introduces the entire series of Whitman poems. Play the cassette, or have a student prepare a reading.

Reteaching Alternatives. Assign a student who shows a good grasp of the poem to play the recording for, and then to tutor, students who are having difficulty with the poem.

Responding to the Poem Text page 332
Analyzing the Poem
Identifying Details

1. Who is "you" in lines 2 and 3? "You" represents all the readers of Whitman's poem, both singly and collectively.

2. What autobiographical facts does the speaker reveal in lines 7–9? The speaker tells us that he is the great-grandchild of American-born ancestors, that he is thirty-seven years old, and that he is in good health. He hopes not to cease his poetic endeavor until death.

Interpreting Meanings

3. What is the connection between the "soul" and "a spear of summer grass" (lines 4–5)? The image suggests delicacy and individuality, and also growth, for both the soul and the grass.

How is the speaker's "loafing" more than mere idleness? By "loafing," Whitman seems to be inviting his soul to grow freely, unfettered by the distractions of work.

4. What other terms could you substitute for "creeds" and "schools" in line 10? Other terms might be philosophies (or religious beliefs) and universities, or schools of thought about poetry.

For what purpose does the speaker hold these "in abeyance"? Whitman seems determined to keep an open mind, in order to be able to absorb all sorts of diverse experiences and opinions.

5. In Whitman's time, as never before, nature was being explored, analyzed, harnessed, exploited, and otherwise "used" to serve humankind. How is this poet going to "use" nature? He is going to "use" it to inspire original poetry and "energy."

How could this statement be seen as a description of the poet's style? Student answers will vary. In general, Whitman's style seems as open and comprehensive as nature itself. He responds to nature and to humanity freely, "without check."

6. What lines of this poem show that the speaker wants to share his being or individuality with all of the natural world? Students may cite lines 3, 6, and 12–13.

What do you think of the idea expressed in line 3? The idea is that the speaker is united with his readers by virtue of being human. Student reactions will vary.

The Elements of Literature: Free Verse Text page 333

Pause for a detailed discussion of this section with your students before they continue reading Whitman. Spend enough time to be sure that students are comfortable with the major terms presented: *free verse, assonance, alliteration, onomatopoeia, parallel structure, imagery, cadence,* and *trochaic tetrameter.*

In answer to the questions posed in the final paragraph: There are thirty-three repetitions of a sibilant consonant sound (*s* or *z*). Examples of parallel structure include the use of "I" plus a verb to open several lines and second halves of lines, and the parallel use of verbs connected by "and" (as in "loafe and invite," "lean and loafe").

Walt Whitman 121

"Song #10"

Text page 334

Objectives

1. To recognize the use of sensory images
2. To analyze cadence
3. To identify tone
4. To analyze the speaker's attitude

Introducing the Poem

This selection is also available on audiocassette, read in a way that will help students identify the change in tone from the first three scenes to the last two. The recording should also help students formulate impressions of the speaker's personality as portrayed in the final stanza (see "Responding" question 6 on text page 335). Again encourage students to listen for Whitman's repetition and rhythmical cadences.

Backgound on the Poem. Historical context is important to "Song #10." By 1848 Whitman was, politically, a "Free-soiler"—a member of a party opposed to the acquisition of more slave territory. In 1848 he was a delegate to the Buffalo [NY] Free-Soil convention, demonstrating that his views on slavery were well-formed before the Civil War.

Teaching Strategies

Providing for Cultural Differences. If you have students who are recent immigrants to this country, you may need to explain that now as in Whitman's day (as evidenced by western movies), the "wild frontier" holds a perennial attraction for Americans; that racial issues addressed by the poem—treatment of American Indians and blacks—have divided Americans since earliest times; and that at Whitman's time anti-slavery people provided for runaway slaves a series of "safe houses" we call "the underground railroad."

Providing for Different Levels of Ability. Present the vocabulary before reading the poem.

Introducing Vocabulary Study. Knowing the meanings of the following words is important to understanding the selection. (The starred word appears in the Glossary.)

scud	l. 6	plasters	l. 22
dumbly*	l. 12	fire-lock	l. 24
limpsy	l. 17		

Reading the Poem. Use the audiocassette that is available for this selection or prepare your own reading in advance. Go to the questions in the text when you are satisfied that students have grasped Whitman's literal meaning.

Reteaching Alternatives. Assign students who read well to prepare a reader's theatre presentation for the class. Audio- or videotape their presentation for use with students who were absent.

Responding to the Poem

Text page 335

Analyzing the Poem

Identifying Details

1. In the five stanzas of this poem, the speaker observes and participates in five far-ranging American scenes. Identify the "scene" in each stanza. The scene in the first stanza is the wilds and the mountains, where the speaker, accompanied by his dog, is hunting. In the second stanza, the setting is aboard a Yankee clipper ship. In the third stanza, the poet is with boatmen and clam-diggers, with whom he has a "good time" around the chowder-kettle. In the fourth, the speaker witnesses the marriage of an Indian girl and a trapper outdoors in the far West. Finally, in the fifth stanza, the speaker is at his own house, where he aids a runaway slave.

2. What *images* of sight, touch, and sound bring the reader into each of these scenes? Among the images students may cite are the following: the images of kindling the fire and cooking (line 4), the picture of the ship under sail (line 6), the description of the Indian girl's father and his friends (line 12), the portrait of the girl (line 14), the motions of the runaway slave "crackling the twigs of the woodpile" (line 16), and the description of the speaker attending to the slave's wounds (line 22).

3. What repetitions of sentence patterns help create a sense of *cadence* in this poem—a rhythmic rise and fall of your voice as the lines are spoken aloud? Student answers will vary. They may mention, for example, the sequence of present participles in lines 4–5 ("kindling... broiling... falling"), or the sequence of verbs connected by "and" in lines 16–22.

4. To read poetry, you need to keep a dictionary handy. What is the meaning of a "Yankee Clipper" and of "scud" (line 6)? A "Yankee Clipper" is a particular type of nineteenth-century sailing ship with tall masts. "Scud" here may mean "misty rain"—or, more probably, simply the swiftly moving waves parted by the ship's prow.

Does "dumbly" in line 12 mean "stupidly" or "mutely"? It means "mutely."

122   A New American Poetry

What do you guess "limpsy" is in line 17? The word is a variation of "limp," in the sense of "weak" or "swaying."

What are "revolving eyes" (line 21) and "galls" (line 22)? "Revolving eyes" refer to the man's eyes rolling in fear or pain; "galls" is equivalent to "chronic sores."

Interpreting Meanings

5. In the first scene, the speaker says that he was "amazed" at his own "lightness and glee." In the second scene, he shouts "joyously from the deck." In the third, he "went and had a good time." In the fourth and fifth scenes, such expressions of personal delight are absent. What is the *tone* of these scenes? How do you account for this? In the fourth scene, the speaker implies an unhappy atmosphere at the wedding with the phrase "dumbly smoking" in line 12. Perhaps the marriage of the trapper and the Indian girl has been forcibly arranged. In the last scene, the pathetic plight of the runaway slave moves the speaker deeply; there is no room for joy.

6. In the last scene, the "runaway slave" is one of thousands who entrusted their lives to the compassion of men and women who might feed and clothe them and otherwise assist their attempts to escape bondage. With this fact in mind, what do you think the stanza—especially the last line—shows about the speaker's character? The stanza shows that the speaker is profoundly sensitive, caring, and compassionate. He reassures the runaway, bathes his bruised body, gives him a room and clean clothes, bandages his wounds, and feeds him. Just as the runaway entrusts himself to the speaker, the speaker exhibits trust: as the last line tell us, he leaves his fire-lock in the corner.

7. How would you describe the speaker's attitude toward the red girl and the runaway slave? He pities both of these figures.

"Song #26"

Text page 336

Objectives

1. To identify examples of parallel sentence construction
2. To identify onomatopoeia

Introducing the Poem

The song "My Favorite Things" from the frequently televised Rodgers and Hammerstein musical, *The Sound of Music* (1965), consists of catalogues followed by the refrain, "These are a few of my favorite things." As an introduction to "Song #26," you might ask students to create a similar list, limiting themselves to "my favorite *sounds.*"

Background on the Poem. The major literary techniques to note in "Song #26" are use of the *catalogue*, evocative *sensory images*, *parallel construction*, and *onomatopoeia*—words with sounds that echo their meaning.

Teaching Strategies

Providing for Cultural Differences. The images catalogued are common to cultures worldwide, with the possible exception of grand opera. If students have little acquaintance with opera, you might play for students a brief operatic selection that offers at least two or three of the elements mentioned by Whitman: violoncello, cornet, choral song, tenor solo, soprano solo.

Providing for Different Levels of Ability. Discuss vocabulary and the allusion to the planet Uranus (see headnote on text page 336) before reading the poem.

Introducing Vocabulary Study. Knowing the meanings of the following words is important to understanding the selection. (Starred words appear in the Glossary. The italicized word has a special meaning, explained in the headnote on text page 336.)

accrue*	l. 1	orbic-flex	l. 21
bravuras	l. 3	wrenches (v.)*	l. 24
disjointed*	l. 8	ardors	l. 24
pallid*	l. 9	indolent*	l. 25
premonitory	l. 11	*fakes*	l. 27

Reading the Poem. A good oral reading will go far in helping students interpret the poem. (This selection is not available on audiocassette.) This selection lends itself to being done as reader's theatre by several students. Whoever reads the poem—students or the teacher—should convey the emotional tone of the various lines. Encourage listeners to note repetition and evocative sights and sounds.

Reteaching Alternatives. Direct students to study text page 333 on free verse, with special attention to the definitions of *alliteration*, *onomatopoeia*, and *imagery*, and then to re-read the poem aloud.

Responding to the Poem   Text page 337
Analyzing the Poem
Identifying Details

1. The speaker says in line 2 that he will let sounds "contribute" to his own song. How does he *describe* the sounds he hears in line 3? Note the alliteration in "bravuras of birds, bustle of growing wheat"; "growing wheat, gossip of flames"; "clack of sticks cooking."

2. What is the sound that the speaker says he loves? The speaker says he loves the sound of the human voice (line 4).

3. What is "honeyed morphine" (line 27)? Morphine is a drug that takes away pain. It may thus be called "honeyed" or sweet because of its analgesic effects. Here Whitman compares its effects to the sound of the music he hears.

4. The sounds in this poem tend to fall into categories. Break Whitman's long *catalogue*—or list—of sounds into these categories: sounds of joy, sorrow, work, art, and nature. Sounds of joy: bravuras of birds (line 2), the sound of the human voice (line 4), the loud laugh of the working people (line 7), the sound of the orchestra (line 22). Sounds of sorrow: the faint tones of the sick (line 8), the ring of alarm-bells (line 11), the slow death march (lines 13–14). Sounds of work: the bustle of growing wheat (line 3), the clack of sticks cooking (line 3), the stevedores and the refrain of the anchor-lifters (line 10), the whirr of the engines and carts (line 11). Sounds of art: the musical instruments (lines 15–17), the chorus of the opera (lines 18–19), the voices of the tenor and the soprano (lines 20–22), the sound of the orchestra (line 23). Sounds of nature: the birds (line 3), the wheat (line 3).

5. How many examples of *parallel sentence construction* can you find in this poem of 29 lines? Students may mention the following examples: the infinitives "to accrue" and "to let" (line 2), the repetition of "I hear" (lines 3–5, 15, 16, 18, 22), the "sounds" (line 6), and the series of clauses beginning with "it" (lines 23–24).

6. What sound in line 3 is an example of *onomatopoeia*—the use of a word with a sound that echoes its very sense? Students should point to the phrase "crackle of sticks cooking my meals."

What open vowel sounds contribute to the majestic orchestral sounds of the last three stanzas? Student answers will vary. They may mention the long "i" sounds in line 23 and the long "a" sounds of line 25, among others.

Interpreting Meanings

7. Whitman's lines are not long or short by accident. He had a reason for stopping each line as he did, or for extending it as long as he did. What long lines suggest a medley of many different sounds? Among such lines are lines 3 and 11.

What does the poet gain by making the last line so short? The last line concisely sums up in one phrase the immense diversity conveyed in the preceding lines of the poem.

8. Whitman had a great love for grand opera, especially Italian opera. In opera, many different characters may sing simultaneously of their own emotions. What makes the mention of an operatic chorus particularly appropriate at lines 18–19? The mention of an operatic chorus is appropriate because Whitman has just catalogued an astounding variety of different sounds, many of them contrasting with each other, in lines 6–17.

9. Why do you think the speaker calls "Being" the "puzzle of puzzles" in the last two lines? Student answers will vary, but in general Whitman regards human existence as a mystery: a vast diversity of often contradictory emotions and experiences. This is perhaps why he calls "being" the "puzzle of puzzles."

10. In the final section of this selection, the speaker describes the physical effect that operatic singing has upon him, and he attempts to suggest its spiritual effect. What is the physical effect? The physical effect is a "wrenching" sensation and a feeling of breathlessness.

What would you say the spiritual effect is? Student answers will vary. Most students will agree that the speaker experiences a form of ecstasy.

From "Song #33"   Text page 338

Objectives

1. To recognize the use of sensory images
2. To analyze line breaks
3. To note changes of tone

Introducing the Poem

The themes of this selection are heroism and empathy. You might ask students to jot down two or three examples of "everyday" heroism that they can identify with.

Background on the Poem. Note especially the evocative sensory images of the selection. You may also wish to remind students of the "underground railroad" of the mid-1800's.

Teaching Strategies

Providing for Cultural Differences. All cultures have the concept of heroism. If you have students from a variety of ethnic backgrounds, having them compose short lists of heroic acts that reflect their own cultures will provide a basis for grasping the poem.

Providing for Different Levels of Ability. Discuss vocabulary before students listen to the poem, following along in the text as it is read.

Introducing Vocabulary Study. Knowing the meanings of the following words is important to understanding the poem. (Starred words appear in the Glossary.) It should suffice to ask the class orally for definitions before the poem is read.

disdain*	l. 12	artillerist	l. 37
taunt*	l. 22	ambulanza	l. 44

Reading the Poem. Use the audiocassette that accompanies the selection, allowing that interpretation to serve as a catalyst for class discussion. The speaker/reader *becomes* each hero conjured up—the sea captain, the hounded slave, the mashed fireman, the old artillerist. This selection is also an especially good one to use in asking students to account for Whitman's line breaks and line lengths.

Reteaching Alternatives. Have small groups of students paraphrase the poem in prose paragraphs.

Responding to the Poem   Text page 340
Analyzing the Poem
Identifying Details

1. "The large hearts of heroes" is the keynote for this passage. What kinds of heroism does the speaker describe here? List the people he identifies with. In the first stanza, the speaker celebrates the selfless courage of the ship's captain who faithfully stuck by his passengers in a ferocious storm and brought the ship through to safety. In the second and third stanzas, the speaker praises the determination of two types of martyrs: those condemned for witchcraft, and the slaves who are hounded runaways. Both sets of martyrs were unfairly persecuted. In the fourth and fifth stanzas, the speaker "becomes" a fireman who has risked death to battle a blaze and has been injured by a collapsing building: this is another example of selfless heroism. Finally, the speaker evokes the heroism of a dying general in war, who urges his troops to "mind the entrenchments" rather than come to his aid.

2. At what moments does the speaker restate the point of "I am the man, I suffer'd, I was there"? The speaker restates this point at several places in the poem: see particularly "I am the hounded slave" (line 17); "I am the mash'd fireman" (line 26); "I am the clock myself" (line 36); "I am an old artillerist" (line 37); "I take part, I see and hear the whole" (line 42).

3. Remembering the historical background against which this poem was written, how would you explain the incident described in lines 17–22? The hounded slave is similar to the "runaway slave" of "#10" (see page 334): he is probably one of the numerous slaves who attempted to escape from the South to the North on the "underground railroad" of the 1840's and 1850's.

What conflict is the poet describing in the account of the old artillerist in lines 37–49? The poet is probably imagining the bombardment of Fort Sumter in April, 1861—the conflict which started the Civil War.

4. What does "mind" mean in the last line? The word means "pay attention to."

5. Find at least five *sentence structures* that Whitman repeats in this poem to create his *rhythm*. Among the repeated sentence structures that students may mention are the following: the clauses beginning with "how" (lines 3–9, the parallel clauses of line 11, the sequence of nouns at the beginning of lines 12–15, the parallel clauses beginning with "I" in lines 37–38, and the series of nouns and phrases in lines 43–47.

6. The poet wants us to share his empathy. What *images* of sight and sound help us feel we also "are there"? Student answers will vary. They may find vivid images of sight and sound almost anywhere in the poem.

Interpreting Meanings

7. How would you describe the speaker's *tone* in this passage—what are his feelings for these "heroes"? Student answers will vary. In general, the speaker's tone is marked by imaginative empathy, admiration for the heroes' courage, and deep compassion for suffering and loss.

8. Notice the alternation of very long lines and very short lines. Can you see the reason for each short line? How would you use your voice in reading each short line aloud? Student answers will vary.

"Song #52"

Text page 341

Objectives

1. To describe a response to the poet's language
2. To write a paragraph as a poem
3. To write an essay comparing and contrasting a poem with an essay
4. To write an essay comparing and contrasting a poem with a psalm

Introducing the Poem

This is the final poem of the 1855 edition of *Leaves of Grass*, Whitman's valedictory to the reader. Have students go back to look at "#1" from "Song of Myself" (page 332) before reading "#52."

Background on the Poem. Whitman shows his awareness of the newness of his kind of poetry, alluding to it as a "barbaric yawp." He characterizes his own oneness with nature through the image of the spotted hawk and his physical continuation in the world through the dirt under his readers' boot soles.

Teaching Strategies

Providing for Cultural Differences. Students of Eastern religions may find the concepts of this poem even easier to grasp than students raised in the Judeo-Christian tradition. Clarify vocabulary, however.

Providing for Different Levels of Ability. Again, the only difficulty may be with vocabulary. Also, have students follow along in the text as the poem is read.

Introducing Vocabulary Study. Knowing the meanings of the following words is important to understanding the poem. (The starred word appears in the Glossary.)

barbaric	l. 1	effuse	l. 8
yawp	l. 1	eddies*	l. 8
send (n.)	l. 4	bequeath	l. 9

Ask students to define the words orally, using the Glossary or dictionaries as necessary. Explain the phrase "filter and fibre your blood" (purify and strengthen your blood).

Reading the Poem. Use the audiocassette reading that accompanies the poem, or prepare your own reading. Check for understanding after the first reading by using the seven response questions on page 342, and then re-read the poem (or replay the cassette).

Reteaching Alternatives. Have students listen to the audiocassette or paraphrase the poem with the aid of a student who understands it.

Responding to the Poem

Text page 342

Analyzing the Poem
Identifying Details

1. **What qualities does the speaker say he shares with the spotted hawk?** He says in lines 2–3 that he is not tamed, that he is untranslatable, and that he sounds a "barbaric yawp."

2. **Beginning with line 9, the speaker makes one of his most direct addresses to his readers. What, in your own words, is his parting message?** Whitman imagines himself as melting into the dirt "to grow from the grass I love." He tells his readers that they may not know or understand him well, but that he will remain—through his poetry—as a salutary influence on them. If readers fail to "reach" him at first, they should be encouraged and search for him in another place; they will eventually find him.

Interpreting Meanings

3. **Considering what you know of the work of poets who preceded him, what does the poet mean when he describes his own poetry as "barbaric yawp"? Do you agree? Describe your response to Whitman's language. Do you think its effect on people has changed with the passage of time?** Student answers will vary.

4. **Could Whitman also be using the phrase "barbaric yawp" to refer to the way the Old World might have regarded the experiment of democracy itself? Explain.** Again, students will have different opinions. Encourage the students to support their answers with specific facts and/or arguments.

5. **What do you think of the poet when he says, in line 10, "look for me under your boot-soles"?** He probably means that he intends his poetry to be as accessible and nearby as the earth or the dust under the bootsoles of the average working person of the day.

126   A New American Poetry

6. The first line of "Song of Myself" is "I celebrate myself, and sing myself"; the last line is "I stop somewhere waiting for you." Taking into account all that you have learned of the poet's character and the range of his poem, tell what you think the last words in the poem reveal about Whitman's intention. The connection of the words "I" (the first word in the first line) and "you" (the final word in the last line) serves as an emblem for Whitman's profound empathy: the ability to inject his own personality into those of other people in order to experience their emotions more deeply. He intends all his readers, as far as possible, to accept his "search" for them and to empathize with him in return.

7. What tense does the poet use in these selections from "Song of Myself"? He consistently uses the present tense.

How would the effect have differed if he had spoken in the past tense? The effect would have lost much of its immediacy and intensity.

Writing About "Song of Myself"
A Creative Response

1. Writing the Essay as a Poem. Suitable sections from Emerson include "I become a transparent eyeball" ("Nature," page 192); and "Trust thyself" and "A foolish consistency" ("Self-Reliance," page 194). Have students experiment until they find a paragraph that works well for them.

Criteria for Evaluating the Assignment. The student has arranged the lines from Emerson to reveal their cadence.

A Critical Response

2. Comparing Whitman to Emerson. Note that students are to use all of the selections from "Song of Myself" in comparing Whitman's message and style with that of Emerson in "Nature." The writing prompt provides an outline for the essay.

Criteria for Evaluating the Assignment. The essay compares Emerson's and Whitman's messages about people and their relationship to nature. The essay also compares the poets' styles and diction. Points are supported by quotes from Emerson's essay and Whitman's poems.

3. Comparing a Poem to a Psalm. Give students copies of Psalm 22 ("My God, my God, why hast thou forsaken me . . . ?") for reference. This psalm, sometimes called a "Suffering Servant" psalm and applied to the crucified Christ, can also apply to any sufferer. Its many parallels with "Song #33" will emerge readily as students complete the suggested chart.

Criteria for Evaluating the Assignment. The essay cites similarities between Psalm 22 and "Song #33" in terms of parallel structure, cadences, message, and tone. Quotes from the psalm and from the poem support the essay's major points.

"On the Beach at Night" Text page 343

Objectives

1. To analyze symbolism
2. To recognize vivid imagery

Introducing the Poem

Ask students how they thought clouds and stars related to each other when they were very small. Did they ever worry, for instance, that the stars were being covered forever by the clouds?

Background on the Poem. The poem may be read on both a literal level (a child on the beach with her father is crying) and on a symbolic level (all life passes except—perhaps—the stars, or maybe the human spirit).

Teaching Strategies

Providing for Cultural Differences. Ask students how they understand the term "immortality." You might also ask them to name some things thought to be immortal by various groups of believers.

Providing for Different Levels of Ability. Have students study the vocabulary words before reading the poem aloud. Students should take notes on words that are new to them.

Introducing Vocabulary Study. Knowing the meanings of the following words is important to understanding the poem. (The starred word appears in the Glossary.)

ravening*	l. 5	pensive	l. 22
athwart	l. 6	indirection	l. 27
ether	l. 7		

Reading the Poem. Rehearse the poem yourself (or with a student who reads well—it is not on the audiocassette), and read it aloud in class. Have students follow in their textbooks. After checking for literal comprehension, have students answer the response questions on page 344.

Reteaching Alternatives. Have students discuss the poem line by line in small groups.

Responding to the Poem Text page 344
Analyzing the Poem
Identifying Details

1. What does *ravening* mean in lines 5 and 17? The word suggests voracious hunger. As Whitman applies it to the clouds, however, it seems to mean "destructive."

2. Why does the child weep silently in lines 11–13? The child weeps because she is afraid that the clouds will "devour" Jupiter and the stars.

3. How does the poet reassure the child in the fourth stanza? The poet tells the child that the clouds will not obscure the bright stars and the planet for long. He tells her to watch again another night, and he asserts that the stars are immortal.

Interpreting Meanings

4. The last stanza implies the poem is intended on a *symbolic*, as well as on a literal, level. What do you think the "ravening clouds" might symbolize? The clouds may symbolize the forces of evil and destruction in the world, which threaten to overwhelm good.

What might Jupiter and the "immortal stars" symbolize? In ancient mythology, Jupiter was worshipped as king of the gods. The Romans pictured him as equitable and just. In general, Jupiter and the immortal stars in this poem are images of light, perhaps symbolizing radiance, justice, and the triumph of good over evil.

5. When the poet says in line 27 that he is giving "the first suggestion, the problem and indirection," it is as if he were teaching the child her first lesson on an important, and possibly difficult subject. What do you think the subject is, and what is the lesson the poet wants to teach the child? Students may have various reactions. From the statement in the last stanza that "something will endure longer even than lustrous Jupiter" (line 30), we may infer that Whitman is talking about the soul—or perhaps about a higher, divine power. The lesson the speaker is teaching the child evidently concerns the profound issues of good and evil, life and death. He reassures the child that the stars, images for good and beauty, are immortal; beyond them, there exists an even more enduring power that watches over the world.

6. What specific *images* help you to visualize what is happening in the sky? Among the images students may mention are the "black masses" (line 5), the transparent "belt of ether" in the east (line 7), the description of the planet Jupiter rising (line 8), and the "delicate sisters" of the Pleiades (line 10).

How do the two figures on the beach contrast with these distant sky images? They seem small and insignificant.

How is this contrast important to the poem? The theme of the poem emphasizes that "something" more immortal than the stars persists in nature and watches over us. This being or entity is immeasurable and powerful, just as the stars seem immeasurable and powerful to us.

7. What do you think he means by the "something" in the last stanza—the "something" that is immortal and will endure? Student answers will vary.

Do you think the lesson he intends for the child is clear? Student answers will vary.

How would you respond to Whitman's main point in this poem? Student answers will vary.

"On the Beach at Night Alone" Text page 345

Objectives

1. To recognize a catalogue constructed of parallel phrases
2. To write an essay comparing two poems

Introducing the Poem

The sea is here used as an archetype—a pattern basic to literature of every culture in every age. In this poem the sea is a creative force, "the old mother," but you might ask

128   A New American Poetry

students why peoples of all cultures would similarly have come to view the sea both as life-giver and as destroyer—the two main uses of the archetype.

Background on the Poem. The catalogue need not be explicated line by line—the overall sweep and inclusiveness of the poem are what matter.

Teaching Strategies

Providing for Cultural Differences. Sea imagery is common to all cultures, although some students may never have visited an ocean. Allow those who have done so, or who have experienced the sea's danger, to describe their experiences.

Providing for Different Levels of Ability. Review the vocabulary before reading the poem. Have students take notes on words that are new to them.

Introducing Vocabulary Study. Knowing the meanings of the following words is important to understanding the poem.

| clef | l. 3 | inanimate | l. 7 |
| similitude | l. 4 | | |

Reading the Poem. Rehearse the poem yourself (or have a student who reads well do so—it is not on the audiocassette), and read it aloud, with students following in their textbooks. Check for literal comprehension, and then discuss with students the questions on page 345.

Reteaching Alternatives. Ask students to imagine themselves alone at the shore on a starry night. What thoughts would they have about living beings in general, and how earth bound creatures relate to the universe? When students have jotted down at least one idea, send them back to the poem to see how Whitman responded in the same circumstances.

Responding to the Poem   Text page 345
Analyzing the Poem
Identifying Details

1. Who is the "old mother"? (The title gives you the clue.) The "old mother" is the sea.

What is her "to and fro"? The "to and fro" is the ebb and flow of the ocean waves or the tides.

2. What is the old mother's "husky song"? The song is probably the noise of the waves.

3. How would you define "similitude"? Student answers will vary. One possible definition is "sameness."

Interpreting Meanings

4. What in human life might the old mother's "to and fro" be compared with? One might compare it to the cycle of birth, life, and death.

5. What does the poet mean by a "vast similitude" that "interlocks" all? He means that everything in nature is bound together.

The *catalogue* that Whitman cites includes many categories. Name some of them. Some of the categories include: celestial bodies, human beings, aspects of culture, and inanimate objects.

6. What distinction can you make between a "vast similitude" that "*interlocks* all" and a "vast similitude" that "*spans*" them? Do the verbs merely suggest two aspects of the same phenomenon? Explain. Student answers will vary. Many students may point out that "spans"—in the sense of "bridges"—has a slightly different (and weaker) meaning than "interlocks"—in the sense of "unifies closely."

7. Why do you think thoughts like these came to the poet while he was on the beach? Student answers will vary.

Writing About the Poem
A Critical Response

Comparing the Poem to "Thanatopsis." Briefly review William Cullen Bryant's "Thanatopsis" (pages 142–144) after the students have completed the "Identifying Details" and "Interpreting Meanings" questions on Whitman's poem. Discuss similarities the students see.

Criteria for Evaluating the Assignment. The essay is brief, but notes similarities in views of the universe. Quotes from the poems support the essay's points.

"When I Heard the Learned Astronomer" — Text page 346

Objectives

1. To interpret the meaning of the poem
2. To write an essay comparing two poems

Introducing the Poem

The poem poses a contrast between the aesthetic and the scientific approach. To anticipate this contrast, ask students to explain the different ways in which an artist and a surgeon would think about the human body.

Background on the Poem. See the headnote on page 346 of the student text.

Teaching Strategies

Providing for Cultural Differences. Cultural differences should pose no problems with this poem.

Providing for Different Levels of Ability. Review the vocabulary before reading the poem. Have students take notes on words that are new to them.

Introducing Vocabulary Study. Knowing the meanings of the following words is important to understanding the poem.

learned (adj.)	l. 1	mystical	l. 7
unaccountable	l. 5		

Reading the Poem. Rehearse the poem yourself (or have a student who reads well do so—it is not on the audiocassette), and read it aloud with students following in their textbooks. Call to students' attention the fact that the poem consists of a single sentence, and ask them to note how the sentence builds to its climax as they hear the poem read.

Reteaching Alternatives. If possible, bring to class a copy of Antoine de Saint-Exupéry's *The Little Prince*. Read students the first eleven paragraphs of Part IV (through the line, "But certainly, for us who understand life, figures are a matter of indifference"). The Little Prince's reaction to a lecturing astronomer exactly parallels that of Whitman's speaker. Then send students back to the poem.

Responding to the Poem — Text page 346
Analyzing the Poem
Identifying Details

1. How does the audience's reaction to the astronomer's lecture differ from the speaker's reaction? The audience applauds enthusiastically, whereas the speaker feels "tired and sick."

Interpreting Meanings

2. Listening to a lecture that he had obviously wanted to attend, the speaker finds it puzzling—"unaccountable"—that he "became tired and sick." What do you think might have been the reason for such an unexpected reaction? Whitman's unease can probably be explained by his feeling that the astronomer has reduced the mystery of the universe to proofs, figures, columns, charts, and diagrams.

How is this reaction typical of the Romantic attitude toward a scientific dissection of nature? Whitman's reaction is typically Romantic in that the Romantics prized mystery, subjectivity, and intuition as ways to higher truth.

3. In terms of the conflict of reality versus imagination, of science versus art, what is the significance of the poem's final line? In general, the final line contrasts silence and mystery with rational discourse and objectivity: Whitman evidently believes that the universe is a far vaster, more mysterious place than the astronomer would say it is.

What do you think the poet gained from watching the stars in "perfect silence" that he couldn't get from the astronomer? He gained peace and a sense of the beautiful majesty of nature.

Writing About the Poem
A Critical Response

Comparing Poems. Note that the assignment asks students to use the speaker from "On the Beach at Night" (page 343) rather than the speaker of ". . . Learned Astronomer."

Criteria for Evaluating the Assignment. The essay is brief, but notes that for the speaker of "On the Beach at Night," the stars lead to thoughts not of orbits and measurements but of the unity of all creation.

"A Sight in Camp in the Daybreak Gray and Dim" — Text page 348

Objectives

1. To identify details of setting
2. To analyze the speaker's tone
3. To analyze response to rhythms, diction, catalogues, subject matter, and tone

Introducing the Poem

Ask students to describe the view of war conveyed in the more serious episodes of the television series "M*A*S*H" or films such as *Platoon* or *The Killing Fields*. Like this poem, such films depict the reality of individual deaths obscured by phrases like "casualty rate."

Background on the Poem. Field hospitals during the Civil War were places of horror since they predated antiseptic practices, and amputation served as the most common solution if an arm or leg were injured. Soldiers were as likely to die from infections acquired in the hospital as from their actual wounds. Note, too, the headnote on page 348—Whitman wrote from personal experience.

Teaching Strategies

Providing for Cultural Differences. Cultural differences should pose no problems with this poem.

Providing for Different Levels of Ability. Point out the inversion that occurs in some sentences (line 3, for example) before reading the poem aloud.

Introducing Vocabulary Study. Students should have no difficulty with vocabulary in this poem.

Reading the Poem. Rehearse the poem yourself (or have a student who reads well do so—it is not on the audiocassette), and read it aloud, with students following in their textbooks. Ask them to listen for the vivid description of the setting.

Reteaching Alternatives. Locate a copy of Wilfred Owen's World War I poem, "Dulce et Decorum Est." Read and discuss it with any student who had difficulty with Whitman's poem, or use it as an enrichment of Whitman's poem for the entire class. (The Latin motto ending Owen's poem, "Dulce et decorum est / Pro patria mori," translates to "It is sweet and right / To die for one's fatherland"—a motto Owen, too, shows to be a false image of war.)

Responding to the Poem — Text page 349
Analyzing the Poem
Identifying Facts

1. Find the details that identify the *setting* of the poem. The hospital tent and the stretchers identify the setting as a battlefield.

2. What is the sight that the speaker sees in the daybreak? He sees three people lying untended on the stretchers.

Describe the three faces he sees. The first is the gaunt and grim face of an elderly man. The second is the innocent face of an adolescent boy. The third face is beautifully calm.

Interpreting Meanings

3. The poem moves from anonymity to identity, from mere "forms," each hidden by an "ample brownish woolen blanket," to individuals with particular physical features. One of these strikes the speaker as having the features of "the Christ himself." Why, given the circumstances of this particular war, might the poet have seen this face on one of the dead soldiers? Student answers will vary. Some students will suggest that the Civil War setting, in which brothers were pitted against brothers, makes the apparition of the face of Christ—who bade men love one another—especially ironic and effective. Others may simply think of bearded faces.

4. The point of the poem is never openly stated; that is, it remains implicit. How would you make the poet's *message* explicit? Students may want to emphasize the fundamental theme of camaraderie and brotherhood in the poem. Whitman's point is that the Civil War has ruthlessly violated the brotherhood of mankind.

Is there any significance to the fact that the "forms" who become persons in the eyes of the speaker are a trio? Explain. Whitman may be using the trio symbolically to evoke the Christian notion of the Trinity: three persons—Father, Son, and Holy Spirit—in one God.

5. Whitman's poetry, technically speaking, is all of a piece—a body of work easily identified by rolling *cadences*, by *catalogues* of things and activities, and by self-assertive expostulations. What most distinguishes one of his poems from another lies in the *tone*: in modulations of voice that indicate his attitude toward different subjects, and in a kind of timing that suggests that the reader is overhearing a man's conversation with himself. How would you describe the tone of this poem? What are the main elements that support your description? The tone is somber, both at the beginning and the end. In the opening lines, Whitman is "sleepless" and walks "slowly" as he spies the forms lying on stretchers. His sympathy for the wounded is clear in the body of the poem. At the end, he evokes the memory of the Crucifixion, as he comments that Christ, "brother of all," has been newly killed in the Civil War, which pitted brother against brother.

The Poems as a Whole

1. Answers will be highly individual. You might have students use this question in small-group discussions.

2. You might divide the class into pairs or triads, and have each such pair or triad offer one image they find particularly evocative.

3. This question makes a good individual assignment as part of a general review of Whitman.

Writing About the Poems
A Creative Response

1. Writing a Free-Verse Poem. Note that students are to select *one* of the lines given (not all four), and to use the poetic elements listed in the prompt.

Critria for Evaluating the Assignment. The poem opens with one of Whitman's lines, and achieves its effect through imagery, sound effects, and at least one form of repetition.

A Critical Response

You may wish to have students write only *one* of the critical writing assignments, but discuss all five in class.

2. Analyzing the Ideas in the Poems. Elicit a listing of the poems in which Whitman most clearly expresses his ideas on "similitudes," the poet's presence, and the role of the imagination. The list will provide students with appropriate sources.

Criteria for Evaluating the Assignment. The essay cites examples to show how Whitman develops the notion of "similitudes," the idea that the poet is "with us," and the idea that imagination can discover truths inaccessible to reason.

3. Explaining the Poet's Statement. Discuss the aspects of Whitman's poems that definitively mark them as American.

Criteria for Evaluating the Assignment. The essay quotes from Whitman's poems to demonstrate that they could have been written only by an American.

4. Contrasting Whitman with a Fireside Poet. The "Fireside Poets" (page 122) are the Boston group of Longfellow, Holmes, Lowell, and Whittier. Make sure students understand Whitman's statement before they review poems by the Fireside group to seek support for it. In their essays, they should replace "I" with "Whitman" to use his statement as their thesis statement.

Criteria for Evaluating the Assignment. The essay contrasts the conventional themes and style of the Fireside Poets with the themes and style of Whitman. Examples from the Fireside Poets and from Whitman support the essay's major points.

5. Comparing Whitman to Taylor and Emerson. Review Taylor's "Upon a Spider Catching a Fly" (page 46) and Emerson's "Nature" (page 191), having students take notes on how each man "reads" nature. Then discuss how Whitman "reads" nature.

Criteria for Evaluating the Assignment. The essay shows similarities and differences in how Taylor, Emerson, and Whitman "read" nature. Examples from the writings of all three men support the essay's major points.

6. Analyzing the Prose. Read and discuss "Primary Sources" (pages 350–351) in class. Have students work together to complete the chart suggested in the writing prompt.

Criteria for Evaluating the Assignment. The essay briefly compares Whitman's prose with his poetry in terms of tone, democratic feelings, use of lists and catalogues, and use of vigorous language.

Extending the Poems

Students who are good oral interpreters may wish to locate, prepare, present, and interpret for the class another Whitman poem: "When lilacs last in the dooryard bloom'd," parts of "Out of the cradle endlessly rocking," or Songs #4, #6, or #8 from "Song of Myself."

Research topics associated with Whitman's era include the Free-Soil political party (of which Whitman was a member), the Underground Railroad, and medical practices during the Civil War period.

In addition to works on Whitman, some students may wish to gain a fuller appreciation of the practicalities of life in the 1860's, as well as the political issues, by reading Gore Vidal's fictional account of Lincoln's presidency, *Lincoln*, and preparing a written or oral report.

Emily Dickinson

Text Page 352

The challenge with Emily Dickinson is to strike a balance between myth and fact. You might assign reading of the text biography (pages 352-353) and "Primary Sources" (371-372), and open class discussion the following day by asking why the following quotation from the Norton Anthology of American Literature is appropriate to Emily Dickinson:

> "[T]o think of Emily Dickinson only as an eccentric recluse is a serious mistake. Like Thoreau, she lived simply and deliberately; she fronted the essential facts of life. In Henry James's phrase, she was one of those on whom nothing was lost."

During discussion, you may wish to supplement the text with some additional information.

Dickinson's frailty has often been exaggerated. She repeatedly insisted that it was not invalidism that led to her seclusion. (It may, nevertheless, interest students to know that in her lifetime, in Massachusetts alone, more than forty percent of all children died of diseases like diphtheria, tuberculosis, "brain fever," and malaria before the age of twelve.) In adulthood Dickinson developed Bright's disease, the kidney disease of which she died, and which may also have caused the eye problems that led to two minimally successful operations during her early thirties. (Her vision problems directly affected her penmanship.)

In childhood Dickinson was a tomboy, much happier romping with her brother Austin (a year older than she; their sister Lavinia was three years younger than Emily) than practicing the domestic and hostessing tasks expected of nineteenth-century women. In her first school she was mischievous enough to be shut up in a dark closet for punishment at least once. In her teens she loved reading forbidden romantic novels, and was part of a chattering group of girls. At Amherst Academy she had the usual schoolgirl crushes on male teachers, and enjoyed her curriculum of classical languages, philosophy, history and rhetoric. In addition, she often joined other girls in trekking up the hill to Amherst College where they were allowed to sit in on college lectures in geology, astronomy, and biology.

After graduation from Amherst Academy, Dickinson so adamantly refused to turn to domestic interests that in 1847 her father sent her to South Hadley Seminary for Women (later Mount Holyoke College). Her career there lasted less than a year. Regardless of her scores in academic subjects, she was not allowed to return because she repeatedly and publicly refused to accept the tenents of the Calvinistic Christian faith.

There is, nevertheless, a deeply religious quality to Dickinson's work. She was influenced by the Puritan philosophy of her times, and metaphysical topics—the origin of the universe, whether or not there is an afterlife, the true nature of God and of the soul—equaled slavery as a topic of everyday discussion. Dickinson, though religious, simply would not yield to any efforts to force her acceptance of a specific body of religious doctrine.

Like religion, literature was a formative influence for Dickinson, as suggested by her letter to Higginson ("Primary Sources," page 371). Her father believed in giving his children books rather than toys, and his home library contained law books, English classics, and a smattering of travel, religious, and natural science books. Dickinson was especially familiar with the Bible, the classics, and Shakespeare, but also valued the work of her contemporaries—Alfred, Lord Tennyson; the Brontë sisters; Robert and Elizabeth Barrett Browning; Thoreau and Emerson.

Biographers have repeatedly attempted to explain Dickinson's seclusion as resulting from a thwarted love affair. In fact, when Dickinson was fourteen, the death of a girlfriend, Sophia Holland, led to so deep a depression that she had to be taken out of school for a time. Dominating her life was her father, Edward (a stern Calvinist, a lawyer who later served a term in Congress). He did drive off some men, including Benjamin Newton, a law student who apprenticed in his office and who later died of tuberculosis (it was he who introduced Emily to the works of Emerson); and college students with whom she shared the excitement of poetry. Overall, however, it appears that after the death of her girlfriend, Dickinson found all partings so traumatic that she chose to withdraw. Others of whom she was fond were Susan Gilbert, who married her brother Austin; the Reverend Charles Wadsworth (see text), to whom she turned for spiritual guidance; and various editors and critics of her poetry, including Higginson and Todd, who edited the first editions of Dickinson's poems after her death.

Some of the problems experienced by Dickinson's early editors were of her making. She wrote on any scrap of paper available—the fish wrapper, an envelope, the grocery list—and filled drawers and bags with these scraps. Sometimes she sewed the scraps together into little books. Another difficulty was her poor handwriting. At other times she could not decide on the exact word and would list several possibilities, making it necessary for the editors to select one. Then, too, her use of "slant" or "off" rhyme, imperfect grammar and spelling, and made-up words made her poems somewhat shocking in her own day.

When Dickinson died, several clergymen participated in a service described as "poetical," and workmen who had served the Dickinsons carried her casket. The cemetery was not the end of Dickinson, however. Her sister Vinnie took bundles of poems (she left some 1,775 poems) to Higginson and Todd, and the small gold and white first volume, published in November 1890, astonished Amherst.

The Boston *Herald,* while commenting that "Madder rhymes one has seldom seen," nevertheless reported that there was in the poems "a fascination, a power, a vision . . . that draws you back." Higginson himself remained "bewildered" by Dickinson's work. William Dean Howells, distinguished novelist and editor, praised the poems as being "true as the grave and certain as mortality. They are each a compressed whole, a sharply finished point . . . If nothing else had come out of our life but this strange poetry, we should feel that in the work of Emily Dickinson, America . . . had made a distinctive addition to the literature of the world."

It was really not until 1955, however, when Dickinson's complete work was made available, that her accomplishment could be fully assessed. She is now seen as a distinctively modern poet who tackles the deepest puzzles of human consciousness and whose work is remarkable for its variety, subtlety, and richness, despite its apparent simplicity. She has been praised by poets as varied as Hart Crane, Allen Tate, and Adrienne Rich; and William Carlos Williams, whose work students will read in Unit Nine, claimed her as his "patron saint."

"Heart! We will forget him!" — Text page 355

Objectives

1. To paraphrase the speaker's words
2. To identify feeling or tone

Introducing the Poem

You might ask students whether they've ever been so emotionally involved with someone or something that they couldn't stop thinking about the person or issue no matter how hard they tried. (General descriptions are sufficient response to prepare students for the poem.)

Background on the Poem. The techniques of apostrophe (direct address to an absent person or an abstract or inanimate entity) and slant rhyme (off rhyme, as with begin/him) appear in this poem. Since critics (and the public) have speculated endlessly on Dickinson's love life, encouraged in part by this poem, it may be more important, however, to remind students that the speaker in a literary work is a creation of the writer—not automatically the writer herself. (The audiocassette accompanying this selection reinforces this point by having four different readers interpret Dickinson's poems.)

Teaching Strategies

Providing for Cultural Differences. The theme of loving and losing someone is universal, as is the conflict between mind and heart.

Providing for Different Levels of Ability. The general concept of the poem is accessible to all, including the symbolic uses of warmth and light.

Introducing Vocabulary Study. No words are difficult.

Reading the Poem. After the brief introductory activities, discuss the headnote on page 355 and then read the poem aloud. Discuss the response questions, and then read

134 A New American Poetry

the poem aloud again or play the audiocassette. (You may wish to discuss all twelve of Dickinson's poems in this text before replaying all of them on the audiocassette.)

Reteaching Alternatives. Ask students to name a popular song (perhaps in the country-western tradition) about trying to forget someone. Discuss it briefly, and then re-read the Dickinson poem.

Responding to the Poem Text page 355
Analyzing the Poem
Identifying Details

1. Assume that the speaker is the mind. What does it order the heart to do? The mind orders the heart to forget the warmth that the beloved gave.

2. Which word describes what "he" gave the heart? "Warmth" (line 3).

Which word describes what "he" gave the mind? "Light" (line 4).

3. Exclamation points punctuate this little poem, as if the poem were saying, "Hurry up! We must get this over with!" **Why is she in such a hurry?** The matter cannot wait because the speaker is half afraid that she will weaken in her resolution to forget the lover.

Interpreting Meanings

4. Why do you think the heart is asked to take the lead in this situation? Students may suggest that the speaker feels it will be harder for the heart than for the mind to forget; therefore, the heart is asked to take the lead.

5. How would you *paraphrase* what the speaker means by warmth and light? Answers may vary. One paraphrase for "warmth" might be "passion"; one paraphrase for "light" might be "intelligence."

6. If you wanted to forget someone, would you first try to forget his or her "warmth" or "light"? Why? Answers will vary.

7. What feeling or *tone* would you say this lyric expresses? Among the suggestions students may offer are: regret, determination, impatience, frustration.

"Success is counted sweetest" Text page 356

Objectives

1. To identify imagery
2. To interpret the meaning of the poem

Introducing the Poem

Ask students whether they have ever achieved something they had been wanting—buying a desired object, winning a certain contest, being invited to a special party—only to find that success did not make them feel as good as they had expected. In retrospect, is there any sense in which they would appreciate the goal more if they *hadn't* achieved it?

Background on the Poem. Concentrate on the message. You might note that Dickinson's use of war imagery doesn't have the immediacy of Whitman's in "A Sight in Camp in the Daybreak Gray and Dim" (text page 348), since she was using war imagery symbolically to convey a different point.

Teaching Strategies

Providing for Cultural Differences. Winning and losing are concepts familar to cultures or worldwide.

Providing for Different Levels of Ability. Dickinson's compression of language and inversion of usual word order (lines 7–8, for example, would normally be expressed "Can so clear[ly] tell the definition of victory") may confuse some students. Check for literal comprehension by asking students to paraphrase the poem (orally) before you assign the response questions.

Introducing Vocabulary Study. Knowing the meanings of the following words is important to understanding the selection. They are defined in text notes.

nectar	l. 3	Host	l. 5
sorest	l. 4		

Reading the Poem. After brief introductory activities, read and discuss the headnote on page 356 and then read the

Emily Dickinson 135

poem aloud. Ask students orally to paraphrase the poem before you assign or discuss the response questions. You may then wish to read the poem aloud again or play the audiocassette.

Reteaching Alternatives. Do a line-by-line, thought-by-thought paraphrase with the students.

Responding to the Poem Text page 356
Analyzing the Poem
Identifying Details

1. According to the poet, who is likely to count success sweetest? The defeated, or those who never succeed, count success sweetest.

2. Purple is a color associated with blood shed in battle. What is the "purple host" in line 5? Purple was the imperial color of ancient Rome. Dickinson associates the conquering army with the Roman host that conquered the known world in ancient times. The word *purple* perhaps also refers to the blood of the defeated.

3. What example does the poet supply to illustrate her statement about those who know success best? She supplies the example of a defeated army.

4. What *image* does the poet present in the last stanza? The last stanza presents the scene of a defeated, dying warrior who hears from a distance the strains of his enemy's triumph.

Interpreting Meanings

5. Two kinds of desire are balanced in the first stanza. How would you define them? What is their relationship to each other? The first kind is abstract—the desire for success. The second kind of desire is concrete—the extreme need of thirst for a "nectar." In both cases the idea of "need" is present. Also, the poet stresses the idea that true understanding of an abstract idea or of a concrete object is possessed only by those who strive for but do not attain it.

6. Do you think the feeling expressed in this poem is valid? Is it common? Explain. Students will have various answers. Encourage them to support their answers with concrete examples.

7. "Victory" is considered in military terms here. Can you think of other circumstances—perhaps a circumstance in your own life—in which the situation in this poem, and its conclusion, might be repeated? Answers will vary, but the theme of the poem can clearly be applied to a wide range of situations, such as sports, job interviews, examinations, and so forth.

"The Soul selects her own Society" Text page 357

Objectives

1. To analyze images
2. To analyze changes in meter
3. To write an essay evaluating a title

Introducing the Poem

Read and discuss the headnote on page 357. The fact that each of us has internal "rules" for selecting friends may be new to some students, but should arouse discussion.

Background on the Poem. This poem is particularly compressed, and students may benefit from inserting omitted words such as "[even if] an Emperor [should] be kneeling" (line 7) or "[She is] Present no more" (line 4).

Teaching Strategies

Providing for Cultural Differences. The theme is universal.

Providing for Different Levels of Ability. Word choice may present some difficulty. Use text notes and response questions 6–8 on page 357.

Introducing Vocabulary Study. No words are difficult in themselves, but see questions 6–8 on page 375 on nuances of meaning.

Reading the Poem. Read the poem aloud, discuss the response questions, and then re-read the poem (or play the audiocassette).

Reteaching Alternatives. Have students work in small groups to paraphrase the poem, with a very capable student

136   A New American Poetry

assigned to each group. Or offer Robert Frost's lines from "Mending Wall" (text page 680) as a discussion topic:

> Before I built a wall I'd ask to know
>
> What I was walling in or walling out.

Then lead students to see a connection between Frost's idea and Dickinson's poem.

Responding to the Poem   Text page 357
Analyzing the Poem
Identifying Details

1. In the first stanza, what does the soul do? The soul decides its preferences and then firmly "shuts the door" on things and people she does not select.

2. What words have to be added to lines 3–4 to make a complete sentence? The subject and the verb ("she is") have to be added.

3. What is the principal *image* of the second stanza? The principal image is that of an emperor or ruler, pausing in a chariot to beg the soul to admit him. He kneels upon the soul's "mat" (perhaps an entrance mat) before her "low gate," but she is unmoved. Dickinson reverses the usual idea of subjects kneeling before an emperor.

4. In stanza 2, where does the poet sacrifice correct syntax in order to make her point? How would you put this stanza into conventional English? In line 7, the phrase "an Emperor be kneeling" displays unusual syntax. A prose paraphrase of the stanza in conventional English might run as follows: "She is unmoved when the chariots pause at her low gate; she would remain unmoved even if an emperor should kneel upon her mat."

5. In the last stanza, what does the soul do? She chooses one person from a vast throng, and then she closes off her attention to everybody else.

Interpreting Meanings

6. "Majority" as used here has at least two meanings. It could mean having reached the full legal age, or having "come into one's own"; or it could mean superiority (an obsolete usage); or it could mean "the greater part of something." What do you think it means? Answers will vary. Many students will suggest that "majority" means "the greater part of something" here.

What kind of person does the adjective "divine" suggest? Student answers will vary.

7. Look up the word *valve* in a dictionary. Do you think the phrase "Valves of her attention" is drawn from the world of organic things (the valves of a clam-shell)? Or from the world of mechanical things (the valves of a faucet)? What do you picture happening here? Answers will vary.

8. The editors changed the word *valves* to the word *lids*. How does this change the *metaphor*? How does it change your *image* of what is happening? The word "lids" metaphorically suggests that the soul has eyes.

9. Look carefully at the *meter* of lines 10 and 12. How does the rhythmical pattern of these lines differ from the corresponding lines in the first and second stanzas? In the first two stanzas, the second and fourth lines each have two stresses in an iambic pattern. But in the last stanza, each of these lines is reduced from four syllables to two syllables, with approximately equal stress.

What is the effect of this difference? The effect is to slow down the rhythm and give the soul's choice an air of unmovable finality.

10. What advantage may lie in a "selection" as strict as this "soul" makes? What are its disadvantages? Students should be encouraged to share their own opinions. The advantage may be the intensity with which the soul can love those whom she singles out. The disadvantage may be that someone, or something, will be prematurely or unfairly excluded.

Writing About the Poem
A Critical Response

Evaluating a Title. Discuss the early editors' choice of "Exclusion" to title the poem, in terms of both its applicability and its limitations. Brainstorm a list of other possible titles (e.g., Choice of the Heart, Choice, It's Personal) which students may use as a starting point for selecting or offering a new title of their own.

Criteria for Evaluating the Assignment. The paragraph evaluates the applicability and limitations of "Exclusion" as a title for "The Soul selects...," and suggests an alternative title that addresses the message of the poem.

The Elements of Literature: Slant Rhyme   Text page 358

Read and discuss this section, and have students look for slant rhymes in the three poems already taken in class. Questions are asked of the students in the final two paragraphs. Answers are matters of opinion, except for the slant rhymes employed in "The Soul selects..." on page 358. The slant rhymes present are Society/Majority, Gate/Mat, nation/attention, and One/Stone.

"A Bird came down the Walk"

Text page 358

Objectives

1. To analyze figures of speech
2. To analyze images

Introducing the Poem

William Carlos Williams, some of whose poems, such as "The Red Wheelbarrow," are pure images, claimed Dickinson as his "patron saint." The sharp images of this poem suggest why.

Background on the Poem. Concentrate on figures of speech and images with this poem. You may also wish to check to see whether students are now catching the slant rhyme.

Teaching Strategies

Providing for Cultural Differences. The topic is approachable by students from any culture.

Providing for Different Levels of Ability. The figures of speech may be difficult for some students to grasp. Handle the response questions either in a full-class discussion or in small-group discussions.

Introducing Vocabulary Study. No words are difficult.

Reading the Poem. Read the poem aloud, have a student who reads well do so, or play the audiocassette. Briefly check for grasp of the main idea—that the poet is describing an encounter with a bird—and *then* discuss the headnote above the poem on page 358. Follow up with discussion of the response questions.

Reteaching Alternatives. Ask students to watch a bird and then give a brief description (orally or in writing) of how it moves and what happens when someone tries to offer it food. Then return to the poem with pauses after each stanza to help students visualize the scene.

Responding to the Poem

Text page 389

Analyzing the Poem
Identifying Details

1. What various things does the bird do while the speaker watches? The bird bites and eats a raw angleworm, and drinks a drop of dew from a blade of grass. Then he hops sideways on the walk to allow a beetle to pass. He glances around rapidly and hurries. He stirs his head cautiously.

2. What happens when the speaker tries to be friendly with the bird? When the speaker offers it a crumb, the bird "unrolls" its feathers and flies away.

3. The poem is purely descriptive until the third stanza, when one daring simile lifts it into the realm of the imagination. What is that *simile* and what two distinct things is it comparing? The simile compares the bird's eyes to "frightened Beads."

4. The two *figures of speech* in lines 15–20 are also strikingly unusual. What is the bird compared to here? The poet compares the bird to a boat; the bird unrolls its feathers and just before it flies away, just as the oars of a boat spread apart to divide the ocean in the act of rowing. Then Dickinson adds another comparison, likening the bird to butterflies that "swim" off "Banks of Noon."

5. Describe how the actions of the bird in the air contrast with its actions on the ground. The bird seems nervous and hurried on the ground. In contrast, when it is in the air, it is graceful and streamlined.

Interpreting Meanings

6. Explain what you think the poet means by "unrolled," "rowed him," "Banks of Noon," and butterflies that "swim." What *images* do these words put in your mind? Dickinson's complex imagery first relates the bird's feathered wings to the oars of a boat, spreading apart to divide the water. The wings "unroll" as if they are to "row" the bird's body, as oars would row a boat. The phrase "Banks of Noon" implies a related image; noon, a time of day, is pictured as a river or stream, upon whose banks butterflies "leap." The butterflies themselves, in their playful movement, are in turn imagined as water creatures that "swim," rather than fly.

7. What kind of ocean do you think would be "Too silver for a seam"? The phrase implies a beautifully calm, tranquil ocean.

8. Beginning with line 15, how many "o" sounds can you hear? The long "o" sounds occur in "unrolled," "rowed," "home," "ocean." Students may also note the "o" sounds in "softer," "oars," and "noon."

What other sounds in lines 15–20 do you think help create a soft, "liquid" music? Answers will vary. Among

138 A New American Poetry

the words that students may note are: "feathers," "silver," "seam," "leap," "plashless," and "swim."

9. Some readers feel that this poem dramatizes the unbridgeable distance between the human world and the natural world. Do you agree? Explain. Student answers will vary.

10. When this poem was first published, it was entitled, "In the Garden." Do you think this title adds or subtracts from the impact of the poem? Explain. Students may be divided on this question. The title "In the Garden" supplies an explicit setting for the poem, and some students may feel that such a title helps to make the poem more concrete. Other students may disagree, arguing that a specific setting detracts from the suggestive power of the poem.

"I died for Beauty—but was scarce"

Text page 360

Objectives

1. To analyze the ue of slant rhymes
2. To identify the poet's message

Introducing the Poem

Read the headnote above the poem and ask students to paraphrase Keats's words. (Keats was one of Dickinson's favorite poets.)

Background on the Poem. Until now **slant rhyme** has merely been identified. In this poem its value in saving a poem from triteness is addressed by response question 4 on page 360.

Teaching Strategies

Providing for Cultural Differences. Although the themes are universal, you may wish to rephrase "truth" and "beauty" to a parallel that gets at the same idea, such as scientific vs. artistic approach, practically vs. aesthetics.

Providing for Different Levels of Ability. Have students work in carefully structured small groups (at least one very able student per group) to answer the response questions.

Introducing Vocabulary Study. No words are difficult.

Reading the Poem. Read the poem through, and then go back to identify the imaginary setting and the main message of the poem. Does Dickinson agree or disagree with the words of Keats in the headnote? Then send students to the response questions on page 360.

Reteaching Alternatives. Have students listen to the poem on the audiocassette and then write a prose paraphrase of the poem.

Responding to the Poem   Text page 360
Analyzing the Poem
Identifying Details

1. What situation does the speaker imagine happening in the first stanza? The speaker imagines that she is dead, having died "for Beauty," and that she is newly laid to rest in the tomb. Next to her, one who has died "for Truth" is buried.

Where is this situation taking place? The setting is a tomb or mausoleum.

2. What do the two speakers have in common that allows one of them to claim that they are "Brethren"? Both speakers died for abstract concepts—truth and beauty—that are really two aspects of the same whole. (This idea echoes John Keats's famous lines at the conclusion of "Ode on a Grecian Urn," quoted in the headnote: "Beauty is truth, truth beauty.")

3. What event is described in the last two lines of the poem? In the third stanza, the speaker pictures a regular series of conversations between the two dead persons. She compares these to the talks kinsmen might have when they meet at night. In the last two lines, the moss of the cemetery reaches the speakers' lips and covers up their names on their tombstones.

4. The *meter* in this poem is so regular and the rhyme arranged so like clockwork that only the use of the two *slant rhymes* saves it from a sing-song quality. Where are the slant rhymes? What sound to you *expect* to hear? The slant rhymes occur in lines 6 and 8 ("replied" and "said") and in lines 10 and 12 ("Rooms" and "names"). In each case, we expect the second word of the pair to echo the end sound of the first word.

Emily Dickinson 139

Interpreting Meanings

5. How does the *slant rhyme* make the last word stand out? Do you think this is an important word? Why? The sound of the last word, "names," clashes a bit with the sound of the word "rooms." This clash helps to draw attention to the word "names." Most students will agree that it is an important word, because a person's name is a clue to his or her identity.

6. What are the "rooms" in lines 4 and 10? The rooms are probably tombs or graves.

7. In the third stanza, "the moss" is real, in the sense that it is a kind of green growth likely to be found in a cemetery, or in any other place of stones and shade. But "the moss" is also a *metaphor*. For what? What is significant in the fact that it covered up the speakers' names? The moss metaphorically suggests a passage of time that results in oblivion. The speaker seems to suggest that death is a kind of oblivion for those who die, who are destined to be forgotten by the living as well.

8. The incident recounted here is imaginary. Nevertheless, Dickinson seems to have a *message* in mind. What would you say that message is? Would you say that it is optimistic or pessimistic? Student opinions will differ. An optimistic interpretation might be that those people who have supported goodness—truth and beauty—during their lives will meet together after death for mutual comfort. Pessimistic interpretations might point to the fact that the poem ends with the apparent oblivion of the speakers.

9. Poetry gives form to feelings. What feelings would you say are expressed in this poem? Students will have various answers. Among the feelings they may suggest are: love, kinship, dedication, regret.

"I heard a Fly buzz—when I died—"   Text page 362

Objectives

1. To analyze tone
2. To analyze word choice

Introducing the Poem

What child—or adult, for that matter—hasn't at some time or other imagined all the people who would come to his or her funeral? Dickinson does the same, but focuses imaginatively on a fly that invades the room.

Background on the Poem. Because of the poem's mention of the anticipated coming of the "King," you may wish to ask students what they have heard to be the common elements of near-death experiences, according to researchers such as Dr. Elisabeth Kubler-Ross (such as joy, a tunnel, bright light). Make sure students understand, however, that this poem creates an *imaginary* experience.

Teaching Strategies

Providing for Cultural Differences. For recent immigrants, you may need to explain American death and burial customs.

Providing for Different Levels of Ability. Students are unlikely to have difficulty with this poem.

Introducing Vocabulary Study. No words are difficult.

Reading the Poem. You might ask two students to rehearse the poem, assuring them that their interpretations may differ. Have one student read the poem to the class before discussion of the response questions; the other, after.

Reteaching Alternatives. Have a student who enjoys the poem play the audiocassette for, and tutor, students who do not understand the poem.

Responding to the Poem   Text page 362
Analyzing the Poem
Identifying Details

1. Paraphrase the statement made in stanza 1. One paraphrase might run as follows: At the moment of my death, I heard a fly's buzzing break the stillness of the room. (Answers will vary.)

2. According to the second and third stanzas, how had the speaker and those around her prepared for death? The speaker had dried her tears, collected her strength for her meeting with the "King" at the Last Judgment, and made her will. The people around her had ceased weeping and had steeled themselves for the final onset of death.

140   A New American Poetry

3. **According to stanza 2, what are the dying person and those around her *expecting* to find in the room? What appears instead?** They are expecting death. Instead, the fly "interposes."

In what way is this appearance *ironic*? It is ironic because the unexpected appearance of a commonplace creature, the fly, reverses momentarily the expectation of a solemn event, death.

4. **Who do you think the "King" of line 7 is?** This is probably God or Christ, whose power will be "witnessed" by the soul of the dead person.

5. **What does the poet mean by the phrase "the Windows failed" in line 15?** The word "windows" is used metaphorically for the light which passes through them. The poet means that at the moment of death her eyes cloud over in darkness.

6. **In order to clarify the syntax, how would you *paraphrase* line 5?** The line might be paraphrased as follows: The people standing in the room had finished weeping and had wiped their eyes.

Interpreting Meanings

7. **In reference to the behavior of storms, what word other than "Heaves" might have been useful in line 4? Why is "Heaves" an appropriate word, in regard to what is happening in the poem?** The speaker might have used a word like "gusts" or "bursts." "Heaves" suggests the bodily agony of a serious illness.

8. **How does the poet use pauses and specific words in lines 12 and 13 to make the appearance of the fly dramatic and lively?** The pause in line 13 divides the description of the fly. The word "interposed" is so unexpected and formal that it is almost comic. In line 13, the phrase "uncertain stumbling Buzz" displays alliteration, assonance, and onomatopoeia.

9. **In the third stanza, the poet speaks of signing away the portion that is "assignable." What portion of the speaker, by implication, is *not* assignable?** She cannot assign her soul, which is spiritual and immortal.

10. **What is the *tone* of the poem—what feeling do you think the poet expresses by inserting the fly into a deathbed scene?** Answers will vary. The contrast between the common household insect and the solemnity of death is highly dramatic. Students may suggest that the tone is semi-serious, semi-comic.

11. **Do you find this poem grotesque or moving? Or do you have some other reaction?** Student answers will vary.

"If you were coming in the Fall"

Text page 363

Objectives

1. To identify similes
2. To paraphrase a stanza
3. To respond to tone

Introducing the Poem

Like most people, teenagers are impatient: they can't wait until Friday, they can't wait until the dance, they can't wait until so-and-so arrives. Discuss with them the added strain created when you don't know the exact arrival time of the event or the person you are awaiting.

Background on the Poem. This is a **metaphysical** poem, one with far-fetched intellectual imagery. A **conceit** is an extended concept or image that gives structure to a metaphysical poem—in this poem, extensions of the time period the speaker can bear to wait. The text headnote (page 363) explains metaphysical poetry.

Teaching Strategies

Providing for Cultural Differences. The concept of waiting for a loved one is universal.

Providing for Different Levels of Ability. Discuss the poem slowly, stanza by stanza.

Introducing Vocabulary Study. Knowing the meanings of the following words is important to understanding the poem. *Goblin* (line 19) and *Van Diemen's Land* (line 12). Van Diemen's Land is defined in response question 3, page 363.

Reading the Poem. Read the poem through entirely, once, and then go back over it stanza by stanza, interpreting each stanza yourself if students are unable to do so. Then re-read the entire poem and move on to the response questions on page 363.

Reteaching Alternatives. Assist students in writing a prose paraphrase of each stanza.

Emily Dickinson 141

Responding to the Poem
Text page 363

Analyzing the Poem

Identifying Details

1. What is the *simile* in the first stanza? What two things are being compared? The poet compares the summer before her lover comes, to a fly which can be easily brushed aside, or dismissed, by a housewife.

2. In the second stanza, what domestic articles are the months compared to? The months are implicitly compared to yarn or clothes, which are wound into balls and stored in separate drawers.

Why does the speaker put them in separate drawers? The vivid detail of the "separate drawers" perhaps implies that they are opened at regular intervals as the months go by, just as we would open drawers to fetch clothes for different seasons.

3. "Van Dieman's Land" in stanza 3 is the old name for Tasmania, the large island south of Australia. It is used to mean those places on the globe furthest away from us. Given this fact, can you *paraphrase* the third stanza? One possibility might be: If you were coming after several centuries, I would count them off on the fingers of my hand until those fingers mingled with the earth and dropped to the place on earth which is furthest away.

4. The fourth stanza contains a daring but simple *simile*. What would the speaker toss away as if it were the rind of an orange? The speaker would toss her life away to taste the "fruit" of eternity, if only she were certain that her lover would come.

5. The speaker's *tone* changes in stanza 5 and her exaggerations disappear. Conscious of how long her hope must be maintained, the speaker is goaded, or pushed and prodded against her will. What is she goaded by? She is goaded by her own uncertainty about how long her wait must be.

Interpreting Meanings

6. How would the bee in the last stanza be different from the fly in the first stanza? The fly is a harmless, petty annoyance; it provokes "half a smile" and "half a spurn," and is easily brushed aside. But the bee "goads" the speaker. The *threat* of its sting is compared to the gnawing uncertainty in the speaker's mind.

7. A goblin is a grotesque creature in folklore. What does it mean that the bee is a "Goblin" and will not "state" its sting? Dickinson uses the word "goblin" to suggest the mysterious fear associated with uncertainty: it is like a ghost or demon. The word goblin is associated with the bee who goads the speaker, and this insect, who will not "state" its sting, is like the nagging uncertainty that plagues the speaker; uncertainty that harms her, but that she has difficulty in clarifying, or "stating."

8. Who might "you" be? How would you describe the speaker's situation, and how does she feel about it? "You" in the poem might be a friend or lover. The speaker's situation is uncertain. She intensely dislikes this uncertainty.

9. If you were the editor of this poem, would you suggest any corrections in spelling? Students may suggest corrections of "your's" to "yours" (line 14) and "it's" to "its" (line 20).

"Because I could not stop for Death—"
Text page 364

Objectives

1. To recognize extended metaphor
2. To recognize irony
3. To write an essay of critical commentary

Introducing the Poem

Read the headnote in the text, page 364. You may wish to assign reading of the poem as homework, to be followed by class discussion of the poem and the response questions.

Background on the Poem. The poem depends on an extended metaphor: Death comes for the speaker in a carriage.

Teaching Strategies

Providing for Cultural Differences. You might discuss the ways different cultures personify death—as a "grim reaper," a rider of a black horse, or something else.

Providing for Different Levels of Ability. Discuss the vocabulary and identify the basic metaphor of the poem before reading and discussing the poem in class.

A New American Poetry

Introducing Vocabulary Study. Knowing the meanings of the following words is important to understanding the poem. The italicized words are defined in text notes.

civility	l. 8	*tulle*	l. 16
gossamer	l. 15	cornice	l. 20
tippet	l. 16	surmised	l. 23

Reading the Poem. Have students read the headnote and the poem itself before class. Then read it aloud in class, discuss the response questions, and assign the writing topic on page 365.

Reteaching Alternatives. Dickinson's punctuation is a source of difficulty to some students. Have students listen to the accompanying audiocassette and punctuate the poem as the reader interprets it. Give the students a copy with altered punctuation and go through the poem again, thought unit by thought unit. Or read an entirely different poem which also personifies death, such as James Weldon Johnson's "Go Down Death," or remind students how Poe personified death in "The Masque of the Red Death" (page 228), and then return to Dickinson's poem.

Responding to the Poem   Text page 365
Analyzing the Poem
Identifying Details

1. How many passengers are in Death's carriage? Who are they? There are three passengers: the speaker, Death, and Immortality.

2. As what kind of person is Death *personified*—what are his characteristics? Death is personified as a courteous suitor who kindly stops to take the speaker for a ride in his carriage.

3. What three things do the riders pass in stanza 3? They pass a school where children play, fields of grain, and the setting sun.

4. What is significant about the fact that the carriage passes the sun in stanza 4? How does the temperature now change? The "passing of the sun" suggests both the coming of night and the darkness of death. The temperature now becomes chilly.

5. What has the speaker surmised, or guessed, in the last stanza? The speaker realizes that this is the day of her death and that the "carriage-ride" is her journey to eternity.

Interpreting Meanings

6. Can you paraphrase the first two lines in a way that emphasizes their *irony*? One possibility might be: Because I was too busy to think about death, he kindly came of his own accord.

What word in line 2 tells you unmistakably that the *tone* is ironic? The ironic word is "kindly."

7. In stanza 2, "civility" means politeness, or formal good manners. How does this kind of behavior on the part of both Death and the speaker extend the *irony* of stanza 1? The notion of "civility"—unexpectedly connected with death—extends the irony of the word "kindly" in the first stanza.

8. Of all the things the poet might have had the carriage pass, why do you think she chooses the children and the grain in stanza 3? Student answers will vary. The children and the grain may be held to suggest growth and life.

How can grain be imagined as "gazing"? The stalks of grain, bowed in one direction or another by the wind, may be imagined as heads with eyes that "gaze."

9. Stanza 5 is a riddle in itself. Can you solve it by identifying what the nearly buried house is? The "house" that is a "swelling in the ground" is the tomb, or mausoleum, of the speaker.

10. Some readers think the concluding stanza subtly introduces a *tone* of terror, because the speaker has suddenly realized she will ride on forever, conscious of being dead. Some think that the whole poem is an expression of trust and even triumph. Which group do you agree with, and why? Student answers will vary.

Writing About the Poem
A Critical Response

Commenting on a Critic. Discuss Kazin's comment and students' ideas on what Dickinson meant by the Eternity the horses were going toward in "Because I could not stop for Death—."

Criteria for Evaluating the Assignment. The paragraph offers a reasonable explanation of what *Dickinson* could have meant by the Eternity toward which the horses were going—not the student's personal beliefs about an afterlife.

Emily Dickinson   143

"I never saw a Moor—"

Text page 366

Objective

1. To interpret the speaker's meanings
2. To analyze word choice

Introducing the Poem

Use the text headnote. You might also quote Blaise Pascal, "The heart has its reasons which Reason does not know," and ask students to apply Pascal's words to the poem—particularly the second stanza.

Background on the Poem. Emphasize grasp of Dickinson's theme or message in this poem.

Teaching Strategies

Providing for Cultural Differences. Cultural differences offer no barrier to understanding the poem.

Providing for Different Levels of Ability. Without changing any of the words, rewrite the poem as short prose paragraphs, restoring normal English word order and observing current rules of capitalization and punctuation. Have students read this prose version and then return to the poem.

Introducing Vocabulary Study. Knowing the meaning of the following words is important to understanding the poem. The italicized word is defined in response question 4 on page 367.

| moor | 1. 1 | *checks* | 1. 8 |
| heather | 1. 3 | | |

Reading the Poem. Read and discuss the headnote, poem, and response questions in class, or assign the entire page as homework.

Reteaching Alternatives. See "Providing for Different Levels of Ability."

Responding to the Poem

Text page 366

Analyzing the Poem

Identifying Details

1. What does the speaker say she has never seen in the first stanza? She has never seen either a moor or the sea. By extension, she has never seen heather or waves.

What does she know in spite of this? In spite of this, she can imagine how the heather must look on a moor and how the billows, or waves, look on the ocean.

2. What does the speaker say she has never done in the second stanza? She says she has never spoken with God or visited heaven.

What is she certain of in spite of this? She is certain that heaven exists, and she says she knows the spot "as if the Checks were given."

Interpreting Meanings

3. Do you think Dickinson is professing a belief in heaven based on religious conviction? Or is she celebrating the power of the imagination to confirm what she could not have experienced during her life? Explain. Students will have various responses. Encourage them to express their own opinions. This may be a good time to discuss with students the notion of ambiguity in poetry. A poem's richness is often increased when we consider multiple interpretations. Perhaps Dickinson left the matter open intentionally.

4. "Checks" were colored railway tickets given to passengers to assure the conductor that they were heading in the right direction. Dickinson's editors wanted to change the word to "charts," which was more conventionally poetic. A *chart* is a map. Which way would you be more likely to get to a destination: by riding on a train with your tickets in hand, or by following a map? Students will probably agree that you would be more likely to get to your destination by riding on a train with your tickets in hand.

"Tell all the Truth"

Text page 367

Objectives

1. To paraphrase a line
2. To interpret a metaphor

Introducing the Poem

See "Reading the Poem," below.

Background on the Poem. In lines 3–4 and 5–6 you may wish to restore normal English word order and supply appropriate words for ones Dickinson omits, for comprehension's sake. Note also the **simile** (truth is like lightning) with which Dickinson expresses her message.

Teaching Strategies

Providing for Cultural Differences. The concept is universal.

Providing for Different Levels of Ability. If you provide missing words and restore normal English word order, students should have no difficulty with the poem.

Introducing Vocabulary Study. Important words are discussed in the response questions.

Reading the Poem. Call students' attention to the headnote and first line of the poem. What is their immediate impression of how the line applies to Dickinson's poetry? Return to the same point immediately after reading the entire poem: students' ideas should change to include Dickinson's messages.

Reteaching Alternatives. See above, "Providing for Different Levels of Ability."

Responding to the Poem Text page 367
Analyzing the Poem
Identifying Details

1. **How would you define the word *slant* as it is used in line 1?** Suggestions might include "distorted," "changed," "toned down."

2. **What is "Circuit"? How would you *paraphrase* line 2?** "Circuit" suggests a way that is circuitous or roundabout. Line 2 might be paraphrased: "If you want to be successful, tell the truth in a roundabout way, rather than directly."

3. **In line 3, what is "too bright for our infirm Delight"?** The surprise of truth is too bright.

4. **Lines 5 and 6 provide an example to illustrate the poet's point about truth. As is typical of Dickinson's technique, she omits several words in these lines. How would you rephrase the lines to make a full sentence?** The lines might be paraphrased as follows: "Truth is so bright and dangerous that it may be compared to lightning: just as lightning is less scary when it is explained carefully and kindly to children, so truth is more approachable from a roundabout way."

Interpreting Meanings

5. **The last two lines explain why the truth must be told "slant." What is the reason?** The reason is that truth is so bright that a direct revelation of it would blind all of us.

   How would you define the words *dazzle* and *blind* here? Student answers will vary.

6. **The poet says that Truth is "bright" and that it can "dazzle." What *metaphor* is implied here—what is Truth being compared with?** Truth is being compared to an intensely bright light.

7. **Can you think of some cases where the truth might be told "slant"? How is this different from a lie?** Student answers will vary. They should be able to supply a number of examples from their reading or from everyday experience.

8. **Do you agree with the poet's message? Explain your response to Dickinson's poem.** Student answers will vary. Encourage a lively discussion.

Emily Dickinson 145

"Apparently with no surprise"

Text page 368

Objectives

1. To recognize use of personification
2. To analyze the theme
3. To recognize tone

Introducing the Poem

Discuss the headnote on page 368 and play the poem on the accompanying audiocassette.

Background on the Poem. Remind students of the definitions of tone, theme, and personification.

Teaching Strategies

Providing for Cultural Differences. The nature images are common to all cultures. The reference to God may arouse discussion.

Providing for Different Levels of Ability. If you paraphrase the poem, students should have no difficulty understanding it.

Introducing Vocabulary Study. No words are difficult.

Reading the Poem. Call attention to the headnote, play the audiocassette, or have a student read the poem, and discuss the response questions.

Reteaching Alternatives. See "Providing for Different Levels of Ability," above.

Responding to the Poem Text page 368
Analyzing the Poem
Identifying Details

1. **What happens in the poem?** The power of the frost "beheads" a happy flower and kills it. Meanwhile, the sun—and by implication, God Himself—take no notice of the event.

2. **What word tells how the sun feels about the incident?** The sun is said to proceed "unmoved."

   How does God feel? God is apparently "approving."

Interpreting Meanings

3. **Who *is* the "blonde Assassin"?** The assassin is the frost, called "blonde" because of its whiteness.

4. **Aside from the use of capital letters, how are the flower, the frost, and the sun *personified* in this poem? What kind of person does each seem to be?** The flower is personified as a laughing, happy child, unaware of the danger that threatens it. The frost is called an "assassin," a grim, powerful figure who beheads the flower. The sun is personified as an impersonal, uncaring figure who "proceeds unmoved" in the task of measuring off "another Day."

5. **What do you think is the *theme* of this poem? Is the theme shocking or reassuring? Explain.** Students will have different opinions. In general, the theme is a detached observation of the cyclical, impersonal ways of nature. It may seem odd, or even shocking, that God apparently "approves" the frost's killing of the flowers. Dickinson probably recognizes God as the creator of all things, but she may wonder that He paradoxically allows the destruction of beauty in nature by natural forces.

6. **A *pun* is a play on words with similar meanings. What pun is in line 6? How would you explain it?** The word "unmoved" could mean "motionless" (in the physical sense) or "without feeling" (in an emotional sense).

7. **The speaker describes how she thinks God feels about the flower's beheading. How do you think the speaker feels?** Student answers will vary. Most students will agree that the speaker sympathizes with the flower and regrets the loss of the flower's beauty.

8. **How does the speaker's attitude toward nature in this poem differ from Emerson's attitude in the selection from "Nature" (pages 191–193)?** Emerson focuses on the positive aspects of nature. In this poem, the speaker focuses on its negative, or apparently unresponsive, aspects.

   Which point of view do you favor, and why? Student answers will vary.

146   A New American Poetry

"To make a prairie it takes a clover and one bee"

Text page 369

Objective

1. To interpret the poet's message

Introducing the Poem

Have students look up the word *revery* as suggested in the headnote.

Background on the Poem. Focus on the message of this poem.

Teaching Strategies

Providing for Cultural Differences. The concept is universal.

Providing for Different Levels of Ability. The poem should be accessible to students of all ability levels.

Introducing Vocabulary Study. Knowing the meaning of the word *revery* (*reverie*) is important to understanding the selection.

Reading the Poem. Have students define *revery*, read the poem, and discuss the response questions.

Reteaching Alternatives. Have an able student repeat the class activities with the student who is having difficulty.

Responding to the Poem
Text page 370
Analyzing the Poem
Identifying Details

1. **Scientifically speaking, how could one bee and one clover "make a prairie"?** The notion is that both bees and clover would eventually multiply.

2. **How, if "bees are few," could "revery" accomplish the same thing?** Dickinson seems to be implying a union between the concrete and the abstract. She celebrates the power of the imagination to create one's own universe, and even implies—in the last two lines—that the imagination is so powerful that "revery alone will do."

Interpreting Meanings

3. **What idea or message about the imagination do you think Dickinson wanted to convey in this poem?** Student answers will vary. Most students will agree that Dickinson is emphasizing the almost infinite power of the imagination.

The Poems as a Whole
Text page 370

1. Student answers will vary. Create a chalkboard chart using "success," "failure," "religion," "love," "death," and "imagination" as the headings. Brainstorm for one (or two) of the categories a short list of what students believe Dickinson says about the topic. Then ask students to cite poems supporting their ideas. Continue with general discussion of the remaining topics, noting that while all readers do not agree on Dickinson's meaning, a valid interpretation must be backed by the poet's words.

2. Student answers will vary.

3. Student answers will vary. Brainstorm one or two metaphors and identify the things being compared; then have students continue on their own.

4. Follow the same procedure as for question 3.

5. Students will have to acknowledge that Dickinson does focus on death and immortality, but beyond that, answers will be personal.

Writing About the Poems
A Creative Response

1. **Writing Quatrains.** Discuss the rhyme schemes common in a quatrain (abab, abcb) and list some rhyming words for the Dickinson starter lines suggested in the prompt. Note that students should consider slant rhyme and irregular meter, like Dickinson, to prevent the quatrain's being mechanical.

Criteria for Evaluating the Assignment. The quatrain has a definite pattern of rhyme and meter, but does not sound sing-song or mechanical.

A Critical Response

Discuss all of the critical writing assignments, although you may wish to permit students to select *one* to write.

2. **Analyzing a Poem.** Use the first stanzas of "Tell All the Truth" (page 367) and "I never saw a Moor" (page 366) to demonstrate, respectively, the 8, 6, 8, 6 syllable count (note: *syllables*, not accents) and the 6, 6, 8, 6 count.

Emily Dickinson 147

Allow students to use these poems in their analysis of two poems showing the 8, 6, 8, 6 pattern and at least one poem showing the 6, 6, 8, 6 pattern.

Criteria for Evaluating the Assignment. The essay correctly cites two Dickinson poems employing the 8, 6, 8, 6 count of syllables; and at least one using the 6, 6, 8, 6 pattern.

3. **Analyzing an Edited Version.** "If you were coming in the Fall" is printed here as it was on page 363, but with the changes made by early editors written in. Discuss the effects of these changes before students write the essay.

Criteria for Evaluating the Assignment. The essay offers logical reasons for the editors' changes and describes the effect of the changes on the poem.

4. **Comparing Poems.** Review Bryant's "Thanatopsis" (page 142) and Taylor's "Upon a Spider Catching a Fly" (page 46) and "God's Determinations Touching His Elect" (page 49) in terms of subject matter, message, tone, metaphor, rhythms, and rhymes before students select the Dickinson poems they wish to compare with those of Bryant and Taylor.

Criteria for Evaluating the Assignment. The essay cites examples from the poems of Dickinson, Bryant, and Taylor to support its major points about how the poems are alike and how they differ in terms of subject matter, message, tone, metaphors, rhythms, and rhymes.

Analyzing Language and Style
Diction and Syntax

As students identify each case of rule-breaking, discuss the effects, and also whether or not Dickinson's eccentric punctuation affects the poem's meaning.

1. No examples appear in the poems in the text.
2. Ask students to supply the subject of the verb *feels*, line 22 (page 264).
3. See poems on pages 363 and 368.
4. Perhaps "Heaves" of storms, page 362.
5. Nearly every poem provides examples of nonstandard punctuation.
6. Most poems also provide examples of omission of articles.
7. For example, *Bretheren* on page 360.

Extending the Poems

Students with a dramatic flair may wish to select from Dickinson's collected works a series of poems on a theme of their choice, and present these poems to the class in Reader's Theatre format.

Interesting research topics include further exploration of the influence of the philosophies of Ralph Waldo Emerson and Henry David Thoreau on Dickinson.

Students intrigued with Dickinson's solitary life may wish to read about the poet herself and about three other unmarried women writers of the same general era, the Brontë sisters (Anne, Charlotte, and Emily), and compare their lives in an oral or written report.

Primary Sources: Higginson's Account of Dickinson   Text page 371

If you did not assign this section in conjunction with reading the biography of Dickinson (pages 352–353), assign it now. It further demonstrates Dickinson's personal eccentricities, comments on her handwriting and appearance, and provides first-hand evidence that in 1862, when she was 32, she sought critical evaluation of her work, experienced illness, and as yet possessed no photograph of herself.

Students having now completed the sections on both Whitman and Dickinson, this is an appropriate time to return to Ezra Pound's poem in the unit introduction (page 325) and to write in their journals a second interpretation of Pound's meaning.

Unit Six: The Rise of Realism:
The Civil War and Post-War Period

Teaching the Rise of Realism Unit

The change from romanticism to realism in American fiction was in large part due to historical and social changes. The Civil War, the growth of the railroads, the telegraph, mass immigration, and rapid industrialization all combined, in the latter half of the nineteenth century, to transform the United States from a mostly agrarian, decentralized nation to an urbanized, more centralized one. Transportation and communication brought people into closer contact with the various regions of the country at precisely the same time that regional differences began to fade away. The result was nostalgia, a feeling that expressed itself in fiction as regionalism, or local color.

The hardships of the Civil War and its aftermath, and the grim conditions that prevailed in the burgeoning urban slums, factories, railroad camps, and mines, impressed themselves upon writers who felt that the depiction of this form of human suffering was an important artistic end in itself. The influence of foreign literature was also important in the development of realism in American writing. American Romanticism had followed in the footsteps of its European models, and when European writers turned to realism, Americans, who at that time still represented the "junior" nation, followed suit. Frank Norris studied Emile Zola. Henry James was influenced by Flaubert and Turgenev in his striving toward ever more subtle psychological realism. Stephen Crane and Joseph Conrad, who knew each other in England, strengthened each other in their development of an impressionistic descriptive style. Kipling was another strong influence on Crane, who took his famous "wafer" simile from a line in *The Light That Failed*: "... the sun shone, a blood-red wafer...." And the journalistic, sentimental, comic melodrama of Dickens influenced a whole generation of writers, from Dostoevsky in Russia to Mark Twain and Bret Harte in the United States.

Objectives of the Rise of Realism Unit

1. To increase reading proficiency and expand vocabulary
2. To gain exposure to notable authors of American realism and their works
3. To define and identify elements of nonfiction, fiction, and spirituals
4. To define and identify significant literary techniques: characterization, theme, figures of speech, tone, point of view, style, theme, and humorous devices (hyperbole, exaggeration, irony)
5. To interpret and respond to autobiography, spirituals, stories, and novels, through analysis of their elements
6. To write original works
7. To analyze the use of regional dialect
8. To practice the following critical thinking and writing skills:
    a. Responding to an idea
    b. Comparing and contrasting two forms of literature
    c. Comparing and contrasting two writers
    d. Analyzing the use of euphemism and irony
    e. Comparing and contrasting tone and theme
    f. Analyzing features of impressionistic style
    g. Analyzing inferences and point of view

Introducing the Rise of Realism Unit

The introduction to the unit in the student text can be divided naturally into two sections: a discussion of the Civil War and its effect on American literature (text pages 376–379) and a discussion of realism and regionalism as literary styles contrasted with romanticism (text pages 380–384). It might be fruitful to study Douglass's "The Battle with Mr. Covey" immediately after the first part of the introduction, since its subject, slavery, has a strong historical bearing on the Civil War, and since, as a nonfictional memoir, it doesn't strictly belong to a fiction-oriented typology of realism versus romanticism. After the Douglass piece, you can then go on to finish the introduction, following it up with Harte's "The Outcasts of Poker Flat," a representative work of regionalism.

If your students have already, in their history courses, studied such topics as the Civil War, slavery, Reconstruction, the expansion and settlement of the frontier, and the rise of industrialism and urbanization after the Civil War, encourage them to bring this knowledge to bear on the development of literature, during your discussion of the introduction to this unit.

Frederick Douglass

"The Battle with Mr. Covey"

Text page 385

Text page 386

Objectives

1. To identify elements of humor
2. To analyze character
3. To write an essay applying meanings
4. To write a paragraph responding to an idea
5. To analyze metaphors

Introducing the Autobiography

In outline form, for your reference, here are the major elements of the autobiography:

- **Characters:** Frederick Douglass, a young slave; Covey, a slaveowner to whom Douglass has been "rented" for a year; Thomas, Douglass's owner; Sandy Jenkins, a fellow-slave owned by Thomas
- **Themes:** the indomitable spirit of freedom rising up against slavery; the inner strength that results from asserting oneself against injustice; the degrading influence of slavery upon slaveowners as well as slaves
- **Point of View:** first-person
- **Significant techniques:** narrative combined with thematic exposition; metaphor
- **Setting:** a slaveowner's farm on the eastern shore of Maryland in the 1830's

Background on the Autobiography

Frederick Douglass was far more than a single-issue crusader. His personal sufferings led him to identify with, and fight for, the rights of the downtrodden in many areas of the world. He was a leader of the women's rights movement, and on the day he died, he spoke at a women's rights meeting with Susan B. Anthony. After escaping to the North, he learned about the kinds of discrimination faced by free black people there, and in an early example of nonviolent civil disobedience, he desegregated the trains in New England by refusing to leave the all-white section until physically carried off. During his career as a writer and lecturer he spoke out for world peace, temperance, Irish freedom, repeal of the corn laws that oppressed English farm laborers, free speech, the abolition of capital punishment, and prison reform.

Summary. After passing out from exhaustion while fanning wheat, Douglass is beaten by Covey and given a severe head wound. He flees seven miles to Thomas's farm, but Thomas refuses to give him sanctuary and orders him to return to Covey. Covey treats him decently at first, because it is Sunday when Douglass returns. Later, however, Covey and a hired hand, Hughes, try to beat and tie Douglass, but he fights back, getting the better of them. For the duration of Douglass's stay, Covey treats him cautiously and nonviolently.

Teaching Strategies

Providing for Cultural Differences. Depending on your area, your class may have students whose family histories include the experience of slavery, as well as students whose ancestors were refugees from various kinds of political, economic, or religious persecution. Students can be encouraged to share their knowledge and their feelings about these historical experiences, and should be led to empathize with the ordeals of peoples of all kinds, and to understand that the American ideal is one of freedom and justice for all.

Providing for Different Levels of Ability. This is a forceful, straightforward narrative, but slower students may have a little trouble with vocabulary, as in the word "intimated" in the first sentence. The custom of slaveowners' "renting" slaves to each other will need to be explained at the outset. The episode concerning Sandy Jenkins's "magic" root is clearly enough narrated, but its significance and tone will probably require a bit of discussion.

Introducing Vocabulary Study. Knowing the meanings of the following words is important to understanding the selection. (Starred words appear in the Glossary. Italicized words either are archaic or have special meaning in context.)

intimate (v.)	386	unaccountable	388
epoch*	386	*afforded*	388
feeble*	386	*impressed* (v.)	388
sundry	388	quailed*	389
entreating*	388	expiring	389

Reading the Autobiography. The selection is short enough and vivid enough to be read at one sitting, either at home or in class. Given the nature of the subject matter, it might be best to ask for volunteers, rather than calling on students, if you have it read aloud.

150   The Rise of Realism

Reading Check. You might want to use the following questions as a reading check. Have students respond *True* or *False*.

1. Frederick Douglass did not know how old he was when the battle with Mr. Covey occurred. ___True___
2. His fellow slave, Bill, joined in the beating to which Douglass was subjected. ___False___
3. The slave Sandy Jenkins had a free wife. ___True___
4. After beating Mr. Covey, Douglass was forced to flee for his life, and went immediately north to freedom. ___False___
5. When Douglass fled to Thomas's farm, Thomas gave him yet another beating. ___False___

Reteaching Alternatives. While the battle of slave against master has universal impact, some students may be slow to grasp the historical particulars of Douglass's experience: the renting of a slave by one farmer to another, the belief in magical talismans, and so forth. These can be clarified during class discussion, but you can reassure your students that these details are not the essence of the narrative: Douglass's battle for his own dignity is. You might ask your students to write in-class paragraphs describing how they would feel if they were slaves and were subjected to the kind of treatment Douglass describes.

Responding to the Autobiography

Text page 390

Analyzing the Autobiography

Identifying Facts

1. What action did Douglass take after being struck by Covey? Douglass decided to enter a complaint with his master. Weak and seriously wounded, he walked seven miles to St. Michael's.

What did Thomas advise Douglass to do? Thomas said that he expected that Douglass deserved the beating. He told Douglass to return to Covey, whom he called a "good man," and to cause no more trouble.

2. Explain how Sandy Jenkins helped Douglass. Sandy told Douglass to return to Covey, carrying a certain root from the woods on his right side. The root would protect Douglass against Covey's violence.

3. Describe what Douglass calls the turning point in his life as a slave. Douglass's stout resistance when Covey and Hughes attempted to tie him up evidently inspired Covey's grudging respect. Douglass says that this episode revived in him his own sense of manhood.

Interpreting Meanings

4. Sandy Jenkins's "root" was a talisman, an object invested with supernatural powers. Explain what Douglass discovered that was even more powerful than the root. According to Douglass, his own fighting spirit was more powerful than the root.

What personal *characteristics* would you say impelled Douglass to revolt against Covey? Students will have various answers. Many students will point to Douglass's fierce determination and pride.

5. What elements of humor are found in Douglass's account of Sandy Jenkins's advice? Explain. Douglass recounts with wry humor how Mr. Covey's apparently gentle behavior on Sunday almost convinced him that the root had supernatural powers.

6. What does this passage reveal about Covey's character? Most students will agree that the passage reveals that Covey was a violent bully. Like many bullies, he became cowed when faced with firm resistance.

7. Explain the distinction between being a slave "in form" and a slave "in fact." By a slave "in form," Douglass means his outer, legal designation as a slave. By saying that he was no longer a slave "in fact," he refers to the pride and independence of his inner spirit.

8. Do you think any aspects of Douglass's narrative are relevant to the problem of racism in modern society? Explain. Students will have various answers. Encourage the students to support their opinions with examples and logical reasoning.

Writing About the Autobiography

A Creative Response

1. Applying Meanings. Skim "Self-Reliance" with your students. They may at first see a contradiction between Douglass's behavior and Emerson's "Accept the place the divine Providence has found for you," but through discussion should realize that, overall, Douglass's narrative exemplifies Emerson's principles: a man "must take himself . . . as his portion"; "Trust thyself"; "Society everywhere is in conspiracy against the manhood of every one of its members"; "Whoso would be a man must be a nonconformist."

Criteria for Evaluating the Assignment. By citing examples and quotations from both Douglass and Emerson, the essay briefly demonstrates that Douglass's realizations and actions support Emerson's philosophy.

Frederick Douglass 151

A Critical Response

2. Responding to an Idea. While responses to the quotation from Douglass will be individual, note that students are asked to comment on its implications, how the quotation is true, and how it is not true.

Criteria for Evaluating the Assignment. The paragraph expresses the student's personal response to Douglass's words, explores the implications of the quotation, and suggests at least one way in which it is true and one in which it is not.

Analyzing Language and Style
Metaphors

1. A fading ambition for freedom is compared with the embers of a dying fire; the battle is compared with a flint or spark that rekindles the fire. Any new fire offers warmth and light—a source of rebirth. Fire is also central to the image of the phoenix, said to die on a pyre and rise again from the ashes.

2. The word "arm" personifies slavery as a cruel taskmaster who inflicts death, wounds or pain (the word "bloody").

3. "It was a glorious resurrection, from the tomb of slavery, to the heaven of freedom" (page 389). Slavery is compared with death; freedom is compared with new life in heaven.

Extending the Autobiography

Several of the writers in previous units have espoused or exemplified freedom, but Douglass is the only one who was actually a slave. Jefferson, in fact, was a slaveowner. Ask your students how they think Douglass would respond to the writings and lives of Bradford, Byrd, Jefferson, Paine, Franklin, Emerson, Thoreau, or Whitman, and how those writers would respond to him. A panel discussion or student-created dramatic sketch might be appropriate.

Spirituals and "Code" Songs

Text page 391

Objectives

1. To write an original stanza resulting from an oral folk tradition
2. To analyze allusions
3. To write an essay comparing the spirituals with the Puritans' writings
4. To write a paragraph describing code songs

Background on the Songs. While Douglass, in the passage on text page 391, emphasizes the melancholy nature of the slaves' songs, another great black leader, W. E. B. Du Bois, while calling them "sorrow songs," thought that they always contained an element of hope that transcended the sorrow: "Through all the sorrow of the Sorrow Songs there breathes... a faith in the ultimate justice of things.... Sometimes it is faith in life, sometimes a faith in death, sometimes assurances of boundless justice in some fair world beyond. But whichever it is, the meaning is always clear: that sometime, somewhere, men will judge men by their souls and not by their skins."

Summary. "*Go Down Moses*": The song retells the story of Moses leading the Hebrews out of Slavery in Egypt. It calls on Moses to "go down" to Egypt and to tell Pharaoh, "Let my people go." "*Follow the Drinking Gourd*": This code song gives directions for escape along a river bank, and tells the listener, "For the old man is a-waiting for to carry you to freedom / If you follow the drinking gourd."

Teaching Strategies

Providing for Cultural Differences. Students may vary in their degree of previous acquaintance with this type of song, and the variation may not be entirely along racial lines. Many spirituals have entered the general heritage of American culture, and some students may be familiar with them as folk songs performed in modern versions. If some of your students have recordings of these or other spirituals at home, you might play them for the class. Some students may be more familiar than others with the Biblical story of Moses, and may be able to clarify it for the rest of the class.

Providing for Different Levels of Ability. The line, "Left foot, peg foot, traveling on" is possibly the most obscure in the two songs. Some folk versions, such as the Weavers's, include an introduction explaining that a peg-legged sailor was supposedly walking along a levee near the fields, singing this song, and that his "peg-foot" left a trail for the slaves to follow. In most respects, though, the songs are clear and straightforward.

Reading the Songs. As the word "songs" implies, these

152   The Rise of Realism

pieces of folk poetry are best appreciated when set to music. Instruments are not necessary, though—they were intended to be sung by unaccompanied voice. There is an accompanying audiocassette selection for "Go Down, Moses." Encourage your students to bring in recordings of these or other spirituals or songs of slavery; your school library may have some as well.

Reteaching Alternatives. The major problem some students may have with these songs is that the lyrics have double meanings. You might ask them to draw a line down the middle of a sheet of paper and paraphrase the songs' literal meaning on one side, their "code" meaning on the other. This can also be done on the chalkboard.

Responding to the Songs   Text page 392

The assignments are interrelated. It would help if you provided copies of the three spirituals listed in assignment 3 before students begin any of the assignments. They will also need Bibles or copies of Exodus 1–14, 2 Kings 2, and Joshua 2. Assignments 1 and 3 require prior discussion of assignments 2, 4, and 5.

Writing About the Songs
A Creative Response

1. Writing a Stanza. After students have analyzed codes as explained in assignment 5, they should write a stanza that echoes the pattern of the song and continues or supplements the directions given in its existing stanzas.

Criteria for Evaluating the Assignment. The four-line stanza uses "Follow the drinking gourd" as the fourth line, fits the meter of the original, and gives directions that follow or fit between the directions already given.

A Critical Response

2. Analyzing Allusions. Allusions not mentioned in the writing prompt are "Israel" and "smite your first-born dead." "Israel" was the alternate name of Jacob, whose twelve sons fathered the twelve Hebrew tribes; by extension it means the entire Hebrew people. "Smite" alludes to ten plagues God inflicts on the hardhearted Egyptians so they will release Israel. The tenth plague is the death of every Egyptian's first-born child (Exodus 11:1–10 and 12:29–30).

Criteria for Evaluating the Assignment. The essay identifies allusions to Israel and the plagues, and explains the parallels a slave would have seen between Moses and a rescuer, Pharaoh and endorsers of slavery, and Egypt and slave-owning states.

3. Reporting on Other Spirituals. You may wish to give students the Biblical chapters containing the allusions, allowing them to focus on interpretation: (a) When Pharaoh's army pursues the Israelites, the Red Sea closes upon and drowns them (Exodus 14:23–31). (b) The prophet Elijah ascends to heaven in a flaming chariot shortly after parting the Jordan (2 Kings 2: 7–11). (c) After the death of Moses, the Israelites cross the parted Jordan and enter the Promised Land, led by Joshua (Joshua 3).

Criteria for Evaluating the Assignment. The essay explains the Biblical allusions and interprets them in a manner consistent with slaves' experiences.

4. Comparing the Spirituals to the Puritans's Writings. You may wish to guide students especially to William Bradford's history (pages 13–20) and Mary Rowlandson's account of her captivity (pages 24–29).

Criteria for Evaluating the Assignment. The essay cites similarities between any two spirituals and the writing of one Puritan writer in use of Biblical narratives and images as "types" of human experiences.

5. Analyzing a Code Song. Review "Follow the Drinking Gourd" in terms of searching for codes.

Criteria for Evaluating the Assignment. The paragraph cites repeated references to "the old man" (an underground railroad guide), and lines about following the riverbank (line 9), passing dead trees (line 10), coming to the end of a river between two hills (line 13), and reaching the confluence of a small river and a larger one (line 16).

Extending the Songs

Douglass compared the slaves' songs with those of the oppressed Irish of his day; others have compared their soulful quality to the music of Russian serfs before their emancipation in 1862, or to Yiddish music of the ghettoes of Europe. There are also interesting similarities and differences between American slavery, and other forms of servitude and oppression in other parts of the world and other eras. Some of your students may be interested in reporting on such institutions as South American peonage, Russian serfdom, feudal European peasanthood, ancient Greek and Roman slavery, and the like.

Spirituals and "Code Songs"   153

Bret Harte

"The Outcasts of Poker Flat"

Objectives

1. To state the theme
2. To write a paragraph identifying actors for an imaginary film
3. To write a report comparing two writers's characters and themes
4. To analyze the use of euphemism and irony

Introducing the Story

In outline form, for your reference, here are the major elements of the story:

- **Characters:** Oakhurst, a gambler; "The Duchess," "Mother Shipton," and Uncle Billy, deportees from the town of Poker Flat; Tom Simson and Piney Woods, a pair of innocent young lovers
- **Conflicts:** people vs. nature, conventional morality vs. inner goodness
- **Point of view:** third-person, omniscient
- **Significant techniques:** euphemistic humor, comic irony, sentimentalism
- **Setting:** California, November and December 1850

Background on the Story. Harte was one of the earliest in a long tradition of American newspapermen-turned-fiction-writers, which continued with Twain, Crane, Hemingway, and John O'Hara. This constituted a parallel literary tradition to the more genteel, philosophical New England tradition that produced Hawthorne and the Transcendentalists. Newspapers carried reports from the frontier back to the cities, and writers such as Harte, aiming at a predominantly male audience, told stories that were considered racy at the time. The use of dialect was favored for its air of authenticity. The exaggeration of the glories of the Old West in these tales was a significant force in the history of the United States, for many a settler from back East was drawn West by the ringing words of newspaper reports and "dime store novels."

The Plot. The law-abiding citizens of Poker Flat cast out a group of people whom they consider immoral. Making camp in the mountains, the outcasts are joined by a pair of innocent young lovers. Then Uncle Billy steals the mules and leaves camp, and the remaining characters are trapped by a snowstorm, which directly or indirectly kills all of them except Tom Simson, who went to get help.

Teaching Strategies

Providing for Cultural Differences. Most students' ideas about the Old West will have been formed from watching Western movies, but in many cases these are not less realistic than Harte's story. Students who are themselves from Old West backgrounds may be able to provide bits of local or family history that may help illuminate Harte's subject from a different angle. Female students may be somewhat troubled by Harte's use of stereotypes such as the prostitute with the heart of gold and the comically innocent young backwoods bride. Remind them that this story was written a long time ago and that its portrayals of the good side of "fallen" women actually seemed forward-thinking for its day.

Providing for Different Levels of Ability. Harte's use of euphemistic humor makes careful vocabulary study important. Students who have trouble with the story's antiquated diction might also be helped if they have a brief synopsis of the plot to refer to. The actual incidents of the plot, and the characters are vividly and schematically drawn. You might want to make a list of the major characters on the chalkboard, and have your students, in discussion, provide brief descriptions of the characters' traits.

Introducing Vocabulary Study. Knowing the meanings of the following words is important to understanding the selection. (Starred words appear in the Glossary. Italicized words either are archaic or have special meaning in context.)

ominous	394	maudlin	396
predisposing	394	impassiveness*	396
conjecture*	394	recumbent	396
spasm	394	equanimity	396
impropriety*	394	comely	397
reimbursing	395	dissuade*	397
equity	395	amicable	397
expatriated	395	sylvan	397
cavalcade	395	jocular	397
coquetry	396	unaffectedly	397
anathema	396	felonious	397
regenerating	396	hypothesis*	398
temperate	396	extemporize	398
prescience	396	*beguiled*	398
bellicose	396	abated*	398

Text page 393

Text page 394

154 The Rise of Realism

debarred	398	replenish	399
vociferation	398	querulously	399
sententiously	398	rend (v.)	400
commiseration	399	asunder	400
malediction	399	travail*	400
vituperative	399		

Reading the Story. The difficult vocabulary and arch, sentimental tone of this story might make it difficult for students to read out loud in a convincing tone. You might want to assign the story as homework, then go over it in class, scene by scene, stopping at points where student questions arise.

Reading Check. You might want to use the following questions as a reading check. Have students respond *True* or *False*.

1. Oakhurst, the gambler, is the only member of the group who survives the snowstorm. _False_
2. Tom Simsom runs away with the mules, leaving his sweetheart behind. _False_
3. The narrator calls Mother Shipton "the strongest and yet the weakest of the outcasts of Poker Flat." _False_
4. Oakhurst once returned to Tom some money he had won from him in a card game. _True_
5. Uncle Billy was run out of Poker Flat on suspicion of stealing gold ore. _True_

Reteaching Alternatives. Class discussion will probably help clear up any remaining questions about plot and character, but students may still have reservations about Harte's style, tone, and themes. You might point out that this story is essentially a precursor of the more realistic works of Twain and Crane. One way of assessing the story might be to have each student draw up a list of what aspects of the story are realistic and what aspects are not; the students's individual reactions can then be compared and refined. This process can also be done on the chalkboard.

Responding to the Story
Text page 400
Analyzing the Story
Identifying Facts

1. Who are the outcasts of Poker Flat? The outcasts are Oakhurst (a gambler), the "Duchess," Mother Shipton, and Uncle Billy (a suspected robber and a drunkard).

2. Why are Oakhurst and the others forced to leave town? They are all targets of the town's determination to exile all "improper persons."

3. Who are Tom Simson and Piney Woods, and where are they going? Tom Simson and Piney Woods are young fiances who have eloped together from Sandy Bar. They are on their way to Poker Flat.

Why is Tom so glad to run into Oakhurst? Tom thinks of Oakhurst as a friend because Oakhurst had returned the money that Tom had lost to him in a card game. He thinks the meeting is lucky because he and Piney, tired out from their journey, can make camp and rest with good company.

4. What *complications* result to make the characters' problem difficult to resolve? Uncle Billy steals the mules, leaving the characters stranded. A heavy snowstorm traps the travelers in the valley. Food and fuel become increasingly more scarce.

5. What has happened to each character by the story's end? Which two might still be alive? Mother Shipton grows ill and dies. The Duchess and Piney Woods perish in the cold. Oakhurst commits suicide with his pistol. Uncle Billy and Tom may still be alive.

Interpreting Meanings

6. When Piney first reveals herself to the group, Oakhurst has a vague idea that the situation is not "fortunate." What might be unfortunate about having Piney and Tom join them? Oakhurst has a premonition that the company may be in for hard times. Apparently, he fears that the two innocent young people may have to share the hardships of the others.

What is Uncle Billy's reaction? Uncle Billy cynically guffaws when Tom makes the innocent mistake of referring to the Duchess as Mrs. Oakhurst.

7. Why doesn't Oakhurst want Piney and Tom to know what Uncle Billy has done? He may be afraid that they will panic.

8. How does each of the outcasts—except for Uncle Billy—change in the course of the story? What causes the changes? The pressure of hardship brings out generosity and self-sacrifice in each of the characters, who were previously cynical and hard-boiled.

What early cues *foreshadow* the fact that Billy might be the one character not to undergo a change? Uncle Billy's alcoholism and cynical attitude toward the innocent young lovers foreshadow that he may not undergo a change.

9. Why does Oakhurst leave the camp with Tom? Oakhurst pretends that he is going only as far as the canyon to see Tom off on the latter's desperate mission to get help. Actually, Oakhurst sees that the situation is hopeless: he is going to the head of the gulch to commit suicide, apart from the others.

In what ways is he the strongest of the outcasts? In what way might he be considered the weakest? Oakhurst organizes the camp and exercises leadership among the outcasts. He is protective toward Tom and Piney Woods, and he conceals Uncle Billy's theft of the mules from them so that they will not panic. On the other hand, Oakhurst yields to despair at the end of the story and commits suicide.

10. What does this story reveal about the power of innocence? Do you find what it says believable? The story shows that the innocence of Tom and Piney Woods had the effect of keeping up the other characters's spirits and of inspiring them to become generous and self-sacrificing. Students will differ on whether or not they think this result is believable.

11. How would you state the *theme* of this story? Do you think the story is strongly moralistic? Explain. One statement of the theme might be: Under the pressure of hardship, even people whom the world at large condemns as "evil" or "improper" can show themselves as generous and humane. The story is certainly somewhat moralistic. Encourage students to discuss the ways in which Harte blends irony, humor, and local color with moralism in the tale.

12. If this story were being told by a contemporary realist, how do you think it might change? A contemporary realist might change some or all of the following: the innocence and purity of the young lovers's relationship; the dramatic changes of heart in the Duchess and Mother Shipton; the descriptions of nature and of the snowstorms; and the melodramatic epitaph of Oakhurst. Encourage students to discuss what form these changes might take.

13. How do you feel about Harte's depiction of the women characters in this story? Can you find any attitudes toward the women that might be labeled sexist today? Student answers will vary. Encourage the students to discuss how they would define "sexism," and then ask them to examine the story for applications of this definition.

Writing About the Story
A Creative Response

1. Casting a Film. You might list the characters on the chalkboard and brainstorm lists of actors for each part.

Criteria for Evaluating the Assignment. The essay consists of one paragraph per character, each paragraph offering reasons for choice of actor that show a grasp of key character traits.

A Critical Response

2. Comparing Depictions of the Frontier. Students may already be familiar with Clark's *The Ox-Bow Incident* and with Schaefer's *Shane*, Western classics. Your librarian may be able to recommend specific works by Johnson and the prolific L'Amour.

Criteria for Evaluating the Assignment. The report analyzes the realism or romanticism with which the writer depicts western themes and characters, and explains whether the work is more or less realistic than Harte's.

Analyzing Language and Style
Euphemisms and Comic Irony

1. **a.** The hanged women had made a career of an "improper" line of work.
   b. They were prostitutes.
2. **a.** It means to form or grow again. In a context such as this, it usually refers to spiritual renewal.
   b. He uses *regenerating* ironically to mean a spurious, hypocritical type of moral rebirth.
3. **a.** A respectable career in law, medicine, or the like.
   b. He is a gambler.
4. **a.** In morality and in the physical strength of youth.
   b. The "angels" are the prostitutes.
5. **a.** The women are making the cabin habitable.
   b. Her experience would be with bordellos, usually considered gaudy and extremely tasteless in decor.
6. **a.** Rouge on the Duchess's cheeks.
   b. Prostitutes used make-up at the time, but "virtuous" women did not.

Extending the Story

Harte's fiction looks backward to Dickens and forward to Twain and Crane. From Dickens, Harte learned a sentimental style of melodrama, leavened by polysyllabic humor, and using eccentric characters who represented fairly specific points on the Victorian moral spectrum. Harte did this, however, without Dickens's verbal and psychological genius. From Harte, the later American realists learned an appreciation of the value of stark incident and realistic local detail. Your more advanced students, for purposes of comparison, might be interested in reading Stephen Crane's two best Western stories, "The Blue Hotel" and "The Bride Comes to Yellow Sky."

Mark Twain

Text page 402

From *Life on the Mississippi*

Text page 404

Objectives

1. To analyze irony
2. To analyze the devices of hyperbole, digression, metaphor, incongruity, and boast
3. To write an exaggerated boast
4. To rewrite regional dialect into standard English

Introducing the Story

In outline form, for your reference, here are the major elements of the selection:

- **Characters:** Huck Finn, Jim, and a group of raftsmen on the Mississippi
- **Conflicts:** boast vs. actuality, fantasy vs. reality, exterior roughness vs. inner decency, fear vs. bravery
- **Point of view:** first-person narrative of Huck Finn, framed by first-person introduction and conclusion in Twain's own voice
- **Significant techniques:** dialect, hyperbole, comic metaphor, incongruity, boasts, digression
- **Setting:** the Mississippi River, just south of Cairo, Illinois, before the Civil War

Background on the Story. Twain worked on *Life on the Mississippi* and *Huckleberry Finn* concurrently, and his notes for the two books overlapped. Indeed, after finishing both, Twain at one time contemplated a sequel in which Huck would become a cabin boy on a Mississippi steamboat.

Twain's books were published on the subscription system, rather than being sold in bookstores and published by the usual trade publishing houses. Traveling salesmen for the subscription publishing company went from door to door, usually in rural areas, selling subscriptions to the book before it came out. The audience for subscription books demanded massive volumes for their money, which explains why *Life on the Mississippi* is padded, not only with an excerpt from one of Twain's other books, but with quotations from earlier travel writers.

The subscription sales for *Life on the Mississippi* were disappointing, but nevertheless the book was the fruit of the greatest creative period of Twain's life.

The Plot. Twain begins by describing the raftsmen and their times in his own words, then introduces a chapter from *Huckleberry Finn* in which Jim sends Huck, at night, to swim over to a raft so he can overhear the raftsmen talking, and thus find out how close they are to Cairo. Huck doesn't find that information, but overhears the raftsmen boasting, fighting, and telling a ghost story. The raftsmen discover and threaten him, but let him go after he talks his way winningly out of the jam.

Teaching Strategies

Providing for Cultural Differences. The amount of explanation you may have to give about the way of life on the Mississippi River will probably vary depending on your region of the country. In the final analysis, of course, all regions of America today are very distant from the antebellum era on the Mississippi. Female students may have more trouble with this selection than male students, since it is very much a boyish adventure episode. You might point out that even in comparison to the life of the average American boy on the Mississippi in the early 1800's, Huck's adventures are an exaggeration, a heightening of reality, rather than a documentation. And it is not difficult to imagine a girl participating in adventures similar to Huck's. (A modern work showing a girl of the 1800's crossing the country with a pet wolf is *The Journey of Natty Gann*.)

Providing for Different Levels of Ability. The historical matter at the beginning of the chapter may be a bit heavy for some students. It can be readily synopsized, the crucial paragraphs being the ones that directly describe the river trade and the boatmen. In the excerpt from *Huckleberry Finn*, the events themselves are quite vivid, but the use of dialect, and some padding, may put a veil between the action and the reader. It will probably be necessary to paraphrase the dialect into standard English to at least some extent, for at least some students, even though a bit of flavor will be lost.

Introducing Vocabulary Study. Knowing the meanings of the following words is important to understanding the selection. (Starred words appear in the Glossary. Italicized words either are archaic or have special meaning in context.)

prodigal	404	row*	407
magnanimous	404	meridians	407
stoicism*	404	*breakdown*	409
dismal*	405		

Reading the Story. The raftsmen's boasts, from the bottom of page 405 through the first paragraph on page 408 in the text, cry out for oral reading, and the surrounding passages describing the fight can be read out loud too. The ghost story, pages 409–411, has some effective and humorous moments, but it may be too long, and too thick with dialect, to be profitably read out loud in its entirety by present-day students. After having the class read the story on their own, you might choose specific passages (such as the comparison of Mississippi and Ohio River waters, from the bottom of page 408 to the top of page 409), for oral repetition.

Reading Check. You might use the following questions as a reading check. Have students respond *True* or *False*.

1. The rafts Twain is describing were a kind of steamboat. False
2. Huck and Jim swam together from their own raft to the boatmen's raft. False
3. Dick Allbright felt that he was pursued by a haunted barrel. True
4. The winner of the fight was the man called Little Davy. True
5. The raftsmen made Huck clean their deck before letting him go. False

Reteaching Alternatives. Extensive paraphrasing will probably be necessary for the central portions of this selection. It would probably be best to divide the class into small groups and have each group paraphrase a portion. The selection breaks naturally into separate units: the introduction in Twain's voice; then Huck's eavesdropping on the boasts and the fight; then the raftsmen's recreations, including singing and conversation, leading up to the ghost story, which can be divided into two or three parts; then the raftsmen's discovery of Huck.

Responding to the Story   Text page 413
Analyzing the Story
Identifying Facts

1. What is Twain's purpose in presenting a chapter from his work in progress? He wants to illustrate "keelboat talk and manners" for his readers.

2. Explain why Huck Finn swims to the huge raft. Describe what he observes when he climbs aboard. Huck and Jim are bound for Cairo, but a fog causes them to pass the city on the river. Huck hopes to eavesdrop on the men's conversation in order to find out their true location. When he climbs aboard, Huck sees from his hiding place a collection of rough men, singing and drinking. The men are fierce-looking and vie with each other in profanity and boasting.

3. Describe how the keelboatmen seem to pass their time. They sing, drink, curse, and tell stories.

Interpreting Meanings

4. List the words Twain uses to describe the keelboatmen in the opening passage of this selection. How is this litany like Whitman's *catalogue* style? (See page 326.) Among the adjectives Twain uses to describe the keelboatmen are the following: rude, uneducated, brave, stoic, coarse, reckless, foul-witted, profane, prodigal, bankrupt, honest, trustworthy, faithful, and magnanimous. The men were heavy drinkers, fighters, and braggarts. This passage resembles Walt Whitman's catalogue style in that it contains a list of vivid, contrasting qualities.

5. In ancient epics and romances, the heroes had supernatural powers and were often identified with forces of nature. Find the *images* and details in the boasts of Bob and the Child of Calamity that show they are the backwoods equivalents of these heroes. Bob claims that he was "sired by a hurricane" and "dam'd (mothered) by an earthquake." He says his relations are diseases (cholera and smallpox), and that he eats alligators and drinks a barrel of whiskey for breakfast. His voice and his glance split the rocks and drown out the thunder, and he drinks blood. The Child of Calamity tries to outdo Bob by bragging that he is superior to the cosmic forces of lightning, thunder, cloud, storm, and ocean. The outlandish hyperbole of the boasts of simple keelboatmen, when compared with the vaunting of mythological heroes, is a source of comic irony.

6. What supernatural elements are in the story of Dick Allbright and the baby? The lightning plays around the barrel as it floats nearby. The appearances of the barrel seem to cause the crewmen to sprain their ankles. Dick Allbright claims that the barrel has been chasing him since he accidentally choked his child, and that every time it appears four men die. At the end of the tale, Allbright jumps overboard with the dead baby in the barrel and is never seen again.

How does this combine "gallows humor" (morbid humor) and pathos? The motifs of Allbright's love for the baby and of its accidental death are pathetic. But the story is dominated by gallows humor, in which the corpse of the dead baby becomes a curse that demands expiation through the deaths of others.

7. In the *Odyssey*, Homer's epic, Odysseus is a prototype of the cunning hero, one who often escapes from tight or dangerous situations by using his wits rather than brute force. Odysseus has been called the master "artificer," meaning that he is a skilled liar. Explain how this boy narrator is also a master "artificer." Huck wins Davy's sympathy by bursting into tears when he is discovered. Then he pretends he has only been on board for a quarter of a minute. The men roar with laughter when Huck tells them that his real name is Charles William Allbright. He then pretends that his name is Aleck Hopkins

158   The Rise of Realism

and that he is bearing a message from his father on a trading-scow. Although the men do not believe him, they good-naturedly let him go, making him promise that he will keep out of scrapes in the future.

8. How would you describe the *characters* of the keelboatmen? Are such character types evident in any occupation in American life today? Explain. Student answers will vary. Ask them to explain their answers with specific examples.

Writing About the Story
A Creative Response

1. Writing an Exaggerated Boast. A review of page 407 and a look ahead to page 510 (Davy Crockett) should establish the idea. You might also brainstorm a list of *types* of braggarts—he-men, scholars, artists, politicians, etc.

Criteria for Evaluating the Assignment. The elements of the paragraph—name, metaphors, humor, claims—work together to create a consistent whole.

2. Rewriting Dialect. Suitable exchanges begin to appear on page 405. Call students' attention to the fact that they are also to comment on what is lost when standard English is substituted in the specific context.

Criteria for Evaluating the Assignment. The selection is accurately rendered in standard English, and the student comments on the resultant loss of liveliness, verve, immediacy, or realism.

Analyzing Language and Style
Dialect and Frontier Humor

1. The assignment is to find five examples each of variation from standard English in (1) vocabulary, (2) pronunciation, and (3) grammar. Answers will vary.

2. These are *hyperbole, metaphors, incongruity, boasts,* and *digressions.* Answers will vary. You might however, suggest starting with the shouting match on page 407.

3. All are used, but *metaphor* and *hyperbole* stand out.

4. Students should be able to come up with many examples of hyperbole, incongruity, and digressions, but may have a harder time finding current examples of metaphor and boasts.

Extending the Story

Interested students should be encouraged to read the rest of the book on their own. The first thirty-one chapters, in particular, are generally considered the high point of *Life on the Mississippi*, containing Twain's classic descriptions of river commerce and steamboat piloting; the later chapters tend to be somewhat padded.

From *The Adventures of Huckleberry Finn*

Text page 414

Objectives

1. To evaluate images and figures of speech
2. To evaluate the use of comic tone
3. To write a paragraph imitating a writer's technique
4. To write a journal entry
5. To write an essay responding to a critic
6. To write an essay analyzing the selection
7. To write an essay evaluating voice
8. To analyze descriptive language

Introducing the Story

In outline form, for your reference, here are the major elements of the selection:

- **Characters:** Huck Finn, the narrator, a fourteen-year-old boy; Pap, his abusive, alcoholic father; Jim, a runaway slave
- **Conflicts:** the individual vs. authority, personal morality vs. social morality, freedom vs. confinement
- **Theme:** the emotional and moral development of a youth into an adult through a series of ordeals that test his ingenuity and spirit
- **Significant techniques:** "voice," dialect, comic irony, colloquial lyricism
- **Point of view:** first-person, major character
- **Setting:** the Mississippi River and environs, 1845

Background on the Story. Twain worked on his masterpiece for six years or more, on and off. His philosophy of composition, for all his books, was to work on a project when he was inspired and to set it aside when inspiration flagged. In the summer of 1883, he experienced the greatest creative surge of his life. He finished a draft of *Huckleberry*

Finn and began revising it. "This summer it is no more trouble for me to write than it is to lie," he told his mother. At the same time he was working on another book, which never panned out, and several of his characteristic, wrongheaded business schemes, among which was a game, "Mark Twain's Memory-Builder," which was similar to today's "Trivial Pursuit."

Although Twain was a world-famous writer and lecturer at the time, the pre-publication outlook for the book was gloomy, because of bad planning, bad luck, and generally hard economic conditions. During the first month after publication, there was little critical response of any kind, and what there was was often negative: the genteel establishment was offended by the book's gritty, vernacular realism. What propelled the book toward success, in fact, was further negative reaction: the Concord, Massachusetts public library banned the book from its shelves. Louisa May Alcott said, "If Mr. Clemens cannot think of something better to tell our pureminded lads and lasses, he had best stop writing for them." The resulting publicity turned the book's fortunes around. Twain wrote to his publisher: "They have expelled Huck from their library as 'trash and suitable only for the slums.' That will sell 25,000 copies for us sure."

The Plot. Pap returns to Huck's room one night in search of the money he heard Huck received. He abuses Huck verbally and physically, and later we see Pap, whom a new judge had tried to reform, lapse into delirium tremens. Huck decides to run away, and covers his trail with pig's blood and other signs of violence so people will think he has been killed. He escapes to Jackson's Island, where he encounters the runaway slave Jim, and promises not to turn him in.

Teaching Strategies

Providing for Cultural Differences. The obviously sensitive area here is that of race. The spelling-out of Jim's dialect may be something of a problem: while it's true that Twain carefully records several different dialects, black and white, in the book, it's also true that the black dialect is made to seem substantially thicker. And Jim's reaction to what he thinks is Huck's "ghost" is an unfortunate piece of stereotypical humor. Nevertheless, Twain depicts Jim, for the most part, as an intelligent, level-headed, and dignified human being, and the book as a whole is a sustained argument against prejudice and inhumanity. It is not a platitude to say that Twain, as an individual and a writer, was essentially fair-minded and decent, and that the elements of racism that we detect, a century later, were vestiges of the times he was brought up in.

Providing for Different Levels of Ability. Less advanced students may have some trouble with the dialect, and also with the rather dense descriptive detail concerning Huck's escape. You might want to introduce each section with a brief paraphrase so the students will recognize the "landmarks" as they come to them. If students find particular passages to be stumbling blocks, you might have them read the passages out loud and work out their own paraphrases, assisted by other students in discussion where necessary.

Introducing Vocabulary Study. Knowing the meanings of the following words is important to understanding the selection. (Starred words appear in the Glossary.)

stanchion*	416	quicksilver	423
skiff	418	brash*	425
whetstone	422		

Reading the Story. The accompanying audiocassette for "Pap starts in on a New Life" provides a good way of accustoming your students to the "sound" and "feel" of Huck's colloquial first-person narration. It might be a good idea to play this for your class on the first day you study the selection, even if they have already read it at home. Depending on time constraints, you may or may not want to ask your class to read other portions out loud as well.

Reading Check. You may want to use the following questions as a reading check. Have students respond *True* or *False*.

1. Huck's father returned in order to give Huck money. ___False___
2. Judge Thatcher took Huck away from Pap and gave him to a guardian. ___True___
3. When Pap got drunk, he usually started to complain about the government. ___True___
4. As part of his deception, Huck bashed the door of his cabin with an axe. ___True___
5. Huck acquired his name because he survived mainly on huckleberries while on Jackson's Island. ___False___

Reteaching Alternatives. Because of the thick nineteenth-century colloquialism of the narrative, some students might not be able to make the imaginative leap toward feeling the true horror of Huck's home situation. You might ask them to write brief descriptions of Pap, and to list the things he does to Huck after returning to Huck's dwelling.

If some students are confused as to why Jim is so frightened of Huck, remind them that Jim is a fugitive slave and subject to the death penalty.

Responding to the Story   Text page 428
Analyzing the Story
Identifying Facts

1. **In the opening scene, explain what Huck's father wants. Why does he abduct Huck?** Huck's father wants him to stop attending school. He abducts Huck in order to ensure that he can control him.

160 The Rise of Realism

2. Describe how Pap treats Huck at the old cabin. Pap locks up the boy and leaves him alone for long periods.

What are Huck's mixed feelings about life with Pap and the widow at this point in the story? On the one hand, Huck is relieved not to have to go to school and to be subject to the widow's discipline. He likes being messy, lazy, and jolly, fishing and smoking. On the other hand, Huck is often lonely and terrified of his father, who often beats him in his drunken rages.

3. Describe the strategy Huck devises to escape from Pap. Huck fools Pap by sawing through a log in the cabin and crawling through the hole to liberty. He collects all the goods that are worth taking from the cabin and carries them to a canoe that he has found and hidden on the river. He shoots a wild pig and uses its blood to stage a "murder scene," so that Pap and others will believe that Huck has been killed; he also creates a false trail with a sack of meal, so that those who hunt for the robbers will be misled.

Where does Huck hide from his pursuers? He hides on Jackson's Island.

4. What had brought Jim to the island? Jim is hiding there as a runaway slave.

Explain what it is that Huck promises Jim. Huck promises Jim that he will not betray his whereabouts.

Interpreting Meanings

5. What do the *images* and *figures of speech* used to describe Pap in the passage beginning "He was almost fifty" on page 414 reveal about Huck's feelings for his father? How would you *characterize* Pap? Among the images and figures of speech that Huck uses to describe Pap are the following: his long greasy hair, his shining eyes, the comparison of his paleness to a tree-toad and a fish-belly, his ragged clothes, his two toes sticking through a boot, and his old slouch hat, which resembles a lid. The language reveals that Huck feels disgust for his father's appearance. Students will generally agree that Pap looks and behaves like a cruel, dissolute character.

6. What is *ironic* about the episode involving Pap and the new judge? The new judge believes that he can make a man of Pap and reform him. He gives Pap new clothes, feeds him, lodges him in his own house, and lectures him on temperance. In an emotional scene, Pap promises that he will turn over a new leaf. That night, however, Pap escapes from his room, trades his new coat for some liquor, and gets "drunk as a fiddler." The new judge says that he reckons that the only way Pap can be reformed is with a shotgun.

What is *ironic* about the title "Pap Starts in on a New Life"? Pap's "change of heart" lasts for barely a day, rather than a lifetime.

7. As Huck tells us about his first few days on the island, his language blends the colloquial with the poetic. From the way he describes the river, woods, and sky, in this and other passages, how do you think Huck feels about his natural surroundings? What details support your interpretation? Student answers will vary. On the one hand, Huck is practical and observant, cleverly evading his pursuers. On the other hand, he uses a variety of poetic phrases to describe his surroundings. Some of the phrases that students may single out include: "Everything was dead quiet, and it looked late, and it *smelt* late;" "The sky looks ever so deep when you lay down on your back in the moonshine; I never knowed it before;" "There was freckled places on the ground where the light sifted down through the leaves...." One especially evocative passage blends sensory details and the hint that Huck is lonesome: "... and so I went and set on the bank and listened to the current swashing along, and counted the stars and drift-logs and rafts that came down, and then went to bed; there ain't no better way to put in time when you are lonesome; you can't say so, you soon get over it."

8. From what you have seen so far, how do Huck's first days on the river contrast with the life he knew with the widow and with Pap? Although Huck is forced to rely entirely on himself, he is now free and uninhibited, either by the widow's efforts to educate him or by Pap's cruelty. His clever strategies to conceal himself and avoid discovery mingle with his wonder at nature to establish an exciting, optimistic tone.

9. Explain how this part of the novel *symbolically* describes Huck's "death" and subsequent "rebirth." In being "reborn," what "bonds" or "chains" has he thrown off? Huck's simulation of his own death is readily apparent in the trick which he uses to fool Pap and get away. He is symbolically reborn on the river, where he throws off the "bonds" of discipline and control—both good (the widow) and bad (Pap).

10. Identify several scenes in this excerpt that might easily have been used as the basis for tragedy. What devices does Mark Twain use to establish and consistently maintain a *comic tone* in this excerpt? Student answers will vary. Pap's drunkenness and cruelty to Huck are not minimized by Twain. But he blends realism with comic detachment by exaggerating Pap's rantings, by inserting the ironic episode of the new judge and showing the judge's naivete, and by making Huck more than a match for Pap. Similarly, Huck's loneliness and desperation are realistically portrayed, but are offset by his spirit of adventure, his practicality, and Twain's descriptions of the river's beauty. The plan with which Huck outwits Pap and the pursuers is somewhat grotesque, in that the boy stages his own "death;" the reader, on the other hand, is brought to sympathize with the boy and to applaud his ingenuity. Toward the end, the ironically comic scene in which Huck and Jim, both scared to death, are reunited helps to distract the reader's attention from Jim's life-and-death situation as a runaway slave. Encourage students to offer other suggestions on Twain's tone in this selection.

11. Explain how the characters and events in this part of Huck's story are relevant to contemporary life. If any events in the chapters you've just read could not happen today, explain the broad ways in which they may still be relevant. Students will have various answers. It would be hard to imagine certain aspects of the tale today: for example, those parts of the story dealing with the river, with the custody of a minor child, or with slavery. On the other hand, some key aspects of Twain's story remain broadly relevant, such as the motifs of child abuse and alcoholism. On the thematic level, Huck's struggle to break away from restraints and to achieve freedom is probably part of every child's psychological make-up at a certain stage.

Writing About the Story
A Creative Response

1. Imitating a Writer's Technique. Carefully analyze the description of Pap on page 414 ("He was most fifty..."), noting Twain's blend of physical description and words conveying attitude.

Criteria for Evaluating the Assignment. The paragraph reveals both a person's appearance (hair, eyes, color, face, and clothes) and how the speaker feels about the person.

2. Writing a Journal Entry. Twain's comment ("Primary Sources," page 429) reveals the later respectability of his model for Huck Finn. It may help students decide what Huck will be like as an old man, but they need not make their own Huck a justice of the peace in Montana.

Criteria for Evaluating the Assignment. The journal entry is a plausible one for a much older Huck Finn. It reveals his age, where he lives, the form of his name he prefers, and his adult interpretation of his boyhood escapades.

A Critical Response

3. Responding to a Critic. Read Young's comment (page 427) and discuss it until students are able to cite specific reasons for agreeing or disagreeing with Young.

Criteria for Evaluating the Assignment. The essay argues for or against Young's claim that repeated exposures to violence, injustice, and brutality "wound" young Huck, citing specific support from the novel.

4. Analyzing the Selection. Review the concepts of realistic and romantic writing (pages 380-381) and "The American Hero in Romantic Fiction" (pages 120-121, preceding Washington Irving).

Criteria for Evaluating the Assignment. The essay cites several elements making Twain's novel realistic, and proposes the romantic solutions Washington Irving might have given Huck for his problems with Pap and his escape to the river.

3. Evaluating "Voice." Review the concept of *voice*. As an example, ask students for instances where they understood more quickly than Huck what was happening.

Criteria for Evaluating the Assignment. The essay briefly analyzes the narrative voice of *Huckleberry Finn* and lists elements Twain would have had to change for an older Huck.

Analyzing Language and Style
Descriptive Language

1. The word *smelt* is an extremely effective choice.
2. Choices will vary, but images should clearly appeal to at least one of the senses. See, for instance, the paragraph on page 425 beginning, "My heart jumped up...."

Extending the Story

What if Bret Harte had written this excerpt from *Huckleberry Finn*? Have students discuss what aspects of Twain's characters, story line, and style might have been changed. What aspects might have remained the same?

Ambrose Bierce

Text page 430

"An Occurrence at Owl Creek Bridge"

Text page 431

Objectives

1. To evaluate theme
2. To analyze the use of cinematic techniques
3. To imitate a writer's technique
4. To write an essay analyzing the use of suspense
5. To write an essay responding to a critical comment

Introducing the Story

In outline form, for your reference, here are the major elements of the story:

- **Characters:** Peyton Farquhar, a Southern planter; and some Union soldiers who have captured him
- **Conflicts:** illusion vs. reality; subjective time vs. objective time
- **Themes:** the intensity of the stream of consciousness within a very few seconds; the disappointment of human dreams by inevitable fate
- **Point of view:** third-person limited, major character
- **Significant techniques:** cinematic style, controlled point of view, suspense, flashback, surprise ending
- **Setting:** Alabama during the Civil War

Background on the Story. This very famous story has perhaps had more influence on genre fiction, such as science fiction, than on "serious" literature. Indeed, it was made into an episode of the old, black and white, half-hour *Twilight Zone* series. Genre writers have often found it easy to adopt Bierce's psychological surprise ending by changing the outer trappings—changing the setting and the costumes. The fact that virtually all of the externals of the story can be altered and its essence still retained may say something about its limitations as a work of literature. It may show that to some extent the story is built around a mere contrivance. On the other hand, there is no doubt that embedded in this contrivance is a forceful psychological truth.

The Plot. Peyton Farquhar, a well-to-do Alabama planter, has been captured by Union forces for attempting to sabotage a bridge, and is being hanged. We see him, through his own point of view, escaping and returning to his home, but at the ending we learn that the escape has been a fantasy, taking place in the few moments during which he has, in reality, been hanged.

Teaching Strategies

Providing for Cultural Differences. The story's point of view makes it seem sympathetic to the Confederate side, but Bierce himself was a much-decorated Union veteran. It seems likely, therefore, that Bierce, true to his nature, was expressing his bitterness at the idea of military partisanship in general, and saying that war, on both sides, is a waste of human life.

Providing for Different Levels of Ability. Less advanced students may not be able to catch on to the surprise ending at first, and after a first reading and discussion, you may want to guide them through the selection again, pointing out the specific places where clues and foreshadowings are presented. Advanced students, on the other hand, may already be familiar with the story, and therefore not surprised by it. They will probably, however, enjoy analyzing Bierce's techniques.

Introducing Vocabulary Study. Knowing the meanings of the following words is important to understanding the selection. (Starred words appear in the Glossary. Italicized words either are archaic or have special meaning in context.)

sentinel	431	periodicity	435
carriage	431	luminous	435
acclivity*	432	oscillation*	435
embrasure*	432	apprise	435
manifestations	432	preternaturally	435
fixity	432	prismatic	435
unsteadfast	434	gesticulated*	436
knell	434	aspirated (adj.)	436
imperious*	434	presaging	436
dictum	434	vortex	436
elude*	435	velocity*	436
ceremoniously	435	interminable	437
poignant	435	ineffable	437
ramification	435		

Reading the Story. The last four paragraphs contain all the essential elements of the contrast between Farquhar's fantasy and the reality of his hanging, as well as Bierce's techniques of foreshadowing and cinematic cutting. You might want to select this passage for reading aloud, but only

Ambrose Bierce 163

after the students have read the story in its entirety by themselves. Otherwise the surprise ending will be given away.

Reading Check. You may want to use the following questions as a reading check. Have students respond *True* or *False*.

1. Farquhar is a Confederate captain who has been captured in a sabotage attempt.   False
2. Farquhar has been condemned to death by firing squad.   False
3. Farquhar was entrapped by a Union scout into sabotaging the bridge.   True
4. In the middle part of the story, Bierce uses flashback to explain why Farquhar is being executed.   True
5. While waiting to be executed, Farquhar is very much disturbed by a sound that turns out to be the ticking of his watch.   True

Reteaching Alternatives. If some students have trouble locating the changes from reality to fantasy in the story, you might have them go over the story paragraph by paragraph, or passage by passage, jotting down, in each case, whether the description is of an external fact or an internal fancy. (Part III of the story is the section where most of the fantasy occurs, the first two parts being rather straightforward.) You might draw a line down the middle of the chalkboard, and for each paragraph in Part III, ask the class to determine whether it belongs on the "fantasy" or "reality" side of the line.

Responding to the Story   Text page 438
Analyzing the Story
Identifying Facts

1. How much time actually elapses between the opening and closing lines of Part III? Probably only several seconds elapse between the time that Farquhar falls through the bridge and his actual death.

2. Describe the *setting* at the opening of the story. What is Peyton Farquhar's situation? The story is set during the Civil War. Soldiers surround a prisoner on a railroad bridge in northern Alabama. Spectators line one bank of the river which is spanned by the bridge. Peyton Farquhar, the prisoner, is about to be hanged.

3. Describe Farquhar's last thoughts. He thinks of his wife and children.

Identify and describe the sound that disturbs the thoughts going through his mind. Farquhar hears a sharp, regular percussion like the sound of a blacksmith's anvil. The sound turns out to be the ticking of his watch in the silence just before the signal is given for the hanging.

4. In the *flashback* of the story's second section, who visits Peyton Farquhar? A gray-clad soldier visits Farquhar at his plantation. The soldier tells him that the Union forces have repaired Owl Creek Bridge, and have issued an order that provides that anyone caught interfering with the bridge will be summarily hanged.

What plan does Farquhar conceive as a result of this visit? Eager to serve the Confederate cause, Farquhar decides to try to elude the guards and burn the bridge.

5. What does Farquhar imagine in the story's last section? Farquhar imagines that he falls into the river with the noose around his neck, frees his hands, and swims underwater to evade the soldiers' bullets. Some distance downstream, he reaches the river bank. He travels through a forest all day and all night to reach the front gate of his own house the next morning. He stretches out his arms to embrace his wife, who is awaiting him.

Ironically, what is his real fate? Farquhar is hanged.

Interpreting Meanings

6. Summarize what you think this story reveals about the psychology of a person facing death. Do you find the psychology believable? Explain. Student answers will vary. The story shows that, despite Farquhar's apparent calm, the unconscious terror of death has the effect of heightening his sense perceptions and of distorting time and distance. The story also shows that at the moment of death we may be prompted to fix our thoughts on those who are dearest to us. Ask students to defend their evaluations of these psychological points.

7. The third part of the story, which occurs within the few seconds before Farquhar dies, is presumably a fantasy. What *point of view* does the writer use here? Bierce uses third-person limited point of view, recounting the events as they are seen by Farquhar in his imagination.

How does Bierce prepare us for the final outcome of the story? Bierce refers several times to the pain in Farquhar's neck and his sense of suffocation. The heightening of sensory details, like the unfamiliar stars and singular noises in the forest, also suggest an unreal, dream-like atmosphere.

8. When you discovered Farquhar had not actually escaped but had only imagined it, what were your own emotions? Student answers will vary. Most students will probably call the end shocking, even though they may have suspected that Farquhar was only imagining his escape.

Did you feel that this outcome was more credible and more powerful than the one you had been led to anticipate? Or did you feel cheated by the surprise ending? Explain your response. Student answers will vary.

9. **Do you think the writer tries to enlist your sympathies toward either the Union or the Confederate side? Or does the story seem to be focused on a more general *theme* about the nature of the war? Cite details from the story to support your response.** Again, students will have different opinions. The description of Farquhar's gentlemanly bearing and the account of the Union soldier's trick both prejudice the reader somewhat toward the Confederate side. On the other hand, Bierce's ironic comment about the "liberal military code" suggests that he thinks war is brutal.

10. **Review the story closely and comment on how Bierce has used a cinematic style, including the following techniques:**
    a. close-up shots
    b. group shots
    c. panoramic shots
    d. fast motion
    e. slowed motion
    f. dream sequences
    g. sound effects
    h. quick cuts
    i. moving camera shots

Discuss how you think the story might be adapted into a movie. The story opens with a "close-up" shot of Peyton Farquhar. Bierce then uses a "group shot" to show the two ends of the railroad bridge. A "panoramic shot" describes the spectators of the execution in the second paragraph. Another "close-up" in the third paragraph gives a physical description of Farquhar. "Slowed motion" appears in Farquhar's hearing the ticking sound of his own watch in Part I and in the fantasy of Part III, while "fast motion" frames Part III in the description of the falling body and Farquhar's death of a broken neck. Much of Part III consists of "dream sequences," while "sound effects" are used in the ticking of the watch and in the reports of the rifles of the soldiers. Encourage students to discuss their movie adaptations in detail.

Writing About the Story
A Creative Response

1. **Imitating a Technique.** It may be helpful for small groups or the class as a whole to list several pressured situations students could use as starting points.

Criteria for Evaluating the Assignment. The account plausibly yet suspensefully narrates the thoughts inside a character's mind over a very short but intensely stressful period of time.

A Critical Response

2. **Analyzing Suspense.** Elicit from the class several examples of how Bierce builds suspense, such as the buildup of a mysterious noise in Part II which turns out to be "the ticking of his watch."

Criteria for Evaluating the Assignment. The essay explains two different methods Bierce uses to increase the reader's suspense in the second and third parts of the story.

3. **Responding to a Critical Comment.** Read Brooks and Warren's comment and make sure students understand their point. Direct students to use supportive details from the story in their essays whether they agree or disagree with Brooks and Warren.

Criteria for Evaluating the Assignment. The essay clearly agrees that the story is not true fiction, or argues that the story uses psychology to reveal something important about Farquhar or human nature in general. In either case, the writer's opinion is supported by details from the story.

Extending the Story

Surprise endings were, in the past, a staple of popular fiction: a few decades ago, *Collier's* magazine relied almost exclusively on stories with surprise or twist endings. Your students may have read such old chestnuts of the genre as O. Henry's "The Last Leaf" and Maupassant's "The Necklace." Ask them what other examples of surprise-ending stories they know of; discuss the advantages and limitations of the device. Such stories have gone out of fashion, but an excellent, very brief one from fairly recent years is the third of John Cheever's "Three Stories" in *The Stories of John Cheever*. J. D. Salinger's "A Perfect Day for Bananafish" and "Pretty Mouth and Green My Eyes" both have surprise endings. Ann Beattie's "Janus" is an excellent, fairly short example of a contemporary story in which the surprise is that there is *no* gimmick ending: the story proceeds as if it might be foreshadowing such an ending, but instead, gives us a richer emotional truth.

Stephen Crane

Text page 439

The Red Badge of Courage

Text page 441

Objectives

1. To read a major American novel
2. To analyze elements of the novel
3. To imitate the writer's style
4. To write a short concluding chapter narrating the protagonist's homecoming
5. To write an essay analyzing theme
6. To write an essay comparing tone and theme
7. To write an essay responding to a critique
8. To write an essay analyzing a major character
9. To analyze features of impressionistic style

Introducing the Novel

In outline form, for your reference, here are the major elements of *The Red Badge of Courage*:

- **Characters:** Henry Fleming, an ordinary soldier, usually called "the youth"; Jim Conklin, "the tall soldier"; Wilson, "the loud soldier"; the tattered soldier
- **Conflicts:** fear vs. bravery, expectation vs. performance, individual action vs. mass action, self-image vs. objective appearance
- **Theme:** the gradual maturation of a young soldier in battle
- **Point of view:** third-person, omniscient, concentrating mostly on the viewpoint of the youth
- **Significant techniques:** simile and metaphor, personification, synesthesia, fragmented dialogue, ironic authorial observations
- **Setting:** an unnamed battle of the Civil War, that may be the battle of Chancellorsville, May 1863

Background on the Novel. *The Red Badge of Courage* was not, strictly speaking, the first realistic fiction about the Civil War (Bierce and J. W. De Forest came earlier) but it was the first to gain wide attention, and thus can be said to have initiated a new phase in American war fiction. Its publication was greeted with the greatest critical enthusiasm, and there was a running debate between British and American reviewers as to which nation had discovered the book first.

A fellow writer, two years younger than Crane, who met him when the book was being syndicated in newspapers, was Willa Cather. She proofread the novel for the *Nebraska State Journal* while she was a junior at Nebraska State University. Cather was struck by the contrast between Crane's shabby attire and his long, delicate hands, and one evening, in the newspaper corridor, Crane spoke confidingly to her in the way people sometimes open their hearts to strangers. In her article, "When I Knew Stephen Crane," she wrote, "I have never known so bitter a heart in any man as he revealed to me that night." She also noticed that Crane seemed aware that he was destined to have a short lifespan. When Cather told him that in ten years he would laugh at his youthful bitterness, he responded, "I can't wait ten years, I haven't time."

The Plot. Henry Fleming, a young, inexperienced soldier, wonders how he will react to the stress of battle. No sooner has he begun to think highly of his military potential, than he finds himself panicking in battle, fleeing helplessly—and the battle is an apparent victory for his side. He gradually makes his way back to his regiment, seeing many of the horrors of war en route. This time, his behavior is more heroic—he fires his gun ferociously, and captures an enemy flag as well—but it is just as automatic and unthinking as his previous cowardly behavior. Even his head wound—his "red badge"—has been obtained in an ironic fashion: he was hit in the head by the rifle butt of a fleeing Union soldier whom he was trying to stop. But at the end, Henry believes that he has been through a trial of fire and has passed a test—that he is a boy no more and has become a man.

Teaching Strategies

Providing for Cultural Differences. Different regions, and different cultures, have different views of the military and different responses to military behavior. Ever since it was first published, some readers have felt that the novel deserved reproach for showing an act of cowardice by its protagonist. Some of your students may share this view; others may feel that it is important for fiction and nonfiction to show that war is an often frightening and inhuman activity rather than a glorious one. You may find some variation according to the sex of your students: your male students, after all, will anticipate that they themselves might someday be called to war, while your female students will feel free of that anxiety (though not free of it on behalf of male relatives and friends). Bear in mind, then, that if some students object to Henry's lack of valor, it may be because they themselves are trying to establish their own self-confidence—just as Henry was doing, before his battle experience. You might point out that virtually all soldiers, including those who fight with genuine courage, feel intense fear before battle, and rightly so, since it is a fearsome experience.

Providing for Different Levels of Ability. Stephen Crane's reluctance to call his characters by name may frustrate some students. You might want to write the names of the main characters on the blackboard, with their identifying sobriquets ("Henry Fleming—the youth," "Jim Conklin—the tall soldier," and so on).

Crane's compact but densely imagistic style may also give some students trouble. Careful attention to "Analyzing Language and Style," text page 509, and to question 12 in "Analyzing the Novel," page 462, question 12 on page 477, questions 7–10 on page 491, and questions 7, 8, 9, 10, and 12 on page 507, should help in dealing with this.

Introducing Vocabulary Study. Knowing the meanings of the following words is important to understanding the selection. (Starred words appear in the Glossary. Italicized words either are archaic or have special meaning in context.)

Chapter 1
lucid	443	effaced	444
assailed (part.)	443	diffidently	444
disdaining	443	martial	445
oblique	443	despondent	446
secular	444	scoffing	447

Chapter 2
adherents	447	kindred (adj.)	450
figuratively	447	ardor	450
derided	447	vindication	450
aflare	449	commiseration	450
dun-colored	450	felicitating	450

Chapter 3
extricated	451	declamation	453
impetus	452	nonchalant	454
rent	453	rending*	454

Chapter 5
| discomfited | 457 | querulous | 458 |

Chapter 6
| redoubtable | 460 | blanched | 460 |

Chapter 7
| sagacious | 463 | | |

Chapter 8
| clangor | 464 | perfunctory | 464 |
| transfixed* | 464 | | |

Chapter 9
| ague | 469 | | |

Chapter 13
| phosphorescent | 479 | languor | 480 |
| ethereal | 479 | | |

Chapter 14
| peremptory | 480 | audacity* | 481 |
| pallid | 480 | deprecatory | 481 |

Chapter 15
lugubrious	482	laggard	482
condescension	482	pompous*	482
retribution	482		

Chapter 16
| temerity | 485 | imprecations | 493 |
| altercation | 486 | superficial | 493 |

Chapter 20
| epithets | 494 | proximity | 496 |
| harangued* | 495 | tableau | 496 |

Chapter 21
| perturbation | 497 | *withal* | 498 |

Chapter 23
| paroxysm | 501 | scathing | 503 |

Chapter 24
| elation | 506 | inconsequent | 506 |
| bludgeon (n.) | 506 | quail (v.) | 506 |

Reading the Novel. You'll probably want to spend several days on this long selection, assigning the reading for homework. The text is divided into four sections, with a "Responding to the Novel" exercise at the end of each: pages 443–462, 463–477, 478–491, and 492–506. Crane's prose is of a uniformly high quality and the action of the novel flows smoothly, but some passages stand out as being especially suitable for intensive study and possibly for reading aloud: Henry's worries about how he will stand up to battle (pages 450–451); his flight (460–461); the "cathedral" scene in which he encounters a soldier's corpse in a chapel-like pine woods (page 464); Chapter 9, containing Jim Conklin's death and the famous line, "The red sun was pasted in the sky like a wafer" (pages 468–470); Chapter 10, the "tattered man" scene (pages 470–471); the scene in which Henry obtains his "red badge" (page 474), Henry's ferocious firing of his rifle (page 488); Henry's capture of the enemy flag (pages 493–494); and Henry's final assessment of his own maturation (page 506).

Reading Check. You may want to use the following questions as a reading check. Have students respond *True* or *False*.

1. Henry's mother sent him to the army camp with socks, a Bible, and a cup of blackberry jam. ___True___

2. The tall soldier was afraid of falling down and being run over by artillery wagons. ___True___

3. Henry has a friendly encounter with the cheery soldier without ever seeing his face. ___True___

4. When Henry fires his rifle at the enemy in a mad fury, his lieutenant berates him for not obeying the "cease fire" order. ___False___

5. At the novel's conclusion, Henry examines his own actions and feelings, and concludes that he still has far to go before he truly becomes a man. ___False___

Reteaching Alternatives. The novel is so successful at transmitting the chaotic welter of sense impressions assailing a young soldier, that some students themselves may find the progression of events chaotic. It might be helpful if you ask them to draw a timeline of the novel—as novelists often do when they plot a book—recording each of the major scenes of combat and personal encounters, and stating how each one affects Henry's state of mind.

Some students may also have trouble interpreting Henry's feelings about his experiences, since they are narrated not only in impressionistic language, but also in impressionistic nineteenth-century language. You might ask students to write a paragraph expressing how they imagine *they* would feel in Henry's situation—for instance, upon encountering a corpse near a battlefield, or fleeing from battle, or seeing a friend die in war, or proving their courage after initial self-doubt. You can then help them compare and contrast their own imagined reactions to Crane's imagining of Henry's reactions.

Responding to the Novel   Text page 462
Analyzing Chapters 1–6
Identifying Facts

1. We don't discover the full name of the main character, Henry Fleming, until long after the opening of the novel. How does the writer usually refer to Henry? Crane usually refers to Henry as "the youth."

2. What rumor does the tall soldier report at the opening of Chapter 1? The tall soldier, Jim Conklin, reports that the army is at last going to move.

How does this news affect Henry? Henry retreats to his hut so that he can be alone. He contemplates the news with a sense of wondrous astonishment.

3. What problem preoccupies Henry in the opening chapters? Henry tries to prove to himself that he would not run from a battle.

How does he try to solve this problem? He tries to measure his own courage by calculations of how his comrades, particularly the tall soldier, might behave in battle. But this expedient fails to resolve his private doubts about his own nerve. He is afraid to confess his doubts to anyone, lest he be mocked.

4. In Chapter 3, why does the youth experience a wave of hatred for the young lieutenant? He feels that the young lieutenant has unjustly reproached him for lagging behind the regiment.

5. What does the loud soldier tell Henry at the end of Chapter 3? The loud soldier tells Henry that he has a premonition of death in this engagement, and he gives Henry a packet of letters to deliver to his family.

6. At the opening of Chapter 6, Henry feels proud and self-satisfied. What *ironic reversal* occurs in this chapter? Henry runs "like a rabbit" when the army is attacked for the second time. Ironically, the line holds, and the general proclaims the engagement a victory at the end of the chapter.

Interpreting Meanings

7. What general impressions of war does Henry have when he enlists? Henry thinks of war as grand, mysterious, and somehow glorious.

Are they romantic, or realistic? These impressions are decidedly romantic, as Henry will shortly discover.

What do you think may be the source of these ideas? Books and newspaper accounts may have been the source of some of these ideas. Henry also may have heard of war exploits by word of mouth.

Are they typical of young people today as well? If they aren't, what has caused the change? Most students will agree that these romantic notions of war would not be typical of young people today. The causes of the change are not far to seek: the development of mass media, and especially of television, has made the violence and destructiveness of warfare particularly graphic.

**8. Henry's mother tells him, "Yer jest one little feller amongst a hull lot of others, and yeh've got to keep quiet an' do what they tell yeh." Pick out some passages that stress the notion of the army as a mass, rather than as a collection of individual soldiers. How is this related to Crane's referring to Henry so often as "the youth,"

168   The Rise of Realism

rather than by name? Numerous passages emphasize the notion of the army as a mass. For example, early in Chapter 2 Crane uses a simile to compare the army to "one of those moving monsters wending with many feet" (page 449). In Chapter 3, Henry feels that his capacity for independent decision and action has been curtailed by the "iron laws of tradition and law on four sides": "He was in a moving box" (page 452). In Chapter 4, the army is described as follows: "A sketch in gray and red dissolved into a moblike body of men who galloped like wild horses" (page 456). Crane refers to Henry as "the youth," rather than by name, to emphasize the young soldier's insignificance in the army as a whole.

What other soldiers play prominent roles in this part of the novel, and how are they referred to? Among the soldiers who play prominent parts are Jim Conklin (referred to as the tall soldier) and Wilson (referred to as the loud soldier). The lieutenant and the general are unnamed.

9. Crane's *style* pushes realism to such limits that it is often called *impressionistic*. He offers us vivid, fragmented images that correspond with the moment-by-moment impressions of the men on the field. How does Crane's use of *vivid metaphors* contribute to this impressionistic style? Select and discuss some examples of metaphors from the opening chapters. Students should be encouraged to offer and discuss a number of representative examples. Among the striking metaphors that contribute to Crane's impressionistic style in these chapters are the following: "In the eastern sky there was a yellow patch like a rug laid for the feet of the coming sun" (page 449); "But the long serpents crawled slowly from hill to hill without bluster of smoke" (pages 449–450); "The blades pressed tenderly against his cheek" (page 450); "The insect voices of the night sang solemnly" (page 451); "They were going to look at war, the red animal—war, the blood-swollen god" (page 453); "It was a flow of blood from the torn body of the brigade" (page 459); "The guns, stolid and undaunted, spoke with dogged valor" (page 461); "Too, he felt a pity for the guns, standing, six good comrades, in a bold row" (page 461).

10. Crane's handling of *dialogue* is also a major feature of his impressionistic style. Why do you think he includes so many snatches of dialogue that are disjointed or fragmented? The disjointed, fragmented snatches of dialogue are presumably intended to capture realistically the real-life experience of the men. This style of dialogue is also especially effective in suggesting the pressures and doubts that the men experience but do not verbalize.

How does Crane's use of *dialect* affect your reading of the novel? Student answers will vary. Ask the students if they think that the use of dialect enhances the realism of the novel.

11. Are the soldiers you have met so far like soldiers in contemporary fiction, in movies, and on TV? Are they like real soldiers you know? Explain your answers. Again, student answers will vary. Encourage the students to use specific examples to support their comparisons.

Responding to the Novel Text page 477
Analyzing Chapters 7–12
Identifying Facts

1. How does Henry try to rationalize his flight in Chapter 7? Henry reasons that the annihilation of the army was imminent. He thus compliments himself on his strategic insight in fleeing from the battle.

What does the sight of the running squirrel do for Henry's image of himself as a deserter? As he watches the squirrel, Henry rationalizes that his flight has been prompted by natural law, where the recognition of danger prompts retreat.

2. Why does the talk of the tattered man so disturb Henry? The tattered man's talk of the soldiers' courage ironically undermines Henry's self-image, since it reminds him of his inner shame and guilt. When the tattered man asks Henry where he has been wounded, the youth becomes acutely embarrassed. In Chapter 10, the tattered man's disordered ramblings on Tom Jamison remind Henry that he has been unable to take care of his friend, Jim Conklin, and the youth grows even more nettled and uncomfortable.

3. What have we learned so far in the novel about Jim Conklin and Henry's relationship to him? Jim Conklin is affable and optimistic, although he has admitted to certain misgivings about his own courage. Henry has known Jim since childhood, and he feels that he is his equal. Nevertheless, there have been several hints in the novel so far that Henry looks up to Jim, in that he measures his own behavior by Jim's standard.

How does Henry try to help Jim in Chapter 9? Henry tries to offer Jim some assistance and comfort as he staggers along, gravely wounded.

4. According to the opening paragraphs of Chapter 9, what is the meaning of the novel's title? The "red badge of courage" refers to a wound received in battle.

5. In Chapter 11, Henry experiences renewed anxiety about his flight. How does he hope he might be vindicated? He thinks that the general retreat of the Union army may vindicate his actions as prophetic and strategic.

6. How does Henry acquire his "red badge"? What is *ironic* about this incident? Henry tries to stop a soldier from fleeing, and the man angrily brings his rifle crashing down on the youth's head. The incident is ironic because the context contains certain parallels to Henry's own wild flight from battle.

7. At the end of Chapter 12, what does Henry suddenly realize about the man with the cheery voice? He realizes that he has not even seen the man's face.

Interpreting Meanings

8. Why is the encounter with the dead soldier, toward the end of Chapter 7, a *turning point* for Henry? Henry shrieks and then stares at the man's grotesque, decomposing body. He then imagines that the corpse may pursue him. The incident is a turning point because it marks Henry's first exposure to death in all its grotesqueness; the sight deepens his guilt at having run away from the battle.

9. What are some of the memorable details describing Jim's death? Among the memorable details are the following: Jim's waxlike features, the description of his gory wound, his spasmodic movements, and his pathetic concern about his body's being crushed by the wagons. Crane compares him, even in the last stages of life, to a specter. Henry watches his death throes, as he falls like a giant tree to the ground.

Jim's death is tragic, but some people feel there is humor in the telling of it. What do you think? Student answers will vary. Encourage them to support their answers with specific references to the text and with logical reasoning.

10. What is *ironic* about Jim's wish to be alone when he dies? Jim's wish is ironic because he dies at the very moment when Henry most needs companionship, due to the youth's guilt at having fled. Although Henry is eager to help Jim, his friend rejects any assistance and wishes to die alone.

How do you think Jim's wish affects Henry? Henry must be deeply affected by Jim's wish to die alone. He must experience inner anguish, as he compares his friend's suffering and heroism with his own cowardice.

11. In his flight, Henry believes that the Union forces are defeated. Why is that important to his self-esteem? The defeat and withdrawal of the Union forces would help Henry to rationalize and come to terms with his own flight.

How is he affected by the discovery that the general is rejoicing in a victory? This discovery ironically reverses Henry's view of himself: he now feels an even more bitter shame and disgust at his own cowardice.

12. Crane often achieves powerful effects with simple, short sentences at the end of an episode or chapter. Analyze and comment on the effect of the following sentences, in context:

a. "A sad silence was upon the little guarding edifice." (Chapter 7) The detached, factual realism of the description contrasts with Henry's emotion at seeing the decomposing corpse of the dead soldier.

b. "The red sun was pasted in the sky like a wafer." (Chapter 9) Here again, a detached, quasi-symbolic vignette abruptly interrupts Henry's emotional outburst after Jim's death. The effect is to contrast human emotion with an impersonal view of nature.

c. "He was a slang phrase." (Chapter 11) The concluding sentence of the chapter serves as a bitter summary of Henry's self-consciousness and guilt.

13. Where in these chapters are you most sympathetic with Henry? Perhaps the most sympathetic portrait of Henry in these chapters is in Chapter 9, where he is genuinely affected by the death agony of his friend, Jim Conklin. Students may also suggest that the portrait of Henry's view of the dead soldier in Chapter 7 inspires sympathy for the protagonist.

Where are you least sympathetic? Henry's rationalizations for his behavior in Chapter 7 result in a somewhat unsympathetic portrait.

Responding to the Novel   Text page 491
Analyzing Chapters 13–18
Identifying Facts

1. What conclusion does the corporal draw about Henry's wound? The corporal concludes that Henry has been grazed by a musket ball in battle.

Does Henry dispute this conclusion? He does not dispute this conclusion.

2. In Chapter 14, what change does Henry notice in Wilson? Henry notices that Wilson, previously the "loud

170 The Rise of Realism

young soldier," now has a more confident, philosophical outlook on his situation: he possesses a "fine reliance."

What is the significance of the packet of letters that Henry carries for him? The letters were confided to Henry early in the novel, when Wilson suffered from premonitions and a lack of confidence (see the end of Chapter 3).

3. How do the comments of the sarcastic man in Chapter 16 make Henry more modest? The man asks Henry sarcastically if he thinks he fought the whole battle yesterday; the effect is to take Henry down a peg.

4. In the major engagement, how does Henry display great courage? He takes up a position and keeps firing, even through the flames and smoke. At the conclusion of the battle, he retires only reluctantly.

How does the lieutenant praise him in Chapter 17? The lieutenant compares Henry to a wild cat. He says that if he had ten thousand like him, he would win the war in a week.

5. What do Henry and Wilson overhear the general discussing in Chapter 18? They overhear the general discussing a charge.

What comment by the officers about the regiment unnerves the young men? The young men are unnerved when they hear the general compare the regiment to mule drivers, many of whom may not survive the charge.

Interpreting Meanings

6. These chapters present a very mixed portrait of Henry. What are some of the positive aspects of his feelings and behavior? What negative aspects make his heroism somewhat ambiguous? Comment specifically on Henry's feeling that "he had performed his mistakes in the dark, so he was still a man" (page 482). How do you respond to Henry's view of Wilson's packet of letters as a "small weapon with which he could prostrate his comrade" (page 482)? Positive aspects of Henry: his courage in Chapter 17. Negative aspects: his acquiescence in the corporal's mistaken conclusion (Chapter 13) and his smugness and condescension in the matter of Wilson's packet of letters (Chapter 15). The two passages cited are also negative, in that they touch on Henry's guilt and insecurity. The second passage even implies that there may be a cruel streak in Henry.

7. Crane often uses *personification* to render battle scenes vividly. Point out some examples of this figure of speech from the opening paragraphs of Chapter 16. Some examples of personification here include: "Later, the cannon had entered the dispute"; "... their voices made a thudding sound"; "before them was a level stretch, peopled with short, deformed stumps"; "The guns were roaring without an instant's pause for breath"; "It seemed that the cannon had come from all parts and were engaged in a stupendous wrangle."

8. Examine the *imagery* of Chapter 17 closely. What details does Crane use to suggest ironically that the soldiers are less than human at the very moment of their greatest courage and victory? Among the details that students may single out are the following: the comparison of the fighters to "animals tossed for a death struggle into a dark pit," the simile comparing Henry to a dog, and Henry's sudden realization that "he had been a barbarian, a beast."

How is the style and meaning of Henry's question on page 483 related to this *irony*: "And, furthermore, how could they kill him who was the chosen of gods and doomed to greatness?" Henry's rhetorical question, which reveals his lack of awareness of his true role, is consistent with the ironies surrounding the army's "heroism." Just as the soldiers' victory contrasts with their portrayal as animals, so does Henry's vision of himself as divinely marked for greatness clash with his real position as a minor cog in the wheel of the army as a whole.

9. *Antithesis* means that a writer presents a pointed contrast for effect. Find the antithesis in the concluding sentence of Chapter 17. How is it similar to the antithesis at the end of Chapter 5? At the end of Chapter 17, Crane contrasts the ominous cloud of smoke from the ruins of battle with the bright sun and the pure, blue sky. The antithesis here is similar to that at the end of Chapter 5, where the serenity of the sky and the sun are contrasted with the destructiveness and bedlam of warfare below on earth.

Find at least two other related examples of this device in the novel so far. Students may mention the striking antithesis at the end of Chapter 12, where Crane contrasts the cheerful soldier's consolation of Henry with the fact that the youth had not even glimpsed the soldier's face, and the juxtaposition of Henry's unawareness and his exaltation as a "knight," near the end of Chapter 17: "They had fallen like paper peaks, and he was now what he called a hero. And he had not been aware of the process. He had slept and, awakening, found himself a knight" (page 488).

10. In Crane's highly compressed style, several figures of speech may be included in one short sentence. Crane is also fond of what is called *synaesthesia*. This means that the same image appeals to two or more of our senses. Analyze and comment on each of the following

images. What figures of speech can you find in them? (*Metaphor*, *simile*, or *personification*) To which senses does each image appeal?

a. "A yellow fog lay wallowing on the treetops." (Chapter 7) The metaphor implicitly compares the fog to a beast like a hippopotamus wallowing in water. The image appeals to the senses of sight and touch.

b. "The trees began softly to sing a hymn of twilight." (Chapter 8) This personification presents the trees as singers of hymns. The image appeals to the senses of sight and hearing.

c. "Far off to the right, through a window in the forest, could be seen a handful of stars lying, like glittering pebbles, on the black level of the night." (Chapter 13) The simile compares the stars in the sky to pebbles lying on a flat surface. The image appeals to the senses of sight and touch.

d. "The distance was splintering and blaring with the noise of fighting." (Chapter 14) The metaphor likens a space to a material that can be "splintered" and to a musical instrument which could be imagined to "blare" with sound. Hearing, sight, and touch are the three senses appealed to in this compressed image.

e. "This din of musketry on the right, growing like a released genie of sound, expressed and emphasized the army's plight." (Chapter 16) The simile compares the sound of the rifles to a magic spirit or genie released from a bottle. The image appeals to the senses of sound and sight.

11. What *point of view* does Crane use in this novel? Crane used the third-person omniscient point of view. He recounts most of the events from the vantage point of the protagonist, Henry Fleming, but he feels perfectly free to add authorial comments on Henry's perceptions.

Responding to the Novel   Text page 507
Analyzing Chapters 19–24
Identifying Facts

1. Describe how Henry behaves in the charge. At first Henry feels jostled and pushed; then he fixes his eye on a distant clump of trees and runs toward it as a goal. As he runs in the vanguard, he looks to be "an insane soldier." Finally the pace of the men slackens. When the lieutenant arrives, he spurs the men on and upbraids Henry, who challenges him in turn.

Why does he abandon his rifle to carry the flag? He feels that the flag has a supernatural power to protect him from the enemy guns.

2. How does Henry feel toward the officer who called him a "mule-driver"? He hates him worse than he hates the enemy.

3. What two extremes of blame and praise does the author present in Chapter 21? The general reproaches the colonel because he thinks the regiment did not advance far enough. At the end of the chapter, some soldiers report that the colonel praised Henry's action in carrying the flag.

4. Describe the capture of the enemy's flag. Henry catches sight of the enemy flag bearer, who is fatally wounded. He thinks that the capture of the enemy's flag would be "high pride." Henry's friend springs forward like a panther and wrenches the flag free, and the Union soldiers throw their caps in the air with a cheer.

5. How does Henry sum up his experience in the last chapter of the novel? He reviews all his actions and, although he is still bothered by his flight in the first engagement and the memory of the tattered man, he decides that he has acquitted himself well.

What kind of life does he now look forward to? He looks forward to a peaceful life of "tranquil skies, fresh meadows," and "cool brooks."

Interpreting Meanings

6. Toward the end of Chapter 19, what emotions does the sight of the flag inspire in Henry? The flag inspires a kind of love in him.

To what is the flag compared? It is compared to a radiant goddess.

How is this incident both a critical *turning point* in the novel and a *symbolic* episode? The incident is a critical turning point because it spurs Henry on to his most outstanding heroic act. Symbolically, the incident suggests that Henry is now motivated by sheer patriotism, rather than an egocentric or self-conscious desire to achieve glory or to avoid shame or guilt.

7. The heat of battle reaches a climax in Chapter 19. Analyze the *imagery* of this chapter closely. What does Crane seem to imply about the men and the physical scene through his choice of images? The men are said to be "moblike" and "barbaric"; there is a "frenzy" in their "furious rush." Like an animal, the regiment "snorted and blew" when the men's pace slackened. When the men started to move again, they "danced and gyrated like tortured savages." Crane's choice of images implies that

172   The Rise of Realism

the physical scene is grotesque, ghastly, and somehow inhuman.

8. Explain how Crane uses *synaesthesia* (see page 491) in the following phrases from Chapter 19: (a) "a blue haze of curses"; (b) "the yellow tongues"; (c) "pulsating saliva." (a) The first image mingles the senses of sight and sound; (b) the second combines taste and sight; (c) the third combines touch, sight, and taste.

9. Crane prepares us for the general's bitter reproaches when he has the youth perceive the warping of space and time in Chapter 21 (see page 497). What is the ironic effect of this paragraph in its context? The paragraph has the effect of reversing Henry's previous opinion about the magnitude of the struggle and of the regiment's achievement.

10. What do you think is the point of the description of the four enemy captives at the end of Chapter 23? The captives present a typical range of attitudes: defiance, shame, stoic resignation, and good fellowship. Perhaps the point is to show that the enemy soldiers are not demons, but very much like the soldiers in the Union army.

Why is the placement of this description, immediately after the capture of the enemy's flag, especially appropriate? It is especially appropriate because it serves to humanize the enemy soldiers, even in defeat.

11. Why do you think Henry is disturbed by the "dogging memory of the tattered soldier" in Chapter 24? He is disturbed by this memory because it reminds him of his shame in the first engagement.

Does he finally succeed in putting this memory to rest? Although the memory is persistent, Henry gradually succeeds in laying it to rest.

12. Analyze the *image* in the last sentence of the novel. How is this concluding sentence similar to, yet different from, other places we have seen where Crane refers to the sky? What may Crane be *symbolically* suggesting in these few words, about the development of Henry and about the *theme* of the novel as a whole? The image portrays a golden ray of sunshine piercing shining through a bank of gray, leaden clouds. The reference to the sky is reminiscent of the concluding sentences of Chapter 5 and Chapter 9; here, however, instead of contrasting the sky with the violence on earth, Crane suggests symbolically a measure of peace and tranquility for Henry.

13. Do you agree that Henry has, in the end, achieved "a quiet manhood, non-assertive but of sturdy and strong blood"? Or do you think this confidence is only temporary? Explain why or why not. Student answers will vary. Encourage the students to support their opinions with references to the novel.

The Novel as a Whole

1. What *is* the red badge of courage? Did Henry win his red badge? Explain. The red badge of courage is an honorable wound in battle that witnesses to a soldier's courage. Henry won his red badge in a rather roundabout, ironic way when he tried to prevent a soldier from retreating: The soldier brought his rifle crashing down on Henry's head. Henry also proves his courage—perhaps more genuinely—in the incidents involving the two flags.

2. Is Henry a *hero* in any conventional sense of the word? How is he similar to, or different from, a mythical hero like Odysseus, or a romance hero like King Arthur, or a tragic hero like Antigone? Is Henry like the heroes you see today in films and in other works of contemporary literature? Most students will agree that Henry, although portrayed as something of an anti-hero in the opening chapters, acquires some of the characteristics of true heroism by the end of the novel. However, Henry is quite different from the heroes of mythology, romance, and tragedy, in that he is a common soldier rather than a "noble" personage who sums up the aspirations of an entire culture. In this sense, Henry resembles the heroes of modern films and contemporary literature, who are apt to be "everyday" people in ordinary circumstances. Encourage students to support their comparisons and evaluations of Henry with specific examples.

3. Chapter 24 of *The Red Badge of Courage* appears to imply that Henry has, by hard-won experience, become truly a man. Do you think the overall portrayal of Henry in the novel justifies the protagonist's own view of himself in the last chapter: "He saw that he was good"? Do you believe Henry has undergone a genuine change of character in the course of the novel? Explain. Student answers will vary, but most students will agree that Henry's exposure to the grim realities of war has caused a profound change in his character.

4. The *setting* of Crane's novel is never precisely specified, but many scholars believe the story is based on events that took place at the Battle of Chancellorsville, fought in the opening days of May, 1863. In that battle, despite major losses, neither side achieved a clear victory. Read about the actual battle and discuss its similarities to the battle in the novel. Encourage students to research the historical battle in an encyclopedia or an American history text. Then have them present their findings to the class in the form of an oral report. The fact that neither side achieves a clear victory perhaps suggests that Crane was more interested in the novel in focusing on the experience of war from the point of view of an ordinary soldier than in dealing with the strategic or political dimensions of the battle.

**5. Imagine that you are directing a filmed version of *The Red Badge of Courage*. What aspects of the novel do you think would lend themselves especially well to a film adaptation? What features or qualities of Crane's style, and of the work's overall effect, would be especially difficult to capture in a filmed version? The battle scenes might lend themselves especially well to a film adaptation. However, it would be difficult in film to capture Henry's inner emotions. It might also be difficult to render the impressionistic effect of the fragmented snatches of dialogue.

6. In the century since *The Red Badge of Courage* was published, many novels, short stories, and movies have been produced about war. How does Crane's story compare with these more recent portrayals of men in battle? You might consider comparing Crane's novel to the following:
   a. Ernest Hemingway, *A Farewell to Arms* (novel)
   b. James Jones, *From Here to Eternity* (novel)
   c. Eric Maria Remargue, *All Quiet on the Western Front* (novel)
   d. Joseph Heller, *Catch-22* (novel)
   e. Leon Uris, *Exodus* (novel)
   f. *Apocalypse Now* (movie)
   g. *Platoon* (movie)
   h. M*A*S*H (TV series)

These comparisons could be assigned to students as individual projects, depending on the students' preferences and familiarity with the works listed.

Walt Whitman, writing before *The Red Badge* was published, said "...the real war will never get in the books" (see page 351). Do you think this is any longer true? Whitman's remark points to the tendency at the time to "prettify" accounts of the war and to color them with political bias. Most students will agree that, since the advent of television, the facts of "real war" are now widely disseminated.

Writing About the Novel
A Creative Response

The creative assignments reinforce different writing skills. The first stresses descriptive writing; the second, ability to extrapolate from what has been revealed and to continue the narrative.

1. Imitating the Writer's Style. You might use as models some of Crane's descriptions such as the opening paragraph of Chapter 3 (page 451), the three paragraphs beginning "The din in front" in Chapter 4 (pages 455–456), or the opening paragraph of Chapter 8 (page 464).

Criteria for Evaluating the Assignment. The scene is described in vivid figurative language and language appealing to the senses—especially vision, by use of color words, and hearing, by use of evocative verbs.

2. Extending the Novel. Remind students that they are writing not as themselves, but as Stephen Crane. The sequel must therefore pick up on hints such as those in Chapters 1 (pages 444–445), 2 (page 450), 10 (pages 470–471), 12 (page 475), and 15 (page 483).

Criteria for Evaluating the Assignment. The homecoming chapter presents a plausible narrative of events and Henry Fleming's reactions to them, considering his new insights into war, cowardice, and heroism.

A Critical Response

Because of the number of critical responses, you may wish to require that students write only one. The assignments do, however, stress different critical thinking and writing skills, and all four should be discussed. An option is to assign small groups the different topics and have the class take notes as each group reports its findings.

3. Analyzing Theme. You may wish briefly to review the contrast between realistic and romantic fiction (page 380) and Crane's use of irony, before students complete the chart suggested in the writing prompt.

Criteria for Evaluating the Assignment. The essay discusses the quote from Chapter 17 in relation to the quest theme of the entire novel, but points out that Crane gives the theme an ironic twist in that Henry Fleming realizes the emptiness of the romantic myth.

4. Comparing Crane's Poetry and Fiction. Read and discuss "War Is Kind," noting the contrast of the martial symbols and military mind set of lines 6–11 ("Hoarse, booming drums....") and 17–22 ("Swift blazing flag...") with the realistic images of shooting, dying, and burial conveyed in lines 1–5, 12–16, and 23–26. Note also the increasingly devastating effect of the refrain, "Do not weep./War is kind"—an ironic exhortation to do and believe the opposite.

Criteria for Evaluating the Assignment. The essay shows awareness that Crane's ironic refrain in "War Is Kind" is applicable to both the poem and the novel, and that Crane urges human beings, though powerless, to rage at the indifferent universe.

5. Responding to a Critique. Discuss Kazin's comment, asking students to state his major points in their own words, before they respond in an essay.

Criteria for Evaluating the Assignment. The essay cites Kazin's main points correctly, and responds with the student's own opinions, supported by citations from the novel.

6. Analyzing Character. Since the prompt specifically requests a five-paragraph essay, you might suggest this pattern: (1) Introductory statement of points essay will make about whom, (2) Analysis of the character's function

174 The Rise of Realism

in the novel, (3)–(4) Explanation of whether the character is flat or fully developed, supported by citations from the novel, and (5) Conclusion/summary.

Criteria for Evaluating the Assignment. The paper is a well-organized five-paragraph essay that analyzes Henry Fleming, Jim Conklin, Wilson, or the tattered man in terms of function in the novel and dimensionality of character; and which supports points made by citing the novel.

Analyzing Language and Style
Impressionism

1. These quotations appear on page 455.

2. Answers will vary. One such passage is the paragraph beginning "The youth in this contemplation...." (page 497). You may also wish to contrast battles viewed from a distance (as in column 2, page 499) with scenes from the thick of battle (as on page 457).

3. Answers will vary. Inversions occur in sentences like, "Then there appeared upon the glazed vacancy of his eyes a diamond point of intelligence" (page 488). Broken-off quotations are also frequently used, as on page 455.

Extending the Novel

You might, if time permits, want to assign each student to locate, read and report on some other novel or memoir about war, comparing and contrasting it with Crane's. In addition to those listed on page 507, some excellent ones are: Walt Whitman, *Specimen Days* (Civil War); Robert Graves, *Goodbye to All That* (World War I); E.E. Cummings, *The Enormous Room* (World War I); John Dos Passos, *Three Soldiers* (World War I); Leo Tolstoy, *Sebastopol Sketches* (Crimean War), Stendhal, *The Charterhouse of Parma*, chapters 3 and 4 (the Napoleonic wars in Italy); Hemingway, *For Whom the Bell Tolls* (Spanish Civil War); William Wharton, *A Midnight Clear* (World War II); Michener, *Tales of the South Pacific* (World War II; the basis for the musical, *South Pacific*); Tim O'Brien, *Going After Cacciato* (Vietnam, fiction); Tim O'Brien, *If I Die in a Combat Zone* (Vietnam, nonfiction); Philip Caputo, *A Rumor of War* (Vietnam); Ron Kovics, *Born on the Fourth of July* (Vietnam); Michael Herr, *Dispatches* (Vietnam); Joseph Ferrandino, *Firefight* (Vietnam).

Exercises in Critical Thinking and Writing   Text page 515
Making Inferences and Analyzing Point of View

In "Analyzing the Story," question 7, text page 438, students are asked to identify the point of view from which the third part of "An Occurrence at Owl Creek Bridge" is told. Before students begin on this writing assignment, you might want to review with them their response to the question and have them support that response with specific details from the story. Then have students discuss whether this third-person point of view is maintained throughout the story. Also, especially if you have discussed the "Background" material on page 81 of this manual with students, they may feel that the purpose of the point of view in this story is primarily to allow for the surprise ending. This is a legitimate response that should be supported, like all responses, with evidence from the text.

Criteria for Evaluating the Assignment. Students' essays do not necessarily have to follow the plan outlined in the writing section, but students should identify the point of view of the story and discuss several inferences the reader must make because of that point of view. Encourage students to use information gathered in the prewriting section to develop their essays.

Unit Seven: *The Moderns: The American Voice in Fiction*   Text page 517

Teaching the Moderns

The event that forms the far boundary for the era of the writers in this unit is World War I. Although America emerged victorious from that war, and—at least in comparison to the European combatants—virtually unscathed, the experience wrought great changes. Even for those who had no direct involvement in it, the war seemed to sever America's past from its present. The values and traditions of the past no longer seemed to answer. New social, sexual, and aesthetic conventions appeared to challenge old ones.

In the literature of the nineteenth century, a cluster of ideas and values, now collectively known as the American dream, played an important role. One element of the dream was the vision of America as a new Eden—innocent, beautiful, rewarding. Another was the optimistic belief that the future held boundless opportunity—that people's lives were bound to get better. A third element was the importance of the individual. All of these ideas were to be challenged and questioned in the light of new philosophies and political movements in the post-war world.

The ideal of the Edenic land is stated by the old man in "The Leader of the People," but scorned by his son-in-law as no longer applicable to modern life. In Faulkner and Hemingway, idyllic nature is cruelly juxtaposed with scenes of human violation—by the Snopeses or by brutal armies. The optimism that was essential to the American dream is satirized in Babbitt's soulless activities and, more sympathetically, in Anderson's "The Egg." Both motifs—Eden and boundless optimism—are sounded in *The Great Gatsby*—the former nostalgically, as for a lost past, the other in Gatsby's absurd but tragic belief that the dream is real and can be lived.

Of the original elements of the American dream, the importance of the individual alone remains a serious concern of the writers in this unit. But this idea has changed also. Instead of Emerson's "single man . . . indomitable on his instincts" to whom, in time, "the huge world will come around," Hemingway's twentieth-century hero relies on his pride in his competence, his will to go on, and his ability to exhibit "grace under pressure." Anderson's hero probes patiently but blindly for meaning in his life; Willa Cather's, William Faulkner's, and Eudora Welty's heroes and heroines are able to prevail because they are "capable of compassion and sacrifice and endurance," as Faulkner puts it in his Nobel acceptance address (page 619).

Modern American writers have explored the predicament of the individual in many different ways, but despite differences in temperament and style, certain common features can be discerned: stories and novels are generally less concerned with plot than with the exploration of theme; a good deal of experimenting is done to find ways of representing the thoughts and feelings of characters without authorial intervention; and a distinctive intensity and singleness of emotion figure as key elements in character. The concern with character of modern American authors demonstrates, as Alfred Kazin observed, "that fiction can elicit and prove the world we share . . . and display the unforeseen possibilities of the human—even when everything seems dead set against it."

Objectives of the Moderns Unit

1. To improve reading proficiency and expand vocabulary
2. To gain exposure to notable authors and their work
3. To identify and define major elements in fiction
4. To identify and define significant literary techniques
5. To express and explain responses to fiction, orally and in writing
6. To evaluate primary sources
7. To analyze the language and style of notable authors
8. To write original works
9. To provide practice in the following critical thinking skills:
   a. Analyzing character
   b. Identifying and stating theme
   c. Inferring the attitude of the writer
   d. Analyzing conflict
   e. Comparing and contrasting works
   f. Responding to a study
   g. Responding to theme
   h. Analyzing character
   i. Analyzing a story

Introducing The Moderns

As an alternative to assigning the introductory essay for this unit at once, you may want to give a brief account of the era and introduce your students at once to the Moderns themselves. (You can then assign the introductory essay after the Hemingway or Steinbeck selections, when students have a firsthand impression of some of the major writers.)

"The Egg," the first story in the unit, brings together some typical features of the work of this group of authors: It takes an ironic view of the Edenic land (a chicken farm in this story), optimism, and self-reliance—all elements of the American dream of the past. "The Egg" also has the advantage of being a funny story, a fact that will help get the unit off to a good start.

Sherwood Anderson

Text page 525

"The Egg"

Text page 526

Objectives

1. To determine the writer's attitude
2. To recognize irony
3. To predict outcomes
4. To identify and interpret symbols
5. To distinguish between external and internal conflict
6. To rewrite a narrative using another point of view
7. To write an essay analyzing conflict

Introducing the Story

The father in "The Egg" is driven by his wife's ambition to undertake ventures in which he has little prospect for success. His ludicrous failure as an entertainer—a role he invents for himself—is an attempt to redeem the frustrations and disappointments of years of chicken farming by making the egg the talisman of success.

Sherwood Anderson's concept of a *grotesque*, a person obsessed by a single idea or motive, is essentially a comic idea, even though the obsession may have tragic consequences, as in many of Anderson's stories. The person who rigidly pursues his or her course regardless of altered circumstances or consequences—like the stately walker whose averted gaze does not detect the banana peel in the path—has been a staple of comedy since the Greeks. The father in "The Egg" has only a mild mania: he mistakes his long acquaintance with eggs for mastery over them. The scene with Joe Kane, which really ends with the father gently placing the triumphant egg on the bedside table, demonstrates in simple form the basic situation of comedy.

In outline form, for your reference, here are the major elements of the story:

- **Protagonist:** the narrator's father
- **Antagonist:** intractable nature, symbolized by the egg
- **Conflict:** person vs. intractable nature
- **Point of view:** first-person
- **Significant technique:** development of theme through a single comic anecdote
- **Setting:** rural Ohio, in the early years of this century

Background on the Story. The frustrations and disappointments of contemporary life play a central role in Anderson's stories and novels. As his concept of the *grotesque* suggests, many of these frustrations result from a character's single-minded pursuit of an idea. So it is with the father in "The Egg." He feels he has paid his dues, through long years of suffering on behalf of eggs and poultry; now he hopes to achieve success through his mastery over the egg. The title of the collection from which this story is taken—*The Triumph of the Egg*—indicates how the father's hopes will be realized.

The Plot. The narrator's father, an easygoing farmhand, marries an ambitious woman who leads him to undertake several ill-fated ventures. After ten or so years of unsuccessful chicken farming, the couple starts a restaurant in a nearby town. There the father conceives the idea of entertaining patrons with masterful tricks involving eggs. He tries his act on Joe Kane, a young man waiting for a train, with comically disastrous results.

Teaching Strategies

Providing for Cultural Differences. Although the rural setting and the details of chicken farming will be unfamiliar to most students, their experience with television and movies should enable them to visualize the setting of the story.

Providing for Different Levels of Ability. Most students will have no difficulty reading "The Egg" in a single sitting. Some, however, may need encouragement to get through the somewhat discursive first half of the story. If you anticipate this problem, you might read the story aloud up to the point where Anderson describes the scene in the restaurant (text page 530, bottom right). From that point, the comic action should carry most readers along.

Introducing Vocabulary Study. Students will benefit from knowing the meanings of the following words before they read the story.

digress	528	incubators	528
duplicity	531	induced	526
embarked	528	monstrosities	531
enterprise	526	nonchalantly	532
grotesques	529	prenatal	530
inarticulate	532	venture	526

Reading the Story. The reading of this story makes a suitable assignment for reading at home or in class. If you assign it for classroom reading, you might ask students to stop at the sentence "There was something prenatal about the way eggs kept themselves connected with the development of his idea" (about one-third of the way down the right-hand column on text page 530). When students have read to this point, ask a volunteer to explain what this sentence means. Try to elicit the explanation that the writer is saying that eggs had a powerful influence on the father's idea as he was first working it out. Ask what kind of idea for entertaining customers the father might have been thinking of. Ask what the idea seemed to involve? (Eggs)

Before they read on, have students write down a prediction about the kind of entertainment the father has in mind and how successful it will be. When students have completed the story, sample the predictions.

Reading Check. You may wish to use the following questions as a reading check. Have students respond *True* or *False.*

1. The narrator's family's first business venture was a chicken farm. *True*
2. His father and mother pooled their savings to buy the farm. *False*
3. The narrator's father had a full head of bushy, unruly hair. *False*
4. The father's greatest treasure was a collection of deformed chicks. *True*
5. The father briefly succeeds in making an egg stand on end. *True*

Reteaching Alternatives. Anderson's reflections upon the troubles of chicken farming contain examples of verbal irony that you may want to examine with your class. Direct students' attention to the long paragraph beginning on text page 528, left-hand column. Ask whether the writer is being entirely serious in this passage. Explain that one kind of verbal irony involves exaggeration, and illustrate with a sentence like "A few hens and now and then a rooster... struggle through to maturity." Ask students if this passage reminds them of the writing of another American author. Possibly a student will recognize a technique often used by Mark Twain.

As an alternative reteaching strategy, ask whether the father in the story reminds the class of a common type in American literature. Students may recognize the well-meaning but ineffectual husband from television sitcoms and the comics. Discuss the ways Anderson manages to make this rather weak character sympathetic.

Responding to the Story   Text page 532
Analyzing the Story
Identifying Facts

1. What change took place in the attitude of his parents shortly after the narrator was born? The narrator's parents became more ambitious: the American passion of "getting up in the world" took hold of them.

2. What tragic facts about chickens caused the narrator to become "a gloomy man inclined to see the darker side of life"? Chickens are often attacked by disease. A few of them survive into maturity, when the hens lay eggs and the whole gloomy cycle is repeated.

3. Why does the family move to Pickleville? The narrator's parents plan to start a restaurant near the train station.

4. What are the "grotesques"? Why are they regarded as the family's greatest treasure? The "grotesques" are malformed chickens born with hideous defects. The narrator's father preserves them in alcohol and carries them with him in jars, because he is convinced that they will prove valuable.

What does Joe Kane seem to think of them? He finds them disgusting.

5. What means does the father decide on to increase business at his restaurant? He decides to become a sort of entertainer.

What dreams does the father have about the restaurant and its effect on the townspeople? He dreams that the restaurant will become successful as a social center for the townspeople, particularly the young people.

6. Describe what happens when the father puts his ideas into practice with Joe Kane. The father tries to perform several "tricks" with an egg for Joe Kane's amusement. First he attempts to stand the egg on its end, and then he heats it in vinegar so that the shell will soften and the egg will fit into a bottle. But the father is nervous and clumsy, and Joe Kane, who is waiting for a train, is easily distracted. When Joe pays no attention, the father becomes angry; when Joe laughs, the father throws the egg at him.

Interpreting Meanings

7. A *symbol* is something used to stand for itself and also for an idea or a force other than itself. A lamb, for example, often symbolizes innocence, and a serpent often symbolizes evil or duplicity. In the hands of a skillful writer, a symbol can have several layers of meaning because its several characteristics can stand for several ideas. A bird, for example, could symbolize

Sherwood Anderson   179

freedom because it can fly; fragility because it can be easily destroyed by larger animals; and beauty because of its song. **What does the egg symbolize in this story? Describe the layers of symbolism you can find in these characteristics of an egg: Life hatches from eggs; the shell is a protective cover; the shell is easily broken.** Eggs have often served as symbols of rebirth and fertility: consider, for example, the folk custom of linking Easter with eggs. In Anderson's story, the symbolism of the protective cover perhaps applies to the father, whose obsession with the restaurant may be a kind of protective mechanism, psychologically insulating him from reality. The fact that the shell is easily broken may symbolize the father's disillusionment, when he fails to "entertain" Joe Kane. The egg symbolism perhaps applies to the story on a more general level: the narrator implicitly draws a parallel between the gloomy life cycle of chickens and the life cycle of humanity in general.

8. Why does Anderson refer to "the triumph of the egg" at the story's end? How would you state the story's *theme*, considering this phrase and the egg's symbolism? The "triumph of the egg" may refer to the narrator's disillusionment with his father's life and with his own. One statement of the story's theme might be as follows: It is inevitable that one generation of human beings will follow another, but it is also inevitable that human beings are doomed to exist in a hard, troubled world.

9. The narrator says of his parents: "The American passion for getting up in the world took possession of them." How does the narrator feel about this passion? The narrator seems skeptical about this passion for "getting ahead"; materialism, he seems to feel, is a dead end.

How would a Romantic writer feel about the father's dream of getting ahead, and what would probably become of that dream? A Romantic writer would probably feel favorably about the father's dream, and in a Romantic version of the story the dream might have been successful.

10. Think of what you know about the narrator's father before the family moves to Pickleville. What evidence is there that his scheme to increase his business is bound to fail? The narrator tells us that the father was self-satisfied and content with his life. The evidence revealing his unambitious nature hints that the restaurant venture is doomed.

Does the father remind you of a common character "type" in American literature? Explain. Student answers will vary. Ask the students to defend their comparisons with specific examples. Certainly the father seems to share some traits with Washington Irving's Rip Van Winkle.

11. Does the narrator's father fit Anderson's definition of the word *grotesque* (page 525)? Explain. Most students will agree that the father does fit the definition, since he is in the grip of the single-minded obsession.

12. Do you think this story, especially its final scene, is pathetic or comical, or a combination of both? Why? Most students will agree that the story is both pathetic and comical. Even though the father is made to appear ridiculous, most readers will sympathize with him.

Writing About the Story
A Creative Response

1. Using Another Point of View. Before students begin to write, elicit from them a short list of scenes where the mother's role is especially important. Briefly review, as well, the relative advantages and disadvantages of first- and third-person point of view.

Criteria for Evaluating the Assignment. The narrative passage develops a scene of "The Egg" from the mother's point of view. It makes effective use of the point of view selected.

A Critical Response

2. Analyzing Conflict. Briefly review the meaning of the terms "internal" and "external" conflict, and have students list all conflicts they noted in "The Egg." Remind them to cite details from the story to support their points.

Criteria for Evaluating the Assignment. The essay consists of three well-developed paragraphs that describe the nature of the conflicts in the story and their resolutions by citing details from the story.

Primary Sources: *"They were not nice little packages...."* Text page 533

So Sherwood Anderson described his stories, going on to say that they were written by "one who did not know the answers." Anderson believed that the "history of life was but a history of moments"; he was convinced that stories that honestly reflected life could not be bound by principles of form or structure—could not be put into "nice little packages." Instead, they must be free to embody the tentative groping of his characters toward meaning and fulfillment.

Sinclair Lewis

From *Babbitt*

Objectives

1. To recognize and appreciate satire
2. To detect affective language
3. To identify clichés
4. To write a speech
5. To write an essay comparing and contrasting two views of self-reliance

Introducing the Speech

Since students will lack experience with the kind of civic club speech that Lewis satirizes here, you may want to describe some of the features of this American art form. Babbitt begins with classic bromides—the joking reference to the impromptu speech tucked into his pocket, the ethnic joke of no particular relevance, the protestation that he doesn't expect to do well as a speaker. Students, if they wished to do so, could find handbooks for speakers in public libraries that recommend such "ice-breaking" devices.

You may want to point out also that Lewis also has a few barbs for the newspaper reporter who wrote up Babbitt's speech. *Livest* for *liveliest, no where west of New York* for *nowhere else...*, the misquotation from Cowper (*the cup that inspired* for *the cups that cheer*), and such infelicities as *Mine host,* suggest that the reporter is as likely a candidate for ridicule as Babbitt himself.

Background on the Speech. *Babbitt* created a sensation when it appeared in 1922, for at that time businessmen enjoyed a mainly positive image in the public mind. (A few years later, President Coolidge was to say, "The business of America is business," a sentiment that Babbitt would have agreed with wholeheartedly.) Although Babbitt is ridiculed for his beliefs and for his way of expressing himself, Lewis obviously feels some sympathy for him. Babbitt emerges in the novel as a man whose individuality has been destroyed by his slavish adherence to conventional values and ideas.

Summary. The major points of Babbitt's speech may be summarized as follows:

Babbitt begins by praising Zenith, the city in which he lives and sells real estate, and goes on to eulogize "our Ideal Citizen" (also referred to as "our Standardized Citizen" and the "Solid American Citizen"), whose attributes are aggressiveness as a businessman, reliability as a family man, innate good taste in the arts, and common sense in politics and religion. Babbitt returns briefly to the theme of praising Zenith (which contains "the second highest business building in any inland city in the entire country") and ends with a diatribe against "liberals," "radicals," and other intellectuals whom Babbitt considers cynical and pessimistic, in which he warns that many of the undesirables are to be found on the faculty of the State University. Babbitt's peroration sees the hope of Zenith and the nation in the "two-fisted Regular Guy," another epithet for the "Ideal Citizen."

Teaching Strategies

Providing for Cultural Differences. While Babbitt's boosterism is exaggerated for satiric purposes, students should understand that it is not outrageously exaggerated. Boosters of towns and cities were less subtle in the early part of this century than they are today, and speeches not unlike this one were probably often heard. Students should note also that in the 1920's, a yearly income of $4,000 to $10,000, which Babbitt's ideal family enjoyed, was a very comfortable one for middle-class families.

Introducing Vocabulary Study. Students will benefit from knowing the meaning of the following words before they read or listen to the selection. (The starred word appears in the Glossary.)

| inebriate* | 535 | intelligentsia | 539 |
| impromptu | 535 | scotched | 539 |

Providing for Different Levels of Ability. Any speech is better to hear than to read, and Babbitt's is no exception. All of your students, but especially those who have reading problems, will benefit from an oral presentation. You might ask several of your better readers to study the speech and then present parts of it to the class.

Reading the Speech. As suggested above, your students will benefit more from hearing this speech than from reading it. You may wish to omit the doggerel poem on text pages 538 and 539. It satirizes the kind of poetry that formerly appeared in newspapers and expresses values that Babbitt approves of, but it adds little to the speech and may distract students' attention from it.

Reading Check. You may wish to use the following questions as a reading check. Have students respond *True* or *False*.

1. Babbitt already enjoys a reputation as an orator before he delivers the Annual Address. *True*
2. Babbitt envies New York for the cultural diversity that the many foreign immigrants living there provide. *False*
3. According to Babbitt, the Second National Tower is the tallest building outside of New York. *False*
4. One of the major products manufactured in Zenith is paper boxes. *True*
5. Even though Babbitt doesn't agree with the "fault-finding" professors at the State University, he defends their right to say what they believe. *False*

Reteaching Alternatives. The reporter who covered Babbitt's speech for the Zenith *Advocate-Times* was obviously favorably impressed. Have students imagine they are writing a review of the speech for the editorial page of another paper. Instead of quoting the speech, as the *Advocate-Times* reporter has done, students can write an account of the speech that challenges Babbitt's values.

Responding to the Speech Text page 540
Analyzing the Speech
Identifying Facts

1. According to Babbitt's description of what Zenith has to accomplish in order to become "perfect" (see page 536), how would he define a "perfect" city? To become perfect, Babbitt says that Zenith will have to plan more paved roads. The "perfect" city, according to Babbitt, is inhabited by ideal citizens who make four to ten thousand a year, drive cars, and live in nice little bungalows at the edge of town.

2. List the phrases Babbitt uses to describe his ideal citizen. What is his attitude toward women? The ideal citizen is busy and energetic, family-oriented, and prosperous. He has judgment in politics and taste in art. Babbitt also calls him the "Sane Citizen," the "Regular Guy," and—most tellingly—the "Standardized Citizen." For Babbitt, the ideal citizen is rigidly conventional. Babbitt pays no attention at all to considering women in his speech: one assumes that their "ideal" role is as housewives and mothers.

3. How would you describe Babbitt's attitude toward European civilization? Toward foreigners? Babbitt generally regards Europe as corrupt and decadent (even though he admits he has never been there). Although he says that "one of the most enthusiastic Rotarians" he ever met spoke with a Scottish accent, he is generally suspicious of foreigners. He loses few opportunities to contrast his vision of the American businessman with his supposedly inferior European counterpart, and at one point he mentions "foreign ideas" and "communism" in the same breath.

Toward higher education? See the response to question 6.

Toward art and literature? Art and literature are praised by Babbitt, but superficially. At one point, for example, he proudly proclaims that the United States has more "reproductions" of the Old Masters than any other country in the world. At another point, he envisions the Ideal Citizen settling back after dinner with "a chapter or two of some good lively Western novel."

4. Find details in the speech that reveal Babbitt's overriding concern with conformity. Students should be able to supply many details that reveal Babbitt's overriding concern with conformity: among such details are his obsession with "standardization," his portrait of the Ideal Citizen with his family, his objections to the liberal university professors, and his long quotation of Chum Frink's doggerel poem.

Interpreting Meanings

5. Although Babbitt pays lip service to friendship and harmony, he reveals a great amount of prejudice and hostility toward certain groups. Who are these groups? Where does Babbitt reveal his bias? Why would a person like Babbitt dislike or distrust these groups? The groups include foreigners, non-Christians, and non-whites. Babbitt indirectly reveals his racism and xenophobia in a number of places—as, for example, when he says that the great cities of New York, Chicago, and Philadelphia are "notoriously so overgrown that no decent white man... would want to live in them." It is also evident that Babbitt distrusts liberals and people and what he calls "cranks": anyone, in other words, who might dare to differ from "standard" American values (as he himself defines them), or who might dare to criticize American industry and progress. Babbitt's dislike and distrust probably stem from his own fears and insecurity.

6. Babbitt delivers this speech sincerely. But Lewis has written it so that we, as readers, feel his mockery of Babbitt. Tell how Babbitt's speech fits the requirements of *satire* (the use of irony or derision to expose folly). Satire pokes fun at the vices and follies of people and institutions in order to reform them. The portrait of Babbitt is to some extent a caricature. Babbitt consistently exposes himself as an advocate of mediocrity, of blindly rigid adherence to conventional dogmas, and of the exaltation of machines and half-formed doctrines above people.

Although he ostensibly believes in family, patriotism, justice, and industry, his picture of the perfect life relies to a great extent on prejudice and jingoism. He consistently emphasizes material objects and ignores the people who own or use them. When he discusses education, for example, he talks about the fine ventilating systems in American high schools, neglecting to mention the teachers, the curriculum, and the students. Babbitt manages to satirize Babbitt, and the system to which he so unthinkingly clings, through the words that come from his own mouth.

In light of the definition of *zenith,* **how is the town's name** *ironic*? "Zenith" means the highest point. The town's name is ironic because none of the achievements that Babbitt mentions would justify any such evaluation of Zenith. The "values" that Babbitt takes so seriously point, rather, toward conformity and mediocrity.

7. The headnote says that Babbitt really yearns for emotion. Do you agree? Do you find any evidence of this in his speech? Explain. Student answers will vary. Some students may point out that Babbitt has a vague longing for emotion in his comments on art, literature, and music. But, since he obviously possesses little firsthand exposure to these things, he remains, for the most part, mired in materialism.

8. How would you account for Babbitt's values? Why do you think he needs conformity and fears what is "different"? What are your own responses to Babbitt as you read this speech? Student answers will vary, but most will agree that—although Babbitt champions many broadly supported values such as family, patriotism, and piety—he does so in a narrow-minded and superficial way. Perhaps his fears of anyone or anything "different" spring from deep-seated insecurities: in the effort to be accepted by his peers, and perhaps to convince himself that his life of dull routine is really heroic, he forces himself to go everyone "one better" in his praise of "standard American values."

Writing About the Speech
A Creative Response

1. Answering Babbitt. Answering the response questions (above) will have established Babbitt's values in students' minds. You may wish to discuss briefly the kinds of values an opponent would offer in their stead, and to suggest that students read their papers aloud and adjust diction and syntax for effective speech.

Criteria for Evaluating the Assignment. The speech presents, in a manner suitable for effective public speaking, values and visions that contrast with Babbitt's.

2. Updating Babbitt. Discuss the kinds of audiences potentially receptive to a revised version of the speech. You may wish to give students photocopies of the speech so that they can make initial revisions directly on the copy.

Criteria for Evaluating the Assignment. The revised speech could plausibly be given today to the audience named by the student.

A Critical Response

3. Comparing and Contrasting the Speech with "Self-Reliance." Briefly review the excerpt from "Self-Reliance" (text page 194) as preparation for students' writing.

Criteria for Evaluating the Assignment. The essay cites both "Self-Reliance" and the excerpt from *Babbitt* in demonstrating that Babbitt's speech distorts Emerson's perceptions of the self-reliant individual, particularly in the area of an individual's conformity with society.

Analyzing Language and Style
Clichés

1. Examples abound. On page 536 alone there appear "lay down the battle-ax," "standing together eye to eye and shoulder to shoulder," "waves of good fellowship," "the wheels of progress," "first and foremost," and "busier than a bird-dog."

2. Babbitt expects unthinking acceptance and approval of his ideas and values.

Willa Cather

Text page 541

"A Wagner Matinée"

Text page 542

Objectives

1. To state the theme
2. To analyze setting
3. To write a paragraph describing a character
4. To analyze imagery
5. To write an essay comparing the responses of two authors to nature

Introducing the Story

The effectiveness of this story depends in large part upon the careful selection and presentation of detail. The hardships of Georgiana's frontier life are suggested by "the tall, unpainted house, with weather-curled boards, ... the crooked-backed ash seedlings where the dishcloths hung to dry; the gaunt, moulting turkeys picking up refuse outside the kitchen door." The elegantly dressed women in the matinee audience wear bodices whose colors are "past counting, the shimmer of fabrics soft and firm, silky and sheer; red, mauve, pink, ... all the colors that an impressionist finds in a sunlit landscape." Most important of all, Georgiana's response to the music is shown through a number of closely observed details—her gripping of the narrator's sleeve, her quick intake of breath, the tears rolling down her cheeks.

In outline form, for your reference, here are the major elements in the story:

- **Protagonist:** Aunt Georgiana
- **Antagonist:** the circumstances that compel her to live on the frontier
- **Conflict:** person vs. circumstances
- **Point of view:** first-person
- **Significant techniques:** careful selection and presentation of detail
- **Setting:** The story itself is set in Boston, but the bleak frontier setting of Georgiana's home, presented in flashbacks, plays an important role in the story.

Background on the Story. This short story reflects several themes that run throughout Cather's work. The tension between the values of home and family and the values of art, paralleled by the contrast between frontier life and the cultural life of Boston, reflects conflicts characters typically experience in Cather's stories and novels. Like the narrator of "A Wagner Matinée," Cather left Nebraska at a fairly early age to experience the thriving cultural life of the city—in her case New York, not Boston.

The Plot. Clark, the narrator, receives a letter from his Uncle Howard in Nebraska informing him that his Aunt Georgiana, Howard's wife, will arrive in Boston shortly on family business and asking him to look after her. Clark arranges for her to stay at his landlady's and sets out to meet Georgiana at the railroad station. Because of Georgiana's love of music, which found expression mainly before her marriage, Clark has planned to take her to a symphony concert. Her dowdy clothing and her worn-out appearance almost lead him to change his plan. He fears that he may reawaken the old conflict between her bleak farm life and her taste for music and civilized life. However, Clark does take Georgiana to the concert, to which she listens enthralled.

Teaching Strategies

Providing for Cultural Differences. Students who have read books from the *Little House* series by Laura Ingalls Wilder or seen episodes of the television series based on them will have a general idea of the stark simplicity of pioneer life. It may, however, be hard for them to imagine the full extent of Georgiana's sacrifice of her music. Remind them that in those days there were no radios or phonograph records and no nearby city with an orchestra. Their understanding of the fact that Georgiana's deprivation was total is the key to their appreciating the effect the concert has on her.

Providing for Different Levels of Ability. Good readers will have no difficulty reading this story at home or in class. However, slow readers will benefit from your breaking the story before the beginning of the first full paragraph in the right-hand column of text page 545. Discuss briefly what they know about Georgiana and her relation to the narrator so far. Call students' attention to the short speech of Georgiana's beginning, "Don't love it so well..." (page 544). Ask what Georgiana's sacrifice was. (Her music) Have students finish the story, or if you prefer, read the last part aloud.

184   The Moderns

Introducing Vocabulary Study. Knowing the meanings of the following words is important to understanding the selection. (Starred words appear in the Glossary.)

inert*	545	sordid	544
inexplicable	543	tentatively*	542
infatuation*	543	trepidation	545
myriad	547	turmoil*	546
reverted	543		

Reading the Story. Students reading at an average or above average level should have no problems reading this story at home or in class. As suggested above, slower students may need a break in the story to sort out what they have learned about Georgiana from the short flashbacks provided. The best place to interrupt the story is just before the concert with the passage beginning, "From the time we entered the concert hall . . ." near the top of the right-hand column on text page 545. Breaking at this point also has the advantage of having students practice predicting outcomes. How will Georgiana respond to the concert after all these years of being deprived of music?

Reading Check. You may want to use the following questions as a reading check. Have students supply the necessary word to fill in the blanks.

1. The narrator's Aunt Georgiana was once a teacher of _____ in Boston. *music*
2. She met her future husband while vacationing in the _____ Mountains of Vermont. *Green*
3. For thirty years, Georgiana has not been farther than fifty miles from the _____. *homestead* or *farm*
4. The concert Clark and Aunt Georgiana attend is scheduled for the _____. *afternoon*
5. The audience at the concert was made up mainly of _____. *women*

Reteaching Alternatives. As an alternative to describing a person's appearance (text page 548), suggest that students write an entry Georgiana might make in her diary after attending the Wagner matinee.

Responding to the Story Text page 548
Analyzing the Story
Identifying Facts

1. **Who is the narrator of the story?** The narrator is Clark, Aunt Georgiana's nephew.

   What message contained in the uncle's letter sets the action in motion? The uncle writes Clark that Georgiana has come into a small inheritance and is coming to Boston to attend to matters connected with the estate.

2. **Numerous *flashbacks* in the story provide information about Aunt Georgiana's life after she moved to Nebraska. Cite some of her hardships and disappointments.** The necessary tasks of farm life kept Georgiana busy from early in the morning to late at night. She washed, cleaned, cooked, and cared for many of the animals. Still, she found time to help Clark with his reading and his music. Other hardships included living in a dugout, getting water from the lagoons where the buffalo drank, and defending against Indian raids. Georgiana's principal disappointment was her separation from her music, which she had loved.

3. **Explain why the narrator feels he owed a great debt to Aunt Georgiana.** He feels he owed her a great debt because she had instilled in him an appreciation for music and literature.

   What special treat has he planned for her in Boston? He has bought tickets for a concert by the Symphony Orchestra.

4. **Describe Aunt Georgiana's reactions to the concert.** At first she seems impassive and out of touch with her surroundings. Little by little, however, she responds to the music, and in the second half of the concert she weeps from emotion.

Interpreting Meanings

5. **What seems to be Clark's attitude toward his uncle Howard?** Clark dislikes Howard.

   Locate the passage in which Cather hints at this attitude. In the first paragraph, Cather hints at this attitude by having the narrator comment that Howard has characteristically delayed writing until the very last minute.

6. **Georgiana says about music, "Don't love it so well, Clark, or it may be taken from you." How do you feel about this attitude toward life and its joys?** Student answers will vary. Most students will probably agree that Georgiana's statement reveals a pessimistic attitude. Ask students to share their responses with the class.

7. **As she often does, Cather uses a male narrator to tell her story. Locate passages in which this first-person narrator actually acts as an *omniscient narrator*. How would you characterize Clark? Can you see any reason why Cather didn't use a woman's voice to tell her story?** The passages describing Aunt Georgiana's feelings at the concert shift to a third-person omniscient point of view. Clark may be characterized as sensitive and supportive in the story. Ask students to discuss if they feel the story would have been more effective if told by a female narrator.

8. Summarize in your own words what Clark "understands" at the end of the story. Student answers will vary. Most students will agree that Clark "understands" that Georgiana clings to the experience of the concert as a symbol of the life she left behind when she settled with Howard in Nebraska. This life has been briefly recalled for Georgiana at the matinee, and, even though she will probably return to Nebraska, a wave of nostalgia sweeps over her.

9. The story contrasts the past and present lives of both Aunt Georgiana and her nephew. On the whole, what seems to be Cather's *theme* in the story? Students will have various answers. One statement of the theme might be prompted by the narrator's words about the soul (page 546): Even after great hardships, human beings have the capacity to endure and to "flower" again.

How does the central episode of the concert, reflected in the title, contribute to this theme? Music serves as the catalyst for Georgiana's "reflowering."

10. Willa Cather was an accomplished musician, and the powerful attraction of music is a theme that often recurs in her fiction. Find the passage in which Cather describes the effect the music might have had on Georgiana's imagination and feelings. Does this story convey some of the emotional effects that anyone might experience in listening to music? The passage occurs in the fourth paragraph from the end. Encourage the students to discuss their emotional responses to music.

11. In contrast to the music and the music hall is the emotional effect of the Nebraska frontier, the *setting* we hear about over and over again in the story. How would you describe the feeling Cather wants us to have for this setting? What specific *images* create this feeling? Students will generally agree that the setting is stark and forbidding: note the "tall, naked house . . . black and grim as a wooden fortress," the "black pond . . . its margin pitted with sun-dried cattle tracks," and the "rain-gullied clay banks." Also note that the story concludes with an unattractive image of "the gaunt, moulting turkeys picking up refuse about the kitchen door."

12. If this story were told by a Romantic, how would Aunt Georgiana's visit to Boston have turned out? A Romantic writer might well have minimized Aunt Georgiana's hardships in Nebraska and idealized her emotions at the concert. Or, possibly, Georgiana would have decided to remain in Boston. Ask students to suggest other possibilities for a Romantic version of the story.

How would a Romantic writer have described the Nebraska farm setting? A Romantic writer would probably have idealized the vast, open prairie and minimized the hardships of daily life.

Writing About the Story
A Creative Response

1. Describing a Character. Draw from the students an awareness of how the paragraph beginning "But Mrs. Springer knew nothing of all this" (page 543) uses carefully chosen physical details to support a single overall impression. Have students choose a real or fictitious person and the characteristics they wish to emphasize, and then list details that convey those characteristics.

Criteria for Evaluating the Assignment. The paragraph conveys specific characteristics of the person described through use of carefully selected details.

A Critical Response

2. Analyzing Imagery. Write on the chalkboard "farm life" and "city life," and have students brainstorm the images that stand out in their minds. Then send them back to the story for confirmation and expansion of the lists.

Criteria for Evaluating the Assignment. The essay contrasts Cather's most prominent images of farm and city life: for example, "black stuff dress" (page 543) vs. "shimmer of fabrics soft and firm" (page 545); "the deluge of sound" (page 547) vs. "the inconceivable silence of the plains" (page 546). It also describes the emotional impact of each set of images.

3. Comparing Responses to Nature. Have students skim pages 208–218 from Thoreau's *Walden*, jotting down events or images revealing Thoreau's experiences with a kindly nature, and ask them how they account for the differences between his experiences and those of Cather's heroine.

Criteria for Evaluating the Assignment. The essay compares and contrasts Thoreau's perceptions of nature with those of Cather's heroine, and offers a plausible explanation for the differences.

Analyzing Language and Style
Figures of Speech

1. The balconies are like terraced gardens. The balconies are filled with colorful clothing, the gardens with flowers.
2. The moving violin necks and bows are compared with tree branches tossing in the wind. Both move together in waves.
3. Strokes of the violin bow are like movements of a

magician's wand. The sounds of the music draw feelings from the narrator's heart, just as the wand pulls ribbons from a hat.
4. Movement of the bows is downward, like rain. The similarity lies in the quick, firm direction of movement.
5. Orchestral sound is compared with a tremendous downpour of rain, the music and rain alike in density, fullness, and brightness.
6. The chairs and stands resemble bare, winter cornstalks. Similarity lies in their emptiness.

Thomas Wolfe

Text page 549

From *Look Homeward, Angel*

Text page 550

Objectives

1. To paraphrase a prose passage
2. To make inferences about character development
3. To write an essay comparing and contrasting descriptions
4. To identify alliteration and figures of speech

Introducing the Chapter

Wolfe's beginning his novel with his hero's earliest American ancestor imitates the chronicle style commonly used by nineteenth-century writers. This device permits the writer to establish the main character's legacy from his ancestors—the talents, physical features, and aspects of character that may have been transmitted to him. When the hero appears, we feel at least partly acquainted with him; as he grows up, we look for aspects of character or temperament that he may have inherited. The disadvantage of the chronicle method is that it is slow to engage the interest of the inexperienced reader. To overcome this problem, you might ask students to be on the lookout as they read for aspects of character that these two ancestors might be likely to pass on to a twentieth-century descendant. Giving them specific details to look for will help to motivate their reading.

Background on the Chapter. Thomas Wolfe lacked the discipline to prune his work and as a result produced vast quantities of manuscript in which purple passages, tediously wordy passages, and intensely moving passages appear side by side. He was extremely fortunate in happening upon an editor like Maxwell Perkins who had the interest and the ability to shape a huge and amorphous manuscript into a coherent and moving novel. Wolfe has enjoyed wide popularity, especially among the young. Less widely read now than in the past, *Look Homeward, Angel* still has the power to move high school students with its intense depiction of the joys and agonies of adolescence.

The Plot. After a brief introductory reflection on the fact that human beings are the products of the accidents and chance encounters that befell their ancestors, this chapter recounts the lives of the grandfather and father of the protagonist of the novel. The former, Gilbert Gaunt, immigrates to America in 1837 and wanders westward to Pennsylvania, making a disreputable living by matching fighting cocks against local contenders. He marries a widow, who has a small farm, and charms the neighbors with stories of his travels and with Shakespearean speeches delivered in the manner of Edmund Kean. Gilbert's second son, Oliver, inherits from his father a passionate hunger for wandering. A chance encounter with Confederate soldiers when he is fifteen leads him south. He becomes apprenticed to a stonecutter in Baltimore and then proceeds farther into the Reconstruction South, settling in a small city and marrying a spinster ten years his senior. In a short time, his drinking causes his business to fail and his wife dies. Oliver resumes his aimless drifting, this time westward. The chapter ends with a description of Oliver's journey by rail and then by horse-drawn wagon toward Altamount, where he is to make a fresh start.

Teaching Strategies

Providing for Cultural Differences. Although the reference to Rebel soldiers on their way to Gettysburg locates the selection in time, you may want to remind students that Reconstruction was a troubled period in the South and that Oliver's ability to gain acceptance in the Southern city was a considerable achievement. Explain also that the Dutch referred to in connection with Gilbert's history are Pennsylvania Dutch—people of German origin—not Dutch from the Netherlands.

Providing for Different Levels of Ability. For less advanced students, you may wish to read these paragraphs aloud with the students following along. Explain that some details, such as the reference to the cock and the soft stone smile of the angel, will become clearer after they have read the selection. Then have the class read the rest of the selection, beginning with the fourth paragraph.

Introducing Vocabulary Study. Knowing the meanings of the following words is important to understanding the selection. (Starred words appear in the Glossary.)

bequeathed*	550	interminable*	552
epithet	551	invective*	551
improvident	550	reproving	552

Reading the Chapter. This short selection is probably best read in class. Your reading the first three paragraphs aloud will help get students started. When all have finished reading the selection, you may want to return to the first three paragraphs again, asking volunteers to explain what the "cry of the cock" and "the soft stone smile of an angel" refer to. (The former refers to the fighting cocks by which the young Gilbert Gaunt made his living; the latter to the angel that attracts Oliver into the trade of stonecutting.)

Reading Check. You may want to use the following questions as a reading check. Have students respond *True* or *False*.

1. Gilbert Gaunt led a disreputable life before settling down in Pennsylvania. *True*
2. The legacy he left his son Oliver was an appetite for travel. *True*
3. Oliver worked as a stonecutter's apprentice until he was able to carve an angel's head. *False*
4. The people in Sydney refused to accept Oliver because he was a Yankee. *False*
5. The town of Altamount was situated in the mountains. *True*

Reteaching Alternatives. Ask students to write a paragraph predicting how the experiences of Gilbert and Oliver Gaunt might be expected to influence the life of the as-yet-unborn protagonist of the novel.

Responding to the Chapter   Text page 553
Analyzing the Chapter
Identifying Facts

1. Where was Oliver's father from, and how did he come to settle in Pennsylvania? Oliver's father, Gilbert Gaunt, came from England to Baltimore on a sailing vessel in 1837. He wandered westward through Pennsylvania and settled there because he was attracted by the plenty of the Dutch farmlands there.

2. Around when and where was Oliver born? How do you know? Oliver must have been born and grown up near Gettysburg, Pennsylvania, shortly before the Civil War. He sees the "dusty Rebels" marching toward Gettysburg.

3. What detail in this first chapter suggests what the book's *title* means? The detail of Oliver noticing the carved angel in a Baltimore shop when he was fifteen leads to his ambition to become a stonecutter. His ambitions suggest that he wants to control his own destiny: to "wreak something dark and unspeakable in him into cold stone."

4. What habits ruin Oliver Gaunt's health? He drinks too much.

5. What effect does the theater have on Oliver? The theater inspires a passionate response from him, and he memorizes many of the rhetorical lines of the plays he sees.

What is the "pentameter curse" on page 552? This refers to the fact that Oliver ranted in blank verse, probably quoting the lines of some of the Shakespearean plays he had seen.

6. What does Wolfe mean on page 552 when he says that Oliver's foot "stayed on the polished rail"? The reference is to the railings in bars or saloons. Wolfe means that Oliver started drinking heavily again.

7. Why does Oliver move to Altamount? After the death of his wife Cynthia and the failure of his business in Sydney, Oliver strikes out for a new life.

Interpreting Meanings

8. *Paraphrase*—restate in your own words—the main idea that is expressed in the second paragraph of the chapter. One paraphrase might be: As individual human beings, we are the sums of all our history and ancestry, and apparently remote connections of time and place have their effect on us.

9. From the details describing what Oliver sees from the train window on the way to Altamount, how would you describe the way he feels about the land? The details, emphasizing poverty and gloom, suggest that Oliver feels despair and disgust.

10. What is the significance of travel in this excerpt, as it affects the characters of Gilbert Gaunt and Oliver Gaunt? Student answers will vary. Most students will agree that travel serves as a way to a new start in life for both characters.

11. What details in this chapter do you think make Wolfe a realistic writer, as well as a Romantic one?

Details that indicate Wolfe's realism include the description of the career of Gilbert Gaunt, the account of Oliver's poor health and its causes, and the description of the train journey.

Writing About the Chapter
A Critical Response

Comparing Two Descriptions. Suitable passages from Irving appear on pages 129–131. Have students select a specific passage of two or three paragraphs before they complete the chart given in the writing prompt.

Criteria for Evaluating the Assignment. The essay cites similarities from the passages by Irving and Wolfe in terms of use of colors, sounds, and smells; mood or atmosphere; and tone—the writer's feeling for the land.

Analyzing Language and Style
Poetic Prose

1. Examples of two alliterative words abound; sentences with three are harder to find. See, for instance, "the profits of a public house which he had purchased" (page 550); "He set up business in Sydney, the little capital city of one of the middle Southern states" (page 551); "the great barns of Pennsylvania, the ripe bending of golden grain" (page 552).

2. Choices will vary. See for instance, "Each of us is all the sums he has not counted" (page 550), "the minute-winning days, like flies, buzz home to death" (page 550), "ghostly hawsers of water" (page 552).

3. Some examples are "buzz" (page 550), "rattled" (page 552), "clacking" (page 552), and "dizzily" (page 552).

F. Scott Fitzgerald Text page 554
"Gatsby's Party" Text page 556

Objectives

1. To analyze ironic tone
2. To analyze theme
3. To write a description of a party
4. To write an essay responding to the story
5. To analyze the use of imagery

Introducing the Story

Although it did not enjoy the instant success accorded Fitzgerald's first novel, *This Side of Paradise*, *The Great Gatsby* has come to be recognized as his finest work. Through the innocent eyes of its narrator, Nick Carraway, Fitzgerald shows us an arresting view of fashionable life in the Twenties and prophetically suggests the toll that its excesses will take. Gatsby's party gives us a miniature view of that world and introduces Gatsby himself in his curious but characteristic role as both host and outsider at his own parties.

In outline form, here are the major elements of the selection:

- **Protagonist:** Jay Gatsby
- **Conflict:** Gatsby's false dream *vs.* reality
- **Point of view:** first-person
- **Significant techniques:** effective use of imagery; use of small vignettes to characterize many different guests at the party
- **Setting:** a mansion on the North Shore of Long Island in the 1920's

Background on the Story. Because of the instant success of *This Side of Paradise*, Scott and Zelda Fitzgerald were able to embark on a life of high living and big spending that established them as representatives of the "Jazz Age." But while Fitzgerald's first novel heralded that age, *The Great Gatsby*, appearing five years later, assesses it and finds it shallow and its promise unfulfilled. Not long after the publication of *Gatsby*, Zelda had to be hospitalized for mental illness, and Scott began a struggle with alcoholism, failing health, debt, and depression that was to end only with his death. The sense of impending disaster that built in *The Great Gatsby* forebodes the future of the celebrated Jazz Age couple.

The Plot. Nick Carraway, the narrator, is invited to a party given by his wealthy neighbor, Jay Gatsby. The party is already in full swing, although most of the guests have come uninvited. Nick attaches himself to Jordan Baker, a professional golfer and the one person at the party he knows. Later, a man about his own age recognizes Nick from a brief encounter during the war and invites Nick to hydroplane with him the next day. The man turns out to be Gatsby. Throughout the party, guests, few of whom seem to know Gatsby, exchange rumors about Gatsby's past and the sources of his wealth. We glimpse Gatsby himself observing his party from the outside but rarely entering into it. The selection ends with a comic scene in which a drunken departing guest knocks a wheel off his car in Gatsby's driveway.

Teaching Strategies

Providing for Cultural Differences. Although the 1920's may be prehistory for today's students, the big, extravagant party is likely to be familiar from movies or television shows.

Providing for Different Levels of Ability. Students should have little difficulty understanding the selection. Less advanced students may need help interpreting Fitzgerald's occasional impressionistic locutions (e.g., "...three men, each one introduced to us as Mr. Mumble"; "I had taken two finger bowls of champagne." Taking these expressions literally would be misleading).

Introducing Vocabulary Study. Students will benefit from knowing the meanings of the following words before they read the selection. (Starred words appear in the Glossary.)

caterwauling*	564	homogeneity	559
constrained*	561	inuendo	556
cordials	556	prodigality	556
echolalia	561	spectroscopic	559

Reading the Chapter. The selection may be assigned for out-of-class reading for good and average readers. Less advanced readers are likely to benefit from reading it in class in two installments. Divide the selection after Gatsby says, "I'm afraid I'm not a very good host" (left column, page 561). Ask students what they have heard about Gatsby before Nick meets him and whether he is what they expected or different. Read aloud the next paragraph, which describes Gatsby's smile, and ask whether it gives them a positive or negative feeling about Gatsby. After a brief discussion, assign the rest of the selection.

Reading Check. You may want to use the following questions as a reading check. Have students respond *True* or *False.*

1. Gatsby's parties were very exclusive and only a favored few got to attend them. *False*
2. Nick had known Jordan Baker before the party. *True*
3. Gatsby was considerably older than Nick. *False*
4. Liquor could not be served because of Prohibition. *False*
5. After the party, Gatsby's driveway is blocked by a disabled car. *True*

Reteaching Alternatives. Fitzgerald scatters details about Gatsby throughout the party scene. As an alternative to one of the writing assignments on text page 564, you might ask students to write a paragraph telling what people say about Gatsby, what is known about him, what he looks like, and how he talks. The details should be culled from the selection.

Responding to the Story   Text page 564
Analyzing the Story
Identifying Facts

1. Parties are notoriously difficult for a fiction writer, requiring, as they so often do, the introduction of many people who may not be relevant to the central conflict and story line. Fitzgerald has overcome those difficulties by using the guests' conversation about their host to create suspense. What are some of the stories these party-goers tell about Gatsby? Not knowing for certain who he is or where he comes from, many of the party-goers tell exaggerated and clearly untrue stories about their host. One says, for example, that she is sure he has killed a man. Another alleges that he was a German spy during the First World War; his friend says that she is equally sure that Gatsby served in the American army during the war. Jordan Baker, in whom Gatsby confides, says she has heard "simply amazing" things, but has sworn not to tell any of them. She also tells Nick that Gatsby once told her that he had attended Oxford University, but that she doubts that he went there.

2. Describe how Nick finally meets his host. What contradictory impressions does Gatsby make on him? At a lull in the party, a young man about Nick's age turns to him and asks if he served in the Third Division during the war. The man invites Nick to try out his new hydroplane with him the following morning. Nick explains that he feels awkward because he is a neighbor, and has not even met the host of the party. It is only then that his new acquaintance tells him, "I'm Gatsby." Nick is struck by the supremely reassuring quality of Gatsby's smile. But he thinks to himself that, were it not for his smile, Gatsby would resemble an "elegant young roughneck" with an almost absurd "formality of speech." He has the impression that Gatsby chooses his words with great care.

190   The Moderns

Interpreting Meanings

3. Toward the end of the party, Fitzgerald deepens the atmosphere of mystery surrounding Gatsby. Cite the details that suggest the mystery. Gatsby is continually interrupted by his butler, who tells him he is wanted for urgent telephone calls from various cities. The impression is that Gatsby is either an important executive—or, just possibly (given the lateness of the hour)—an underworld figure. The aura of mystery is also emphasized by Jordan Baker, who tells Nick that Gatsby has told her an "amazing" story, but then refuses to reveal any details.

4. Events at Gatsby's party at first appear as random and meaningless, but clearly the writer has a plan in mind. Which incidents at the party might *foreshadow* disaster? What human characteristics do you think might cause the disaster? The incidents involving the drunken guests, especially "Owl Eyes," might foreshadow disaster. The human characteristics that may be involved are excess, superficiality, and carelessness.

5. Fitzgerald achieves much of his ironic tone by juxtaposing the opulence of the setting with the snobbery and vulgarity of the guests. What incidents and snatches of dialogue seem to you especially effective in making this ironic point? Student answers will vary. Many may point out that most of the party-goers are portrayed as crude freeloaders, who lack either an invitation or any human interest in their host or each other. They are there to see and to be seen, and to overindulge in Gatsby's apparently unlimited supply of food and drink. Their stories and fragments of conversation are confused and inaccurate; even the comparatively subdued contingent from East Egg, representing "the staid nobility of the country-side" (as opposed to the social climbers), are portrayed as snobs. The drunken Owl Eyes, who is astonished that Gatsby's library books are real, is himself a boorish lout who proclaims he has been drunk for a week. Although we have the impression that Gatsby throws parties to entertain, and perhaps to impress, his guests, the guests themselves are shown to be even more "on the make" than their host.

6. Although the image of Gatsby dominates the chapter from beginning to end, the actual character figures in only a few brief scenes. How does Fitzgerald combine irony with compassion in his presentation of the *character* of Gatsby? The casual, almost imperceptible entrance of Gatsby into the narrative is highly effective in this scene. In one stroke, Fitzgerald manages to blend irony (everyone is enjoying the party, but not even Nick can recognize the host) with a more delicate pathos: in his formal politeness, Gatsby seems insecure, fragile—a figure who, whatever his true nature, is immediately set apart from the wild hubbub of the crowd. During the performance of Vladimir Tostoff's *Jazz History of the World*, Nick catches a glimpse of Gatsby, standing alone on the marble steps of his mansion and surveying the scene. Nick can see "nothing sinister" about him; indeed, he rather sympathizes with Gatsby's loneliness as he reflects that the host neither drinks nor dances. Gatsby is polite and correct as he bids Nick and the others good night. As Nick turns away from the house and crosses the lawn to his cottage, he sees the figure of his host once more, standing on the mansion's porch and raising his arm in a "formal gesture of farewell" to the guests. Here again, Nick is struck by a sense of Gatsby's "complete isolation."

7. Fitzgerald has been said to write of "the romance of money." Do you see that *theme* reflected in this extract? In what ways does this party scene also suggest that "the romance of money" is a false dream? Student answers will vary. The opulence of the party and the party-goers' efforts to impress one another certainly suggest the "romance of money." Fitzgerald's implications that the characters are living in an illusory world suggest that this romance is a false dream.

Writing About the Story
A Creative Response

1. Describing a Party. Have students analyze Fitzgerald's first six paragraphs, jotting notes on adaptations needed to fit a party in their own social circles.

Criteria for Evaluating the Assignment. While the essay may be shorter than Fitzgerald's six paragraphs, it evocatively describes the contemporary setting, character types, hosts, food, and music.

A Critical Response

2. Responding to the Story. Elicit from students familiar with the television show *Lifestyles of the Rich and Famous*, details about the lives of the rich in our own time. Briefly discuss similarities to or differences from the society described by Fitzgerald.

Criteria for Evaluating the Assignment. The essay uses telling details in comparing the society of the wealthy in 1925 with that of today, and comments on the points of relevance to contemporary life that appear in the description of Gatsby's party.

Analyzing Language and Style
Imagery

1. Choices will vary, but must create impressions of sight, sound, smell, taste, or touch.
2. Answers will depend on passages chosen to answer item 1. For example, "The lights grow brighter as the earth *lurches* away from the sun" (page 556) appeals to the senses of touch and sight.
3. Answers will vary. See, for example, "pastry pigs and

turkeys bewitched to a dark gold," "shawls beyond the dreams of Castile," and "the opera of voices" (page 556).

4. Answers will vary. See, for example, "stiff, red hands" and "dugout in the red hillside" (page 543); a "kit of mackerel...which would spoil" (page 545) and "a cornfield that stretched to daybreak" (page 546).

5. Answers will depend on those to item 4. The examples above appeal to the senses of touch, smell, and sight.

Primary Sources: A Letter to His Daughter
Text page 565

Fitzgerald was always keen on giving improving advice to others, and his only daughter, Scotty, was a natural recipient. The litany of things to worry about or not to worry about that ends this letter to Scotty at camp is basically serious advice, with a few bits of jocular counsel thrown in.

Ernest Hemingway
Text page 566

From *A Farewell to Arms*
Text page 568

Objectives

1. To analyze the use of imagery to create a sense of incongruity
2. To identify and respond to understatement

Introducing the Chapter

In this selection, Hemingway juxtaposes an idyllic natural setting and the trappings of war—far-off artillery, passing trucks filled with troops and supplies, soldiers marching to the front. The suggestion is that war is a harsh violation of the natural world. The seasons change from late summer to winter and the soldiers and officers pass on their way to the mountains, but otherwise nothing much happens. The chapter ends with the laconic observation that a cholera epidemic broke out but was checked and "only" seven thousand died of it.

The style, which became a Hemingway trademark, consists mainly of loose compound sentences with the clauses joined by *and* or occasionally a semicolon. Dependent clauses are used sparingly, as though to subordinate one element to another would be an unjustifiable imposition of the writer's judgment on his material.

Background on the Chapter. The setting for *A Farewell to Arms* is northern Italy during World War I. An ally of Germany and Austria-Hungary before the outbreak of war, Italy was persuaded by offers of vast territorial gains to enter the war on the Allied side in 1915. Fighting between the Austro-Hungarian and Italian armies was inconclusive until the Italians were routed at Caparetto in late 1917. The retreat from Caparetto figures prominently in a later part of the novel.

Teaching Strategies

Providing for Cultural Differences. You will probably need to inform your students that Italy fought on the Allied side in World War I and that the enemy on the other side of the mountains is the Austro-Hungarian army. The little king, who can scarcely be seen between the two officers, is Victor Emmanuel III of Italy.

Providing for Different Levels of Ability. Students should have no difficulty in reading this short chapter. Make sure that students recognize the ironic understatement in the final sentence.

Reading the Chapter. If possible, read this short selection aloud. Students will get a better sense of the flavor and rhythm of the Hemingway style if they hear it as they read along.

Reading Check. You may want to use the following questions as a reading check. Have students respond *True* or *False*.

1. It is spring when the chapter opens. *False*
2. The narrator's house was within sight of the mountains. *True*

3. The plain between the river and the mountains was rich with crops. *True*
4. The king was easy to recognize because of his immense size. *False*
5. An epidemic of cholera in the army broke out that winter. *True*

Reteaching Alternatives. You may want to have students examine Hemingway's style a little more closely. Put the long last sentence of the first paragraph on the board and mark off the independent clauses joined by *and*'s. Point out the superficial resemblance to a young child's sentence structure (e.g., "We went to the circus and we saw some clowns and there were elephants..."), which gives each item equal emphasis. Hemingway also avoids telling the reader which idea is more important than another, but his naive-seeming style is very carefully crafted.

Responding to the Chapter Text page 569
Analyzing the Chapter
Identifying Facts

1. What season opens the chapter? At the opening of the chapter, it is late summer.

What seasonal changes occur throughout the chapter? The leaves fall from the trees as summer yields to autumn. Finally, the rains come more frequently, as autumn turns to winter.

During what season does the chapter end? It is winter.

2. Hemingway is known for his sense of *incongruity*—an awareness that things which are seen together often do not "fit together" in a way we think is harmonious or appropriate. (A flower growing out of a cannon, or a child holding a weapon, would be examples of incongruity.) In this chapter, Hemingway describes two categories of *imagery* to create a sense of incongruity about the *setting*. What are the two categories? Make a list of at least six images that fit under each category. The two categories of imagery comprise word pictures of peaceful, everyday life and word pictures of war and destruction. Images of peaceful life: the blue, clear water, the falling leaves, the plain rich with crops, the orchards of fruit trees, the cool nights, the mountains, and the rain. Images of war: the dust raised by the marching troops, the artillery flashes, the sound of the motor tractors, the guns and ammunition of the troops, the small gray motor cars carrying officers, and the deaths from cholera.

Interpreting Meanings

3. Incongruity can create many effects—Hemingway often uses it to suggest a feeling of stress. Why would the incongruous images in this scene create a sense of stress? The incongruous images create stress because they convey that the war and its effects intrude on the idyllic scene of Italian village life.

4. Hemingway is said to be a Romantic when he looks on the natural world. Do you see evidence of that in his description of nature here? Most students will agree that the description of the setting is somewhat Romantic.

What is his attitude toward the war? Does he present the military situation as heroic or as something else? Explain. Hemingway does not seem to present the military situation as heroic; rather, he seems to describe it as a violent, unwanted intrusion on the natural world.

5. Like many modern writers, Hemingway uses understatement. An *understatement* describes a situation in terms much more restrained than the situation warrants. What understatement concludes the chapter? What emotional response do you have when the full meaning of this sinks in? The understatement concluding the chapter is the fact that "only" seven thousand soldiers died of cholera that winter. In fact, this is a very large number; when the full meaning of this understatement sinks in, we are left to wonder at the destruction that the disease caused.

"In Another Country" Text page 570

Objectives

1. To identify the narrator's attitude
2. To state the theme
3. To write a description of a setting
4. To write an essay responding to the theme
5. To write an essay comparing stories

Introducing the Story

Hemingway was himself wounded during his tour of duty as an ambulance driver in World War I, and this experience is reflected in several of his novels and in stories like this one. In this story, the wounded soldiers are isolated. The war goes on, but they do not "go to it any more." They are honored with citations and receive medical treatment but hold a pessimistic view of the meaning of their sacrifice and the possibility of a cure.

In outline form, here are the major elements of the story:

- **Protagonist:** unnamed narrator
- **Conflict:** person *vs.* hopelessness and disillusionment brought on by war
- **Point of view:** first-person
- **Significant technique:** first-person narrative with minimal expression of feeling or attitude by the narrator
- **Setting:** Milan, Italy, during World War I

Background on the Story. Like *A Farewell to Arms*, this story is set in northern Italy during World War I. Milan is several hundred miles away from the area along the Austro-Hungarian border where most of the fighting was taking place.

The Plot. The narrator, a wounded officer in the Italian army, receives physical therapy along with other outpatients at a hospital in Milan. The doctor in charge is enthusiastic about the new machines used in their therapy, but the patients remain skeptical. The narrator becomes friendly with three Italian officers, who are fellow patients, but they become somewhat distant when they learn that the narrator has received his decorations mainly because he is an American serving in the Italian army. He also meets an older man, a major, who had been a great fencer, but now has a withered hand as a result of his wound. The major helps the narrator with his Italian and is generally friendly. One day, however, he speaks harshly and rudely to the narrator. We learn that the major's young wife has just died of pneumonia. When the major later returns for treatment, he spends his time looking out the window.

Teaching Strategies

Providing for Cultural Differences. Explain to students that mechanical devices for physical therapy, common today, were mainly quite primitive eighty years ago. Probably the narrator, the major, and the other patients were justified in their skepticism. Students may also wonder about the "communist quarter," which the soldiers pass through on their way to the Café Cova. The quarter was populated mainly by working class people, among whom many were proponents of Communism. Communists were opposed to the war, a fact that accounts in part for their hostility to the young officers.

Providing for Different Levels of Ability. Less advanced students may need your help in understanding the occasional irony in the selection. For example, the observation that the plastic surgery for the boy with no nose was not successful because "he came from a very old family and they could never get the nose exactly right," is an ironic reference to the importance a notable family places on such hereditary features. Similarly, when the narrator tells the major that he finds Italian very easy, the major's reply, "Why, then do you not take up the use of grammar?" is an ironic putdown. Situational irony occurs when the major, who has been careful not to marry until he was invalided out of the army, loses his young wife to pneumonia.

Reading the Story. You might choose several students to read portions of the story aloud. Ask students to listen for the distinctive tone and sentence length. By breaking the reading after the first paragraph in the right-hand column on text page 571 and just before the last paragraph in the right-hand column of page 572, you will easily be able to point up the instances of verbal irony mentioned above.

Reading Check. You may want to use the following questions as a reading check. Have students respond with a word or phrase.

1. The hospital in the story is located in _____. *Milan*
2. The doctor who treats the narrator and the other soldiers is particularly proud of his _____. *machines*
3. Before the war, the major had been a very great _____. *fencer*
4. The narrator's problems with learning Italian involve its _____. *grammar*
5. The major's wife dies of _____. *pneumonia*

Reteaching Alternatives. As a prewriting assignment in preparation for the imitation of Hemingway's style, suggest that students try combining the following short sentences into one "Hemingway" sentence: *The fields were green. There were small green shoots on the vines. The trees along the road had small leaves. A breeze came from the sea.* (The Hemingway original, from Chapter 3 of *A Farewell to Arms:* "The fields were green and there were small green shoots on the vines, the trees along the road had small leaves and a breeze came from the sea.") Compare students' imitations for sentence length, structure, and tone.

Responding to the Story   Text page 573
Analyzing the Story
Identifying Facts

1. Who are the main *characters* in this story, and where is the story *set* (time, place, and season)? The story is set in Milan in northern Italy during World War I, in the fall. The narrator, a wounded American soldier, tells of a doctor, an Italian major with an injured hand, three young army

194   The Moderns

veterans, and a youth who wore a black handkerchief across his face because his nose had been smashed.

2. Describe what has happened to each of the characters. What "wounds" has each suffered in the war? The major, who has been a great fencer, has suffered a serious injury to one of his hands. The army veterans have all been wounded in various ways. The narrator has sustained a wound in the knee. The youth with a black handkerchief has had his nose smashed. In addition to their physical wounds, the characters seem psychologically "wounded" by disillusionment and despair.

3. The patients are the wounded heroes of a nation at war. But why did the people in the wine shops hate them? They hated them because the patients had been officers; the people in the communist quarter used to call, "Down with the officers!"

What details suggest that the young soldiers are isolated from the real life of the Cova district? The description of the walks to the hospital, when the four young men would have to jostle people to get by, suggest that the soldiers are isolated from the real life of the Cova district.

4. Within the fraternity of the war wounded, there seem to be two grades of heroism. How is the narrator different from his companions on the level of heroism? Why does he say "I was not a hawk"? The narrator feels that the three young men have thoroughly deserved their medals and that his own medals were awarded to him only because he was an American. He says, "I was not a hawk" because he secretly doubts that he would have been as brave as the other soldiers.

5. The major with the small hand is at first sympathetic and kindly, but his nature turns to bitterness with his loss. What is his loss? His young wife has died suddenly of pneumonia.

How does he hope to protect himself from this kind of loss? The major cannot resign himself to his grief. He tells the narrator never to get married.

Interpreting Meanings

6. The machines keep appearing in this story. What are these machines that are to make "all the difference"? Apparently, the machines are exercise machines that are supposed to strengthen gradually the atrophied muscles of the wounded.

How are the machines a reflection of people's attempts to recover what they have lost? The machines represent the hopes of the wounded soldiers to return to a normal life. The doctor tells the narrator, for example, that he will play football again "like a champion," despite his wounded knee.

7. What is the significance of the new photos in front of the major's machine at the story's end? The new photos, depicting all sorts of wounds before patients had been "cured" by the machines, are supposed to give the major some renewed hope. But the major takes no notice of the photographs, and only stares out of the window.

8. What do you think the narrator's *attitude* is toward these machines? By repeatedly quoting the doctor and by telling us that the machines are new and evidently unproved, the narrator implies a skeptical attitude.

9. How many things can you name that these characters have lost? The characters have all lost, at least temporarily, their physical health and vigor. In addition, the major has lost his wife to pneumonia. On an emotional level, it is implied that the characters have lost their sense of optimism and their feeling of "belonging" to a social community.

How does the opening description of the *setting* reinforce this sense of loss and death? The opening description, emphasizing the cold and the darkness and featuring the images of the dead foxes and deer, emphasizes the sense of loss and death.

10. What different meanings can you attach to the word *country* in the title? What does it literally mean? What other "country" or countries could it refer to? The word *country* in the title literally refers to the narrator's position as an American in a foreign country. But perhaps the word could also refer to a psychological "country"—a state of mind of hopelessness and disillusionment, brought about by the destructive effects of war.

11. How would you state the *theme* of "In Another Country"? What is Hemingway saying about patriotism, heroism, and the trust one should put in love for another human being? Answers will vary. But the theme of the story centers on human loneliness in the face of overwhelming odds: the destruction of war, social conflict, and the loss of those we love and trust. The frustration and pessimism of the story seem summarized by the major's bitter remark that a man "should find things he cannot lose." Hemingway seems pessimistic about patriotism, heroism, and trust. The narrator doubts his own heroism, realizing that his citations for bravery are somehow false. In the major, the author portrays a character who feels betrayed by fate. Students will have various opinions on Hemingway's philosophy.

Writing About the Story
A Creative Response

1. Describing a Setting. Have students brainstorm individually or in small groups the words they associate with each season. When the words begin to spark ideas, the students should begin to write.

Criteria for Evaluating the Assignment. Through evocative word choice and images, the paragraph describes a season in a manner that conveys an impression of life and hope or death and loss.

A Critical Response

2. Responding to Theme. Elicit from the class several statements of theme, or offer one of your own as a basis of discussion. Guide students to citing the story as they attack or support the suggested theme statements.

Criteria for Evaluating the Assignment. The essay cites, for "In Another Country," a theme that is supported by events and details of the story; and explains the student's personal response to that theme.

3. Comparing Stories. Since Crane's novel has the space to expand more fully on war themes than does Hemingway's story, you may wish to narrow the topic to a comparison of **theme** and **tone** specifically in relation to war injuries, decorations and heroism.

Criteria for Evaluating the Assignment. The essay cites similarities between Crane's novel and Hemingway's story in terms of their **themes** and **tones,** citing details from each work to support points made.

"The End of Something"
Text page 574

Objectives

1. To identify and interpret key images
2. To state the theme of the story
3. To write an imitation of Hemingway's style
4. To write an essay responding to a critic
5. To analyze elements of style in two writers

Introducing the Story

The stories collected in *In Our Time*, from which this selection is taken, are mainly about Nick Adams. Some deal with Nick's early life in upper Michigan; others with his return there after World War I, in which he was wounded—like the character in "In Another Country." Interspersed among the stories in *In Our Time* are brief interludes labeled "Chapters." The italicized paragraph that introduces this selection is an example. These interludes are mainly unrelated to the stories that precede or follow, although one of them describes a scene just after Nick has been seriously wounded. Graphically depicting scenes of war, bull fighting, or other violence, these interludes taken together give the title of the collection an ironic meaning.

In outline form, for your reference, here are the major elements in the story:

- **Protagonist:** Nick Adams
- **Conflict:** need to end relationship vs. regret at hurting Marjorie
- **Point of view:** third-person limited
- **Significant technique:** presentation of emotional scene mainly through dialogue
- **Setting:** a bay and its shoreline in northern Michigan

Background on the Story. This story is part of the chronicle of Nick Adams as related in the collection *In Our Time*. Several characteristic Hemingway themes appear: the wounded hero (Nick's wound is described in one of the interludes in *In Our Time*); autobiographical details from the author's early life in Michigan; the preoccupation with doing ordinary things neatly and well (e.g., Nick's advice on preparing the perch for bait); the alienation felt by a soldier returning from war.

The Plot. Nick Adams and his girl go fishing on Hortons Bay. They have no luck and land the boat on a point where they set up night lines for trout and build a fire. Nick seems irritable and when Marjorie insists on knowing what is bothering him, he tells her that nothing—including being in love—is any fun anymore. Marjorie leaves. Presently, Bill, a friend who seems to know that Nick was going to break up with Majorie comes along. Nick remains very depressed.

Teaching Strategies

Providing for Cultural Differences. Explain that the italicized paragraph that introduces the story describes an event occurring in World War I in France, instead of Italy, the setting of the first two selections in this group.

Providing for Different Levels of Ability. Since the important event in this story is implied rather than described, some less mature students may not realize exactly what happens. To avoid having anyone miss the point, you might have students read silently up through the last complete paragraph in the right-hand column of text page 575. Ask students what they think the relationship between Nick and Marjorie is. Is she his girl, his sister, or just a friend? Help students arrive at the conclusion that Nick and Marjorie have been in love. Then assign the rest of the story.

Reading the Story. Read the italicized introductory paragraph aloud to the class. Ask where and when this scene takes place. Elicit the response that the scene is France during World War I. Suggest that students keep this violent preface in mind as they read the story and then decide later what relevance, if any, the war scene has to the story.

Reading Check. You may want to use the following questions as a reading check. Have students respond with short answers.

1. What kind of fish are Nick and Majorie trying to catch? *Trout*
2. What does Marjorie call "our old ruin"? *The remains of the sawmill*
3. What specific instruction does Nick give Marjorie? *How to prepare the perch as bait*
4. How does Marjorie get back home? *She takes the boat.*
5. Who appears after Majorie has left? *Nick's friend Bill*

Responding to the Story Text page 576
Analyzing the Story
Identifying Facts

1. **The title "The End of Something" goes out of its way to be uncommitted about what has ended. On one level, what has ended for Hortons Bay?** Hortons Bay, once a thriving mill town, is now almost abandoned.

   On another level, what has ended for Marjorie and Nick? Nick's love for Marjorie has ended.

   On yet another level, what has wholly ended in Nick? Nick's pleasure in living has ended. He says: "I feel as though everything has gone to hell inside of me."

2. **What is the substance of the quarrel between Nick and Marjorie?** Student answers will vary, since the story is noncommittal on the surface. But Nick is obviously suffering from a deep, inner malaise—a nameless anxiety which he cannot define or describe. The joy has gone out of his life: he predicts that the fish will not strike, he says he does not feel like eating, and he bitterly comments to Marjorie, "I've taught you everything"—presumably about fishing and the wilderness. He tells Marjorie, "It isn't fun any more. Not any of it." Perhaps he means their friendship, perhaps he means life itself. The cause of Nick's dreadful anxiety is probably the war, as he tries to get over the nightmare memories of death and destruction.

3. **What is Bill's role when he turns up at the end?** Bill is one of Nick's friends. But Nick rejects Bill's companionship at the end of the story, apparently because the parting with Marjorie has upset him so much.

Interpreting Meanings

4. **What comment of Marjorie's shows a romantic nature?** She says that she knows there is going to be a moon.

   Does Nick also reveal a romantic nature? Explain. Most students will agree that Nick—although he may once have had a romantic nature—certainly does not display it in the story. He seems to take no pleasure in the setting, in fishing, or in Marjorie's company.

5. **At first there doesn't seem to be a relation between the prefatory note about a bloody wartime incident and this rather painful yet peaceful incident on the shore of an American lake, but clearly Hemingway intends one. If that wartime memory is Nick's, how does it relate to the rest of the story?** The prefatory note, a brief vignette of killing on a mass scale, provides a clue to Nick's deep depression in the body of the story. Assuming that the narrative "I" in the note is the same person as Nick, and that they are both bound up with the persona of Hemingway himself, the story poignantly records the mental and emotional devastation of a veteran, returned home from World War I and trying vainly to piece together his life. If students comment that this picture is quite different from more conventional portrayals of heroic homecomings from war, you may want to discuss with them the idea of "shell shock," and to remind them of the more recent, familiar accounts of Vietnam veterans who have struggled to put the war behind them.

6. **What *images* of violence or savagery are also part of this peaceful scene?** Among such images are the word pictures in the first paragraph, describing the end of Hortons Bay as a lumber town.

7. **How could the sawmill that was shipped away on a schooner be seen as a *metaphor* for a *theme* of this story? How would you state the story's theme?** Perhaps the sawmill, which gave life to the town, might be seen as a metaphor for the soldiers, including Nick, who were "shipped away" (transported) to World War I in Europe. The traumatic experiences of the war, in turn, led to the interior "death" of even those soldiers who returned; their spiritual malaise may be compared with the death of the town. One statement of Hemingway's theme might be as follows: The effects of war are not limited to physical death and destruction, but also include spiritual despair and the death of emotions.

8. **The word *ending* is key to the story's meaning. Is there any hint at all that something is also beginning? Explain.** Perhaps the final appearance of Bill indicates that Nick may find a path out of his distress through friendship with him.

Ernest Hemingway

9. "You are all a lost generation," remarked Gertrude Stein to Ernest Hemingway. (See page 567.) Do these Hemingway stories reveal any aspects of that "lost generation"? Do they explain in any way why that generation was "lost"? Could the label in any way apply to life today? Most students will agree that these three stories are thematically unified, in that they touch on the anxiety and despair produced in the "lost generation" by World War I. In "In Another Country" and "The End of Something," we see how that despair, even after the war, seriously affects interpersonal relationships. Encourage students to offer their own opinions of the links between the stories and to support these opinions with specific references to the texts.

Writing About the Stories
A Creative Response

1. Imitating Hemingway's Style. Before students attempt this assignment, have them do the "Analyzing Language and Style" exercises on the same page.

Criteria for Evaluating the Assignment. In rewriting a passage from Irving, Poe, or Melville, the student has evoked Hemingway's style particularly through use of simple sentences, compound sentences connected by *and*, stress on verbs and nouns to carry the story, understatement, repetition, and detached tone.

A Critical Response

2. Responding to a Critic. Briefly discuss Kazin's comments and aspects of "disorder" in "In Another Country" and "The End of Something."

Criteria for Evaluating the Assignment. The essay clearly agrees or disagrees with Kazin that Hemingway was a great expresser "of enduring disorder," and cites details from both stories to support the position taken.

Analyzing Language and Style
The Plain Style

Answers will vary (especially in how individuals respond to each style), but, in general, students should note the following points:

1. Fitzgerald's sentences range through every grammatical form from the simple to the compound-complex, while Hemingway tends to use simple sentences, compound sentences joined by *and,* or complex sentences using *that.*
2. Fitzgerald uses more adjectives than Hemingway does.
3. Both use color.
4. Fitzgerald uses a greater range of figures of speech than does Hemingway, who mainly uses short similes.
5. Sensory imagery is present in both writers, but it is more elaborate in Fitzgerald.
6. Fitzgerald's tone is less detached and distant than Hemingway's.

Primary Sources: Nobel Prize Acceptance Speech, 1954   Text page 577

In this short speech, Hemingway makes this statement: "For a true writer each book should be a new beginning where he tries again for something that is beyond attainment." Many critics think that Hemingway did not follow this precept himself, but rather stuck to a kind of writing that he knew he could do well. As William Faulkner said of Hemingway: ". . . he stayed within what he knew. He did it fine, but he didn't try for the impossible."

John Steinbeck   Text page 578

"The Leader of the People"   Text page 579

Objectives

1. To analyze character
2. To analyze ironies
3. To state the theme
4. To write a paragraph using another point of view
5. To write an essay comparing and contrasting characters
6. To write an essay comparing themes

198   The Moderns

Introducing the Story

This story, set in Steinbeck's native Salinas Valley pits the hunger for heroism and great achievement of an old man and his grandson Jody against banal reality. The Westward movement, in which Jody's grandfather played an important role, was one of the truly heroic chapters in American history. The fact that the old man's life has seemed anticlimactic ever since that long trek ended and that he is eager to relive those days through his stories is understandable and touching. Of course, the irritation of Jody's father at having to hear the same stories over and over is understandable also—especially since his own life is by comparison prosaic and unheroic.

You may want to tell your students that Steinbeck's most famous book—*The Grapes of Wrath*—is the epic account of another Westward movement—this one undertaken by depression-broken families who hoped to improve their lot in California.

In outline form, for your reference, here are the major elements in the story:

- **Protagonist:** Jody's grandfather
- **Antagonist:** Jody's father, Carl Tiflin
- **Conflict:** hunger for heroic achievement vs. reality
- **Point of view:** third-person, limited
- **Setting:** Salinas Valley in the early 1900's

The Plot. When Jody's grandfather plans a visit to the family, Jody eagerly anticipates hearing some of the heroic stories the old man is fond of telling about his experiences as leader of a wagon train across the west to California. Jody's father, Carl, is impatient with the old man's stories, but grudgingly allows him to tell them at dinner. The next morning, however, Carl angrily complains about having to listen to the old man, only to be overheard by the old man as he comes to breakfast. Carl tries to apologize, but the damage is done: the old man realizes that the sense of the heroic that he had hoped to evoke with his stories has died out along with the dream of "Westering." Jody comforts the old man by bringing him a lemonade.

Teaching Strategies

Providing for Cultural Differences. The time at which the story takes place is not indicated, except by the fact that Jody's grandfather travels by horse cart and, as we later learn, was a wagon train leader during the Westward movement. Explain to students that a general migration westward took place in the mid-nineteenth century, and in this the old man took an important part. His advanced age at the time of the story and his reference to the drought of 1887 suggest that the events take place in the early years of this century.

Providing for Different Levels of Ability. Less advanced students may benefit from having the first half of the story (through the bottom of page 582) read aloud. Then you can discuss briefly the differing attitudes toward the old man held by Jody and his mother and father. Once you are sure students understand the general situation, assign the rest of the story for in-class reading.

Introducing Vocabulary Study. Students will benefit from knowing the meanings of the following words before they read the story. (Starred words appear in the Glossary.)

arrogant*	579	rancor	581
dirge*	585	unseemly*	581
Piutes	583		

Reading the Story. Most students will have no difficulty reading this story in a single sitting, either at home or in class. If you have many less advanced students, try dividing the story as suggested above, with the first half being read aloud.

Reading Check. You may wish to use the following questions as a reading check. Have students respond with a word or phrase.

1. As a younger man, Jody's grandfather was the leader of a _____. *wagon train*
2. Jody was looking forward to killing the _____ that lived under the haystack. *mice*
3. Billy Buck is the name of a _____ on Jody's father's ranch. *ranch hand* or *hand*
4. The people in the wagon train used steel plates as protection against _____. *Indians*
5. Jody's grandfather overhears _____ saying that nobody wanted to hear his stories over and over. *Carl* or *Jody's father*

Responding to the Story Text page 588
Analyzing the Story
Identifying Facts

1. Explain why Jody looks forward to his grandfather's visit. Jody seems to enjoy his grandfather's company, and he looks forward to hearing again Grandfather's exciting stories about Indians and crossing the plains. When he meets Grandfather as the old man arrives, Jody invites him to share in the mouse hunt.

In contrast, how do his father and mother feel? Jody's parents are not nearly as excited as the little boy about Grandfather's arrival, although Mrs. Tiflin softens her attitude a bit by remarking that Grandfather does not come to see them that often.

John Steinbeck 199

2. According to Mrs. Tiflin, why does her father still talk about leading the wagon train west? She says that it is the only exciting thing he has ever done in his life.

3. What is the subject of Grandfather's stories? Grandfather tells about leading a wagon train across the plains to the West Coast. The crossing involved much hardship and danger.

In what way was he the "leader of the people"? Grandfather was entrusted by the other settlers with overall responsibility for the crossing. He had to ensure that the people had enough to eat and that they could defend themselves against Indian raids. Steinbeck indirectly suggests that Grandfather was also a leader in a metaphorical sense—as an aspiring, daring young man, he had participated in a heroic age of the American past, an age which now seems ended forever.

4. Steinbeck uses an old fictional device when he has Grandfather overhear something that he was not intended to hear. How does Carl insult the old man, and how does this exchange between the two older men affect Jody? Carl insults Grandfather by saying that he should forget his stories; no one wants to hear them told over and over. Carl's subsequent apology to Grandfather makes Jody feel ashamed.

Interpreting Meanings

5. What seems to have been the true significance of "the crossing" for Jody's grandfather? After the scene between Grandfather and Carl in the kitchen, Grandfather sadly explains to Jody that he hadn't realized people would grow tired of hearing about the crossing. He says that what mattered to the travelers was not the destination itself, but the act of "westering"—of steadily pushing forward across the continent. He speaks of the settlers collectively as a "big beast." When the beast reached the Pacific Ocean, there was no place left to go; sadly, Grandfather says that "westering has died out of the people." In Grandfather's mind, westering seems symbolic of the frontier dream—and, in a larger sense, of an aspiring state of mind among Americans. Both he and Jody, in contrast to Carl, have the intuition that such aspirations were linked with heroism.

6. Carl Tiflin is strongly intolerant of his father-in-law's oft-told stories. Do you think it is just boredom that provokes Carl's anger? Or could he be taking the stories as some reflection on his own life? What might that be? Student answers will vary. Carl is presented as narrow-minded, unimaginative, and slightly tyrannical. Perhaps his intolerance of his father-in-law stems from an unconscious comparison of Grandfather's moment of glory with his own dull routine.

7. Jody is the one character who can't get enough of his grandfather's old stories. Why does he have the appetite for them? The child is portrayed as imaginative and romantic; Grandfather's stories appeal to him because of his ambition for some sort of heroism.

8. Given what he says and does and given the way other characters respond to him, how would you *characterize* Billy Buck? Grandfather says that Billy Buck is one of the few men of the new generation who haven't "gone soft." All the characters, including Carl, seem to like Billy Buck; he is responsible, respectful, and solid.

What do their actions with the moth (page 583) reveal about the characters of Billy and Carl? Their actions with the moth reveal a streak of cruelty in both characters.

9. How does Jody in the early part of the story show a streak of cruelty, perhaps like his father's? Jody picks up a stone to throw at the cat. He also seems obsessed with chasing and killing the mice.

What is the significance of his decision to give up the mice hunt? Jody feels that paying attention to his grandfather, who has been insulted by Carl, is more important than pursuing the mice hunt.

10. The story is full of *ironies*. How does Steinbeck ironically characterize the modern age by the use of the mice hunt? Steinbeck has Grandfather imply the softness and puniness of the modern age by making him say, "Have the people of this generation come down to hunting mice?" (page 582).

11. There are several *conflicts* in "The Leader of the People,"—between Carl Tiflin and his wife, between Jody and his father, and between Jody's father and his grandfather. Describe the source of each conflict. Which interests you the most? Would you say this story is more about family relationships, or more about the changing attitudes of each new generation? The source of the conflict between Carl and his wife is Grandfather's visit. Although Mrs. Tiflin does not pay much attention any more to her father's stories, she insists that her husband show the old man some respect. The source of the conflict between Carl and his father is Carl's determination to control his son and to keep him in his place: note the ironic epithet "Big-Britches" for Jody. Jody's evident pleasure in Grandfather's visit and in his stories also annoys Carl. The source of the conflict between Carl and Grandfather is that Carl is bored and annoyed by Grandfather's obsession with the past. Students will differ on which conflict interests them most and about the generational significance of the clashes in the story.

**12. What would you say is the *theme* of this story? Do you believe, as Jody's grandfather does, that there are no longer any frontiers for young Americans? If you

200 The Moderns

disagree, where would you look for modern frontiers? One statement of the theme of the story might run as follows: The imaginative hunger of the human spirit for heroism and great achievement must inevitably clash with harsh, almost brutal realities. Students will differ in their opinions on whether or not any more frontiers exist for young Americans. Certainly, some students may suggest that there are still frontiers of knowledge to conquer. Ask the students to back up their opinions with logical reasoning.

Writing About the Story
A Creative Response

1. Using Another Point of View. Note that Jody is to write when he is ten years older than his age in the story. Ask students to cite some specific lessons they believe he learned, before they begin to write.

Criteria for Evaluating the Assignment. The paragraph is written in first-person as Jody, ten years later. It reveals what he learned from his experiences with his grandfather the day his grandfather overheard Carl.

A Critical Response

2. Comparing and Contrasting Characters. Students may wish to work together on charts of what each character looks like and says, how he behaves, and how others feel about him, before they begin to write.

Criteria for Evaluating the Assignment. The essay characterizes each man on the basis of what he says and does, how he behaves, and how others respond to him. Three key adjectives describe each man. Points are supported by details from the story.

3. Comparing Themes. Have students work in small groups, or consult their notebooks for work already done on the theme of each story, in order to list themes that touch on lost opportunities for heroism.

Criteria for Evaluating the Assignment. The essay correctly identifies two stories that touch on the theme of lost opportunities for heroism and cites details from the stories that support this interpretation.

Analyzing Language and Style
Figures of Speech

Paraphrases will vary. The figures of speech to be identified are as follows:

1. personification
2. metaphor
3. personification
4. oxymoron
5. metaphor
6. hyperbole
7. simile
8. metaphor/hyperbole

"The Migrant Way to the West" 　　　　　Text page 589

Objectives

1. To recognize in word choice indications of the writer's purpose
2. To write an essay comparing imagery

Introducing the Chapter

During the 1930's, thousands of families who had lost their farms because of droughts or the Depression trekked westward in hopes of finding a new and better future. Their quest parallels that of the settlers who traveled West in such wagon trains as the one Jody's grandfather led in "A Leader of the People." The differences, however, were striking. This "Westering" of the thirties was born of despair; instead of relatively well-planned communal projects, as the wagon trains had to be, these farm families started out mainly as isolated families. This chapter from *The Grapes of Wrath* tells of some of the needs and pressures that meld individual families into small traveling "worlds."

Background on the Chapter

John Steinbeck joined some Oklahoma farmers in the 1930's and spent the next two years living and working with them. Steinbeck drew upon these experiences to write his powerful novel *The Grapes of Wrath*, from which this excerpt is taken. This novel, which won the Pulitzer Prize in 1940, was both widely praised and widely attacked. It was by far the most popular of the protest novels of the 1930's.

The Plot. The chapter recounts how individual migrant families learned to integrate with other families to form and reform small worlds. These communities developed their own informal laws and shared experiences, food, joys, and sorrows. As they moved westward, these families changed from farmers, concerned about rainfall, crops, and dust, into migrants, concerned only with the obstacles to their journey.

Teaching Strategies

Providing for Cultural Differences. Explain to students that farmers in California held out the hope to these desperate people of being able to earn decent wages and to buy land. These promises were made to obtain a pool of cheap labor, and those who believed in them were cruelly exploited. Students should know that these people who were bravely struggling to reach California were destined to endure great hardships there.

Providing for Different Levels of Ability. All students should be able to read the chapter, either in class or as a homework assignment. However, less advanced students may fail to understand that the selection describes the way in which family units learn to integrate themselves with groups made up of others like themselves to improve their chances for survival. Discussing the final paragraph of the selection should help to bring out this important point.

Introducing Vocabulary Study. Students will benefit from knowing the meanings of the following words before they read the selection.

apprehended   592   integrated   592

Reading the Chapter. In order for students to appreciate the epic quality that Steinbeck is trying to achieve in this extract from *The Grapes of Wrath*, you might read or have it read aloud. Perceptive students may recognize that the number of sentences and paragraphs beginning with *and* have a Biblical ring. (Have students compare the formal, epic tone of this selection with the relaxed, informal style of the previous selection.)

Reading Check. You may want to use the following questions as a reading check. Have students respond *True* or *False*.

1. Each migrant family tried to keep to itself as much as possible. *False*
2. The worst punishment meted out by groups of migrants was ostracism. *True*
3. Each member of a migrant family had his or her own duties. *True*
4. When the baby in a migrant family died, it was buried in a potter's field. *False*
5. The migrant men still worried mainly about droughts and floods endangering their farms. *False*

Reteaching Alternatives. Have students compare the "Biblical" style of this selection with Hemingway's plain style. Have them compare sentence length, number of simple and compound sentences vs. complex ones, and level of abstraction.

Responding to the Chapter   Text page 592
Analyzing the Chapter
Identifying Facts

1. What economic conditions caused the migrants to move West? The loss of their farms during the Depression caused the migrants to move West.

2. We learn that the migrants developed a new social order and new rules of behavior on the road. What are some of these? Some of the rules include: the right to privacy, the right of the hungry to be fed, the necessity to keep the drinking water clean, and the prohibitions against rape, adultery, theft, and murder.

Interpreting Meanings

3. What specific words and comparisons in the first paragraph reveal that the journey of the migrants is not presented in romantic, heroic terms? Among such words and comparisons in the first paragraph are the following: "crawled," "scuttled like bugs," "clustered like bugs," "sadness and worry and defeat."

Yet, **in what ways does Steinbeck present the migrants as admirable?** He presents the migrants as admirable in that, for the most part, they are persistent in clinging to their goal and generous in helping each other out.

4. Explain what Steinbeck means when he says that these people changed "as only in the whole universe man can change" (page 592). Is this a positive or negative remark about people? The remark signifies that human beings have a unique capacity for adapting themselves to changing circumstances. On the whole, Steinbeck's statement is positive.

5. Do you think from this extract that Steinbeck saw people as essentially good and moral, or as essentially evil and corrupt? Support your answer with references to the chapter. Based on the evidence of this extract, Steinbeck seems to view people as essentially good and moral. He emphasizes the interdependence of the migrants as they move West: they listen to each other's stories, establish rules for a new social "community," and aid each other in hunger, disease, and death.

6. What are the differences and likenesses between the migrants' journey west and the westering described by Grandfather in "The Leader of the People" (page 579)? Both journeys involve danger and hardship, and in both journeys the travelers are spurred on by the hope of a "promised land" in the West. But the migrants' journey in "The Migrant Way to the West" is distinctly less "heroic" than the journey described by Grandfather several generations earlier.

7. What groups can you cite that separate and come together as the migrants do in this account? Explain the tie that keeps these groups "together." Student answers will vary. Urge the students to offer specific examples.

8. On the basis of this chapter, explain why you believe *The Grapes of Wrath* was either an attack on, or an affirmation of, traditional American values. Again, student answers will vary. But most students will point to the chapter's emphasis on cooperation, order, hard work, and ambition as an affirmation of traditional American values.

Writing About the Chapter
A Critical Response

Comparing Imagery. Make sure students notice that the writing prompt has two parts: first they are to relate the image from "The Leader of the People" to images of this chapter from *The Grapes of Wrath*; and, second, they are to comment on what these images may reveal about Steinbeck's feelings about the power of the individual versus that of the group.

Criteria for Evaluating the Assignment. The essay relates images such as those of how camps formed (*The Grapes of Wrath*) to the image of "a whole bunch of people made into one crawling beast" from "The Leader of the People," and speculates on Steinbeck's feelings about the power of the individual versus that of the group, citing details from the story or the chapter to support points made.

Primary Sources: Nobel Prize Acceptance Speech, 1962   Text page 593

Calling man himself "our greatest hazard and our only hope," Steinbeck sees literature as a medium for understanding which he hopes can bring about the perfectability of humans. Indeed, Steinbeck says that a writer who does not believe that the perfectability of humans is possible "has no dedication nor any membership in literature." The statement reflects Steinbeck's warm, somewhat sentimental view of human nature, but most will agree that the requirement he sets for "membership in literature" is extreme. It would exclude many great writers—Hawthorne, Melville, and Faulkner, to name only Americans.

James Thurber   Text page 594
"The Secret Life of Walter Mitty"   Text page 595

Objectives

1. To analyze the use of free association
2. To identify the central irony
3. To recognize parody
4. To write an essay analyzing characters
5. To write an essay comparing stories

Introducing the Story

James Thurber had an acute sense of the absurdity of an ordinary, domesticated husband, imagining himself in such heroic roles as navy commander, surgeon, and World War I ace; yet he also had a sympathy for this pathetic longing to be dashing, dramatic, and important. In this story, Walter Mitty's imagination soars the moment it is given a chance, letting him briefly plan one dramatic role after another, only to be dragged back to reality by his wife, a cocky parking attendant, or the recollection of a forgotten item on his shopping list.

In outline form, for your reference, here are the major elements of the story:

- **Protagonist:** Walter Mitty
- **Antagonist:** his wife
- **Conflict:** daydream vs. reality
- **Point of view:** third-person, limited
- **Significant technique:** clever use of free association
- **Setting:** Waterbury, Connecticut, in the 1930's

Background on the Story. Explain to students that James Thurber produced a number of stories and cartoons that feature a kind of anti-hero who finds it difficult to assert himself. Walter Mitty, the protagonist of this story, shares the predicament—sneered at by parking lot attendants, ridiculed by a passing pedestrian for muttering "puppy biscuit" out loud, and browbeaten by his wife. Walter is able to escape from uncomfortable reality, at least for a few moments at a time, into one of many fantasy roles in which he is always dashing, competent, and admired.

The Plot. On a shopping expedition with his domineering wife, Walter Mitty escapes from reality from time to time into a fantasy life rich in drama and adventure. Driving to Waterbury, he imagines himself piloting a giant navy seaplane through a fierce storm, until his wife rebukes him for speeding. Passing a hospital triggers the fantasy that he is Dr. Mitty, the famous surgeon who can do anything, including repairing a complicated life-support system with a borrowed fountain pen. Later adventures find Mitty being tried for his life in a courtroom, flying a crucial mission as a World War I ace, and finally standing with his back to the wall, disdainfully facing a firing squad. Each daydream is triggered by a sight or sound or trivial event, and each is cut short by rude summons back to reality.

Teaching Strategies

Providing for Cultural Differences. Explain to students that when this story was written in 1932, *hydroplane* was the name for a seaplane, not a boat with hydrofoils, and that fifty-five miles per hour was quite fast. You may want to tell them also that Mitty's fantasies mainly parody radio melodramas popular in the 1930's and 1940's. Because the medium was radio, these dramas depended heavily on sound effects and dialogue to tell their stories. The recurring sound effect, "ta-pocketa-pocketa," in Mitty's daydreams reflects this feature.

Providing for Different Levels of Ability. Students should be able to read and enjoy this story either as a homework or in-class assignment.

Introducing Vocabulary Study. Students will benefit from knowing the following words before they read the story. (Starred words appear in the Glossary.)

| craven* | 596 | inscrutable | 598 |
| fleeting* | 597 | rakishly* | 595 |

Thurber uses a mix of real and bogus medical terms in the Dr. Mitty episode: *obstreosis* and *ductal tract* are nonsense terms, but *streptothricosis* is actually the name of an infection caused by a fungus (all three occur on page 595); *coreopsis* (596) is a wildflower, not a morbid condition. Similarly, when Mitty is reviewing his mental shopping list (596), *carborundum*, *initiative*, and *referendum* are real words, but not the names of things likely to be found on a shopping list.

Reading the Story. Try reading the first paragraph to the class, as the headnote suggests, and ask students what they think the story will be about. If you have time, read the entire story aloud, or have some of your better readers do the reading. Students will enjoy sharing the story.

Reading Check. You may wish to use the following questions as a reading check. Have students respond *True* or *False*.

1. Mrs. Mitty reminds Walter to buy a snow shovel. *False*
2. As Dr. Mitty, Walter repairs the anesthetizer with a metal coat hanger. *False*
3. One item on Walter's shopping list is puppy biscuits. *True*
4. One of the roles Walter imagines himself in is that of a crusading district attorney. *False*
5. An article about German air power triggers Mitty's fantasy about being a World War I ace. *True*

Reteaching Alternatives. You might have students try writing an updated Mitty fantasy, using the jargon from a current television program or movie—e.g., Mitty could be a police lieutenant, a computer expert, or a private eye.

Responding to the Story   Text page 598
Analyzing the Story
Identifying Facts

1. **Describe the *setting* of Walter Mitty's everyday life.** Walter Mitty leads a routine, dull existence in suburban Connecticut. He is on a shopping expedition with his wife.

   In contrast, what are the settings of his secret life? Mitty imagines himself as a heroic figure in a variety of romantic daydreams. In the first fantasy, at the opening of the story, he is a Navy pilot fearlessly commanding his plane in a dangerous storm. He then imagines himself as a world-famous surgeon, implored by the other doctors to supervise a tricky operation on a celebrated patient. In the third fantasy, Mitty is a star defense witness at a murder trial. Then he is Captain Mitty, bravely risking his life on a crucial wartime mission. Finally, he imagines himself as a prisoner about to be executed by a firing squad.

2. What errands is Mitty on in his real life? His errands include getting some overshoes and buying puppy biscuit.

What deeds does he perform in his secret life? He commands a war plane, performs a tricky surgical operation, testifies at a murder trial, and executes a critical wartime mission.

3. Thurber makes use of a psychological technique known as *free association*, in which words and sounds from real life become associated with elements of Mitty's daydreams. How does each daydream begin, and what sends Mitty into it? What decidedly unheroic events snap Mitty out of his reveries? Thurber ingeniously uses association to guide the flow of the story from incidents in Mitty's real world to the dream episodes and back again. For example, the notion of speed at the opening of the story connects Mitty's fantasy of the Navy plane with Mrs. Mitty's unheroic reproach, "Not so fast! You're driving too fast!" The mention of gloves is associated with "Dr. Mitty's" surgical gloves in the episode of the operating room. This episode ends with the parking lot attendant jarring Mitty back to reality. Mitty's remark to himself that he will wear his right arm in a sling is interwoven with a detail in the courtroom episode. The insult at the end of that fantasy, "You miserable cur!", leads directly into Mitty remembering (in real life) that he needs to buy puppy biscuit. As Mitty leafs through a magazine in the hotel lobby, he sees an article about the German air force; the headline leads into his fantasy about piloting a bomber to destroy an enemy ammunition dump.

Interpreting Meanings

4. What is the central *irony* of Mitty's life? Is this irony humorous, serious, or partly both? Explain. The central irony stems from the extreme gulf separating Mitty's real world from his fantasy world. Whereas Mitty imagines himself as heroically courageous and universally admired, in real life he is timid, insecure, and henpecked by his wife. Student interpretations of the tone of the irony will differ. On the surface, the story is humorous in its consistent emphasis on the incongruity of Mitty's daydreams. Some students may feel that there is an element of pathos in the portrait of Mitty's need to escape from reality, and some may point to the rather unsympathetic portrayal of the nagging Mrs. Mitty.

5. *Parody* is the satirical imitation of someone's speech, manners, or ideas. Where does Thurber use parody in this story? Who or what are the targets of the satire? Most obviously, Thurber parodies technical jargon, as with the phrase "obstreosis of the ductal tract" in the hospital fantasy. But we should also notice that Mitty's fantasies themselves are broad parodies of stereotyped situations and characters: the intrepid flight commander leading his anxious crew through a storm, for example, or the surgeon with nerves of steel, or the dramatic revelation at a courtroom trial and Mitty's chivalrous defense of the "lovely, dark-haired girl" in his arms. The dialogue that Mitty imagines in these scenes (including lines for himself such as "We're going through!" and "You miserable cur!" and "We only live once . . . Or do we?") almost seems a parody of lines from adventure movies. Ask the students if they have seen any films starring Humphrey Bogart; those who have will easily recognize the ethos of Mitty's fantasies.

6. Walter Mitty could be seen as one of a line of archetypal American characters that begins with Ben Franklin's "self-made man." What does Mitty's life reveal about the opportunities offered for heroism today? What is your opinion of Thurber's message here? Mitty's life reveals that there are few opportunities offered for heroism today. Thurber implies that heroism exists primarily in the realm of fantasy. Students will differ in their opinions of Thurber's message.

7. Could Mitty be a disappointed romantic? Explain. Most students will agree that Mitty could be regarded as a disappointed romantic. His life of dull routine fails to correspond to his interior image of himself as dashing, heroic, and glorious.

Writing About the Story
A Critical Response

1. Analyzing Characters. Brainstorm a list of popular Mr. and Mrs. Mitty types, ranging from Dagwood and Blondie to couples in current movies and TV shows. Identify the key traits of Mr. and Mrs. Mitty, and reevaluate the list of current couples for how well they fit the type.

Criteria for Evaluating the Assignment. The essay analyzes the key traits that make Mr. and Mrs. Walter Mitty stock American character types, and cites several couples of that type found in today's popular movies and television shows.

2. Comparing Stories. Call students' attention to the fact that the writing prompt outlines what the essay of comparison and contrast is to contain.

Criteria for Evaluating the Assignment. The essay shows similarities and differences between the Van Winkle and Mitty stories in terms of the four characters' strengths and weaknesses, sources of the couples' conflicts, how the conflicts are resolved, the husband-wife relationships, and story tone.

Primary Sources: The New Yorker's Farewell
Text page 599

The New Yorker is noted for graceful, touching eulogies for deceased workers and staff members, and E.B. White was perhaps the best to attempt this difficult kind of writing. This tribute suggests the scope of Thurber's comic genius without ever falling into extravagance or sentimentality. The sentence "During his happiest years, Thurber did not write the way a surgeon operated, he wrote the way a child skips rope, the way a mouse dances" is pure White and one that Thurber would have admired.

Katherine Anne Porter
Text page 600

"The Grave"
Text page 601

Objectives

1. To recognize irony
2. To state the theme
3. To write an essay responding to a critical comment
4. To recognize and interpret imagery and symbolism

Introducing the Story

This story describes a young girl's rite of passage as she suddenly grasps the meaning of life and death. The sight of the unborn rabbits is an experience that provides Miranda with a sudden insight into the very nature of reality.

In outline form, for your reference, here are the major elements of the story:

- **Protagonist:** Miranda
- **Conflict:** innocence vs. experience
- **Point of view:** third-person, omniscient
- **Setting:** rural Texas, 1903
- **Significant technique:** use of imagery to suggest a state of mind

Background on the Story. This story concerns Miranda, the autobiographical heroine of a number of Katherine Anne Porter's stories. These stories record Miranda's progress from innocence to experience and her questioning of the network of custom and obligation in which she finds herself. Like Miranda, Porter grew up in rural Texas about the turn of the century.

The Plot. Miranda and her brother, who are out hunting rabbits, pause to explore what had been the family cemetery until the bodies were removed preparatory to the sale of the land. In the empty graves they find two treasures: a gold wedding ring and the screw head for a coffin decorated with a silver dove. The children resume their hunt and soon see a rabbit, which Paul kills. On skinning the rabbit, Paul discovers that it is a female carrying a number of fetuses. The sight of the unborn rabbits gives Miranda a sudden insight into the reality of death, which her exploration of an open grave had not.

Teaching Strategies

Providing for Cultural Differences. Since the burial of family members on private property is now extremely rare, students should be told that this practice was once common, particularly in the South.

Providing for Different Levels of Ability. Less advanced students may need your help in understanding the effect the sight of the unborn rabbits has on Miranda. Through discussion you can help these students see that Miranda is not merely repelled by the sight of blood, but rather shaken by a sudden insight into the reality of life and death.

Introducing Vocabulary Study. Students will benefit from knowing the meanings of the following words before they read the story. (Starred words appear in the Glossary.)

covetousness	601	intuitions*	603
exasperating*	602	oddments	601

206   The Moderns

Reading the Story. This short story is best read in class if there is ample time for discussion. As suggested above, less advanced students are likely to have difficulty grasping the significance of Miranda's experience.

Reading Check. You may wish to use the following questions as a reading check. Have students respond with short answers.

1. Why does Paul object to having Miranda fire her rifle at the same time he does? *Miranda always claims any game they get firing at the same moment.*
2. What is the silver dove? *The head of a coffin screw*
3. Why was the family cemetery abandoned? *The family had sold the property on which it was located.*
4. Whose shot kills the rabbit? *Paul's*
5. Why does Paul skin the rabbit? *Miranda uses the fur to make coats for her dolls.*

Reteaching Alternatives. You may wish to explore with your students the central irony of the story. The children climb in and out of graves, find mementos of dead ancestors but give death no thought. Then, the killing of the pregnant rabbit after they have left the cemetery brings home the reality of life, birth, and death. Have students review the definition of situational irony in *A Handbook of Literary Terms.*

Responding to the Story   Text page 604
Analyzing the Story
Identifying Facts

1. When and where does the major incident of the story take place? The major incident occurs in 1903 at a graveyard in Texas.

How old are Miranda and Paul? Miranda is nine years old, and Paul is twelve.

2. What are they hunting? They are hunting doves and rabbits.

How are their feelings about hunting different? Paul takes hunting very seriously and is a good shot. Miranda is not especially interested in hitting any targets; she likes walking around in the open air.

3. What does Miranda discover in the grave she explores? What does Paul find? Miranda discovers a silver dove (which is really a coffin screw) and Paul finds a gold ring.

What do they do with the things they find? After a little bickering, they trade.

4. What does Miranda want to do about her clothing after she puts the ring on? (How does the ring make her think of her role as a woman?) She wants to take a cold bath, dust herself with some of her older sister's talcum powder, and put on the thinnest, prettiest dress she owns.

5. At first Miranda is excited by her discovery of the rabbit's young ones. What changes her feelings, so that she begins to tremble? How does Porter go on to describe what Miranda discovers about herself? Miranda sees that the young ones are covered with blood, and she begins to tremble. Porter goes on to indicate that Miranda intuitively understands her own budding womanhood and the process of reproduction.

6. The *setting* of the story changes in the final paragraph. **Where and when does it take place?** The final scene takes place on a market street "in a strange city of a strange country." This scene occurs nearly twenty years after the principal episode in the story.

How is this scene connected with the incident involving the rabbit? Certain sense images link the scene in Miranda's mind to that long-ago day when she and her brother had explored the graves.

Interpreting Meanings

7. How do you think the incident with the rabbit relates to the discovery of the dove and the ring? (Think about where the dove and the ring had really come from, and whether the rabbit changed the children's feelings about their treasures, which they had initially regarded only with delight.) The dove and the ring come from graves, and they are symbolically related to death. On the other hand, the incident with the rabbit symbolically suggests both birth and death.

8. Chart the changes in Miranda's feelings from the beginning to the end of this story. Be sure you are clear on what causes the changes. At the beginning of the story, Miranda shares Paul's excitement in exploring the graves and his delight at finding a "treasure." While the two children are hunting, Miranda's mood gives way to a dreamy lack of interest; her thoughts touch on her unconventional way of dressing and on the romantic yearnings inspired by the ring. When Paul displays the dead rabbit, Miranda admires his facility in skinning it. She stares at the unborn baby rabbits in wonder; but then she trembles as she sees the blood that surrounds them. For reasons that she can't completely understand, she now knows that she has an intuitive insight about her own body, and perhaps about birth and death. In agitation, she rejects the skin of the rabbit. Promising never to tell that Paul has killed a pregnant animal, she represses the "whole worrisome affair" after a few days. But, suddenly, nearly twenty years later, a combination of images recalls the memory of the incident.

9. Why do you think Paul insists that Miranda not tell their father about the rabbit he has killed? He insists that

Katherine Anne Porter   207

Miranda not tell because it is against the traditional code of hunters to kill a pregnant animal. Perhaps he is also afraid of getting into trouble with the father for showing Miranda things that she should not see, given her age.

10. What do you think Miranda and her brother discover about birth and life and death on that long-ago day? The encounters of the two children show them that birth and death—though bewildering and sometimes frightening—are inescapable and natural.

11. How would you state the story's *theme*? Student answers will vary. One statement of the theme might run as follows: Everyone experiences a moment of direct confrontation with the inescapable facts of life in nature, birth and death, and this moment makes an indelible impression on the memory.

Writing About the Story
A Critical Response

Responding to a Critical Comment. Discuss both the critics' remark, and what the divisions of a three-paragraph response essay might be.

Criteria for Evaluating the Assignment. The essay consists of three well-developed paragraphs that state an opinion on the critics' remark, and cite passages from the story to support the writer's opinions.

Analyzing Language and Style
Imagery and Symbolism

1. *Miranda* means "admiring" or "to be admired." The name also evokes the Miranda of Shakespeare's *The Tempest,* who gazed with awe on the visitors to her island.

2. Interpretations of summer symbolism will vary. Some may suggest a time of freedom or waiting before the maturity of fall.

3. A dove usually symbolizes peace. A wedding ring usually symbolizes unity or endless commitment.

4. The final image, her brother's face, is a face of experience by comparison with Miranda's at that time. The tray of sweets is similarly an image of experience. Answers will vary about the definitions of innocence and experience. In terms of this story, awareness of sexuality and how children are born represents experience; lack of that knowledge represents innocence.

William Faulkner   Text page 605

"Spotted Horses"   Text page 607

Objectives

1. To analyze character
2. To recognize comic comparisons
3. To write a tall tale
4. To write an essay responding to a critic
5. To write an essay comparing two writers
6. To recognize uses of dialect

208   The Moderns

Introducing the Story

Make sure that all students read the headnote which includes Malcolm Cowley's account of the Snopes family in general and Flem in particular.

In outline form, for your reference, here are the major elements in the story:

- **Protagonist:** Flem Snopes
- **Conflict:** sharp dealer vs. his victims
- **Point of view:** first-person (minor character)
- **Significant techniques:** skillful use of regional speech; use of exaggeration and irony in spinning a tall tale
- **Setting:** Frenchman's Bend, Yoknapatawpha County, Mississippi, late nineteenth century

Background on the Story. Students should have at least a general acquaintance with Faulkner's Yoknapatawpha County and its main inhabitants, including the insufferable Snopes clan. Read aloud at least the following excerpts from the introductory material on pages 605–06: the second paragraph (605); the passage beginning with the first complete paragaph on page 606 and ending with the last complete paragraph in the left-hand column.

The Plot. Flem Snopes, absent from Frenchman's Bend for almost a year, reappears in the company of a Texan bringing about two dozen wild ponies. The next morning, the Texan auctions off the horses. Eck Snopes, Flem's cousin, is given a horse in return for starting the bidding. Henry Armstid, a poverty-stricken farmer ignores his wife's protests and bids five dollars of her money for a horse. Other local men buy horses until all have been sold. Sympathizing with Mrs. Armstid's plight, the Texan tries to give the money back to her. Henry, however, is adamant about keeping the horse. The Texan says he will give the five dollars to Flem Snopes to return to her the next day. Henry goes into the corral to get his horse and the whole herd escapes. Bedlam ensues: one horse gets into the boarding house, another upsets a wagon on a bridge; the purchasers spend the night trying to catch their horses. The Armstids stay at the boarding house while Henry recovers from being run over by the horses. Mrs. Armstid reluctantly approaches Flem Snopes to recover her five dollars, but he claims that the Texan took the money with him. As a "generous" gesture, Snopes give Mrs. Armstid a nickel bag of candy for her children.

Teaching Strategies

Providing for Cultural Differences. Remind students that this story is supposed to take place in the late nineteenth century and that the five dollars that figures in it was a far more significant sum then than it is now. You may also want to explain that sharecropping means working farm land as a tenant for part of the crop.

Providing for Different Levels of Ability. Good readers can read the story in a single assignment. Less advanced readers, who may have some problems with some of the regional speech, will probably benefit from breaking the story into two parts. If you choose this course, ending the first assignment at the end of Part III (page 612) makes a convenient division.

Reading the Story. Read at least the first two paragraphs aloud to your class to let them sample the flavor of the regional dialect. If you have the time, you can ask some of your better readers to read additional portions of the story aloud.

Reading Check. You may want to use the following questions as a reading check. Have students respond *True* or *False*.

1. The horses that Flem and the Texan bring to town have never been broken. *True*
2. Flem Snopes takes an active part in the auction. *False*
3. Henry Armstid is presented as an extremely sympathetic character. *False*
4. During the escape of the horses, Henry Armstid breaks his leg. *True*
5. Flem Snopes gives Mrs. Armstid back her five dollars. *False*

Reteaching Alternatives. As a possible alternative to comparing "Spotted Horses" with Twain's "The Raftsman," you may prefer to read to the class Twain's "The Genuine Mexican Plug." The parallels between the two accounts of unmanageable horses may make such features of the tall tale as comic irony and overstatement easy for students to recognize.

Responding to the Story   Text page 618
Analyzing the Story
Identifying Facts

1. In Section I, what facts do we learn about the *character* Flem Snopes? Flem comes from a lowly origin as a member of a large clan of share-croppers and tenant farmers. But he is different from the rest of the Snopeses: Flem is ambitious and brazen, smart, cunning, and utterly without compunction. He cheats his neighbors and kinfolk alike, and he manages to get away with it. Early in the story we learn that he has secured a position as clerk at Jody Varner's general store. Flem emerges the victor in the battle for Eula Varner's hand, thus securing his social and financial position in the town.

How long will it take Flem to gain control of Jody Varner's business? The narrator says that within ten years Jody Varner will be clerking for Flem.

2. Describe all those spotted horses. What comic *comparisons* does the writer use to help us visualize them? The narrator says that the horses are colored like parrots and are as quiet as doves, although they would kill you "quick as a rattlesnake." Not one of the horses has eyes of the same color.

What details immediately establish the fact that the "spotted varmints" are dangerous? One of the horses cuts the vest off the Texas man. The narrator tells us that, during the night, the horses bite, kick, and squeal, and that they strike their hoofs against the barn, producing a noise like a pistol shot.

3. In Section II, why doesn't Mrs. Armstid want her husband to buy one of the horses? The Armstids are desperately poor and cannot afford to buy a horse.

4. Who is Eck Snopes? Eck is Flem's cousin and the father of the little boy, Ad.

How does he start the bidding at the auction? At the Texas man's prompting, Eck says he will bid a dollar on one of the horses.

5. Explain how the townspeople are swindled by the Texas man at the auction. When the townspeople try to claim the horses they have bought from the Texas man at the auction, it turns out that the horses are wild ponies, who scatter all over the countryside. Eck Snopes is the only man able to corner his horse, but the horse breaks its neck.

6. What problem is faced by Henry Armstid in Section III? Henry tries in vain to tame his horse and take it home.

What does the Texas man tell Mrs. Armstid? He tells Mrs. Armstid that she can collect her money on Saturday from Flem Snopes.

7. Describe how Mrs. Littlejohn deals with the horse in her house in Section IV. She cracks it across the head with a scrubbing-board.

What advice does she give Mrs. Armstid? She says that Mrs. Armstid should ask Flem to return her money, even though she doubts that Flem will give it back.

8. In Section VI, when Mrs. Armstid tries to collect her five dollars from Flem Snopes, how does Flem react? Flem first tries to ignore Mrs. Armstid. He then tells her that the man from Texas has left town, and that he must have forgotten to give Flem the five dollars.

What does the generous Flem finally give her instead? Flem gives her a small bag of candy as a present for the Armstid children. The narrator ironically reflects that the candy belonged to Jody Varner and that he bets Flem still owes Varner a nickel.

Interpreting Meanings

9. Describe the *character* of Flem Snopes, basing your answer on his words and actions, and on the comments of other characters, including the narrator. Flem is cunning, brazen, and ambitious. His own relatives seem to hold him in awe: even as he cheats them, they are forced to admire him. The townspeople's attitude is summed up in the conversation between Mrs. Armstid and Mrs. Littlejohn, when the latter says that she doubts Flem will return the five dollars. The narrator's efforts to shame Flem into returning the money are depicted as useless. Flem calmly denies any knowledge of the whole affair, signaling his contempt by spitting across the porch into the road. At the end of the story, the narrator must reluctantly agree with I. O. Snopes, who says that the townspeople may as well stop trying to "get ahead of Flem," since Flem is too smart for them.

How do you know that Flem was really involved in the scam of the horses? Faulkner never explicitly states that Flem was involved, since the trick on the townspeople depends on Flem's covert collaboration with the Texas man. Nevertheless, the first and last sentences of the story broadly hint at Flem's involvement, and the narrator notes that Flem and the man from Texas ride into town together with the horses. Flem is careful to keep out of sight during the auction itself; but the fact that another Snopes, Flem's cousin Eck, starts the bidding is suspicious. On the whole, there seems to be no doubt of Flem's involvement: the man from Texas probably shared the proceeds from the auction with him.

10. What sort of person is Mrs. Armstid? What does her way of rolling her hands in her dress tell us about her? Mrs. Armstid is timid and unsure of herself. The habit of rolling her hands in her dress indicates that she has a worried, anxious personality.

11. How do the citizens of Yoknapatawpha County view greed and the ability, so highly developed in Flem, at "skunning" or "trimming" someone in a deal? The townspeople seem to view these characteristics with a certain wry, ironic admiration.

12. Reread the scene in which Mrs. Armstid and Mrs. Littlejohn are washing dishes in Section V. What details make this one of the story's funniest scenes? Student answers will vary. The loud noise of the dishes at the end of the incident comically suggests Mrs. Littlejohn's frustration with the timid and indecisive Mrs. Armstid.

13. Although the story deals mostly with men, the women are important characters. Are the women more or less admirable than the men? Who is more romantic and who is more realistic—the men or the women?

Explain. Student answers will vary. By and large, the men are more "romantically" portrayed as naive dreamers; the principal women—Mrs. Littlejohn and Mrs. Armstid—are practical and realistic.

14. How did you feel about these characters? Are they universal types—that is, could the story have taken place in any part of the country, or world? Most students will agree that the characters, even though drawn with much local color, are universal types: Flem is the con-man, Henry Armstid is the gullible victim, Mrs. Armstid is the timid and long-suffering wife, Mrs. Littlejohn is the practical realist, and the narrator is the wry, detached observer.

15. Which parts of the story could have been serious, or pathetic, if the story had been told by a writer with a serious theme in mind? Henry Armstid's injury could have been serious or pathetic; likewise, Flem's rejection of Mrs. Armstid could have been depicted as malicious and cruel.

Writing About the Story
A Creative Response

1. Writing a Tall Tale. Previous work with boasts (page 413) may help students create characters for this assignment. You may also wish to brainstorm lists of characters and situations that would make good tall tales.

Criteria for Evaluating the Assignment. The tall tale shows a character type from the student's part of the world in action. The tale uses exaggeration and is comical in tone.

A Critical Response

2. Responding to a Critic. Before students begin to write, discuss Cowley's comment on Faulkner with them, checking for grasp of Cowley's literal meaning.

Criteria for Evaluating the Assignment. The essay notes the applicability of Cowley's comment to "Spotted Horses," and correctly identifies "poetic," "mythic" and "epical" elements of the story. The essay also notes that the story has the ring of a legend, and supports all points made with details from the story.

3. Comparing Two Writers. Have students work in small groups to complete the suggested comparison chart on Twain's and Faulkner's humorous stories.

Criteria for Evaluating the Assignment. The essay cites details from Twain's "The Raftsmen" and Faulkner's "Spotted Horses" which show similarities between the stories in terms of trickster, boaster, exaggeration, comic descriptions, understatement, dialect, and elements of farce.

Analyzing Language and Style

Answers will vary. These are a few examples.

1. Example: "outen" (page 607) for "out of"
2. Examples: "mought" (609) and "frailed [the tar]" (612), clear from context
3. Example: "But wasn't nobody surprised at that." (Page 609)
4. Noun singulars and plurals: gal, gals (girl, girls); cattymounts (catamounts); agreement of nouns and verbs: "Its legs was braced" (page 610); tenses of verbs: "Folks never knowed" (page 608); forms of pronouns: "hisself," "ourn," "hisn"
5. "She looked like a old snag still standing up and moving along on a high water." (Page 617)

Interpretations about the story's opening words will vary, but most students will have heard a "down home" accent on television.

Primary Sources: Nobel Prize Acceptance Speech, 1950   Text page 619

In this speech, Faulkner, like Steinbeck, sees literature as being important to human survival. But unlike his fellow Nobel laureate, Faulkner does not expect literature to perfect human beings. He says: "I believe that man will not merely endure: he will prevail. . . . He is immortal . . . because he has a soul, a spirit capable of compassion and sacrifice and endurance." For Faulkner, the writer's duty is to lift man's heart, and literature is one of "the pillars to help him endure and prevail."

William Faulkner   211

Flannery O'Connor

Text page 620

"The Life You Save May Be Your Own"

Text page 621

Objectives

1. To recognize foreshadowing in details of setting, characterization, and dialogue
2. To identify irony
3. To state the theme
4. To write a new ending
5. To write an essay expressing an opinion
6. To write an essay analyzing the story

Introducing the Story

This story is one of exploitation. Mr. Shiftlet arrives at the place, looks around to see what he can take, and decides on the old car that hasn't run for years. The old woman sees him as a match for her idiot daughter. Both characters display the selfishness to which the highway slogan in the title appeals.

In outline form, for your reference, here are the major elements in the story:

- **Protagonist:** Mr. Shiftlet
- **Antagonist:** the elder Lucynell Crater
- **Conflict:** one selfish person vs. another
- **Point of view:** third-person, omniscient
- **Setting:** rural Georgia in the 1940's

Background on the Story. Flannery O'Connor was a devout Roman Catholic all her life, and her strong beliefs are reflected in all of her stories. She also had a predilection for the grotesque and the violent—features that place most of her writing in the category of Southern Gothic. The violence is absent from this story, but the grotesques are on hand.

The Plot. Tom T. Shiftlet appears at the Crater place and accepts meals and a bed (in an out-of-commission car) in return for handyman chores. In a short time, he greatly improves the appearance of the place and teaches Lucynell, the idiot daughter, to say "bird," her first and only word. Lucynell (senior) proposes that Shiftlet marry her daughter Lucynell and he agrees, on condition that the old woman stake him to enough money to stay a night in a good hotel and get something to eat. She agrees, reluctantly, to give him $17.50 for these amenities. Shiftlet and Lucynell are married at the courthouse and drop off her mother. After driving a hundred miles or so, Shiftlet stops at a diner and leaves Lucynell there, asleep at the counter. Shiftlet drives on. At the end of the story, ominous storm clouds descend in front of the car and behind it.

Teaching Strategies

Providing for Cultural Differences. Help students place this story in the 1940's, when the $17.50 that old Lucynell grudgingly gives Shiftlet would go further than it would today.

Providing for Different Levels of Ability. Less advanced students may need help in appreciating the ironic humor in the story. Help them focus on specific instances.

Reading the Story. All students will be able to understand the main events in the narrative, but, as suggested above, some may fail to appreciate the humor. Reading at least part of the story aloud will help students become familiar with the tone. If you read from the beginning, the middle of the righthand column on page 624 offers a good stopping point. (An audiocassette recording of this entire story is available. Three performers take the roles of the narrator, Mr. Shiftlet, and Lucynell Crater.)

Reading Check. You may want to use the following questions as a reading check. Have students respond *True* or *False*.

1. Tom Shiftlet is interested in the Crater car from the beginning. *True*
2. Lucynell, the daughter, is just over sixteen years old. *False*
3. Shiftlet claims to have been a gospel singer at one time. *True*
4. The first word that young Lucynell learns to say "sugarpie." *False*
5. Shiftlet tells Mrs. Crater that he needs money to buy a suit to get married in. *False*

Reteaching Alternatives. You may wish to assign the extracts from O'Connor's letters that appear in "Primary Sources" on text page 629. Have students write an essay describing what the television producers are doing to the author's story and her attitude toward them.

Responding to the Story   Text page 628
Analyzing the Story
Identifying Facts

1. Describe the improvements Mr. Shiftlet makes in the Craters' place during his first week there. Shiftlet fixes the roof of the garden house and repairs the front and back steps; he builds a new hog pen and restores a fence; he teaches Lucynell to say the word "bird"; and he begins to repair the automobile.

2. Explain how Mr. Shiftlet seems to want to exploit the Craters. Shiftlet's continual interest in the car foreshadows the end of the story, when he abandons Lucynell and drives to Mobile. He succeeds in getting old Lucynell to pay for the new parts for the car, and he manages to persuade her to give him some money for the wedding trip.

How does the older Lucynell want to exploit Mr. Shiftlet? Old Lucynell sees in Shiftlet a solution to her problem in marrying off her innocent, speechless daughter.

3. What has become of young Lucynell and Mr. Shiftlet by the story's end? Shiftlet, who has married Lucynell, abandons her while she is asleep at the Hot Spot Cafe and drives off to Mobile.

Interpreting Meanings

4. In the opening pages of the story, what details of *setting*, of *characterization*, and of *dialogue* carry potentially ominous or menacing undertones? Among the details students may mention are the following. *Setting:* the sunset is described as "piercing"; the old woman and her daughter live alone in a "desolate spot"; the sun appears precariously balanced on the peak of a small mountain. *Physical description of the characters:* the strange behavior of young Lucynell; the characterization of Shiftlet as a tramp; old Lucynell rising "with one hand fisted on her hip"; Shiftlet's "long black slick hair" and his "steel-trap jaw"; his look of "composed dissatisfaction" and his peculiar pose against the sky so that his figure forms "a crooked cross"; Shiftlet's "pale sharp glance" and his frequent notice of the automobile; his actions with the burning match; the mention of "the trigger that moved up and down in his neck" (suggesting part of a gun). *Dialogue:* evasion by both Shiftlet and old Lucynell; Shiftlet's mention of surgery on the human heart in Atlanta; his statements that "the world is almost rotten," "people'll do anything anyways," and "people don't care how they lie."

5. What is the significance of the remarks made by the hitchhiker just before he leaps from the moving car? In general, the boy's insults form an abrupt counterpoint to Mr. Shiflet's mawkishly sentimental statement about his mother.

What are we to make of the fact that Mr. Shiftlet feels that "the rottenness of the world" is about to engulf him? What *irony* do you sense in Mr. Shiftlet's realization? Mr. Shiftlet is able to see rottenness in others, but not in himself. His melodramatic observations about other people's dishonesty and materialism clash with the fact that he has just behaved badly by abandoning Lucynell and stealing the automobile.

6. The ending of the story focuses on Mr. Shiftlet, rather than on the two Lucynells. Explain how you think the writer means us to regard him. Is he a prophet or a demon? Consider why O'Connor points out, early in the story, that Shiftlet's figure "formed a crooked cross" (page 623). Encourage the students to put forward and defend their opinions about this complex character. Most students will agree that O'Connor intends for us to be repelled by Shiftlet: some students may observe that his name slyly suggests "shiftly" or "shiftless." On the other hand, O'Connor paints a complex portrait. When Mr. Shiftlet declares, for example, that he possesses a "moral intelligence," is he totally wrong? Or is it simply that his deeds in the story (and probably in his past life, as well) do not measure up to the ideals that he so slickly invokes? The description, early in the story, of his figure as a crooked cross against the evening sky seems both symbolic and ambivalent. O'Connor may have meant that Shiftlet is both Christ-like and deeply flawed—perhaps he is an emblem of all those flawed human beings who know the good but somehow lack the faith or character to practice it.

7. What is the significance of the peculiar clouds and the storm pursuing Mr. Shiftlet toward Mobile at the end of the story? Student answers will vary. Most will agree that the description at the end of the story implies that Shiftlet will somehow be punished for his insensitivity and selfishness in stealing the car and abandoning young Lucynell.

8. How would the story's *theme* and *effect* have changed if Mr. Shiftlet had returned to the café for Lucynell? How do you feel about the way the story ended? Student answers will vary. Most will agree that it would have been out of character for Shiftlet to have returned to the helpless Lucynell: the story reveals him as tricky, greedy, pompous, and morally weak.

9. **Do you sense *irony* in the story's title?** Students should first identify the context of the title phrase's occurrence within the story. Mr. Shiftlet sees the words on a road sign immediately after he leaves young Lucynell at the Hot Spot cafe and before he picks up the hitchhiker. The irony of the title may be variously explained. If students examine closely the familiar road-side warning, they may note an almost casual selfishness (why not say, for example, that you might save *another* person's life if you drive safely?). This selfishness mingles with an ostensibly public-spirited concern for highway safety. Encourage students to discuss parallels with the character of Shiftlet, as it is presented in the story.

How would you state the story's *theme*, using the warning expressed in the title? One statement of O'Connor's theme might run as follows: Most people, whatever they say to the contrary, are really preoccupied with their own self-interest.

10. **Can you see any relationship between Mr. Shiftlet and Flem Snopes in "Spotted Horses" (page 607)? Explain.** Students may note a number of similarities between the two figures: both Flem Snopes and Mr. Shiftlet are greedy, selfish characters who do not scruple to cheat other people in order to get ahead. Both characters are described with more than a touch of wry, ironic humor.

11. **Are there any "heroes" in this story? Do you think it is a story about innocence vs. evil? Or do you think it is a story about a world in which everyone is a rogue? Explain.** Student answers will vary. Ask the students to support their interpretations with logical reasoning and with references to the text.

12. **Think of this story in relation to other stories you have read. What is your response to O'Connor's characters and theme? What do you think of her *tone*?** Students should be encouraged to analyze the tone of the story carefully. Ask students to discuss how O'Connor mingles irony, broad humor, and pathos with the grotesque. Then encourage students to apply their conclusions to an evaluation of O'Connor's characters and theme.

Writing About the Story
A Creative Response

1. **Extending the Story.** Discuss endings consistent with Lucynell's handicaps and human nature in general.

Criteria for Evaluating the Assignment. The ending is appropriate to Lucynell and human nature in general.

A Critical Response

2. **Expressing an Opinion.** Assign "Primary Sources" or discuss the page (629) in class. Students should have no problem engaging in lively discussion of the essay aspects listed in the writing prompt.

Criteria for Evaluating the Assignment. The essay shows a grasp both of O'Connor's story and of the realities of schools, movies and television in reasons cited for (a) why the TV producers would change the story, (b) whether it would be popular if dramatized on TV or made into a movie today, and (c) why a textbook would omit the last paragraph.

3. **Analyzing the Story.** Read and discuss "Elements of Literature: The Four 'Modes' of Fiction" (page 630) before students do this assignment. Lead the class to see that the story is indeed an ironic parody of a romance, and then to account for the reversals listed, in their essays.

Criteria for Evaluating the Assignment. The essay identifies O'Connor's story as an ironic parody of a romance and cites details from the story in offering reasonable explanations for reversals of (a) the nurturing mother, (b) the beautiful, innocent young woman, (c) the charming prince who is the rescuer, and (d) the fairy-tale kingdom setting.

Analyzing Language and Style
Connotations

1. Answers will vary. Some include "jutting steel-trap jaw" (page 621), "his clay-colored eyes" (page 623), "the trigger that moved up and down in his neck" (page 624), "smile stretched like a weary snake" (page 626).
2. "A cloud . . . shaped like a *turnip*"; "a *guffawing* peal of thunder . . ." (page 627).
3. The question refers to the figures of speech from item 1 and the words from item 2. They suggest that Shiftlet is anything but a knight in shining armor.
4. He should become a far more savory character.

Primary Sources: The Adventures of Mr. Shiftlet
Text page 629

These excerpts from Flannery O'Connor's letters give a goodhumored account of mischances involving "The Life You Save May Be Your Own," including the prospect of Gene Kelly's playing Shiftlet and the discovery that the last paragraph has been omitted when the story was reprinted in a school anthology.

214 The Moderns

| Elements of Literature: The Four "Modes" of Fiction | Text page 630 |

Read and discuss this section before students attempt the third writing assignment on page 628—analyzing Flannery O'Connor's "The Life You Save May Be Your Own." The final question on this page—*What modes do you think the other stories in this unit are written in?*—could serve as a general review question to be addressed in small groups.

| Primary Sources: "Is Phoenix Jackson's Grandson Really Dead?" | Text page 637 |

This essay was occasioned by questions from students and teachers concerning "The Worn Path," of which Welty's favorite is the one that provides the title. The essay gives students a rare opportunity to analyze a story in the light of the author's own explication of its meaning.

Eudora Welty
Text page 631

"A Worn Path"
Text page 632

Objectives

1. To make inferences from details of description
2. To analyze character
3. To recognize situational irony
4. To recognize the importance of setting
5. To state the theme of the story
6. To write a new ending
7. To write an essay analyzing a character's journey
8. To write an essay analyzing character

Introducing the Story

Tell students that the story they are about to read concerns a very old woman who periodically makes a long journey to a city on foot. You may wish to remind them that from earliest times storytellers have used a journey as a metaphor for life—Ulysses's journey to Ithica, Gulliver's travels, and Huck Finn's raft trip down the Mississippi are only a few examples. Have them consider to what extent Phoenix Jackson's journey is a symbolic one.

In outline form, for your reference, here are the major elements of the story:

- **Protagonist:** Phoenix Jackson
- **Antagonist:** obstacles to her journey
- **Conflict:** person vs. obstacle to the journey
- **Point of view:** limited third-person
- **Significant technique:** development of theme through journey motif
- **Setting:** Mississippi in the Depression era

Background on the Story. As Eudora Welty explains in the short essay that follows this story, "A Worn Path" was inspired by the sight of an old woman walking slowly across the winter landscape. Welty then invented the errand that would make her go on her journey and the passing adventures that make the story.

The Plot. Phoenix Jackson makes a long journey on foot through woods, across fields, and along country roads until she reaches Natchez. On her way, she is frightened by a scarecrow and a dog, aided but patronized by a hunter, and patronized again by a receptionist at the doctor's office that is her destination. She has traveled there to obtain medicine for her grandson. With a nickel the receptionist gives her and another the hunter dropped, Phoenix plans to buy a paper windmill for her grandson before she starts back.

Teaching Strategies

Providing for Cultural Differences. Reminding students that the story takes place during the Depression, when a nickel went a long way, will help them to understand that the receptionist's gift to Phoenix is not as miserly as it might now appear.

Providing for Different Levels of Ability. All students can easily manage this story either as homework or as an in-class assignment.

Introducing Vocabulary Study. Students will benefit from knowing the meanings of the following words before they read the story. (Starred words appear in the Glossary.)

| illumined* | 632 | obstinate | 636 |
| lolling* | 634 | | |

Reading the Story. Before assigning the story, you may want to read aloud the first three paragraphs, which describe Phoenix Jackson. Ask students to summarize what they know about her and to speculate briefly on what errand brings her on this journey. Then assign the story for in-class reading.

Reading Check. You may want to use the following questions as a reading check. Have students respond *True* or *False*.

1. The story takes place in winter. *True*
2. Phoenix often talks to herself as she walks along. *True*
3. Her destination is a general store in a nearby town. *False*
4. A hunter gives Phoenix some money. *False*
5. Her grandson suffers from a throat ailment. *True*

Reteaching Alternatives. As an alternative to the writing assignments on page 637, you may wish to have students write an essay on the journey as a metaphor for life.

Responding to the Story   Text page 636
Analyzing the Story
Identifying Facts

1. Describe the purpose of Phoenix Jackson's journey. Phoenix travels from her home, far out in the country, into the town of Natchez to collect medicine for her grandson, who suffers chronic throat trouble because he has swallowed lye.

On her way to Natchez, what obstacles does she overcome? Because she is so old, Phoenix must face obstacles of the terrain: walking uphill, crossing a creek on a log, getting through a barbed wire fence, and trying to fend off a dog.

2. Explain how Phoenix acquires the two nickels. Phoenix retrieves one of the nickels when the man she meets on the road drops it. The doctor's attendant gives her the other nickel.

How does she intend to spend them? She intends to buy a paper windmill for her grandson.

3. What is the result of Phoenix's long and perilous journey through the woods? Does she get what she wants? Explain. The result is successful, in that Phoenix receives the medicine and prepares to buy her grandson a gift.

Interpreting Meanings

4. Phoenix Jackson, the central figure of this story, is surely memorable. How do Welty's descriptions of her *appearance*, *speech*, and *behavior* identify her with the world of nature and with time itself? Numerous personifications of animals and features of the landscape during Phoenix's journey help to identify the old woman with nature. She is identified with time because of her great age: she tells the hunter that there is "no telling" how old she is. By comparing the wrinkles of Phoenix's forehead to a small tree, the author suggests flourishing, natural growth; this impression is reinforced when Welty speaks of the "golden color" underlying the old woman's skin.

5. Describe what her encounters with the little boy offering marble cake, with the buzzard, with the scarecrow, with the bramblebush, and finally with the hunter tell us about Phoenix's *character*. The imagined encounter with the little boy offering marble cake shows that Phoenix is polite and gracious. The question she asks the buzzard, "Who you watching?", indicates that she is imaginative, and perhaps a bit superstitious. The encounter with the scarecrow, when Phoenix tries to dance, shows that she has a sense of humor. The encounter with the bramblebush, in which Phoenix says that she thought "you was a pretty little *green* bush," perhaps suggests that Phoenix is inclined to be optimistic and to look on the bright side of things. Finally, her encounter with the hunter shows that Phoenix is courageous and dignified—perhaps also a bit sly, since she creates a diversion so that she can pick up the nickel the hunter has dropped.

6. Would you describe Phoenix as a heroine, in the traditional sense of the word? Why? Student answers will differ. Most students will agree that Phoenix is heroic in her courage, persistence, dignity, and steadfast love.

7. What do you suppose possessed the hunter to point his gun at the old woman? Perhaps the hunter was having a "joke" at the old woman's expense.

Do you think the hunter deliberately lies about not having any money? Or is there another explanation? Perhaps the hunter does not even realize he has dropped the nickel; for him, in contrast to Phoenix, a nickel may have been a negligible amount of money.

8. What is ironic about the reason the hunter suggests for Phoenix's long journey? It is ironic that the hunter suggests that Phoenix is going to town to see Santa Claus because, in reality, Phoenix is on an errand of love. By bringing the medicine and a present to her grandson, she *becomes* the spirit of love and charity, symbolically represented by Santa Claus at Christmas.

Do many people treat Phoenix condescendingly? Why? The hunter and the nurses at the hospital treat Phoenix condescendingly because she is old, poor, and black.

9. Explain the significance of Phoenix's name. Why is it an appropriate name for her? The phoenix is a mythical bird which was said to be periodically reborn from its own ashes: it is thus a symbol of renewal and regeneration. Within the context of the story, it is an appropriate name for the old woman who travels to town, since she is associated with love and healing.

10. Describe the story's seasonal *setting*, and explain its significance. By setting the story at Christmastime, Welty provides a religious resonance for her theme of love and rebirth.

Does Welty use the setting to make us feel *irony* in the nurses' attitude? Explain. The nurses' detached, condescending attitude ironically clashes with the true, loving spirit of Christmas.

11. When the nurse gives Phoenix the medicine, she says, "Charity," and makes a check mark in her book. Given the character of Phoenix, what is *ironic* about the nurse's statement and action? Phoenix's act of charity is performed at great sacrifice, whereas the nurse seems to treat "charity" in an offhand and impersonal fashion.

12. When you grasped the purpose of Phoenix's long journey to Natchez, what did you discover about her life? Is it a fulfilled one? Is it tragic? Explain. Most students will agree that Phoenix, in her harmony with nature and her great love for her grandson, is shown to lead a fulfilled, rather than a tragic, life.

13. What do you think is Welty's *theme* in "A Worn Path"? Put another way, what "worn path" is open to us all? The title perhaps suggests that Phoenix has made the journey to town many times over; the path from her home to the doctor's office is thus "well worn." Metaphorically, the title may also suggest the habitual "path" of love in Phoenix's mind and heart. This, in turn, suggests Welty's theme: that the path of love—"worn" because it entails sacrifice and needs to be trodden again and again—is open to us all.

Writing About the Story

Have students read and discuss "Primary Sources: 'Is Phoenix Jackson's Grandson Really Dead?'" (pages 637–638)—as preparation for the first three writing assignments.

A Creative Response

1. Extending the Story. Welty's essay should lead to a farily philosophical discussion of whether it is better for the child to be dead or alive when Phoenix Jackson reaches home.

Criteria for Evaluating the Assignment. The ending "works"; that is, whether the grandson is dead or alive, the ending retains the characterization of Phoenix and the importance of her journey.

A Critical Response

2. Analyzing the Journey. Set the pattern for the assignment by eliciting from the class examples of the first two categories, *dreams* and *harassments*.

Criteria for Evaluating the Assignment. The essay cites those elements of Phoenix Jackson's journey which can be categorized as (a) dreams, (b) harassments, (c) small triumphs, (d) jolts to her pride, (e) flights of fancy to console her, (f) scary encounters, (g) a cause to be ashamed, and (h) a moment to dance and preen.

3. Responding to a Comment. The assignment requires students to interpret a metaphor. Answers will vary.

Criteria for Evaluating the Assignment. The paragraph provides a reasonable explanation of Welty's term, "the habit of love," and of why this habit is better compared with a worn path than with a new road, rocket path, or crystal stairway.

4. Analyzing Character. Most students will see that Phoenix is essentially timeless.

Criteria for Evaluating the Assignment. Whether the essay presents Phoenix Jackson as someone who changes or as an essentially timeless character, it cites details from the story to support the position taken.

The American Language

Text page 642

1. Students should collect as many slang terms as they can for the following words. They should then discuss the metaphors on which the slang terms are based. Sample answers might include the following:

car: wheels, jalopy, buggy, limo, chariot

failing: flunking, punting

getting angry: blowing a fuse, blowing up, hitting the ceiling

going to sleep: catching some z's, hitting the sack, taking a cat-nap, drifting off, out like a light

2. Students should identify the form of figurative language that each of the following words or phrases is based on. They should then provide another example of slang using the same kind of figure of speech.

chicken: metaphor for cowardice

stuffed shirt: metaphor for pomposity

hit the ceiling: hyperbole for getting angry

out like a light: simile for going to sleep

to talk someone's ear off: hyperbole for garulousness

tenderfoot: metaphor for inexperience

rubberneck: metaphor for slowing down to look at an accident out of curiosity

to put on ice: metaphor for postponement

Student examples of other slang phrases based on the same figure of speech will vary.

3. Students should use a dictionary to identify the full forms of the following clipped forms.

ad lib: ad libitum

bus: omnibus

car: cart

cello: violoncello

flu: influenza

gym: gymnasium

lunch: luncheon

pep: pepper

prop: property

4. Students should check the etymology of each of the following standard words that were once considered slang. They should then try to propose reasons why each word developed its current meaning.

bleachers: containers, like vats or tanks, used for bleaching

bore: to make a hole with a sharp instrument

club: a short spar on a ship

freshman: a student in the first year of a course

glib: slippery

handsome: easy to handle

kidnap: nab

tidy: seasonable

trip: step lightly

Students' speculations on the development of the current meanings of the words will vary.

5. Students should explain in plain English each of the following terms of sports argot.

a. *winning streak:* series of consecutive victories
   snapped: interrupted
b. *fast-break:* sudden offensive on the run
c. *benched:* relegated to the player's bench and so not in the game
   hauled down: established
d. *popped out:* hit a short fly ball that was caught for an out
e. *punched:* struggled with force and vigor

Exercises in Critical Thinking and Writing   Text page 643

Making Generalizations

In this exercise, students are asked to use the critical thinking skill of generalizing as they discuss in an essay the theme of either Faulkner's "Spotted Horses" or O'Connor's "The Life You Save May Be Your Own." You might begin reviewing generalizations by discussing the five statements under the section "Background," text page 643. Statements 1, 3 and 4 are matters of opinion. Statement 2 could be proved only if students knew the total number of both men and women who write poetry, statement 5 only if students knew the number of symbols used by all writers throughout time. In the prewriting stage, you might consider in class discussion especially questions 3 and 5 in the section "Prewriting," text page 644.

Criteria for Evaluating the Assignment. The theme, as students discuss it in the essay, is a generalization about human nature and is not limited to the specific events and characters of the story. The theme expresses the complexity of human experience; it is not a moral lesson.

218   The Moderns

Unit Eight: *Poetry: Voices of American Character* Text page 645

Teaching the Poetry Unit

The strength and the limitation of the poets in this unit is that they wrote realistically about the lives of ordinary Americans. Their poems tend to be vignettes or anecdotes, comparable in power and intent to good short stories. Many of these poems are written in the third-person, and even those written in first-person are often about characters who are clearly external to the poet. These poems, then, might be considered a kind of "verse fiction."

The contrast with the American poetry that came afterward is stark. From the 1920's on, the best American poetry has been concerned mainly with advancing the art form itself—with making new explorations of technique, and broadening the range of verbal effects available—and the subject matter has consisted largely of introspection about the poet's most subtle feelings, or at least the feelings of a character (like Eliot's Prufrock) who was clearly a stand-in for the poet. This change was equivalent to the change that occurred in the visual arts at the same time, when painters became preoccupied mostly with technique, and no longer thought it important to reproduce faithfully a representational subject.

The inescapable fact, then, is that with the exception of Frost, these poets may not seem, to some readers, so challenging, or so impressive, as Pound, Eliot, and Stevens. The poets in this unit represent, to many critics, an unexperimental, undaring period in American poetry, a fallow period before a period of tremendously exciting growth. Paradoxically, however, this makes them readily accessible to the high-school-age reader. In many respects, you can approach the poems in this unit almost as though they were works of prose fiction: analyses of character and of social message will be of primary importance, and even the analyses of language will involve discussions of characters' voices, in the main, rather than of linguistic innovations. The purely formal discussions, meanwhile, will tend to involve conventional schemes of rhyme and meter, or, as in the case of Masters and Jeffers, a kind of free verse that seems secondary to the poet's message.

These qualities also create a resemblance between the poems in this unit and the lyrics of songs. The best contemporary rock lyricists, such as Bruce Springsteen, Suzanne Vega, Paul Simon, and Robbie Robertson, tend to write verse vignettes that are strong character studies of American lives, in the vernacular, usually in a simple, voice-oriented free verse, and with rhymes that range from the achingly obvious to the strikingly clever. Some of the poems in this unit are, themselves, good candidates for musical settings, and indeed, Paul Simon once recorded Robinson's "Richard Cory" as a song.

It is important to note that several of the poets in this unit had careers that were artificially and tragically stunted by the social conditions of their day. Black poets such as Paul Laurence Dunbar, James Weldon Johnson, and Countee Cullen were highly gifted, and yet their careers were filled with frustration. Even when they achieved some success, they found themselves in a kind of artistic ghetto, pressured to produce work that would not be threatening to the white intelligentsia: either stereotypical dialect poems, or verses in conventional schemes of rhyme and meter that tamed the anger and pain in their message.

All the poets in this unit did, however, produce some moving, lyrical expressions of the human condition. The characters they created still live, and their wisdom still impresses. We return to them for the reassurance that the pain of human life can be partially healed through song.

*O*bjectives *of the Poetry Unit*

1. To improve reading proficiency and expand vocabulary
2. To gain exposure to notable poets and their works
3. To define and identify the elements of poetry
4. To define and identify significant literary techniques
5. To respond to poetry orally and in writing
6. To analyze the language and style of notable poets
7. To analyze primary sources
8. To practice the following critical thinking and writing skills:
   a. Analyzing a poem
   b. Comparing and contrasting poems
   c. Analyzing imagery
   d. Responding to a poem's theme
   e. Comparing authors' attitudes
   f. Comparing sermons
   g. Responding to critics

*I*ntroducing *the Poetry Unit.* You might prefer not to belabor the technical, prosodic terms, having to do with rhyme and meter, at this point. Many students will have been exposed to them already, and while a certain amount of repetition is necessary to learning, these verse forms themselves have by now come to seem of largely antiquarian interest. Indeed, a good case could be made for the proposition that conventionality of form weakens most of the rhymed and metered poems in this unit. (You will, however, probably want to discuss blank verse when you come to Frost's poems.) At the beginning of the unit, it might be best to stress the rich geographical and ethnic variety exemplified here and the interesting range of characters we come to know. You might give your students brief "coming attractions" about some of these characters: James Weldon Johnson's preacher who orates beautifully on the death of Sister Caroline; Robert Frost's broken-down hired man, Silas, and the farm couple who discuss his fate; Edgar Lee Masters's tombstone-carver, Richard Bone, who tells us his thoughts from his own grave. Then, go directly to the first poem.

Edwin Arlington Robinson

Text page 651

Reading About the Poet

Robinson is an example of a poet who found his distinctive style early on, stayed with it throughout his career, and did not seem to be affected by changing trends or by the advances made by younger poets. His reputation today is neither much higher nor much lower than it was in his own lifetime. He is, thus, another of the great solitaries of American literature, belonging to no school, but occupying solidly his own niche.

After becoming known for brief character portraits of New Englanders, he produced a book-length poem, *Captain Craig* (1902), which is similar in subject and style; most critics, though, agree that it is padded, and that it would have benefitted from being held to the length of his previous vignettes. More successful were *Lancelot* and *Tristram* (1927), which retell the Arthurian legends, showing us heroes and lovers searching for light in a dark world. Robinson regarded *Tristram* as his masterpiece. Robinson seems to have been born, or at least early bred, to an introspective, sober temperament and a pessimistic but still hopeful view of the world; it makes his work somewhat less than viscerally thrilling, perhaps, but always intelligent and serious.

"Richard Cory"

Text page 652

Objectives

1. To recognize irony
2. To describe tone
3. To identify the moral

Introducing the Poem

This poem, like "Miniver Cheevy," was originally published in *The Children of the Night* (1897) the volume that can be considered Robinson's *Spoon River Anthology:* a collection of character portraits from his fictitious "Tilbury Town." Among his characters are a miser, Aaron Stark, who laughs at those who pity him; a butcher, Reuben Bright, who tears down his own slaughterhouse in grief over his wife's death; Annandale, a derelict who is a victim of euthanasia. The critic Stanley T. Williams says, "These hard little poems are specimens of human experience in a world in which agony is real and happiness but a wish.... They are microfilms needing only the illumination of the reader's experience to be projected as reality."

The Literal Meaning. Richard Cory was rich and envied, but, for unspecified reasons, he shot himself.

Teaching Strategies

Providing for Cultural Differences. Students from lower socio-economic backgrounds may not feel much grief at Richard Cory's plight; on the other hand, students from higher socio-economic backgrounds may resent the implication that wealth is a sign of hidden guilt.

Providing for Different Levels of Ability. This poem is easier to read than "Miniver Cheevy," both because it lacks the antiquarian allusions and because it is written in the first-person, plural voice of an ordinary American community. The phrases, "imperially slim" and "he fluttered pulses" may give some students problems.

Reteaching Alternatives. While the surface events of the poem are easy to understand, some students may feel uncomfortable about the fact that Robinson provides no specific motivation for his character's suicide. You might point out that this is deliberate: Robinson is showing us that Richard Cory's outer grandeur hides anguish, but he leaves the specific nature of that anguish up to the reader's imagination.

Responding to the Poem Text page 652
Analyzing the Poem
Identifying Details

1. What advantages does Richard Cory have that make the townspeople envy him? Richard Cory is rich, graceful, handsome, and polite.

2. What contrasting picture of their own lives is presented in the fourth stanza? Most of the townspeople are poor. They are often forced to go without meat and they "curse the bread" of their monotonous, daily diet.

3. List all the details in the poem revealing that the townspeople regarded Richard Cory with awe and a sense of inferiority. Among such words and phrases are the following: "imperially slim" (line 4), "fluttered pulses" (line 7), "he glittered when he walked" (line 8), "richer than a king" (line 9), "admirably schooled in every grace" (line 10), and lines 11–12.

How would you define the word *human* in line 6? Student answers will vary. In context, the word seems to mean "polite," "sympathetic," or "down-to-earth."

Interpreting Meanings

4. What is *ironic* in the fact that Richard Cory took his own life? The irony consists in the speaker's (and our) reversal of expectation: Whereas Richard Cory seemed to enjoy every blessing, he was inwardly so unhappy that he committed suicide.

What irony is there in the fact that the night was calm? The irony proceeds from the contrast between the tranquil night, on which nothing noteworthy might be expected to happen, and the sudden violence of Cory's self-inflicted death.

5. What aspects of Richard Cory's life are *not* mentioned? Nothing is said about Richard Cory's family or friends.

How might these hidden or overlooked areas account for his fate? Student answers may vary. Some may speculate that Cory's suicide resulted from extreme loneliness; others may guess that his fate was the result of some private tragedy, perhaps involving his family, that was concealed from the townspeople.

6. How would you describe the speaker's *tone*? Most students will agree that the tone of the speaker is admiring toward Richard Cory.

Does the contrast between the tone of the speaker and the tragic nature of the story heighten the poem's emotional effect? Explain why or why not. The tone of awe and admiration contrasts with the sudden, unexpected revelation of Cory's suicide in the poem's last line. Especially effective is the juxtaposition of the informal, almost casual phrase, "one calm summer night" (line 15), with the report of Cory's suicide in the final line. The impact of that report is so sudden that it almost resembles the sound of a gunshot, or the bullet that ended Cory's life.

7. What *moral* or lesson might be found in the tale of Richard Cory? Student answers may vary. The poem suggests that appearances may often be deceptive. Cory's wealth and genteel manner gave the townspeople no hint of the inner anguish which, "one calm summer night," led to his suicide.

Do the poem and its moral have relevance to our experience today? Most students will agree that the moral is relevant, especially in a culture which discourages displays of emotion or hints of weakness.

8. Read Robinson's own comments on "Richard Cory" on the opposite page. What do you think he means when he says there's a lot of "humanity" in the poem? Student answers will vary. Many students will suggest that Robinson means that the underlying situation of the poem—the cleft between appearance and reality—is more a part of the human condition than people might at first suspect.

Why do you think it made his correspondent feel "cold"? The correspondent was probably shocked by Richard Cory's violent, sudden death.

How do you respond to the poem? Student answers will vary.

"Miniver Cheevy"   Text page 654

Objectives

1. To describe change in tone
2. To write a letter using another point of view
3. To write a letter answering the speaker
4. To write an essay responding to the poems
5. To write an essay comparing and contrasting two poems

Introducing the Poem

While the poem is not autobiographical, Robinson, who was later to write three books based on Arthurian legends, must have empathized with Miniver, who "dreamed of Thebes and Camelot." The mocking humor aimed at Miniver seems less harsh if we understand that the poet is being to some extent self-deprecatory.

The name "Miniver" is a strong dactyl—an accented syllable followed by two unaccented ones—but the bulk of the poem itself is iambic. This combination produces a bouncy rhythm, with the first two syllables of his name functioning as a trochee (´ ˘) and leading into iambs.

The Literal Meaning. Miniver Cheevy daydreams about bygone eras, and drinks.

Teaching Strategies

Providing for Cultural Differences. The romance of Thebes and Camelot is even further from us today than it was in Miniver's time. Some students, therefore, may not be able to relate to Miniver's plight, thinking it a case of musty antiquarianism. A good modern-day analogy would be with a teenager of the 1980's who wished he or she had been a teenager in the 1960's.

Providing for Different Levels of Ability. The literary allusions and Romantic trappings make this poem more difficult than it need be, and the bouncy rhythm makes it easy for the hasty reader to overlook the fact that this is a poem about a distressed and downtrodden person. The last stanza serves as a kind of summation. After discussing it with the class, you might then go back and give the preceding stanzas a reappraisal.

Reading the Poem. You might begin by asking your students if they have ever wanted to live in a different time or place. Which ones? You might make a list on the chalkboard, and conduct a preference poll. You can then point out that a longing for other times is an almost universal human phenomenon, of which Miniver Cheevy is the classic example in American literature.

Reteaching Alternatives. If, after reading and discussing the poem, some students can't penetrate its verbiage, you might have them write the numbers 1 through 8 on a sheet of paper and state, in one simple sentence, what character trait of Miniver's each stanza depicts.

Responding to the Poem   Text page 654
Analyzing the Poem
Identifying Details

1. Briefly summarize Miniver Cheevy's reasons for weeping that he was ever born. Miniver wishes that he had been born in one of the more graceful, "civilized" eras of the past. He regards the present era as vulgar and uncultured. There is a hint in lines 25–26 that he affects a scornful attitude toward money; yet he resents being without it.

2. "Romance" and "Art" are *personified* in the fourth stanza. According to Miniver, what has happened to Romance and Art in his own time? He thinks that Romance and Art have been neglected: Romance is now "on the town" (that is, it depends on public charity), and Art is a "vagrant."

3. How does the disappointed Miniver cope with his lot in life? He sighs, makes money, and drinks too much.

Interpreting Meanings

4. What does "child of scorn" mean? The phrase means that Miniver is habitually scornful, as if he had been born of ill-tempered parents—or even been the child of "Scorn" personified.

5. Do Miniver's problems really stem from his having been "born too late"? Explain. Students will have various responses. But the exaggeration of Miniver's yearning for the past seems to point to a warped nature. He is one of those people who is unable to find any pleasure in life, and so tries to escape from it in a flurry of scorn. By rejecting the present and dreaming of an impossible return to the

222   Voices of American Character

past, Miniver has cut himself off from an active life and from fulfilling human relationships.

6. What is the effect of the abbreviated rhythm in the fourth line of each stanza? Student answers may vary. In general, however, the shorter rhythm of each fourth line produces a clipped, ironic effect.

7. Point out three details in the poem that make Miniver appear ridiculous. Among the details that make Miniver appear slightly ridiculous are the following: "dancing" at the dream of a "warrior bold" (lines 7–8), sinning "incessantly" as a member of the Medici family (lines 19–20), missing the "medieval grace of iron clothing," or suits of armor (lines 23–24).

How would you describe the change in *tone* in the last stanza, and how does this change affect the poem's meaning? It is only in the last stanza that we learn that Miniver's health is deteriorating: his unhappiness and alienation have led to coughing and constant drinking. Robinson thus combines the irony of the previous stanzas with a note of sympathy in the final four lines, as he allows the reader to understand the physical effects of Miniver Cheevy's obsession.

8. Do you think "Miniver Cheevys" are found in contemporary life? What sorts of worlds do they mourn for? Most students will probably agree that "Miniver Cheevys" are as common in the contemporary world as in any other period. Encourage students to discuss in special detail the second half of the question: What sorts of different worlds do these dissatisfied people long for? Does the yearning for a different world suggest anything significant to students about the nature of our world? Are "Miniver Cheevys" necessarily deluded in their desire to escape from the world that surrounds them?

9. Compare Walter Mitty (page 595) to Miniver Cheevy. Students should have little trouble participating in a lively discussion. Although both characters are dreamers, it is clear that they have quite different personalities: Whereas Miniver Cheevy is cranky, self-destructive, and possibly neurotic, Mitty is (at least to outward appearances) mild-mannered and submissive.

Writing About the Poems
A Creative Response

1. Using Another Point of View. Discuss with students the clues to Cory's views contained in the poem "Richard Cory."

Criteria for Evaluating the Assignment. Whether in verse or in prose, the first-person account fits the character of Richard Cory as revealed in the poem. It reports, especially, what Cory thinks of the people who look up to him.

2. Answering a Speaker. Have students list the elements of the poem that indicate Miniver Cheevy's obsession with the past, and brainstorm modern parallels of equal interest which they could suggest to him.

Criteria for Evaluating the Assignment. The paper is in the form of a letter to Miniver Cheevy. It gives him advice on how to free himself from his nostalgic thoughts.

A Critical Response

3. Responding to the Poems. Note that the writing prompt offers students a choice of ways in which to compare "Miniver Cheevy" and "Richard Cory." Discuss all five areas but allow students to respond in terms of the areas most interesting to them.

Criteria for Evaluating the Assignment. The paper responds to "Miniver Cheevy" and "Richard Cory" and uses quotes from the poems to support its comments on one or more of the following areas: characterization, tone, verse forms, use of irony, or view of life and human nature.

4. Comparing Characters. Have students review the passages from Emerson (pages 187–203) and Thoreau (204–225) for comments on human nature suitable to this assignment.

Criteria for Evaluating the Assignment. The essay shows how Robinson's characters—Richard Cory and Miniver Cheevy—are distortions of an ideal proposed by Emerson or Thoreau. The essay also shows how Richard Cory and Miniver Cheevy are similar to and different from each other.

Analyzing Language and Style
Connotations

1. Crown, imperially, arrayed, glittered, grace.
2. Hair, undeniably, dressed, was neat, skill. The poem loses interest and color.
3. A titled person; a well-educated person.
4. Its assonance; the effect of Cory's "descending" to a lesser place.

Extending the Poems

Robinson, whose career began in the 1890's, has certain affinities with the Naturalists, though he is not usually classed as one of them. You might have students compare and contrast his bleak view of human life with that of Stephen Crane, using Crane's poem, "War Is Kind" (text page 508) as an example. Robinson was only two years older than Crane.

Edgar Lee Masters   Text page 656

Reading About the Poet

Like Robinson, Masters is remembered mostly for character portraits in verse; the differences between the two artists in other respects, however, are deep. Robinson was a stylist and prosodist of the highest caliber who managed to infuse conventional forms with a degree of new life at a time when they were on the wane. Masters was an indifferent stylist whose attempts at traditional verse were undistinguished and whose free verse has a prosy plainness. Robinson was first and foremost a poet, and his single-minded pursuit of that calling left him impoverished and insecure through much of his life; Masters was a lawyer who worked in poetry as an avocation. Masters's one notable book of poetry, *Spoon River Anthology,* can be compared with Robinson's long roster of distinguished, if little read, volumes.

In his one great book, however, Masters produced one of the landmarks of twentieth-century American literature. It is more a thematic landmark than a poetic one. It did not influence the art of writing verse. It did serve as a touchstone for later works—often works of prose, like *Winesburg, Ohio*—that critically and realistically show the unhappiness underneath the facades of ordinary small-town Americans.

"Richard Bone"   Text page 657

Objectives

1. To identify analogy
2. To invent names for fictional characters that reflect their traits

Introducing the Poem

"Richard Bone" can be considered the keynote poem of *Spoon River Anthology,* since it is about a carver of epitaphs and Masters himself is writing epitaphs on the lives of his characters. Here we find the crucial idea of the pleasant facade that conceals the unpleasant truth about people's lives. Here, too, we see the plainness of Masters's free verse style in contrast with the more flowing styles of Whitman or Jeffers, of the more highly charged style of Dickinson. An interesting exercise might be to rearrange the typography of the poem so that the lines end on different words. Doing so would not make much difference; in fact, a general shortening of lines might strengthen the poem.

The Literal Meaning. Richard Bone makes a living carving epitaphs to order, though he knows he is carving falsehoods.

Teaching Strategies

Providing for Cultural Differences. Depending upon your region, your students may or may not be very receptive to the idea that conventional small-town life hides a multitude of hypocrisies. The important point here is that although Masters is writing about a single fictitious town, his unveiling of the facade of society has universal applications.

224   Voices of American Character

Providing for Different Levels of Ability. The last five lines of the poem are the most intellectually challenging, particularly the clause, "And made myself party to the false chronicles / Of the Stones," and the idea of a historian writing without really knowing the truth. Advanced students may want to discuss the difference between mere inability to know the full truth, and hypocrisy.

Reading the Poem. You might have a student volunteer read the poem aloud. If the poem gives some students problems of comprehension, you might want to reread it aloud yourself, stopping to answer questions at the points where they arise.

Reteaching Alternatives. If some students still have trouble understanding the poem, you might ask them to write their own paraphrase of it, in one or two brief sentences.

Responding to the Poem   Text page 657
Analyzing the Poem
Identifying Details

1. What does Richard Bone come to realize about the town of Spoon River? Bone realizes that the pious epitaphs he carved on the tombstones of his clients were very often far from the truth.

Explain why he keeps on carving false sentiments. Bone was probably afraid to dispute his clients; his living depended on their good will.

2. What *analogy*, or comparison, does the speaker draw in the poem's last three lines? Bone compares himself to an historian who is either ignorant of the truth or corrupt.

Interpreting Meanings

3. In line 11, the speaker says he knew "how near to the life" were his epitaphs. How do you know he means "how *far* from the life"? Would the latter choice of words have been as effective? Why or why not? The choice of the words "how near to the life" ironically emphasizes the gap between illusion and reality represented by the idealized epitaphs. The more predictable phrase "how far from the life" would probably not have been as effective, since it would not underline Bone's sudden realization.

4. What does Bone mean when he says he made himself "party to" the false chronicles of the stones? The phrase "made myself party to the false chronicles" suggests that Bone thinks of himself as an accomplice in some sort of crime, for which he now feels guilty.

5. Is Richard Bone making too much of his job? Or is there a more universal message in this poem? Explain. Student answers will vary. Some will feel that the dead stonecutter's lament for his hypocrisy in life is poignant; others may question why, if he had convictions, he didn't stand up for them. This dilemma, some students may suggest, may comprise the poem's universal message.

Writing About the Poem
A Creative Response

Inventing Names for Characters. Discuss the examples given in the prompt—the medieval quality of the name "Miniver"; the pun in "Loman"—to be sure students grasp the point.

Criteria for Evaluating the Assignment. The surnames invented by the students clearly suit a self-doubting person, a natural leader, a patriot, and a person lacking a sense of humor. The student is able to explain his or her choices if at first the intent is not clear.

"Lucinda Matlock"   Text page 658

Objectives

1. To explain the theme
2. To analyze the poet's attitude

Introducing the Poem

The characterization in this poem is much stronger than in the preceding one. Where the voice of Richard Bone primarily expresses a theme, without providing details of the

Edgar Lee Masters 225

speaker's private life, the voice of Lucinda Matlock bursts with energy and tells us, in line after vividly detailed line, of the specific pleasures and duties of her ninety-six years. Because of the cataloguing of events and scenes, this poem moves at a much more energetic pace than the shorter "Richard Bone."

The Literal Meaning. A woman reminisces about her ninety-six years and scolds the younger generation.

Teaching Strategies

Providing for Cultural Differences. The poem speaks of a way of life that has passed: playing snap-out, spinning, weaving, gathering medicinal herbs. Some of your students have had this kind of nostalgic past in their family backgrounds; students of more recent immigrant background or of urban minority background, may see Lucinda Matlock as an arrogant representative of a privileged group. Her vigor in old age, however, is a leavening factor that should transcend cultural boundaries.

Providing for Different Levels of Ability. Some students may be less excited by the characterization than others. The essential facts of Lucinda Matlock's life, however, should not pose a comprehension problem.

Introducing Vocabulary Study. Knowing the meanings of the following words is important to understanding the selection.

    repose (n.)   l. 17   degenerate (adj.)   l. 20

Reading the Poem. This poem is a natural for an energetic female student to read aloud.

Reteaching Alternatives. You might ask your students to think of their own grandmothers or great-grandmothers. How were they similar to Lucinda Matlock? How were they different? You might then ask them to write a brief description of Lucinda's character in a short paragraph.

Responding to the Poem   Text page 658
Analyzing the Poem
Identifying Details

1. List the simple pleasures and pastimes the speaker mentions in describing her life. She mentions dances, games, moonlit drives, gathering shells and flowers, and rambles and singing in the fields.

What hardships has she experienced? She has raised twelve children and seen eight of them die before she was sixty years old; she has performed all the household chores and worked in the garden; she has nursed the sick.

Interpreting Meanings

2. Explain why the speaker feels that the younger generation is "degenerate." She accuses the younger generation of complaining too much and of yielding to sorrow, anger, and discontent.

Is it fair for her to imply that their own lives could be as happy as hers? Or has she simply been lucky in the circumstances of her life? Student answers will vary. Encourage them to express and defend their opinions. Obviously, to some extent, Lucinda Matlock has been lucky; but she has also had a considerable share of hardship and pain.

3. The poem's *theme* is summed up in the last line. Explain the meaning of this final statement. Lucinda Matlock seems to mean that life cannot be loved and enjoyed unless we fully "live it": that is, plunge ourselves into its mixture of pleasures and hardships.

What two meanings do you give to the word *life*? The first meaning might be "vitality" or "energy"; the second meaning is the root meaning, "human existence."

4. What do you feel is Masters's own attitude toward Lucinda Matlock? Does he regard her as a judgmental old lady, or as a voice of wisdom? Give evidence from the poem to support your view. Student answers will vary. In general, Masters seems to admire Lucinda Matlock's joyful acceptance of simple pleasures and her stoic endurance of hardships. Her view is that both happiness and sadness are inevitably part of life. It does no good to give way to anger and to let hopes droop if we are discontented; the road to a full enjoyment of life is, quite simply, the living of it.

5. If it were possible to ask the "sons and daughters" to speak in their own defense, what might they say? Student answers will vary. Urge the students to base their suggestions for a "defense" on hints offered in the poem.

"'Butch' Weldy"

Text page 660

Objectives

1. To identify simile and irony
2. To describe tone
3. To write a paragraph comparing two poems

Introducing the Poem

It is important for the students to understand that Butch Weldy's industrial accident took place at a time when workers' compensation laws, safety codes, and the laws of liability in general, were much more primitive than today, and when industrial workers were not protected by unions as we know them.

The Literal Meaning. "Butch" Weldy was horribly injured in an industrial accident.

Teaching Strategies

Providing for Cultural Differences. Students of working-class backgrounds may be able to identify with the subject of this poem more readily than students of upper-class backgrounds.

Providing for Different Levels of Ability. Some students may require a rereading and a paraphrase before they can accurately visualize the accident and comprehend the trial verdict. Students with legal ambitions may be particularly interested in this poem, and helpful in discussion.

Reading the Poem. This poem is a natural for a male student to read aloud.

Reteaching Alernatives. Ask your students how they would feel if they suffered an accident like Butch's. (They would probably feel anger, bitterness, despair.) You can then point out that Butch, too, undoubtedly feels these emotions, but that they are expressed obliquely in the poem.

Primary Sources: The Genesis of Spoon River

Text page 661

The fictitious small town has a long and honorable tradition in American literature: Masters's Spoon River, Anderson's Winesburg, Faulkner's Jefferson, Robinson's Tilbury Town, Bret Harte's Poker Flat, Updike's Olinger, Crane's Whilomville. Then there are the real towns that have been raised to almost mythic status by individual writers: Steinbeck's Salinas, Twain's Hannibal. Based on the readings by these authors that students have done, they might glean details about the towns and then write descriptions of one or more of them.

Responding to the Poem

Text page 661

Analyzing the Poem

Identifying Details

1. Describe "Butch" Weldy's accident. While filling the tank at the canning factory with gasoline, Butch was the victim of an explosion, ignited by a blowfire which someone had left going. The explosion resulted in two broken legs and permanent blindness.

2. When Butch talks about what happened to him, he produces a horrifying *simile*. What is it? He compares his burnt eyes to a couple of eggs (line 13).

3. Explain why the Circuit Judge decided that Old Rhodes's son didn't have to compensate Butch for the accident. The judge reasoned that the explosion was caused by a fellow laborer; Rhodes's son was therefore not responsible.

Interpreting Meanings

4. When a person says that he has "steadied down," what is he implying about his former way of life? Perhaps he implies that he formerly led a rather wild life.

What *irony* do you feel when you consider that this horrible accident took place *after* Butch settled down? The irony results from a reversal of expectation. Whereas such an accident might have been predictable if Butch were living an unruly life, it was surprising in the context of a "steady" life with a regular job and good habits.

5. How do you think Butch feels about the accident that ruined his life? Student answers will vary. As the speaker in the poem, Butch seems stoic; but the sharply edged vignette at the end of the poem of him repeating, "I didn't know him at all," betrays his emotion.

6. Do you think Masters shares Butch's feelings about the accident and about the decision made by the judge? Describe what you think Masters's own *tone* is in this poem. Some students may argue that Masters, as well as Butch, seems bitter: Hints in the poem suggest, for example, that Butch received no compensation because of influence-peddling.

Edgar Lee Masters 227

7. *Spoon River Anthology* was published in 1915. Could something like Butch's accident happen today? Most students will agree that, no matter how well protected the modern workplace is, industrial accidents may always happen. Encourage the students to find and describe specific examples.

What do you think a contemporary court of law would do for a victim like Butch? Butch would probably be awarded workman's compensation, and possibly a handsome negligence settlement. Ask the students to defend their opinions.

Writing About the Poems
A Critical Response

Comparing and Contrasting Poems. Discuss both "'Butch' Weldy" and "Mrs. George Reece," especially in terms of characters and message.

Criteria for Evaluating the Assignment. The paper shows both similarities and differences between the two poems, especially in terms of characters and message.

Extending the Poems

Some of your students might be interested in writing their own "Spoon Rivers" about their home towns, or about fictitious towns they make up from their own knowledge of life. They can create a set of characters from contemporary America—whether small-town or not—and write brief portraits in simple free verse.

Paul Laurence Dunbar   Text page 662

Reading About the Poet

Dunbar was the son of a fugitive slave who had fought on the Union side in the Civil War. He won high academic honors in an otherwise all-white high school, but because his skin was very dark, he was subject to further discrimination even within the boundaries of those jobs available to black men at the time, and could only find work as an elevator operator. Later, at the age of twenty-one, he was more fortunate in landing a job as Frederick Douglass's assistant at the Haiti Pavilion at the 1893 Chicago World's Fair. (Douglass was then the American consul to Haiti.) Dunbar benefitted from the inspiration of being near the great man, but perhaps more, he desperately needed the five dollar weekly wage from this temporary job.

William Dean Howells, who had championed Twain, James, and Crane early in their careers, was largely responsible for bringing Dunbar's work before the public, but he did so in a rather patronizing manner: His introduction to *Lyrics of Lowly Life* praises Dunbar for depicting the emotional and intellectual limitations of blacks. It's not surprising, then, that Dunbar felt considerable ambivalence about his popular success.

"The Haunted Oak"   Text page 663

Objectives

1. To analyze symbols
2. To explain the use of meter, rhyme, and repetition
3. To describe tone
4. To write a paragraph analyzing imagery
5. To analyze the use of archaic diction

Introducing the Poem

This poem deals with lynching in the form of a traditional ballad, with old-fashioned poetic diction and the deliberate use of archaic words like "trow." It raises the interesting question of whether the poetic technique is suited to its subject. On one hand, the form creates a certain mood of timeless outrage that expresses the poet's feelings; on the other hand, the reader may be left with a sense that Dunbar has decked the subject out in inappropriate garb, prettifying it for a genteel audience, by presenting the symbolic utterances of a personified hanging tree rather than the realistic horror of a lynching.

The Literal Meaning. An oak that has been used for lynching tells its feelings.

Teaching Strategies

Providing for Cultural Differences. Black students, white students, and students in different parts of the country may react to this poem in different ways. Among black literary critics, too, there is disagreement about whether to honor Dunbar as a forerunner or reprehend him for indulging in highly stereotyped dialect depictions of black life. While "The Haunted Oak" is not in dialect, and does express anger at injustice, students of all kinds may feel that it is a rather tame protest because of its conventional, artificial form.

Providing for Different Levels of Ability. Less advanced students may have difficulty penetrating the deliberate antiquity of the poem's style. Careful attention to "Analyzing Language and Style," page 664, should help them substitute modern words for the archaic ones.

Introducing Vocabulary Study. Knowing the meanings of the following words is important to understanding the selection. (The starred word appears in the Glossary. Italicized words are archaic.)

| *pray* | l. 1 | smote* | l. 19 |
| *trow* | l. 5 | *nigh* | l. 20 |

Reading the Poem. In order to emphasize the speaker change after the first stanza, you might want to have one student read that stanza aloud—or read it aloud yourself—and another student read the rest of the poem.

Reteaching Alternatives. Because of the use of archaic diction, a line-by-line paraphrase may be necessary for quite a few students. You might divide the class into nine groups—one for each stanza—and have the whole class share the paraphrases they have arrived at.

Responding to the Poem Text page 663

Analyzing the Poem
Identifying Details

1. What characteristics of the tree have prompted the opening questions? The tree is bare; as the speaker passes beneath it, a shudder runs through him.

2. What causes the "gurgling moan" in line 10? The moan comes from the victim who is hanged from the tree.

Who is the "judge" in line 29, and what punishment is visited upon him? The "judge" may have been the leader of the lynching party. He is punished throughout his life by a terrible sense of guilt for his crime.

3. In your own words, what is the answer to the question asked in the first stanza? Student answers will vary. One possibility might be: "My bough will never blossom with leaves because it is cursed by the hanging of an innocent victim."

Interpreting Meanings

4. What does the first stanza contribute to the dramatic thrust of the poem? What would be lost if the poem were to begin with stanza 2? The first stanza establishes a dramatic dialogue between the questioner and the tree; it also contributes to the poem's setting and to a sense of foreboding and suspense. If the poem had begun with the second stanza, these elements would have been lost.

How would the words spoken by the tree be affected? These words would lack a dramatic context.

5. In the final stanza, what larger *symbolic* meaning do the oak tree and its leafless bough assume? The last stanza implies that it is not only the tree, but also the speaker and (by extension) all humanity that must feel the dreadful responsibility for the murder of an innocent victim by lynching.

What symbolic meanings do the words "curse" (line 28) and "haunted" take on in the context of the final stanza? In this context, "curse" and "haunted" assume a more general, symbolic meaning. If the oak tree is regarded as a symbol of nature as a whole, including human life, the "curse" on the bough symbolizes a terrible violation of nature. Humanity must always be "haunted" by shame for the heinous persecution by white men of innocent black victims.

6. Explain how Dunbar's use of *meter, rhyme,* and *repetition* give his poem the effect of a traditional ballad. Why is this form especially appropriate, given the poem's content? The meter and rhyme of the poem are those

Paul Laurence Dunbar   229

of the traditional ballad stanza; the rhyme scheme is abcb, with four strong beats in the first and third lines, and three strong beats in the second and fourth lines. Repetition is especially marked in the final two stanzas ("And ever... And ever...," "rides by, rides by," "haunted"). The form is appropriate because the poem—like many ballads—combines a narrative of a violent act, committed sometime in the past, with motifs of the supernatural (a speaking tree, a haunted bough). Dunbar uses these devices to underline a profound, moral lesson.

7. How would you describe the *tone* of the oak tree's story? Students may suggest that the tone combines grief with indignation.

Given the nature of the story, would you have expected a more bitter tone? Explain. Students' answers will vary.

Writing About the Poem
A Creative Response

1. Setting the Poem to Music. Students of music may be able to name an existing tune to which the poem can be set.

Criteria for Evaluating the Assignment. The student can explain why the tune is suitable for "The Haunted Oak."

A Critical Response

2. Analyzing Imagery. Have students list and discuss the images they find in "The Haunted Oak," and draw some conclusions about the imagery, before they begin to write.

Criteria for Evaluating the Assignment. The essay comments on the use of imagery in "The Haunted Oak" and cites examples of images that involve sight, hearing, and touch.

Analyzing Language and Style
Archaic Diction

1. Pray (line 1), trow (line 5), sore (line 11), smote on (line 19), nigh (line 20), throe (line 23).
2. "Let us *pray*" (speak to God). My broken arm is *sore* (it hurts). The others are rarely used.
3. Please (line 1), believe (line 5), severely (line 11), struck (line 19), near (line 20), agony (line 23). The effect is to modernize the poem, but only in part, leaving expressions such as "set him fast in jail" sounding as if they come from another era (as they do).

Primary Sources: Dunbar and Dialect Poetry   Text page 664

The comparison between Dunbar's dialect poems and James Weldon Johnson's folk poems is interesting. Using stereotyped dialect, Dunbar achieved results that can be seen as demeaning. Using standard English filled with the rhythms and idioms of black speech, Johnson produced moving and authentic, though sometimes somewhat watered-down, folk poems with engaging characters and stirring depictions of black religious life.

Edna St. Vincent Millay   Text page 665

Reading About the Poet

Nowadays Millay's name is better known than her work. Overshadowed by the more powerful, more original poets of the generation that followed her, she is now regarded as a minor lyricist. It would be a mistake, however, to view her as a prissy or genteel poet. She was in the vanguard of her age in matters of women's rights, took public stands on many issues of the day, and led a life that was free-spirited and eventful. The contrast with Emily Dickinson is interesting: The recluse of Amherst was a dazzlingly original poet, while Millay, the Greenwich Village personality, was quite conservative in her literary stance.

Despite her lack of depth and complexity, Millay was a highly accomplished craftsman with a knack for simple, evocative descriptions of nature and the emotions of love. She was particularly adept at the sonnet form, and her 1931 volume of sonnets, *Fatal Interview*, helped revive that form in her time. She was a favorite poet of young people in an era when it was widely believed that young people could solve the problems of injustice and change the world for the better.

230   Voices of American Character

"Recuerdo"

Text page 666

Objectives

1. To identify metaphor
2. To describe meter and rhyme scheme
3. To analyze connotations

Introducing the Poem

This poem is a model of simplicity in its use of language. In the entire poem there are only two words of more than two syllables: "underneath" and "bucketful." The same two lines are used to begin each stanza. And the reiteration of very common words—"we," "very," "and"—gives the poem rhythm and melodic charm. Not every poem on every subject, of course, can be quite so simple. But "Recuerdo" provides a good lesson for students, showing that poetic description does not necessarily imply abstruseness or overblown effects.

The Literal Meaning. The speaker recalls a happy youthful experience of riding a ferry with a friend.

Teaching Strategies

Providing for Cultural Differences. There is a certain air of slumming in this description of two young lovers on a ferry, bestowing kindness on a poor woman by purchasing her apples and pears. Students from some backgrounds may identify more with the old woman than with the young lovers. You might point out that the young lovers themselves are only of modest means, as the remark in the last line, "we gave her all our money but our subway fares" implies.

Providing for Different Levels of Ability. Your less advanced students will probably understand this poem as well as any they read. You may encounter some resistance in persuading your more advanced students of the virtue of its simplicity.

Reading the Poem. You might ask your students to think of good times they've had with people they've loved—very simple activities like taking a walk or a ride, looking at nature or buildings or people. This, you can then inform them, is exactly the kind of experience, and emotion, Millay is evoking. (An audiocassette recording accompanies this poem.)

Reteaching Alternatives. You needn't belabor the poem, but you might ask students, after reading the poem, to locate for themselves the specific, straightforward descriptions of lying on a hilltop, eating fruit, and so forth.

Responding to the Poem

Text page 666

Analyzing the Poem

Identifying Details

1. What details describe what the speaker and her friend did this night? Line 2 describes an all-night trip on a ferry boat. The couple watched the sunrise (lines 11–12). At the end of their trip, they met a shawl-covered woman (line 15), to whom they gave the apples and the pears they had bought (line 17), as well as all the money they had on them (line 18).

Interpreting Meanings

2. Who do you think the "we" in the poem are? The speaker never identifies the other person in the poem, but the context suggests that it is a man with whom she is romantically involved.

What do lines 4–5 suggest about their feelings for one another? The lines have romantic connotations: They give us a picture of two lovers looking into a fire, leaning toward each other across a table, and lying in the moonlight on a hilltop.

3. Why do you think they gave all their money to the "shawl-covered head"? Students' answers will vary. Most students will agree that the couple are in a happy, carefree, generous mood.

What does this action say about the power of love? It implies that love can inspire sympathy and generosity. It also shows that one part of being in love is the need to share that love with someone else, even if it be a stranger.

4. Identify the *metaphor* in line 12. Describe what this image reveals about the speaker's feelings. The sun is compared to a bucket that rises slowly from the sea, containing "gold" rather than water. The image contributes to a portrait of the speaker as romantic and highly emotional; her feelings are almost ecstatic.

5. Read the poem aloud, using the tone and pacing of natural speech. Then describe the poem's *meter* and *rhyme scheme*. What use of repetition contributes to the poem's *mood*? Students will have various responses. Be sure that the students are able to identify the rocking, lilting rhythm of the poem.

Edna St. Vincent Millay 231

Analyzing Language and Style
Imagery and Feelings

1. "Shrieking," "shrilling."
2. "An overripe orange," "a putrid lemon," "a damaged coin."
3. "A stringy-haired head."
4. She could have snarled or spat at the people and snatched at the apples and pears instead of thanking them.

"Dirge Without Music"   Text page 668

Objectives

1. To examine the poem's attitude toward death
2. To analyze the use of rhythm and rhyme
3. To write an imaginary conversation between two speakers
4. To write an essay responding to a poem
5. To compare and contrast two poems

Introducing the Poem

In stark contrast to "Recuerdo," "Dirge Without Music" is the meditation of a mature person on sorrows to come, rather than a still-young poet's memory of joys past. As the title implies, Millay deliberately left the poem bereft of verbal music—its long lines read much like prose.

During her own later years, Millay was in poor health and drank excessively, perhaps to numb the grief she felt after the deaths of several friends and relatives. After her husband's death in 1949, she was alone for the remaining year of her life.

The Literal Meaning. The speaker voices her refusal to be resigned to death.

Teaching Strategies

Providing for Cultural Differences. Millay's view of death was somber and offered no hope of immortality. Students from strongly religious backgrounds may want to offer more optimistic views.

Providing for Different Levels of Ability. Some students may have trouble appreciating the quiet mournfulness of the poem's tone. You might point out that despite its lack of verbal pyrotechnics, this is a poem of strong grief rather than resignation: Indeed, the phrase, "I am not resigned," is used three times.

Introducing Vocabulary Study. Knowing the meanings of the following words is important to understanding the poem. (The starred word is listed in the Glosssary.)

    resigned   l. 4   indiscriminate*   l. 6

Reteaching Alternatives. In discussion, or in brief, in-class written exercises, you might ask your students to pinpoint those phrases where Millay most specifically characterizes the qualities of the people she misses; then, those phrases where she most specifically expresses her own reaction.

Responding to the Poem   Text page 668
Analyzing the Poem
Identifying Details

1. In the first stanza, the speaker mourns the loss of "the wise and the lovely." Whose loss does she mourn in stanza 2? Stanza 4? In the second stanza the speaker mourns the loss of lovers and thinkers. In the fourth, she mourns the beautiful, the tender, and the kind; and also, the intelligent, the witty, and the brave.

Interpreting Meanings

2. What phrase best expresses the speaker's attitude toward death? Students will have various answers. Many students will suggest that the defiance expressed in the penultimate phrase, "I do not approve," best expresses the speaker's attitude. Others may suggest the phrase, "I am not resigned" (lines 4 and 16).

232   Voices of American Character

3. Explain what the speaker means by the statement in line 8 that "the best" is lost after death. What is "the best," in her opinion? In the speaker's opinion, the best is the living, breathing presence in the world of lovers and thinkers.

Do you agree that "the best is lost" in death? Student answers will vary.

4. What comparison does the speaker make in lines 10–12? Explain her point here. The remains of the dead fertilize the ground and "help to feed the roses." The speaker compares the light in the eyes of a lost loved one to the elegance and fragrance of these flowers, saying that she values the eyes of her love more than all the roses in the world.

How does the beauty and delicacy of the flower image help to drive home this point? The delicacy of the image emphasizes the elusive, precious, and fragile character of human life.

5. The last line almost echoes the sentiment of the first, except that the speaker adds another note when she states, "I do not approve." How does this new sentiment affect the *tone* and meaning of the poem? This sentiment injects a further note of bitterness, as if the speaker had been asked to "approve" of death and had politely, but firmly, declined. The sentiment stems from a strongly assertive, individualistic personality, who refuses to conform to fate or to traditional precepts of resignation and acceptance.

6. Although this poem contains certain patterns of *rhythm* and *rhyme*, Millay tries not to allow these sound effects to create "music" for her dirge, or "lament." Do you think she avoids creating a lilting, musical effect? Explain what you think *is* the effect of the poem's sound. Millay uses slant rhymes, internal rhymes, and long, irregularly syncopated phrases to emphasize the speaker's anguished quarrel with death. The jerky interruptions of the rhythm in stanza 3 are especially effective, as are the three brief, complete sentences that occupy the poem's last line.

7. Describe what might have prompted Millay to write this poem. Students may suggest that the loss of a loved one would be the most likely occasion for the poem.

8. Are this speaker's feelings about death widely shared? Explain. Student answers will vary. Most students will probably agree that the speaker's sentiments have many parallels among people whom the students know.

Writing About the Poems
A Creative Response

1. Writing a Conversation. Topics that allow the speakers to show contrasting attitudes toward life would include the meaning of life or the value of small joys. Have students brainstorm other topics that would work.

Criteria for Evaluating the Assignment. The conversation reveals attitudes appropriate to the speakers in Millay's "Recuerdo" and "Dirge Without Music."

A Critical Response

2. Responding to the Poem. Discuss both sides of the issue in class until reasons have emerged for each side of the question.

Criteria for Evaluating the Assignment. The essay gives reasons in support of its contention that "Dirge Without Music" expresses either an immature or a mature attitude toward death.

3. Comparing and Contrasting Poems. Since students have reviewed "Thanatopsis" for other comparative essays, they may be able to complete the chart with no lengthy review of that poem. Have students work together on the chart.

Criteria for Evaluating the Assignment. The essay shows similarities or differences between Bryant's "Thanatopsis" and Millay's "Dirge Without Music" in terms of speaker, subject, message, tone, rhythm, and rhyme.

Primary Sources: "The brawny male sends his picture"   Text page 669

Though Millay may not have deliberately tried to hide the fact that she was a woman when she entered the poetry contest, it can't be denied that literary critics and judges have in the past been known to respond more favorably to the works of men. As a result, some female writers have used male pen names. A very famous one of Millay's generation was Isak Dinesen, author of *Out of Africa*. The greatest, of course, was Mary Anne Evans—better known as George Eliot.

Robert Frost

Text page 670

Reading About the Poet

Frost's poetry invites interesting comparisons with some of the poets your students are already familiar with. Like Emerson, he was a New England nature poet, but unlike Emerson, he was not a mystic. Frost found beauty in nature, and sought repose there, but did not seek in it an intimate contact with a transcendent spiritual force. While he makes rich use of nature in his imagery, his fundamental concern is with the choices and predicaments that make for happiness or unhappiness in human lives.

In his use of dramatic monologues and character studies, he resembles Masters and Robinson, but his style is much more skillful than the former's, and yet his language is much less "literary" than the latter's. In addition, unlike Masters and Robinson—and also unlike Sherwood Anderson, Erskine Caldwell, William Faulkner, and a good many other regionalists—Frost has not mapped out and identified a specific, unified location for his work. He has no "Spoon River" or "Tilbury Town" or "Yoknapatawpha County." Most of his poems take place within a New England landscape, but exact locations are left vague, and the poems do not contain cross-references to each other. This deprives him of the advantage of using a clearly demarcated microcosm, but in a larger sense it may give his poems a more mythic aura. Frost's farms, hills, pastures, woods, are universal settings, regionally accented but not parochial.

In the rhythms of his poetry, Frost tried to capture the rhythms of ordinary talk: what he called "sound-posture." He made this task more difficult for himself by refusing to write in free verse, at a time when most of the important new American poets were turning to that form. But Frost attempted to harmonize the rhythms of speech with the traditional meters of English verse. When successful, this attempt produced a highly sophisticated, complex, and supple versification with a simple vocabulary.

Frost's poems generally "grow" in theme from beginning to end, mimicking the process of human observation and thought. They often begin with a deceptively quiet description of a natural phenomenon or a situation, then proceed to develop it in such a way that we begin to see the symbolic applications. The last line or two of a Frost poem is often a culminating, if oblique, disclosure of a piece of wisdom gained from thought or experience.

"Design"

Text page 672

Objectives

1. To identify similes
2. To analyze the rhyme scheme
3. To write an essay responding to a critic
4. To contrast the use of imagery in three selections
5. To write an essay comparing two poems

Introducing the Poem

This poem was originally printed in an anthology in 1922, yet Frost himself did not include it in any of his own volumes until 1936.

The poem deals with the most serious theme of cosmic design versus cosmic accident, yet it also contains sparks of Frost's quirky humor. The description of the spider in the first line, especially the word "dimple," makes it sound somewhat like a baby, and line 5, "Mixed ready to begin the morning right," contains unmistakable echos of breakfast food advertisements. Frost may have been implying a correspondence between what he finds appalling in nature and in humanity.

The Literal Meaning. The speaker describes seeing a white spider holding a white moth atop a white flower, and wonders about the philosophical implications.

Teaching Strategies

Providing for Cultural Differences. The poem's emphasis on the color white (the word is used five times in fourteen lines) may make nonwhite students uncomfortable, but in fact there are no racial overtones in the poem. There is, however, a comparison to be made with Melville's symbolic use of the color in *Moby-Dick*.

Providing for Different Levels of Ability. Though the

234   Voices of American Character

poem's vocabulary is not difficult, it is an intellectually challenging piece at any level. In the octave, Frost describes a delicate but gruesome scene of a white spider gripping a white moth on a white flower; in the sestet, he asks what force brought them there, and whether cosmic design works on even such a small scale as this, and why the universe is so often appalling. These questions are similar to those Blake asked in "The Tyger."

Introducing Vocabulary Study. Knowing the meaning of the following words is important to understanding the selection. (The italicized word is archaic.)

thither   l. 12   appall   l. 13

Reading the Poem. You might ask your students whether they have ever looked at small, seemingly innocent flora and fauna—insects, birds, small animals—and been appalled by the cruelty that occurs in apparently peaceful backyards and fields. You can then inform them that this is precisely the kind of experience Frost is writing about. (An audiocassette recording accompanies this poem.)

Reteaching Alternatives. The first eight lines paint a picture, and it might help some students if you actually draw a quick picture of the spider, moth, and flower, on the chalkboard. The last six lines pose questions about what brought the creatures to the flower, and whether it was a matter of chance or design. These questions can be paraphrased by your more advanced students during discussion.

Responding to the Poem   Text page 673
Analyzing the Poem
Identifying Details

1. Identify the three "characters" discussed in the poem. The three "characters" are a spider, a moth, and a flowering plant called the heal-all.

What color is each one? Each character is white.

What is happening to the three characters? The moth is trapped and killed by the spider on the heal-all.

2. Identify each of the *similes* in the *octave* (first eight lines) of the sonnet. The moth is compared to a "white piece of rigid satin cloth" (line 3). The combination of the three characters is compared to the "ingredients of a witches' broth" (line 6). Finally, the wings of the dead moth are compared to a paper kite (line 8).

3. Briefly stated, tell what questions the poet asks in the *sestet* (last six lines) of the sonnet. The poet tries to probe the intentions of nature in his questions. He wonders what sinister "design" brought the moth to its death on the flower.

Interpreting Meanings

4. Look up the word "character" in a dictionary. Which definitions of the word might Frost be applying in line 4? The meanings that Frost might be applying may include: a distinctive mark, a personage in a drama, a genetic attribute, and —most generally—a sign.

How does each definition affect the meaning of the line? Have the students apply each definition in turn to the context.

What justifies the poet's description of these things as "characters of death and blight"? The destruction of the moth by the spider justifies the reference to death. The word "blight," meaning plague or destruction, is ironically juxtaposed with the connotations of "white" and the salutary qualities of the heal-all, to which curative powers were attributed.

5. In line 13, the poet answers his own questions with another question. In your own words, explain how this question answers the previous one. The question of line 13 suggests that it is a "design of darkness"—or some sinister plan of nature—that has resulted in the moth's death.

6. In line 14, Frost qualifies his answer with a reservation, beginning with a crucial "if." What final question remains in his mind? The final question hints at an even more frightening possibility: that the moth's death is not the result of a malevolent design in nature, but simply a random event in an indifferent universe—a universe governed by no design whatever.

How would you define a "design of darkness"? The phrase might be defined as a "sinister plan of nature"—or even, perhaps, as a reference to some diabolical "design" of hell.

7. How does the last line affect the whole *tone* and meaning of the poem? The last line introduces a chilling note of doubt: that the "small" events of nature are not governed by any kind of plan, but simply play themselves out in a random fashion.

8. Describe the *rhyme scheme* of the poem. In your view, how does Frost's use of a very limited number of rhymes affect the poem's *tone*? The rhyme scheme is as follows: abab, abab, aca, aca. The limited number of rhymes focuses the reader's attention on the color "white," the word used to set up the most common end-rhyme in line 1. The form also has the effect of tightly compressing the description of an apparently insignificant event, and of forcing the reader to ponder that event's wider implications.

9. How would a Puritan writer from Unit One have answered the questions Frost asks in the poem? A Puritan writer might have agreed with Frost that the playing out of death in nature could represent an allegory for man;

Robert Frost   235

but no Puritan writer would have answered Frost that the universe was randomly governed.

How would the Rationalists from Unit Two, or a scientist, answer them? Most students would agree that the Rationalists would have accepted the phenomenon as purely scientific. A Rationalist thinker would also have insisted that an orderly, generally benevolent "design" governed natural phenomena.

10. Do you see any similarities between Frost's use of the color white in this poem and Melville's use of white in *Moby-Dick*? (See page 297.) Why do you think each writer chose this color? Encourage students to review the relevant sections of *Moby-Dick* before they launch a class discussion. In fact, Frost's use of the color here is rather similar to Melville's. In both cases, the usual connotations of the color white—innocence and purity—are sharply reversed, and our attention is directed to a terrifying blankness, or absence of color.

Writing About the Poems
A Critical Response

1. Responding to a Critic. Read and discuss Perrine's comment on Frost's "Design," checking for understanding.

Criteria for Evaluating the Assignment. The essay argues that in "Design," Frost does or does not pose "the problem of evil," and gives reasons for the stance taken.

2. Contrasting Three Selections. Note that the assignment calls for attention to the *differences* in use of spider imagery by Taylor, Edwards, and Frost. Discuss the use each writer makes of the spider until students begin to formulate the differences into generalizations.

Criteria for Evaluating the Assignment. The essay cites details from Taylor, Edwards, and Frost to support major points made about differences among the three writers in their use of the spider image.

3. Comparing Poems. Briefly review what each of the five listed poems is "about" before students make their selection and begin to complete the chart.

Criteria for Evaluating the Assignment. The essay briefly states similarities between Frost's "Design" and one of the other poems listed in terms of rhyme, rhythm, figures of speech, tone, and message.

"Neither Out Far Nor in Deep" — Text page 674

Objectives

1. To analyze irony and symbolism
2. To recast the poem into the second person
3. To write a paragraph comparing literary works
4. To write a paragraph comparing two poems

Introducing the Poem

This is a poem about which critics have disagreed, so you may expect your students to disagree also. Randall Jarrell considered it a profound statement, in a restrained tone, of the essential limitations of mankind, but William H. Pritchard feels that Jarrell himself may have been going out too far and in too deep in interpreting it, while Richard Poirier sees it as a comic indictment of human conformity, and Rolfe Humphries complained of its lack of "lyric" quality. The poem invites lively discussion by being carefully suspended between tones.

The Literal Meaning. The speaker describes people on a beach, watching the ocean.

Teaching Strategies

Providing for Cultural Differences. This poem makes no reference to any specific culture. It is not recognizably set in Frost's New England or any other specific location.

Providing for Different Levels of Ability. As in many of Frost's poems, the words of this poem, taken one by one, are not hard to understand; the difficulty lies in discerning what's beneath the placid surface. The last stanza is the most thematically explicit part of the poem, and the final two lines will probably require some paraphrasing.

Reading the Poem. Frost himself, during his numerous public readings, enjoyed reading the same poem aloud two or three times to make sure the audience "got it," and you may want to do that with this poem, as well as with some of his other short, cryptic lyrics, such as "Design," "Once By the Pacific," and "Nothing Gold Can Stay." (An audiocassette recording accompanies this poem.)

236 Voices of American Character

Reteaching Alternatives. You might ask the students to restate the poem in a short prose paragraph.

Responding to the Poem   Text page 674
Analyzing the Poem
Identifying Details

1. What phenomenon of human behavior does the poet observe in the first stanza? The poet describes people on the beach who turn their backs to the land and gaze out at the water.

According to line 9, why does this behavior seem surprising? The behavior is surprising because, although the variety of the land might be expected to capture the people's interest, they persist in looking out over the sea all day.

2. What is the one *simile* that gives an imaginative lift to the stark, flat landscape and seascape the poem depicts? The simile occurs in lines 7 and 8, where the puddles of water at the shoreline are said to reflect the figure of a standing gull "like glass."

Interpreting Meanings

3. In what way are lines 11–12 tinged with *irony*? The speaker in the poem notes that the land may seem to be more interesting than the sea—but that, "whatever the truth may be," people insist on looking at the water, because it "comes ashore." Ironically, people seem more fascinated by the monotonous lapping of the shore by the waves than in the land itself.

4. On a literal level, why is it that the people in the poem can look neither "out far" nor "in deep"? They cannot penetrate the opacity of the water by the shoreline, and they cannot distinguish the water clearly when it meets the horizon, far out to sea.

What more general human limitations might be *symbolized* by our inability to probe the distance and depth of the sea? Student answers may vary, but in general the poet seems to mean that people are limited in the depth and breadth of their perceptions in everyday life.

5. What might the sea and the land *symbolize* in this poem? Again, student answers may vary. But the sea could be understood as a symbol for the future in humanity's collective experience and in the particular experience of every individual; the land could symbolize the more familiar territory of the past and the present.

What larger meaning might the "watch" (line 16) take on? In the symbolic context suggested above, the "watch" might be a figure of speech for every individual's monitoring of his or her own life as it wends toward death.

6. Comment on the poet's *tone* in the last line. Does he admire the watchers for keeping their vigil in spite of all obstacles? Does he feel scorn or pity for their failure to recognize their limitations? Do you have some other interpretation? Explain. Student answers will vary. In general, Frost's tone seems detached and neutral: His poem is a commentary on the human tendency to regard the future with uncertainty, curiosity, or apprehension, often at the expense of enjoying a full life in the present.

Writing About the Poem
A Creative Response

Revising the Poem. Make the change to second person in the first stanza, asking students to supply other changes needed for smoothness, and discuss the effect on the tone of the poem. Assign use of the final stanza for the essay.

Criteria for Evaluating the Assignment. The essay changes the final stanza of "Neither Out Far . . ." to second person and makes other changes necessary for smoothness. The essay explains how the stanza differs from Frost's in tone.

A Critical Response

1. Comparing Literary Works. Briefly review Ishmael's reflections and discuss their similarity to Frost's.

Criteria for Evaluating the Assignment. The paragraph states similarities between Ishmael's reflections on the human response to the sea in *Moby-Dick* and Frost's views in "Neither Out Far Nor in Deep."

2. Comparing Poems. Review Whitman's poem "On the Beach at Night Alone" in a brief class discussion.

Criteria for Evaluating the Assignment. The paragraph notes similarities between Frost's and Whitman's messages, their poetic forms, and the overall effect of their poems.

"Birches"   Text page 676

Objectives

1. To find examples of metaphor, simile, and onomatopoeia
2. To identify similes
3. To summarize the poem as a parable
4. To write a paragraph or poem using an everyday sight to comment on a larger subject
5. To write a paragraph comparing writings
6. To write a paragraph comparing attitudes
7. To write an essay responding to the poem

Introducing the Poem

Frost wrote this poem during his stay in England, when he was feeling homesick for New England. The critic John Kemp, in *Robert Frost and New England*, identifies "Birches" as the first poem in which, rather than describing nature impersonally and realistically, Frost adopts the voice of a Yankee sage purveying wisdom—a trend Kemp regrets.

It is important to keep in mind that the birches Frost speaks about have not in fact been swung by a boy. That is merely what he says "I should prefer" (line 23). In fact, they have been bent by an ice storm.

The Literal Meaning. Seeing birches bent by an ice storm, the speaker wishes a boy has swung them. He dreams of becoming a birch-swinger himself.

Teaching Strategies

Providing for Cultural Differences. Students who are not from rural New England may have a hard time visualizing, or even believing in, the idea of a young person swinging a birch tree, but it is a realistic fact. Students from all regions, however, will have had the experience of climbing trees.

Providing for Different Levels of Ability. The major difficulty in this poem is the shift from fact to fantasy, from earthbound description to celestial hypothesizing. The speaker first, on seeing the bent birches, enjoys imagining that a boy has swung them, but in lines 5–20, he returns to a factual description of an ice storm. He then whisks reality aside in favor of his preference for imagination, and from line 43 to the end of the poem, he makes birch-swinging a metaphor for life, death, and rebirth.

Introducing Vocabulary Study. Knowing the meanings of the following words is important to understanding the selection. (The starred word is listed in the Glossary.)

    crazes (v.)   l. 9   arching*   l. 17

Reading the Poem. You'll probably want to preface the reading of the poem with a discussion of the practice of birch-swinging Frost describes. For purposes of reading the poem aloud, you can divide the poem into parts: lines 1 to the middle of line 5 (which you might want to read yourself to get things started), from there through line 20, line 21 to the middle of line 32, from there through line 40, from line 41 through line 49, and from line 50 to the end.

Reteaching Alternatives. Through class discussion, you might make a list on the chalkboard of the traits Frost assigns to the birches and to the boy swinging them, and alongside each entry, write down the thematic meaning it takes on in context.

Responding to the Poem   Text page 677
Analyzing the Poem
Identifying Details

1. Describe the scenario that the speaker imagines when he sees birch trees. When he sees the birch trees bend in a high wind, the speaker likes to imagine that some boy has been swinging them.

What realistic objection to his idea does he recognize in lines 4–5? He realizes that, whereas the trees may bend back after someone swings on them, an ice storm bends them down permanently.

What "matter of fact" does "Truth" break in with in lines 5–20? The matter of fact is the realistic description of an actual ice storm.

2. In lines 48–49, what does the speaker say he would like to do? He says he would like to get away from earth for a while, and then return to it.

How does he relate this wish to swinging a birch tree? Swinging on the birch tree is a metaphor for a temporary absence from the ground (the earth) and then a return to it.

Interpreting Meanings

3. Find at least three examples of *metaphor* and *onomatopoeia* in the poem. Examples of metaphor: the trees clicking upon themselves (line 7), the stir crazing the tree's

238   Voices of American Character

enamel (line 9), the trees shedding crystal shells (line 10), the implied comparison in the "heaps of broken glass" and the shattering of the "inner dome of heaven" (lines 12–13). Examples of onomatopoeia include: "stir cracks and crazes" (line 9); "crystal shells" (line 10), "shattering and avalanching on the snow crust" (line 11).

4. Two strong *similes* give the poem a richness that is both imaginative and the result of close observation. What are these similes? At lines 19–20, the bent trunks of the birch trees, from which the leaves grow trailing on the ground, are compared to girls on their hands and knees, who fling their wet hair over their heads to let it dry in the sun. The comparison suggests an attitude of affection and tenderness. At lines 44–47, the speaker compares life to a "pathless wood," and he speaks metaphorically of life's troubles as cobwebs which "burn" and "tickle" the face. Pain, and the grief it causes, are said to result from a twig lashing an eye open, and thus bringing tears. The speaker uses these images to describe depression, grief, and weariness.

5. What does the playful activity of swinging birches seem to *symbolize* in the poem? The playful activity of swinging on birches assumes a symbolic meaning for the speaker: In the exhilaration of physically reaching toward heaven and returning again to earth, he sees a metaphor for his own spiritual needs.

6. A *parable* is a short story in which an ordinary event from everyday life is used to teach a much wider moral or religious lesson. Summarize in your own words what you think the moral or message of Frost's parable is. Students may suggest various possibilities. In general, the message of the parable seems to be that we can be periodically refreshed by "breaking away" from the routines of life, and then returning to those routines with renewed optimism and energy.

7. Describe the complex, conflicting attitudes toward life revealed through this parable about birch-swinging. On the one hand, the speaker affirms his commitment to life in lines 50–53: He says he does not wish to escape the earth permanently, since it is "the right place for love." But the speaker is sensitive to the bruises and hurts of life, from which we all need occasionally to escape.

Writing About the Poem

Assignments 1, 2, and 3 relate Frost's work to earlier traditions. You may wish to allow students to choose *one* as an essay topic. Assignment 4 analyzes Frost's poetic theory.

A Creative Response

1. Reading Nature. By now students have seen Americans from earlier eras move from observing nature to moral or philosophical comment. They should need no further models.

Criteria for Evaluating the Assignment. The paragraph or poem moves from an everyday sight or event to comment on a much larger subject.

A Critical Response

2. Comparing Writings. Discuss how the Puritans "read" moral significance in nature, how Romantics "read" philosophical observations in nature, and how Frost may fit into one of these traditions.

Criteria for Evaluating the Assignment. The essay defines the tradition to which Frost seems to belong and offers cogent reasons in support of that position.

3. Comparing Attitudes. Review the Puritan tendency to see moral or religious lessons in natural events.

Criteria for Evaluating the Assignment. The paragraph explains how a Puritan would relate the bending of birches to human moral attitudes or behavior.

4. Responding to the Poem. Clarify Frost's meaning as necessary, especially the words *delight* and *wisdom*.

Criteria for Evaluating the Assignment. The essay defines *delight* and *wisdom*, and briefly argues whether or not "Birches" begins "in delight" and ends "in wisdom."

"Mending Wall" Text page 678

Objectives

1. To explain simile
2. To interpret symbolism
3. To change the poem's voice
4. To write a paragraph comparing two poems

Introducing the Poem

The famous refrain, "Good fences make good neighbors," contains several possible levels of ironic meaning in this poem. As is pointed out in question 10, text page 680, the character who needs the wall less is the one who initiates the yearly mending. Critic Richard Poirer suggests that

Robert Frost 239

even if good fences don't make good neighbors, good fence-*making* does.

The poem is also notable for its wonderfully flexible use of blank verse. A line-by-line scansion of at least part of the work would be appropriate for teachers and classes who are interested in that aspect of technique.

The Literal Meaning. Each spring, two neighbors mend the stone wall separating their property, after the freezing of the ground has displaced some stones.

Teaching Strategies

Providing for Cultural Differences. As in many Frost poems, students from rural or New England backgrounds are likely to be quickest to respond to the setting of this poem. Fences and walls, however, are important features of urban and suburban settings as well.

Providing for Different Levels of Ability. There are no words of more than two syllables in this 45-line poem, but Frost's simplicity of diction sometimes creates its own kind of opacity. Slower students will require a paraphrase of the key line, "Something there is that doesn't love a wall."

Reading the Poem. You might begin by asking your students what kinds of walls—tangible or intangible—separate them from their neighbors. Some students may have houses with fences; others may lack fences around theirs. What effects do fences, or the lack of them, have on their daily lives?

Reteaching Alternatives. You might ask your students to retell the poem in the form of a short prose paragraph in the voice of the speaker, describing wall-mending and saying how he feels about wall-mending and about his neighbor.

Responding to the Poem Text page 680
Analyzing the Poem
Identifying Details

1. What makes the speaker say that "something" doesn't love a wall? The speaker observes nature's tendency to force up roots and boulders to disturb the walls that human beings construct on their land. Symbolically, the speaker may be referring to the human tendency to resent or to minimize the importance of barriers between people.

Besides this "something," who else sometimes knocks down walls? The speaker says that hunters often destroy walls.

2. Describe what is happening in lines 13–16. The speaker and his neighbor each walk down their respective sides of the wall, picking up and restoring the boulders that have fallen on their property.

According to the speaker, why is rebuilding the wall merely a game (lines 23–26)? The speaker does not take the wall's rebuilding seriously because he sees no need for a physical barrier between his property and that of his neighbor; the neighbor raises pine trees, while the speaker owns an apple orchard. Even without a wall, the two different species of trees will never interfere with each other.

3. What question does the speaker think should be settled before building a wall, according to lines 32–34? The speaker says that, before he built a wall, he would like to know what he was walling in and walling out, and to whom he was like to give offense.

4. Why would the speaker say "Elves" (line 36)? The reference to the mischievous sprites of mythology suits the speaker's quizzical sense of humor.

5. From whom did the neighbor get his saying "Good fences make good neighbors"? The saying came from the neighbor's father.

Interpreting Meanings

6. In lines 23–27, what two different personality types or temperaments might be dramatized? The speaker seems open, curious, and playful. His neighbor seems taciturn, reserved, and conservative.

7. Why do you think the speaker would rather his neighbor said "Elves" (lines 37–38)? The speaker seems to long for emotional common ground with his neighbor: He would like his neighbor to share his sense of humor.

8. The speaker says in lines 41–42 that the neighboring farmer moves in a "darkness" that is "not of woods only and the shade of trees." What else might this darkness be? Explain the significance of the *simile* in line 40. The speaker only hints at the answer, but the comparison mentioning an "old-stone savage armed" in line 40 suggests that the speaker thinks of his neighbor as narrow-minded and primitive. Perhaps he refers to a spiritual or emotional "darkness," which may have blinded his neighbor to the virtues and pleasures of friendship.

9. What might the wall *symbolize*? In your view, what philosophies about human social relations does the poem explore? The wall may symbolize the barriers which human beings erect, between themselves and their fellows.

10. How do you explain the fact that the man who doesn't see the need for a wall is the one who, every spring, is the first to call upon his neighbor and so make sure the wall is rebuilt? Might he want something more from his neighbor than merely a hand with repair work? Perhaps he uses the wall-mending as an excuse to find companionship with his neighbor.

11. Which of these two men is in greater harmony with nature, in your opinion? Why do you think so? Student answers will vary. Many students will suggest that the

240 Voices of American Character

speaker is in greater harmony with nature, since he seems sympathetic and observant.

12. When the speaker repeats his neighbor's statement in the poem's last line, does he mean to emphasize his neighbor's stubborness? Or does he somewhat reluctantly mean to recognize that there's wisdom in the statement? Students may support either of these alternatives. The poet seems intentionally to have left the meaning of this repetition ambiguous.

13. Do *you* believe that "good fences make good neighbors"? Why or why not? Student answers will vary. Encourage the students to support their responses with specific, cogent reasoning and examples.

Writing About the Poem
A Creative Response

1. Changing the Poem's Voice. Discuss the possible responses a neighbor might make to the speaker's musings. Allow students to respond in verse or in prose.

Criteria for Evaluating the Assignment. The paragraph or poem responds to the speaker's musings on the idea of walls, from the neighbor's point of view.

A Critical Response

2. Comparing Poems. Briefly call to mind Dickinson's main point in "The Soul selects...," and discuss any connections the students see with "Mending Wall."

Criteria for Evaluating the Assignment. The paragraph states whether or not "Mending Wall" has anything in common with Dickinson's poem and cites details to support the points made.

"Once by the Pacific" Text page 681

Objectives

1. To identify personification
2. To interpret symbolism
3. To write an essay comparing two poems

Introducing the Poem

This is a poem of vague prophecy, and Frost himself used it as evidence that he had prophesied a wide variety of unhappy events in his own and his friends' lives. His manuscript of the poem bore the notation, "as of 1880," possibly indicating that the poem's mood sprang from an experience on the California coast when Frost was six years old. Technically, the poem is a sonnet in rhymed couplets.

The Literal Meaning. The speaker describes a frightening storm seen once on the Pacific coast, and compares it to the end of the world.

Teaching Strategies

Providing for Cultural Differences. Students who have lived near a seacoast may be able to contribute their personal experiences of witnessing ocean storms.

Providing for Different Levels of Ability Some students may need help with the hair simile in lines 5 and 6, with the progression shore-cliff-continent in lines 8 and 9, with the phrase "a night of dark intent" in line 10, and with the phrase, "God's last *Put out the Light*" in line 14.

Reading the Poem. The poem is short enough to be read aloud by a well-prepared student. (An audiocassette recording accompanies this poem.)

Reteaching Alternatives. You might ask your class to compare this poem with the other short Frost poem about the ocean they have read, "Neither Out Far Nor in Deep" (text page 674), possibly writing a brief statement of the symbolism of each and sharing these with each other in discussion.

Responding to the Poem Text page 681
Analyzing the Poem
Identifying Details

1. Identify at least three examples of *personification* in the poem. Examples include: waves looking over others in line 2, waves thinking in lines 3–4, clouds like locks of hair on a person's head in lines 5–6, the shore being lucky in line 8, a night of dark intent in line 10.

Interpreting Meanings

2. What does the scene remind the speaker of? The

Robert Frost 241

scene reminds the speaker of some future disaster or calamity.

3. Explain what you think the speaker means by "a night of dark intent...not only a night, an age" (lines 10–11). The speaker is not specific, but these phrases seem to portend the advent of some dreadful calamity, either natural or human-made, which will wipe out civilization as we know it.

Whose "intent" is he referring to? This is left unclear: Perhaps the speaker is referring to nature, to God, or to some mysterious, impersonal force.

4. Who do you think is the "someone" who "had better be prepared for rage" (line 12)? Again, the speaker's lack of a specific reference contributes to the sinister, menacing tone. Perhaps the speaker means "mankind" in general by the word "someone."

Whose "rage"? Students may suggest that the rage is divine, or perhaps they may argue that it is a metaphorical rage of natural forces.

5. Besides ocean water, what else might be "broken" during that rage? Student answers may vary. Possible answers include houses, lives, cities, or human life itself.

6. "*Put out the light*" is something anyone might say on an ordinary evening at home. How does the use of this casual, domestic phrase make the poem's message even more chilling? What would you say that message is? The informality of the phrase contrasts with the context, in which it is associated with God. If God commanded at the Creation, "Let there be light," his command to "Put out the light" may possibly refer to the extinction of humanity and the world. Note also a secondary allusion to Shakespeare, *Othello* V ii.7, in which the jealous Othello compares the act of snuffing out a candle to the murder of his wife, Desdemona.

7. The poem's *title* suggests that Frost is describing a scene he once saw as he gazed at the Pacific Ocean. What larger "moment" might this scene *symbolize*? Encourage students to present and defend their responses. One possibility is an apocalyptic vision of the end of the world. Another is the emotion experienced by someone who has witnessed the awful destructive power of nature, gathering its forces to strike a blow at the "artificial" world of man.

8. Do you view this poem as a warning? Or do you think Frost is just expressing a certain philosophy of life? Explain what the warning might be, or discuss the philosophy. Students may be divided in their responses. Those who see the poem as a warning might suggest that Frost intends to address it to human beings who spoil the environment or who imperil the continuation of human life by the manufacture of nuclear weapons. Those students who see the poem as the expression of a grimly pessimistic philosophy should state what factors may have been involved in the formation of that philosophy.

Writing About the Poem
A Critical Response

Comparing Poems. Reread Whitman's poem, and have students work together to complete the chart suggested in the writing prompt. Direct them to use at least three of the items from the chart in their essays.

Criteria for Evaluating the Assignment. The essay compares Frost's "Once by the Pacific" with Whitman's "On the Beach at Night" in terms of three or more of the following: message, use of symbols, tone, use of rhythms and rhymes, or use of imagery.

"The Death of the Hired Man" Text page 682

Objectives

1. To identify and interpret imagery
2. To analyze irony
3. To state the poem's message
4. To write a paragraph re-setting the poem in contemporary times
5. To write an essay analyzing three characters
6. To analyze the use of blank verse

Introducing the Poem

This poem includes two of Frost's most famous sayings—the two definitions of "home" in lines 118–120—and there is a school of criticism, typified by Richard Poirier and Louise Bogan, that views Frost's pose as "Yankee sage" as a regrettable concession to the tastes of the mass audience, and wishes he had stuck with impersonal nature realism. However, William H. Pritchard asserts that Frost considered it "a challenge...to bring out an interplay of sympathy and judgment by setting in motion the contrasting voices of man and woman," as well as to write a long poem consisting mostly of the sounds of plain speech, but with passages of more elevated diction to prevent monotony.

The Literal Meaning. A farm couple discuss an old, worn-out hired hand who has returned to their farm for shelter. Checking on his condition, they find him dead.

Teaching Strategies

Providing for Cultural Differences. Students from farm areas will identify most readily with the subject of this poem, although farming methods, and the relations between employers and employees, have progressed since the poem was written.

Providing for Different Levels of Ability. The sheer length of this poem may daunt your less advanced students, but you might point out that it is essentially a short story in verse, and not long by those standards.

Introducing Vocabulary Study. Knowing the meanings of the following words is important to understanding the selection. (Starred words appear in the Glossary. The italicized word either is archaic, or has special meaning in context.)

beholden*   l. 21   piqued*   l. 73

Reading the Poem. Given its length, you might want to assign this poem as homework. If you have it read aloud, you might have a female student read Mary's dialogue, a male student read Warren's, and a third student, or yourself, read the narration.

Reteaching Alternatives. This poem is about relationships of duty and of emotion, and about how both elements enter into the creation of a home. While the hired man's relationship to the farm couple is the catalyst for the drama, Mary's and Warren's relationship to each other is at least as important. You might ask your students to discuss what the drama of the hired man's arrival shows us about the couple's relationship, with its elements of duty and emotion.

Responding to the Poem   Text page 687
Analyzing the Poem
Identifying Details

1. Describe the basic problem facing Warren, Mary, and Silas. The basic problem facing the three characters is what to do with Silas, now that he wants to return to work.

2. Why is Warren reluctant to hire Silas? Warren is reluctant to hire him because, last haying season, Silas asked for fixed wages and then left Warren unexpectedly, just when Warren needed him the most.

3. What is Silas's attitude toward Harold Wilson, the college boy about whom he reminisces? Silas is piqued that the lad is so wrapped up in education. Harold Wilson studies Latin and is the "fool of books," in Silas's opinion. Silas regrets that he never succeeded in convincing Harold that he could find water with a hazel prong.

What does he wish he could teach the boy, and why? Silas wishes he could show Harold how to build a load of hay, so that the boy could "be some good perhaps to someone in the world." Harold may have book-learning; but Silas wants to teach him some practical countryman's skills.

4. What explanation does Mary suggest for the fact that Silas never talks about his brother? Mary suggests that Silas is too proud to call on his brother for help.

5. Identify four remarks that reveal Mary's tenderness for Silas. Remarks that indicate Mary's tenderness for Silas occur in line 7 ("Be kind"), line 31 ("Sh! not so loud: he'll hear you"), lines 49–50 ("Surely you won't grudge the poor old man / Some humble way to save his self-respect"), line 76 ("I sympathize"), line 99 ("Poor Silas, so concerned for other folk"), and line 158 ("You mustn't laugh at him").

Interpreting Meanings

6. Describe how Warren's attitude toward Silas differs from Mary's. Warren remembers with irritation that Silas left him in an awkward spot during the last haying season. Whereas Mary sees Silas as a human being who has "come home to die," Warren at first regards him as an embarrassing nuisance. He mentions that he steered clear of Silas's disputes with the young college boy, Harold Wilson. He wonders why Silas's relatives cannot, or will not, take care of the old man. But as the dialogue continues, Warren is forced to admit that Silas has never harmed anyone.

Do you think Warren's feelings about Silas are mixed? Give evidence from the poem to support your opinion. On the one hand, Warren regards Silas as eccentric and undependable, and he seems put off by Mary's insistence that he take the old man in. On the other hand, Warren admits that Silas is skilled at his job and is basically harmless.

7. After a quick narrative introduction, dialogue carries the story until it is more than half told. The narrator reenters in line 103. Identify the details in lines 103–110 that create a vivid *image* of the *setting*? These lines describe the setting moon, whose light falls on Mary's apron in her lap. Mary extends her hand to the morning-glories, as if she plays on a stringed instrument of "tenderness" as she tries to persuade her husband to be kind to Silas.

Robert Frost   243

Besides contributing to atmosphere, what does this passage tell us about Mary's *character*? The passage shows Mary's innate qualities of pity, understanding, tenderness, and tact.

8. Find the two definitions of "home" offered in the poem. One critic has said that one definition is based on law and duty, the other on mercy. Which is which, and do you agree with the critic's observation? At line 118, Warren defines "home" in a limited, rather negative way—as the place where, "when you have to go there, they have to take you in." In the following lines, Mary defines the concept of "home" in a more positive, giving fashion—as "something you somehow haven't to deserve." Warren implies that Silas's relatives have a duty to accept him. Mary asserts that duty and merit should be irrelevant to Silas's treatment at home, where he should be accepted out of love, with no implications that his comparative failure in life has brought him shame. Most students will agree with the critic's observation.

Which definition do you favor? Ask the students to justify their preferences with reasons, examples, or incidents.

9. When the conclusion of a play, story, or poem seems to be "inevitable," we take a kind of satisfaction in knowing that no other ending would do. Does the conclusion in this poem strike you as inevitable? Why or why not? Student answers will vary. Encourage them to support their opinions with specific references to the poem.

What would your feelings have been if, instead of "Dead" in answer to Mary's question, Warren had answered "Asleep," or "Sharpening his scythe"? Most students will agree that either of these answers would have been anticlimactic.

10. Consider this possible *irony* in the poem: Warren and Mary, able to hire Silas and to become controlling factors in his life, are here themselves controlled by Silas's independence. Do you think the poet is pointing out that, in the long run, it is the free spirit who has the power to dominate those who "live by the rules"? Do you think this idea is true or false? Explain your answer. Ask the students to consider carefully the two parts of the question. When students have determined their view of Frost's attitude about the power of the "free spirit," they may go on to discuss whether or not they agree with this attitude.

11. State in your own words the poem's *message*. Do you think this message has any particular importance in today's world? Student answers will vary. One possible paraphrase of the poem's message is the importance of respect and compassion for our fellow human beings, no matter how independent or eccentric they may seem. Most students will agree that the poem is relevant to today's world.

12. How did you feel about each of the three characters in this poem? Students' answers will vary. Encourage the students to compile a chart of personality traits for each of the three major characters before they discuss their responses to them.

Writing About the Poem
A Creative Response

1. Extending the Poem. Write on the chalkboard "city," "rural area," "suburb," "modern farm," and "migrant camp," and brainstorm for each heading some of the changes that would have to be made in conflict, characters, and resolution to accommodate the altered setting.

Criteria for Evaluating the Assignment. The paragraph selects a new setting for "The Death of the Hired Man" and explains changes that would have to occur in conflict, characters, and resolution.

A Critical Response

2. Analyzing Characters. Discuss the prompt fully, noting that it lists the characters to be analyzed (one paragraph each) and the aspects of characterization to be covered.

Criteria for Evaluating the Assignment. The essay devotes one paragraph each to Silas, Mary, and Warren. It analyzes each character's values, the character's conflict and handling of it, the effect the character has on others, and any changes the character undergoes.

Analyzing Language and Style
Blank Verse

1. Students are to recite the first ten lines aloud.
2. In the first ten lines, lines 4, 6, 7, 8, 9, and 10 scan as iambic pentameter; lines 1, 2, 3, and 5 vary the meter.
3. At times Frost ends a sentence in mid-line or breaks a line into dialogue between two speakers. These seem to be deliberate "stops" of "the rope" rather than examples of Frost's "tripping" himself.
4. Choices will vary. Some rearrangement of words and number of lines might occur, as in this revision of lines 78–81:
   He mentally associates Harold with Latin.
   He asked me what I thought of Harold's claim
   To study Latin because he likes it,
   As he likes the violin—
   What kind of argument is that?
5. Students will vary in agreeing or in not agreeing with Frost.

"Nothing Gold Can Stay"

Text page 688

Objectives

1. To analyze symbolism.
2. To analyze sound, rhythm, and tone
3. To write a paraphrase
4. To write a paragraph comparing two poems

Introducing the Poem

Some of your students may already know this poem from S. E. Hinton's popular "young adult" novel *The Outsiders,* or from the successful movie that was made of it. In *The Outsiders,* when Ponyboy Curtis and Johnny Cade are watching a sunset, Ponyboy recites this poem, which becomes a repeated motif in the story. When Johnny dies, he tells Ponyboy to "stay gold."

The poem was part of a section of short lyrics, called "Grace Notes," in Frost's 1923 volume, *New Hampshire.* The section included several of his best poems, such as "To Earthward" and "Stopping By Woods on a Snowy Evening."

The Literal Meaning. Spring greenery, flowers, Eden, and dawn are four "gold" things that did not stay.

Teaching Strategies

Providing for Cultural Differences. The story of the loss of Eden and the Greek myth of the Golden Age may need a brief reintroduction for some students.

Providing for Different Levels of Ability. The fact that the word "gold" is used here metaphorically may give some students trouble at first. The word is used to mean anything precious; thus, the first green buds of spring may, metaphorically, be "gold."

Introducing Vocabulary Study. Knowing the meanings of the following words is important to understanding the selection.

  hue   l. 2   subsides   l. 5

Reading the Poem. This poem is not only short enough to be read by one student in less than a minute, but it is also short enough to memorize, if you feel your class would benefit. (An audiocassette recording accompanies this poem.)

Reteaching Alternatives. You might ask your students to write a paragraph about anything they have experienced and enjoyed that has not stayed.

Responding to the Poem

Text page 688

Analyzing the Poem

Identifying Details

1. Identify four specific things in the poem that cannot, or did not, "stay." They are: nature's "first green" (line 1), the flower of nature's "early leaf" (line 3), the paradise of Eden (line 6), and the golden dawn (line 7).

Interpreting Meanings

2. Think of what the very first buds of leaves look like in spring, and explain what line 1 means. The first buds of leaves in spring often have a gold tinge: the first line means that the "green" of the leaves starts in "gold" buds.

3. Explain the natural process described in line 5. The first few leaves of spring give way to a profusion of leaves in summer.

4. What Biblical event is *alluded* to in line 6? Line 6 refers to the Biblical account of humanity's loss of Eden through Adam and Eve's sin of disobedience.

What state of mind or situation might "Eden" *symbolize* here? Eden may symbolize a blissful, untroubled, "golden" existence.

5. "Gold" as used here is not the precious metal, but an idea. What different ideas might "gold" *symbolize?* Among the different ideas that students may suggest are preciousness, perfection, value, nature's beauty, and wealth (both in its material and spiritual aspects).

Why can't "gold" stay—or do you disagree? The speaker of the poem implies that "gold"—as an idea—is transient due to the nature of things. The seasons wax and wane; humans lost the paradise of Eden; day is followed by night. Students should be encouraged to discuss the main idea of the poem, and to state whether or not they agree, and why.

6. Show how its *rhymes* and *rhythm* conribute to this poem's compactness and completeness. How do *alliteration, slant rhyme,* and other *sound echoes* also contribute to the poem's tightly-woven effect? Examples of alliteration include: "green is gold" (line 1), "her hardest hue to hold" (line 2), "dawn goes down to day" (line 7).

Robert Frost 245

Slant rhyme: "flower" and "hour" (lines 3–4). Other sound echoes: "only so" (line 4), "Eden . . . grief" (line 6).

7. How would you describe the speaker's *tone*? The tone seems bitter-sweet, or melancholy. Encourage students to defend their responses.

Writing About the Poem
A Creative Response

1. Paraphrasing. Thorough discussion of questions 1–5 ("Identifying Details," "Interpreting Meanings") must precede attempts to paraphrase the poem. Prepare your own paraphrase ahead of time to gain awareness of difficult spots.

Criteria for Evaluating the Assignment. All key ideas of the poem are present in the paraphrase.

A Critical Response

2. Comparing Poems. Briefly review use of "gold" as a symbol in "Eldorado" and "Miniver Cheevy." Suggest that students chart the elements for "Nothing Gold Can Stay" and either "Eldorado" or "Minister Cheevy" before writing.

Criteria for Evaluating the Assignment. The paragraph tells how Frost's poem is similar to or different from Poe's or Robinson's poem in terms of use of gold as an image and symbol, message, tone, and poetic form and technique.

Extending the Poems

The statement, "Nothing Gold Can Stay," invites the rejoinder, "What about great poetry?" You might discuss with your class the idea that literature, and all art, is an attempt to disprove Frost's assertion.

Primary Sources: "I must have the pulse beat of rhythm . . ." Text page 689

Frost's comments would make a good basis for discussion or for a brief essay on your students' own views of free verse compared to metered verse. You might ask whether they feel Frost was contradicting himself. In the first paragraph, he praises Whitman and castigates the American literary world for being slow to accept him. Isn't Frost showing the same kind of fearfulness in his reluctance to accept the free verse of his own time? You might want to save a full discussion of this question until after your students have read the free verse poets in Unit Nine. They can then determine for themselves whether free verse was largely a momentary effect without staying power.

John Crowe Ransom   Text page 690

Reading About the Poet

Ransom's *Selected Poems,* published in 1945, contain only forty-two poems: Ransom weeded out from his early work everything he considered less than first-rate. The critic Willard Thorp says, "It would be difficult to name a single volume by an American poet in which the quality is so consistently high."

Ransom was part of a great Southern renaissance in American writing that began in the 1920's and had affiliations with the Modernist movement in art throughout the Western world but retained an identity of its own. Most of the participants in this renaissance were descendants of landowning families that had suffered reversals in the Civil War and Reconstruction, but were regaining enough ground, in the new century's prosperity, to send their children to college. Before that generation, literature among the Southern gentry had been an amateur pursuit—admired, but practiced as a pastime like sports, rather than as a profession. The generation of the Fugitives deliberately set out to become professional writers in opposition to the traditions of their families. Among them were William Faulkner, Robert Penn Warren, Tennessee Williams, Thomas Wolfe, Katherine Anne Porter, Margaret Mitchell, and many others.

"Bells for John Whiteside's Daughter"

Text page 691

Objectives

1. To identify a simile
2. To analyze tone

Introducing the Poem

The duality of Ransom's tone has often been noted by critics: He combines wit and tenderness, amalgamating the two into an irony that distances itself from feelings without denying them. Babette Deutsch puts it this way: "Whatever his subject... his tone is right. The glint of irony is there, deepened as well as softened by a sensitiveness without a grain of sentimentality."

The Literal Meaning. The speakers, in first-person plural, recall the frolicsome behaviour of a young girl whose funeral they are attending.

Teaching Strategies

Providing for Cultural Differences. Although Ransom is very much a Southern poet, there is nothing specifically Southern about the setting of this poem. Some students may be puzzled at the lightness of the tone for such a melancholy subject.

Providing for Different Levels of Ability. The rhyme scheme in this poem is simple enough for less advanced students to grasp, yet varied enough to interest advanced students.

Introducing Vocabulary Study. Knowing the meanings of the following words is important to understanding the selection. (Starred words are listed in the Glossary.)

| bruited | l. 5 | scuttle* | l. 15 |
| harried* | l. 8 | vexed* | l. 19 |

Reading the Poem. You may want to warn your students that they are about to read a rather light-hearted poem about the death of a child. You can then inform them that the lightness comes from the fact that the speaker dwells on the child's light-hearted activities during her life.

Reteaching Alternatives. You might ask your students to visualize who is speaking the poem. It is not an "I"; it is a "we." Who are they? What are they doing? What is the occasion?

Responding to the Poem

Text page 691

Analyzing the Poem
Identifying Details

1. **What characteristics of John Whiteside's daughter make the speaker astonished at her present "brown study"?** The speed of her little body and the lightness of the daughter's footfall make her "brown study," or apparent state of being lost in thought, astonishing.

Interpreting Meanings

2. **What kind of "wars" might the little girl have carried on?** She played with the geese, chasing them toward the pond. She may also have carried on playful "wars" with siblings or with friends of her own age.

   When you "take arms" against your own shadow, what do you do? You chase your shadow.

3. **Identify the *simile* that describes the geese in the third stanza. What is meant by their "snow"?** The geese are compared to a snow cloud, trailing snow on the grass. Their "snow" refers to their white feathers.

4. **What action of the little girl caused the geese to cry, "Alas"?** The little girl chased them with a rod, and forced them to scuttle to the pond.

   What additional overtones does this cry take on, given the poem's subject? The cry becomes associated with the lament for the little girl's death in the last stanza.

5. **What *is* the child's "brown study"? What details in the last stanza make clear what has happened to her?** Her "brown study" is her appearance in death, which resembles the state of being lost in thought. Details in the last stanza that make this clear are the funeral bells (line 17) and the reference to the little girl, "lying so primly propped" (line 20).

6. **In the last stanza, what word does the speaker use to describe people's emotions at the little girl's "brown study"? Why is this word a surprising choice?** The speaker uses the word "vexed" (line 19). It is a surprising choice because a reader might expect a stronger word, such as "mournful" or "grief-stricken."

7. **Point out other words and details that give the poem an almost light *tone*. Do you think that this tone suggests a lack of feeling, or does it, in an unsentimental way,**

John Crowe Ransom   247

convey the speaker's affection and sadness? Give reasons for your opinion. Some words and details in the poem that give it an almost light tone include: "lightness in her footfall" (line 21), the bruiting of "wars" (line 5), the portrait of the little girl chasing the geese with a stick, the personification of the geese, the reference to a "little lady" (lines 13–14), and the use of the word "scuttle" (line 15). Students will have various opinions on this tone's effect. Most students will agree that the informal details express a genuine, if unsentimental, grief for the girl's death.

8. What are the bells ringing for in the last stanza? The bells ring for the child's funeral service.

"Parting, Without a Sequel"

Text page 692

Objectives

1. To analyze conflict and symbols
2. To evaluate the use of rhyme
3. To write an essay comparing two poems
4. To study the multiple meanings of words
5. To respond to critical commentary

Introducing the Poem

This is a more difficult poem than "Bells for John Whiteside's Daughter." That poem presents a situation that is unambiguous in itself, but toward which the speaker has a complex reaction. In "Parting, Without a Sequel," the situation itself is ambiguous: A woman sends a man a letter of rejection, but we can sense her grief in the very act of sending it. Also, "Bells for John Whiteside's Daughter" gives us a picture of what has been lost, but "Parting, Without a Sequel" gives us no details at all about the quality of the relationship that is being ended. On the other hand, once the emotions in "Parting, Without a Sequel" are clarified, your students may be able to sympathize with them more than with the emotions in "Bells for John Whiteside's Daughter."

The Literal Meaning. A woman sends a rejecting note to a lover, and simultaneously grieves about it.

Teaching Strategies

Providing for Cultural Differences. This poem does not refer to a specific region or culture; the situation and emotions, however, arise from a tradition of genteel romance. Some students may find the heroine's self-imposed grief self-indulgent compared with their own problems. You might point out that love affairs, with their ambivalent partings, occur in all cultures.

Providing for Different Levels of Ability. Since much of the story of the poem is between the lines, less advanced students may need to be directed to the places where it can be discerned. Close attention to the "Analyzing the Poem" questions, text page 693, should help.

Introducing Vocabulary Study. Knowing the meanings of the following words is important to understanding the selection. (The starred word is listed in the Glossary.)

venomous*	l. 3	stoical	l. 15
functioner	l. 6	wan	l. 19
vaunting	l. 13		

Reading the Poem. You might want to study both Ransom poems in the same lesson.

Reteaching Alternatives. You might ask each student to write a one- or two-sentence synopsis of the poem.

Responding to the Poem

Text page 693

Analyzing the Poem
Identifying Details

1. What decisive action has the poem's main character just taken? She has sent a letter to her sweetheart to break off their relationship.

2. The driving force in this poem is a *conflict* within the main character herself. What details reveal her anger? Details revealing the woman's anger include the following: the fact that the man has "richly deserved" the letter (line 2), the woman's paleness and the mention of the "ruin of

248 Voices of American Character

her younger years" in the third stanza, the detail of the "agitation of the rain" in line 17, and the concluding portrait of the woman, "hot as fever and cold as any icicle" (lines 23–24).

What evidence reveals that she has mixed feelings about her decision? In the second stanza, she hopes that the messenger may lose the letter and never deliver it; in the fourth stanza, she uncertainly seeks advice from her father's oak tree; in the last stanza, the reference to her as both hot and cold graphically exposes her ambivalence.

Interpreting Meanings

3. Identify the "blue-capped functioner of doom" in line 6. He is the messenger who will deliver the letter in which she finally breaks from her sweetheart.

Why do you think he is described as "leering"? A groom may be both a bridegroom and (in the old sense of the word) a servant; the fact that the messenger "leers" at the woman emphasizes her distaste for both the man and his errand.

4. Why do you think the main character hopes this person might lose her letter? This hope reflects her conflict: Even as she sends the letter, part of her wishes that she had never written it, or that it might be lost and never delivered.

5. In what fashion does the oak tree "speak" to the daughter in the fifth stanza, and what message does the tree convey? The tree speaks "low and gentle" (line 18). It reproaches the young woman for her decision.

What qualities associated with an oak tree might make it an appropriate *symbol* for the woman's father? An oak tree is generally large, sturdy, and shady. Its protective strength makes it an apt symbol for the woman's father.

6. Why do you think the messenger's track is described as a "serpent's track" in line 22 instead of, for example, a snail's track or just a wheel track? The phrase "serpent's track" may connote the venomous hatred of the woman's letter, carried by the messenger on the bicycle. It is almost as if the messenger resembles a snake as he proceeds on his errand. The alternative phrases would not be nearly so suggestive.

In what sense does the track go on "forever"? Students will have various opinions. In one sense, the track goes on "forever" because the decision expressed in the letter is definitive and complete: The woman will never see her sweetheart again. Then again, if we associate the mention of the serpent with the serpent in the Biblical account of Eden, there is another, more philosophical overtone: We are, as human beings, forever to be the heirs of strife.

7. How could someone be "hot as fever" and "cold as an icicle" at the same time? What does this suggest the letter writer is feeling? The heat suggests the intensity of the woman's emotion, whereas the coldness suggests her feelings of apprehension. The two phrases combine to evoke the conflict that the woman is experiencing.

8. While *rhyme* can add music to poetry, it can also create wry humor. What ingenious and funny three-syllable rhyme ends the poem? The poem ends with the quixotic rhyme of "bicycle" and "icicle."

Do you think the poet is making a comment by ending this serious, unhappy story on a slightly ridiculous note? Student responses will vary. The ingenious, amusing rhyme creates a note of detachment—as if to say, perhaps, that the young woman's situation is neither unique nor remarkable. The poet does not deny her individual anguish, but he hints at a philosophical interpretation of it.

9. What is the significance of the poem's title? Do you think there usually *is* a "sequel" to stories of unrequited love? Student responses will vary. Urge the students to defend their opinions.

Writing About the Poem
A Critical Response

1. Comparing Poems. Review both Ransom's poem and Lowell's "She Came and She Went" in terms of emotions expressed and view of death revealed. Note that students are to compare speakers' emotions and views on death.

Criteria for Evaluating the Assignment. The essay cites examples from the two poems to support comments on similarities found in the emotions expressed and the views of death revealed.

2. Filling in Meanings. Read the prompt aloud and have students silently jot down the first answers to the questions that come to mind. Then read the answers aloud and discuss them until students know the positions they wish to take in their essays.

Criteria for Evaluating the Assignment. The essay analyzes "Parting, Without a Sequel," in terms of age of the speaker, whether the oak tree represents her father, and attitude of the poet. The essay cites details from the poem to support its interpretation.

3. Comparing Poems. Briefly review Dickinson's poem. Students may wish to chart its similarities with Ransom's poem as they have done for similar assignments.

Criteria for Evaluating the Assignment. The essay cites similarities between Dickinson's "Heart! We will forget him" and Ransom's "Parting, Without a Sequel," in terms of messages, speakers, authors' tone, and imagery.

John Crowe Ransom

4. **Responding to a Critic.** Discuss Young's comment and students' first impressions in terms of Ransom's poems. They should review both poems before writing the essay.

Criteria for Evaluating the Assignment. The essay argues that Young's evaluation of Ransom's poems does or does not fit "Bells for John Whiteside's Daughter" or "Parting, Without a Sequel," and cites the poem to support its points.

Analyzing Language and Style
Multiple Meanings of Words

1. Letters of the alphabet. Ransom is also revealing the letter writer's anger.

2. Bridegroom, stable hand, manservant. "Manservant" applies to line 7, with "bridegroom" echoed also.

3. Sickly and pale. Both the archaic and the modern meanings are appropriate for line 19.

4. A *seer* is a visionary or prophet. The pun is likely.

5. *Vaunting* (line 13) means prideful, boastful, or in a display of vanity. It does shed some mockery on the tree's advice.

Extending Ransom's Poems

Earlier in this unit, your students have read another poem about an oak tree that speaks: Dunbar's "The Haunted Oak" (text page 693). This could be the basis of a compare-and-contrast exercise.

Robinson Jeffers
Text page 694

Reading About the Poet

Jeffers, though a contemporary of many other great American poets, worked in isolation throughout his career. He belonged to no poetic school or movement, and lived in and wrote about a region of the country that seemed quite remote at the time. He became well known for the experimentalism of his free verse, the unrelieved bleakness of his view of human life, and the lurid plots of his long narrative poems, many of which were taken from Greek myths. Today, he is still admired as someone who took Whitman's brand of free verse and developed out of it a strong, majestic line of his own; and as the producer of some moving, well-observed lyrics about the California coast. In general, however, critics today respond bleakly to Jeffers's bleakness, seeing it as the mere symptom of a gloomy personal temperament rather than a convincingly thought-out view of life. They also tend to agree that the piling-on of gore and horror in the plots of his long narrative poems was not a sufficient subsitute for dramatic skill, and that his insistent preaching of pessimism often weighed down his verse. An early champion of his, Babette Deutsch, later said, "Bitter earnestness was apt to make for flat assertion."

"Shine, Perishing Republic"
Text page 695

Objectives

1. To interpret implied metaphor and tone
2. To respond to the poem's message

Introducing the Poem

Although this poem is pessimistic in its view of American society, Jeffers uttered some more optimistic words about democracy in 1940, during the only speaking tour of his life. "Our democracy," he said, "has provided, and still provides, the greatest freedom for the greatest number of people.... It means an attitude of mind—tolerance, disregard of class distinction, a recognition that each person... is equal to any other person. It means: no snobbery, and no flunkyism...."

The Literal Meaning. The speaker, disgusted with human society, counsels his sons to "keep their distance" from it, but praises America as "a mortal splendor."

250   Voices of American Character

Teaching Strategies

Providing for Cultural Differences. This poem is apt to stimulate a variety of emotional responses. Students from working-class backgrounds may see Jeffers's bitterness as the fruit of privilege; some other students may share his dissident views. The best approach is probably to welcome all views as making for lively discussion.

Providing for Different Levels of Ability. Jeffers is one of the more difficult poets in this unit, and you'll probably have to go through the poem slowly, stopping to define words and explain ideas and images.

Introducing Vocabulary Study. Knowing the meanings of the following words is important to understanding the selection. (Starred words appear in the Glossary.)

| vulgarity | l. 1 | decadence* | l. 4 |
| exultances* | l. 4 | compulsory | l. 8 |

Reading the Poem. You'll probably need to go through the poem twice, first reading the poem aloud, or having a student read it, in its entirety, and then reading it once more with pauses for discussion whenever there are questions.

Reteaching Alternatives. This poem presents an idea that will challenge idealistic high school students: the idea that one should retreat from humanity rather than trying to help it. At the same time, Jeffers is not recommending hedonism. You might want to use the novelty of his message as a focus for discussion, or as a topic for brief replies in essay form.

Responding to the Poem   Text page 695
Analyzing the Poem
Identifying Details

1. To whom is the poem addressed? The speaker addresses the poem to his children.

Which line tells you? Lines 7 and 9 show that the poem is addressed to the speaker's sons.

2. In stanza 4, the speaker suggests that his children, and by extension all children, need not surrender to corruption. What alternative does he say is open to them? He says that they can go to the "mountains" rather than to the "cities." He seems to mean that they can live an independent, individualist life in a rugged, natural setting, removed from the mass concentrations of urban society.

3. In contrast to the familiar exhortation to "love thy neighbor," the fifth stanza offers quite different advice. What reason does the speaker give in this stanza for warning his listeners to "be in nothing so moderate as in love of man"? The speaker warns his listeners to be wary of their fellow men; "man," he says, is "a clever servant, insufferable master" (line 9).

Interpreting Meanings

4. The first stanza contains an *implied metaphor*. What is America compared to? America is compared to a "molten mass" in a mold. Details that extend the metaphor include the following: the mold is said to be "vulgarity"; America itself "thickens" to empire; protest is "only a bubble" in the vast melting pot; the mass (or majority) of America "hardens."

What does "vulgarity" mean? "Vulgarity" is probably a pejorative term here, referring to the common, undesirable choices of the majority.

Why is it so bad that the republic thickens to *empire*? Jeffers may have in mind the shift from republicanism at the beginning of America's existence as a nation in the eighteenth century to world domination as one of the superpowers in the twentieth century.

5. What attitude toward America does the second stanza express? The second stanza seems to imply that America's decadence is part of a natural cycle. The speaker refers to flowering, fruit, rot, and earth—which again produces flowers in the spring. Ripeness and decadence are thus part of nature's course.

6. If you were to read the poem aloud, in what *tone* would you read the words "shine, perishing republic"? Student answers will vary.

7. What is the speaker's attitude in the last stanza? The speaker reveals a negative, pessimistic attitude.

Do you think he really means what he says in line 9? Students will be divided in their responses. Some students may doubt that the speaker really means what he says—the students may suggest that this sentiment is rhetorical exaggeration to emphasize the underlying theme of the poem.

8. What does the speaker seem to think is the cause of the republic's condition? The speaker seems to blame conformity, massiveness, power, and intolerance as factors that are responsible for America's decadent condition.

9. How would you respond to the poet's message? Student answers will vary. Ask the students to support their responses with specific, cogent reasoning.

Robinson Jeffers   251

"Love the Wild Swan"

Text page 696

Objectives

1. To interpret symbolism and extended metaphor
2. To rewrite the poem in the form of a dialogue
3. To write an essay responding to the poem
4. To identify different types of rhymes

Introducing the Poem

The poem is a sonnet in the form of an interior monologue. It thus presents a different side of Jeffers, who was known primarily for his experiments in free verse. "Love the Wild Swan" shows him as a highly competent technician in traditional rhyme and meter.

The Literal Meaning. In the octave, the poet bemoans the inadequacy of his verse to capture the beauty of the world. In the sestet, he corrects himself, saying that the beauty of the world is not to be captured but to be loved.

Teaching Strategies

Providing for Cultural Differences. The poem makes instinctive use of the thematic traditions of Western literature: the wild swan as a symbol of beauty, the hunt as a metaphor for the poetic act. Students from other cultural backgrounds may be accustomed to thinking of poetry in different ways: poetry as ritual or celebration, perhaps, rather than as hunt. This cultural difference in attitudes toward art might lead to interesting, enriching discussions.

Providing for Different Levels of Ability. Despite its beautiful sensory images, this is very much a poem of abstract ideas. More advanced students may relish the chance to make the connections between Jeffers's images and his message; less advanced students will need help, particularly with lines 2–3, 5–6, and 10–13.

Reading the Poem. Since the poem is in the form of a statement and response, it would be natural to ask one student to read the first eight lines aloud and another student to read the last six lines.

Reteaching Alternatives. The poem is about the frustration of being unable to achieve all that one hopes to achieve in one's work, and the consolation that one is able to achieve part of it anyway. You might ask your students to discuss, or write a paragraph about, experiences of this kind that they themselves have had.

Responding to the Poem

Text page 697

Analyzing the Poem
Identifying Details

1. What complaint does the speaker make in the poem's first four lines? He feels that his verses are inadequate to capture the splendor of nature.

2. What adjectives in lines 1–8 emphasize the speaker's feeling of weakness and failure? Adjectives that capture this feeling include: "pale," "brittle," "cracked," "twilight," and "unlucky."

3. What response is made to the speaker's complaint in the *sestet*, the last six lines of the sonnet? Another voice consoles the speaker, telling him that the fault is not within himself: No poetry can capture the range and magnificence of nature. The speaker should at least be grateful that his senses can apprehend the "wild swan" of the world.

Interpreting Meanings

4. What might "cracked and twilight mirrors" *symbolize* in line 5? Mirrors that are "cracked" and "twilight" cannot reflect objects clearly; in a symbolic sense, the poet's powers are inadequate to describe nature because the poet's perceptions are flawed and fuzzy, or unclear.

Who is the "unlucky hunter," and what are his "bullets of wax"? The unlucky hunter represents the poet in search of nature, and his bullets of wax are ineffective weapons.

5. This sonnet's *sestet* presents an *extended metaphor* in which the world is compared to a wild swan. What details extend this metaphor? Details that extend the metaphor include: the "white breast" of the swan (line 10), the "flame" of the bird's brilliance (line 11), the "music" of the swan's song (line 14), and the "thunder of the wings" (line 14).

What attitude toward the world does this comparison suggest? The comparison suggests an attitude of wonder at the elusive range, beauty, and variety of the natural world.

6. What might the "flame" in line 11 be? Why might "better mirrors" crack in it? The flame in line 11 may suggest the vitality and brilliance of the natural world, as symbolized by the wild swan. The fact that "better mirrors" might crack in it may indicate that, however sharp a poet's skills may be, he or she can never fully reflect the beauty of nature.

252 Voices of American Character

7. Why does the speaker hesitate in the middle of line 12? What other word than "self" might he be reaching for? Perhaps the speaker meant at first to say "verses," or "poetry."

Writing About the Poems
A Creative Response

1. Rephrasing a Poem. "Identifying Details" questions 1 and 3 (page 697) clarify parts spoken by the two different speakers in "Love the Wild Swan." On the basis of their words, discuss the likely attributes of the two speakers.

Criteria for Evaluating the Assignment. The paper includes a brief description of each speaker, and rewrites the poem as a dialogue between them.

A Critical Response

2. Responding to the Poem. "Identifying Details" questions 1, 2, and 3 (page 697) will assist students in summarizing the content of "Shine, Perishing Republic." Discuss aspects of contemporary life to which views expressed in the poem do or do not apply.

Criteria for Evaluating the Assignment. The essay summarizes views expressed in Jeffers's poem and states whether or not these views are still valid. Main points are supported by references to the poem and to the contemporary life.

Analyzing Language and Style
Rhymes

1. Breast/least, can/swan.
2. Catch/wax.
3. Word/bird.

Extending the Poems

The task Jeffers undertook for himself in writing free verse was as difficult as writing regular metered verse: He sought to set up a kind of pulsebeat rhythm based on the number of accents per line, with the unaccented syllables also assisting in carrying the rhythm forward. If time permits, you might have your students write a brief poem in free verse with an accented-syllable basis, using some aspect of nature as a subject.

James Weldon Johnson
Text page 698

"Go Down Death"
Text page 699

Objectives

1. To identify similes
2. To write a speech
3. To write an essay comparing sermons
4. To compare and contrast poems
5. To identify the influence of Whitman on the poet's style

Introducing the Poem

In an anthology he edited in 1922 called *The Book of Negro Poetry,* Johnson wrote: "What the colored poet in the United States needs to do is . . . find a form that will express the racial spirit by symbols from within rather than by symbols from without, such as the mere mutilation of English spelling and pronunciation. He needs a form that is freer and larger than dialect . . . a form expressing the imagery, the idioms . . . of the Negro, but which will also be capable of voicing the deepest and highest emotions and aspirations, and allow for the widest range of subjects and the widest scope of treatment."

To a considerable degree, he succeeded in finding such a form in *God's Trombones,* his book of poetic sermons in the voices of black preachers.

The Literal Meaning. The preacher, speaking at Sister Caroline's funeral, tells how God called Death to come for Sister Caroline so that she could attain rest.

James Weldon Johnson 253

Teaching Strategies

Providing for Cultural Differences. Black students may be able to comment knowledgeably on the realistic aspects of this sermon-in-verse. Students from all backgrounds, however, will be able to enjoy the richness of its expression and characterization, and the solemn power of its emotion.

Providing for Different Levels of Ability. The important point for students to understand is that this is an oration in the voice of a preacher, not a narration in the voice of an impersonal narrator. The preacher, who knew Sister Caroline, is speaking to a church audience who also knew her.

Reading the Poem. If possible, have your students read silently along with the audiocassette recording to gain the full impact of this powerful oration.

Reteaching Alternatives. You might ask the students to write brief character descriptions of Sister Caroline based on what they learn in the poem, and brief descriptions of the preacher from what is implied by his words and his voice.

Responding to the Poem   Text page 702
Analyzing the Poem
Identifying Details

1. Where is God in stanza 2, and where is Death in stanza 3? God is in heaven, and Death is in a "shadowy place" (line 2), waiting with his pale, white horses.

 According to stanza 5, where is Sister Caroline? Sister Caroline lies on a bed of pain in Savannah, Georgia.

2. How does Sister Caroline respond to Death's arrival in stanza 7? She greets Death calmly and like a "welcome friend" who comes to take her home.

3. Point out at least three *similes* that help to suggest the power and magnificence of the workings of heaven. The similes include the comparison of the angel's voice to a clap of thunder (line 18), the comparison of the foam from Death's horse to a comet (line 47), and the comparison of Death himself to a falling star (line 55).

Interpreting Meanings

4. Does the speaker portray God and Jesus as distant, forbidding figures, or as familiar, gentle ones? Point out at least four details that support your interpretation. Most students will agree that the portrait of God and Jesus stresses mercy and gentleness. Details supporting this interpretation include the pity that touches God's heart (lines 12–13), God's compassion for Sister Caroline's weariness (lines 35–39), the mention of the "loving breast" of Jesus (line 69), and the portrait of Jesus rocking Sister Caroline in his arms (lines 70–75).

5. Death riding a pale horse is a legendary figure in literature and art. Sometimes referred to as the Grim Reaper, he is often pictured as a skeleton on horseback carrying a scythe (a tool used to cut down hay and grass). While most of these traditional representations of death are fearful, the one in this poem is not. How does the poet transform this conventionally horrifying image into an almost comforting one? Death is depicted as God's speedy and obedient servant. It is clear in the poem that his function is to release Sister Caroline from hardships, weariness, and illness, and to reunite her with God and with Jesus. Thus, Sister Caroline greets Death as a friend, rather than as a dreaded enemy. The description of Death's journey in the sixth stanza contains no foreboding or suspense; rather, the poet employs striking imagery to emphasize the heavens' beauty. Finally, it is said in the eighth stanza that Death handles Sister Caroline gently: He "took her up like a baby," and she felt no chill in his icy arms.

6. Johnson was a highly sophisticated writer. Why do you think he uses the informal language of folk tradition for this poem? Student answers will vary. Some will suggest that Johnson uses folk tradition as a means to "humanize" the Bible's teachings about everlasting life. Others may point out that the syntax and diction of folk tradition possess a simple, quiet dignity that is entirely appropriate to Johnson's subject in the poem.

7. Why do you think Death rides a "pale" or white horse? Where else have you seen the color white used in a similar *symbolic* way? Student answers will vary. Remind the students of the use of the color white by Herman Melville in *Moby-Dick* and by Robert Frost in "Design" (page 672).

Writing About the Poem
A Creative Response

1. Extending the Poem. "Interpreting Meanings" question 5 (page 702) can help students refine their picture of Death as drawn by Johnson. Suggest that students read their papers aloud and revise them before making the final copy.

Criteria for Evaluating the Assignment. The paper reads well as a speech. It is appropriate to the character of Death as drawn by Johnson in "Go Down Death."

A Critical Response

2. Comparing Sermons. Note that students are to seek both similarities and differences between Edwards's sermon and Johnson's poem in terms of imagery, figures of speech, message, tone, audience, and purpose.

Criteria for Evaluating the Assignment. The essay compares and contrasts Edwards's and Johnson's sermons in terms of imagery, figures of speech, message, tone, audience, and purpose. The essay cites examples to support points made.

3. Comparing and Contrasting Poems. Briefly review Millay's "Dirge Without Music." Direct students' attention to the questions contained in the writing prompt.

Criteria for Evaluating the Assignment. The essay compares and contrasts attitudes toward death expressed in Johnson's "Go Down Death" and Millay's "Dirge Without Music" in terms of emotions conveyed by the speakers, aspects of life stressed by each speaker, and view taken on what happens to people after death.

Analyzing Language and Style
Free Verse and the Orator's Style

1. For example: Line 1 uses repetition (Weep not, weep not), and lines 2, 3, and 7 each begin with "She is."

2. For example: "Left-lonesome daughter" (line 4); "She's only just gone home" (line 5).

3. For example: Lines 16 (long) and 17 (very short); and lines 47–49 (short/long/short).

Extending the Poem

You might ask your students to write poems of their own in the forms of speeches. They need not be religious sermons and need not be on the subject of death.

Primary Sources: God's Trombones   Text page 703

The passage describes one kind of community leader, one kind of preacher. You might ask students to contrast this person with community and religious leaders they have known in their own experience.

Claude McKay   Text page 704

Reading About the Poet

McKay, born in Jamaica, spent much of his life traveling. He emigrated to the American heartland to go to college, and then lived and worked in New England and New York, and visited England (where he met George Bernard Shaw), then the Soviet Union and France. Though his creative drive waned in his later years, he still produced important work in nonfiction, particularly his autobiography, *A Long Way From Home.*

"America"   Text page 705

Objectives

1. To interpret images
2. To analyze a paradox
3. To capture the poet's feelings in a phrase
4. To compare and contrast two poems

Introducing the Poem

"America" is a sonnet in iambic pentameter, with the rhyme scheme abab cdcd efef gg.

The Literal Meaning. The speaker says that although America makes him bitter, he thrives on its vigor, and looks calmly ahead to a future against injustice.

Teaching Strategies

Providing for Cultural Differences. Students from various cultures may have a wide variety of reactions to the bitterness expressed in this poem. You may want to act as moderator in the airing of views from all sides.

Providing for Different Levels of Ability. Less advanced students may be somewhat daunted by the richness of the poem's imagery. Virtually every line contains a simile or metaphor; you might work with students on creating paraphrases.

Introducing Vocabulary Study. Knowing the meanings of the following words will help students understand the selection.

| front (v.) | l. 8 |
| jeer (n.) | l. 10 |

Reading the Poem. After reading the poem aloud the first time, you might want to go over it with students on a line-by-line basis.

Reteaching Alternatives. Question 1 under "Writing About the Poem," text page 705, provides a creative way of paraphrasing McKay's message.

Responding to the Poem   Text page 707
Analyzing the Poem
Identifying Details

1. In lines 1–3, what treatment does the poet say he receives from America? He says that America makes him bitter and that it threatens to strangle him.

2. What qualities of America cause the speaker to love her anyway? The speaker praises America's vigor, strength, and bigness—qualities which give the speaker strength to protest against injustice.

Interpreting Meanings

3. America is *personified* in this poem as an entity both cruel and powerful. What *images* suggest America's cruelty and injustice? Such images include: "tiger's tooth" (line 2), the mention of "hate" (line 6), the portrait of a rebel confronting a "king in state" (line 8), and the mention of "walls" (line 9).

What images convey her power? In addition to some of the preceding references, students may add the mention of "tides" of vigor in line 5, the reference to America's "bigness" sweeping "like a flood" (line 7), and the reference to "might and granite wonders" (line 12).

4. A rebel with "not a shred / Of terror, malice, not a word of jeer" might seem to be a rebel without a rebellion. How does the poem resolve this *paradox* or apparent contradiction? The speaker is a philosophical rebel who combines nonviolence with protest against injustice and cruelty. Remind the students of the nonviolent philosophy of Dr. Martin Luther King, Jr., perhaps the greatest leader of the Civil Rights movement of the 1950's and 1960's. The poem's speaker resembles Dr. King in that he refuses to repay injustice and cruelty with "terror" or "malice."

5. What does the speaker see happening to America as he gazes into "the days ahead"? He sees America's great and powerful works, "her might and granite wonders," being destroyed by Time.

How would you explain this projected fate? The concluding line, with its mention of "priceless treasures sinking in the sand," suggests that unless Americans can come together and make an end of racial injustice, the country will resemble a desert, where priceless resources will be wasted.

6. How does the speaker's attitude toward America compare with that of the speaker of "Shine, Perishing Republic" (page 695)? Ask students to defend their comparisons with specific references to both poems.

Writing About the Poem
A Creative Response

1. Capturing the Poet's Feelings. Brainstorm, uncritically, some possible slogans (for bumper stickers) and some poster illustrations. When ideas die down, go back and evaluate the appropriateness of each idea to McKay's intent.

Criteria for Evaluating the Assignment. The bumper sticker or poster captures the main idea expressed in the poem.

A Critical Response

2. Comparing and Contrasting Poems. Read and discuss Shelley's "Ozymandias" in terms of similarities to and differences from McKay's "America." Note that both are sonnets, though they use different rhyme patterns.

Criteria for Evaluating the Assignment. The essay compares and contrasts Shelley's and McKay's poems in terms of form, subject, point of view, and emotion. The essay cites examples to support points made.

Extending the Poem

Students may wish to write a brief poem or prose paragraph answering, either pro or con, McKay's message.

Langston Hughes

Text page 706

Reading About the Poet

Hughes was the most famous black poet of the first half of this century. The story of his discovery by Vachel Lindsay in a Washington, D.C., restaurant where Hughes bussed tables became something of a literary legend. During the 1940's he created the fictional character of Jess B. Semple, who came to be called Simple, and whose humorous urban wisdom represents, in the view of many critics, his most enduring achievement.

"Harlem"

Text page 707

Objectives

1. To evaluate the use of free verse
2. To write a news report based on the poem
3. To write an essay comparing two poems

Introducing the Poem

The poem is in free verse with short, forceful lines in colloquial speech.

The Literal Meeting. The speaker describes Harlem as "on the edge of hell" and expresses the economic hardships and emotional response of its residents.

Teaching Strategies

Providing for Cultural Differences. The poem is about black life in Harlem in the Depression, a time when a penny's increase in the price of bread (line 10) was significant. For students from all cultures, this historical difference between now and then will at first be difficult to understand.

Providing for Different Levels of Ability. This straightforward poem should pose few problems of literal comprehension. More advanced students may enjoy discussing the factors, such as sentence rhythm and line length, that make this a poetic rendering of colloquial speech rather than a mere prose transcription.

Reading the Poem. You might want to combine this poem in the same lesson with Hughes's "I, Too" (page 708).

Reteaching Alternatives. Students might enjoy analyzing how this poem manages to combine a light, humane tone with authentic social protest in the space of a few short lines. The poem exemplifies the elusive quality of simplicity in art.

Responding to the Poem

Text page 707

Analyzing the Poem

Identifying Details

1. Name the specific hardships and injustices that the people of Harlem remember, according to the speaker in the poem. The people remember lies that they were told, physical abuse, poverty, and their inability to get a job because they were "colored."

Interpreting Meanings

2. What ideas about Harlem does the speaker suggest when he says that it is "on the edge of hell"? Student answers will vary. Some will note that the image suggests misery and torment, with no relief or escape. Others may suggest that the image contains a warning: In its misery, and in the boiling resentment of its citizens, Harlem is close to a violent destruction or flare-up, which might resemble "hell."

3. Do you interpret the poem's final stanza as an expression of powerlessness, or as a threat? Defend your opinion. Students may have various opinions. Remind them that Hughes may have intended both interpretations—and that these interpretations are not necessarily contradictory.

4. "Harlem" is written in *free verse*. How does the poet's use of short, colloquial lines not only imitate real speech, but also help to convey the speaker's feelings? The simple, colloquial diction and the plain syntax directly confront the reader, powerfully reinforcing the poem's brutal realism.

Writing About the Poem
A Creative Response

1. Writing a News Report. Suggest that students choose a specific newspaper or television show (for example, "Sixty Minutes") in order to better choose their attitude.

Criteria for Evaluating the Assignment. The paragraph is suited to the medium chosen by the student and reflects at least one point made by Hughes in "Harlem."

A Critical Response

2. Comparing Poems. Discuss the questions given in the writing prompt, and direct students to structure their essays around answers to the questions.

Criteria for Evaluating the Assignment. The essay compares Hughes's "Harlem" and McKay's "America" in terms of form, diction, and imagery used to describe the situation of black Americans; states each poet's apparent response to oppression; and states which poem the writer finds more effective as protest, and why.

"I, Too" Text page 708

Objectives

1. To identify details
2. To analyze tone

Introducing the Poem

This brief poem of only sixty-two words, in eighteen very short lines of free verse, is a powerful expression of hope for the end of racism.

The Literal Meaning. The speaker says that although he is "the darker brother," he too is part of America and will "be at the table" in the future.

Teaching Strategies

Providing for Cultural Differences. Students of various cultural backgrounds may wish to tell how their forebears felt about being included in American society.

Providing for Different Levels of Ability. Be sure the students understand that the kitchen referred to in the poem is a metaphor for American society with its abundance.

Reading the Poem. You may want to combine "I, Too" in the same lesson with "Harlem" (page 707).

Reteaching Alternatives. Students may wish to write poetic or prose responses to the speaker of the poem.

Responding to the Poem Text page 708
Analyzing the Poem
Identifying Details

1. Where does the speaker say he is sent "when company comes"? He says he is sent to eat in the kitchen.

What does he say his place will be "tomorrow"? He says he will be at the table then, and that no one will dare to send him away to the kitchen to eat.

Interpreting Meanings

2. Who are "they" in line 3? "They" refers to white people, as is evident from line 2, where the speaker refers to himself as "the darker brother."

What realization does the speaker predict will eventually cause "them" to feel shame? The speaker predicts that white people will eventually grow to recognize the speaker's "beauty"—for he, too, is "America." This is another way of saying that white people will at last be able to recognize their own country in its totality. They will honor the beauty and inherent dignity of every individual, regardless of race.

3. This poem clearly describes the effects of racism, yet there is optimism and forgiveness in the speaker's *tone*. What details in the poem suggest a view of America as one family that will eventually realize the injustice of

258   Voices of American Character

discrimination? Details suggesting the view of America as one family include the central image of a family at the dinner table, the references to the kitchen and to the arrival of "company," and the reference to "the dark brother" (line 2).

4. The poem's last line is almost an echo of its first. What change has been made in the last line? The poet has substituted the word "am" for the word "sing."

What message is highlighted by this change? The identification of the speaker with America highlights the meaning that all citizens, black and white, are a part of the national "family."

How would the poem have been affected if these two lines were reversed? The poem would lose much of its force.

5. Do you think the prophecy in this poem (written in 1922) has in any way come true? In what ways has it not come true? Student answers will vary.

"The Weary Blues"

Text page 710

Objectives

1. To analyze mood
2. To identify alliteration, onomatopoeia, and similes
3. To create a melody for the poem
4. To write an essay comparing two poems

Introducing the Poem

The poem freely adapts the rhyme scheme of the typical blues lyric, based on rhymed couplets. In lines 19–22 and 25–30 there is a poem-within-the-poem: a blues lyric sung by a fictitious musician.

The Literal Meaning. The speaker describes hearing a black piano player sing the blues in a Harlem cafe.

Teaching Strategies

Providing for Cultural Differences. Blues music has penetrated into many different areas of American popular culture, including rock music, country and western, and soul music. You might ask your students what kinds of music they like and whether there's any blues influence in it.

Providing for Different Levels of Ability. Some students may need help identifying the changes of speakers in the poem.

Introducing Vocabulary Study. Knowing the meanings of the following words will help students understand the selection. (Starred words appear in the Glossary.)

| syncopated | l. 1 | pallor* | l. 5 |
| croon* | l. 2 | melancholy | l. 17 |

Reading the Poem. The audiocassette of "The Weary Blues" would make a good culmination for a lesson beginning with the previous Hughes poems. Otherwise, you might have a small group of students rehearse and present a choral reading of the poem.

Reteaching Alternatives. The last line of the poem is a subtle counterpoint to the more upbeat, joyous lines. You might ask students to read that concluding line again and discuss what it says about the singer's life.

Responding to the Poem

Text page 711

Analyzing the Poem
Identifying Details

1. What are some of the words in the poem that help to create a slow, weary, melancholy *mood*? Such words include: "droning" and "drowsy" (line 1), "rocking" and "mellow" (line 2), "pale dull pallor" (line 5), "lazy sway" (line 6), "Weary Blues" (line 8), "moan" (lines 10 and 18), "melancholy" (line 17), "troubles" (line 22), lines 29–30, line 35.

Interpreting Meanings

2. How does the message of the blues singer's first verse contrast with that of his second? The first verse stresses individualism and optimism; although he is alone, the speaker says he is going to "quit his frowning" and "put his troubles on the shelf." But in the second verse, the singer gives way to sadness, saying he is no longer happy and wishes that he were dead.

Langston Hughes 259

3. Describe how the poem's structure suggests the rhythm of blues music. Students will have various answers. The repetition of words and phrases and the syncopation of longer lines with shorter ones contribute to this effect.

Point out examples of *alliteration* and *onomatopoeia* that also add to the poem's wailing, musical effect. Examples include: "droning a drowsy" (line 1), "pale dull pallor of an old gas light" (line 5), "lazy sway" (line 6), "poor piano moan with melody" (line 10), "sad raggy tune like a musical fool" (line 13), "thump, thump, thump" (line 23).

4. How would you describe the emotional effect of the *image* in line 32? The effect is ominous and foreboding; the extinction of the stars and the moon seem to hint that the singer dies, literally or figuratively.

5. What *similes* in the poem's last line describe how the singer sleeps? The speaker says that the singer sleeps "like a rock" or like "a man that's dead."

What do you think are the implications of the last five words? The final five words imply that the singer, although he makes a living by entertaining others, has himself given up hope; his spirit is dead.

Writing About the Poems
A Creative Response

1. Creating Music for a Poem. Music students or a music teacher on your faculty may be able to suggest an existing passage to which the poem can be set, or record an original sung version of several lines.

***C**riteria for Evaluating the Assignment.* The music is appropriate to the mood and content of Hughes's lines.

A Critical Response

2. Comparing the Voices in Two Poems. Refer students back to the "Responding to the Poem" questions on Hughes's "Harlem" and "I, Too."

***C**riteria for Evaluating the Assignment.* The essay briefly compares the speakers in Hughes's "Harlem" and "I, Too," stating how they are a similar and how they differ.

3. Comparing Poems. Given a quick review of Whitman's poem, students should readily see how Hughes's "The Weary Blues" emulates Whitman's style but updates his content.

***C**riteria for Evaluating the Assignment.* The essay briefly explains how Hughes's "The Weary Blues" echoes and comments on Whitman's "I Hear America Singing."

Extending the Poems

You might read aloud to students the following poem by Langston Hughes and have them compare it with the work of Whitman.

The Negro Speaks of Rivers

I've known rivers:
I've known rivers ancient as the world and
   older than the flow of human blood in
   human veins.

My soul has grown deep like the rivers.

I bathed in the Euphrates when dawns were
   young.
I built my hut near the Congo and it
   lulled me to sleep.
I looked upon the Nile and raised the pyramids
   above it.
I heard the singing of the Mississippi when
   Abe Lincoln went down to New Orleans, and
   I've seen its muddy bottom all gold in
   the sunset.

I've known rivers:
Ancient, dusky rivers.

My soul has grown deep like the rivers.

Countee Cullen

Text page 712

Reading About the Poet

Cullen's career paralleled Hughes's in many ways: They both worked in similar genres at similar times. But Cullen was more ambivalent about race than Hughes, while Hughes embraced the subject. For instance, Hughes's play, *Mulatto*, had a long, successful Broadway run during the Depression, while Cullen's play, *The Medea*, was about the ancient world and not meant to be acted on the stage.

"Tableau"

Text page 713

Objectives

1. To identify metaphors
2. To interpret the poem's meaning

Introducing the Poem

The poem is in three quatrains, the lines alternating between iambic tetrameter and iambic trimeter. The rhyme scheme is abab cdcd efef.

The Literal Meaning. A black youth and a white youth walk arm in arm down a street, drawing stares from black and white alike.

Teaching Strategies

Providing for Cultural Differences. The poem speaks of a time when a black boy and a white boy walking together would draw stares. You might ask your students how such a sight would be greeted in their localities today, and how it might have been greeted two generations ago, when this poem was written.

Providing for Different Levels of Ability. The scene described is very simple, but some attention to vocabulary study will probably be necessary, and the brilliant metaphor about lightning and thunder, lines 11–12, may need paraphrasing for some students.

Introducing Vocabulary Study. Knowing the meanings of the following words is necessary to understanding the selection. (Starred words appear in the Glossary.)

sable* (adj.)	l. 4	oblivious*	l. 9
indignant	l. 7		

Reading the Poem. The two very short Cullen poems can be discussed in a single lesson, each read by one student.

Reteaching Alternatives. You might ask students to remember scenes they have witnessed where the race of the participants made an unnecessary difference. Ask how they felt about the incidents.

Responding to the Poem

Text page 713

Analyzing the Poem

Identifying Details

1. What *metaphors* describe the two boys in stanza 1? The white boy is indirectly compared to the "golden splendor of the day" (line 3), while the black boy is called "the sable pride of night" (line 4).

2. How do the "dark folk" and "fair folk" feel about what the boys are doing? They are "indignant" (line 7).

3. How do the boys respond? They are "oblivious"; they pay the critics no mind.

Interpreting Meanings

4. In stanza 3, who or what is the "lightning brilliant as a sword"? The lightning refers to the boys' unexpected courage in risking an interracial friendship; the poet indirectly compares their boldness to the brilliance of a lightning bolt.

Who or what is the "path of thunder"? The "path of thunder" also refers to the example of the boys' friendship. Their boldness clearly runs the risk of upsetting established conventions—and such boldness, although salutary, may be ominous, and even dangerous, for a time.

5. **Why should such a modest and commonplace thing as the friendship between two boys evoke such a dramatic statement? What larger topic is the poem really about?** Encourage students to express their own opinions. Remind them that Cullen is using the boys as a symbol for a commentary on one of America's most profound social problems.

"Incident"

Text page 715

Objectives

1. To interpret irony
2. To write a dialogue between two characters
3. To write a list of camera shots for a screenplay of the poem
4. To write an essay comparing the language of two poems

Introducing the Poem

The poem is in three quatrains, the second and fourth lines of each quatrain rhyming with each other. Iambic tetrameter alternates with iambic trimeter, creating a sing-song rhythm appropriate to the children described in the poem.

The Literal Meaning. The speaker recalls an incident when he was eight and another child called him "nigger."

Teaching Strategies

Providing for Cultural Differences. Racial and ethnic slurs are less common now than they used to be, but are still traumatic to those who are their targets. If students in your class have been exposed to such words, they may be unwilling to talk about the experience. This should be respected as a sign of sensitivity, not criticized as recalcitrance.

Providing for Different Levels of Ability. This poem is written in a deliberately nursery-rhyme-like style befitting the subject and making the racial slur stand out in stark contrast. Its powerful message requires no abstruse interpretation either for more advanced or less advanced students.

Reading the Poem. Your choice of a student reader for this poem will require discretion. It should be read simply and straightforwardly, so that the racial epithet will have the proper unsettling effect.

Reteaching Alternatives. You might point out that for different ethnic groups, different words would be substituted for the last word on line 8—all equally senseless.

Responding to the Poem

Text page 715

Analyzing the Poem
Identifying Details

1. **Which line reveals the speaker's mood at the beginning of the incident?** Line 2 says that the speaker was filled with "glee" in his head and his heart. He was in a happy, carefree mood.

2. **How many people are involved in the incident? Who are they?** Two people are involved in the incident: the eight-year-old narrator, and another boy of about his own age.

3. **What is the incident?** The incident is the racial insult that the other boy gives to the narrator. The narrator smiles at the other boy, but the boy pokes out his tongue and calls the narrator "Nigger."

Interpreting Meanings

4. **What might lead an eight-year-old boy to insult another child in the way described here?** Students will have various responses, including parental example and peer pressure. Encourage them to discuss their opinions.

In what way might a child's prejudice be even more disturbing than an adult's? Again, students may react differently, and even disagree. But a child's prejudice might be more disturbing because it exhibits a vicious aspect of prejudice—namely, that it can repeat itself in cycles, being accepted uncritically and unthinkingly from generation to generation.

5. **What *ironic overtones* does the title have? Is this really only an "incident"?** Even though the speaker is reporting an event from his childhood, it is clear that the insult he received left a bitter, lasting impression. To call it

262 Voices of American Character

a mere "incident" is thus an ironic characterization—since such a title understates the trauma the speaker suffered. Some students may add that newspapers commonly use euphemisms such as the term "incident" in their headlines or reports of what, in fact, were traumatic events, at least for the people involved.

6. The speaker never directly states his emotional response to the experience. How does the last stanza indirectly make clear the impression the event had on him? By telling us that this incident was the only thing he could remember about Baltimore in his seven months there, the speaker indirectly emphasizes his profound sense of injury.

7. How did the incident affect you? Students' answers will vary. Ask the students to compare their reactions to the reaction of the narrator/speaker, as it is evoked in the poem.

Writing About the Poem
A Creative Response

1. Writing Dialogue. Clarify the writing prompt: The two boys walking together in "Tableau" are discussing what happened to the black child in "Incident." The child on the bus may or may not be the black boy (of "Tableau") himself.

Criteria for Evaluating the Assignment. The dialogue reveals the friendship between the boys, their feelings about the incident, and their growing awareness of prejudice.

2. Planning a Screenplay. Technical phrases that might assist students include: "Panoramic shot of...," "closeup," "tight closeup," and "camera follows as...."

Criteria for Evaluating the Assignment. The sequence of shots covers the entire content of "Incident"—old Baltimore, the people on the bus, the children on the bus, the faces and reactions of the two children.

3. Setting the Poem to Music. Music students may be able to suggest an existing melody to which "Incident" can be set, or to create an original tune for it.

Criteria for Evaluating the Assignment. The music is appropriate to the mood and content of Cullen's poem.

A Critical Response

4. Comparing Poems. Students may wish to copy the two poems and place them side by side.

Criteria for Evaluating the Assignment. The essay briefly shows how Cullen used word choice and sentence structure to create different effects in "Tableau" and "Incident."

Extending the Poems

Interested students may want to compare and contrast the works of the black writers in this unit with those of contemporary black writers. Robert Hayden and Gwendolyn Brooks are black poets included in Unit Thirteen. Alice Walker, also represented by a poem in Unit Thirteen, is best known as a novelist. In addition to Andrea Lee and James Alan McPherson (Unit Eleven), prominent contemporary black fiction writers include Toni Morrison, Gloria Naylor, Ishmael Reed, and John A. Williams.

The American Language Text page 720

1. Students are to choose between dialect names for the same object. Answers will vary.

2. Students are to read the passages reproducing several American dialects and then answer the questions that follow.

a. What variations from standard pronunciation do the spellings indicate? In the first passage, examples include holt, sich, k'n, preachin's, workin', and missionaryin. In the second passage, examples include settin', theayter, gettin', w'ile, openin', and aw de cologne. In the third passage, examples include axin', talkin', bout, and goin. In the fourth passage, examples include comin, O, and em's.

b. Is each writer consistent in his or her spelling variations? Can you propose reasons for any inconsistencies? Students may suggest slight inconsistencies: For example, in the Twain passage, the final "g" of the present participle is sometimes indicated with an apostrophe and sometimes not. Reasons for inconsistencies will vary.

c. What nonstandard or slang words and phrases are used by each speaker? What do these words mean? Sample answers: In the first passage, the speaker uses "considerable" (a lot), "line" (occupation), and "missionaryin" (attempting to convert people to a religious faith or creed). In the second passage, the speaker uses "settin'" (sitting), "come" (came), "my right first name" (my actual first name). In the third passage, the speaker uses "axin" (asking), "to figure" (to calculate), "run" (ran), "stare" (stared), "goin rip" (going to rip). In the fourth passage, the speaker uses "copy" (connection), "10-4" (O.K.), "handle" (name), "copy you clear" (hear you clearly), "Smokey Bear" and "Smokies" (police).

d. Are the speakers ungrammatical at any points? Students should be able to furnish numerous examples: See the answers under item c above.

e. Do you find any examples of "eye-dialect"—a word spelled the way it is sounded in standard pronunciation? (An example would be *sez* for *says*.) Can you suggest any reasons why a writer would use eye-dialect? Examples of eye-dialect include "aw de cologne" in the second passage, and perhaps "O" (for *old*) in the fourth passage. Students' reasons will vary. In general, a writer might use eye-dialect to hint that the speaker might lack enough formal education to know the correct spelling of a word.

f. Which passage reproduces the dialect of a group, not of a region? The last passage reproduces the dialect of truckers.

Exercises in Critical Thinking and Writing Text page 721

Interpreting and Responding to a Poem

For some students the poem, "Only the Polished Skeleton," that students are asked to interpret in this exercise might prove less accessible than a somewhat more concrete poem. For these students, you might review the biographical material on Countee Cullen, text page 712, and have students reread "Incident," text page 715, in which Cullen describes the effect of a racially motivated incident on a young child. With this background, you might point out to students that many critics see racial themes in "Only the Polished Skeleton." According to these critics, Cullen expresses racial bitterness in his statement of what is necessary for the body ("heat") and mind to survive and that only upon death can the individual "rest at ease." Help students to understand the contrast in the poem by pointing out the word "only" at the beginning of the last stanza.

Criteria for Evaluating the Assignment. Although students' essays do not necessarily have to follow the plan suggested in the "Writing" section, the essays should indicate, through paraphrase, students' literal comprehension of the poem. Students' interpretations of the poem's meaning should be supported with details from the poem and should be consistent with the literal meaning of the poem.

Unit Nine: *Imagism and Symbolism*

Text page 723

Teaching the Imagism and Symbolism Unit

The Imagist movement, proclaimed by Ezra Pound, lasted less than ten years, from 1909 to 1917, but it had significant consequences. Imagism expanded the subject matter of poetry, emphasized the exact word over the decorative word, and helped to make free verse respectable. Imagism was part of a broader movement, Symbolism, which had started in France in the late nineteenth century and began to influence American poetry in the early decades of the twentieth century. Symbolists stressed the importance of the sound, or music, of verse and, like the Imagists, believed that any subject matter is suitable for poetry.

Since the poems are so often cryptic or ambiguous, Imagism and Symbolism make real demands on the reader. To students in search of the one right answer for every question, such poetry can be a revelation (if multiple interpretations are accepted) or an ordeal (if hard-and-fast answers are demanded). During the study of this unit, your students may be comforted to learn that some critics have called Imagism "the cult of unintelligibility" and Symbolism a haven for the "rimed rebus." For this reason, the text material—the unit introduction, author biographies, and special features—are important to an understanding of the poetry. A brief review of Romanticism and Realism—students might review the introductions to units Three and Six—can also help remind students of what poets in the early twentieth century were reacting to and rebelling against.

Many of the poems in this unit will be more understandable and enjoyable to students if read aloud. Poets have often asserted the importance of oral reading, especially for free verse. Amy Lowell, a leader of the Imagist movement, was one such poet, as critic Richard Benvenuto noted:

> [O]ne of her deepest convictions . . . is that poetry is an oral art, that poems are a form of speech and must be heard to be completely understood. . . . "To understand *vers libre* [free verse]," she said, one must "allow the lines to flow as they will when read aloud by an intelligent reader. Then new rhythms will become evident—satisfying and delightful. For this poetry definitely harks back to the old oral tradition; it is written to be spoken."

In this unit, students should gain a working knowledge of the meanings of the terms *imagism* and *symbolism*, but they should also keep in mind that poets and poems are more important than labels. Each poet is a creative individual, not just a representative of a particular *-ism*. Since great poets can seldom be slotted into neat categories for analysis, students will find far more diversity than uniformity in the seven poets who appear here.

*O*bjectives of the Imagism and Symbolism Unit

1. To improve reading proficiency and expand vocabulary
2. To gain exposure to notable poets and their works
3. To define and identify elements of poetry: figures of speech (simile, metaphor, extended metaphor), symbol, imagery, sound effects (rhythms, meter, free verse), pun, paradox, epithets, apostrophe, mood, and tone.
4. To respond to poetry orally and in writing
5. To evaluate primary sources
6. To analyze language and style
7. To write original works
8. To practice the following critical thinking and writing skills:
   a. Explaining poetic images
   b. Comparing a poem with a prose text
   c. Comparing and contrasting poems
   d. Evaluating a character
   e. Comparing characters
   f. Responding to a criticism
   g. Interpreting a poem's message
   h. Analyzing a poem

*I*ntroducing the Imagism and Symbolism Unit

To show students graphically what poets of the early 1900's were trying to achieve—and to show the interrelatedness of the arts—you might introduce the unit with a series of prints or color slides showing the progression of modern painting. Begin with the impressionists of the late nineteenth century—Renoir, Seurat. Go on to the post-impressionists—Gauguin, Toulouse-Lautrec. Conclude with the abstract artists of the twentieth century—Mondrian, Miro. Point out to students (although they will surely see it for themselves) that the paintings in this sequence become increasingly hard to interpret. Indicate to them that a parallel situation developed in poetry during this period.

Rather than art, or in addition to art, you might want to play recordings of some of the music of Debussy and Stravinsky—music that Amy Lowell claims is "an immediate prototype of imagism." She even attempts to prove it poetically in her poem "Stravinsky's Three Pieces 'Grotesques,' For String Quartet" (from Lowell's *Men, Women and Ghosts*). If you can obtain both the poem and the recording, you might want to see if students feel she has succeeded in reproducing "the effect," as she says, of Stravinsky's music.

Ezra Pound   Text page 729

"The River-Merchant's Wife: A Letter"   Text page 730

"The Garden"   Text page 734

Objectives

1. To identify images
2. To analyze mood
3. To identify a simile and a pun
4. To create a single concrete image
5. To write a paragraph explaining three images as objective correlatives

Introducing the Poem

Significant techniques in these poems include the clear images conveying emotions and meanings, such as "on bamboo stilts," "climb the lookout," and "skein of loose silk blown against a wall." Also significant is the use of free verse.

Background on the Poems. Your students may be interested in this description by Richard Aldington, a British Imagist, of how the movement began:

> [T]he Imagist movement was born in a teashop—in the Royal Borough of Kensington [England]. For some time Ezra had been butting in on our studies and poetic productions, with alternate encouragements and the reverse, according to his mood. H.D. [Hilda Doolittle] produced some poems which I thought excellent, and she either handed or mailed them to Ezra. Presently each of us received a ukaze to attend the Kensington bunshop. Ezra was so much worked up by these poems of H.D.'s that he removed his pince-nez and informed us that we were Imagists.

The Literal Meaning. "*The River-Merchant's Wife*": In the first stanza of this poem, the speaker (who is a girl) and the boy who is "playing house" are children. In the next stanza, at the age of fourteen, she is married to the boy. By fifteen she is devoted to him. In the third stanza, when he is sixteen—and evidently a river-merchant, judging by the title of the poem—he goes by river to a distant region. He has been gone for five months. The images in the last stanza show her to be sad. She says she will go to meet him if she knows when he is coming. "*The Garden*:" A woman, dying of "emotional anemia," is walking in Kensington Gardens. She is surrounded by a rabble who will inherit the earth. The woman has little future and, in her isolation, is "almost afraid" that the speaker will talk to her.

Teaching Strategies

Providing for Cultural Differences. Most students will find marriage at fourteen and business travel at sixteen to be rather unusual. Ask them in what century they think the events in the poem occur. (A good guess would be the eighth century.) Ask them why they think the girl married the young river-merchant. (Apparently it was an arranged marriage.) You might want to discuss the matter of arranged marriages. Do they ever occur today? (Yes, in some cultures.)

Providing for Different Levels of Ability. "The River-Merchant's Wife," which deals with love and loss, should be comprehensible to students at all levels. "The Garden," which, broadly interpreted, seems to concern social classes in England, is not so easy. While you may want to have less advanced students read the first poem on their own, you will probably want to work through the second poem with them in class.

Introducing Vocabulary Study. Knowing the meanings of the following words is important to understanding the poems. (Starred words appear in the Glossary.)

"The River Merchant's Wife"
| lookout | l. 14 | eddies | l. 16 |

"The Garden"
| skein* | l. 1 | anemia* | l. 4 |
| exquisite | l. 9 | indiscretion | l. 12 |

Advise students to keep in mind Pound's insistence on the exact word; then ask them to find three synonyms, if possible, for each of the vocabulary words. Tell them to keep their lists until each poem is discussed in class. At that time, have students try to determine whether any of Pound's words seem to have satisfactory substitutes.

Reading the Poems. Read or have a student read each poem aloud in class. (An audiocassette recording accompanies this poem.) With "The River-Merchant's Wife," go back through it, asking questions about each event in the girl's life and about her relationship to her husband. Before reading "The Garden," you might want to discuss social classes (especially the titled gentry) as they existed in their heyday in England prior to World War I. Students may not be aware of the rigid class distinctions of that time and place.

Reteaching Alternatives. Have one or more interviewers ask questions of the river-merchant's wife and the well-bred lady in Kensington Gardens. The student playing each part should respond to questions in a way consistent with the content of the poem. The interviewer(s) should try to bring out as much information as the poems contain.

"The River-Merchant's Wife"

Responding to the Poem   Text page 732
Analyzing the Poem
Identifying Details

1. What events are referred to in stanzas 1–4? In the first stanza, the girl (who is the speaker) and the boy play together as small children in the village of Chokan. In the second stanza, the speaker is fourteen when she marries the boy, her "Lord." She is bashful and silent. But a year later, in the third stanza, when she is fifteen, she "stopped scowling." In the fourth stanza, when the speaker is sixteen, her husband departs on a long journey on the river; he has now been gone for five months.

2. In the last stanza, what does the wife promise to do? If her husband will send her advance news of his return on the river Kiang, she will come to meet him at Cho-fu-Sa.

Interpreting Meanings

3. How is the third stanza a turning point in the poem? In the third stanza, the speaker's outlook on her marriage changes from shy silence to deep commitment. She "stopped scowling" and began to wish that she and her husband would be united forever, even in death.

In line 14, what is the wife indirectly expressing? Answers will vary. To "climb the lookout" might represent being on watch for her husband's return, or it may be more deeply symbolic of her anxiety of what the future might bring. Either way, the wife seems indirectly to be expressing her faith and confidence in her husband and in her marriage. She wishes her dust and his to "be mingled... Forever and forever and forever."

4. What image suggests that the husband was reluctant to leave home? The speaker says in line 19 that her husband dragged his feet when he left.

5. How is the season of the year appropriate to the mood of the poem? The season of autumn, in which the mosses grow deep and leaves fall, seems appropriate to the speaker's melancholy mood.

6. What "hurts" the young wife in line 25, and why? The "paired butterflies" hurt her. Perhaps that they are in pairs painfully reminds her of her separation from her absent husband.

Why does she say, after only five months, that she grows "older" (line 25)? The separation from her husband must make five months seem like a much longer span of time—a span that makes her conscious of aging.

7. Why do you think the husband left? Do you think he is ever going to return? What may have delayed him? Answers will vary. According to the title of the poem, the husband is a river-merchant. Presumably he left to do business on the river. There is no indication in the poem of how long he expected to be away, so it is hard to know if he is likely to return. He could have been injured, or he could have been delayed by floods. Encourage students to construct imaginative scenarios to explain what may have delayed him.

8. Do you think this letter was ever sent? Answers will vary. Many students may suggest that the letter form is simply a convention adopted for the expression of the speaker's emotions.

The Elements of Literature:
The Objective Correlative   Text page 733

Discuss this page in class, asking two or three students to explain the term *objective correlative* in their own words. Some students may feel that interpreting objective correlatives requires the ability to read the poet's mind. How can a

Ezra Pound   267

reader know what emotion the poet believes a particular object or emotion represents? In the most abstruse Imagist poetry, the reader may not know. But in Pound's "The River-Merchant's Wife" there are many contextual clues. You may want to have students work in pairs or small groups to find the objective correlatives in the poem.

"The Garden"

Responding to the Poem   Text page 734
Analyzing the Poem
Identifying Details

1. What simile describes the woman in the first stanza? She is described as being "like a skein of loose silk blown against a wall."

2. What contrast is set up in the first two stanzas? The phrase "a skein of loose silk" in the first line of the first stanza suggests both the woman's elegance and her fragility. In the second stanza, the poet gives us a contrasting picture of vitality and durability in the "infants of the very poor."

Interpreting Meanings

3. How would you explain the phrase "emotional anemia"? The phrase implies the inability or unwillingness to feel or express emotions.

How would that cause someone to die "piecemeal"? Just as severe anemia could induce a slow death physically, emotional anemia is causing the woman to die a slow death spiritually.

4. The phrase "They shall inherit the earth" comes from the New Testament of the Bible (Matthew 5:5). What does the phrase mean in this context? In Matthew 5:5, in the Sermon on the Mount, Jesus says that the "meek" (or "gentle in spirit") shall inherit the earth. The New Testament passage contrasts the humble with the powerful, implying that the humble will ultimately triumph. In "The Garden," however, the speaker's attitude seems more ambivalent. He scornfully refers to the "rabble" of poor children as "filthy" and "unkillable," suggesting that he has a mixture of emotions and attitudes about the poor. He does not seem to like them very much, but believes that they will indeed inherit the earth from those who were once powerful but are now emotionally anemic.

5. Use a dictionary to find several meanings for *breeding*. Then identify the *pun* in line 8. How does the pun affect the contrast made in the first two stanzas? The "end of breeding" could refer to breeding as "ancestry" or "observance of the proprieties"; thus, the woman might be envisioned as a perfect example of aristocratic elegance. On the other hand, breeding might be taken as "propagation of the species." Because the woman is so devoid of emotions, she can be thought of as spiritually and perhaps physically sterile. Either meaning sets up a contrast with the vigorous, "unkillable" generations of the poor.

6. Why do you think the speaker says he would be committing an indiscretion if he engages the woman in conversation? Answers will vary. Perhaps he fears she will be surprised and put off by his audacity. Since she is "dressed for show" (Samain) and evidently out of touch with the vital, pulsating world, it might be an "indiscretion" to talk with her and cause reality to intrude.

7. This is a poem about individuals, but it is also about something broader. What is Pound's true subject? Answers will vary. Some may conclude that Pound's true subject has to do with the contrast in social classes. Others may argue that the true subject is the barriers that we erect against forthright communication. Let students argue and defend their own opinions.

8. Think about the contrast in the first two stanzas. What similar contrast can you think of from your own experience? Encourage students to be as specific as possible in their answers.

Writing About the Poems
A Creative Response

1. Creating an Image. Brainstorm a list of topics, both negative and positive, likely to arouse strong feelings—recent events or local issues that make your students happy, angry, elated, or frustrated. Elicit images for a few of these—a baby's rattle in a mud puddle, for example, to express sorrow about a burnt-out home—and then let students continue on their own.

Criteria for Evaluating the Assignment. The sentence or phrase presents an image that evokes feelings, but does not directly state the feeling intended.

A Critical Response

2. Explaining Images. Have students go through both poems and list all the images that seem to be objective correlatives, perhaps working in pairs and discussing the images until they know which three they wish to write about.

Criteria for Evaluating the Assignment. The paper presents three images from Pound's "The River-Merchant's

268   Imagism and Symbolism

Wife" or "The Garden" and offers an appropriate explanation of how each image is used as an objective correlative to convey emotion indirectly.

Extending the Poems

Ezra Pound felt that Walt Whitman was the one significant poet of the late nineteenth century. In Pound's well-known poem, "A Pact," published in 1913, he acknowledges his debt to Whitman, but with certain reservations. Ask students to interpret "A Pact":

I make a pact with you, Walt Whitman—
I have detested you long enough.
I come to you as a grown child
Who has had a pig-headed father;
I am old enough now to make friends.
It was you who broke the new wood,
Now is a time for carving.
We have one sap and one root—
Let there be commerce between us.

William Carlos Williams   Text page 735

"The Red Wheelbarrow"   Text Page 736

"The Great Figure"   Text page 737

"Tract"   Text page 738

"Spring and All"   Text page 740

Objectives

1. To explain the metaphorical use of a word
2. To identify images
3. To summarize the speaker's main idea
4. To describe specific images
5. To interpret paradox
6. To retitle poems
7. To write an essay analyzing poems

Introducing the Poems

Background on the Poems. The first half of the twentieth century was a time of experimentation in poetry. Some poets, like Picasso in painting, went through various phases and were involved in more than one movement. Williams is one such poet. You might point out to students that, as a consequence, he may seem to be an Imagist in one poem and not an Imagist in another. As a young man and a traditionalist, Williams came under the influence of Pound and Imagism. Later, believing that Imagism had "dribbled off into so-called 'free verse,'" he embraced what he called Objectivism, a movement that one unsympathetic critic saw as a "craze for actuality."

The Literal Meanings. "*The Red Wheelbarrow*": The speaker sees an image on which "so much depends"—a rain-glazed wheelbarrow and white chickens. "*The Great Figure*": At night the speaker sees a gold figure 5 on a fire truck whose gong is clanging, siren howling, and wheels rumbling. "*Tract*": The speaker tells the townspeople how to perform a funeral. The hearse should not be black or white, but instead should be weathered like a farm wagon, with gilt wheels or no wheels. It should have no glass, no upholstery—no frills. There should be no wreaths. The driver should not wear a silk hat or sit high up on the wagon. He should walk beside the hearse. The mourners should walk behind it, or if they ride, they should not protect themselves from the weather. "*Spring and All*": A cold wind blows near the contagious hospital. Bushes and trees along the road look brown and lifeless. With spring, the grass and leaves begin to awaken.

Teaching Strategies

Providing for Cultural Differences. The poem "Tract" concerns American funerals—specifically the hearse and cortege—in the early 1900's. All students can benefit from a discussion of how funerals today differ from the kind Williams is describing. Apart from the time difference, funerals differ considerably from culture to culture. If you have students from different cultural backgrounds in your class, you may want to see if they can describe funeral customs other than that of today's limousine hearse with an automobile procession following it.

Providing for Different Levels of Ability. At all levels you may hear the objection, "But this isn't poetry!" You may want to point out to students that good free verse is very carefully crafted. Also, point out to students that Williams, like Pound and other poets in this unit, had little use for "pseudo-poets" who thought that free verse removed barriers, lowered standards, and, in general, made randomly reformatted prose into poetry. With less advanced students, you will probably have to explain in class what Williams is trying to do.

Introducing Vocabulary Study. Knowing the meanings of the following words is important to understanding the poems. (Starred words appear in the glossary.)

"Tract"
| gilt | l. 12 | understrapper | l. 53 |
| dray | l. 15 | | |

"Spring and All"
| mottled* | l. 3 |

A *dray* is usually drawn by a horse. Ask students if they can think of five other words that involve horse-drawn means of transportation and are used much less today than they once were. The words will probably not be archaic, but merely in less frequent use now than formerly. (Some possibilities: *buggy, gig, surrey, dogcart, stagecoach, carriage, buckboard, coach-and-four, wainwright, wheelwright*)

Reading the Poems. All the poems will be more comprehensible if you read them aloud in class. (An audiocassette recording accompanies "Spring and All.") Before reading the first two, have students close their eyes and try to visualize the scenes: (1) morning on a farm, with a light rain falling; from the kitchen window, they see a wheelbarrow and a chicken; (2) a city at night with rain falling; a fire truck passes. Before reading "Tract," discuss the introductory note. Have students suggest some of the ways in which a modern limousine hearse resembles a horse-drawn hearse

and some of the ways in which it differs. Introduce "Spring and All" with a few questions about spring. What does spring bring? How is spring usually treated by poets? Why might spring be less significant in some areas than it is in New Jersey, where the poet lived? Be sure that students mention rebirth, genesis, and awakening in connection with spring.

Reteaching Alternatives. Assign a capable student to each of the four Williams poems. Have each student read the poem in class and explain what it means to him or her. Since this assignment follows detailed discussions of both the poems and the accompanying questions and other material, students should have something meaningful to say. If not, suggest that they do some library research to obtain further information on Williams and his poetry.

A Comment on the Poem   Text page 736

Whatever the level of your students, you may want to read and discuss this comment in class. William Carlos Williams is a pivotal figure in modern poetry, and "The Red Wheelbarrow," despite its brevity, is a major poem. If students are to appreciate the free-verse forms being written today, they need to understand that William's poem is neither a trick nor a fraud.

"The Great Figure"

Responding to the Poem   Text page 737
Analyzing the Poem
Interpreting Meanings

1. What one word is used *metaphorically* to describe the fire truck as if it were a person? The word is *tense*.

2. Which *images* recreate specific sights and sounds? The images are the rain and the lights (lines 1–2), the figure 5 in gold on the red truck (lines 3–6), the gong clangs (line 10), the siren howls (line 11), the rumbling wheels (line 12), and the dark city (line 13).

3. Did you think the "great figure" was going to be the number 5 on an ordinary old fire truck? What is suggested by the term "great figure"? Most students will admit to a sense of surprise, since the term would ordinarily mean a human being—a celebrity perhaps.

4. How do you think the speaker feels about this brief scene? Answers will vary. Ask students to try to describe the tone of the poem.

270 Imagism and Symbolism

"Tract"

Responding to the Poem
Text page 739
Analyzing the Poem
Identifying Details

1. Name all the different aspects of a funeral mentioned by the speaker. What does he advise the townspeople to do about each aspect of the ritual? The speaker first mentions the hearse. He advises the townspeople that it should be kept simple: neither white nor black—not polished, but weathered like a farm wagon. The hearse should have no glass windows, upholstery, or little "brass rollers," or "small easy wheels on the bottom." Next, the speaker turns to the wreaths of flowers that are conventional at funerals. He tells the townspeople to substitute a "common memento" for flowers, an object connected with the deceased in a concrete, meaningful way—such as old clothes or a few books. In lines 45–46, the speaker treats the subject of the driver. He angrily objects to the driver's conspicuous position and silk hat, advising the townspeople to "bring him down" and make him walk by the side of the wagon. Finally, the speaker advises the townspeople themselves to walk behind the wagon with "some show of inconvenience"; "to sit openly—/to the weather as to grief"; and to "share" themselves spiritually with each other.

2. When the speaker calls for "gilt wheels" in line 12 is he being inconsistent? What might such prominent wheels contribute to the funeral scene? The speaker does not seem really inconsistent, since he remarks parenthetically that fresh gilt could be applied "at small expense." Perhaps the gilt wheels would emphasize the transitional nature of a funeral—a passage from this life to the next. In fact, the speaker would just as soon have no wheels at all, putting the deceased on a dray next to the earth into which he or she will soon be going.

3. What two kinds of rain is the speaker talking about in lines 23 and 24? The rain in line 23 is literal rain; the rain in line 24 is metaphorical for the loads of earth and pebbles that will "rain" down on the coffin as it is covered up in the ground at the burial site.

In making his suggestions for a funeral, is the speaker exhibiting cruelty or disrespect toward the dead? Answers will vary. Most students will agree that the speaker is displaying no disrespect for the dead. He is simply focusing his attention on the appropriate reactions of the living to a funeral. Some may argue that if the driver gets down from his high perch and the mourners walk behind the hearse, the dead person will be more fittingly honored.

What is the purpose in calling for all this plainness, and even pain and discomfort for the participants? The speaker's purpose seems to be to remind the participants that a funeral should honor or at least emphasize the deceased, rather than necessarily make the survivors feel good.

4. Assume that the speaker is talking about much more than funerals. What might the "rough plain hearse" represent? If we assume that the funeral in the poem may symbolize the art of poetry, then the "rough plain hearse" may stand for the outward appearance of a painting, a poem, a piece of music, etc.

What might the driver in lines 45–56 represent? Why would the speaker get so angry when he's talking about the driver? Answers will vary. The speaker's purpose in this "tract" is to urge his fellow townspeople to focus on the objective reality of a funeral: the nature of the deceased and the true feelings of the surviving mourners. The prominence afforded the wagon driver in conventional funerals irritates the speaker so much because it distracts the participants' attention from the true nature of the occasion. Perhaps there is an oblique reference, in the figure of the driver, to the poet or artist. Just as the driver should not allow his prominence to interfere with a funeral, neither should the poet or artist interfere. He or she should work humbly and inconspicuously, recording objective reality with as little interference as possible.

5. Throughout the poem, the speaker talks of simplicity and honest grief. Then he closes by saying, "share with us—it will be money/in your pockets." Do you think this seemingly hard-boiled promise reflects cynicism on the part of the speaker? Or can the promise of "money in your pockets" be interpreted in more than one way? Answers will vary, depending on whether students interpret the word *money* literally or metaphorically. Williams may mean no more than the fact that sharing enriches those who share, both materially and spiritually.

6. Summarize this speaker's *main idea* about art, even about the way poetry should be written. Assuming that the poem is about poetry as well as about funerals, do you think Williams follows his own directions? The speaker believes that poetry, like funerals, should be as plain and unembellished as possible. The personality of the poet, like the driver, should remain unobtrusive and in the background. In general, the speaker urges a realistic, objective view of his fellow human beings. A funeral serves as a means of expressing feelings honestly for one another. Such an occasion, like art itself, perhaps, is too important to be overlaid with conventional symbolism and irrelevant show. Most students will agree that Williams has succeeded in following his own directions in "Tract."

7. What do you think about this "tract"? Do you agree with its advice on ritual and art, or do you prefer richness rather than plainness? Answers will vary. Encourage students to include specific examples in their discussion.

"Spring and All"

Responding to the Poem   Text page 741
Analyzing the Poem
Identifying Details

1. Describe the specific *images* the speaker sees by the road in the first three stanzas. In these stanzas, the speaker sees blue mottled clouds; broad muddy fields, brown with dried weeds; patches of standing water; bushes and small trees with dead leaves, and leafless vines. He feels a cold wind.

2. Is the "contagious hospital" merely incidental in the poem, since the poet would have gone there in the course of his daily rounds? Or does the reference contribute something important to the poem? What would have been lost if the poet had said "by the road to the library," for example? The fact that the hospital is for "contagious" patients opens the poem on a melancholy, almost ominous note. On the other hand, contagion, like death, seems an inevitable part of life for the speaker. If his purpose in the poem is to emphasize the remarkable "awakening" of spring and life from winter and apparent death, then the last two lines seem a pointed, formal contrast with the first. Contagious infections are part of the human life cycle; but so is the "rooting," "gripping down," and "awakening" of new life. All these associations and speculations would be absent if the poet had used the phrase "by the road to the library."

3. The first stanzas are about plants. The pronoun in line 16, however, may refer to more than plants. What broader meaning might the word *they* have? The word *they* could be an anticipatory reference to the grass, wildcarrot leaf, and the "objects" mentioned in lines 20–22. But perhaps Williams also means human beings in infancy, since he refers to them entering the "new world naked" and characterizes them as "uncertain" in line 17.

4. Reread the last stanza. Which two meanings of the word *still* make line 25 a *paradox*? The word *still* could mean "nevertheless" or it could mean "motionless." With the meaning "motionless," Williams draws our attention to the paradox that things that are apparently "still" may yet be in the process of profound change.

5. In the course of his career, Williams delivered thousands of babies. Can you see any connection between that fact and the last three stanzas of the poem? What specific references would apply equally to the coming of spring and the birth of an infant? Most students will readily see the connection. The specific references include the description of them entering the world naked (line 16) and the beginning of awakening (line 27). We might even associate the word *rooted* (line 26) with a newborn infant's connection to its mother by the umbilical cord.

6. In its treatment of spring, how does this poem differ from a typical Romantic poem? By drawing attention through numerous details to the apparent bleakness of the landscape in very early spring, Williams departs from the usual Romantic description of later spring, which would typically emphasize warmth, flowers, and bright colors.

7. What is the significance of the full title of the poem? Answers will vary. The phrase "and all" is perhaps a suggestion that the process of spring—considered as either the annual rebirth of nature or as the marvel of human birth—needs to be thought of in its total context, which includes the cycle of the seasons and human life and death. Adding the phrase "and all" to the title, therefore, emphasizes Williams's focus on the coming of spring as part of a total process.

Writing About the Poems
A Creative Response

1. Retitling Poems. Have pairs or small groups of students select images and argue their appropriateness before students individually submit titles for the poems.

Criteria for Evaluating the Assignment. The new titles apply unmistakably to one poem or the other: for example, "No Upholstery" (line 27) for "Tract"; "Enter Naked" (line 16) for "Spring and All." It's all right if more than one student suggests the same titles.

A Critical Response

2. Analyzing a Poem. You may wish first to ask students what they perceive Williams's beliefs "about people, art, or life in general" to be, and then ask which images from the poems support their opinions.

Criteria for Evaluating the Assignment. The essay is at least one paragraph long. It names a poem by Williams, identifies three or more concrete objects from the poem, and explains how Williams uses these objects to make statements about people, art, or life in general.

Primary Sources:
Williams Talks About Poetry   Text page 741

This excerpt from Williams's *Autobiography* demonstrates his own doubts about the value of his poetry, the responses of critics of the time, and the difficulty involved in creating genuine imagist poetry—not just chopped-up prose. Suggest that students read it for insight into the poet.

Extending the Poems

Since many of Williams's poems are short and visually striking, you may want to choose a few additional ones to read and discuss in class. Among the most appropriate and most frequently anthologized are "Classic Scene," "The Crowd at the Ball Game," "Drink," "Pastoral," and "The Poor." (All of these except "The Poor" are included in *The Oxford Book of American Verse,* edited by F. O. Matthiessen.)

Marianne Moore   Text page 742

"The Steeple-Jack"   Text page 743

Objectives

1. To analyze a poem with unconventional meter and rhyme
2. To recognize images
3. To describe tone
4. To imitate a poet's technique
5. To compare a poem to a prose text
6. To use a dictionary to check precise meanings

Introducing the Poem

Significant techniques in this poem include Moore's use of vivid visual images, such as "waves as formal as the scales/on a fish" and "a sea the purple of a peacock's neck." The poem is also noted for its unusual meter and rhyme. There is a fixed syllable count for each line; the second and fifth lines of each stanza have end rhymes.

Background on the Poem. Students who think of a poem as a fixed and unchanging entity may be surprised that Marianne Moore created three versions of "The Steeple-Jack." The first published version contains twelve stanzas. When Moore prepared the poem for publication in *Selected Poems* (1935), she cut it to eight stanzas. Three decades later, for *A Marianne Moore Reader* (1961), she restored the cut stanzas and added another. The latest version, containing thirteen stanzas, is the one included in this book.

The Literal Meaning. The poem pictures a pleasant coastal town in which Dürer might have liked to live. A note of fantasy is sounded with the "eight stranded whales." The second stanza portrays the flight of seagulls, while the third describes the color of the sea and pictures fish nets and a huge lobster. A storm is shown, followed by a virtual catalog of local vegetation, then a shorter list of fauna. Next, the poem introduces Ambrose, a college student who knows the town well, including the church steeple on which C.J. Poole, a steeplejack, is working. The town has the church portico as a haven. It also has a schoolhouse and other buildings, along with a schooner. This is a safe town, despite the steeple-jack's danger sign below him on the sidewalk.

Teaching Strategies

Providing for Cultural Differences. Most students will have seen colored photographs of old New England towns in which the church steeple is a focal point. If you think anyone in your classes may be unfamiliar with such a scene, it might be a good idea to bring in photos of some New England coastal towns and discuss their principal features. Most will have (whether shown or not) a tall-spired church, often Congregational; a cemetery, usually near the church; a schoolhouse; a village green or common, typically with public buildings facing it; and a harbor with boats. A few towns will have, as Moore's does, a nearby lighthouse, and all will have houses and stores.

Providing for Different Levels of Ability. All levels should be able to relate to the concrete images in the poem: the seagulls, the lobster, the flowers, the students, the boats, the steeple. Only minimal interpretation is called for, and more advanced students should have little difficulty handling the poem. With less advanced students you may want to provide help with paraphrasing and interpreting.

Reading the Poem. You may want to get prints or slides of suitable examples of Dürer's work. A variety of subjects is ideal, with each picture showing the intricate detail for which Dürer is famous. Ask students why Dürer might "have seen a reason for living" in a particular kind of town. (Presumably because of its richness and variety of subject matter for his art.) Then ask what a poet, like Marianne Moore, might admire in the work of an artist like Dürer. (The exact and detailed representation of what the artist observed.) This introduction could lead to a review of earlier discussions about the Imagists' passion for vividness and exactness. Point out to students that Imagists must be highly skilled at writing description—it is their modus operandi.

Reteaching Alternatives. Rather than rereading the poem, try having students paraphrase it orally in class. Go through the poem phrase by phrase, image by image, having students "translate" the poem into conversational language and explaining whatever in it may be unclear—for example, the references to Dürer, the fantasy quality of eight stranded whales, the primitive-art aspect of waves that look like fish scales. Once you are into the poem, students may see possible meanings for images that you and others have not seen.

Responding to the Poem   Text page 746
Analyzing the Poem
Identifying Details

1. In "The Steeple-Jack," (as in many of Moore's poems), conventional poetic meter and free verse are replaced by the strict count of *syllables*. Count the number of syllables in each line of the first stanza. Then do the same with the following stanzas. Is the pattern repeated? The pattern is repeated as follows: 11 syllables in the first lines of each stanza, 10 in the second, 14 in the third, 8 in the fourth, 8 in the fifth, and 3 in the sixth.

In which stanza does Moore introduce a new pattern of syllables? In the fourth stanza, the sixth line has 4 syllables rather than 3 ("side flowers and"). The 4-syllable pattern is repeated in the next stanza ("at the back door"), after which the pattern reverts to 3 syllables in each sixth line.

2. The poem is unified by an unusual *rhyme scheme*. To discover what it is, find the two lines that rhyme in the first stanza. Then examine the following stanzas to see if you can find a pattern of rhyme. The rhyme scheme is as follows: abcdbe.

3. What details in the poem suggest the location of the town? Many details suggest that this is a coastal town. Among the references in the first three stanzas are the following: the eight stranded whales referred to in line 2; the "sweet sea air" in line 3; the view of the sea's waves in lines 4–6; the mention of the seagulls in line 7; the lighthouse in line 9; and the references to lobsters and nets in lines 16–17. Since we are in a northern climate (see lines 36–38), and since a prominent part of the landscape is the church steeple, Moore's town is probably in New England.

4. List as many *images* as you can that help you see, hear, and smell the town. Students' answers may include the following: the sweet sea air (line 3); the vignette of the seagulls (line 7); the color of the sea (line 13); the lobster and the fish nets (line 18); the flowers and trees in the fog (line 24); the cats (line 40); the newt (line 42); the boats (line 48); the church spire (line 54); the black and white sign of C. J. Poole (line 59); the whitewashed columns of the church (line 61); the gilded star (line 77).

5. What does the speaker think of this town? The speaker evidently approves of the town. She says "it could not be dangerous to be living/in a town/like this."

Interpreting Meanings

6. What role does Ambrose play in the poem? The college student Ambrose is introduced in line 45 as an appreciative observer of town life who likes "an elegance of which the source is not bravado." Perhaps this use of a relatively young observer suggests the continuing, understated beauty of the town, where living could not be dangerous and where simple people seem at home.

7. Considering the poem's title, why would Moore take so long to bring in C. J. Poole? Moore apparently wants to establish the setting as precisely and vividly as she can, using carefully chosen concrete details and objects, before she presents human characters in the poem. (In motion picture and TV terminology, this would be called an "establishing shot.")

Why do you think the poem is named for him? Answers will vary. On the one hand, the steeple-jack is somewhat removed from real life. The speaker says of him that he "might be part of a novel," and she identifies him through his painted sign. On the other hand, she describes him as at home in the town, and she associates him with the gilding of the star on the steeple, a star linked with the notion of hope. Then, too, from the steeple, Poole would have a bird's-eye view of the town and would be able to take in all the details that the speaker introduces.

8. What is the nature of the confusion referred to in the fourth stanza? The "confusion" is apparently the welter of sense impressions and details of this town taken in by the speaker-observer.

9. Explain the significance of the fact that the hero, the student, and the steeple-jack are all "at home." Three people of widely different backgrounds (and, presumably, personalities) can call the town home because of the tolerance and diversity that exist there.

10. Explain what you think is the significance of the star at the poem's end. The star evidently symbolizes hope—hope for the town and perhaps for humankind in general.

11. How would you describe the *tone* of this poem? How did it make you feel about this town? Answers will vary. Most students will agree that the tone of the poem is pleasant and comforting. They will probably have a favorable impression of the town. Any reasonable answer should be accepted, of course. Students can be asked to point to specific words, phrases, and lines to support their answers.

12. How does Moore's view of a small Maine town contrast with Edwin Arlington Robinson's character studies of people who live in another Maine town? (See page 651.) Answers will vary somewhat. Students should note, however, the difference between the hypocrisy and destructiveness of small-town life represented in Robinson's poems and the town of "simple people" with a star that "stands for hope" depicted in Moore's poem.

Writing About the Poem
A Creative Response

1. Imitating the Poet's Technique. Note that students are to concentrate not on Moore's syllable count and rhyme pattern, but on her catalogue of sights, sounds, and smells. Elicit a list of local places—perhaps a farmer's market, a junkyard, a mall—with vivid sights, sounds, and smells. Allow students to use one of these places or a different one for their own responses.

Criteria for Evaluating the Assignment. The poem or paragraph catalogues sights, smells, and sounds evocative of a specific place.

A Critical Response

2. Comparing the Poem to a Prose Text. As preparation for writing this paragraph, have students skim pages 535–540 and list a number of concrete items that prove Zenith's perfection to Babbitt. They should next compare this list with the list of images found in response to question 4.

Criteria for Evaluating the Assignment. The paragraph states how Babbitt's and Moore's views of the ideal town differ, and cites specific details or categories of details from the speech and the poem (for example, appliances versus flowers) to demonstrate that difference.

Analyzing Language and Style
Precise Meanings

Tyrol: Region of the eastern Alps in Austria or Italy

salpiglossis: a Chilean herb with strikingly colored, funnel-shaped flowers

lichens: plants composed of symbiotic algae and fungi growing on a solid surface, such as a rock

bracts: leaves from the axil of which a flower may arise

banyan: large tree from the branches of which shoots grow down to the soil and form secondary trunks

portico: a colonnade or covered walk at the entrance of a building

fluted: marked by grooves

Primary Sources: Animals and Athletes   Text page 746

You may want to go over Marianne Moore's statements in class to make sure that students understand them. Point out not only that was Moore a baseball fan, but that she wrote a number of poems about baseball, including "Baseball and Writing." The Imagists, by opening up the subject matter of poetry, brought baseball and other sports a literary respectability they had not had before. Ernest Lawrence Thayer's "Casey at the Bat" appeared in 1888, but it is a comic poem. William Carlos Williams's "The Crowd at the Ball Game"—to take one example—appeared in 1923 and is a serious work of art.

Extending the Poem

Have a number of volunteers do library research on Marianne Moore's poetry, locating some critical comments, if they can, on "The Steeple-Jack." Ask the researchers to read in class the critical commentary they have found. See whether other students agree or disagree with what is said.

Carl Sandburg

Text page 747

"Chicago" — Text page 749

"Limited" — Text page 751

Objectives

1. To recognize and interpret epithets
2. To identify the central image
3. To identify examples of parallelism
4. To write an apostrophe to a place
5. To write an essay comparing and contrasting poems by different poets
6. To analyze paradox and irony

Introducing the Poems

A significant technique in "Chicago" is the use of epithets to convey meaning, such as "Hog Butcher of the World," "Stacker of Wheat," and "City of the Big Shoulders." The central image of "Chicago" is indirectly expressed through these epithets, which express a tough, active man, and the participles ("flinging," "shoveling," "bragging") that suggest someone boisterous. The images near the end of the poem—a young man, an unbeaten fighter, youthful laughter—indicate a young man. In "Limited," the main idea of the poem is implicit through that one word: the *limited* life of manufactured products (the train); *limited* life of human beings (men and women on train; man in smoker); *limited* perception of man on train ("Omaha").

Background on the Poems. Sandburg ends his "Notes for a Preface" in his *Complete Poems* with a one-paragraph biographical sketch. Students may appreciate his observations on writing:

> I am still studying verbs and the mystery of how they connect nouns. I am more suspicious of adjectives than at any other time in all my born days. I have forgotten the meaning of twenty or thirty of my poems written thirty or forty years ago . . . All my life I have been trying to learn to read, to see and hear, and to write . . . It could be, in the grace of God, I shall live to be eighty-nine, as did Hokusai, and speaking my farewell to earthly scenes, I might paraphrase: "If God had let me live five years longer I should have been a writer."

The Literal Meanings. "*Chicago*": The poet addresses the city in a series of apostrophes. He then notes the unfavorable things that people say about Chicago. He accepts the arguments of these critics, but gives "them back the sneer" by picturing the city as vibrantly alive and constantly in motion. He ends by saying that Chicago is proud to be all the things apostrophized in the first stanza. "*Limited*": The speaker is on one of the nation's best trains, crossing the prairie. There are fifteen cars with a thousand people in them. He says in parentheses that the train will become scrap and the passengers will die. A man, asked where he is going, answers, "Omaha."

Teaching Strategies

Providing for Cultural Differences. Many students will benefit from a brief discussion of Chicago in the early twentieth century. By 1900, Chicago's population made it the "Second City" after New York (a title it can no longer claim), with more than a million and a half people. It was also, as the poem says, a meat-packing and food-processing center, a railroad hub, and a city of heavy industry. In 1900, New York, with more than twice the population of Chicago, was the financial and publishing capital of the nation; Chicago was—in Sandburg's poem and in fact—a newer, rawer, brawnier place.

Providing for Different Levels of Ability. Students should not have much difficulty with "Chicago," but less advanced students may need some help with "Limited." In teaching "Limited," focus on the title—on the word *limited*. Ask for a definition. Have students name things that are limited. (In the broadest sense, everything except infinity has limits.)

Reading the Poems. In the 1950's and 1960's college students queued up to get tickets to Sandburg's touring performances. He recited his own poetry and sang his songs, strumming the guitar. One of his best-known poems, "Fog," is mentioned in the introductory biography. You may want to read the poem aloud to your students.

276 Imagism and Symbolism

Fog

The fog comes
on little cat feet.

It sits looking
over harbor and city
on silent haunches
and then moves on.

This poem caused quite a stir when it was published, many people claiming it was not a poem at all. You might ask your students to answer the question, "Is 'Fog' a poem?" Why or why not? What comparison is Sandburg making? How effective do your students find this comparison?

You will want to read aloud, or have students read aloud, both "Chicago" and "Limited." In "Limited" make sure that students see the point at which the speaker's mind takes a philosophical turn. What is the speaker thinking about when he asks, "Where are you going?"

Reteaching Alternatives. Consider asking students to suggest (or perhaps bring in recordings of) songs about various cities in the United States. See how many the class can find. From the familiar "New York, New York" to less well known songs such as "Gary, Indiana" from *The Music Man,* there are a great many possibilities. Have students compare what they learn about each city from its song with what they learn about Chicago from Sandburg's poem.

"Chicago"

Responding to the Poem Text page 750
Analyzing the Poem
Identifying Details

1. Sandburg opens with a litany of *epithets,* or descriptive phrases, about Chicago. What does each of these epithets reveal about the city and the various activities that make up its economy? "Hog Butcher" refers to Chicago's preeminence as a meat-packing center; "Tool Maker" refers to Chicago's manufacturing, to its heavy industry; "Stacker of Wheat" refers to Chicago's position as a center of grain processing; "Player with Railroads" and "Nation's Freight Handler" refer to Chicago's prominence as a rail hub.

2. What do people tell the speaker about Chicago? What is the speaker's answer to each of these comments about the city? People tell the speaker that the city is wicked, crooked, and brutal. The speaker agrees with each of these comments, mentioning prostitutes, murders by gunmen who are then freed, and the hunger of women and children.

Interpreting Meanings

3. Many different images contribute to this portrait of Chicago, but its central *image* is never named. To what is Chicago really being compared? How is this image introduced and extended? The central image is that of a lusty young man. The image is introduced in the opening apostrophes, culminating with "City of the Big Shoulders." Later the city/man is pictured "Flinging magnetic curses," "Bareheaded," "Shoveling," "Wrecking," "Planning," and so on. Its youth is emphasized in the simile "as a young man laughs" and in the metaphor of an unbeaten fighter. The conclusion contains a reference to the "brawling laughter of youth."

4. What are the city's main strengths and main weaknesses, according to Sandburg? The city's main strengths seem to be vitality, industry, pride, and endurance. The city's main weaknesses include wickedness, crime, brutality, and perhaps dirt.

On balance, what seems to be his attitude toward the city: Does he think it is boastful? Defensive? One-sided? Naive? Proud? Which attitude do you think the poet would most want to emphasize? Answers will vary. The poet emphasizes both the city's vitality—its "aliveness"—and its pride.

5. How does the long list in the last line help to unify the poem? The last line repeats the apostrophes of lines 1–3.

6. Find at least four examples of *parallelism* in the poem. How does this parallelism affect the poem's rhythm? Answers will vary. Examples of parallelism include the repetition of apostrophes in lines 1–5; the repeated structure of "they tell me" in lines 6–8; the succession of participles in lines 13–17; the repetition of the word *under* in lines 18, 19, and 21. Parallelism contributes to the declamatory rhythm of the poem, as if the speaker were formally addressing the city.

7. Which features of Chicago do you think have changed since this poem was written in 1914? Answers will vary. The stockyards are now an industrial park. Finance and wholesaling are more important now than they were in 1914. Heavy industry is less so. The gas lamps are gone.

Which features mentioned in the poem might still be part of the life of the city? The city is still the world's greatest railhead and a leading manufacturing center. Many of the details concerning jobs are still valid. Like most big cities, Chicago has its share of painted women, gangsters, and hunger.

8. What would you say to those critics who have claimed that Sandburg's poetry is full of bluster and proclamations at the expense of thought? Answers will vary. Remind students that they are basing their views on a single example of Sandburg's poetry. Urge them to defend their views with specific references to the poem.

Writing About the Poem
A Creative Response

1. Writing an Apostrophe. Clarify the meaning of *epithet* (a characteristic word or phrase replacing the name of a person or thing), and ask students to identify the city meant by the epithet "The Big Apple" (New York). Do local promotional epithets already exist for their city? What epithets could they propose? Guide students to focus on key geographical, sociological, political, or industrial features of the city.

*C*riteria for Evaluating the Assignment. The five or more epithets listed are appropriate for the intended city, and they could be used like Sandburg's five opening lines.

A Critical Response

2. Comparing and Contrasting Poems. Have students work in pairs or small groups to complete the suggested chart on Whitman's and Sandburg's poems.

*C*riteria for Evaluating the Assignment. The essay is well organized, states both similarities and differences between Whitman's "I Hear America Singing" and Sandburg's "Chicago," and cites specific details from each poem to support its major points.

"Limited"

Responding to the Poem Text page 752
Analyzing the Poem
Identifying Details

1. Where is the speaker of the poem? The speaker is crossing the prairie of the American Midwest in a fast train.

2. What does the speaker predict will happen to the train and its passengers? The speaker says that both the passengers and the coaches will one day be scrap, rust and ashes.

Interpreting Meanings

3. What does the word *crack* mean in line 1? The word means "fine" or "excellent."

4. What phrase in line 1 prepares the reader for the *paradox*, or self-contradiction, that underlies the whole poem? The paradoxical phrase "limited express" prepares the reader for the self-contradiction underlying the whole poem.

5. In your own words, state the *main idea* of this poem, using the word *limited*. The main idea is that people and the objects they create have a *limited* time on earth. The express train is not merely *limited* in the sense of being higher priced and somewhat exclusive; it also has a limited lifespan. So do the people riding it.

6. Do you think there is a double meaning in the speaker's question in line 4? If so, what *irony* do you sense in the other passenger's answer: "Omaha"? Answers will vary. Most students will see the double meaning of the speaker's question. The man in the smoker responds literally and sensibly to the question. The irony arises because of the speaker's parenthetical thought (which the man cannot know) about the transience of trains and life. That thought almost leads one to expect the man in the smoker to respond, "Heaven," or something such. In a sense, this is dramatic irony—the reader knows something that a character (the man in the smoker) does not.

7. What connections can you see between this poem and Robert Frost's "Nothing Gold Can Stay" (page 688)? Student answers will vary. Most students will agree that transience is the central theme of both poems. Encourage students to be as specific as possible in their comparisons of the two works.

8. How could the poem's details be up-dated? Perhaps the traveler could be pictured on a supersonic aircraft. Encourage students to offer imaginative suggestions.

Primary Sources:
"Rhymes are iron fetters" Text page 752

Since some students are likely to feel that "real" poetry demands rhyme, you may want to have a class discussion about Sandburg's and Holmes's view of rhyme. Does the passage suggest that good poetry *cannot* be written in rhyme? (It may seem to, but surely neither Sandburg nor Holmes would have maintained that position.) Does it mean that better poetry can be written in free verse? (Again, it seems to; and Sandburg, if not Holmes, probably would have taken that position.) What do your students believe? Some will undoubtedly agree with Robert Frost that writing free verse is like playing tennis with the net down. Others may think that Sandburg, with Holmes's help, has made a convincing case for free verse and against rhyme.

278 Imagism and Symbolism

Extending the Poem

Carl Sandburg's *Complete Poems*, published in 1950, contains many excellent poems. If you can obtain the book, you might want to read in class "When Death Came April Twelve, 1945." Ask students what kind of poem it is. (An elegy) See if anyone knows offhand who died on April 12, 1945. (President Franklin D. Roosevelt) If not, see if they can discover the answer from context, pointing to the clues that helped them. (For example, "frontline tanks nearing Berlin," "The Commander," "battle stations over the South Pacific")

E. E. Cummings   Text page 753

"nobody loses all the time"   Text page 754

"what if a much of a which of a wind"   Text page 756

Objectives

1. To write a paragraph in the poet's style
2. To compare poems by two different poets
3. To identify images
4. To describe the rhyme scheme
5. To write a paragraph comparing two poems
6. To compare a poem with a statement
7. To analyze the poet's diction

Introducing the Poems

Cummings's poetry is known for its "thought groups" unmarked by punctuation or line endings, such as parenthetical phrases not set off ("to use a highfalootin phrase," "to wit") and sentence endings not indicated by periods. As students will quickly note, the poems are also marked by unusual capitalization and punctuation and by parts of speech used as other parts of speech.

Background on the Poems. Since many of your students are likely to question Cummings's eccentricities of style, you may want to present a critic's defense of them. Norman Friedman, author of a critical biography of Cummings, writes:

> To break lines and words on the page, to use capitals and lower case letters where they don't belong, to insert parentheses anywhere and everywhere, to scatter punctuation marks apparently at random—what uses can these serve? There is ... the "feel" of the poem as it lies on the page. To me at least there is a pleasurable tactility in these devices, a sense of visual structure as in a painting ... [T]he best reason [is] that typography may not be pronounceable but it does affect the way we read. Pause and emphasis are supported by these devices; the meaning of words and lines is underscored; but most importantly of all, meanings are created as the reader's mind is slowed in its progress through the poem and forced to go back and forth....This is what any good poem asks of the reader and Cummings is simply extending this request by making it explicit.

The Literal Meanings. "*nobody loses all the time*": The speaker's Uncle Sol foolishly went into farming. He failed at raising vegetables, chickens, and skunks, because the chickens ate the vegetables, the skunks ate the chickens, and the skunks died. Sol then drowned himself. At the impressive funeral, everyone cried. Finally, Uncle Sol went into the earth and started a worm farm. "*what if a much of a which of a wind*": If the universe is destroyed, "the single secret will still be man." If the world freezes over, the stouthearted will survive to "cry hello" to spring. No matter how many people are destroyed, the human spirit will prevail.

Teaching Strategies

Providing for Cultural Differences. Students whose first language is not English may have difficulty interpreting Cummings's poetry, especially "what if a much of a which of a wind." The best solution may be to read both poems aloud in class and to discuss each of them briefly, using the questions in the text and offering help when needed.

Providing for Different Levels of Ability. Most students will understand the sequence of events in "nobody loses all the time" and will appreciate the black humor of the ending. Less advanced students may find "what if a much of a which of a wind" confusing and perhaps annoying. Probably the best approach with these students is to read the poem to them—it is lyrically beautiful—and not press for much interpretation.

Introducing Vocabulary Study. Knowing the meanings of the following words is important to understanding the poems (Starred words appear in the Glossary. The italicized word either is archaic or has special meaning in context.)

"nobody loses all the time"
vaudeville	l. 5	auspicious*	l. 29
highfalootin	l. 9	scrumptious	l. 30
Victor Victrola	l. 28	splendiferous	l. 30

"what if a much of a which of a wind"
| awry* | l. 4 | stifles | l. 12 |

In Cummings's poetry, many apparent vocabulary problems stem from syntax. Readers are not accustomed to having adverbs function as nouns, for instance, and may not know how to "define" words in out-of-place positions. Ask students to find at least three words in Cummings's "what if a much of a which of a wind" that are in positions usually requiring other parts of speech. (Possible answers: *seem* [l. 5]; *keen* [l. 9]; *ago* [l. 12]) Some students may choose *much* or *which* from the title. Accept either answer. Point out, however, that *much* does sometimes function as a noun, although it is not idiomatic for *much* to be preceded by *a*. A similar problem exists with *which;* a pronoun can follow the preposition *of,* but *which* would not be preceded by *a*.

Reading the Poems. (An audiocassette recording accompanies "what if a much of a which of a wind.") Have students look at the poems before reading them. Ask: Do these look to you like poems? Why or why not? What punctuation and capitalization do you find in the poems? How does it differ from ordinary punctuation and capitalization? Do you see any logic in the line breaks? Why do you think a poet would write this way? When students read the poems, have them pay attention to tone. Ask them what kind of poet seems to be revealed by the two poems. Use the questions to work through each poem's meaning. Do not try to analyze the meaning of every word or every line in "what if a much of a which of a wind." Knowing the general idea of the poem, appreciating its lyricism, and experiencing the feelings being conveyed are the desirable outcomes.

Reteaching Alternatives. You might ask half the class to write a four- or five-sentence prose summary of "nobody loses all the time." Ask the other half to write a similar summary of "what of a much of a which of a wind." Form a committee to choose the two best summaries and then write them on the chalkboard. Have the whole class discuss any additions, corrections, or improvements that should be made in the summaries.

"nobody loses all the time"

Responding to the Poem Text page 755
Analyzing the Poem
Interpreting Meanings

1. What does the title mean? The title means that even born failures like Uncle Sol attain some success, even if only by the law of averages, and even if the success is not what they would have liked.

Do you see any significance in the fact that the sun is often called "old sol"? Answers will vary. Since this is a humorous poem, the pun Sol/sol may suggest the downward-tending course—as in the sun setting—of poor Uncle Sol. Then, too, Sol is a rather sunny character, despite his repeated failures, as indicated by his singing and his insistence on farming.

2. When we read Cummings's collected works, we realize that he used many different borrowed or imitated voices to reveal the characters of the speakers in his poems. From what you hear, and overhear, in this monologue, what sort of person would you say we are listening to? Is he or she aware of the *irony* that runs through the story? When does the irony become clear? Answers will vary. The speaker is a kind of breathless narrator of Sol's life. He seems to come from the city, since he regards farming as "that possibly most inexcusable of all . . . luxuries." The speaker mixes formal language ("to wit," "be it needlessly added") with colloquial language ("highfalootin," "splendiferous"). Something of a cynic, the speaker seems keenly aware of the irony of the story, playing up that irony with rhetorical flourishes. Even so, the full irony of the story does not become clear until the last four lines.

3. This poem is about the career of a "born failure." What else is it about? Answers will vary. Some students may say that the poem uses black humor to mock our often euphemistic outlook on death. Urge students to discuss their ideas with specific reference to the poem. What, besides the opinion of "everybody," really indicates that Uncle Sol had wasted his life? Is the speaker—surely not Cummings—something of a smart aleck himself, passing an unfair judgment on Sol? Does the description of Uncle Sol's

280 Imagism and Symbolism

funeral, with the mourners crying "like the Missouri," satirize hypocrisy?

4. Do you find a hint of cruelty in the poem? Do you think that it is intentional, or is it accidental? Why do we laugh at the last line, when we should shudder at it? Most students will agree that there is a hint of cruelty. If so, the cruelty is certainly unintentional on Cummings's part, although it might possibly be intentional on the part of his speaker/narrator. Perhaps Cummings intended to shock his readers and to shake up their perceptions of failure, death, and grief. We laugh at the last line because of the irony of Uncle Sol's end and because of the tongue-in-cheek tone of the speaker throughout the poem.

Writing About the Poem
A Creative Response

1. Writing in Cummings's Style. To demonstrate the idea, you might take a short "human interest" story used as a filler in a recent newspaper, and have students direct you in breaking lines and omitting punctuation as you rewrite it on the chalkboard or overhead projector.

Criteria for Evaluating the Assignment. The material falls into reasonable thought groupings which suggest, by context, the omitted punctuation. The starting material may be original or from a newspaper.

A Critical Response

2. Comparing and Contrasting Poems. Note that students are asked to compare and contrast "nobody loses all the time" and "Richard Cory" not in terms of message, but in use of rhyme, meter, and tone. Clarify the assignment as necessary, especially the term *tone* (author's attitude).

Criteria for Evaluating the Assignment. The paper states that the poems are similar in use of an ironic tone, but different in rhyme and meter. Specific details from the poems are used to support the points made.

"what if a much of a which of a wind"

Responding to the Poem   Text page 757
Analyzing the Poem
Identifying Details

1. If the world is blown away, what will still survive? Even if the world is blown away, the secret of human existence will remain.

2. Who "shall cry hello to the spring" if the world freezes over? People "whose hearts are mountains, roots are trees" will survive to greet the spring.

3. What will happen if the universe is blown up? Even if the universe is blown up, the human spirit will remain.

4. What *images* describe the seasons of the year in the first two stanzas? In line 2, "summer's a lie" is revealed by the winds of later summer or autumn (note the "dizzying leaves" and the red color suggested by "bloodies" in line 3). In lines 9–10, the setting is evidently winter, with "lean wind" that "flays/screaming hills with sleet and snow." At the end of the second stanza, in line 16, the end of winter is greeted by those who cry "hello to the spring."

How does the third stanza deal with time on a different scale? In the first two stanzas, the poem concentrates on the cycle of the seasons. In the third stanza, however, it focuses on eternity ("dawn of a doom"), using such words as *forever, nowhere, never,* and *nothing.*

5. Describe the *rhyme scheme* of the poem. How does Cummings make use of *slant rhyme*? The rhyme scheme of each stanza is as follows: abcbddac. Slant rhyme is used in lines 3 and 8 (*sun* and *man*), lines 5 and 6 (*seem* and *time*), lines 1 and 7 (*wind* and *drowned*), lines 9 and 15 (*flays* and *trees*), lines 19 and 24 (*grave* and *live*), lines 21 and 22 (*twice* and *was*), and lines 17 and 25 (*dream* and *home*). Cummings also uses internal rhyme and assonance.

Interpreting Meanings

6. What common human fears does Cummings refer to in the first six lines of each stanza? In the first lines of each stanza, Cummings refers to the fears of disappointment, loss, death, and oblivion.

How does he comment on those fears in the last two lines of each stanza? In each stanza, the last two lines respond to those fears with expressions of affirmation, faith, and confidence in life.

7. What is the effect of the direct reference to "me and you" in line 20? This direct reference helps to make the poem's appeal more immediate and personal.

8. What do you think Cummings means by the last two lines? Is he celebrating life or death? Explain. Answers will vary. A possible paraphrase: Eternity and the unknown universe are the home to which we are all eventually going; the more who go there, the greater the number of souls—

E. E. Cummings   281

and perhaps the greater the joy—we will find there. Most students will agree that the last two lines comprise a life-affirming statement.

Writing About the Poem
A Critical Response

1. Comparing Poems. With so many points of comparison to be drawn, students may wish to construct a data chart similar to that used on page 750. This time the poets are Whitman and Cummings, and the left-hand headings are (1) theme or message, (2) imagery, (3) tone, (4) form, and (5) structure.

Criteria for Evaluating the Assignment. The essay cites how the poems are similar in the five areas listed above. Specific details from Whitman's "On the Beach at Night" and Cummings's "what if a much of a which of a wind" are used to support the points made.

2. Comparing the Poems to a Statement. Have students read and discuss Cummings's points in "Miracles are to come," and selected statements that relate to the messages of his poems.

Criteria for Evaluating the Assignment. The paper identifies statements which can reasonably be interpreted as similar to the messages of Cummings's poems, and cites details from the poems to support points made.

Analyzing Language and Style
Diction

1. Pretentious, pompous
2. Deceptively splendid
3. Answers will vary; "pompous" and "glittering" are apt.
4. "Wept a river of tears" is one of many possibilities.
5. The diction, including the frequent alliteration (line 17) and internal rhyme (line 9), suggests a down-to-earth person who is playful despite danger. This contributes to a tone that is, overall, positive.
6. Answers will vary on what the words mean when used as nouns. Some possible answers are given in parentheses: *seem* (emptiness); *ago* (oblivion); *blind* (blindness); *soon* (immediate future); *never* (annihilation); *isn't* (non-life, death); *was* (a thing of the past).

Primary Sources: "Miracles are to come" — Text page 757

Students will need to analyze this excerpt by Cummings in order to respond to the second writing assignment. Though by now they should be aware of Cummings's unusual punctuation, you may also wish to point out the delightful single words "mostpeople" and "squarerootofminusone."

T. S. Eliot — Text page 758
"The Love Song of J. Alfred Prufrock" — Text page 760

Objectives

1. To identify figurative language
2. To interpret an extended metaphor
3. To analyze setting
4. To paraphrase lines
5. To write a dialogue between the speaker and another person
6. To imitate the poet's writing style
7. To write an essay evaluating a character
8. To write an essay comparing two characters
9. To write an essay responding to a critic
10. To analyze the use of rhythms, rhymes, metaphors, and allusions

Introducing the Poem

In addition to the many literary and Biblical allusions, this poem also has many memorable figures of speech, such as the simile comparing the evening sky to "a patient etherized upon a table" and the metaphor comparing the yellow fog to a cat. In addition, students might note the many images that reveal the character of the speaker: Prufrock's fear of his bald spot; Prufrock "pinned and wriggling on the wall"; and Prufrock wondering if he dares to eat a peach.

Background on the Poem. Eliot wrote "The Love Song of J. Alfred Prufrock" in 1911, but it was not published until 1915. The reactions that readers had to it before its publication may interest your students (whose own reactions may be closer to Harold Monro's than Ezra Pound's):

> But if he [Eliot] was unhappy and nervous about his own work, there were others whose faith in his abilities was more marked. Conrad Aiken [a well-known poet] had his own copy of "The Love Song of J. Alfred Prufrock"; he had come to England the year before and, with touching loyalty, had shown the poem to anyone he thought might be interested. Rupert Brooke had introduced him to Harold Monro, the owner of the Poetry Bookshop, but Monro handed the poem back to him saying that it was "absolutely insane." Indeed those of markedly English taste found it quite odd.... But Aiken also spoke about his friend's work to Ezra Pound, a fellow American who took an interest in such things.... and Pound [when he read the poem] told him, "This is as good as anything I've ever seen...."

The Literal Meaning. The speaker in the poem, Prufrock, invites the reader to go through half-deserted streets with him. Immediately, Prufrock interrupts the journey with an observation about women who speak of Michelangelo. Then he describes the evening fog and introduces his obsession with time. After another mention of the women and Michelangelo, he conveys a picture of his self-consciousness, his boredom, and his apparent fear of women. He laments that he should have been a silent sea crab. Next, he illustrates, through an incident after tea, his inability to communicate with another person. He wonders if he should, like Lazarus, arise from the dead, but he cannot. He compares his irresolution to Hamlet's. He laments growing old. Although he wants to be able to live a full, romantic life, he is unable to do so.

Teaching Strategies

Providing for Cultural Differences. All students, whatever their cultural backgrounds, will benefit from a brief consideration of T. S. Eliot's own cultural background. Eliot was an expatriate—many consider him a British, rather than an American, author—who found much that he disliked in England as well as in the United States. Students should bear in mind that a poet, like readers of poetry, is a product of the culture in which he or she lives. Some of that culture is sure to be evident in the poetry, even if the poet is alienated from the norms of the place and time in which he or she lives.

Providing for Different Levels of Ability. With less advanced students, you may simply want to tell them about "Prufrock," read the poem to them, and explain some of the major parts. Tell them that they will notice how Prufrock's thoughts seem to skip around. Ask them if their own thoughts ever tend to skip around. You should probably not expect these students to answer all the questions at the end of the poem. If you want to reduce that number, the following five questions are among the easiest: 1, 3 (first two parts), 5, 13, 20. All students will benefit from the commentary on text page 764, the side notes, and the questions. Remind them that Eliot expected readers to have to work to understand his poetry.

Introducing Vocabulary Study. Knowing the meanings of the following words is important to understanding the poem. (Starred words appear in the Glossary.)

etherized	l. 3	marmalade	l. 88
insidious	l. 9	deferential*	l. 115
formulated	l. 56	politic*	l. 116
digress	l. 66	meticulous*	l. 116

You may want to have your students write a sentence using each of the eight words correctly.

Reading the Poem. After you have talked about Eliot and "Prufrock," read the poem aloud in class. For homework, you might have students review the poem, read "A Commentary on the Poem," and think about the responding questions. Unless you handle "Prufrock" as an extended project, you may not want them to write the answers to all the responding questions on text pages 765–767, but merely be able to discuss them in class. Begin the next day with a second oral reading of the poem, this time perhaps by a well-prepared student. Go over the side notes before proceeding to the 26 questions at the end.

Reteaching Alternatives. You might assign each stanza (even the two-line stanzas) to a different student. Have each student study his or her stanza carefully and be prepared both to read it in class and to explain its meaning in his or her own words. The stanzas should be read in the same order as they appear in the poem. Advise students that a great deal has been written on T. S. Eliot's poetry and on "Prufrock" specifically. If they can obtain help in the library, the infusion of some critics' views on Eliot and "Prufrock" will add greatly to the discussion.

Responding to the Poem Text page 765
Analyzing the Poem
Interpreting Meanings

1. The very name "J. Alfred Prufrock" gives us clues to the character of our "hero." Think of "prude" and "prudence." Think of what you associate with a "frock"—in terms of costume, in terms of religion. What hints to the man's personality might these details supply? Answers will vary somewhat. The associations of "prude" suggest that the "hero" may be shy, squeamish, or sexually insecure. "Prudence" would imply that he is cautious, perhaps overly timid. The word *frock* in terms of costume may suggest that the "hero" is, or perceives himself to be, somewhat effeminate. The word *frock* in terms of religion suggests that he might be monkish and withdrawn. Encourage students to offer other suggestions.

2. How could the famous *simile* in lines 2–3 reveal that the speaker's mind or will is paralyzed? (What kinds of things are the evening sky and sunset usually compared with?) Since sunset is often associated with fire, the comparison to an anesthetized patient on an operating table comes as a surprise. The simile suggests that Prufrock may regard himself as an invalid, or as someone who has been numbed by anxiety or indecisiveness.

3. What is the speaker inviting someone to do in lines 1–12? The speaker is proposing to the reader (or someone else—even himself) a journey through the city streets on some kind of visit. The destination is left unclear.

What kind of place are they going to travel through? From the details in lines 4–7, it seems that they are going to travel through a rundown, unattractive quarter of a large city: note the "one-night cheap hotels" and the restaurants with sawdust on the floor.

How could some of these *images* also suggest a journey through someone's *mind,* as well as a physical journey? The comparison of the half-deserted streets to a "tedious argument" in line 8 offers the possibility that this journey may be mental or figurative as well as physical.

4. Think about what the name Michelangelo contributes to the transitional passage in lines 13–14. What would be the effect, if, for instance, the women were "talking of Joe DiMaggio" or "discussing detergents"? The students will have various answers. In general, the name "Michelangelo" connotes an image of cultivated, refined (perhaps overrefined) conversation.

5. In lines 15–22, we have one of the most famous *extended metaphors* in modern poetry. What is being directly compared with what? How many details extend the metaphor? In these lines the "yellow fog" and "yellow smoke" of the city on an October night are being compared to an animal, probably a cat. Among the details extending the metaphor are the following: the fog, like the animal, "rubs its back" (line 15) and "rubs its muzzle" (line 16); it licks its tongue (line 17); it lets the soot fall "upon its back" (line 19); it slips by the terrace and makes "a sudden leap" (line 20); it sees the softness of the night (line 21); it curls around the house and falls asleep (line 22).

6. While the setting of this poem is more a state of mind than a place, certain stanzas and passages provide clues to where we are. This stanza (lines 15–22) is one of them. What does it reveal about time and place? From these lines, we recognize that it is an urban setting, probably London. The time is an October night.

What is the significance, for the poem, of the time of year it names? Why would another time of year (say, spring) be less appropriate for Prufrock's journey? The fact that the time of year is autumn emphasizes Prufrock's melancholy, his sense of anxiety about the passage of time, and his own mortality. Spring, with its usual associations of hope and rebirth, would be much less appropriate.

7. Psychologically speaking, what do you do when you "prepare a face to meet the faces that you meet"? (Think of all the people in the range of your acquaintance. Do you prepare a new face for each of them?) What might line 27 reveal about Prufrock's ego, or sense of self? When you "prepare a face" to meet people, you are probably anxious or self-conscious about how they will perceive or judge you. Line 27 reveals that Prufrock is timid and insecure.

8. The self-consciousness of the speaker is nowhere more evident than in lines 37–44. What is he self-conscious and worried about in these lines? He is self-conscious and worried about his physical appearance, especially as he grows older. He mentions that his hair will be thinning and that, despite his correct attire, people will notice that his arms and legs are growing thin with age.

9. In line 51, Prufrock says, "I have measured out my life with coffee spoons." What does this imply about the way he has lived? (To answer this question, take into account the fact that "coffeehouses" have long been an important feature of life in England and on the continent of Europe.) The sentence implies that he has spent much time in coffeehouses or at other people's salons. Perhaps it suggests that he lives alone, and that he is bored and lonely.

What other "measuring devices" would suggest a more exciting life? Answers will vary. Certainly the fact that it is coffee (rather than something stronger) that Prufrock drinks suggests a tame, socially correct sort of life. A "dram" or a "pint" might suggest a less ordered life. If he measured out his life in hundred-yard dashes, he would surely be more active. Encourage students to name a variety of measuring devices that would add excitement to Prufrock's life.

10. Lines 56–60 contain another *extended metaphor*. To what does the speaker compare himself? The speaker compares himself to an insect which has been pinned on a surface such as a wall, to be displayed or analyzed.

Which of the following words would best describe his self-characterization here: Trapped? Victimized? Humiliated? Exposed? Students may consider all of these words appropriate. Ask them to make and defend a single choice.

11. In line 62 Prufrock begins to think about women. What other references does he make to women in the

284   Imagism and Symbolism

poem? Lines 13–14 (repeated in lines 35–36) offer a vignette of cultivated society women discussing art. At line 75 the speaker pictures himself having tea with a woman—a scene that continues through line 110. Finally, at line 124 the speaker refers to mermaids, saying that he does not think they will sing to him.

How do you think he feels about women and his attractiveness to them? Prufrock seems to feel timid in the presence of women and insecure about his attractiveness or his ability to deal with them.

12. The setting and people described in lines 70–72 (in the form of a question) are considerably different from the settings and people familiar to Prufrock. How is this place different? In contrast to the upper-class settings familiar to Prufrock, these details suggest a working-class neighborhood.

What might this experience with another segment of city life tell us about Prufrock? Answers will vary. Perhaps this experience suggests that Prufrock has had diverse experiences but that, in spite of his acquaintance with different social strata, he cannot feel at home anywhere; he always feels alienated.

13. In lines 73–74, we have a critical point in the poem. The speaker reaches for a *metaphor* that will most pointedly dramatize his sense of alienation. The one he chooses is extreme and bizarre. Yet, by this time we know him so well we are not surprised by his attempts to express his remoteness from the rest of the world. Can you explain why Prufrock thinks he should have been a crab at the bottom of the sea? The metaphor is a striking expression of Prufrock's self-consciousness, timidity, and alienation.

14. Which statement in the stanza beginning "And the afternoon" (line 75) best explains Prufrock's emotional difficulty? The concluding statement, "I was afraid" (line 86), best explains Prufrock's emotional difficulty.

15. Lines 87–98 echo the widely heard complaint that a "lack of communication" between people is the cause of misunderstanding. What do you think Prufrock would like to tell people? Answers will vary. Many students will suggest that Prufrock would like to confide his hopes and fears. However, he feels compelled to be silent because he is afraid others might misunderstand him or see him as weak.

Do you think part of the problem lies in the contrast between the grandeur of Prufrock's expectations and the triviality of people's responses to them? Answers will vary. Urge students to defend their opinions.

16. In lines 94–104, Prufrock summarizes his life and reaches a point of exasperation that seems close to surrender: "It is impossible to say just what I mean!" What sort of life does he seem to have led? Prufrock seems to have led a lonely, alienated life of dull routine. Although he is socially observant, he feels that other people either ignore or dismiss him; certainly they fail to understand him.

17. Then, *ironically*—in a poem loaded with irony—he does exactly what he believes is "impossible" by stating what he means in a brilliant visual metaphor that exposes him, body and soul, with the force of an X-ray. What is the metaphor? How is he afraid people will respond to his exposure? The metaphor compares his inner thoughts and emotions, or "nerves," to patterns illuminated by a magic lantern on a screen. Prufrock is afraid that people will respond by ignoring or dismissing his sensitivities. He will thus have exposed his inner secrets only to be humiliated or brushed off.

18. In lines 111–119, how does the speaker characterize himself? Is he sincere, or is he mocking himself? In these lines, the speaker characterizes himself as an actor playing a minor role (an "attendant lord") in a Shakespearean drama. The tone seems slightly self-mocking.

19. After all his questions and speculations, the speaker finally arrives at decisiveness in line 121. Explain how he sees his role in life. Do you think he has overcome his doubts, or is he now just ignoring them? Prufrock now admits that he is aging, and he goes on to picture himself as an elderly man, wearing the bottoms of his trousers rolled, carefully parting his hair to conceal his growing baldness, and worrying about his digestion. Most students will agree that he has not overcome his doubts in these lines; he seems to be merely transposing these doubts to a different context.

20. In line 122, the speaker asks two questions. How would you characterize someone who worries about the part in his hair and about what he should dare to eat? Most students will probably agree that such a person might be characterized as elderly and timid.

21. What do you associate with mermaids (lines 124–125)? What could they represent for the speaker? Mermaids carry associations of mysterious, mythical beauty.

Why does he believe that they will not sing for him? Prufrock believes they will not sing for him because he will be old and unattractive. Perhaps there is a further suggestion that he will have lost his powers of imagination.

22. In lines 125–128, the speaker thinks that the mermaids are indifferent to him; and yet he is held by the romantic vision they embody. For what we know of our hero by this time, can you say why he is so fascinated by the sound and sight of such mythological creatures? Answers will vary. Some students may suggest that, even as Prufrock portrays himself as alienated and disillusioned, he desperately *wants* to believe in romance—if only as an escape from the dull routine and bleakness of his everyday life.

23. By means of *paraphrase*, can you restate the meaning of lines 129–131? When "human voices wake us," what do we "drown" in? A paraphrase might be: We have nurtured illusions for a long time, until reality has awakened us from our dream.

24. Think about the poem as a journey, a quest that begins with an invitation to join the man who makes it. What has the journey finally led us to? Can you formulate an answer in a single statement? Do you think it's possible that the point of the poem is not so much an answer arrived at as an experience lived? Answers will vary. If Prufrock has achieved a resolution, it seems to be a decidedly pessimistic one—the last phrase of the poem suggests death by drowning, not only for Prufrock, but for everyone. In the end, Prufrock appears to resign himself to old age and the timorousness of his own nature; he does not think the mermaids will sing to him. But the poem's resonances transcend the particular personality of its hero, as many students will see. This is a portrait of a modern "Everyman," whose struggle and ultimate failure to experience genuine feeling is the true subject.

25. Why do you think Eliot called this a "love song"? How is it different from the usual love song? Eliot's intention in the title is almost certainly ironic, since the poem differs so markedly from the usual love song. Rather than being a romantic serenade, the poem expresses indecisiveness and alienation. Prufrock is unable to love.

26. This is one of the most famous poems of the twentieth century. Explain why it has been described as a reflection of spiritual emptiness and emotional paralysis. Do you think its depiction of modern life is accurate? Students should be able to point to a number of examples in the poem that suggest spiritual emptiness and emotional paralysis. Ask students to defend their judgments of the poem's applicability to modern life.

Writing About the Poem
A Creative Response

Your most able students should be able to handle assignment 1; less able students may prefer assignment 2.

1. Writing a Dialogue. If you want your students to make the dialogue between Prufrock and Emerson, review Emerson's advice in "Self-Reliance." Students might also enjoy having Prufrock talk with a counselor or psychologist.

Criteria for Evaluating the Assignment. The conversation reveals the self-consciousness and inadequacy Prufrock feels, as conveyed by the poem, and perhaps paraphrases or uses specific lines from the poem. The second speaker is completely in character as Emerson or the speaker of the student's choice.

2. Imitating Eliot's Style. As data for the assignment, discuss the thoughts that go through a person's mind when he or she thinks an invitation may not be accepted.

Criteria for Evaluating the Assignment. The monologue reflects the random process characteristic of such thinking and reveals the thinker's feelings and fears. It begins with the words, "Let us go then, you and I."

A Critical Response

Assignments 3 through 6 all evaluate Prufrock's character, but do so in different ways. You may wish to discuss all four assignments, but allow students to choose one on which to write.

3. Evaluating a Character. The writing prompt outlines the contents of the essay. Elicit some immediate reactions to the three aspects suggested.

Criteria for Evaluating the Assignment. The essay cites details from the poem in order to explain (a) how Prufrock sees himself, (b) how he thinks others see him, and (c) how he wants others to see him. The essay concludes with a statement of whether or not the student can sympathize with Prufrock.

4. Comparing Characters. Students will need to have read the Walter Mitty story in order to complete this assignment. Although the prompt suggests that either answer is all right—that Prufrock is or is not a Mitty type—note that it directs students to make lists of similarities and differences and to choose the more persuasive list.

Criteria for Evaluating the Assignment. The essay shows insight into the fact that Prufrock never imagines his own greatness, despite comparisons with John the Baptist and Hamlet, whereas Mitty constantly does so.

5. Responding to a Critic. Read and discuss Pound's comment, together with directions preceding and following it. Note that students are to comment on whether it is possible to interpret the poem as ending on a note of triumph, and to give an opinion of the stanza on Hamlet.

Criteria for Evaluating the Assignment. The essay offers cogent reasons for believing the poem does or does not end on a note of triumph, and states the student's opinion on the stanza referring to Hamlet.

6. Interpreting Prufrock's Age. Clarify the assignment: have students write either an essay showing different arguments for *all three ages* (60, 40, or 20), or an essay arguing in favor of *only one of the ages* listed.

Criteria for Evaluating the Assignment. The essay offers cogent details from the poem to support its interpretation of Prufrock's age.

Analyzing Language and Style
Rhythms, Rhymes, and Metaphors

1. Metrical feet per line vary from 3 to 4, 5, or 6. The lines easiest to scan are lines 1 and 12 (trochaic tetrameter) and 11 (iambic trimeter).

2. Repetition within stanzas unifies stanzas (for example, "time" in lines 26–34); repetition of "In the room the women come and go/Talking of Michelangelo" serves as a refrain and warning of scene change.

3. Rhyme is used throughout the poem. Some examples of end rhyme: Stanza one uses *I/sky, streets/retreats, hotels/shells, argument/intent, is it/visit.* Lines 41–44 repeat one rhyme, *thin/chin/pin/thin.* Internal rhymes are far fewer but include "decisions and revisions" (line 48), "days and ways" (line 60).

4. Choices will vary. Some probabilities include "When the evening is spread out against the sky / Like a patient etherized upon a table" (lines 2–3); "I have measured out my life with coffee spoons" (line 51); "And when I am . . . sprawling on a pin, / . . . wriggling on the wall" (lines 57–58).

5. Answers will depend on responses to question 4. The figures of speech quoted above use "things" from modern life rather than elements from the world of nature.

Allusions

1. The speaker lives in his own kind of hell.

2. Knowledge of the great painter suggests sophisticated, "cultured" women.

3. There will be a time for philosophical considerations.

4. The speaker feels as if he's been dissected but will never really suffer such a prophet's fate.

5. Would it really matter if one could grasp the meaning of the universe?

6. These blasé people wouldn't be interested even in the observations of someone who came back from the dead.

7. The speaker does not see himself as wrestling with the meaning of existence so profoundly as Hamlet did.

8. The speaker knows how to play up to somebody important.

Extending the Poem

Your students might enjoy discussing a possible historical parallel between modern poetry and rock music. Many early readers of Imagist poetry and free verse were convinced that it was a fad, and a most annoying fad at that. They assumed that such poetry would quickly wither away. Much the same thing happened with rock music. Traditionalists disliked early rock and predicted its rapid demise, but here, too, the critics were wrong. Just as today's poetry shows the continuing influence of Imagism and Symbolism, rock music now dominates the popular music scene. You might want to find out whether your students regard this Imagist/rock parallel as valid.

Wallace Stevens   Text page 768

"The Death of a Soldier"   Text page 770

"Anecdote of the Jar"   Text page 770

Objectives

1. To interpret symbols
2. To recognize the nature of an elegy
3. To write an essay comparing two poems
4. To write a paragraph analyzing a poem's message
5. To determine the precise meanings of words

Introducing the Poems

In these poems students should note the use of symbols to stand for abstract ideas. Autumn, with its falling leaves, might represent falling soldiers; the jar is often seen to stand either for anything made by humans or for art; the wilderness, on the other hand, probably symbolizes untamed nature or possibly, even, chaos. In addition, you might want students to consider the poet's precise word choice to convey possible ambiguous intended meanings.

Background on the Poems. Students may think that literary critics have all the answers and tend to be in general agreement about specific poets and their poems. If so, the following anecdote may enlighten them.

Reviewing *Parts of a World* [1942] by Wallace Stevens ... Horace Gregory raised the question: "Is Mr. Stevens a philosopher? Can we hook ladders to his Prester John's balloon with the hope of landing safely on a terrain peopled by Zeno, ... Socrates, ... William James ... ?" Gregory thought not. "I would go further," he wrote, "and insist that Mr. Stevens is not an intellectual...."

The same week ... Mary Colum reviewed the same volume in *The New York Times Book Review*. "The mind that the author projects into such careful and measured language [she wrote] is the philosophic speculative mind where the passions are of the intellectual ... order." She quoted as representative a short passage ... and said: "It reads a little like a piece of Thomas Aquinas."

The Literal Meanings. "*The Death of a Soldier*": A soldier dies. No pomp is called for; death has no memorial. The autumn wind may stop, but the clouds keep moving. "*Anecdote of the Jar*": The speaker placed a round jar on a hill in Tennessee. The "slovenly wilderness" surrounded the jar, but the jar won out—it "took dominion everywhere."

Teaching Strategies

Providing for Cultural Differences Different cultures place different values on the lives of soldiers and on the encroachment of things human-made on the natural—the subject matter of the two poems by Wallace Stevens. Even in classes without significant cultural differences, you may want to have students discuss these two topics. The United States builds a monument listing the name of every soldier killed in Vietnam. How do other nations and cultures—the North Vietnamese, for example, or the Iranians—memorialize their war dead, if at all? the United States worries about losing its natural environment to rampant development. How do other nations and cultures view such development?

Providing for Different Levels of Ability. The broad ideas in the poems are not hard to grasp, although the poems do permit a range of specific interpretations and speculations. Encourage more advanced students, or ones especially interested in poetry, to read more of Wallace Stevens's poems.

Introducing Vocabulary Study. Knowing the meanings of the following words is important to understanding the poem. (The starred word appears in the Glossary.)

"The Death of a Soldier"
   personage   l. 4

"Anecdote of the Jar"
   slovenly*   l. 3

A vocabulary assignment—"Precise Meanings"—appears on text page 772 under "Analyzing Language and Style."

Reading the Poems. The two Stevens poems can be handled in one class period. Before beginning, you might point out to students that highly symbolic poetry is by that very fact susceptible to more than one interpretation. Symbols can be slippery. There is seldom one "right" answer for what a symbol means. For this reason, it is wise to accept any student's interpretation not absolutely inconsistent with the text of the poem. You will probably want to spend more time on "Anecdote of the Jar" than on "The Death of a Soldier." If students cannot interpret the "jar" as a symbol, tell them that it seems to be a human creation—whatever it may be, leaving the interpretation of the "wilderness" open. There are varying interpretations of "slovenly" as well. In one interpretation, nature is already slovenly; in the other, nature becomes slovenly only after the "jar" is placed there. This difference is important in deciding what the poem "means." Also, have students think about the various literal definitions of the word *jar*. Could its various meanings as a verb ("to be out of harmony" is one meaning) have anything to do with the interpretation of the poem?

Reteaching Alternatives. You might ask two students who have differing interpretations of each poem to debate their ideas informally. If they can find support for their views in the interpretations of critics, that will help bolster their position. A number of critical studies of Stevens's poetry have been published.

"The Death of a Soldier"

Responding to the Poem   Text page 770
Analyzing the Poem
Identifying Details

1. According to the first two lines, what happens in the season of autumn? The speaker says that life contracts, or grows shorter, and death is expected.

2. What is a "three-days personage" (line 4)? Answers may vary. Some students may recall that a typical military term is a "three-day [or weekend] pass," by means of which persons in the armed forces enjoy a brief period of liberty. Others may see the expression as an oblique allusion to the three days between Christ's death on the cross and His resurrection.

288   Imagism and Symbolism

3. This soldier does not impose his "separation" on the world and does not call for "pomp." What other "soldiers" might do so? This question is very much open to individual interpretation. Some students may answer that generals, heroes, and other "important" soldiers might require pomp, such as elaborate funeral services, but that the soldier in this poem gets only anonymity. He may be the "Unknown Soldier" as an abstract ideal.

4. According to lines 8–12, what happens in autumn? According to these lines, the clouds pass through the sky in the direction they were going, even though the wind stops.

Interpreting Meanings

5. How, in a "season of autumn," can life be considered to contract? By analogy with the shortening days and the closing of the year in autumn, life can be said to "contract," or become briefer.

6. What do you think the clouds might symbolize? Answers will vary. The clouds may symbolize continuation of life even though one individual dies. They may symbolize the indifference of the world to the central self. They may symbolize human beings' inevitable mortality. Any reasonable interpretation should be accepted—there is no one answer.

7. Stevens seems to present a human death as no more than an anonymous incident in relation to death's "absolute" force and the indifference of nature. **In what sense may "The Death of a Soldier" be considered an *elegy*? Do you think the poem provides the solace and affirmation that most elegies offer?** Answers may vary. Most students will probably agree that the poem fits the definition of an elegy. Some students may offer the view that the consolation is provided by the speaker's sympathy for the death of the unknown soldier, even as he contrasts his death with those deaths calling for pomp. Others may argue that the continuation of nature, oblivious as it may be to one individual's death, is in itself a form of consolation for the speaker. Urge students to defend and support their opinions.

"Anecdote of the Jar"

Responding to the Poem   Text page 772
Analyzing the Poem
Identifying Details

1. Describe what the speaker does in the first stanza. The speaker places a jar on a hill in Tennessee.

What adjective does the speaker use to describe the jar? The adjective is *round*.

How does he describe the wilderness in which he places the jar? He says the wilderness is "slovenly."

2. In the second stanza, what effect does the jar have on the wilderness? It civilizes or tames the wilderness.

3. What does the jar "take" in stanza 3? What does it *not* give? The jar takes "dominion everywhere": that is, it rules its environment. It does not give "of bird or bush": that is, it has no connection with the untamed wilderness.

Interpreting Meanings

4. How would you paraphrase lines 11–12? Answers will vary. One paraphrase might be this: The jar, unlike anything else in the environment, has no connection with its natural surroundings.

5. The "jar" is, on one level, a ceramic or clay vessel, designed by human ingenuity, and shaped by human hands. By extension, it might *symbolize* anything made or devised by humans. The jar contrasts with what simply arises out of the vast abundance of nature. The "slovenly wilderness," for example, is nature in its raw state, untamed by efforts to turn it into pastures or farmlands, or even parking lots to serve the customers of supermarkets. **What, in your view, is the meaning of the jar's "dominion" over the wilderness (line 9)?** Answers will vary. The "dominion" is all-encompassing (note the word *everywhere* in line 9). It seems to be a civilizing force, but at the same time (perhaps ominously) it poses a constant threat to the world of nature, since it does not "give of bird or bush" (line 11). The speaker's ambivalence is possibly revealed by the adjectives he applies to the jar: *gray* and *bare*. Although the jar may be a symbol of human ingenuity and progress, it may also seem sterile and unappealing when compared to the wilderness.

6. Could the jar symbolize poetry, religion, law, and other human endeavors? Explain your answer with reference to details in the poem. Most students will probably agree that these and other interpretations are possible. The symbols in the poem can only be interpreted, never finally explained.

7. What might the "wilderness" *symbolize*? The wilderness may symbolize nature in its raw, untamed state. If a student believes that the jar represents art, religion, law, or some other codifying human endeavor, then the wilderness could represent something as abstract as "chaos."

8. Do the details in this poem still puzzle you? If so, tell what they are. Considering what you know now about the poem, try to analyze why these details still puzzle you. Answers will vary.

Writing About the Poems
A Critical Response

1. Comparing Poems. Have students review both Melville's "Art" (page 319) and Stevens's "Anecdote of the Jar" before they summarize either poet's views.

Criteria for Evaluating the Assignment. The paragraph or brief essay cites Melville as commenting on the powerful, paradoxical forces that meet and meld in poetry, and Stevens as commenting on the power of poetry to serve as the focal point of everything around it.

2. Analyzing the Poem's Message. Two legitimate interpretations of the poem are given in the writing prompt. You may wish to have students who strongly favor the different views conduct a sort of mini-debate for the class.

Criteria for Evaluating the Assignment. Whether the essay argues that the jar symbolizes the way art gives order and meaning to nature or that the jar symbolizes human interference with nature, cogent reasons and details from the poem are used to support the argument.

Analyzing Language and Style
Precise Meanings

1. *Contracts* means "shrinks, draws together." "Life contracts" suggests a shriveling up as contrasted with death, which is conveyed by "life is extinguished."

2. Answers will vary. Possibilities include *vase, stone, monument,* etc. Another meaning of *jar* is "disharmony."

3. *Slovenly* means "lazily slipshod." It is usually applied to people and therefore does personify nature.

4. *Port* can mean "harbor, haven, gate, door, passageway," or "hole."

Primary Sources: Poetry and Meaning Text page 772

In this excerpt Stevens explains why it is difficult to say what a poem means. You may wish to compare the "man walking" with the literal words of a poem and the "shadow" with the deliberately ambiguous, multiple meanings a poem may imply.

Extending the Poems

Have students discuss the following critical comments about "Anecdote of the Jar" from Susan B. Weston's *Wallace Stevens: An Introduction to the Poetry.*

1. "True, there are allegorical dimensions to the two images, with the jar suggesting man, imagination, and art, and the wilderness suggesting nature, reality, and unordered chaos."

2. "The poem's first line—'I placed a jar'—suggests the importance of the gesture to the speaker: the placing, focusing activity of mind organizing the 'wilderness.'"

3. "In spite of the ease with which we label Stevens' particulars, though, the poems are rarely adequately summed up by a single abstract assertion, for Steven' ambiguous syntax and his titles generally create a richness not apparent at first glance."

Exercises in Critical Thinking and Writing Text page 773

Analyzing a Poem

In this exercise, students are asked to analyze either of two poems, an Imagist poem by Wallace Stevens or a Symbolist poem by Marianne Moore. If time that students can devote to their essays is limited, you might want to narrow the focus of the assignment to one or two of the elements that contribute to the poem's meaning, rather than to all of the elements. During the prewriting stage, you might discuss with students the images of "Disillusionment of Ten O'Clock," pointing out that the words *haunted* and *dream* both indicate that the poem is about the imagination (or lack of it). With "Poetry," you might point out the importance of reading the poem for its literal meaning about the speaker's attitude toward poetry. In fact, she makes statements throughout the poem with which students should readily identify, such as "We do not admire what we do not understand." It might help students to know that the reference to "business documents and school-books" refers to the poet's belief that it is difficult to distinguish between poetry and prose and that "literalists of the imagination" refers to poets such as Yeats who believed that his poetic visions and symbols represented divine ideas that should not be obscured with too much attention to style.

Criteria for Evaluating the Assignment. Students should demonstrate in their essays, through praphrase, that they understand the literal meaning of the poem. In addition, essays should analyze one or more elements significant to the poem by illustrating how that element contributes to the overall meaning and effect of the poem. Finally, students should discuss their affective response to the poem.

Unit Ten: *American Drama*

Text page 775

Teaching the American Drama Unit

The unit introduction covers the principles of drama and the history of American drama thoroughly. Whether you use individual reading, teacher-led discussion, or small-group discussions with the unit material, students should note the following points:

(1) Play-writing differs from other genres of writing in that a play is not finished until the words and gestures the playwright has imagined come to life on stage—a process involving also a director, actors, set and costume designers, stagehands, musicians, and electricians ("The Elements of Drama" introductory paragraph, text page 776).

(2) Good plays make dramatic use of **conflict**, a struggle that has the viewer rooting for someone, usually the **protagonist** (the major character who drives the action). Conflict may be **external** (coming from the side opposing the protagonist) or **internal** (within the protagonist). **Exposition** or the giving of background information must enable the viewer actively to *participate* in the performance ("The Basic Principles of Drama," text pages 776–778).

(3) It is almost a miracle if a new play is produced in the United States today because only Broadway plays earn enough to allow a playwright to remain dedicated to writing, and the route to Broadway is difficult. Involved are the playwright, his or her agent, a producer's ability to raise half a million dollars or more to finance the play, a director, actors, tryouts of the play off Broadway, and finally success—or failure—on Broadway ("How a Play Is Produced," text pages 778–779).

(4) Historically, Eugene O'Neill (1888—1953) is considered the first important American playwright. Before him, American drama consisted of shows, entertainments, melodramas and farces, often presented by touring companies ("The History of American Drama," introductory paragraph, text page 780).

(5) "Drama travels in the caboose of literature" (Robert Sherwood): that is, it is slow to adopt new attitudes and methods, perhaps because drama is a social art: people may stalk out of a theatre when presented with something they would read—even enjoy—in private ("Theatre as a Social Art," text page 781).

(6) European drama, which greatly influenced American drama, matured earlier. Of special importance were the Norwegian Henrik Ibsen (1828–1906), who tackled subjects like guilt, sexuality, and mental illness; the Swede August Strindburg (1849–1912), who brought psychological complexity to his characters; and the Russian Anton Chekhov (1860–1904), who focused on the inner emotions and concerns of daily life ("The Influence of Ibsen, Strindberg, and Chekhov," text page 781).

(7) Early twentieth-century American drama was dominated by **realism**: the illusion that watching a play is looking at life through a missing "fourth wall." Eugene O'Neill tried to reveal more than realism can by experimenting with masks and asides. He was helped by the Provincetown Players in New York's Greenwich Village, who formed in 1916 to produce plays the commercial theatre would not touch. A similar group was the Washington Square Players, formed in 1917 ("American Realism and Eugene O'Neill," text page 782).

(8) The dominant American dramatists since World War II have been Arthur Miller (born 1915) and Tennessee Williams (1911–1983), who combine realism with poetic expression. Miller focuses on society's impact on his character's lives, while Williams probes his characters psychologically. Miller's great plays include *The Death of a Salesman* (1949), *All My Sons* (1947), and *The Crucible* (1953). Williams's include *The Glass Menagerie* (1944), *A Streetcar Named Desire* (1947), and *Summer and Smoke* (1948). ("Arthur Miller and Tennessee Williams," text pages 782–784).

(9) Realism was originally a revolt against mid-nineteenth century theatricalism. There is currently a swing back to **theatricalism**, which emphasizes stage effects and imaginative settings. **Expressionist** (**Theatre of the Absurd**) playwrights aimed not so much to tell a story as to reveal their characters' inner consciousness. They include Samuel Beckett and Eugene Ionesco of Europe, and the American, Edward Albee (born 1928). Thanks to such experimental drama, playwrights now have considerable freedom ("The Revolt Against Realism," text pages 784–785).

*O*bjectives of the American Drama Unit

1. To improve reading proficiency and expand vocabulary
2. To gain exposure to two notable playwrights and one of each of their plays
3. To define and identify the elements of drama
4. To define and identify significant literary techniques
5. To interpret and respond to drama, orally and in writing, through analysis of its elements

6. To practice the following critical thinking and writing skills:
   a. Responding to conflict
   b. Responding to "biographical criticism"
   c. Evaluating versions of a play
   d. Analyzing the use of light
   e. Comparing a play with memoirs
   f. Predicting a character's development
   g. Evaluating a play

Tennessee Williams

Text page 786

The Glass Menagerie

Text page 787

Objectives

1. To recognize dramatic situation
2. To evaluate the use of suspense
3. To analyze the use of basic dramatic elements
4. To discuss symbolism
5. To write an imaginary letter written by a character
6. To write an essay responding to the play's conflict
7. To write an essay responding to the "biographical criticism"
8. To evaluate different versions of the play
9. To write an essay analyzing the use of light
10. To write an essay comparing the play to the memoirs

Introducing the Play

The major elements of the play are listed here in outline form, for your reference. Note that a case can be made, however, for *either* Amanda, Tom, or Laura as **protagonist**.

- **Protagonist:** Amanda Wingfield
- **Antagonist:** Tom Wingfield
- **Conflicts:** person vs. person; internal
- **Significant techniques:** episodic ("memory") structure, symbolism
- **Setting:** tenement apartment, Midwestern city (St. Louis, MO) in the Depression era of the early 1930's
- **Theme:** illusion versus reality

Background on the Playwright. Williams was born March 26, 1911, as Thomas Lanier Williams, in the rectory of his grandfather's Episcopal church in Columbus, Mississippi. Both of his parents—Edwina Dakins and Cornelius Coffin Williams—came from proud American lineages. Because Cornelius traveled for the phone company, young Tom, his mother, and his sister, Rose (two years his senior), lived with Edwina's parents in a warm, genteel environment rich in status ("the minister's family") if not wealth. A darker element was Tom's childhood case of diphtheria which led to eye and kidney problems, delicate treatment as a child, and life-long hypochondria.

In 1919 Tom, Edwina, and Rose moved to St. Louis to join Cornelius, promoted to a settlement management position with the International Shoe Company. Relocation to a noisy industrial town where other children (and their own father) ridiculed their accents and quiet ways devastated the shy Tom and Rose. Meanwhile Edwina was often ill after the birth of another son, Dakin, in 1919; and Cornelius's unsettled behavior pattern led to violent arguments. The family also moved repeatedly (Tom had lived in 16 places by age 15), Edwina constantly seeking a properly "aristocratic" home.

Tom reacted to a traumatic environment by turning to an imaginative inner life—he graduated 53rd in a high school class of 83. But his grandparents and father sent him to the University of Missouri at Columbia, noted for journalism and obligatory ROTC training. Classmates found the slim, five-foot-six-inch Tom shy, but enjoyed his wit and good humor, and ribbed him about the absentmindedness arising from his preoccupation with writing. Again, however, Tom let his grades slide. After three years, his father cited Tom's *F*'s in ROTC as a reason to pull him out of college (the real reason appears to have been money).

During the next two or three years Tom worked for the shoe company, days, and wrote feverishly, nights. Meanwhile his beloved sister Rose, who had already been institutionalized twice, grew more and more emotionally unbalanced. But it was Tom who collapsed—from too little sleep, too much smoking and caffeine, and turmoil about personal feelings he could not yet handle. He recuperated rapidly with his grandparents (then in Memphis), and began to view himself as a new kind of Williams—one that flourished in Tennessee.

After a brief stint at Washington University in St. Louis, Tom was associated with a writing group at the State University of Iowa by the time his parents solved Rose's problems by means of a prefrontal lobotomy—an irreversible operation that left her calm but irrational the rest of her life. Tom finally earned his B.A. and left college in 1938, but the horror of his sister's fate never left him. He devotedly visited her and saw to her needs all his life.

For *Tennessee* Williams, as Tom renamed himself, the next six years were a precarious mix of odd jobs, small writing prizes, little-theatre productions of a few plays, and itinerant movement—New Orleans, southern California, Mexico, New York. A cataract on his left eye (he later had four surgeries) kept him out of World War II.

Background on the Play. Williams's first professionally produced play, *Battle of Angels* (1940), was not a success, but a six months' screenwriting job in the MGM movie mill enabled him to complete *The Gentleman Caller*, soon retitled *The Glass Menagerie* (1944)—his first success. Surprisingly, critics kept the play alive in its three-month Chicago debut, and its longer New York run established, at age 34, Williams's name and fortune. As the noted critic Brooks Atkinson observed, *The Glass Menagerie* glowed with "pity for people, coolness of perspective [and] poetic grace." Other successes followed, notably, *A Streetcar Named Desire* (1947), *Summer and Smoke* (1948), *Cat on A Hot Tin Roof* (1955) and *The Night of the Iguana* (1961), all of which were also filmed. But as biographer Donald Spoto notes, "... nothing Tennessee Williams ever wrote after *The Glass Menagerie* has its wholeness of sentiment, its breadth of spirit and its unangry, quiet voice about the great reach of small lives." A 1980 recipient of the highest American civilian honor, the Medal of Freedom, Williams remains the foremost American dramatist of the post-World War II era.

Summary. *Scenes 1 and 2.* Amanda Wingfield fantasizes that her daughter, Laura, will one day have a normal life despite her leg brace and her having quit her business classes out of inability to cope. *Scenes 3 and 4.* Amanda's son Tom dreams of leaving home, and escapes his troubles by going to the movies every night. Tom appeases Amanda by agreeing to bring a friend home from work. *Scenes 5 and 6.* Amanda is excited about Jim O'Connor's coming, but when Laura realizes he is the same Jim O'Connor she admired in high school, she gets sick and hides in the other room. *Scene 7.* Jim treats Laura so gently she opens up enough to try to waltz. She gives Jim the glass unicorn accidentally broken in their clumsy dance; he apologizes for being unable to come again because he is engaged. Amanda furiously accuses Tom of deliberately choosing an ineligible caller, and he leaves home, always to remember his sister's uncertain future.

Teaching Strategies

Providing for Cultural Differences. The "Southern belle" concept that figures strongly in the characterization of Amanda may need explanation—a genteel way of life where the social graces and hospitality are of the utmost importance, social life revolves around the front parlor, and young men and women play elaborate flirtation games conducted with exquisite politeness.

Providing for Different Levels of Ability. Vocabulary should be studied before each set of scenes. Complete the response questions on each set of scenes before moving on.

Introducing Vocabulary Study. Knowing the meanings of the words listed below is important to understanding the play. (Starred words appear in the Glossary. *Italicized* words are defined in text notes.)

Scenes 1 and 2 (Pages 788–795)

automatism*	788	interfused*	788
beaux	791	mastication	790
blanc mange	790	matriculating	789
cloche	792	murky*	788
conglomerations*	788	paranoia	788
emissary*	790	*portieres*	788
fluidity*	788	symptomatic*	788
implacable*	788	tenement*	788
ineluctably	788	vivacity*	795

Scenes 3 and 4 (Pages 796–803)

aghast*	798	preoccupied*	796
averted*	798	querulous	801
fiasco*	796	sublimations	796
motley*	799	turgid*	797

Scenes 5 and 6 (Pages 804–814)

cotillion	809	*paragon*	812
emulate	804	supercilious	806
incandescent	811	translucent*	808

Scene 7 (Pages 815–826)

indolently	818

Reading the Play. You might want to assign parts to your best readers and read the play aloud. Group Scenes 1 and 2, 3 and 4, and 5 and 6. Take Scene 7 by itself. (If you have many good readers, you may wish to assign alternate casts for different sets of scenes.) Briefly check comprehension of each set of scenes before moving on. After correcting misconceptions, begin to discuss the response questions

Tennessee Williams 293

from the text or assign them as homework. At the beginning of the next class period, briefly discuss this work before continuing the play.

Reading Check. You may wish to use the following questions to check literal comprehension of each set of scenes. Have the students respond *True* or *False*.

Scenes 1 and 3

1. Tom and Laura's father will be home soon. __False__
2. Amanda delights in talking about her popularity in her youth. __True__
3. Laura is doing well in typing and shorthand. __False__
4. The nickname "Blue Roses" comes from "pleurosis." __True__
5. Laura is crippled and sensitive about it. __True__

Scenes 3 and 4

1. Amanda sells magazine subscriptions by telephone. __True__
2. Tom escapes his troubles by going to the movies. __True__
3. Amanda angrily breaks Laura's glass ornaments. __False__
4. Amanda nags Tom to provide for Laura's future. __True__
5. Amanda praises Tom for his totally unselfish concern for her needs and Laura's. __False__

Scenes 5 and 6

1. Tom realizes that Laura lives in a world of her own. __True__
2. Amanda tells Laura to wish upon the moon for a job. __False__
3. Jim O'Connor has not achieved the greatness that his high school achievements seemed to promise. __True__
4. Tom thanks Jim for his warning and promises to buckle down and take his job seriously. __False__
5. Laura is too nervous and sick to eat dinner. __True__

Scene 7

1. The reason Amanda first lights a candle is that she finds candles more romantic than electric lights. __False__
2. Jim treats Laura with kindness and consideration. __True__
3. Attempting to dance, Jim and Laura knock down a shelf of Laura's glass ornaments. __False__
4. Jim kisses Laura but apologizes for doing so. __True__
5. Amanda accuses Tom of deliberately tricking her by bringing home an engaged man. __True__

Reteaching Alternatives. If possible, audio- or videotape the in-class reading of the play. Use this tape to help students interpret the play as they follow in their texts.

Responding to the Play   Text page 795
Analyzing Scenes 1 and 2
Identifying Facts

1. Tom's opening speech sketches the social background of the play and introduces the main characters. What basic information does Tom provide in this speech about his family? About the gentleman caller? About the nature of the play itself? Tom tells us that his family is "set apart" from the real world; that the gentleman caller who appears in the final scenes is an "emissary" from the real world; that his father abandoned his family a long time ago. Tom says that the play is a memory play, that it is sentimental and not realistic, and that—despite the "pleasant disguise of illusion"—the play deals with the truth.

2. In Scene 1, how do we know that there is tension among the family members? Who seems to cause the tension? Amanda is the cause of the tension. She nags Tom, criticizing the way he eats and the fact that he smokes too much; she tells her son that he is "not excused from this table." Amanda glorifies and romanticizes her youth in a way that irritates Tom, for she has told the same stories dozens of times. She keeps talking about Laura's gentleman callers as if they were a reality, when she knows that no callers are coming—and we can guess that this must upset her daughter.

3. A play is put in motion by some element that upsets the situation at the beginning of the story. The new element here arrives in Scene 2. What is it? How does it upset the opening situation, and how does it set the play in motion? Amanda discovers that Laura has not been attending her classes at the business school. The opening situation is upset because in it Amanda believes that Laura will be able to get a job and to take care of herself in the future. Because Amanda realizes that this is no longer likely, she vows to find a nice young man for Laura to marry, and it is this search for the gentleman caller that sets the action in motion.

4. In Scene 2, what does Laura say and do to reveal that she is "set apart" from the real world? Laura is painfully shy, so much so that she throws up on her first day at business school and never returns. She escapes the real world by spending her days in the art museum, at the zoo, at the movies, and at the tropical flower house. She seems to have no sense of the need to find a way to earn money in order to support herself and to help support the family. Also, she makes no attempt to establish relationships with

294   American Drama

people outside her home. She seems satisfied with an "odd" way of life, and she makes no attempt to change it.

5. What is the significance of the "blue roses" that appear on the screen at the start of Scene 2? "Blue Roses" is the nickname Jim gave to Laura when they were in high school.

Interpreting Meanings

6. At this point in the play, does Amanda seem to be a weak or a strong character? Student responses will vary, but most will view Amanda as a strong character, intent on dominating her adult children.

Does she arouse your sympathy, or do you think Williams wants you to dislike her? Explain. Again, student answers may vary. In Scene 1, Amanda seems pitiful and boastful, living in the past; however, she is also annoying and irritating. In Scene 2, she seems more sympathetic, momentarily "beaten" by life. We see her caught in bitter circumstances; she seems to be doing her best to cope.

7. How do we know that the boy in the yearbook was important to Laura? Laura has already shown herself to be painfully shy; she lives a completely isolated life, except for her relationship with her family. But she keeps her yearbook with Jim's picture underneath her glass menagerie, which is her most precious possession, and she speaks warmly of Jim and his accomplishments. Laura's talk about Jim, in fact, shows her at her liveliest thus far in the play.

Why doesn't Amanda seem particularly interested in this young man? Amanda loses interest in Jim when she finds out that he was only a slight acquaintance of Laura's and that he is not a potential gentleman caller, since he is probably married.

8. In *The Glass Menagerie*, Tennessee Williams has created "theater poetry" by using various arts besides language. For example, he used the two transparencies at the beginning of the play to enhance the idea that this is a memory play. Check through the stage directions and dialogue to find other uses of visual and sound effects which, combined with words, help to create "theater poetry." The scenes are dimly lighted; the picture of the father on the living room wall is referred to and spotlighted. Laura plays old records on the phonograph and escapes to the glass menagerie; the typing table, the typewriter, and the typewriter chart represents Amanda's goal for Laura—a goal that Laura rejects.

Do any of these effects add a touch of humor to the play? The screen image of "blue roses," which we find out was Jim's misunderstanding of "pleurosis" is both poignant and humorous.

9. Few people have Laura's specific physical handicap. Do you think most people can identify with her? Why or why not? Student answers will vary. But most students will agree that Laura's shyness makes her easy to identify with, since most people have experienced shyness at one point or other in their lives.

Analyzing Scenes 3 and 4 Text page 803
Identifying Facts

1. In Scene 2, we saw that Amanda was in *conflict* with Laura. Who is in conflict in Scene 3? The conflict is between Amanda and Tom.

What starts the conflict, and what is it about? Amanda begins nagging Tom about the lighting and about sitting up straight. Just as in the scene at the dinner table, she chides Tom as if he were a child. Despite repeated reminders from Tom and from Laura that Tom is trying to write, nothing stops Amanda. Tom explodes in anger, accuses her of confiscating his library books, and ends by calling her an "ugly babbling old witch." Amanda accuses Tom of being impudent, of jeopardizing his job and their security by getting too little sleep, and of lying about where he goes at night.

2. Each of the Wingfields escapes from unpleasant reality into a comforting, private world. In Scene 1, Amanda escapes from her present circumstances by remembering and talking about her past youth, her beauty, and her romantic successes. How does Laura escape the real world? Laura escapes by polishing her glass menagerie, by listening to old phonograph records, and by visiting the zoo, the art museum, and the plant house.

What does Tom do to escape from his unhappiness? Tom uses movies and drinking as his means of escape. Presumably, he also escapes through his writing, but so far we have no indication of how serious a writer he is, or of how much time he spends writing.

3. What part does Laura play in the angry argument between Tom and Amanda? Laura has only two lines in this scene and plays no part in the argument. Her first line occurs at the beginning of the scene when she cautions Amanda not to bother Tom because he is trying to write. Her second line, at the end of the scene, expresses her grief at the breaking of the glass animals.

4. What does Amanda ask Tom to do? Amanda asks Tom to find a nice young man for Laura.

Tennessee Williams

Interpreting Meanings

5. In the conflict between Tom and Amanda in Scene 3, which character do you sympathize with, and why? What does Williams want us to feel about Amanda? Most students will agree that our sympathies are with Tom. Amanda is offensive in treating Tom like a small child, and she is annoyingly intrusive when he is trying to write. Even when Tom asks her politely to stop interrupting, she does not let up. We cannot, however, feel that Amanda is evil or despicable, since she does her best to cope with her difficult life and has obviously succeeded in raising her children to adulthood. Also, her nagging of Tom and the plans she makes for Laura are motivated by a desire for her children's well-being.

6. How is Laura's relationship with Tom different from her relationship with Amanda? Laura is at ease with Tom, and not afraid of what he will say or do. Unlike Amanda, Laura trusts Tom and believes his stories about where he has been. Also, she seems considerate of Tom's needs (cautioning Amanda that he is trying to write), and she is not harshly judgmental of his actions. Toward Amanda, on the other hand, Laura seems dependent and fearful.

How can we tell that Tom is truly fond of Laura? The moment at the end of Scene 3, when Tom accidentally smashes Laura's glass collection, reveals Tom's depth of feeling for Laura.

7. Amanda often refers to her absent husband, and his grinning picture is highlighted at various points during the play. What does the photograph represent to Amanda? To Tom? To Amanda, the photo is a constant reminder of the wrong choice she made for a husband—when she might have had so many other successful men. The photo reminds Amanda, as well, of the reason for her finding herself in such difficult circumstances—her husband abandoned her and the children. Tom is surely angry at his father, because if the father had not abandoned the family, Tom would not be trapped as he is. The photo is also a constant reminder to Tom of what seems to be the only way out of his "trap": abandoning the family.

How is the photo a constant threat to Amanda and Laura's survival? The possibility of Tom's leaving—just like his father—constitutes a threat to the survival of Amanda and Laura, for the family is barely surviving with Tom's salary.

8. The outburst of anger that ends Scene 3 marks the emotional peak of the play so far. How has the playwright prepared us for Tom's anger and Amanda's accusations? In Scene 1, the bickering between Tom and Amanda has prepared us for conflict and tension between them, although in the opening scene this tension is on a low emotional level. Scene 1 also shows us Amanda treating Tom as if he were a child, which she also does at the beginning of Scene 3. Scene 2 also helps us to understand Amanda's anxiety about the future—her worries about who will provide for Laura and for herself.

Analyzing Scenes 5 and 6   Text page 814
Identifying Facts

1. In Scene 5, Tom displays an attitude toward his mother that we have not seen before. Describe that attitude, and find the lines of dialogue that reveal it. Tom is sympathetic and patient. The stage directions instruct him to speak gently at the beginning of the scene, and he shows patience in response to the same type of nagging that he found so annoying in Scenes 1 and 3.

Cite two lines of dialogue from this scene that show that Amanda is also trying to behave differently toward Tom. Amanda tries to show approval: "You just keep on trying and you're bound to succeed"; "Both my children are—they're very precious children and I've got a lot to be thankful for." She tries to keep the peace: "I—I'm not criticizing, understand that!" She is more honest with Tom than we have ever seen her: about loving his father and about her fears for Laura and her understanding of Tom's desire to join the Merchant Marine.

2. What does Amanda ask Tom to do at the end of this scene? She asks him to bring home from the warehouse a gentleman caller for Laura.

3. In Scene 6, we hear that the much-talked-about gentleman caller is finally about to arrive. Before we meet him, what information does Tom give us about him? He is a shipping clerk at Tom's warehouse and earns about eighty-five dollars a month. His name is James D. O'Connor, and he goes to night school to study public speaking and radio engineering. He is not especially handsome, according to Tom.

How does Amanda react to this new information about the gentleman caller? She is very excited, but also upset that the gentleman caller is coming so soon. She makes plans about how to fix up the house. She also seems to assume that the gentleman caller will fall in love with Laura and will marry her.

4. In Scene 5, Tom gives his mother two realistic warnings to counter Amanda's pleasant fantasy of the gentleman caller. What are these warnings? How does Amanda react to them? Tom tells Amanda that a lot of boys meet girls whom they don't marry. He also reminds Amanda that Laura is crippled and very different from other girls—even peculiar. Amanda does not even respond to Tom's first warning; she complains that he can never stick

296   American Drama

to a subject. And she completely denies, as we have seen her do earlier in the play, that Laura is crippled. She tells Tom not to refer to Laura as peculiar, but she does not respond when he defines exactly how she is peculiar.

5. How does Amanda transform herself for the gentleman caller? Amanda transforms herself with a ball dress, resurrected from the days of her youth.

How is her attitude about their guest different from Laura's? Amanda joyfully, but somewhat unrealistically, looks forward to the gentleman caller's visit as the start of a campaign to get Laura married. Laura is nervous and shy.

6. What is Laura's reaction when she learns the identity of the gentleman caller? She is acutely embarrassed and says she will not come to the table.

How does Amanda respond to this reaction? Amanda reacts sternly, saying that Laura will not be excused.

Interpreting Meanings

7. At the beginning of Scene 5, both Tom and Amanda try to make peace. Why do they begin to argue again? Amanda cannot seem to stop her nagging—about going to the movies—and her criticism of Tom. Amanda means to ask Tom to bring home a friend for dinner (a gentleman caller), but before she gets to that, she accuses Tom of selfishness, and he becomes very angry. The reader and the audience have the feeling that Amanda's accusations have been repeated many times before.

8. The basic *dramatic situation* from which a play can grow involves a person or persons whom we care about, who are in more or less desperate situations with a great deal at stake. Such characters decide to act and then actually take steps to achieve their "wants." Discuss how these dramatic elements are used up to this point in *The Glass Menagerie*. Amanda feels desperate because Laura cannot take care of herself, and she realizes that Tom wants to leave them to join the Merchant Marine. Without Tom's salary, she and Laura will not be able to survive, so Amanda takes steps to get Laura married. Tom is equally desperate—to leave the family and his job in the warehouse. He wants adventure, but so far the only step he has taken to achieve his desire is to receive a letter from the Merchant Marine. Laura does not seem desperate; she only wants to be left alone.

9. In most plays, suspense is preferable to surprise. If we reach the top of a hill and look down to see two trains at the moment they crash, it is a *surprise* and it is shocking. But dramatically, it would be more effective if, as we neared the top of the hill, we saw the trains approaching each other on the same track from perhaps a mile apart. This would be *suspense*: we are very anxious about what will happen next. How has Tennessee Williams used suspense in the play up to now? Williams uses suspense as he carefully, almost logically, prepares us for the arrival of the gentleman caller. This motif is first referred to in Tom's opening speech as narrator. Scene 1 (Amanda's reminiscences of seventeen gentleman callers), Scene 2 (Amanda's conclusion that only marriage will do for Laura), Tom's speech as the narrator at the opening of Scene 3, and his angry reference to Amanda's gentleman callers at the end of that scene—all of these keep the theme or motif of the gentleman caller constantly before us. Although we know that a gentleman caller will arrive, we don't know who he will be, what he'll be like, why he will come, or what will happen between him and Laura. All of these still unanswered questions create suspense.

10. We have seen that Amanda is a complex *character*—not easily described as either "good" or "bad." What aspect of her character do we see in Scene 6? Do you feel sympathetic toward her? Explain. Amanda seems sympathetic in this scene. When she figures out that Tom could save $4.50 a month by not smoking, she graciously admits that that "wouldn't be very much." In this scene, Amanda also seems to show a sincere wish for her children's happiness. She is probably more likeable here than at any other time so far in the play.

11. What are your feelings for the gentleman caller at this point in the play? Most students will probably react sympathetically to Jim, since he is walking into a situation that he knows little about.

How do you feel about Tom? Student answers will vary.

Analyzing Scene 7   Text page 827
Identifying Facts

1. What does Williams achieve in the way of "theater poetry" by having Tom neglect to pay the light bill? The lights go out at the beginning of Scene 7, so that the long scene with the gentleman caller is acted by candlelight. This gives a mysterious, romantic air to the scene, and it also creates the opportunity for a powerful ending for the play—as Laura blows the candles out, perhaps symbolically suggesting the end to a very special day (like a birthday), or perhaps hinting at the extinction of any hopes Tom (and we) may have cherished for Laura's happiness.

2. What happens to make us think at first that Jim O'Connor's visit may work out as Amanda hopes? Jim is charming and honest with Laura. He seems to understand her feelings and not think of her as "peculiar." He gets Laura to relax and to talk. They dance and kiss, and it seems for a moment as if a romance might be possible.

Explain how the evening ends in disappointment for Laura and Amanda. Jim tells Laura and Amanda about his engagement to Betty, and says he can never come back again.

Interpreting Meanings

3. The gentleman-caller scene is a perfect little play within a play. Tell how the *basic dramatic elements* are used in this scene: characters we care about, placed in a situation where much is at stake, taking steps to get what they want. What we hope for in this scene is that there will be a romance between Jim and Laura. Certainly, much is at stake—Laura's whole future. Jim is the only man she ever liked, and suddenly, by coincidence, he turns up at her house—unaware that Amanda has planned for her to "trap" him. At the beginning of Scene 7, Laura is lying on the daybed, sick with nervousness. She is shy and apprehensive as Jim brings her the glass of wine, but she begins to relax as she talks to him, even telling him of her admiration for him in high school. Laura accepts a stick of gum, shares some painful memories, and listens to his advice. Most of all, she remains—she does not run away. She dances, they kiss: our hopes are at their highest. Suddenly, there is a reversal when Jim announces his engagement to Betty. Laura is disappointed, gives Jim the unicorn, and retreats to her menagerie. Amanda is told the bad news, and Jim leaves. In anger, Amanda lashes out at Tom for playing such a trick on them, and then Tom leaves. Things have, indeed, turned out badly.

4. One of the basic elements of drama is *progression*, or change. Trace the progression of the relationship between Jim and Laura in this scene. Laura is shy and apprehensive when Jim arrives, but little by little his charm succeeds in thawing her reserve. She shares memories with him and listens to his advice. We can see that she is romantically attracted to him when they dance. But Jim's announcement of his engagement shatters our (and Laura's) hopes.

5. How did you feel about Jim O'Connor in this scene? Student answers will vary. Jim is obviously a confident extrovert, and he gives the introverted, shy Laura good advice about improving her self-confidence. He is open, polite, and unaffected, and many students will agree that he is likeable. Others may criticize Jim as rather unimaginative, at least compared to the other characters. He also seems somewhat materialistic and self-satisfied.

6. Why does Laura say about the broken horn on the unicorn: "Maybe it's a blessing in disguise"? In this statement, perhaps Laura is speculating that the loss of the horn, which differentiated the unicorn from the other animals, has made the creature more "normal"—symbolizing, in turn, Laura's own hopes to become less painfully shy and more like other people.

7. What does Tom mean at the end when he talks about Laura blowing out her candles? The statement is ambiguous: it might refer to the end of a special day, or it might signal the end of Laura's hopes for a normal life.

The Play as a Whole

1. Williams has written of his own sister's collection of glass animals:
> By poetic association they came to represent, in my memory, all the softest emotions that belong to recollection of things past. They stood for all the small and tender things that relieve the austere pattern of life and make it endurable to the sensitive.—Tennessee Williams

Discuss the *symbolism* of the glass menagerie in relation to Laura. How, for example, does Laura resemble the glass animals? From our impressions of Laura in the opening scene, we can say that she resembles the glass animals in that she is shy, fragile, and easily hurt; she is also naive and innocent. At the beginning of Scene 6, she is transformed into a pretty young woman. The stage directions says that she "... is like a piece of translucent glass touched by light, given a momentary radiance, not actual, not lasting." This description suggestively foreshadows the outcome of the play.

What does the unicorn represent at first, and what does it represent once its horn has been broken? Like Laura, the unicorn is different from all the others around it. Laura tells Jim that the unicorn is her favorite animal—thus implying an awareness on her own part that she is "set apart" from the rest of the world. Like Laura herself, the unicorn is a fantasy animal, living in a fantasy world. But once the unicorn's horn is broken, it becomes like all the other animals. Paradoxically, Laura does not grieve at Jim's accidental breaking of the horn; she seems to recognize that Jim may have been the means of restoring her (and the unicorn) to "normalcy." By giving the unicorn to Jim as a souvenir, Laura implicitly entrusts him with her favorite possession, as well as—symbolically—with herself.

2. Discuss the way Williams uses the following motifs or props in the play as *symbols*. What does each one represent? How do they relate to the play's theme?

The movies symbolize escape from painful reality for Tom.

The fire escape is also an escape for Tom: this is where he goes to smoke.

The Paradise Music Hall symbolizes romance and adventure for Tom, as he recalls hearing the music from across the alley and seeing young couples kiss.

Laura's leg brace is a visible reminder of her physical handicap and, therefore, of her "difference" from others.

3. **Why do you think Williams chose the line from Cummings's poem (see page 787) to open his play?** The epigraph from Cummings underlines the pathos and fragility of Laura's world.

4. **The *climax* of a play is the high point of the story—its most intensely emotional moment. What scene do you think marks the climax of *The Glass Menagerie*?** Students should agree that Scene 7 marks the play's climax. We have two reasons to hope that Jim will fall in love with Laura. One is Amanda's intense wish to have Laura married to a "nice young man." The other, quite separate wish is Laura's own. Jim is the only man she has ever cared about, and she has never before expressed her feelings to him. She does so in this scene, and he seems to respond—with a dance, a kiss—until suddenly our hopes, and Laura's, are dashed with the announcement of his engagement. Jim seems, on balance, a likeable character. He is honest, caring, sincere, willing to help, on the right track for getting ahead—although some observant students may question how well such a practical temperament as his would have meshed with Laura's dreamy, romantic outlook on life.

5. **In any story, complexity makes for interesting characters. In good drama, we rarely find a "good guy" pitted against a "bad guy"; the best drama often occurs when both people in a conflict are right. Do you sympathize with Amanda, even though she causes her children to suffer?** We sympathize with Amanda, above all, because she wants her children to be happy. She wants Laura to have a normal life and to be well taken care of, and she wants Tom to have ambition and a better life (the night school course in accounting). Amanda also fears that Tom will take to drink as an escape, and she doesn't want that. Because of her own experiences as an abandoned wife living in poverty, Amanda knows about life's difficult realities. She has coped as best she could—selling magazines, working in a department store—to support the family. It is her fear of poverty, alcoholism, and dependence that causes her to establish goals for her children that are not theirs. Amanda manages to save enough money for Laura's business course, and we admire her for her ability to cope and survive. At the end of the play, Williams says that Amanda has "dignity and tragic beauty," and that is why we sympathize with her.

Do you think Tom and Laura are both "wrong" and "right"? Explain your responses. Tom wants to write and to see the world—goals that are understandable and perfectly acceptable. But he is "wrong" because in order to achieve his goals he must abandon his mother and his sister. Laura wants peace in the household, and she also wants to be left alone. For a brief moment at the end of the play, she also appears to want a relationship with Jim. But she is "wrong" because she has not taken responsibility for her own life. She needs to find a way to support herself and to be with people—or she is destined to be dependent. Her decision to withdraw completely from life outside the household makes her seem emotionally ill.

6. **One critic has said that *The Glass Menagerie* shows us a series of contrasts between (a) the dreamer and the doer, (b) the past and the present, (c) fantasy and reality, (d) psychological and physical handicaps, and (e) the desire for escape and the awareness of responsibilities. Choose one of these contrasts, and trace the way it's developed in the play.** Student answers will vary, depending on which contrast students select. Urge them to illustrate their analysis thoroughly, with specific references to the play.

7. **Williams keeps indicating that music called "The Glass Menagerie" is heard. Locate the places in the play where the music is called for. Discuss in a group the kind of music you think should be provided. If there are musicians in your class, they might compose "The Glass Menagerie" music.** Student answers will vary.

Writing About the Play

The six writing assignments differ in the critical thinking and writing skills demanded of the student. All should, therefore, be discussed, even if students write only one or two of the essays. Topics 3 and 6 are the most similar, in that both use biographical data, but even with these two topics, only the first analyzes the relevance of biographical information to a literary work.

A Creative Response

1. **Extending the Play.** Discuss the probable contents of such a letter—Laura's and Amanda's feelings? their household worries? appearance of some new benefactor? concerns about Tom?—but allow students to choose contents that seem most appropriate to them.

Criteria for Evaluating the Assignment. Whatever the letter's contents, it echoes Laura's attitudes and phrasing, and at least hints at the home situation without Tom.

A Critical Response

2. **Responding to the Play.** This topic centers on an internal conflict faced not only by Tom, but also by many grown children. Plausible arguments can be made for either side of the issue. Note that students should both discuss the issue in general, and state whether they believe Tom was right or wrong in leaving for the Merchant Marine.

Criteria for Evaluating the Assignment. Whatever

Tennessee Williams 299

stance is taken, the student offers cogent reasons or arguments in favor of the stance, and judges the rightness or wrongness of Tom's action in a manner consistent with the stance.

3. Commenting on "Biographical Criticism." Read and discuss Brendan Gill's remarks and the entire writing prompt, clarifying the dual issue: Is such biographical criticism *necessary*? Is it *helpful*? With your guidance, students should come to see that a work of art is an entity understandably apart from the author's life. Nevertheless, one's enjoyment or appreciation of a work can be enhanced by awareness of events in an author's life.

Criteria for Evaluating the Assignment. The essay clearly states the student's opinion on both the *necessity* and the *helpfulness* of biographical criticism. These opinions are clarified by references to Tennessee Williams and *The Glass Menagerie*, *or* to the lives and works of other authors.

4. Evaluating Different Versions of the Play. You may wish first to elicit from the class explicit statements of the theme and mood of the play, and then focus discussion on how theme and mood would change if Laura's emergence from her fragile world were *not* left in doubt, or if the narrative lines spoken by Tom, in uniform, were omitted.

Criteria for Evaluating the Assignment. The essay shows a grasp of the **theme** and **mood** of the play in (1) its statement of opinion on the film ending (Laura happily preparing for another caller), (2) its statement of opinion on the 1973 television changes (nearly entire omission of Tom's speeches), and (3) its explanation of how *each* set of changes affects theme and mood.

5. Describing the Use of Lights. Discuss a few of Williams's explicit comments on lighting (for example, pages 790, column 1; 796, column 2; and 797, column 1), and have students locate and analyze additional examples before they begin to write.

Criteria for Evaluating the Assignment. The essay cites specific passages from the play to support its explanation of how lighting *creates mood* and *contributes to the theme of illusion versus reality*.

6. Comparing the Play to the Memoirs. Have students read "Primary Source: The Model for Laura" (page 829), and discuss it as a class or in small groups before they fill out the information chart suggested in the writing prompt.

Criteria for Evaluating the Assignment. The essay identifies similarities in *characters*, *setting*, and *conflict* between Williams's play and his memoirs on himself and his sister Rose. The essay cites specific details to support its points.

Extending the Play

Consider having students research and report on the life of Tennessee Williams and his importance to American drama (see reading list) or read another famous American play and compare and contrast it with *The Glass Menagerie*.

Students who are musically inclined may wish to prepare the tape of "background music" for selected scenes, play the tape for the class, and explain their rationale.

You may wish to have students compare and contrast a movie version of the play with the printed version. (The 1950 movie, which changes the ending, stars Jane Wyman, Kirk Douglas, Gertrude Lawrence, and Arthur Kennedy; the 1987 version, which omits some of Tom's narration, features Joanne Woodward, John Malkovich, Karen Allen, and James Naughton.)

Students might also read and/or view another prize-winning Williams play: (1) *A Streetcar Named Desire* (Pulitzer Prize, 1947)—a 1951 movie with Vivien Leigh as Blanche DuBois, and Marlon Brando as Stanley Kowalski; a 1984 TV movie with Ann-Margaret as Blanche. (2) *Cat on a Hot Tin Roof* (Pulitzer Prize, 1955)—a 1958 movie with Burl Ives, Elizabeth Taylor, Paul Newman, and Judith Anderson.

A Reading List

Harry Rasky, *Tennessee Williams: A Portrait in Laughter and Lamentation* (1986). A perceptive account of Williams's life, works, attitudes and beliefs, built upon the Canadian filmmaker's interviews with Williams in 1972 and ten years' subsequent acquaintance. Photos.

Donald Spoto, *The Kindness of Strangers: The Life of Tennessee Williams* (1985). A thorough, well-documented, well-balanced biography. Photos.

Tennessee Williams, *Memoirs* (1972, 1975). Many photos. Disorganized impressions of family and friends.

A Viewing List

The filmed plays of Tennessee Williams noted above.

Tennessee Williams's South. A 90-minute documentary by Harry Rasky, first aired by the Canadian Broadcasting Corporation March 26, 1973. Definitive presentation on Williams's life, works, attitudes, and beliefs, combining conversations, scenes from his plays reenacted by high-calibre actors, and Williams's readings of some of his own work. Williams said of this film, "Let this be my epitaph!"

Lorraine Hansberry

Text page 830

A Raisin in the Sun

Text page 831

Objectives

1. To identify conflicts
2. To recognize revelation of character through actions
3. To analyze reversals
4. To interpret symbols
5. To identify dynamic and static characters
6. To analyze theme
7. To discuss the use of suspense
8. To write an essay projecting a character's development
9. To write an essay evaluating the play

Introducing the Play

These are the major elements of the play, in outline form, for your reference:

- **Protagonist:** Lena (Mama) Younger
- **Antagonist:** Walter Lee Younger
- **Conflicts:** person vs. person; internal
- **Significant techniques:** foreshadowing and reversals
- **Settings:** a rundown apartment, Chicago's Southside, between 1945 ("the end of World War II") and 1959
- **Theme:** the triumph of courage over character flaws and societal injustice

Background on the Play. Have students read and discuss the text introduction (page 830) which describes Hansberry's life and the effect of her work on the American theatre. Note that the final quotation was spoken six years before Hansberry died of cancer, at a time when she had no reason to expect to die young.

In addition to the comment of Woodie King in the text, you may wish to quote James Baldwin, who said of this play, "Never before, in the entire history of the American theater, had so much of the truth of black people's lives been seen on the stage." Critics in general also praised the play. Walter Kerr of the *New York Herald Tribune* called it "an honest, intelligible, and moving experience." Wrote Frank Ashton of the *New York World-Telegram & Sun*, "It is honest drama, catching up real people.... It will make you proud of human beings."

Background on the Playwright. You might also comment on Hansberry's awareness that to siblings seven, ten, and twelve years older, she was a nuisance, so she learned to play alone. In *To Be Young, Gifted and Black* she writes, too, of childhood games ("Captain, may I?"), the whole family sleeping in the park on sweltering Chicago summer nights, the howling mob that surrounded their house when they moved into a hostile white neighborhood, the way other children at school beat her up when her mother sent her to kindergarten—in the midst of the depression—wearing a white fur coat (giving her a lasting hatred of symbols of wealth.) Herself from a middle-class home, she envied latch-key ghetto children the yellow door keys they wore on strings around their necks.

In her twenties, attending the Art Institute in New York, Hansberry shared an apartment on the lower East Side with three other girls—because, she explains, it was too crowded in black Harlem, even for those who *wanted* to move there. She was earning $31.70 a week as a typist-receptionist, attending black movement meetings many nights, ushering at rallies, going for long walks in Harlem just to talk to people, and—always—writing and dreaming about making a contribution to American theatre. By 1954 she was married to Robert Nemiroff, a songwriter and music publisher, and living with him in a small Greenwich Village walk-up apartment. They were still there when *A Raisin in the Sun* proved a phenomenal success.

Later Hansberry and Nemiroff moved to the country, and Hansberry continued the rest of her life to write, and to speak for the black movement. In January 1964 she was excited about her play *The Sign in Sidney Brustein's Window* (1964); by July she knew something was seriously wrong with her health. James Baldwin reports having seen Hansberry in the hospital as she was dying: "She did not seem frightened or sad, only exasperated that her body no longer obeyed her; she smiled and waved."

After her death in 1965, Hansberry's husband arranged a collection of her letters, poems, and dramatic scenes into a seven-and-a-half hour radio presentation, *Lorraine Hansberry in Her Own Words* (WBAI, 1967); then into the play, *To Be Young, Gifted and Black* (Cherry Lane Theatre, New York City, January 2, 1969), which ran for twelve months; and finally into a book of the same title (1970)—a work offering insight into the black experience of mid-century America.

Summary. *Act One.* The Younger family dreams of change to come from a ten-thousand dollar insurance check. Walter wants to invest in a liquor store, Beneatha in medical education, and Ruth discovers she is pregnant. *Act Two.* Mama, seeing change in living circumstances as vital, uses thirty-five hundred dollars as a down payment on a house in a white neighborhood. She instructs her son Walter to set aside $3,500 for Beneatha's medical education and to take charge of the remaining $3,000. Walter invests all $6,500 with a man who runs off with it. *Act Three.* In despair, Walter proposes accepting the white community's offer to buy off their move into the new neighborhood. Mama successfully challenges his pride, and Walter refuses the offer.

Teaching Strategies

Providing for Cultural Differences. Students need to grasp the enormity of a $10,000 check in the 1940's and 1950's. $6,000 to $10,000 a year was an extremely good salary, comparable to $25,000 or $35,000 in the 1980's. You may also wish to comment on *dialects* of English (or remind students of page 413 after the Twain selections—dialects differ from standard English in vocabulary, pronunciation and grammar) and the fact that black English obeys highly complex rules of its own.

Providing for Different Levels of Ability. If the play is presented well, it will be accessible to students at all levels of ability.

Introducing Vocabulary Study. Knowing the meanings of the following words is important to understanding the play. (*Italicized* words are defined in text notes.) You might consider having students work in pairs to define and use the words for each act before you read that act in class.

Act One (Pages 832–852)

assimilationism	847	oppression	834
deferred	831	permeated	836
futile	841	raucous	842
furtively	841	savor	841
graft	836	sophisticate	846
heathenism	845	stupor	833
indestructible	832	tyranny	844
indictment	833	vengeance	847
indifference	833	vindicated	834
mutilate	846		

Act Two (Pages 853–873)

facetiousness	868	*Prometheus*	857
incredulity	832	scrutinize	856

Act Three (Pages 874–882)

ominous	874	retrogression	875
replenish	875	*Titan*	876

Reading the Play You might begin by reading and discussing the introduction on Lorraine Hansberry and the play (page 830). After the play, read and discuss "A Comment on the Play" (page 883) and "Primary Sources" (page 884) before students write about the play.

Depending upon your class, you will probably want students to read the play aloud. If possible, arrange to have students listen to the audiocassette (from Act III) that accompanies this play, or, if you have a student who is especially good at the phrasing and accents required, have that student work with the other students. If you use readers, have the class listen as the readers sit facing the class to present the play. You might pause for a reading check after each act, begin the response questions in class, and assign the remaining response questions as homework. Review this work before continuing with the play the next day. If you will not be reading the play in class, you might assign the reading as homework and do reading checks and the response questions in class.

Reading Check. You may wish to use the following questions to check comprehension after each act.

Act One Have students respond with short answers.

1. What is the amount of the insurance check Mama expects to receive? $10,000
2. What does Walter want to invest the money in?   A liquor store
3. What does Beneatha want to become?   A doctor
4. What does Mama want to use the money for?   A house
5. What news about Ruth stuns Walter?   She is pregnant.

Act Two Have students respond *True* or *False*.

1. George Murchison enjoys and approves of Walter's and Beneatha's African act.   False
2. Mama has put a down payment on a house in a white area called Clybourne Park.   True
3. Mama says Walter can do anything he wants with the remaining $6,500.   False
4. Walter and Beneatha accept Mr. Linder's offer for the house.   False
5. One of Walter's partners runs off with the money Walter invested with him.   True

Act Three Have students respond *True* or *False*.

1. Asagai thinks Beneatha has given up her dreams too easily.   True
2. Asagai invites Beneatha to come to Africa with him.   True
3. Walter asks Mr. Lindner to come to the apartment.   True
4. Mama is proud of the manner in which Walter plans to accept Mr. Lindner's offer.   False

302   American Drama

5. Walter accepts the money from Mr. Lindner.   False

Reteaching Alternatives. Play the audiocassette, an excerpt which runs from Walter's angry exit in Act III, Scene 2 (page 878) to the end of the play, while students follow along. Discuss how the recording helps a reader imagine the play, and then return to other parts of the play that the student finds difficult.

Responding to the Play   Text page 852
Analyzing Act One
Identifying Details

1. In the fourth speech of the play, the line "Check coming today?" arouses our interest and curiosity. Trace the development of the check in this act as it moves from something that arouses our curiosity to something that becomes the central plot issue of the play. Our curiosity is first aroused when Walter asks if the check is coming, and Ruth tells him that it is due tomorrow and not to talk to her about money. It is clear that the Youngers do not have much money, although we do not yet know what type of check Walter is expecting. Then Travis enters and mentions the check. In the following dialogue, Ruth refuses to give him fifty cents for school (she says they haven't got the money), and tells Travis not to ask Mama for it. But Walter, much to Ruth's annoyance, gives his son a dollar. Then Walter reveals his "investment" plan to Ruth, and urges her to try to persuade Mama. When Beneatha enters, the check is again mentioned: Beneatha says the money will belong to Mama, while Walter accuses her of accepting money to finance her education. In this scene, we learn that Mama will receive the money from an insurance policy, following the death of her husband. When Mama enters, she and Ruth discuss the money and Mama declares that she will not help Walter to finance a liquor store, because that sort of business goes against her convictions. Mama also says that she will put away part of the ten thousand dollars for Beneatha's education; she rejects the idea of taking a trip herself; and she introduces the plan of buying a small house and moving from the apartment—a plan which Ruth subtly encourages. In Scene 2, Walter refers to the check when he talks to Willy Harris on the telephone. The whole family is eagerly awaiting the mailman's arrival. Later in the scene, Travis enters excitedly with the check, and Mama opens the envelope.

2. In a play, our attention is held by people in *conflict*. Look carefully at the opening scene through Walter's exit (page 839). Point out the number of subjects, large and small, over which the characters argue. Walter argues with Ruth over the length of time Travis stays in the bathroom. They then have a small argument over Walter's smoking in the morning. Ruth and Travis argue over the fifty cents which Travis wants to take to school, but mother and son then make up. Walter and Ruth argue over the "investment" plan in the liquor store, and Walter accuses Ruth of not supporting him. When Beneatha enters, she and Walter argue over the use of the insurance money, with Walter accusing Beneatha of being selfish.

3. Walter expresses his "dream" in Scene 1. What does he want to do with Mama's money? He wants to invest in a liquor store together with several friends.

How does his dream *conflict* with Beneatha's ambition? Beneatha wants to be a doctor, and she needs money for her education.

4. At the end of Scene 2, why is Mama so angry with Walter? Mama calls Walter a disgrace to his father's memory because he will not pay attention to his wife, who is pregnant and thinking of destroying the child.

Interpreting Meanings

5. It has been said that to enjoy a play we must believe what is happening and care about the characters. Is the action of the play believable so far? Explain your answer. Student answers will vary, but most will agree that the setting, characters, and motivations are realistic and believable.

6. At the end of Act I, which character are you "rooting" for most, and why? Again, student answers may vary. Some will probably be on Walter's side, arguing that he ought to have a chance to achieve his dream. Others may well side with Beneatha, who—despite her excesses—cherishes a worthy ambition. Still others will be on the side of Mama in her struggle to keep the family together and to prevent Ruth from taking the life of an unwanted child. Still others may be "rooting" for Ruth, who has displayed considerable patience and wisdom in this act.

7. There has been a considerable build-up for Mama's entrance, which occurs late in Scene 1. What are we told about Mama before she appears? We are told that Mama is about to receive the check; Walter implies that Mama will listen more to Ruth than she will to Walter himself, and that it is prudent to approach her indirectly; Ruth tells Travis not to bother his grandmother for the fifty cents that he wants; Ruth cautions Walter and Beneatha not to argue because their mother will hear them.

In a play, showing is better than telling. When she makes her entrance, Mama immediately shows us in small ways what kind of woman and mother she is. What does she do, and what do her actions reveal about her *character*? Mama enters with great dignity in her bearing. Her features express nobility and strength, and the stage directions suggest that she has a heroic quality. Her voice is soft. In her first line, she expresses concern about the "slamming doors" that must have been the sign of an argument. In her second speech, she shows that she is indeed a concerned, loving mother: she tells Ruth that she looks peaked and offers to iron some of the clothes, and she reminds Beneatha to put on her robe so that she will not catch cold. She even expresses solicitude about her "old plant." When she sees Travis' messy bed, she emphasizes that he is a little boy, her "baby," who tries.

8. It is important that we know the strength of Mama's religious beliefs because it is these beliefs that influence her decision not to give Walter the money. How does the playwright show us how strong Mama's beliefs are? We are shown the strength of Mama's religious beliefs in the scene with Beneatha. When her daughter claims that she doesn't accept the idea of the existence of God, Mama firmly reminds her that—while she remains in Mama's house—Beneatha will acknowledge God.

9. The character of Asagai, introduced in Scene 2, gives us a different perspective on life in the Younger household. What does Asagai represent? Asagai represents a different, more international viewpoint on the black experience. He is a Nigerian student in Chicago—well-traveled, liberal, and passionately convinced that the true roots and identity of blacks are to be found in Africa. Asagai believes that American blacks should not yield to "assimilationism." It is obvious that he likes Beneatha, but it is also implied that her attraction to him is perhaps more intellectual than romantic or emotional.

How is he contrasted with George Murchison, Beneatha's other admirer? Whereas Asagai opposes assimilationism, George, who is the child of wealthy and successful black parents, seems to have given up his roots and joined the "mainstream" of conventional American society. Beneatha resents the fact that George does not take her ambition to be a doctor seriously, and she accuses the Murchison family of being "snobbish."

10. What dramatic questions have been posed in this first act? What possible answers could each question have? Among the dramatic questions the playwright raises are: How will the conflict over the insurance money be resolved? What will Ruth do about her pregnancy? How will things work out for Beneatha and Asagai? Will Mama succeed in her efforts to keep the family together? Students will have various possible answers for each question.

Analyzing Act Two   Text page 873
Identifying Facts

1. In Scene 1, how does Walter react to Beneatha's version of an African dance and chant? Walter, who has had too much to drink, at first seems sarcastic in his reaction to Beneatha's music and her costume. But in his exaggerated routine, which imitates African political rhetoric, Walter soon seems more African than American.

How does George Murchison react to both Walter and Beneatha? George seems mystified; he is unable to understand either Walter's behavior or Beneatha's costume, and he urges her to change her clothes so that they can go to the theater.

2. At the end of Scene 1, we find out what Mama has done with the insurance money. What is Ruth's reaction to Mama's news? Ruth is ecstatically happy that Mama has made a down payment on a house.

What hints have we had earlier that this is what Ruth wanted all along? In Act I, we have seen that Ruth subtly tried to encourage Mama when Mama speculated that it might be possible for the Youngers to move out of the dreary apartment.

3. How does Walter react to Mama's announcement? Walter is furious that Mama has refused to back him in his investment plan.

What is the problem with the new house? The new house is in an overwhelmingly white neighborhood, where the residents are known to be hostile to blacks.

4. In Scene 2, what does Mama say and do that makes Walter feel differently about his future? Mama tells Walter that she has been mistaken in not backing him more, but she explains to him that she has never had any money to give him because of the family's poverty. She tells him that she has always felt that there was nothing as precious to her as her children. Therefore, she gives Walter the $6,500 that is left over after the down payment. She tells him to deposit $3,000 of this money in the bank for Beneatha's medical education; with the rest of the money, he is to start an account in his own name. Mama tells Walter that she trusts him to spend the money as he decides since he should now be the head of the family.

In Scene 3, what are we told and shown that convinces us that Walter has changed? Walter enters in a happy mood, singing and snapping his fingers. He plays music on the phonograph and dances with Ruth, and his first speeches seem to indicate that he has gotten over his bitterness on the question of race. He carries a large box, which—as we later find out—is a present for Mama.

5. What is the purpose of Mr. Lindner's visit to the Younger family? The ostensible purpose is to welcome the Youngers to the neighborhood. But it gradually becomes clear that Lindner has another, more ominous purpose in mind. He reveals that the folks of Clybourne Park do not want blacks to move into the neighborhood, and are willing to offer the Youngers a substantial sum to buy them out.

How does Walter react when he realizes what Mr. Lindner really wants? Walter angrily rejects Lindner's proposal and tells him to get out.

6. What bad news does Bobo bring to the family at the end of Scene 3? Bobo fearfully tells Walter that their

304 American Drama

supposed friend and partner, Willy Harris, has absconded with all their money.

Interpreting Meanings

7. In Scene 1, why does George address Walter as "Prometheus"? Since Prometheus was the mythical Greek hero who defied the gods and suffered torture as a result, George implies that Walter's rantings are proud, vain and wrongheaded.

8. Walter asks Ruth, "What is it gets into people ought to be close?" When they try to talk about why they are having such problems, they reach no conclusion. What do you think the playwright wants us to understand as the cause of their problems? Student answers will vary. But the basic conflict between Walter and Ruth—the conflict that is the seed of their growing apart—is the result of Walter's materialistic ambition, which has almost completely overwhelmed his duties and sense of tenderness as a father and as a husband.

9. Beneatha is a serious character, but she also becomes comic through her excesses. Discuss how she can be seen as a comic *character*. Is she a convincing character, or a stereotype? Explain. Beneatha's ambition to become a doctor is serious, and the audience will probably sympathize with her. But it is also clear that Beneatha is somewhat immature, allowing herself to become passionately involved in various passing fancies. For example, in Act I we are told that her guitar lessons are likely to be just a fad. In her eagerness to learn about the roots of blacks in Africa, Beneatha's posturing in native costume and her rigidity in "talking down" to the rest of the family seem more than a bit comic. Most students will agree that the relatively complex portrayal of Beneatha prevents her from being merely a stereotype.

10. To which character does Mama first reveal her news in Scene 1? Why? Mama first reveals her news to Travis, her grandson. Her reason appears to be linked with one of her major goals: the stability and continuity of family life. She tells Travis that one day the house will be his.

11. Scene 3 is full of *reversals*, in which sudden shifts take place in the fortunes of the main characters. Discuss the reversals in this scene. The first major reversal occurs in connection with Lindner's visit. Whereas it first appears that Lindner's purpose is to welcome the Youngers to their new neighborhood, it turns out that his true goal is to propose a "buy out" of their new house, since they are not welcome in Clybourne Park. When informed of this development, Mama is at first disturbed, but her consternation is followed by pleasure and joy when Walter, Ruth, Beneatha, and Travis give her their presents. This light moment, however, is soon shattered when Bobo enters with the terrible news that Willy Harris has stolen the money that Bobo and Walter had entrusted to him to use in Springfield. Walter, practically speechless, admits to Mama that he never deposited Beneatha's school money in the bank; Mama beats Walter. Remembering her dead husband, Mama prays to God for strength, and then crumples on the floor.

What is the mood at the beginning of this scene and at the end? At the beginning of the scene, the mood is joyful and expectant. At the end, all seems to have been lost.

12. How do you feel about the various characters at this point in the play? Are you rooting for any particular character? Have your sympathies switched from one character to another? Explain. Student answers will vary. Encourage the students to support their responses with specific references to the play.

Analyzing Act Three   Text page 883
Identifying Details

1. In their long scene at the beginning of this act, Beneatha and Asagai discuss his vision of Africa's future. How does Asagai view his role in Africa? Asagai says that his role is to lead his people out of ignorance and to aid their progress.

What does he ask Beneatha to do? He asks Beneatha to return to Nigeria with him as his wife.

2. Why does Walter call Mr. Lindner? At this point, Walter plans to recoup the stolen money by accepting Lindner's proposal for a buy-out of the new house.

Why do Ruth, Mama, and Beneatha object to his plan? They object to his plan because it involves a complete surrender of human dignity.

3. The scene with Mr. Lindner is the *climax* of the play. What happens during this scene that ends our doubts and worries about the Younger family's future? Walter finally stands up for his own dignity and that of his family. He turns away from material ambition and asserts his essential humanity by telling Lindner that the Youngers will not accept his proposal.

4. What do the closing stage directions suggest about Mama's frame of mind just before the final curtain? By having Mama look around at the walls of the apartment, the playwright suggests that she is nostalgic about the past and her many years of married life with Big Walter. As the heaving rises in her and she puts her fist in her mouth, her actions may suggest that she is fearful of the future, of the unknown. But she pulls on her coat, pats her hat, and makes her exit toward new surroundings. As she re-enters for a moment to collect her plant, we are reminded of her nurturing qualities—over and over, during the play, she has displayed tenderness toward the plant, a small growing thing which she has "mothered."

Interpreting Meanings

5. A movable object on stage is called a *prop*, (short for *property*). We have seen in the *The Glass Menagerie* that a prop, such as the glass unicorn, may serve as the *symbol* that stands for much more than the object itself. There is a similar prop in this play. What is it, and what does it symbolize? The prop is Mama's plant, which is a symbol for the constant, loving tenderness with which Mama nourishes all who surround her.

6. In a play, certain characters change and grow as a result of their experiences. These are *dynamic* characters. *Static* characters remain essentially the same throughout the play; they do not change in any important way. Which characters in this play are dynamic characters? Student answers may vary, but they should agree that both Mama and Walter are dynamic characters. Mama learns to understand Walter's torment, and she changes as she trusts and supports him more vigorously. Walter learns that, in order to "be a man," he must stand up for his own dignity and must pay more attention to the needs of his wife and children, rather than narrowly fixing his dreams on material success.

Which are static? Students will probably agree that the minor characters in the play—Asagai, Travis, George, Bobo, and Lindner—are all static characters. Students may have various opinions about Ruth and Beneatha. Essentially, however, both of these figures are the same at the end of the play as at the beginning. Ruth is identified with enduring, family values; Beneatha, in her fascination with Asagai's proposal to go to Africa (which is firmly rejected by Mama, at least for the time being), remains somewhat immature.

7. How are the play's title and the poem by Langston Hughes (page 831) related to the play's *theme*? The poem by Langston Hughes implies that a dream which is too long "deferred" may be the cause of torment, suffering, or violence. The poem most obviously relates to the suffering of Walter in the play. But the play's major theme—that the values of dignity and of love are enduring and triumphant—is somewhat different from the theme of the poem, which ends on an ominous, menacing tone.

Which characters in the play have had their "dreams deferred"? Which characters have dreams that come true? Most of the characters in the play have had their dreams deferred in one way or another. Walter has long dreamed of material success and social status. Mama and Ruth dream of holding the family together. Asagai dreams of leading his people toward progress in Africa, and Beneatha dreams of becoming a doctor. By the end of the play, none of these characters has fully achieved his or her dream. But it is strongly implied that the dreams of Mama and Ruth are about to be fulfilled.

8. During the course of the play, we learn that Mama believes there are several absolutely essential things in life. What would you say Mama's values are? Find passages in the play to support your answer. Three essential values for Mama are religion, love, and human dignity. She reveals the depth of her religious beliefs in Act I, when she firmly reprimands Beneatha for saying that God does not exist. In Act III, she tells Walter that her family, which came from five generations of slaves and sharecroppers, has never allowed anyone to rob them of their dignity with a bribe. And finally, a little later in Act III, Mama defends Walter to Beneatha, reminding her that "there is always something left to love."

9. Discuss the playwright's use of *suspense* in Act Three. What is it that we fear will happen? We fear that Walter will "sell out" by making the deal with Lindner.

How does the playwright draw out the action so that our suspense will be heightened? At first we do not know Walter's plan; we only see him as he listens to the conversation between Asagai and Beneatha, and then frantically searches for the piece of paper with Lindner's telephone number. When Walter reveals his plan to Mama and Beneatha, his excitement rises to a fever pitch as he bitterly parodies the actions of a defeated black man, begging a white master for mercy. As he breaks down and retires to the bedroom, we are almost convinced that Walter is unbalanced, and that he will not heed Mama's words about human dignity. Then the moving men arrive, almost simultaneously with Lindner, and the suspense is intensified since a decision must be made. Mama orders Travis to remain in the room, as Walter has to confront Lindner. Walter starts out with an apologetic, almost humble tone—but then asserts the pride of the family and finally rejects Lindner's offer.

10. Both Mama and Walter seem "defeated" for a while in Act Three. However, we know from the play's general tone that it cannot end in defeat for these good people. In a way, we "enjoy" their defeat and despair because we sense that the playwright is preparing us for another *reversal*. What is it that rouses each character from defeat to the joyful, triumphant note on which the play ends? For Walter, the element that rescues him from defeat is a basic realization of his own dignity and pride. Mama, in turn, has made this realization possible when she objects to his plan to debase himself and his family by making the deal with Lindner. Although Mama herself seems broken and defeated, her strong sense of love and support for her children rescues her: this is most visible in the short scene with Beneatha, as she tells her daughter that "there is always something left to love."

Writing About the Play

The three assignments differ in focus. You might discuss all three, even if students write only one essay.

A Creative Response

1. Extending the Play. Discuss the depth of Walter's realization of new values, and brainstorm some possibilities for his future, depending on how well those values have "taken."

Criteria for Evaluating the Assignment. The essay consists of at least three paragraphs that plausibly describe what happens to Walter after the family moves to Clybourne Park.

A Critical Response

2. Responding to the Characters. The questions in the writing prompt move from the concerns of Beneatha and Asagai to the basic issue of cultural identity versus assimilation. If your students are quite diverse in background, encourage those from minority cultures to speak on the issue. Note that at least three stances are possible—first, a stance favoring total commitment to ethnic identity; second, a stance arguing for total assimilation; and third, a position favoring adaptation in some ways but retention of key cultural values as well.

Criteria for Evaluating the Assignment. The essay clearly states the student's opinions on (1) Beneatha's and Asagai's feelings about heritage, (2) the importance of an individual's retaining cultural identity, and (3) whether or to what degree assimilation should be our goal as Americans. Cogent reasons are offered in support of positions taken.

3. Evaluating the Play. Read the writing prompt with your students, but before they make decisions about the universality of the play, read also "Primary Sources: A Letter from the Playwright" at the bottom of the page. Hansberry's statement of the point she hoped to make may suggest directions for response on this topic.

Criteria for Evaluating the Assignment. The essay clearly states the writer's belief that Hansberry has or has not succeeded in saying something universal about human beings, and cites reasons or details from the play to support that belief.

Extending the Play

If possible, arrange a viewing of the perceptive film version of *A Raisin in the Sun* (1961) with its cast of Sidney Poitier, Claudia McNeil, Ruby Dee, Diana Sands, Ivan Dixon, John Fiedler, and Louis Gossett. Have students explain its effect on their interpretation of the play.

A number of African peoples and leaders are cited in footnotes to Act II (see especially page 855). Have students research these peoples and their accomplishments, or study and report on *Roots* (1976), Alex Haley's search for cultural identity.

Students might also compare and contrast selected portions of Hansberry's autobiographical collection, *To Be Young, Gifted and Black*, with autobiographical works by James Baldwin, Alex Haley, or Richard Wright; compare and contrast *A Raisin in the Sun* with fictional works by Alice Walker or Richard Wright; compare and contrast *A Raisin in the Sun* with another Hansberry play.

To compare and contrast the lives of American blacks with lives of those in the Union of South Africa, suggest a study of Alan Paton's novel *Cry, the Beloved Country* (1948) or John Briley's novelization (1987) of Richard Attenborough's film of the Stephen Biko story, *Cry Freedom* (1987).

Exercises in Critical Thinking and Writing Text page 885

Evaluating a Play

The assignment here is for students to write an essay analyzing and evaluating one of the two plays in this unit. In preparation, you might want students to read sample reviews of either stage or television plays from library or students' own sources. As students discuss the reviews, you might have them point out which comments seem objective, based on criteria listed under "Guidelines for Evaluating the Play," text page 885, and which comments seem more subjective. Also, if time and resources permit, a good preparation for this assignment is a class viewing and discussion of a videotaped production of a play. During discussion of the two plays in this unit, students will probably have reviewed the elements of drama that appear in the chart on text page 885; if not, you may want them to do so now.

Criteria for Evaluating the Assignment. Students' essays arrive at an overall evaluation of the play through an analysis of the elements of drama—characters, plot, setting and theme—as they contribute to the overall effectiveness of the play. Throughout the essay, specific examples are used to support the overall evaluation stated in the first paragraph. The essay concludes with the student's subjective response to the play. The response is supported with reasons.

Unit Eleven: *Fiction 1945 to the Present*

Teaching the Fiction Unit

The stories in this unit are most notable for their diversity—diversity of style, of form, of technique, of artistic philosophy, of subject matter. Reading them will give your students a good idea of the many alternative modes of narrative that are now available to the fiction writer. Your more advanced students will find these stories springboards from which they can explore more widely in the world of postwar fiction. For instance, after reading Donald Barthelme's "Game," they might read not only other stories of his, but also stories by fellow-experimentalists such as John Barth, Vladimir Nabokov, and William H. Gass. After reading stories by Isaac Bashevis Singer and Bernard Malamud, interested students may wish to make the acquaintance of other Jewish writers, such as Philip Roth, Leonard Michaels, and Bruce Jay Friedman.

Among the postwar trends students might find interesting are "metafiction" and "magic realism." Both of these, in somewhat different ways, depart from the traditional form of realistic storytelling. Metafiction is a style of experimental fiction in which narrative form is itself part of the subject matter of the story. A metafictional story comments not only upon its ostensible subject matter, but also upon the art of fiction itself. Many of Donald Barthelme's stories are allegorical fragments in which Barthelme comments upon what he believes to be the exhaustion of realistic modes of storytelling. His story "The Tolstoy Museum," for instance, explicitly pays homage to the traditional realists, represented by Leo Tolstoy, but implies that their approach to fiction is now suited only to museums—to a memorialized past. The Barthelme story in this unit, "Game," text page 926, does not make an explicit metafictional statement, but it continues Barthelme's investigation of the absurdity of modern life, the fragmenting of personality, and the breakdown of old belief-systems. In many respects it resembles a traditional type of science fiction story about the threat of nuclear war; however, Barthelme's sophisticated style and parodistic use of banal figures of speech make it a comment not only on the possible destruction of the contemporary world, but also about its ongoing mode of existence.

Where metafiction is directly descended from the modernistic experiments of writers such as James Joyce, Gertrude Stein, and Samuel Beckett, magic realism tries to infuse new vigor into storytelling by using the age-old devices of fable, fairy tale, and legend. Works of magic realism are usually set in a recognizably "realistic" setting rendered in skillful detail, but within which the laws of realism are occasionally suspended to create a dreamlike effect. In Isaac Bashevis Singer's story, "The Key," text page 895, the setting is an absolutely authentic New York City tenement apartment building, but a supernatural element, which in turn is a convincing outgrowth of the protagonist's state of mind, expands the dimensions of the story at the end. Mark Helprin's "Tamar," text page 932, takes place in a lovingly detailed London before World War II, but a dreamlike air pervades the piece, abetted by a rather light-headed narrator, and in marked contrast to the seriousness of his mission. In Bernard Malamud's "The Magic Barrel," nothing occurs that defies the laws of nature, but an air of allegorical improbability, perhaps partly influenced by Hawthorne, lends both charm and meaning to the work.

Other writers in this unit deal with a more straightforward kind of reality, and in their works we find a variety of American ethnic experiences expressing themselves and enriching our literature and our national life. John Updike's "Son" shows us three generations of white Protestant males in the space of a few short pages, transmitting love from one to the other at the same time that they experience conflict. Though the story is realistic, it makes use of metafiction devices in its shifting time scheme and somewhat ambiguous way of identifying characters. Mario Suarez's "Maestria" is about Chicanos in Arizona; Anne Tyler's "Your Place is Empty" is about culture clash between an American woman and her Middle Eastern mother-in-law. James Alan McPherson contrasts the attitudes of Northern and Southern black people in the past, while Andrea Lee's "New African" is about a middle class black family in Pennsylvania.

After your class reads the stories in this unit, you may want to devote a bit of time to reviewing the many kinds of narrative technique, the different approaches to storytelling, that they have found there, and to comparing and contrasting the effects, strengths, and limitations of these forms of narration.

Objectives of the Fiction Unit

1. To expand vocabulary and increase reading proficiency
2. To gain exposure to notable authors of fiction and their works
3. To define and identify elements of fiction
4. To define and identify significant literary techniques: figurative language, imagery, symbolism, paradox, repetition, and irony

5. To interpret and respond to fiction, orally and in writing, through analysis of its elements
6. To write original works of fiction
7. To analyze the language and style of authors of fiction
8. To practice the following critical thinking and writing skills:
   a. Analyzing theme
   b. Comparing and contrasting works of literature
   c. Responding to literary criticism
   d. Analyzing the writer's method
   e. Responding to a title
   f. Analyzing humor
   g. Analyzing generalizations
   h. Forming generalizations
   i. Evaluating a story's ending

Introducing the Fiction Unit

You might want to give your students a preview of the many worlds, both cultural and stylistic, they will find in this unit. There will be continuity with previous units—the black experience, the Vietnam War, the immigrant experience, the Chicano experience, the Anglo-Saxon Protestant experience, all appeared in works previously studied—but what is new in this unit is a freedom in the authors' handling of the techniques of narrative. Authors such as John Updike have availed themselves of the entire range of techniques of modern fiction, from the most conventional realism to the fragmentations of metafiction.

You might pose this to your students as an imaginative exercise: have them imagine that no one has ever written stories before, and that they are inventing the art of fiction. If they could start from scratch, what kind of structure would they provide for stories? What kind of narrative would do justice to the complexity of American life today? Would it be the conventional story form with a clearcut beginning, middle, and ending? Or would a story begin anywhere and end anywhere? Or is there some third alternative? Your students will doubtless not be able to arrive at final answers to these questions, since writers and literary critics through the past two generations have not arrived at final answers either. But you can inform them that all writers in this unit have striven, in their different ways, to arrive at a way of storytelling that does justice to the increasing complexity of contemporary life.

Isaac Bashevis Singer

Text page 894

"The Key"

Text page 895

Introducing the Story

In outline form, for your reference, here are the major elements in the story:

- **Protagonist:** Bessie Popkin
- **Antagonist:** "Human tormenters...demons, imps, Evil Powers"
- **Conflict:** person vs. irrational fear and mistrust
- **Point of view:** third-person limited (omniscient narrator)
- **Significant techniques:** foreshadowing, figurative language, irony
- **Setting:** Upper West Side of New York City, the present

Background on the Story. Students may be interested to know that although Singer writes in Yiddish, he takes an active interest in the translations of his stories into English, usually as a collaborator. That situation, which is quite unusual, means that Singer's stories in English have, in the words of one critic, the author's "fortifying approval." The novelist Saul Bellow has acted as one of Singer's translators.

The Plot. Bessie Popkin, an elderly, reclusive widow who is suspicious of her neighbors and afraid of supernatural forces, gets dressed and walks a short distance to a supermaket on Broadway. It is dusk when Bessie returns home, puts the groceries down by the door to her apartment, and starts to unlock the door. The key breaks. Bessie, desperate, does not dare turn to anyone for help. She leaves the grocery bag by the door and goes outside. Not knowing what to do, she wanders the streets. At last she falls asleep on the steps of a church. During the night, she sees miraculous signs from another world. In the morning, she feels "no longer alone." People seem friendlier, even the Irish super, supposedly "her deadly enemy." The super opens the door for her. A woman in a nearby apartment has kept Bessie's perishable groceries in her refrigerator. Bessie lies down in her apartment and sees a vision of her dead husband, Sam. She hears the words spoken many years ago by a hotel owner on her honeymoon, "You don't need no key here."

Teaching Strategies

Providing for Cultural Differences. Be sure students understand the reasons for Bessie's fears, exaggerated as some of those fears are. She is old and alone in a neighborhood that is no longer familiar to her. Her pocketbook has been stolen three times. She is Jewish, perhaps an immigrant, in a section of New York City that once had many Jewish residents, nearly all of whom have now moved away. Discuss in class what it would be like to be old and alone, living in a high-crime area of a large city.

Providing for Different Levels of Ability. Less advanced readers may need help in understanding the third-person limited point of view in the story. Have a student or students read the first three paragraphs in class. Discuss with them how much of what Bessie views as fact really *is* fact. Point out that Singer is giving his readers Bessie's perceptions of reality, not reality itself.

Introducing Vocabulary Study. Knowing the meanings of the following words is important to understanding the poem. (The italicized word either is archaic or has special meaning in context.)

tormentors	895	entity	898
rancid	895	uncanny	898
liquidated	895	intercede	899
rheumatism	896	depleted	900
papaya	896	anesthesia	900
super	898	clandestine	900
constricted	898	intonation	901

Ask volunteers to suggest a definition for each word. Students can be assigned to check these definitions against actual dictionary definitions. Write a final, accurate definition for each word on the chalkboard. Make sure that each definition matches the specific meaning of the word in the context of the story.

Reading the Story. This story implicitly raises the question of what families and society should do for their senior citizens. You may want to discuss the question in class before students read the story. Should children provide a home for their aged parents? Are retirement communities a good idea? Is rent control or subsidized housing—which may permit older people to remain in familiar surroundings—a good idea?

Reading Check. You might want to use the following questions as a reading check. Have students choose the letter of the word or phrase that best completes each sentence.

1. Bessie Popkin keeps her stocks and bonds (a) in a safe-deposit box (b) among the logs in the fireplace (c) in her clothes closet (d) in a church near Central Park. ___(b)___

2. Bessie loses her place in line at the supermarket because (a) she has forgotten to get oatmeal (b) she has misplaced her purse (c) a man pushes ahead of her (d) the store will not accept food stamps. ___(a)___

3. After Bessie's key breaks, she (a) returns the groceries to the store (b) takes the groceries to the super (c) leaves the groceries near her door (d) gives the groceries to a neighbor. ___(c)___

4. During her night on the church steps, Bessie sees (a) a white butterfly (b) a yellow cat (c) a policeman (d) a vision of Sam. ___(a)___

5. While Bessie is away, a woman in a nearby apartment (a) steals her groceries (b) reports her missing (c) opens the door with a passkey (d) stores the butter and milk in her refrigerator. ___(d)___

Reteaching Alternatives. Have students search for examples of foreshadowing in the story. One instance of foreshadowing is identified in "Interpreting Meanings," question 7, text page 901, and there are a number of others. Students should look particularly for examples indicating that Bessie's surroundings are not so grim and unfriendly as she thinks and that Bessie may die at the end of the story.

Responding to the Story   Text page 901
Analyzing the Story
Identifying Facts

1. Describe the ways in which Bessie Popkin has isolated herself from her neighbors. Bessie is almost paranoid in her fear and suspicion of those around her. She has had her purse stolen three times by muggers, and she lives in constant fear, not only of her neighbors and people on the street, but also of the supernatural—"demons, imps, Evil Powers."

Find the details that reveal that Bessie sees her *setting* as hostile and inhuman. She suspects her neighbors of entering her apartment when she is not there, in order to steal or disarrange her belongings. She no longer uses the telephone because of the disturbing calls she used to receive. The errand boy from the grocery store tried to burn her belongings with a cigarette. The superintendent has infested her apartment with rats and cockroaches in an effort to evict her. Bessie hides her money and valuables in various places. She fortifies her apartment as if against an armed assault. She regards the people on the street suspiciously. She is afraid of the dogs and cats, the street traffic, and the noise. The city seems to her hot, dirty, and menacing.

Isaac Bashevis Singer   311

2. Describe Bessie's *conflicts*. Bessie's basic conflicts arise from fear and mistrust of those around her. She is in conflict with her environment. She is obsessed by the suspicion that she will be exploited or victimized.

3. The key to the turning point of the story is an actual key. Explain how Bessie's suspicions shut her out of even her own home. What is she now forced to do? When the key breaks in the lock, Bessie realizes that her chances of getting into her own apartment are slim. Because of her suspicions, she has ordered a new combination lock, which she is sure no master key will open. The neighbors and the superintendent will not help her, she thinks, because they are her enemies. She has no money to pay a locksmith, because she never carries any more money than she needs. Bessie is now forced to leave her food in the corridor, descend to the street, and wander all night, until she is so tired that she falls asleep on the steps of a church.

4. Describe the miraculous signs from another world that Bessie sees during the night. She sees a white butterfly, which she interprets as the soul of a newborn baby. She also sees a "ball of fire," a kind of soap bubble floating in the air, which she thinks is the soul of someone who has just died.

5. As Bessie goes home in the morning, how does the storyteller let us know that she is "cleansed," that she now sees the world in a new light? Bessie is sympathetic with the pigeon she sees, wondering how it can survive the rain, cold, and snow. She is confident that she can go home, and that people will not leave her in the streets. She no longer feels alone. As she watches people going to work, they seem to her "silent and strangely peaceful, as if they, too, had gone through a night of soul-searching and come out of it cleansed." She admires the fact that they have risen so early to go to work, and she is forced to admit that not everyone in the neighborhood is a gangster or a murderer. Bessie tries to smile in response to a young man who nods good morning to her.

6. What happens to Bessie at the end of the story? She experiences great weakness and a kind of seizure, as if she has been put under anesthesia. Then she has a vision of her dead husband, Sam, who walks with her. She hears the words she had heard on the night of her honeymoon, words about not needing a key. The storyteller implies that Bessie dies and goes to heaven.

Interpreting Meanings

7. As Bessie puts her head to the door on page 898, she hears a murmur. What is the sound? Answers will vary. The noise seems to Bessie to be the sound of an "entity imprisoned in the walls or the water pipes." Since Bessie has made herself a virtual prisoner in her own apartment, she may be hearing the "sound" of her own soul. In any case, it is strongly suggested that the murmur has a supernatural origin.

How does this *foreshadow* the ending? The sound at this point foreshadows Bessie's encounter with the supernatural at the end of the story, when, at the moment of her death, she has a vision of her husband Sam.

8. As Part 2 opens, Bessie awakens on the church steps. The first sign of a figurative "awakening" occurs when we read that she "gaped [because] she had almost forgotten that there was a sky, a moon, stars. Years had passed and she never looked up—always down." What does this last statement mean literally? The literal meaning is that Bessie had been watching only earthbound things—the people and events in the city.

Given what you know of Bessie, explain what it means *figuratively*. Answers will vary. In general, students will probably agree that the statement suggests that Bessie has concentrated on mean-spirited, mundane matters. She has been preoccupied with fear and suspicion. She has neglected her responsibilities and her religious faith. She has not "looked up" figuratively, for she has avoided anything that might inspire love or hope.

9. We generally think of *comedies* as stories with happy endings. But comedy can also encompass many other kinds of plots. One critic, Northrop Frye, says that the theme of comedy is the integration of society: By the end of most comedies, a character is incorporated into a community. Given this theory, do you think Singer's story qualifies as an example of comedy? Explain why or why not. Answers will vary. Singer's story does seem to fulfill Frye's description of comedy, since the eventual redemption of Bessie involves her reintegration into society. At the end of the story, when Bessie dies, Singer even suggests that Sam leads her into heaven. Although most students will say that they see little that is obviously "funny" about the story, the plot's resolution is fundamentally comic.

10. How does Singer seem to feel about his characters— would you say he is sympathetic to them, or does he view them with irony and amusement? Answers will vary. Most students will probably agree that the tone of the story is affectionate, but that Singer injects many notes of irony and amusement.

How do you feel about the people in "The Key"? Answers will vary. Ask students to support their opinions with specific references to the text.

Writing About the Story
A Creative Response

1. Adopting Another Point of View. List with the class the other characters (including animals), and briefly review the kinds of observations each might make about Bessie.

Criteria for Evaluating the Assignment. The paper is two or three paragraphs long and remains consistently in first-person point of view as a character of the story. Observations made about Bessie and her problems are appropriate for the character.

A Critical Response

2. Analyzing the Theme. As preparation for writing, elicit from the class the meaning of *reckoning* (a settling of accounts), how Bessie has lived without a reckoning, the confession she makes, the meaning of the story's title ("The Key"), and some possible theme statements (on the lines of reawakening and/or reintegration into the community).

Criteria for Evaluating the Assignment. The essay interprets the proverb about reckoning and confession in terms of Bessie's experiences, the symbolic meaning of the story's title, and the story's overall theme of redemption or reawakening to community.

3. Relating the Speech to the Story. Have students read and discuss the excerpt from Singer's Nobel Prize Acceptance Speech (page 902), restating some of his major points—for example, "True art uplifts the spirit," "Modern man has lost faith in everything," "Literature is capable of offering new perspectives to the reader." Have each student select three points that seem especially relevant to the story "The Key."

Criteria for Evaluating the Assignment. The essay shows a grasp of Singer's main points and accurately applies three points from the Nobel speech to the story, "The Key." The essay cites elements of the story that illustrate Singer's points.

4. Comparing Stories. Similarities between the stories should leap to the students' minds, beginning with the characters themselves—old women who are somehow journeying. Have them list from memory the similarities they see in (a) character, (b) perilous journey, (c) triumphant resolution, and (d) theme involving love, and then turn to the stories for supporting details.

Criteria for Evaluating the Assignment. The essay cites significant elements of both stories to illustrate the stories' similarities in character, perilous journey, triumphant resolution, and theme involving love.

Analyzing Language and Style
Imagery

1. Some images appeal to more than one sense. This is a guide:

   Sight: torn newspapers, cigarette butts, hopping pigeons, blazing sky, golden dust, artificial grass, carved coconuts, black and white children
   Smell: stink of asphalt, gasoline, rotten fruit, excrement of dogs
   Hearing: truck blaring shrill songs, deafening campaign information
   Taste: papaya and pineapple juice
   Touch: crush of passers-by, sweated shirts, children splashing in water, hair that stood up like wires

2. Answers will vary. Some students will find the scene exhilarating; others will empathize with the sensory overload for a recluse like Bessie.

3. Answers will vary, although most students will see how Bessie could perceive her surroundings as dangerous and degenerating.

Primary Sources: Nobel Prize Acceptance Speech, December 8, 1978   Text page 902

In view of the length and importance of this source, you may want to handle it as if it were a regular literary selection. Certainly, Singer's speech warrants some classroom time and attention, if your teaching schedule permits. Here are a few questions for students to consider:

1. Why, according to Singer, do people who are in despair over leadership in modern society often look up to the writer?
2. What is Singer's personal view about God?
3. Why is the pessimism of the creative person a positive virtue rather than a sign of decadence?
4. What, according to Singer, is the important lesson the Jewish ghetto taught to the people who lived there?
5. Why does Singer feel there is reason to hope that the Yiddish language, called by some a dead language, will survive?

Extending the Story

Isaac Bashevis Singer is not the only important writer in Yiddish; in fact, Singer's older brother, I. J. Singer, is also a notable writer in the classical Yiddish tradition, while Sholem Aleichem was for many years better known than either of the Singers. You may want to suggest that some or all of your students do further research on Yiddish literature. Have two or three students present their findings orally in class.

Bernard Malamud

Text page 903

"The Magic Barrel"

Text page 904

Objectives

1. To analyze the thematic elements of the story
2. To explain a paradox
3. To write a paragraph extending the story into the future
4. To compare two stories that have similar endings
5. To respond to critical comments about the author and his work
6. To interpret the story's ambiguous ending

Introducing the Story

In outline form, for your reference, here are the major elements in the story:

- **Protagonist:** Leo Finkle
- **Antagonist:** Pinye Salzman
- **Conflict:** person vs. ambivalence of human nature
- **Point of view:** omniscient
- **Significant techniques:** realistic dialogue, paradox, ambiguity
- **Setting:** uptown New York City, not long ago

Background on the Story. Your students may find this critical commentary by F. W. Dupee helpful to an understanding of the story.

> ...Malamud's Jewish community is chiefly composed of people of Eastern European origin... [T]hey tend to retain, morally speaking, their immigrant status. Life is centered at home and in the workshop and remains tough and full of threats. The atmosphere is not that of the 1930's Depression alone... but that of the hard times immanent in the nature of things. His people may prosper for a while and within limits. But memories and connections continue to bind them to the Old World, in some cases to the world of the Old Testament where Jacob labors for Laban and Job suffers for everyone.

The Plot. Leo Finkle, a twenty-seven-year-old rabbinical student, calls in a matchmaker, Pinye Salzman, to find him a suitable wife. Leo rejects all six possibilities that Pinye suggests. Dismissing Pinye, Leo thereafter feels miserable. Soon the matchmaker reappears, recommending Lily Hirschorn, a schoolteacher Finkle had already turned down as too old. She is only twenty-nine, Pinye lies. They date, Lily presses Leo about becoming a rabbi, and he admits that "I came to God not because I loved Him, but because I did not." After rejecting Lily, Leo once again sinks into despair. Pinye next leaves a packet of photographs that Leo refuses to look at for months. Finally, he does, and falls immediately, hopelessly in love with the woman in one of them. He seeks out Pinye, who tells him that it was a mistake to have included this picture of "my baby, my Stella, she should burn in hell." Stella is "dead" to Pinye. Leo persists, and a meeting under a street lamp is arranged. Leo approaches Stella "with flowers outthrust." Salzman, hiding around the corner, chants prayers for the dead.

Teaching Strategies

Providing for Cultural Differences. When Pinye Salzman says of his daughter Stella that "to me she is dead now," non-Jewish students may not know exactly what he means. He does not mean (as we soon learn) that she is physically dead. She is "dead" only in the sense the Pinye has completely severed any relations with her. He does not see her, does not talk to her, and in no way acknowledges her existence. For Salzman's daughter to be "dead" to him, she presumably has done something that he regards as very bad—something seriously offensive to his religious beliefs or principles. The offense is never specified. Since the ending of the story depends on this meaning of "dead," you will want to discuss the word briefly before students begin to read.

Providing for Different Levels of Ability. This is a sophisticated story, but most students should be able to handle it. With less advanced students, you may want to assign the reading in two parts, so that you can review the first part and answer any questions or clear up any misunderstandings before students reach the end. A good place to break is at page 909, after Leo's date with Lily.

Introducing Vocabulary Study. Knowing the meanings of the following words is important to understanding the story. (Starred words appear in the Glossary.)

rabbinical	905	protestations	907
portfolio*	905	fedora	908
menagerie	905	trepidation*	908
dowry*	906	cloven-hoofed	908
imperceptible	906	enamored	909
upbraided*	907	machinations	909

314 Fiction 1945 to the Present

starkly*	909	realms*	911
waylaid*	910	loft	911
abjectly	910	asthmatic	911
sanctified	910	vestibule	912

After students have defined the words, either in class or as homework, use the twenty-word list as a spelling check. You might dictate the list as a written quiz, or use it more informally in some variation of a spelldown.

Reading the Story. Use the headnote on page 904 to prepare students for reading. Ask them if they have ever come across a fictional (or real-life) matchmaker before. Some may mention computer dating services. Others may suggest oversolicitous relatives or friends who try to "fix up" one person with another. Probably some will mention Yente, the matchmaker, who plays an important role in the 1960's Broadway musical *Fiddler on the Roof.*

Reading Check. You might want to use the following questions as a reading check. Have students fill in the blanks.

1. The favorite food of Pinye Salzman, the matchmaker, is _____.   *fish*
2. Leo wants Pinye to call him "Mr. Finkle," because he has not yet become _____.   *a rabbi*
3. At first Leo is not interested in "Lily H.," the high school teacher, saying that she is _____.   *too old*
4. In response to Lily's questions, Leo says that he decided to study at Yeshiva because he was *not* enamored of _____.   *God*
5. At the very end of the story, Pinye Salzman is chanting prayers for _____.   *the dead*

Reteaching Alternatives. The following scenes in the story are excellent for dramatizing:

- The first meeting between Leo and Pinye (pages 905–907)
- The second meeting between Leo and Pinye (pages 907–908)
- Leo and Lily's date (pages 908–909)
- The third meeting between Leo and Pinye (page 910)
- The conversation between Leo and Mrs. Salzman (pages 911–912)
- The first meeting between Leo and Pinye concerning Stella's picture (page 912)
- The final meeting in the cafeteria between Leo and Pinye (pages 912–913)

Choose one or more of these scenes and have selected students present them as stage dialogue. Although the text in the book can be used as a script (if students have practiced), the assignment will go more smoothly if the excerpts are retyped in the form of a script. If they are, be sure to leave in descriptions that serve as stage directions—for example, "He shook his head." If more than one scene is presented, you will want to follow the plot sequence of the story.

Responding to the Story   Text page 914

Analyzing the Story

Identifying Facts

1. Almost like an old folk tale, this story opens with a paragraph that summarizes the problem. According to this paragraph, who is the story's protagonist, what does he want, and what steps does he take to get what he wants? The protagonist is a young rabbinical student named Leo Finkle, who lives in New York City. About to be ordained, he thinks it will be easier to find employment with a congregation if he is married. After two days of thinking about the matter, he answers the advertisement of a marriage broker named Pinye Salzman in the *Jewish Daily Forward.*

2. Another character—Pinye Salzman—is introduced in the second paragraph. Find the descriptive details that seem to hint that there is something tragic in Salzman's past. Salzman appears one night "out of the dark," perhaps implying adverse circumstances or a tragic past. His hat is old and his overcoat fits badly. He smells of fish, and his eyes are mournful, reflecting a "depth of sadness."

3. From his reactions to Salzman's clients, what do you discover about the kind of woman Finkle wants to marry? Leo does not want to marry a widow, nor does he want a woman who is "too old," namely older than himself. He wants a young and pretty woman who believes in romantic love. Because of his suspicions and insecurity, however, Leo wonders why even the most eligible of Salzman's clients would have consulted a marriage broker in the first place.

Explain what Finkle discovers about himself after the experience with Lily. Leo discovers a truth about himself when he tells Lily that he is not a "talented religious person." He admits that he came to God because he did *not* love Him. Leo also realizes with horror that, besides not loving God, he has never loved anyone, apart from his parents. He has called in the marriage broker to find him a bride because he is incapable of finding one on his own. He seems to be loveless and unloved.

4. Explain why Finkle falls in love with the woman in the photograph. The woman gives him an impression of youth and spring flowers. It seems to Leo that this woman, like him, has somehow suffered deeply. He has an impression of evil, but feels only this woman might understand and possibly even love him.

What clues hint at her identity? Leo notices that the woman's eyes are "hauntingly familiar, yet absolutely

Bernard Malamud   315

strange." He has the impression that he has met her before. He even thinks that he might recall her name. These clues hint that the woman is related to Salzman.

Interpreting Meanings

5. What do you think caused Stella's father to regard her as dead? Answers will vary. Somehow Stella has brought "disgrace" on her family, at least in her father's eyes. Perhaps she ran away from home with a man. Perhaps she gave birth to an illegitimate child. The storyteller leaves the matter unresolved.

6. Finkle confesses to Lily, "I came to God not because I loved Him, but because I did not." How would you explain this *paradox*, or seeming contradiction? Answers will vary. Perhaps Salzman is indirectly acknowledging that he undertook his studies after a period of sin or recklessness, in an effort to assuage his guilt or as some kind of penance. Perhaps he implies that some kind of heavenly grace attracted him, as if for salvation, to the service of God.

How does Finkle's confession support the *theme* of the story as a whole? The theme of the story involves the power of love and the onset of maturity. To love sincerely, one must first be honest about what one loves or does not love. Finkle's confession provides him with sudden answers to unasked questions about his relation to God and his relation to women. His new maturity, resulting from this self-knowledge, leads him to opt for romantic love rather than a matchmaker-arranged marriage.

7. Why do you think Finkle pictures in Stella his own redemption? What does he want to be redeemed *from*? Answers will vary. In general, students will probably agree that Finkle sees in Stella the possibility of love, understanding, and the good that may come out of suffering or evil. In Stella, Finkle envisions a future built upon love, as opposed to a selfish and loveless past. Finkle believes that, with her, he can be redeemed from loneliness, unhappiness, and alienation.

8. What do you think of the last scene in the story? Answers will vary. The last paragraph in the story pictures Salzman "around the corner...leaning against a wall, [chanting] prayers for the dead." Perhaps the most obvious interpretation is that he is now praying for his "dead" daughter's redemption. Although he still rejects her because of the shame she presumably brought on the family, he nonetheless hopes to see her saved. There are other plausible interpretations, too. If Salzman set up this Leo-Stella match intentionally, as Finkle rather suspects, then Salzman could be praying for himself. After all, if he really planned it, and if he knows that the new rabbi is headed for trouble with Stella, he himself would have a reason for shame and guilt. Salzman could even be chanting for Finkle's "dead" past—or for his "dead" future with this "animal" Stella

who "should burn in hell." Accept any reasonable interpretation.

Do you think that Salzman arranged a marriage for Finkle after all? Explain. Answers will vary. The speed with which Salzman arrives at Finkle's apartment may imply that he intended Finkle to see his daughter's picture. His explanation that the picture was included in the envelope "accidentally" may be disingenuous. On the other hand, some students may argue that Salzman is as sincere as he appears to be in opposing a meeting between Stella and Finkle.

9. What seasons open and close the story? The story opens in winter and closes in spring.

In terms of the story's *plot*, what significance can you see in these seasonal settings? This combination of settings suggests a parallel in nature for the progress of the story's plot from suffering to happiness, from loneliness to romantic love, from symbolic "death" to symbolic "rebirth."

10. Explain the story's title. The title of the story, "The Magic Barrel" refers literally to the barrel (perhaps nonexistent) in which Salzman, the marriage broker, says he keeps his files of eligible women. In a broader sense, the title symbolizes the strange way in which chance (or Salzman's cleverness) has brought Leo Finkle and Stella together.

Writing About the Story
A Creative Response

1. Extending the Story. Note that in twenty years the characters will be in their forties—usually a strong, settled period in an adult's life. Brainstorm multiple possibilities for Leo and Stella, but caution students then to think critically and to choose one they can justify in terms of qualities of character revealed in the story.

Criteria for Evaluating the Assignment. The future predicted for Leo and Stella is reasonable in terms of the problems encountered in any marriage and in terms of Malamud's characterizations of Leo and Stella.

A Critical Response

2. Comparing Two Stories. Discuss the manner in which each story uses the four elements listed in the writing prompt. Encourage students to base their essays on the two elements for which they find the strongest degrees of similarity.

Criteria for Evaluating the Assignment. The essay cites similarities between "The Key" and "The Magic Barrel" in terms of any *two* elements: (a) comic plot ending with characters uniting, (b) use of visions and dreams, (c) an isolated person's redemption by love, (d) a setting transformed by love. References to the stories support all generalizations.

3. Responding to a Critic. Read both comments and elicit comments on how they could apply to "The Magic Barrel." Direct students to choose the comment which they can most clearly relate to the plot, characters, *or* theme of "The Magic Barrel."

Criteria for Evaluating the Assignment. The paragraph deals with either Lelchuk's comment about moral purpose or Roth's comment about being human and humane. It cites the plot, characters, *or* theme of "The Magic Barrel" to show that the comment does or does not apply to the story.

Extending the Story

You might ask students to write the dialogue that occurs as soon as Leo gives Stella the bouquet of flowers. Do violins and lit candles continue to revolve in the sky? Does the meeting go well? Do Leo and Stella find it easy to talk to each other? Students should make their dialogues and the accompanying text show the outcome of this first conversation.

John Updike

Text page 915

"Son"

Text page 916

Objectives

1. To identify changing time periods in the story
2. To interpret theme
3. To describe tone
4. To imitate the structure of the story
5. To write an essay analyzing the writer's method
6. To identify examples of the writer's pictorial style
7. To rewrite prose into poetry

Introducing the Story

In outline form, for your reference, here are the major elements in the story:

- **Protagonist:** narrator ("I")
- **Antagonist:** narrator's son ("He")
- **Conflict:** father vs. son; also son vs. father
- **Point of view:** mainly first-person; one section third-person limited
- **Significant techniques:** shifting times and points of view; pictorial style of writing
- **Setting:** various places and times: begins and ends at home, in the present; ranges backward in time and brings in other locales

Background on the Story. You may want to emphasize a point made in the brief biography of John Updike on text page 915. One of the most prolific of contemporary authors, Updike writes not only superb short stories but also highly regarded criticism, poetry, and novels. While a number of modern writers have established comparable reputations in one or two of those fields, few have achieved Updike's high repute in so many.

The Plot. The plot of this story is summarized in the response to "Responding to the Story," question 1, on page 316 of this manual.

Teaching Strategies

Providing for Cultural Differences. Relations between generations are probably strained at times in all cultures. You may want to point out that Updike's fiction often comes close to being autobiographical. Since Updike is such a careful observer, with virtually total recall, he presents a very accurate picture of American middle-class life in the second half of the twentieth century.

Providing for Different Levels of Ability. This story requires thoughtful reading, but most students should be able to figure out its backward-moving chronology in the early sections. If you think less advanced students will have

John Updike 317

difficulty in following the sequences of events, point out that the eight sections of the story are shown by page breaks or by extra space. Advise them, too, to watch for the dates—1973, 1949, 1913, 1887–1889—for they provide useful keys. If you think it necessary, you may wish to read the plot summary to students as a preview, pausing to explain more fully the progress at each stage of the story.

Introducing Vocabulary Study. Knowing the meanings of the following words is important to understanding the poem. (Starred words appear in the Glossary.)

symmetrical*	916	antagonists*	916
leonine*	916	anarchy	917
charade	916	jaunty*	918
convolution	916	camaraderie*	918
submissive*	916	claxon*	918
maternally	916	nimbly*	918
mincingly	916	siblings	919

Reading the Story. A brief discussion of genealogy makes a good introduction to this story. You might ask your students if they have heard of *Roots*, Alex Haley's fictionalized account of his black heritage, which became a tremendously popular television miniseries and caused an upsurge of interest in genealogy among Americans generally. Ask your students how much they know about their grandparents, great-grandparents, and so on. As they will see in the story, Updike (or his narrator) has great curiosity about family history.

Reading Check. You might want to use the following questions as a reading check. Have students respond *True* or *False*.

1. The narrator's son is at odds with his father and mother, but he gets along well with his sisters and brother. _____ False
2. The narrator's father is less aggressive and sharp-tongued than his mother. _____ True
3. When the narrator's father was a boy, he was bitter at having to work to help support the family. _____ True
4. The narrator's son is an eager but not very talented soccer player. _____ False
5. When the narrator enforces justice on his son, the son at first smiles, and then becomes angry. _____ True

Reteaching Alternatives. You may find it helpful to read this story in class, asking and answering questions after each of the eight sections. Emphasize to students that the narrator is in a familiar position—caught between the older generation, about which he or she knows some but not all, and the younger generation, about which he or she also knows some but not all.

318 Fiction 1945 to the Present

Responding to the Story Text page 919
Analyzing the Story
Identifying Facts

1. This story consists of eight related sections. Identify the time period of each section, and the son or family the narrator is talking about. In the first section, we are in 1973, as a father talks in the first person about his sixteen-year-old son. The second section involves action occurring nearly twenty-five years earlier (in 1949) and is written with a limited, third-person point of view. The main character is in high school: it is implied that this student is the person who develops into the father in the first section. The third section, which reverts to first-person narration, concerns a boy who returns from his paper route in the year 1913 or so. This boy is the narrator's own father, seen when young. In the fourth section, also written in the first person, we have a discussion of letters written by the narrator's grandfather, when he was a young man in the late 1880's. The events in the fifth section occur in approximately the same time period as those in the first section, and have the same first-person point of view. The narrator discusses his son's physical vigor and success on the soccer team. The sixth section concerns a trip that the narrator's parents take in order to hear their son, now a celebrated author, give a reading. In the seventh section, the narrator's father recounts for his son a conversation about religious vocations that he had with his own father. Finally, in the eighth section, we revert to a scene in the same time period as the opening of the story, with the narrator called upon to punish his son for bullying the latter's younger brother.

2. Find passages in each section where the narrator reveals the private thoughts of his characters. Students may identify such passages in virtually every section of the story.

3. What test faces the father-narrator in the last section of the story? When the narrator must punish his son, he has to face the boy's defiant rebellion.

How does his son respond to the father's discipline? The son smiles at his father and then rushes from the room, slamming the door and shouting obscenities. Later, in his room, he plays his guitar as a gesture of defiance.

Interpreting Meanings

4. This story includes a variety of incidents that range over many different periods. What *thematic* thread unifies the story? Answers will vary. In general, Updike's unifying theme seems to be the ambivalent relationship between fathers and sons. Fathers want to see their sons grow up to be capable and independent, and yet they are fearful of being supplanted. Sons are dependent on their fathers' love and support, but need to assert their own independence. Updike's story explores this bittersweet relationship from both viewpoints over the course of four generations.

5. Hope is a recurring subject in this story. In what ways are the various characters' hopes for each other disappointed? The narrator is clearly disappointed that he and his son do not get along better. He also recalls the trying circumstances of his own childhood, when his father and mother bickered, and he daydreamed about a way of escape from the contentious household. The narrator also recalls his father at a later stage in life, being depressed by memories of *his* father's disappointment at the failure to feel a genuine calling for the Christian ministry.

How are they fulfilled? The narrator admires his son's physical vigor and accomplishment, and he envies the camaraderie his son shares with his school teammates. The narrator's own parents are clearly proud of his success as a writer, since they drive "across the state of Pennsylvania" to hear him read in Pittsburgh. Students may suggest other examples.

6. Updike uses the phrase "the social contract" several times in the course of this story. What do you think he means by this phrase, within the context of the story? The phrase seems to suggest the roles that society has assigned to family members: fathers should be the breadwinners, mothers should be submissive and maternal, and children should love, respect, and obey their parents.

Would he probably say that this contract is or is not honored between fathers and sons? Students will have various opinions. Although Updike writes with deep affection of family ties across the generations, he does not minimize marital and generational discord. There are several examples of "subversion" in the contract—mainly the rebellion of sons against their fathers. The narrator rebelled against his parents, at least to some extent; and the narrator is acutely aware of his son's rebellion against him.

7. At the end of the story, why does the narrator refer to his own son as "our visitor, our prisoner"? The phrase illustrates the narrator's ambiguous feelings about his son's actions and attitudes. He thinks of his son as a "visitor" because, in all likelihood, the boy (like a visitor) is residing with them only temporarily, as a kind of guest. The son is a "prisoner" because the norms of society have dictated that, until he reaches a certain age, he remains partially deprived of his liberty and is kept under certain restraints.

How does this phrase relate to the *theme* of the story? Answers will vary. In general, the phrase underlines the narrator's paradoxical sense of irony and wonder, affection and alienation, in his meditation on the relationships of fathers and sons.

8. Do you think this story could be entitled "Fathers"? Explain why or why not. Students will have various answers. Ask them to explain what might be gained (or lost) with such a title.

9. How would you describe the narrator's *tone* in telling this story? Answers will vary. Many adjectives, such as *bittersweet*, *nostalgic*, and *paradoxical* can accurately describe the tone of the story. Ask students to defend their description of the narrator's tone by citing specific words and phrases from the story.

How does he feel about the people in this family? Despite the inevitable conflicts and irritations, there is little doubt that he loves the members of his family, past and present.

10. Did you find Updike's portrayal of the relationships between parents and children believable? Did you sympathize with these characters? Do you think the story affects every reader the same way? Answers will vary. Some students may suggest that the story will affect parents differently than it affects sons or daughters. If you get that answer, ask students to explain why.

Writing About the Story
A Creative Response

1. Imitating the Story's Structure. Success with this assignment depends on prior careful analysis of sections of the Updike story and what they reveal about characters' private thoughts—see response questions 1 and 2. With this background, students may wish to base their episodes on the first three paragraphs of the story.

Criteria for Evaluating the Assignment. The story is titled "Daughters" and consists of three or more episodes. It imitates Updike in how it reveals the private thoughts and feelings of three generations of women.

A Critical Response

2. Analyzing the Writer's Method. Question 10 on the believability of the relationships portrayed by Updike offers especially good preparation for this assignment.

Criteria for Evaluating the Assignment. The essay states whether Updike writes about parent-child relationships sentimentally or realistically, and correctly interprets and uses details from two different parent-child relationships in the story in order to support this opinion.

Analyzing Language and Style
A "Pictorial" Style

1. Choices will vary. These are examples:
   a. The son playing soccer (page 918).
   b. Town as sepia postcard (page 918).
   c. "I am envious" (page 918).

John Updike 319

2. The simile is "burdock stalks like the beginnings of an alphabet." The words "holding" and "pondering" personify the apple tree.
3. Responses will vary. Allow students to move about in the paragraph, using nonconsecutive sentences which still make sense poetically.

Extending the Story

Have students write a one-paragraph critical review of "Son," modeled after reviews in such publications as *Book Review Digest*, *The New Yorker*, or even *Time* or *Newsweek*.

Mario Suarez

Text page 920

"Maestria"

Text page 921

Objectives

1. To analyze tone
2. To write a character description
3. To write an essay analyzing the story

Introducing the Story

In outline form, for your reference, here are the major elements in the story:

- **Protagonist:** Gonzalo Pereda
- **Antagonist:** owners of fighting cocks that oppose Killer
- **Conflict:** person vs. fate
- **Point of view:** omniscient
- **Significant techniques:** expository beginning and ending, comic tone, irony
- **Setting:** Southwestern United States, time unspecified (probably 1940's or 1950's)

Background on the Story. Cockfighting is a very old activity, having been practiced in Persia, Greece, and Rome. Often opposed by church and humane groups, it is now outlawed in the United States. The first state to make it illegal was Massachusetts in 1836.

The Plot. Gonzalo Pereda keeps a saddle shop, but his real interest lies in his stable of fighting roosters. One day he receives a gift from a friend in Chihuahua, Mexico—a murderous-looking fowl, which Pereda and his son name "Killer." Killer wins his first six fights easily, and Pereda prepares to send a photograph of the triumphant rooster to *Hook and Gaff* magazine. That afternoon, however, Killer loses his seventh fight and barely escapes with his life. Pereda takes great pains in caring for the injured rooster, and Killer recovers. To increase the rooster's blood, Pereda decides to feed him bits of liver. On the second bit of liver, Killer chokes and dies. The narrator compares the rooster's plight to the plight of the *maestros* and to the concept of *maestria*.

Teaching Strategies

Providing for Cultural Differences. Depending on their cultural backgrounds, students may or may not approve of Pereda's leisure-time activity, the object of which is to have one rooster kill another. You may wish to discuss the varying attitudes that people have concerning the use of animals in deadly entertainments, attitudes based largely upon time and place. You may want to mention bear-baiting (common in England in Elizabethan times), bullfighting (still widely practiced in Latin countries), and cockfighting (typically outlawed in the United States but not in many Latin countries).

Providing for Different Levels of Ability. Few students should have difficulty with this story, although with less advanced students you will want to go over carefully the connection that Suarez makes between the fate of *maestria* and the fate of Killer. Point out that the entire episode about Killer begins with the words "for example" and that the story ends with a lament for the passing of a way of life.

Introducing Vocabulary Study. Knowing the meanings of the following words is important to understanding the poem. (The starred word appears in the Glossary.)

pending*	921	gladiator	923
Valentino	922	convalescence	923
commotion	923	Spartan	924
Waterloo	923	fluency	924

In defining the three proper nouns, ask students to explain the story behind each word and to use each word in an original sentence. For example:

320   Fiction 1945 to the Present

- Carlos is good-looking, but he's no Valentino.
- Maria met her Waterloo on Miss Pollara's algebra test.
- Jason is a Spartan when it comes to pregame conditioning.

Reading the Story. In class, read the headnote to this story on text page 921 before students begin their reading. You may not want to go into the details of cockfighting at any length, but the headnote information is basic to an understanding of the story. When you discuss the headnote, you may find that students have differing opinions on sports (including boxing) in which the aim is for one opponent to hurt another. They may also have differing opinions about the use of animals in human pursuits without regard for the animals' suffering (including some kinds of research). Both of these topics have relevance to the story.

Reading Check. You might want to use the following questions as a reading check. Have students choose the letter of the word or phrase that best completes each sentence.

1. When good times returned after the depression, many *maestros* (a) returned to Mexico (b) moved to Chicago (c) went to work for large companies (d) opened small businesses.   (c)
2. Gonzalo Pereda (a) keeps a stable of fighting roosters (b) owns an unsuccessful saddle shop (c) loses his savings in the depression (d) buys Killer from a man in Mexico.   (a)
3. After Killer's sixth victory, Pereda's daughter (a) goes to her first cockfight (b) asks her father to retire Killer (c) sells Killer to a dealer (d) takes photos of Killer.   (d)
4. Pereda first tries to get the injured Killer to eat (a) baby-chicken feed (b) oats (c) liver (d) ice cream.   (a)
5. When Killer dies, Pereda places him in (a) a miniature, flag-draped coffin (b) an unmarked grave (c) a garbage can (d) a shipping carton.   (c)

Reteaching Alternatives. Have students compare the protagonist in "Maestria" with the protagonist in Issac Bashevis Singer's "The Key." What similarities and differences do they see between Gonzalo Pereda and Bessie Popkin?

Responding to the Story   Text page 924
Analyzing the Story
Identifying Facts

1. **What is a *maestro*?** A *maestro* is a master of a trade or craft.

What examples in the first paragraph illustrate the powerful meaning of the word? The author offers examples of a shoemaker, a musician, and a thief.

2. **What is Gonzalo Pereda's trade?** Gonzalo keeps a little saddle shop.

Is he more serious about his trade or about his roosters? Explain. He feels that life is too short to become too serious about business. Every afternoon he hurries home to feed his stable of fighting roosters.

3. **Ironically, how does Pereda's prize rooster perish?** The rooster, named Killer, perishes when Gonzalo tries to feed it a piece of liver to strengthen it.

4. **How is the plight of the *maestros* like that of Killer?** The plight of the *maestros* is like that of Killer in that the *maestros* are dying out.

Interpreting Meanings

5. **How do the last three sentences of the first paragraph prepare the reader for the comic *tone* of the story?** In these sentences, the author tells us that the title of *maestro* is sometimes used harmlessly to refer to those who don't deserve it.

6. **The story's *tone* is also revealed in some of the *maestro*'s remarks about his rooster. Why is it comically ironic that Pereda should call Killer "cute?"** The adjective is ironic because Killer is actually aggressive and bad-tempered.

What is ironic about the words "His beloved Killer"? The phrase is almost oxymoronic, in that love and killing are diametrically opposed notions.

7. **All in all, do you think the writer seems to share the old men's feelings about *maestria*? Explain.** Student answers will vary. Most students will agree that Gonzalo Pereda is a rather disreputable example of *maestria*, in that he devotes most of his energy to cockfighting. On the other hand, there are some serious overtones to the story's conclusion, where the old men lament the gradual eclipse of Hispanic culture in America.

Writing About the Story
A Creative Response

1. **Describing a Character.** Discuss the fact that a *maestro* may come from any walk of life, and need not be famous. Note too that the character described may be imaginary. Elicit from the class a list of suggestions for use as a starting point—someone who creates beautiful calligraphy, for instance, or a person who can fix anything.

Criteria for Evaluating the Assignment. Details of the description fully justify the title *maestro* for the real or imagined person who is described.

A Critical Response

2. Analyzing the Story. Response question 4, which compares the plight of the *maestros* to that of Killer, is good preparation for this assignment.

Criteria for Evaluating the Assignment. The essay consists of at least one well-developed paragraph which gives a logical explanation of the significance of Killer's death in relation to the old men who cherish *maestria*.

Extending the Story

In the story, the reader learns nothing of the rooster that nearly killed the supposedly invincible Killer, nor do we learn about his owner. Have students write a narrative from the point of view of the owner of the victorious rooster as he returns home after the fight. Who is the owner? What does he do for a living? What is his rooster's name? How many fights has his rooster won? How does the owner feel about his rooster beating Killer? How does he feel about Pereda stopping the fight? Encourage students to use their imaginations fully, but, at the same time, to keep their narratives within the general setting and circumstances created by Suarez in "Maestria."

Donald Barthelme

Text page 925

"Game"

Text page 926

Objectives

1. To identify narrator, setting, conflict, and resolution
2. To analyze the use of repetition as a literary device
3. To state the theme
4. To write a new beginning for the story
5. To write a paragraph extending the story into the future
6. To write an essay comparing the story to a poem

Introducing the Story

In outline form, for your reference, here are the major elements in the story:

- **Protagonist:** narrator ("I")
- **Antagonist:** Shotwell
- **Conflict:** person vs. person; person vs. irrationality; person vs. bureaucracy
- **Point of view:** first-person
- **Significant techniques:** fragmentary approach; repetition as literary device
- **Setting:** underground control room in western state; the present

Background on the Story. Your students may be interested in critic Lois Gordon's description of the kinds of characters found in Barthelme's short stories:

> If literature at one time presumably reflected life, Barthelme reverses the formula. His figures have in great part become the media, the art and slogans—the words—about them. They mouth technology, although they are utterly ignorant as to what it means; they explain everything and approach every experience with strategy and skill, with the statistics of management and survival, or the rationalizations of historical precedent. They accept roles—is it not one's greatest goal to be Mick Jagger or Blondie, the Brut man or the Breck girl?—and they admire expertise, as though it had divine authority. Indeed they give credence and praise to authorized texts and media personalities, as they once did to God.

Since Gordon's description was written in 1981, and since recognizable names change so fast in popular culture, you may want to ask students for suggestions on updating Mick Jagger, Blondie, "the Brut man," and "the Breck girl."

The Plot. The unnamed narrator (a first lieutenant) is annoyed because Shotwell (a captain) insists on keeping his jacks and rubber ball to himself. The two of them are in an underground missile-site control center, assigned to watch a console for "certain events" to take place. If the events occur, both men are to turn keys simultaneously in the appropriate locks, whereupon "the bird" flies—presumably, a nuclear missile is launched. The two men were supposed to have been been relieved after twelve hours ("twelve hours on, twelve hours off"), but an oversight has occurred—or else the two are the unwitting subjects of a government experiment—and they have now been underground for 133 days. The bird has not flown; the men have suspended the rules of "normality"; and both are acting strangely. Shotwell plays with his jacks and studies a textbook on marketing; the narrator scratches long descriptions of natural forms (including, oddly, a baseball bat) on the walls with a large diamond. Each is armed with two guns, and each is authorized to shoot the other for acting strangely. Yet neither man can launch the bird by himself—the locks are too far apart for simultaneous turning. The narrator suspects that Shotwell, infantile and desperate, wants him to cooperate in turning the keys. The narrator may do it, he suggests, but only if he is allowed to play with the jacks. "That is fair," he says. "I am not well."

Teaching Strategies

Providing for Cultural Differences. The military has a culture of its own, which you may want to discuss with students before they begin reading. Discipline is extremely important. Obeying orders is vital. Rank determines power. Certain freedoms do not exist. (In "Game," for example, the two men are locked like prisoners in their underground room.) A few students will probably have parents or older brothers or sisters in military service and can share some of the differences between military and civilian life that they have heard described. Understanding the culture of the military is important to understanding Barthelme's story.

Providing for Different Levels of Ability. With less advanced students, you may want to read this story aloud in class. It is not very long, and the comparatively slow pace of oral reading (vis-à-vis even careful silent reading) is a plus. Moreover, you can stop and explain along the way, if necessary.

Introducing Vocabulary Study. Knowing the meanings of the following words is important to understanding the story. (Starred words appear in the Glossary.)

sated	926	sensors	927
ruse*	926	acrimoniously*	927
norms*	926	solitaire	927
precedence*	926	overtures	927
concession	926	stolid*	928
exemplary*	927		

Meanings for many of the words in this list can be inferred from their context. Locate each word in the story and read aloud not only the sentence in which the word appears, but also the preceding and following sentences. Based on this information, ask students to guess at the word's meaning, while a volunteer checks the dictionary definition. You may also want to note the number of times *stolid* is used in the last paragraphs of the story and ask students why the author places such emphasis on this word.

Reading the Story. Some of your students have undoubtedly seen the movie *War Games*. Discuss the movie in class prior to assigning the story. Have students note the similarity of titles. Ask students particularly about the opening of the movie, which presents a situation that involves a decision to launch nuclear missiles. Students who have seen the movie, or heard it discussed, will have a clearer picture of what Shotwell and the unnamed narrator in "Game" are doing in their underground room.

Reading Checks. You might want to use the following questions as a reading check. Have students respond *True* or *False*.

1. The narrator has no interest in Shotwell's jacks and wishes Shotwell would not play with them. _False_
2. In the 133 days the two men have spent underground, the bird has not flown. _True_
3. By the agreement of January 1, Shotwell, although a colonel, has agreed to put aside considerations of rank. _False_
4. Shotwell successfully picks the lock on the narrator's attaché case and gains possession of the .38. _False_
5. The narrator does not know what city the bird is targeted to hit. _True_

Reteaching Alternatives. You might have one student play the part of the narrator and another the part of Shotwell. Then have another student act as a psychologist who visits the underground room. The psychologist volunteers no information from the outside, but asks the two characters questions about their thoughts, behavior, and feelings. The psychologist/interviewer should prepare a list of at least ten questions probing the characters' thoughts and motivation. The narrator and Shotwell should base their answers on details from the story. Others in the class can challenge any answer that does not seem to be supported by the evidence in the story.

Responding to the Story   Text page 929
Analyzing the Story
Identifying Facts

1. Despite his experimentation, Barthelme still uses the essential elements of fiction. Who is the *narrator* of this

Donald Barthelme   323

story? The narrator is a military officer, assigned to some sort of top-secret duty in connection with nuclear forces.

What is the *setting*? The setting is an underground control room, somewhere in one of the Western states.

What is the narrator's problem, or *conflict*? His external conflict is caused by his enforced confinement and by Shotwell's bizarre behavior. His internal conflict arises from his own anxiety, and perhaps from his fear that he is becoming unstable under pressure.

2. Is there a *resolution* to the conflict? No; by the end of the story the narrator seems as unnerved and anxious as ever.

Interpreting Meanings

3. Which details in the first three paragraphs suggest the state of Shotwell's and the narrator's minds? Shotwell and the narrator are evidently in an underground control room on a military assignment. The monotony of their duty, which is to watch a console and be ready to initiate a missile attack, has apparently affected their stability—Shotwell plays with jacks and a rubber ball, continually repeating childish phrases, and he will not share his "toys" with the narrator.

How would you explain the men's strange behavior? Both Shotwell and the narrator show signs of extreme stress. They are no longer able to think clearly or logically, and have relaxed the rules that initially governed their behavior. In their extreme condition, with blurred and numbed minds, they unconsciously, and desperately, seek some change in their situation.

What do you think has happened before the story begins? Student responses will vary. The story suggests that both Shotwell and the narrator are serving in the military but have been abandoned or forgotten, rather than relieved of duty after a reasonable length of time.

4. What is the "bird"? It is never stated directly, but the "bird" seems to be a missile, probably armed with a nuclear warhead.

5. What might be the oversight that has led to the men's confinement? Answers will vary; the men who were supposed to relieve Shotwell and the narrator have not arrived.

6. The narrator is apprehensive that Shotwell has "something in mind." Does the story offer a clue as to what that "something" might be? Explain. By mentioning that Shotwell is trying to span the distance between the two locks with his outstretched arms, the narrator implies that Shotwell may intend to start a nuclear war by firing the "bird" on his own.

7. The writer uses a great deal of *repetition* in this story. What phrases are most often repeated? Phrases that are often repeated include the following: "Owing to an oversight . . . ," "I am not well," "He has something in mind," and "Shotwell is not himself."

How does this repetition contribute to the characterization? The use of repetition underlines the numbness and horror of the situation. It suggests that the mental stability of the characters is slowly disintegrating, as they become more and more like children who are unable to think properly. Repetition also implies that the monotony and strain of the characters' situation are slowly altering their personalities. Barthelme's theme is the frightening potential of nuclear war to destroy the world; his use of repetition emphasizes that his characters' connection with nuclear war dehumanizes them, even though no missiles have yet been fired.

8. What "repetition" of history is suggested by the narrator's drawings on the walls? The implication is that these drawings are like the primitive scratchings of early humans on the walls of caves. Should a nuclear war occur, the drawings might serve to give future beings, thousands of years from now, some idea of our civilization. The ironic implication is that the two men in the story, preoccupied with the game of jacks and the "war-game" of watching the console, have regressed to a primitive state of existence.

9. What would you say is Barthelme's *theme* in this story? How does the *title* suggest the theme? Most students will agree that Barthelme's underlying meaning is the terrifying danger of nuclear war. The title, "Game," underscores this danger with its connotations of "war games."

Writing About the Story
A Creative Response

1. Writing the Beginning. Discuss the probabilities—a world already destroyed? A simple paperwork foulup? An experiment like the one the narrator hypothesizes? Allow students to write the paragraph as an omniscient statement of facts *or* in an absurdist style similar to Barthelme's.

***C*riteria for Evaluating the Assignment.** The paragraph accounts for the characters' having been left underground for 133 days.

2. Extending the Story. Discuss the implications of the "overtures" being made by Shotwell, and how those implications relate to the explanation the student has already offered for the two men's being left underground so long. This paragraph should be consistent with the first.

***C*riteria for Evaluating the Assignment.** The extension connects logically with the explanation offered earlier. (For example, if the abandonment was an experiment, the men may now be serving in different installations, having been rescued before they could use their keys.)

A Critical Response

3. Comparing the Story to a Poem. Discuss Auden's "The Unknown Citizen," focusing in particular on the coldness and inhumanity of the world described. You might ask students to read the "he" of the poem as "Shotwell" or "the narrator," and then ask how many lines still "work." (All fit except lines 7–8 and those on marriage, which cannot be deduced from Barthelme's story).

Criteria for Evaluating the Assignment. The essay argues in a well-organized manner that Barthelme's and Auden's characters live in remarkably similar worlds—ones which ignore their humanity. The essay cites specific details from both the story and the poem to support points made.

Extending the Story

You might have students write a news article to fit this headline:

TWO OFFICERS GAIN FREEDOM
AFTER HARROWING 150 DAYS
IN UNDERGROUND CONTROL ROOM

The Elements of Literature: Satire Text page 930

This explanation of satire can be handled as if it were a literary selection. Ask students to be prepared to define in class the five literary terms included: **satire**, **irony**, **hyperbole**, **incongruity**, and **fantasy**. Also ask them to answer, orally or on paper, the two questions in the final paragraph:

What absurd ideas do you find in Barthelme's satire? Answers will vary. Some possibilities: A captain in the armed forces carries a set of jacks and a rubber ball in his attaché case. Both men are carrying supposedly concealed weapons that the other knows about. A twelve-hour stint underground has been extended to 133 days. Using a diamond, the narrator scratches a 4500-word description of the baseball bat on the south wall of the room.

Do the narrator and Shotwell respond to their limited world in the way that Twain's raftsmen do, or are they more the Walter Mitty type? Answers will vary. Some students may point to elements of both types of response in the narrator and Shotwell. As military men with their finger on the nuclear trigger, and with instructions to shoot the other in the case of strange behavior, they are presumably not timid, fantasizing men. The military must have regarded them as raftsmen types. On the other hand, their childish behavior after confinement suggests men who are cowed, if not by women, then by adversity. Like Mitty, they do not maturely face the reality of their situation.

Mark Helprin Text page 931

"Tamar" Text page 932

Objectives

1. To identify and interpret paradoxes
2. To write a journal entry based on the story
3. To write an essay explaining a statement
4. To write an essay responding to the title
5. To analyze metaphors, similes, and personification

Introducing the Story

In outline form, for your reference, here are the major elements in the story:

- **Protagonist:** narrator ("I")
- **Antagonist:** broadly—isolation of well-to-do British Jews from plight of Jews on the Continent; narrowly—Tamar

Mark Helprin 325

- **Conflict:** person vs. illusions
- **Point of view:** first-person
- **Significant techniques:** paradox; use of descriptive detail and figurative language
- **Setting:** London, just before Christmas, 1938

Background on the Story. Students should be aware that, at the time of the story, the modern state of Israel did not exist, and European Jews had no homeland to which they could flee. Although Jews had been struggling for a Jewish state in Palestine since the late nineteenth century, they had not achieved their goal prior to World War II. Jews and Arabs coexisted uneasily in Palestine during the period when the narrator of the story was living there.

The Plot. The narrator, a thirty-two-year-old Jewish man, is in London before World War II, trying to set up a system so that Jews in Germany and Austria can sell their works of art in a way that will not seriously depress prices. One quarter of each sale is to go to help Jews escape the Nazis. Just before Christmas, 1938, he attends a party given by a Jewish art dealer. Arriving late, he is seated with the adolescents, one of whom is Tamar, a beautiful girl of seventeen with a brace on her upper teeth. They are attracted to each other, but the narrator feels that her youth allows him to talk openly with her, and he does. He tells imaginative tales of his exploits in Palestine. She, living "in a world of vulnerable beauty," talks blithely of studying art restoration in Brussels, or even possibly in Rome, "if Fascism flies out the window." Through the next six years of war, the narrator treasures the memory of this dinner party, a moment when the world, like Tamar, was fleetingly beautiful and "not quite real."

Teaching Strategies

Providing for Cultural Differences. Although the story of the Holocaust is well known, you may want to review it as important background for the story. Jewish students, in particular, can probably provide information on the flight of Jews from Europe, the concentration camps, and the genocide. The narrator in the story, entranced by the beauty of Tamar, beguiled by the prosperity and complacency of British Jews, nevertheless sees quite clearly what they do not see—the horror to come.

Providing for Different Levels of Ability. Less advanced students may feel that not much happens in the story. Point out to them that good fiction can be a serious exploration of life. Tell them that in "Tamar" the hero discovers something of great importance to him—and, by extension, to everyone—in one apparently trivial conversation with a young girl at dinner. Suggest to them that a quiet story like "Tamar" can illuminate matters of great importance, often better than an action-packed adventure story.

Introducing Vocabulary Study. Knowing the meanings of the following words is important to understanding the story. (Starred words appear in the Glossary.)

divulge*	933	ell	934
immoderate	933	theologians	935
vulnerability*	933	gregariousness	935
chafing*	933	caldron	935
intricacies	933	parry	935
incalculably	933	ostentatious*	936
apotheosis*	934	dissertation*	937
disheveled	934	alpine	937

You might assign four of these words to each of four groups. Have the groups define their words, and then use each word correctly in an original sentence. Finally, have a spokesperson for each group write the four definitions on the chalkboard and read the accompanying sentences. Other members of the class may question the correctness of the defintions or sentences.

Reading the Story. In introducing the story, ask students if they can recall a moment of insight in their lives—a sudden realization of some truth of which they were previously unaware. Mention that many fine stories, including "Tamar," are based on such an experience. You may want to advise students to be aware of figurative language as they read the story. The author uses it so well, and it is so much a part of his style, that an inattentive reader can easily skip over the marvelous use of similes, metaphors, and personification.

Reading Check. You might want to use the following questions as a reading check. Have students choose the letter of the word or phrase that best completes each sentence.

1. The narrator hopes to use part of the money from the sale of art owned by Jews to (a) oppose Hitler's policies (b) help finance the state of Israel (c) aid Jews in escaping from Central Europe (d) fund the British army. (c)

2. In anticipation of meeting "the most eminent Jew in all the British empire," the narrator (a) goes to the opera (b) buys a new suit (c) cancels an appointment (d) loses sleep. (b)

3. The narrator arrives late at the art dealer's house because he has (a) missed his bus (b) lost his invitation (c) been at another party (d) left his hotel without the address. (d)

4. Tamar is all of the following *except* (a) the host's daughter (b) eighteen years old (c) Jewish (d) beautiful. (b)

5. The narrator believes he might not have known Tamar so well except for (a) the woolly-haired boy (b) Erika, the opera singer (c) a slim bit of wire (d) the war. (c)

326 Fiction 1945 to the Present

Reteaching Alternatives. Put the following factual questions on the board or dictate them to the class. Ask students to reread (or skim) the story and write their answers to the questions in complete sentences.

1. What does the narrator admire about the Jewish upper class in Great Britain? (He admires their bravery.)

2. Where has the narrator spent the last two years before coming to London? (He has spent the last two years in Palestine, in the Negev desert region.)

3. Who, besides the narrator, are seated at the children's table? (There are four red-headed girl cousins, a boy with dark woolly hair, a fat boy who wants to be an opera singer, and Tamar.)

4. Why does Tamar doubt the truth of the narrator's story about his capturing a group of Bedouins? (She thinks he would have gotten water from them rather than continuing to go thirsty.)

5. What happened to the paintings for which the narrator was trying to stabilize the market? (Most of the paintings survived the war.)

Responding to the Story Text page 938
Analyzing the Story
Identifying Facts

1. Explain why the narrator is in London at the beginning of the story, and what he is hoping to do. The narrator is in London to organize a network for the sale of paintings and works of art belonging to the Jews of Germany and Austria. A portion of the proceeds from these sales will be used to establish an escape fund, so that the Jews can flee Nazi persecution before World War II.

2. Find passages that reveal his attitude toward the well-to-do Jews in London society. What does he think they have failed to understand? The narrator evidently enjoys the grandeur and relative tranquility of London society. He feels he understands the Jewish upper classes in London: he admires their bravery, even as he is distressed by their blindness (their lack of foresight). Because of his mission, he is invited to many of the great houses in England, and he tells us that he revels in the splendor of the parties. But he feels that these Jews have failed to understand the Nazi threat; he says that he has heard from people in the Warsaw ghetto that the Nazis are killing Jews in Poland.

3. What do you learn about Tamar's appearance, her age, and her dreams? According to the narrator, Tamar is a black-haired and black-eyed girl of seventeen, although she looks older. She wears a white silk blouse and a string of matched pearls. She dreams of studying art restoration in Brussels.

What effect does the thin silver wire have on the narrator? The thin silver wire that Tamar wears to straighten her upper teeth shows the narrator that the girl is an adolescent. He feels more comfortable and secure with her, and he decides that he can talk to her.

Interpreting Meanings

4. How would you explain Tamar's attraction to the narrator? What can we infer when Tamar blushes at the reference to Romeo and Juliet? Tamar's beauty and poise make a deep impression on the narrator. He finds her romantically captivating. The blush at the reference to Romeo and Juliet connotes embarrassment at the notion of first love.

5. What does Erika, the opera singer, have to do with the story of Tamar? The narrator tells us that he fell in love with Erika from afar at the age of fifteen. He wanted to run away with her to South America or the South Seas. The function of this episode is probably to underline the narrator's romantic, imaginative sensibility.

6. What effect does Helprin achieve by wrapping the story of Tamar inside an account of the Nazis and the war? What passages of the story remind us, ironically, of what is about to happen in Europe? Students will have various opinions. The narrator's meeting with Tamar and his ignorance of her eventual fate are all the more poignant because of his knowledge (and ours) of the Holocaust that was imminent. The passages of the story that ironically remind us of the Holocaust in Europe occur in the third and in the last paragraphs.

7. What larger group of people might be represented by Herr Dennis and his family and friends? Again, students will have various responses. The narrator's comment that the Jewish upper classes in England possessed both "bravery" and "blindness" perhaps implies that Herr Dennis and his family—for all their wealth and culture—are symbolic of many Jews before World War II who were blind to the horrors of persecution in Europe. Note that the narrator describes himself, near the end of the story, as "in a dream within a dream."

What do you think the children's table itself stand for in the narrator's memory? The children's table reminds the narrator of the young people's vulnerability and—perhaps—of his own youth. In particular, he associates this memory with Tamar.

8. The narrator uses a number of *paradoxes*, or apparent contradictions, to sum up the story in the last two paragraphs. Identify each paradox. The narrator says that all connections are temporary, "and, therefore, can be enjoyed in their fullness even after the most insubstantial touch." He is aware of the contradiction between the luxury

Mark Helprin 327

and beauty of his surroundings on that night and the horror of Europe on the verge of war—the "dark image of a smoky continent." Thinking of the "vulnerable beauty" of Tamar's world, the narrator speculates that "things are most beautiful when they are not quite real." These paradoxes suggest that reality is painful for the narrator; he would prefer to take pleasure in a world that "deepens and becomes art."

9. What does "the world deepens and becomes art" mean? Explain the outlook on life that the narrator seems to be describing in the last passage. What is your response to what he says here? Students answers will vary. In general, the narrator seems to use the beautiful memory of Tamar as an idealistic, stylized counterpart to the ensuing war; Tamar becomes associated with art, which acts as an exorcism of, or an antidote to, the hard facts of reality.

10. Is this a romantic love story? Or is it a story about the redemptive power of beauty and art? Explain. Student answers will vary. Urge the students to support their answers with specific references to the text.

Writing About the Story
A Creative Response

1. Writing a Journal Entry. Response questions 3 and 4 provide good preparation for this assignment.

Criteria for Evaluating the Assignment. The journal entries are consistent with the intelligence, sensitivity, and education of Tamar as revealed in the story.

A Critical Response

2. Explaining a Statement. Response question 2 also deals with the narrator's feelings about his time in London, but response to the assignment requires additional discussion of the entire issue of what was happening to Jews during World War II, and the degree to which a scheme such as the one the narrator was promoting could really help.

Criteria for Evaluating the Assignment. The paragraph provides a plausible explanation of the line, "I have since forgiven myself," placing it into the context of what was happening to Jewish people in Europe during World War II.

3. Responding to a Title. An earlier question that will help students examine the centrality of Tamar to the story is number 6. It may help them to evaluate the rightness of the title "Tamar" if you have them try out other titles, such as "Rescue Scheme" or "London Break."

Criteria for Evaluating the Assignment. The essay gives cogent reasons for citing "Tamar" as a good or poor title for the story. The reasons demonstrate an understanding of the point of the story.

Analyzing Language and Style
Figurative Language

1. a. Sharply V-shaped valleys thick with pine trees
   b. It has military connotations—sleeve stripes.
2. a. Self-important manner
   b. It's a monster that needs clothing.
   c. He recognizes his own swelled head.
3. a. London was like a fantasy land to him.
   b. His purpose had to do with war and inhumanity.
4. a. A place of illusion
   b. A church is serious, subdued; a palace is elegant.
5. a. Sadness, melancholy
   b. Answers will vary.
6. a. *Snakes* suggests danger and/or evil.
   b. A yellow dog rubbing its muzzle against buildings The effect is tamer, friendlier.
7. Jews were taken by surprise and hunted down like animals for slaughter.
8. a. A miniature person being carried on a platter
   b. He feels like an exhibit about to be devoured.
9. They "spoke as seriously as very old theologians"; "pieced together their sentences with . . . care, the way new skaters skate"; "breathed in relief, not unlike students of a difficult Oriental language, who must recite in class." The narrator sympathizes with their lack of ease with him.
10. The extended simile describing the narrator's meeting with Tamar involves crosscurrented waves near a beach running into each other, then falling back in tranquility. This figure of speech suggests a sudden, natural meeting of elemental forces. In the most personal sense, it seems to suggest love at first sight. In a broader sense, it teaches the narrator an important lesson about life.

Extending the Story

Ask your students to assume that Tamar survived World War II and went on to a highly successful career. Have them write a brief one-paragraph biography of Tamar, who is now seventy years old and known worldwide. They will have to make up virtually all the facts in the biography, including Tamar's last name.

Tim O'Brien

Text page 940

"Speaking of Courage"

Text page 941

Objectives

1. To interpret the meanings of symbols
2. To recognize irony in dialogue
3. To analyze a character's internal conflict
4. To write an essay explaining the use of contrast in two stories
5. To write dialogue for a television interview
6. To write an essay comparing and contrasting two stories

Introducing the Story

In outline form, for your reference, here are the major elements in the story:

- **Protagonist:** Paul Berlin
- **Antagonist:** memories of the Vietnam war
- **Conflict:** person vs. self-image
- **Point of view:** third-person limited
- **Significant techniques:** use of symbolism; ironic dialogue; repetition to convey internal conflict
- **Setting:** small Midwestern town, recent Fourth of July

Background on the Story. At the height of the Vietnam war in 1969, there were 550,000 American troops there; consequently, there are a great many Vietnam veterans in the United States today. You may want to discuss the Vietnam war briefly before assigning the reading. However, as O'Brien implies, the incident in the clay tunnel, on which the question of courage turns, could have occurred in almost any war.

The Plot. On Independence Day, Paul Berlin, a Vietnam veteran, drives around the same small Midwestern lake time after time, thinking about his early life in town, the present scene, and, most persistently, his wartime experiences. He received seven medals, none of them for valor, and he would like to tell someone how he almost won the Silver Star. As he circles the lake, he sees the same sights again and again—two boys walking, a stalled motorboat on the lake, and two mud hens. His thoughts keep returning to an incident in a tunnel in Vietnam in which Frenchie Tucker was shot through the neck. It was then that Berlin missed his opportunity to be brave, refusing to advance in the same tunnel where Frenchie had been shot. Berlin keeps thinking about this, about other details of the war, and about how nobody cares or wants to listen. Finally, he goes to an A&W drive-in. After honking his horn, he is told by an annoyed carhop that he has to order on an intercom. He does so, the order-taker using army jargon. He returns to the lake, drives around it some more, and then, when the Fourth of July fireworks start, stops near a picnic shelter, walks down to the beach, and watches them.

Teaching Strategies

Providing for Cultural Differences. As the controversial Vietnam war recedes into history, people in the United States think less about it than they once did, and some students may imagine that everyone now views the war in a similar way. But people who lived through the war—especially American military personnel—sometimes have continuing strong feelings about it. Ask your students if they have heard any such strong feelings expressed recently. What were those feelings? What was the occasion for expressing them?

Providing for Different Levels of Ability. Most students should be able to handle this story without difficulty. Less advanced students can concentrate their efforts on the details of Paul Berlin's actions at the time Frenchie Tucker was shot. Tell them to view their search as a detective's investigation. The narrator presents the story in fragments, and is never totally clear about the specifics of the whole incident. Nevertheless, a careful search for clues will fill in most of the details. Ask students to point to sentences in the story that support their view of what happened.

Introducing Vocabulary Study. Knowing the meanings of the following words is important to understanding the story. (Starred words appear in the Glossary.)

affluent*	941	deft	946
tepid*	941	tactile*	946
mesmerizing	941	carhop	946
causeway	943	intercom	946
sociology	945	bandshell	946

After students have defined the ten words, ask them to write a meaningful paragraph in which they use as many of the words as possible.

***Reading** the Story.* Use the headnote on page 941 to prepare students for reading. With better classes, you might want to discuss why so many of today's best short stories are published in "little" or literary magazines, such as *The Massachusetts Review*, rather than in mass-circulation magazines. (Very few major magazines these days publish quality short fiction. *The New Yorker*, *The Atlantic Monthly*, and *Esquire* are three exceptions.)

***Reading** Check.* You might want to use the following questions as a reading check. Have students respond *True* or *False*.

1. Most of the houses along the lake are old, rather shabby, and in need of paint. _____False_____
2. Paul Berlin received seven medals in the war, but none of them was for valor. _____True_____
3. The day Berlin could have won his Silver Star was the day Frenchie Tucker was shot through the neck. _____True_____
4. In Vietnam, Berlin learned that a man can die from fright. _____True_____
5. At the end of the story, the man whose motorboat was stalled has finally gotten the engine going. _____False_____

***Reteaching** Alternatives.* Paul Berlin insists that he wants to tell his story to someone. Have your students imagine that the town council, believing the Vietnam war to be inadequately understood, asks him to speak from the bandshell at next year's Memorial Day services. Then have students write the speech that Berlin might deliver.

Responding to the Story Text page 947
Analyzing the Story
Identifying Facts

1. Describe the story's *setting*. The story takes place on a summer Sunday near a lake in Paul Berlin's home town in Iowa, some time after Paul has returned from his tour of duty in Vietnam.

In contrast, what sights, sounds, and smells does Paul remember from his time in Vietnam? He remembers the sounds from the mortars, the smell of sulfur, and the sight of the walls of a tunnel.

2. What does Paul wish his father would do? Paul wishes that his father would talk openly with him about the war.

3. List the things Paul has learned as a result of the war. He learned how to tell time without a watch and how to step lightly. He learned the difference between friendly and enemy mortars. He also learned that it is a lie that only stupid men are brave, and he learned that a man can die of fright.

According to Paul, why don't people want to hear about the war? People don't want to hear about the war because nobody believes that it was a war like other wars.

4. Explain what Frenchie Tucker did in Vietnam. What happened to him as a result? Frenchie Tucker was ordered to crawl into a clay tunnel where he was shot in the neck.

5. What does Paul wish he had done in Vietnam? He wishes that he had been a hero and won medals for valor.

What does he want to tell his father? He wants to tell his father stories about what really happened in Vietnam.

Interpreting Meanings

6. Why do you think it is so difficult for Paul and his father to talk? Having actually served in war, both father and son know that courage, discussed so glibly by others, is a complex phenomenon, bound up with memories of fear and pain.

What does Paul mean when he says that his father "knew the truth already"? What *truth* does his father know? How does he know it? The father knows the grim facts of war already because he has served in "another war"—probably World War II.

7. Discuss the *symbolic* meaning of the repeated circular action in the story, and of the repeated references to time. The circular action underlines Paul's aimless, shocked state of mind. Paul's acute awareness of the passage of time contrasts with his lack of ambition to fill the time—as he drives aimlessly around.

8. What is the *symbolic* meaning of the date in the story's context? Independence Day is normally a day of national pride and celebration. But by revealing what many have called the "post-Vietnam syndrome" in Paul Berlin, the author seems to imply that service in the armed forces sometimes takes a terrible, invisible toll on Americans who are outwardly "heroic," "courageous," and "patriotic."

9. Given his experiences, what is *ironic* about the military language in Paul's conversation with the disembodied voice on the drive-in's intercom system? The use of the terminology ironically juxtaposes a trivial scene (ordering food at a drive-in restaurant) with the extremely sober circumstances of armed combat.

10. Find the passages where Paul mentions conversations about God. What purpose do you think these passages serve? The passages occur in the second paragraph of the story, where Paul recalls his driving around with his high school friends. He remembers in particular one friend named Max Arnold, who loved to discuss opinions on the existence of God. Ironically, Max was drowned in the lake, and so was never sent to Vietnam. Students will differ in their conclusions about the purpose of

330 Fiction 1945 to the Present

these passages. Ask the students to support their judgments with logical reasoning.

11. Do you think Paul's *internal conflict* has been resolved by the end of the story? Explain. Most students will agree that Paul has not resolved his internal conflict, even though he admires the fireworks in his own small town.

12. Do you think Paul is or is not a courageous person? Explain your answer. Students will have various answers, although most will agree that, on balance, Paul is depicted as courageous. Urge them to explain and support their opinions.

Writing About the Story
A Creative Response

1. Inventing an Interview. Assuming that the interviewer is not a Vietnam veteran, brainstorm with the class some typical questions such a person would ask, and the points at which the interviewer would cut off Paul's responses, looking for brief, quotable sentences for TV.

Criteria for Evaluating the Assignment. The dialogue reads like those typically seen on television news, allowing Paul scant time really to get at the meat of what it was like in Vietnam. The dialogue may use some actual quotes from the story.

A Critical Response

2. Comparing Stories. Briefly discuss the contrasts in setting, characterization, and tone used in both stories. Notes students have taken in answering the response questions for the stories will be helpful. It may also prove helpful for students to construct a chart of the elements, as is suggested for the third writing assignment on this page.

Criteria for Evaluating the Assignment. The essay explains that the stories are alike in the technique of using contrasts in setting, characterization, and tone. (For example, for setting, the essay points out that "Tamar" contrasts London with concentration camps, and "Speaking of Courage" contrasts Vietnam with a small Midwestern town.) The essay is arranged in a logical, coherent manner. That is, it either shows how contrasts are used for all three areas first in one story and then the other, or it moves from story to story for each element.

3. Comparing and Contrasting Stories. Have students work in groups to complete the chart suggested in the writing assignment.

Criteria for Evaluating the Assignment. The essay is arranged in a coherent, logical manner for a paper of comparison/contrast. That is, it presents all of the information on one story first, and then does the same for the other story; or it deals with one element at a time (setting, conflict, resolution, tone, theme), commenting first on one story and then on the other, always in the same order.

Extending the Story

Ask your students to suppose that Paul Berlin, still unhappy about his performance in the war, writes a letter to Stink Harris of his old platoon. He asks Stink to tell him what the rest of the platoon thought of his actions on the day Frenchie Tucker was shot. Were they disappointed in him? Did any of the other men dare to go into the tunnel? Did Stink dare? Have students write Stink Harris's reply to Paul Berlin. Stink can express any view he wishes that is not inconsistent with the story. In other words, he can add details to those given by Berlin, but he cannot change the details already in the story.

James Alan McPherson
Text page 948

"Why I Like Country Music"
Text page 949

Objectives

1. To describe the conflict
2. To analyze the effect of the audience on the tone
3. To write a characterization using an anecdote
4. To write an essay analyzing a character
5. To write an essay analyzing the sources of humor

Introducing the Story

In outline form, for your reference, here are the major elements in the story:

- **Protagonist:** narrator ("I")
- **Antagonist:** Leon Pugh (narrator's wife Gloria might also be considered an antagonist because of her disdain for country music)
- **Conflict:** person vs. person; person vs. alien "superior" (Northern) culture
- **Point of view:** first-person
- **Significant techniques:** conversational tone; mix of realism and romanticism; realistic dialogue
- **Setting:** small town in South Carolina, many years ago

Background on the Story: An underlying conflict in the story is the one between "Yankee and Confederate folkways." Your students should be aware of the "Historical Event" on which so much of the animosity is based. In the Civil War, many free blacks served as Union soldiers. Then, for the twelve years of Reconstruction after the Civil War, troops of the victorious Northern armies occupied the South, during which time blacks achieved some degree of power and influence. When Northern troops were withdrawn in 1877, however, Southern whites were determined, insofar as possible, to stamp out the changes wrought by the war. They succeeded to a great extent, but not fully, and the long-term result was, as McPherson says in his story, "a synthesis of two traditions no longer supportive of each other."

The Plot. The narrator, a black from the South, decides to tell his wife Gloria, a third-generation Northern black, why he likes country music. Appearing next as a fourth-grade student in Mrs. Esther Clay Boswell's class in a small town in South Carolina, the narrator is shyly enamored of Gweneth Lawson, a pretty, Brooklyn-born classmate. The teacher, a strict, perceptive woman, dominates her class, although lively Leon Pugh—the narrator's rival for Gweneth's attention—always manages to make his presence known. When assignments are made for the big square-dancing event on May first, neither the narrator nor Leon is in Gweneth's group. The narrator tries to get reassigned, and does, only to have Mrs. Boswell's further changes result in Leon and Gweneth being paired as square dancers. The narrator is disappointed, but nothing changes the arrangement until the last minute. Leon wears spurs to the square dance; Mrs. Boswell finds them dangerous and sends Leon off to the lunchroom to have them removed. With Gweneth standing alone, the narrator makes his move. He dances, smiles, and laughs with her. Now, years later, he thinks of Gweneth when he hears country music. "Go on!" his wife protests.

Teaching Strategies

Providing for Cultural Differences. You will want to impress on students that the story itself exemplifies a cultural difference. The narrator, who comes from the South, likes a certain kind of country music because of a childhood connection it has for him. His wife Gloria, a Northerner, cannot believe he likes it. Since popular music is close to the hearts of many students, you may be able to provoke a lively discussion of musical likes and dislikes. If you wish, have students try to discover what relevance, if any, musical taste has to where people live, how old they are, what they do in their leisure time, and other cultural factors.

Providing for Different Levels of Ability. Most students should have no difficulty with this selection. It is relatively long, though, and less advanced students may benefit if you make the story a two-day reading assignment, with discussion preceding their reading the second half of the story. A good place for a break is on page 954, just after the author describes the "ironic mixture of Yankee and Confederate folkways" and first mentions the "ritual plaiting of the Maypole and square dancing."

Introducing Vocabulary Study. Knowing the meanings of the following words is important to understanding the story.

bebop	949	helpmeet	952
buckdancing	949	bounteous	953
capitulated	949	Cavalier	954
provincial	950	negated	954
envoys	950	billowy	954
plaited	950	jitterbugging	955
condescension	950	crinoline	956
infatuation	952	promenade	957

As you work with the vocabulary for the story, ask students who are familiar with music to explain words that name particular kinds of music (*blues*, *bluegrass*, *bebop*, *hillbilly*). Then have students find, at the very end of the story, words that name particular kinds of dancing (*hustle*, *hump*, *Ibo highlife*). Again, ask for definitions. Students may look up the remaining words independently.

Reading the Story. Introduce the story by asking students to try to recall their own fourth-grade experiences. Who were their teachers? What subjects did they study? What were some seasonal activities? Who were the class leaders? Have them recall any specific experiences that they can. A discussion along these lines can provide a good lead-in for the story, which involves the narrator as a fourth-grader.

Reading Check. You might want to use the following items as a reading check. Have students choose the letter of the word or phrase that best completes each sentence.

Fiction 1945 to the Present

1. According to the narrator, the only dance form he ever mastered is (a) the jitterbug (b) the square dance (c) the hustle (d) the waltz. _(b)_
2. Gweneth Lawson's perfume or lotion has the odor of (a) lemons (b) roses (c) a pine forest (d) gardenias. _(a)_
3. One of Leon Pugh's advantages over the narrator is that he has a big brother from (a) South Philadelphia (b) Atlanta (c) Jamaica (d) the Bronx. _(d)_
4. To join the Maypole team with Gweneth, the narrator enlists the aid of (a) his father (b) Queen Rose Phipps (c) Mrs. Boswell (d) Clarence Buford. _(a)_
5. The narrator gets to dance with Gweneth because Leon Pugh (a) is sick (b) wears spurs (c) argues with Mrs. Boswell (d) will not wear his cowboy hat. _(b)_

Reteaching Alternatives. Ask students to list all the characters who play any significant part in the story, and then have them describe each character in a single sentence. (Lists should include the following people: the narrator; his wife Gloria; Gweneth Lawson; Mrs. Esther Clay Boswell; Clarence Buford; Leon Pugh; Queen Rose Phipps; the narrator's father.)

Responding to the Story   Text page 958
Analyzing the Story
Identifying Facts

1. Explain why the narrator has such positive feelings about country music, even though his wife and most of his friends and acquaintances don't care for it. Country music reminds the narrator of his school days, when he was infatuated with his classmate Gweneth Lawson in the fourth grade and square-danced with her.

2. What does the narrator remember best about Gweneth Lawson? He remembers her prettiness, her braids, the colors of the clothes she wore, and the lemony smell of her perfume or lotion.

Who is his rival for Gweneth's attentions? The narrator's worldly wise classmate, Leon Pugh, is also interested in Gweneth.

3. Describe Mrs. Boswell's teaching method. Mrs. Boswell, the narrator's fourth-grade teacher, is a stern disciplinarian who discourages daydreaming and crying in class. She employs a Socratic method with her students, asking them questions which often mystify them.

How does this method affect the action of the story? The narrator says that Mrs. Boswell had apparently understood his infatuation with Gweneth. At first, the teacher seems to thwart the narrator when she shifts the membership of the teams for the Maypole celebration. At the last moment, however, Mrs. Boswell orders Leon Pugh to remove the spurs on his costume, thereby allowing the narrator to dance with Gweneth.

4. What does the main character want? He wants to attract Gweneth's attention and to be her friend, since he idolizes her.

What actions does he take to get what he wants? He tells Mrs. Boswell that he wants to be excused from square dancing on May Day and join the Maypole team.

What twist of fate helps him? Mrs. Boswell notices the spurs on Leon's costume and sends him to the lunchroom to have them removed. Then the narrator takes Leon's place in the square dancing with Gweneth.

5. Describe the broader *conflict* in this story—the one that exists between North and South, "country" and New York. The narrator tells us that he grew up in South Carolina; his wife, to whom he addresses this account of why he likes country music, was reared in the North. Gweneth Lawson and Leon Pugh's older brother were also from the North, and they appeared exotic to the narrator when the latter was a child. Numerous details concerning habits, attitudes, and clothes supplement the conflict, or contrast, between North and South in the story.

6. What is the answer to the "Why" in the title? Country music reminds the narrator of Gweneth Lawson, his childhood love.

Interpreting Meanings

7. How would you interpret the narrator's statement at the story's end: that he is no mere arithmetician in the art of square dancing—that he is into the "calculus" of it? The remark is a lightly ironic metaphor that emphasizes how important the narrator's memories of square dancing with Gweneth Lawson are.

8. Would you classify the story as a *comedy* (page 901)? Remember that a comedy often deals with a character who ends up being accepted into a community, and that it may or may not be overwhelmingly funny. Students will probably differ in their answers, but most will agree that the story is comic. The narrator emerges as an unlikely hero: shy, awkward, and a little bit spoiled. Nevertheless, he manages to achieve his dream—a dance with Gweneth Lawson in the fourth grade.

9. To whom is the story addressed? The narrator addresses the story to his wife, Gloria.

What effect does this audience have on the *tone* of the story? Our knowledge of the narrator's audience enhances the story's humorous tone.

10. Does the story tend to be romantic or realistic? Cite specific elements in the story to support your opinion. Students will have various opinions. On the one hand, the

James Alan McPherson

story emphasizes the narrator's immature infatuation with a fourth-grade classmate, and it abundantly illustrates his romantic sensibility; on the other hand, "Why I Like Country Music" is a vividly realistic evocation of childhood in a certain time and place. Urge students to explain and support their own opinions.

11. Children and dialect are both difficult to portray realistically and convincingly. How would you rate McPherson's characterizations and dialogue? Student answers will vary. Most students will agree that McPherson shows himself very able in both literary elements in the story.

Writing About the Story
A Creative Response

1. Writing a Characterization. Note that the time need not be the present—the student can write about someone who created a lasting impression when the student was a small child. The central idea is use of an anecdote to illustrate a key trait of that person.

Criteria for Evaluating the Assignment. The essay consists of at least one well-developed paragraph. It creates a vivid characterization through use of an anecdote which provides insight into a key trait of the person.

A Critical Response

2. Analyzing a Character. Point out that the writing assignment offers a way to organize notes for this essay: the student should look for details about the character's appearance, speech, and actions; and about how others respond to the character; and any direct comments made by the writer. Clarify the word *credibility* (believability) if necessary.

Criteria for Evaluating the Assignment. The essay draws an accurate portrait of the character, with support for generalizations offered through citation of details from the story on the character's appearance, speech and actions, the responses of others, and authorial comment. The essay ends with the student's personal response to the character and an assessment of the character's credibility.

3. Analyzing Humor. You may wish to divide the class into groups of six students each, with one student in each group seeking examples of one of the types of humor listed. Groups can then share the data and discuss which elements contribute most to the humor of the story.

Criteria for Evaluating the Assignment. The essay takes into account the six listed elements of humor (exaggeration, self mockery, comic irony, incongruity, comic descriptions, and understatement) in its analysis of the sources of humor in McPherson's story. Specific examples from the story support the student's major points.

Extending the Story

Suggest to students that they write a three-paragraph account of the May Day square dance from the first-person point of view of Leon Pugh. In the first paragraph, Pugh should describe his cowboy outfit and his feelings about the dance. In the second paragraph, he should discuss Mrs. Boswell's objections to his spurs, and how he reacts. In the third paragraph, he should explain how he feels about the narrator (students can give the narrator a name) when he realizes he has lost Gweneth for the duration of the dance.

Anne Tyler
Text page 959

"Your Place Is Empty"
Text page 960

Objectives

1. To interpret the meanings of flashbacks
2. To analyze conflict
3. To recognize the gradual shift in tone
4. To state the theme
5. To write the events of an incident from another point of view
6. To write an essay comparing two stories
7. To write an essay discussing cultural differences

Introducing the Story

In outline form, for your reference, here are the major elements in the story:

- **Protagonist:** Mrs. Ardavi

334   Fiction 1945 to the Present

- **Antagonist:** narrowly: Elizabeth, and, to a lesser degree, Hassan; broadly: Western culture
- **Conflict:** cultural, between Iranian (Islamic) ways and American ways; generational, between mother and daughter-in-law
- **Point of view:** omniscient for brief opening; third-person limited thereafter
- **Significant techniques:** flashbacks; changing tone as story progresses
- **Setting:** city in the United States, the present

Background on the Story. Remind your students that Anne Tyler is married to an Iranian psychiatrist who was educated in the United States and now lives here. She is therefore writing from direct personal knowledge, rather than simply inventing this story wholly from her imagination. Since student writers are so often told, "Write what you know," you may want to use this opportunity to review the stories in this unit to see how many are either semi-autobiographical or based on direct personal knowledge.

The Plot. Elizabeth, the American wife of an Iranian-American doctor, prepares for her mother-in-law's visit from Iran by fixing up a room for her and learning some Persian phrases. Elizabeth expects a three-month visit; her husband, Hassan, has said six months; and Mrs. Ardavi, the mother-in-law, plans on a year. From the very beginning, things go awry as Mrs. Ardavi makes a series of moves to revamp the "unclean" American household. During this time, flashbacks fill in details of Mrs. Ardavi's life in Iran. Relations between Elizabeth and her mother-in-law become increasingly strained, nearing the breaking point when the older woman blames Elizabeth for causing her granddaughter's ear infection. The end comes after less than five months when Elizabeth opens a box that Mrs. Ardavi had brought and is greeted by a cloud of insects. Hassan gently delivers an ultimatum, and Mrs. Ardavi prepares to leave for Iran, still "undeniably a foreigner."

Teaching Strategies

Providing for Cultural Differences. This story is *about* cultural differences. You will want to indicate to your students that people tend to favor their own culture, in large part because they are familiar with it; to them, it inevitably seems "right." You may find it useful to write the word "Iran" on the board and ask students to characterize how Iranian culture differs from Western culture.

Providing for Different Levels of Ability. With less advanced students you may want to read the plot summary in the manual before assigning any reading. You won't be giving away any real surprises, and you will be providing students with a framework on which to base their reading.

Introducing Vocabulary Study. Knowing the meanings of the following words is important to understanding the story.

opaque	961	pathetically	968
kashk	964	paisley	969
bunions	964	wincing	969
curlicued	965	spatulas	970
saffron	965	resolutely	971

Because students' oral vocabulary is generally larger than their reading vocabulary, you might check for familiarity by writing the words on the board and dictating the following definitions. Have students match the words and definitions.

a. cloth having a colorful abstract pattern (paisley)
b. purple-flowered crocus (saffron)
c. kitchen utensils having a broad, flat blade, used for spreading, scooping, or lifting (spatulas)
d. hard white balls of yogurt curd (kashk)
e. painful, inflamed swelling on the foot (bunions)

Reading the Story. In view of the Iran hostage crisis of 1979–81, and the subsequently unfriendly American relations with Iran, you might want to introduce this story with a look at other nations with which the United States has had both good and poor relations. Ask students to name as many such nations as they can. (Some possibilities: Great Britain, our enemy in the American Revolution and the War of 1812; Spain in the Spanish-American War; Germany, Turkey, Bulgaria (and others) in world wars I and II; Japan and Italy in World War II; the USSR in the Cold War; Cuba before and after Fidel Castro. Point out that the nature of international politics is that yesterday's enemy can be today's friend, and vice versa.)

After students have read the story in its entirety, you might use the accompanying audiocassette recording to spark a discussion of Tyler's use of foreshadowing.

Reading Check. You might want to use the following items as a reading check. Have students fill in the blanks.

1. When Mrs. Ardavi first sees Hilary, she wants to place _____ around her neck.   *a medal*
2. Mrs. Ardavi will not eat _____, although she is intrigued by its smell.   *bacon*
3. Hassan was annoyed when his mother withheld the truth about the _____ of his brother Ali.   *death*
4. When Hilary gets an ear infection, Mrs. Ardavi says it was because she did not _____.   *wear a hat*
5. To get his mother out of the house, Hassan tells her it is the American custom for guests to stay in the host's home for only _____.   *three months*

Reteaching Alternatives. Elizabeth and Hassan have many conversations in English so that Mrs. Ardavi cannot understand them. A conversation of this kind is mentioned

Anne Tyler 335

on page 965, following one of Mrs. Ardavi's big meals. Another occurs on pages 967–968 at the dentist's office. Have students playing the parts of Elizabeth and Hassan carry on a plausible dialogue that might have taken place on either (or both) of these occasions. Before beginning, have students review the story carefully up to the point of the dialogue. What they say should reflect the situation at the time they are talking.

Responding to the Story Text page 971
Analyzing the Story
Identifying Facts

1. Describe the reunion of Hassan and his mother at the airport. Mrs. Ardavi has naively cherished the notion that her son Hassan will be waiting for her beside the plane, and she is confused and frustrated when she has to make her way alone through immigration, customs, and the baggage claim. She knows no English, and communication is very difficult for her. When she is finally reunited with Hassan, she does not recognize him: he has aged and put on weight, and his clothes are unfamiliar and American. It is only when she smells him as he kisses her that she really believes that this is her son, whom she has not seen in twelve years.

Explain why Mrs. Ardavi is embarrassed and disappointed on the way to her son's home. Mrs. Ardavi is nervous about her appearance: her kerchief and the bad state of her teeth embarrass her. Her son's silence is frustrating to her; she had expected him to be curious about the doings of their large, extended family in Iran. But he concentrates on his driving, asking nothing. Mrs. Ardavi becomes cross, and refuses to speak even when she is tempted to comment on the sights.

2. What is the first thing Mrs. Ardavi wants to do when she arrives at Hassan's house? She wants to see Hilary, her grandchild, who is asleep.

3. In what specific ways does Mrs. Ardavi find it hard to adapt to life in America? Numerous details suggest that Mrs. Ardavi finds it difficult to adapt. For example, she is frustrated by the language barrier, and she seems too old to retain the English words that she painstakingly tries to learn. She cannot understand many of the television programs that the family watches. She objects to the food, which upsets her intestines. She finds Americans curiously undemonstrative. She also sleeps badly; in this strange environment, she is disturbed by worries about the past and the future.

4. What facts do you learn about Mrs. Ardavi in the various *flashbacks*? Important flashbacks include scenes relating to Mrs. Ardavi's childhood, to her marriage and the death of her husband, and to her other sons, Babak and Ali. These flashbacks reveal that Mrs. Ardavi is a complex character, who has known both joy and suffering and who has been both loving and selfish. For example, her childhood is described as scarred by tragedy: her father was a womanizer, and her mother died in childbirth when Mrs. Ardavi was ten. She grew up in a household where children were slapped. Her father evidently preferred her brothers, a fact that "crushed her even after all these years." Mrs. Ardavi resents the early death of her husband, whom she had not loved during their marriage; she was widowed after only six years of marriage. Mrs. Ardavi worries whether or not she was too harsh with her eldest son, Ali, who died four years ago of a brain hemorrhage, the victim of an unhappy marriage. She also regrets not having told Hassan directly of his brother's death. She wonders whether or not she will be able to continue living with her youngest son, Babak, and his wife. All of these flashbacks contribute to a complex portrait of Mrs. Ardavi.

5. List the signs of tension that develop between Mrs. Ardavi and Elizabeth. Mrs. Ardavi interferes with the preparation of food and with Elizabeth's care of Hilary. Even though she apparently means well, she becomes a classic "meddling mother-in-law."

Is Mrs. Ardavi as aware of these signs as the reader is? Mrs. Ardavi is obviously not as aware as the reader is of these signs.

What is the eventual outcome of this *conflict* between the two women? Elizabeth becomes gradually more and more angry. The end result is that Hassan must indirectly ask his mother to leave.

Interpreting Meanings

6. In what ways is the *conflict* in this story the result of a clash of cultures? Clearly, the conflict in the story arises in great part because Mrs. Ardavi, set in her ways, cannot adjust to the customs of American culture. Although Elizabeth, on the other side, makes an effort to welcome Mrs. Ardavi, she is unable to adjust to some Iranian ways.

In what ways is it a clash of generations? The central conflict of the story is also generational: Mrs. Ardavi's inability to understand that her son Hassan has chosen a new way of life, and Hassan's inability, or refusal, to compromise that way of life in order to humor his mother.

7. Describe the difference in *tone* between the beginning of the story and its end. The tone at the beginning of the story is noticeably light, even comic. At the end of the story, the tone is dark, verging on tragedy.

How does this contrast comment on Mrs. Ardavi's visit? Students will have various responses. Most will agree that the contrast strongly hints that Mrs. Ardavi's visit was a failure. Mrs. Ardavi is unable to adjust to American ways, and her actions alienate her son and daughter-in-law. She is caught up in brooding about the past and worrying over the future, and she is set in her ways: these traits of personality make her rather unattractively selfish and stubborn. Ironically, she thinks to herself that Hassan, her son, is overly stubborn; but it is Hassan who, most of all, tries to keep the peace and make the visit work by mediating between his mother and his wife. However, even though Mrs. Ardavi is inflexible and "difficult," the author creates sympathy for her by emphasizing her loneliness.

8. What does Mrs. Ardavi mean when she writes to her son, "Your place is empty"? The phrase "your place is empty" occurred repeatedly in letters that Mrs. Ardavi wrote to her son. In those letters Mrs. Ardavi sadly told him how much she missed him; it is implied that she was urging him to come home to Iran. The literal meaning of the phrase is probably that Hassan's place at the family table is empty, since he is absent.

What additional meaning does this take on as the story ends? As the story ends with the portrait of Mrs. Ardavi's lonely departure to the plane, we realize that mother and son will probably never see each other again; Hassan's place will be forever "empty" in Iran. Mother and son seem irrevocably estranged, a fact which is underlined in the story's last phrase, when Mrs. Ardavi is described as "undeniably a foreigner." The phrase is ironic in that the expectations raised by the story—of a reunion that will bridge differences and end the physical separation of mother and son—are never fulfilled. In the end, the emotional barriers between Mrs. Ardavi and Hassan have proved too great, and the visit fails. Mrs. Ardavi will almost certainly never come to America again, and Hassan will never return to Iran.

9. How would you describe the relationship between Hassan and his mother? Students will have various answers. In general, the relationship is flawed by an inability to communicate. Mrs. Ardavi refuses to understand and accept the fact that her son has adopted the ways of a different culture.

Which character do you feel most sympathy for in this story? Students will have various responses. Some will feel sympathetic with Mrs. Ardavi, who is old and continually frustrated by cultural ways she does not understand; others will feel sympathy with Hassan, who is caught in a most difficult conflict of loyalties, or with Elizabeth.

Do you think the writer "stacks the deck" for or against any of the characters? Explain. Student answers will vary. Ask the students to back up their opinions with references to the story.

10. What would you say is the *theme* of this story? Is the story about a universal human experience, or is it only about people at this time, and in this place? Explain. The theme of the story seems to be that the passage of time, geographical separation, and a conflict of cultures may drive a wedge between even the closest relatives—for example, a mother and a son. Most students will agree that the theme is universal.

Writing About the Story

A Creative Response

1. Taking Another Point of View. List scenes that lend themselves to this assignment—Mrs. Ardavi's arrival, assembling the clothes drying rack, Mrs. Ardavi's taking over the kitchen, going to the park, and so on. Discuss also Elizabeth's attempts to understand her mother-in-law.

Criteria for Evaluating the Assignment. The narration keeps facts of the event the same, but focuses on Elizabeth, revealing thoughts and feelings consistent with the story's characterization of Elizabeth.

A Critical Response

2. Comparing Two Stories. Note that the assignment focuses on parent-child tensions—in this story, Mrs. Ardavi and her son Hassan or even Ali or Babak; in Updike's story, more than one generation. Have students list the relationships from both stories so that they can make generalizations about common tensions.

Criteria for Evaluating the Assignment. The essay consists of at least one well-developed paragraph which cites similarities in parent-child tensions between Tyler's and Updike's stories. Generalizations are supported by references to the stories.

3. Responding to the Story. At first, students may see Mrs. Ardavi's ways as simply "foreign"; the opening question of the assignment leads them to discern values such as genuine concern about others' well-being, a more relaxed pace of life, maintenance of spiritual or moral standards. The prompt goes on, however, to direct students' attention to two points: *differences* between the two cultures and the student's *personal* response.

Criteria for Evaluating the Assignment. In at least one well-developed paragraph, the essay comments on two or three basic differences between the two cultures, shows some understanding of both cultures, and states the student's personal response to the differences.

Extending the Story

Have your students suppose that on the flight back to Iran Mrs. Ardavi sits next to another Iranian woman who is just returning from a six months' stay at *her* daughter-in-law's house. They converse. The other woman's stay may have been similar to Mrs. Ardavi's or totally different. In the form of dialogue for a play, have students write the conversation between the two women. You might then have two students do a dramatic reading of what you consider to be the best dialogue.

Andrea Lee

"New African"

Objectives

1. To describe details of setting
2. To recognize and interpret conflict
3. To infer themes
4. To write a paragraph imitating the writer's style
5. To write an essay analyzing a character
6. To write an essay making generalizations about stories

Introducing the Story

In outline form, for your reference, here are the major elements in the story:

- **Protagonist:** Sarah Ashley
- **Antagonist:** narrowly: aunts and others urging baptism; broadly: conformity
- **Conflict:** person vs. family and community expectations
- **Point of view:** first-person
- **Significant techniques:** detailed description of setting; exploration of theme through childhood memoir
- **Setting:** New African Baptist Church, South Philadelphia, summer, 1963

Background on the Story. This is a story about asserting independence and the need to find one's own identity, a theme as old as the *Odyssey* and a theme with which our students can readily identify. In preparation for reading this story, you might discuss with students the fact that a young adult asserting his or her independence might seem to be rejecting family and community values, but that, in reality, deeply ingrained values are seldom lost—often, in fact, they become even more meaningful in light of the new maturity. In "New African," a young girl has conflicting feelings about her church and asserts her independence from it. In doing so, she is supported by the love of her father, who is the minister, and the love of the congregation. At the end of the story, there is every indication that she, too, will find her "New African."

Although there are references in the story to the civil rights movement, your students may not realize just how important the movement was in the summer of 1963. At the time of the church service Lee describes, Dr. Martin Luther King, Jr.—a Baptist minister like Sarah Ashley's father—was at the height of his influence and prestige. On August 28, 1963, King delivered his famous "I have a dream" speech at the demonstration capping the massive March on Washington where two hundred thousand people heard his impassioned plea for equal rights. Because of the quiet, personal tone of Lee's story, students may not realize (any more than Sarah did at the time) how crucial the civil rights work of her father presumably was in that activist summer of 1963.

The Plot. Sarah Ashley, a ten-year-old black girl, is in church in South Philadelphia, listening to a sermon given by her father, a Baptist minister. She is restless and vaguely resentful that her aunts and various members of the congregation keep encouraging her to be baptized. Matthew, Sarah's older brother, has been baptized and seems to have a sense of superiority as a result. As the sermon ends and the total-immersion baptism begins, Sarah sits on the lap of "Aunt" Bessie, a woman who often takes care of Sarah and Matthew when their parents are away. At the end of the baptismal ceremony, Aunt Bessie tells Sarah to "step forward." Sarah refuses, a struggle ensues, and she flees to her mother's side. Neither her father nor mother ever insists that she accept baptism, and she continues to go to New African, grateful for the gift of independence her father has granted her.

Teaching Strategies

Providing for Cultural Differences. Some students may wonder about the ceremony of baptism as Lee describes it. There are two points about this view of baptism, both central to the story, that you may wish to discuss: the belief that the ceremony should not be performed on nonbelievers and the insistence on the body's total immersion during the baptism ceremony—thus the "pool" in the church.

Providing for Different Levels of Ability. Most students should be able to read this story without difficulty. With less advanced students, you might want to read the story aloud in class, pasuing at the end of each section to have students discuss insights into Sarah and her attitude toward both the church and her father and make predictions about Sarah's actions in the next section. More advanced students might discuss how the story would differ if it were told from the viewpoint of Sarah's father.

Fiction 1945 to the Present

Introducing Vocabulary Study. Knowing the meanings of the following words is important to understanding the story.

cicadas	974	efficacy	977
miasma	974	wistfulness	977
lassitude	974	virtuosity	978
crescent	976	incantatory	978
balkiness	976	reproving	978
secular	977	sedate	980
minutist	977	coquettish	980
sanctified	977	sacrilege	981

After students have determined the meanings of the words, use the words *secular*, *sanctified*, *incantatory*, and *sacrilege* as the basis for a concept-formation exercise. Students should be able to predict that the story is about, or includes, religion.

Reading the Story. As the headnote on page 974 suggests, it may be a good idea to review the section on Puritan beliefs in Unit 1 (page 6). Ask students if they know what happened to the Puritans. (Puritanism as a political force died out in New England in the late 1600's, but Puritan churches, mainly Congregational at the outset—and, more importantly, Puritan beliefs and attitudes—still exist and exert great influence. Baptists gained attention early in American history when Roger Williams and his followers in Rhode Island rejected the Puritan/Calvinist doctrine of infant baptism and established a church in 1639.) Tell students that they will be reading about a Baptist church service. Have them notice how it differs, if at all, from services with which they may be familiar.

Reading Check. You might want ot use the following items as a reading check. Have students respond *True* or *False*.

1. The New African Baptist Church is located in a run-down area of New York City. _False_
2. Sarah feels that a person needs only a slight nudge toward religion in order to be baptized. _False_
3. Reverend Ashley directs his sermon toward the white college students in the congregation, but he clearly dislikes the way they dress. _False_
4. Sarah observes the baptism from the front pew of the church. _True_
5. Aunt Bessie relents when Sarah makes it clear that she does not want to be baptized. _False_

Reteaching Alternatives. Have students compare the protagonist in "New African" with the protagonist in James Alan McPherson's "Why I Like Country Music." What similarities and differences do they see between Sarah Ashley and the "I" narrator in McPherson's story?

Responding to the Story   Text page 982
Analyzing the Story
Identifying Facts

1. Describe the *setting* as it is presented in the opening of the story. The narrator, a black woman, recalls a hot summer Sunday in 1963, when she was sitting uncomfortably with her family at a long service in the New African Baptist Church in Philadelphia. She was ten years old at the time. Her father was the pastor of the church.

What details in the first three paragraphs help you feel the summer heat of the city? Students may mention the heat of the big electric fans in the church, the fact that the Rev. Ashley mops his brow and drinks glasses of ice water, the narrator's wish to go home and put on her shorts, and the ladies fanning themselves.

2. In what ways does Sarah feel her brother growing away from her? What passages show that she regards him as more "acceptable" than she is? Sarah thinks that Matthew has a superior attitude, now that he has been baptized. She is perhaps a bit jealous of her brother's image as "proper" in the eyes of the congregation.

3. Find the passages throughout the story that reveal Sarah's conflicting feelings about the church. Sarah is bored and longs to go home and play in the tree house that she has built with her brother Matthew, who is two years older. She feels claustrophobic in church, and she slouches in the pew with her mother and her aunts. Her brother is not sympathetic, since he has just been baptized and is now remarkably tolerant of long church services. But as she watches her father, Sarah clearly admires him.

Why has she refused to go for baptism? She refuses baptism because she does not feel the call.

Interpreting Meanings

4. Is there a *resolution* to Sarah's *conflict* by the story's end? Explain. Most students will agree that there is a resolution to Sarah's conflict. Although she never indicates what her religious beliefs are, she is grateful to her father for not forcing her to form them when she was a child.

5. In refusing to be baptized, what do you think Sarah is really objecting to? She is really objecting to having her own religion chosen for her.

How would you explain the feeling of being "misplaced," which she experiences at the story's end? She feels puzzled and disoriented because, although she thinks her parents may punish her for "misconduct" in church, they say and do nothing to reprimand her.

Andrea Lee   339

6. From what Sarah says about him, how would you *characterize* her father? The Rev. Ashley is an inspiring preacher, a social activist, and a gifted debater. From what Sarah says about him, her father is obviously an extrovert. But he is also remarkably patient and restrained with his daughter; he does not try to force his religious beliefs on her.

What does Sarah mean in the tribute she pays to her father in the story's last sentence? Sarah respects her father because he allowed her the freedom to choose her own personal beliefs.

7. What *conflicts* between generations and cultures do you infer from this story? Student answers will vary. Among the conflicts they may mention are the following: children vs. parents, traditional attitudes vs. questioning and independence, and old Southern vs. modern urban.

8. How does the *title* of the story relate to these conflicts? Who is really the "new" African in the story? The "new" African in the story seems to be the narrator, who challenges many of the traditional expectations of her parents' generation.

9. This story is presented as a memoir of childhood. Do you think the writer's main purpose is to present a realistic record of a single experience in 1963? Or does she evoke a more profound set of *themes* about being a young black female in 1963? Support your answer with specific references to the story. Again, students will have various responses. Certain details in the story—for example, the author's comments on the social background of the congregation and her fear that her father could never be "well pleased" in her—suggest that Sarah feels out of tune with the church. She is female and young, and she feels that pride of place is given to males—her brother Matthew, for example. Aunt Bessie's praise of rich white people and their manners makes Sarah uncomfortable, and she resents the pressure of many of her relatives for her to be baptized. Students may suggest that the story is really about a young person's struggle to be loved and to fit in without compromising her integrity.

Writing About the Story
A Creative Response

1. Imitating the Writer's Style. Analyze the opening paragraph with your students, leading them to note its attention to the season, the day of the week, the people present, the sensory details that make the reader feel everything that is happening.

Criteria for Evaluating the Assignment. The paragraph identifies the situation, what the young person is wearing, what he or she sees, hears, and smells, and what the person thinks and feels about the event. All details work together to create a specific overall tone.

A Critical Response

2. Analyzing Character. This assignment lends itself to a prewriting activity done in small groups, with different members of groups seeking specific details that characterize either Sarah or her father, and the group then sharing information and agreeing upon key points of characterization.

Criteria for Evaluating the Assignment. The analysis of Sarah or the Reverend Ashley makes generalizations about the character and supports them with details about the character's appearance, speech, or actions, how others respond to the character, the character's private thoughts and feelings, or direct comment from the writer.

3. Making Generalizations About the Stories. Clarify the difference between theme (a statement or judgment about life) and subject (the topic of a story) before students begin to review the stories in terms of the three areas listed.

Criteria for Evaluating the Assignment. The thesis statement or opening paragraph identifies areas the essay will explore or makes generalizations about the stories. The body of the essay explores use of family as a subject, use of generational conflict, and use of love as part of the theme, through references to specific stories in the unit. The essay need not refer to all ten stories, but does make use of at least three to five stories.

Extending the Story

Have students assume that Sarah Ashley, as a teenager, has recently joined your class. You have just assigned a topic for a brief (perhaps three-paragraph) essay: "America's Greatest Hero." Ask your students to write, not their own essay, but Sarah Ashley's essay on the topic. They should base their conclusions on what they have learned about Sarah in "New African" and their style, insofar as possible, on Andrea Lee's.

The American Language

Text page 983

1. **Students are to look through the Yellow Pages or some other business directory to find at least three examples of euphemistic titles for occupations or businesses. They should then say what ordinary word each example is replacing.** Answers will vary.

2. **Students are to invent an "upgraded" word for each of a number of titles.** Answers will vary. Sample answers are provided.

student: learning participant

automobile: transport device

baby sitter: infant custodian

apartment house: residential cluster

3. **Students are to place the words in each of the following pairs under either *Plain* or *Fancy*. They should then write *L* next to each word if it comes from Latin and *AS* next to the word if it comes from Anglo-Saxon.**

Plain	*Fancy*
eat (AS)	dine (L)
win (AS)	achieve (L)
pig (AS)	pork (L)
calf (AS)	veal (L)
spit (AS)	expectorate (L)
cheap (AS)	inexpensive (L)
cow (AS)	beef (L)
work (AS)	career (L)
father (AS)	parent (L)

4. **Students are to write their own definition of each of the following bureaucratic euphemisms.** Answers will vary. Sample answers are provided.

armed conflict: war

unlawful deprivation of life: murder

dependent upon distilled spirits: drunk

a controlled-substance abuser: a drug addict

Exercises in Critical Thinking and Writing

Text page 988

Evaluating a Story's Ending

This assignment asks students to evaluate the ending of one of the ten stories in the unit. It is important that students note a major point given in "Background"—a writer may deliberately choose not to provide closure on all conflicts, but to leave some of them unresolved. To help students choose a story, you might list the ten stories on the board or give students a list of the authors and titles with spaces left for students to briefly recall and jot down the ending of each story. After choosing the story that most interests them, students can then continue, individually or in small groups, with the notetaking questions in the second column and the directions for organizing the essay.

Criteria for Evaluating the Assignment. The essay as a whole is coherent and well organized. If students followed the plan suggested under "Writing," the opening paragraph mentions the title, author, and subject of the story, and summarizes its ending. The second paragraph comments on the writer's use of foreshadowing in its explanation of why the student did or did not find the outcome logical or inevitable. The third paragraph evaluates how well the ending fits the story's theme and characters by showing how at least one alternative ending would have been more or less satisfying. The fourth paragraph discusses the student's emotional response to the story and brings the paper to a satisfying close.

Unit Twelve: *Modern Nonfiction*

Text page 989

Teaching the Modern Nonfiction Unit

Although the essays and journalistic pieces of American writers since World War II have been notable for their high literary quality and for the new respect they have won for the genre of nonfiction, you needn't present this to your students as a wholly unprecedented phenomenon; in fact, nonfiction thrived in the United States before there was much fiction to speak of. This early flowering is probably the fruit of our pragmatic heritage: during the early development of our country, fiction was viewed as something of a frivolity, while nonfiction writers dealt with the most pressing issues of nation-building. Even such a great literary artist as Herman Melville came to prominence in the early years of his career not because of his bold imagination or his towering metaphysical insights, but because he reported to the American audience, with a memoirist's eye, on what it had been like to live among a tribe of South Sea islanders. And Mark Twain was a great reporter, in *Life on the Mississippi* and *Roughing It,* before he flowered as the creator of Huckleberry Finn.

While you won't want to get bogged down in review work, this unit, coming near the end of the year's work, might be a good place to cast a brief backward glance at some of the earlier nonfiction, to help prepare your students for what is to come. They'll find that the rich vein of autobiographical writing in American literature proceeds—despite the differences in subject matter—from Benjamin Franklin to Richard Wright. N. Scott Momaday's observations on American Indian culture can be compared and contrasted with the observations of white writers of the Colonial period, such as William Bradford, Mary Rowlandson, William Byrd, and, again, Franklin. Michael Herr's reportage from Vietnam is descended from a long and honorable line of wartime writing not only in nonfiction like Whitman's *Specimen Days,* but also in fiction such as Crane's *The Red Badge of Courage.* Contemporary essayists who write personally about the natural world, such as Annie Dillard and Lewis Thomas, are the direct literary descendants of Henry David Thoreau. Baldwin and Wright, meanwhile, owe much to the writers of the Harlem Renaissance in Unit Eight.

At the same time, you'll want to direct your students' attention to what is genuinely new in the nonfiction of recent decades. There is, for example, a brash willingness to place the individual writer's consciousness at the heart of the work, rather than maintaining a stance of objectivity. There is a willingness to try new forms—to mix fiction and nonfiction as Maxine Hong Kingston does, or expository prose and lyrical prose-poems as in the book-length version of *The Way to Rainy Mountain.* In the journalism of Hersey and Herr, there is a strong quality which the earlier writers, at the beginning of a new nation's history, had not had time yet to develop: there is a dry disillusionment with war—a cold but hopeful realism that replaces the naiveté of a belief in war's glories. And in the personal odyssey of William Least Heat Moon, we find another quality which, by definition, cannot be found in the infancy of a republic: nostalgia.

Because the contemporary essay is such a personal form, and because it doesn't require the imposition of an artificial structure—a plot—upon its material, it is particularly adaptable to student writing assignments. Some of your students may have already had experience writing journalism for the school newspaper; all of them have had practice at writing expository essays. In this unit more than in other units, they'll have the feeling that in writing about the selections, they are practicing the same skills as the writers of the selections themselves: observing, evaluating, criticizing, explaining, stating their views.

*O*bjectives of the Nonfiction Unit

1. To expand vocabulary and increase reading proficiency
2. To gain exposure to notable authors of nonfiction and their works
3. To define and identify elements of nonfiction
4. To define and identify significant literature techniques: figurative language, comic imagery, symbolism, puns, allusions, hyperbole, concrete detail, subjectivity and objectivity, and irony
5. To interpret and respond to nonfiction, orally and in writing, through analysis of its elements
6. To analyze the language and style of authors of nonfiction
7. To practice the following critical thinking and writing skills:
   a. Analyzing an essay
   b. Analyzing style, atmosphere, character, and suspense
   c. Comparing and contrasting two works of literature
   d. Responding to a critical statement
   e. Imitating a writer's technique
   f. Evaluating fact and opinion in nonfiction

*I*ntroducing the Modern Nonfiction Unit

Nonfiction is part of all our lives even if we are not literary specialists, in a way quite different from fiction. We come to know the outside world largely through the words of journalists and essayists. We learn about wars, elections, famines, economic upheavals, sporting events, without personally witnessing them; and we trust—or have to decide how much to trust—the writers and reporters who give us the information. In introducing this unit, you might ask your students to try to visualize how their knowledge of the world would be different if they had never had any access to nonfiction writing. They'll probably agree that their knowledge of global and governmental affairs would be extremely limited. You might then inform students that nonfiction not only acquaints us with outside events, but it also acquaints us with the minds of the people writing it. If your students keep a journal, you might ask them to write and share entries expressing their personal reactions to public events that have affected their lives or to phenomena of nature or of family history that have been meaningful to them. The results will very likely be in the spirit of this unit.

E. B. White

Text page 993

"Death of a Pig"

Text page 994

Objectives

1. To analyze tone and character
2. To analyze theme
3. To analyze the use of anthropomorphism
4. To write a recollection of an animal
5. To write an essay analyzing the writer's style
6. To write an essay describing a character
7. To write an essay explaining an allusion

Introducing the Essay

White's essay has become a classic because of the poignant, universal themes he develops from a seemingly homely and perhaps even comical subject, the premature death of a pig he had been raising for meat. In the same sentence—for example, the last sentence in the essay—White pokes gentle fun at the antics of a pet dog, and summons up the ache of grief at mortality. In examining this selection, you'll probably want to make your students aware of the subtlety and richness of these variations in tone, and the contrast between the barnyard subject matter and the sublime reflections it arouses.

Background on the Essay. White's style and career are inseparable from the style and the history of *The New Yorker* magazine, but "Death of a Pig," doubtless because of its subject matter, did not first appear in that publication; it was first published in *The Atlantic Monthly.* Nevertheless, you might want to tell your students briefly about the extraordinary influence *The New Yorker* has had on contemporary American nonfiction and fiction, publishing writers like Salinger, Capote, Hersey, John McPhee, John Cheever, John Updike, and many others. The magazine's nonfiction, in particular, is notable for its smooth, balanced, genteel style, its graceful fluency, and its nearly continuous irony flowing underneath a surface of impeccably researched and presented facts. You might want to obtain a recent issue of the magazine and read a few paragraphs of its nonfiction aloud to your class, so they can see that White's style is partly individual and partly generic.

Summary. White raised a pig in hopes of butchering it for meat, but it became severely constipated and died despite White's own efforts and those of a veterinarian.

Teaching Strategies

Providing for Cultural Differences. Rural and urban students may react to this essay in different ways. Rural students may bring to it a fuller understanding of the livestock-raising processes involved, but because of familiarity with the mundane aspects of White's narrative, they may be reluctant to go along with the larger themes. Urban students, for whom the whole subject of pig-raising is only metaphorical anyway, may be more receptive to White's eagerness to philosophize. All students will probably need a brief explanation of the old rural type of crank-operated telephone, with eavesdropping operator—now seen only in old movies.

Providing for Different Levels of Ability. White's style is fairly simple but his wry stance and euphemistic style of humor may need some interpretation for less advanced students. More advanced students will enjoy the pleasing flow of White's sentences, with their judicious variations

344   Modern Nonfiction

in pace, tone, and diction. Almost any passage in the essay can be profitably used as the basis of a stylistic analysis.

Introducing Vocabulary Study. Students will benefit from knowing the meanings of the following words before they read the selection. (Starred words appear in the Glossary.)

premeditated	994	corrosive	997
slapstick	994	inextricably	997
desultory*	996	paraphernalia	998
unseasonable	996	imminence*	998
transitory	996	bereavement	999

Two especially important words on this list are "transitory"—which relates to White's renewed understanding of the transitoriness of all life—and "inextricably," which expresses the connection he feels between the sadness of the pig's fate and that of all living things.

Reading the Essay. You might ask your students whether they have ever been present at, or been affected by, the death of an animal. In certain circumstances, this can be a deeply poignant experience. You might ask whether these experiences made your students feel that they were learning anything general about the nature of life.

Reading Check. You might use the following questions as a check for literal comprehension. Have students respond *True* or *False*.

1. White's dog Fred held the enema bag. True
2. White says he will never forget the third night of the vigil, when the pig died. False
3. White was worried about catching a skin disease from the pig. True
4. The veterinarian gave the pig an injection to end his misery. False
5. The pig's death later became a great subject of jokes among White's neighbors. False

Reteaching Alternatives. To help clarify the themes of the essay, you might ask your students, individually, to write one-paragraph summaries of how White tended his sick pig and how he apparently felt about the experience.

Responding to the Essay Text page 999
Analyzing the Essay
Identifying Facts

1. Why does the narrator want to write about the pig? White says that things might easily have turned out differently: he might have died and the pig might have lived, and then there would be no one left to write about the story. He also says that he sympathized with the pig, since it suffered in a "suffering world."

In the second paragraph, what comparison does he use to describe the process of raising a pig? White compares the process to a play (a tragedy) with actors—a well-recognized and approved script, in which each participant has his own motives and actions.

2. How does the narrator come to regard the pig's suffering and death? The narrator suddenly comes to see himself as "cast" in the role of the pig's friend and physician. He finds himself sympathetic with the pig's suffering, and he dreads its death.

Find the passages where he identifies with the pig. White identifies with the pig when he tries to feed it supper and it won't eat; when he sees its pink throat and it screams in pain; when he scratches the pig and feels its ears; when he tends the pig like an ill patient. The narrator cries when the pig dies, and says that he will visit its grave on "flagless memorial days."

Interpreting Meanings

3. How often does Fred the dachshund appear? Fred is present at the treatments and at the burial of the pig.

What is Fred's importance in the essay? Fred becomes a figure of black humor in the essay—a sort of disturbing, lugubrious presence which contrasts with the sympathetic narrator. Some students may offer the opinion that the rather grotesque portrayal of Fred prevents the essay from becoming mawkish or sentimental.

4. Find the passages where Fred is described as if he were human. Among such passages are the introduction of Fred as "vile," the description of the dog as making "professional calls," the mention of Fred "supervising" the digging of the grave, and the reference to him at the pig's funeral as the "dishonorable pallbearer." At the end of the essay, Fred is said to be able to direct mourners to the pig's grave.

White refers to his pet as a "vile" dachshund. Does White really dislike Fred? How would you describe his feelings toward his nosy dog? Students will probably agree that White does not really hate his dog. He is amused by the dog's nosiness and curiosity, and a bit annoyed at Fred's evident lack of sympathy for the pig.

5. Why were White's feelings about life—its sorrows and uncertainties—shaken by the death of his pig? He seems shaken because the pig's illness and death come to seem like a symbol of unforeseen suffering and death in the human lot.

What examples of *hyperbole* (exaggeration) does he use to illustrate his shaken feelings? White calls the incident a "tragedy." He says he mourned the pig's death with "deep hemorrhagic in-tears."

E. B. White   345

6. Why do you think White and Fred will visit the grave? What will they learn there? Student answers will vary. They might go to remember the pig. They may learn some things about themselves.

7. Where does White explain his *purpose* in writing this essay? How would you explain this statement of purpose? White explains his purpose in the first three paragraphs. His purpose might be explained as follows: he wants to record the death of his pig because its circumstances led him to reflect on life in a "suffering world."

8. What passage or sentences would you say are key to this essay and its *theme*? Students may point to the third paragraph, where White mentions the fact that the pig had become precious to him because it suffered.

9. How did you respond to the essay—to its animal and its human characters? Student answers will vary. Ask them to defend their responses with logical reasoning and with specific references to the text of the essay.

Writing About the Essay
A Creative Response

1. Imitating White's Technique. The assignment has a delightful latitude, allowing students to work with anything from their own pet to an imaginary unicorn, griffon, or creature of their own devising. Brainstorm a list of possibilities to give students this range.

Criteria for Evaluating the Assignment. The essay reflects White's influence in the way the animal is given a consistent, appropriate, human personality.

A Critical Response

2. Analyzing Style. Have students work in groups to find examples of and to discuss how comic metaphors, comic images, irony, exaggeration, and puns help White to create his overall humorous effect. Direct them to cite specific examples in their essays.

Criteria for Evaluating the Essay. In a well-organized manner, the essay cites specific details from the essay to demonstrate how White's humor makes use of the elements of comic metaphors, comic images, irony, exaggeration, and puns.

3. Describing a Character. Response questions 3 and 4 provide data for this writing assignment on Fred the dachshund. Briefly review the appropriate paragraphs.

Criteria for Evaluating the Essay. The essay describes the character of Fred the dachshund not as the student imagines it, but as White creates it. Generalizations are supported by details from the essay on Fred's appearance, interests, and responses to the pig's problems.

4. Explaining Allusion. Review response questions 6 and 7 on the theme of White's essay, and lead students to recall that allusions usually enlarge upon, enhance, or ironically highlight an idea. If Donne's "Meditation XVII" is not readily available, give your students copies of these lines: ". . . all mankind is of one author and is one volume; when one man dies, one chapter is not torn out of the book, but translated into a better language; and every chapter must be so translated." "No man is an island, entire of itself; every man is a piece of the continent, a part of the main. . . . Any man's death diminishes me because I am involved in mankind, and therefore never send to know for whom the bell tolls; it tolls for thee."

Criteria for Evaluating the Assignment. The essay cites the use of the allusion on page 998 as enlarging upon the theme that the death of the pig led the writer to reflect on human experience, and also as a humorous extension of the personification of the pig.

Extending the Essay

White's essay finds universal echoes of mortality in the death of a farm animal; here is a poem by Gerard Manley Hopkins, written in 1880, that finds the same echoes in the fall of a leaf, seen by a child. Have students compare and contrast the theme of mortality as it is expressed in the essay and the poem.

Spring and Fall:
To a Young Child

Margaret, are you grieving

Over Goldengrove unleaving?

Leaves, like the things of man, you

With your fresh thoughts care for, can you?

Ah! as the heart grows older

It will come to such sights colder

By and by, nor spare a sigh

Though worlds of wanwood leafmeal lie;

And yet you will weep and know why.

Now no matter, child, the name;

Sorrow's springs are the same.

Nor mouth had, no nor mind, expressed

What heart heard of, ghost guessed:

It is the blight man was born for,

It is Margaret you mourn for.

Lewis Thomas

"Ceti"

Objectives

1. To identify the tone
2. To write an essay expressing a personal point of view
3. To write a paragraph evaluating the essay
4. To analyze the use of specialized and informal language

Introducing the Essay

Thomas's essay resembles E. B. White's in the sense that both move from the particular to the general. White's "Death of a Pig" begins with some very specific memories of pig-raising and of discovering the pig to be ill, and moves in to become, by implication, a meditation on mortality in general. Thomas's "Ceti" begins with a description of a single scientific conference and goes on to discuss the nature of life and the self-image of the human race. This is a natural format for essays: the writer's attention is caught by a specific phenomenon, and he or she proceeds to muse upon that phenomenon until arriving at general conclusions, thus making the phenomenon seem larger and more meaningful than it was at first glance. The same kind of developmental structure is often used, also, in poetry. Robert Frost was indirectly commenting on this when he said that a poem should "begin in delight and end in wisdom," and many of his poems, such as "Birches" and "Mending Wall," display this sort of structure.

Background on the Essay. As is often the case in journalism, the form of this essay was dictated to some extent by the practical demands of a specific periodical. When Lewis Thomas began his career as an essayist by publishing individual pieces as columns in *The New England Journal of Medicine,* he was required to produce an essay of a certain length, on a certain kind of topic, at regular intervals. Because readers responded well, and because the author's turn of mind suited the journalistic form, Thomas's writing flourished.

Among other excellent contemporary essayists in the sciences, whom your students might be interested in discovering, are Stephen Jay Gould, Oliver Sacks, Richard Selzer, Arthur C. Clarke, Nigel Calder, Carl Sagan, Douglas Hofstadter, and Barry Lopez.

Summary. In 1972 an international conference, intentionally called the Conference on Communication with Extraterrestrial Intelligence (CETI), was held to plan efforts to probe Tau Ceti and other stars for possible electromagnetic messages. Thomas discusses how the human race might react to the discovery of life elsewhere, and muses on what questions we might ask an extraterrestrial species and what artifacts of our civilization we might want to transmit to it.

Teaching Strategies

Providing for Cultural Differences. This essay provides a good opportunity for your more scientifically oriented students to become interested in literature, and for your more literary-minded students to see the poetic side of science. Lewis Thomas himself is an excellent role model for young people, since his career has bridged the "two cultures"—science and the humanities—that C. P. Snow described a generation ago.

Providing for Different Levels of Ability. Thomas uses a number of scientific terms in this essay—"anaerobic," "pili," "ganglions," and so forth—but they are defined in footnotes at the bottoms of the text pages. Your more advanced students will probably be excited by Thomas's speculations, particularly those in the second half of the essay, where he speculates on how we might present ourselves and our civilization to extraterrestrials. Less advanced students may find the beginning of the essay, with its description of a scientific conference, a bit dry, and they may need a paraphrase of his description of the "morphogenesis" of the earth, text page 1002.

Introducing Vocabulary Study. Knowing the meanings of the following words will help students understand the selection. (Starred words appear in the Glossary.)

plausible*	1001	protocol*	1002
acronym*	1001	filaments	1002
suffused*	1002	amenities*	1002

Reading the Essay. Though the essay is short, its scientific contents make it a bit thorny for oral reading. You might want to have your students read it for homework, and then have students read the most intriguing or most troublesome paragraphs out loud in class.

Reading Check. You might want to use the following items as a test for literal comprehension. Have students complete the statements with words or phrases that express the sense of the answers below.

1. Scientists are interested in the nearby star Tau Ceti because <u>it is a plausible candidate for the existence of life</u>.
2. First contact with extraterrestrial species is likely to be made through the medium of <u>radioastronomy</u>.
3. Two-way conversation with extraterrestrials would be made difficult because <u>there would be very long pauses between messages</u>.
4. Thomas says that the safest and most attractive message for earthlings to send would be <u>music</u>.
5. Thomas says that if we sent messages to extraterrestrials about our current affairs, they would become <u>out of date, embarrassing</u> by the time we received a reply.

Reteaching Alternatives. Probably the most crucial area of attention in this essay is the second half, where Thomas discusses what messages we might send to other species and what questions we might ask of them. You might point out to students that this topic, while it may someday become a reality, is essentially a metaphor by means of which Thomas asks some basic questions: What are we human beings? How would our civilization look to outsiders? What should we be proud of in our achievements, and what embarrassed by? What might we want to learn that we don't yet know? These questions are of great importance for the survival of life on this planet, whether or not life exists on others.

Responding to the Essay Text page 1003
Analyzing the Essay
Identifying Facts

1. What does the essay's title refer to? CETI is an acronym, referring to a conference on the Communication with Extraterrestrial Intelligence, held in 1972.

2. What technique has recently been proposed for human communication with life outside the solar system? Participants at an international conference have proposed that radioastronomy offers the best chance of communicating with any life that may exist outside the solar system.

3. What practical problem will have to be faced by the CETI participants in such communication? Since the target for communication, the relatively nearby star Tau Ceti, is one hundred light years from Earth, answers to the messages sent from Earth will not be received for two centuries after the messages are sent. The time lag will thus make meaningful communication difficult.

4. How does Thomas suggest that this problem could be solved? The author suggests that it would be best to send nonverbal messages at first: he suggests (if technology permits) that the best thing to do would be to beam the music of Bach into space.

Interpreting Meanings

5. In what kind of *tone* does Thomas close the essay? Although the essay largely depends on the "assumption" that intelligent life exists outside the solar system, and that such beings would be able to respond to messages from Earth, at the very end Thomas stops us short by suggesting that if we did in fact receive an answer ("Yes, hello"), we might "want to stop there and think...for quite a long time." The implication is that such a discovery would deliver a major shock to our sense of uniqueness as the only intelligent, living beings in the universe. The tone is humorous and whimsical.

6. When Thomas says we should beam Bach into outer space, he adds, "We would be bragging, of course." What does he mean? Thomas amplifies his meaning when he says, a little later on, "We could tell the harder truths later." He implies that, although the music of Bach was one of humanity's most glorious creations, there have been others in which we can take considerably less pride.

7. What different aspects of our humanity does Thomas suggest in the questions he thinks we might ask, such as "Do you always tell the truth? Do you cry?" What do these questions reveal about our natures? Student answers will vary. In general, Thomas points through these questions to the fact that human beings are fallible, vulnerable, and prone to evil or deception.

8. Think of the other essayists you have read: Franklin, Emerson, and Thoreau, for example. Would you describe Thomas as a rationalist, like Franklin, or as a Romantic idealist, like Emerson and Thoreau? Or is it impossible to categorize this essay? Students will probably agree that it is relatively difficult to categorize the essay, since it contains both rationalist and Romantic elements.

9. Would you take issue with any of Thomas's points in this essay? Student answers will vary. Ask the students whether or not they agree with Thomas's points about human failings and flaws in human nature.

Writing About the Essay
A Creative Response

1. Expressing Your Point of View. Use Lewis's partial list of questions in his next-to-last paragraph as a springboard for further questions. Analyze what importance the answers to Lewis's questions would have, and the kinds of information the students consider equally, or more, important, as guidelines for creating further questions. Note that the writing prompt tells students how to organize their three paragraphs.

Criteria for Evaluating the Assignment. The first paragraph lists defensible questions to be asked of intelligent extraterrestrials. The second paragraph explains what "news of ourselves" to send. The third paragraph explains what "harder truths" we might need to tell these beings later.

A Critical Response

2. Evaluating the Essay. Make sure students understand that, in addition to determining the main topic of Lewis's essay and what it "teaches," they are to *evaluate* the essay—make a judgment on its overall value or effectiveness.

Criteria for Evaluating the Assignment. The paragraph correctly cites Lewis's topic as how to communicate with intelligent extraterrestrials and what he "teaches" as the difficulty of establishing criteria for the information and questions to be sent. It offers a judgment on the overall value or effectiveness of Lewis's essay.

Extending the Essay

As a creative exercise, you might ask your students to bring to mind some topic that they have learned about in one of their science courses, and write a brief essay developing the implications of the topic for humanity.

Russell Baker

Text page 1004

"Little Red Riding Hood Revisited"

Text page 1005

Objectives

1. To interpret irony
2. To rephrase slang, jargon, and pleonasm
3. To imitate the writer's technique
4. To analyze the use of jargon

Introducing the Essay

In the brief space of a newspaper column, Russell Baker pokes serious fun at the mutilation of the English language by the forces of institutional obfuscation. Starting with the phrase, "Once upon a point in time," he weaves into the familiar fairy tale the stock pleonasms and linguistic barbarities of politicians, law enforcement officers ("alleged perpetrator"), social scientists ("attained interface"), lawyers, ("a third party, heretofore unnoted in the record"), advertisers ("dramatic relief for stomach discontent"), and the simply semiliterate ("What a phenomena!"). In addition to decrying the distortion of language, Baker implicitly criticizes the bureaucratic officiousness and widespread intellectual sloppiness that have made them possible.

Background on the Essay. Russell Baker is one of a number of journalists who have in recent years raised alarms about the deterioration of our language at the hands of bureaucratic institutions and the mass media. Another *New York Times* columnist, William Safire, regularly writes on this subject, collecting instances of poor usage from far and wide; and Edwin Newman has written several books on the subject, including *Strictly Speaking*. You might keep in mind that for the most part, Baker is not objecting to simple usage errors of colloquial speech but to genteelisms—the kinds of mistakes committed by the half-educated in the belief that they sound official, important, or impressive.

Summary. Baker retells the folk tale of Little Red Riding Hood in the inflated rhetoric of the modern bureaucracy.

Teaching Strategies

Providing for Cultural Differences. A satire of the jargon of contemporary institutions is likely to mean most to those who are familiar with those institutions. This selection was written for a column in *The New York Times,* a newspaper with a predominantly middle-class readership, and it will probably strike the deepest chord in students who stay abreast of public affairs, and whose parents may be in the professions Baker satirizes. Students who may not hear standard English spoken in their homes may not "get" a satire that implicitly measures bureaucratic English against standard English.

Providing for Different Levels of Ability. More advanced students will probably relish Baker's pleonasms and feel that he is speaking for them. Less advanced students may have to be shown the ways in which this essay deviates from good English: for instance, that "a phenomena" is incorrect and that "residing at a place of residence" is redundant.

Introducing Vocabulary Study. Knowing the meanings of the following words will help students understand the essay.

accessible	1005	malaise	1006
indeterminate	1005	manifest (adj.)	1006
implementing	1005	masticating	1006
incursion	1005	propriety	1006
interface	1005	ingestion	1006
alienation	1005	alleviated	1007
consignment	1005	intervention	1007

The list of vocabulary words for this very short selection is very long because the use of big words is itself the topic of the satire. Vocabulary study, then, is part of the fabric of reading the essay. You will probably want to stop at several points during the reading of the selection to explain difficult words and phrases.

Reading the Essay. Although this piece is short, it will benefit from being read slowly, perhaps one paragraph per student if you are having it read aloud. Paraphrase and definition will doubtless be natural accompaniments, since part of Baker's aim is to make us "translate" his pleonasms into clear English as we go along.

Reading Check. You might want to use the following as a check for literal comprehension. Have the students respond *True* or *False*.

1. The wolf was "a mass of repressed hostility intertwined with acute alienation."   True
2. Little Red Riding Hood was carrying "a consignment of foodstuffs."   True
3. Red Riding Hood said, "Grandmother, your ocular implements are of an extraordinary order of magnitude."   True
4. Grandma was put in a television commercial for a headache remedy.   False
5. The ingestion of one grandmother exceeded the wolf's recommended cholesterol intake.   True

Reteaching Alternatives. If oral paraphrasing of the essay leaves some students still confused, question 1 of "Analyzing Language and Style," text page 1007, which asks for a written paraphrase, is a suitable assignment.

Responding to the Essay   Text page 1007
Analyzing the Essay
Identifying Facts

1. In the first paragraph, how does the writer state his *purpose*? He says that he is making the classics more accessible to modern readers by translating them into contemporary language.

Interpreting Meanings

2. When was it first clear to you that the statement of purpose was *ironic*? Some students may claim they recognized the irony as early as Baker's first sentence, with the use of the words "translating" and "modern American language." For most students, the irony will have been apparent by the end of the second paragraph.

3. Baker finds several kinds of language misuse to mock in this updated fairy tale. Identify at least one example each of *slang*, *jargon*, and *pleonasm* (redundancy, or the use of more words than is necessary for the expression of an idea). How could each passage be stated in plain speech? Students will have various answers. Examples of slang include "you dig," "I hear you loud and clear, kid," "new choppers." Examples of jargon include: "daily recommended cholesterol intake," "attained interface with an alleged perpetrator," "a mass of repressed hostility intertwined with acute alienation," "sight systems," "miracle masticating products." Examples of pleonasm: "residing at a place of residence," "and all that," "her mission consisted of taking her to and with," "the time was now, the hour had struck." Students will have various opinions on the inappropriateness of each example. In general, by deliberately including these misuses of language, Baker violates the principles of clarity and coherence in writing, and he amusingly combines different levels of language which are ordinarily kept separate.

4. The "modern American language" that Baker mocks here is often guilty of using words to obscure unpleasant reality. This use of a word or phrase that is less offensive than another is called *euphemism*; an example is the use of the phrase "passed away" instead of the more straightforward verb "died." What euphemisms can you find in this story? What unpleasant reality is each attempting to hide? Among the euphemisms students may mention in the essay are the following: "senior citizen" (for "old woman"), "alleged perpetrator" (for "criminal"), "repressed hostility" (for "hatred"), and "stomach discontent" (for "indigestion").

5. Who or what are Baker's real targets in this *satire*? (Can you find barbs aimed at the fields of politics, sociology, medicine, law, and psychology?) Student answers will vary. The students should be able to illustrate barbs at each of the fields mentioned with numerous phrases in the essay.

Writing About the Essay
A Creative Response

Imitating Baker's Technique. Brainstorm a list of other popular fairy tales—Cinderella, Snow White, Goldilocks, and such—as source material.

Criteria for Evaluating the Assignment. Like Baker, the student uses a mixture of slang, jargon, verbosity and euphemisms in the retelling of a fairy tale.

Analyzing Language and Style
Jargon

1. Student choices will vary. The rewritten paragraphs should be entirely free of jargon. For example, the sentence used in this assignment would read, "Halfway to her grandmother's house, Little Red Riding Hood met a criminal."

2. *Jargon* is derived from a Middle French word meaning "a chattering." The origin is appropriate because jargon outside its specialized field is meaningless, like chatter.

Extending the Essay

You might ask students to clip from periodicals, or write down from newscasts, examples of misused English that they read or hear. This can become an ongoing project, with all members of the class sharing their findings in a notebook or on a bulletin board, or sending their clippings to the school newspaper for publication.

"School vs. Education"

Text page 1008

Objectives

1. To identify hyperbole
2. To state the theme
3. To write a "letter to the editor" responding to the essay
4. To support an assertion with examples
5. To interpret irony

Introducing the Essay

Part of the art of being a social gadfly consists of perceiving the obvious and calling attention to it in a more pungent way than has usually been done before. When Baker, for instance, says that from television, young children learn "how to pick a lock, commit a fairly elaborate bank holdup, prevent wetness all day long, get the laundry twice as white, and kill people with a variety of sophisticated armaments," he is saying, in an oversimplified way, what everyone already knows about the contents of television, but he is saying it memorably. The oversimplification, too, is part of the effect, the vivid rhetoric inviting us to stop and say, "Yes, that's the way it is."

Backgound on the Essay. Debates on the nature of American education have been raging for decades, and Baker is by no means the first to point out that schools teach students how to take tests rather than how to love knowledge. Nor does he propose specific solutions in this essay: that is the preserve of writers of books on education. Baker's role is limited to that of social gadfly, attempting to make us think, discuss, and perhaps come up with our own solutions.

Summary. Baker describes some of the deplorable things young children see and hear on television and in the home, and the test-taking skills they learn in school, and draws an implied comparison between this and true education.

Teaching Strategies

Providing for Cultural Differences. The essay mentions the disruption that can occur in schools torn by racial strife, an aspect of contemporary education that some students in some schools may have experienced personally, while others may have only heard of it on the news. Baker does not address specific conflicts in specific local situations, but, by means of mordant satire, makes the point that racial unrest is a very unfortunate part of some American educational settings. Since most American students have not directly witnessed such conflicts, the essay may make them feel that much better about their own schools; for those who have, the essay may provide a useful opportunity to discuss the problem.

Providing for Different Levels of Ability. The essay refers to the fact that students are, indeed, at different levels of ability and experience different educational fates. This can be a chance to draw your less advanced students into the discussion, by having them respond to Baker's assertions.

Introducing Vocabulary Study. Knowing the meanings of the following words will help students understand the selection. (Starred words are listed in the Glossary.)

cohesion*   1008   pigmentation*   1008

Reading the Essay. Since the essay takes a swipe at the educational establishment, it might be a good idea for you—as the representative of that establishment—to read it aloud to the class, as a way of showing receptiveness to Baker's challenge.

Reading Check. You might use the following as a check for literal comprehension. Have students complete the statements with words or phrases that express the sense of the answers below.

1. According to Baker, during the first six years of life a child learns most from <u>watching its parents; watching television</u>.
2. According to Baker, during formal education a student learns that life is for <u>testing</u>.
3. Baker says the point of school is to equip the child for <u>college</u>.
4. The competitive testing becomes keenest for entrance to <u>graduate school</u>.
5. Baker says that after the former students have attained worldly success, they may one day have the leisure and inclination to <u>read books</u>.

Reteaching Alternatives. This essay is likely to spark lively discussion, since it touches upon an experience—school—in which all students are immersed. You may, if you choose, want to open up the discussion to include the students' own views on what is right and what is wrong about American education as they've known it.

Responding to the Essay   Text page 1009
Analyzing the Essay
Identifying Facts

1. **What does Baker claim is "the point" of lower education in America?** Baker claims that the point of lower education is to equip children to enter college.

 Of higher education? Of graduate school? Higher education, according to Baker, prepares students to enter graduate school, and graduate school provides them with "valuable certificates to prosper in medicine, at the bar, and in the corporate boardroom."

Interpreting Meanings

2. **Baker remarks *satirically* on the so-called "skills" a preschooler receives. What are these skills, and what do they say about the society in which the child is growing up?** Some of the skills Baker mentions are picking a lock, robbing a bank, getting the laundry twice as white, warfare, smoking and drinking, using profane language, and speeding in a car. Baker says that, to learn these skills, children merely have to watch television and imitate their parents. He implies that the society the children are growing up in is violent and abusive.

 Do you agree with Baker's points? Why or why not? Student answers will vary. Encourage the students to support their opinions.

3. **Much of Baker's humor derives from his gift for *hyperbole*, or exaggeration for effect. What are some examples of comic hyperbole in this essay?** Student answers will vary. Most of them will agree that Baker's introductory paragraphs, on the "skills" learned by preschool children, contain many examples of hyperbole. Remind students that Baker's purpose is satirical.

 Do you think these points would be more effectively made in a serious essay? Why or why not? Student answers will vary. Most students will probably agree that the same points might sound too critical or pessimistic if they were presented in a serious essay.

4. **What is the significance of the essay's title? How would you state Baker's main *theme*, or message?** By including the expression "vs." in the title, Baker implies that school and education are opposed or antithetical concepts—whereas, in reality, one should be the vehicle for the other. The message is that education in our schools should reflect better values.

5. **According to Baker, what do American schoolchildren *not* learn during their formal education?** They do not learn to open a book with a curious mind, and thus to start actually to be educated.

 Do you agree with him? Why or why not? Student answers will vary. Encourage the students to support their opinions.

Writing About the Essay
A Creative Response

1. **Answering the Writer.** Have students look at the kinds and lengths of letters actually published in newspapers: they must be short and to the point.

352   Modern Nonfiction

Criteria for Evaluating the Assignment. Whatever the student thinks of Baker's essay, the paragraph is appropriate for a letter to the editor and shows a recognition both of Baker's serious intent and his satirical style.

A Critical Response

2. Supporting an Assertion with Examples. Cull from the essay several points, such as "Teachers show children you should belong to a union"; "Television teaches crime"; "Parents teach prejudice." Ask students about their own experiences which support or refute these points.

Criteria for Evaluating the Assignment. The essay correctly cites at least one point from Baker's "School vs. Education" and explains personal expriences which either cogently support or cogently refute Baker's contention(s).

Analyzing Language and Style
Irony

1. One would expect parents to teach their children positive moral values.
2. The topic sentence comes at the end of the paragraph, thus summarizing strikes and race riots—not an academic focus—as the true beginning of "formal education."
3. Success means the answer the tester wants to hear—not necessarily the *right* answer.

Extending the Essay

You might want to give your students some practice writing newspaper-style columns by having them pick topics of their own choice, either from current events, school events, or American cultural life, and writing brief essays in which they reveal the foibles of the subject, in a style similar to Baker's.

Richard Wright

Text page 1010

From *Black Boy*

Text page 1011

Objectives

1. To analyze imagery
2. To analyze character
3. To write a monologue from another point of view
4. To write an essay comparing and contrasting the styles and themes of two writers
5. To write a paragraph anaylzing the use of dialogue

Introducing the Autobiography

In outline form, for your reference, here are the main elements of the autobiography:

- **Main characters:** Richard; Richard's mother and father; a gang of boys; Miss Simon, director of the orphanage
- **Conflicts:** fear vs. the conquest of fear; deprivation vs. fulfillment; injustice vs. justice
- **Themes:** maturation through struggle; family strife as an outgrowth of poverty; the oppression of black people

- **Point of view:** first-person
- **Significant techniques:** naturalistic detail; vivid dialogue
- **Setting:** Memphis, Tennessee, early 20th century

Background on the Autobiography. Wright said that he hit upon the idea of writing his autobiography after delivering a lecture about his life and about black life at Fisk University in 1942, when he was newly famous from the success of his novel *Native Son.* He found that his honest words about the feelings of black people startled both the black and white members of the audiences, simply because such things had not often been publicly expressed up till that time. In *Black Boy,* Wright memorably recounts how his discovery of literature helped him find his direction in life, and how a Catholic white man, who was also a victim of discrimination, lent him his library card at a time when blacks were not allowed to use the public library.

Summary. After Wright's father left home, his mother tried to keep her family together, but their poverty was such that there was often no food in the house, and finally she had to send Richard to an orphanage, where conditions were not much better. Richard ran away but was returned and beaten. His father refused to provide for his children. Wright describes seeing his father later in life, and forgiving him, but remaining aware of the unbridgeable distance between them.

Teaching Strategies

Providing for Cultural Differences. This selection may have special meaning for some black students, and you might want to encourage them to share their feelings, bearing in mind that such feelings may be too powerful for them to talk about comfortably. However, the power of Wright's narrative transcends race, and even students from middle-class or privileged backgrounds may empathize with the sufferings of a young boy who is confused about his parents' conflicts, frightened of neighborhood bullies, and tyrannized by a Dickensian orphanage director.

Providing for Different Levels of Ability. Wright's style is direct and forceful, though the passing of four decades may make it seem a trifle old-fashioned to today's students. More advanced students might be interested in comparing this selection to works of realism and naturalism studied in earlier units. Less advanced students will probably handle the dialogue sections more easily than the passages of narrative; the latter, you might briefly paraphrase in the normal course of discussion.

Introducing Vocabulary Study. Knowing the meanings of the following words will help students understand the selection.

enthralled (v.)	1011	ardently	1014
gauntly	1012	copiously	1014
clamor	1012	spurned	1015
dispirited	1012	vindictive	1016
retaliate	1013	elapse	1018

It is worth noting that most of these words are words of feeling (*dispirited*, *ardently*) or words of action that directly imply feeling (*spurned*, *retaliate*). Help students prepare for reading the selection by asking them to predict what kind of life might lead a writer to rely heavily on words of such strong emotion.

Reading Check. You might use the following questions as a check for literal comprehension. Have students respond *True* or *False*.

1. This selection takes place in Atlanta, Georgia. ___False___
2. Richard's mother wouldn't let him back in the house until he faced down the bullies. ___True___
3. The judge made Richard's father contribute money to his family's support. ___False___
4. As a bedtime snack the orphanage children were given bread and molasses. ___True___
5. Richard's mother told him not to take the nickel his father offered him. ___True___

Reteaching Alternatives. Despite deprivation, young Richard often displays pride and defiance in this narrative—for instance, on page 1014, when he doesn't want to eat his soup because the preacher is eating a lot of chicken. You might want to discuss how Wright dramatizes this character trait through specific incidents, and how he shows us the way his mother nurtured those traits in him by forcing him to be strong.

Responding to the Autobiography   Text page 1019
Analyzing the Autobiography
Identifying Facts

1. In most of this excerpt, Wright works in swift strokes to draw sharp *images* or pictures of his life. One such picture, for example, shows the boy and his mother confronting his father in court. Another shows the boy standing by Miss Simon's desk in the orphanage. What other important pictures are created in these extracts from the autobiography? Among the other important pictures that Wright creates are the description of himself as a hungry boy, the incident with the gang, the picture of dinner with the preacher, and the pictures of the father and the strange woman, and of Wright's meeting with his sharecropper father twenty-five years later.

2. What details does Wright use to make the reader feel the hunger he experienced as a boy? He mentions his waking up at night, the clamor in his stomach, his dizziness and listlessness.

3. Why did Richard associate his father with his pangs of hunger? He concluded that his father's frequent absences from home were associated with the family's poverty and hunger.

4. How did Richard win the right to the streets of Memphis? He fought back with a stick against the other boys in the gang.

5. Wright speaks of how "the personality of my father first came fully into the orbit of my concern" (pages 1011–1012). What *is* that personality? How does his father behave in the courtroom scene and in the later confrontation with Wright, his mother, and the strange woman? The father is fat, strict with the boy, lazy, and drinks too much. Richard is afraid of him. In the courtroom scene and in the later confrontation with Wright, his mother, and the strange woman, the father behaves in an off-hand, irresponsible fashion. He seems indifferent to the family's plight.

6. What does Wright realize about his father in the last

354   Modern Nonfiction

passage? He realizes that he and his father are "forever strangers" and that his father could never understand him.

How was the city's effect on his father different from its effect on Wright himself? Whereas his father failed in the city, the city has borne the narrator "toward alien and undreamed-of shores of knowing."

Interpreting Meanings

7. When his mother gives Richard a heavy stick and sends him back to confront the street bullies, what lesson is she trying to teach him? She is trying to teach him that, to grow up, he needs to be able to take care of and defend himself.

Do you think she was right? Was there anything else she could have done instead? Student answers will vary. Ask students to support their responses.

8. Why can't Richard eat his soup when the preacher is devouring the fried chicken? What does this detail reveal about the boy's *character*? The boy cannot eat because he resents the preacher's greed and selfishness. The detail reveals that Richard can be angry, righteous, and stubborn.

9. What sad events finally forced Richard's mother to send her sons to an orphanage? Richard's father deserted the family. His mother ran out of money and could not afford to pay the rent on their dingy flat.

If Wright had been living in a contemporary city, what might have happened to him and his family? Student answers will vary. It is possible that the family could have gone on some sort of public assistance program.

10. One of the most painful *images* in this excerpt is the one of the young boy pulling grass at the orphanage. Wright makes no direct comment on this scene, except to describe his physical sensations. What might he have said? Do you wish he had said it, or do you think it wasn't necessary? What feelings does this scene evoke in you? Student answers will vary. Most students will agree that the image is so powerful by itself that it is more effective without any comment from the narrator.

11. Remembering his father and the strange woman, "their faces lit by the dancing flames," Wright says that he felt that in later life this scene "possessed some vital meaning which always eluded me." What do you think he means? He probably means that he realized subconsciously that his father had forsaken the family for good.

Writing About Autobiography

A Creative Response

1. Experimenting with Point of View. Remind students that an interior monologue should reveal what is happening as well as Richard's mother's feelings and opinions about the events. It will take several paragraphs to develop. The second option calls for a series of paragraphs of the "I remember him as..." type that you hear when people are interviewed after the death of a famous person.

*C*riteria for Evaluating the Assignment. If the paper is an interior monologue, it believably interprets Richard's mother's recollections of and feelings about some of the same events Richard reports. If the paper is a series of comments from different people, the tone and content change appropriately for each speaker.

A Critical Response

2. Comparing and Contrasting Two Writers. Have students list the items to look for (theme, sentence structure, dialogue, use of detail, tone of voice, how the piece affected them) before they turn to Twain's *Huckleberry Finn* or Toth's *Ivy Days* to take notes. They should make similar notes on the Wright selection and draw conclusions about similarities and differences before they begin to write.

*C*riteria for Evaluating the Assignment. The essay follows a coherent pattern of comparison/contrast, such as dealing first with similarities and then with differences, or going through the list of items point-by-point and stating whether the other writer and Wright are similar or different on each point. For each point made, details from both the other writer and Wright support the student's conclusion.

Analyzing Language and Style
Dialogue

Have students first list scenes that lend themselves to this assignment—for example, the discussion about hunger or the dinner with the preacher. Whichever incident the student chooses, the paper comments on

1. the contribution of dialogue to the scene's total effect and the characterization of people involved, and
2. how effective the scene would have been without dialogue.

Extending the Essay

Interested students may want to read the rest of *Black Boy* and other works by Richard Wright: the novel *Native Son*, excellent short stories like "Long Black Song" and "Fire and Cloud," and works of nonfiction such as "Blueprint for Negro Writing" and "Joe Louis Discovers Dynamite." The latter is a fascinating and moving piece of reportage on the galvanizing effect Joe Louis's 1935 prize fight victory over Max Baer had on the self-image of American blacks. It, and the other short pieces mentioned above, are collected in the *Richard Wright Reader*.

N. Scott Momaday

Text page 1020

From *The Way to Rainy Mountain*

Text page 1021

Objectives

1. To interpret symbolism
2. To write an imagistic description
3. To write an essay evaluating the use of setting
4. To write a paragraph responding to a statement
5. To examine the use of poetic prose

Introducing the Essay

In outline form, for your reference, here are the major elements of the selection:

- **Characters:** M. Scott Momaday; his grandmother; the Kiowa people
- **Themes:** the search for one's ethnic roots; the veneration of the past through memory
- **Point of view:** first-person reminiscence
- **Significant techniques:** poetic prose, flashback
- **Setting:** Oklahoma, Montana, and points between

Background on the Essay. You might want to emphasize to your students that Momaday is talking about two distinct cultural transformations undergone by the Kiowa people at two different—though not widely separated—times in history. Until approximately the mid-seventeenth century, the Kiowa lived in the rugged mountains of western Montana, at the headwaters of the Yellowstone River. For some undetermined reason, they migrated down from that terrain onto the plains, where they took up a new way of life, becoming expert horsemen, buffalo hunters, and warriors. This plains culture, the period of Kiowa predominance, lasted only a century, when they had to undergo another transformation: battle against white soldiers and adaptation to the massive white presence.

Teaching Strategies

Providing for Cultural Differences. This selection will have special meaning for American Indian students, and for other students whose forebears were involved in the settling of the West. If your class includes such students, this will be a good chance for them to share their knowledge of such events. Other students may have a somewhat romanticized view of American Indians, derived from Hollywood, and this essay will serve to help them appreciate the reality and humanity of one particular Native American culture, and by extension, any culture that differs from their own.

Providing for Different Levels of Ability. More advanced students will savor Momaday's prose and his skillful way of handling shifts of time and place. Less advanced students will probably have trouble with precisely those aspects of the selection. You might encourage students to raise their questions of comprehension during the course of discussion, so that those students who don't have difficulty with the given passages can transmit their understanding to the others.

Introducing Vocabulary Study. Knowing the meanings of the following words will help students understand the selection.

knoll	1022	tenuous	1023
linear	1022	inherently	1024
isolate (adj.)	1022	opaque	1024
luxuriant	1023	enmities	1024
solstice	1023	deicide	1024

Several of these words—*knoll, luxuriant, solstice*—are descriptive of natural phenomena and contribute to the lyrical beauty of Momaday's writing. You might want to define them as you come upon them in your class's reading of the text, and examine how they function in context.

Reading the Essay. This brief, evocative selection, which winds in and out of various times and places, is perfect for being read aloud, one paragraph per student. (An audiocassette recording of an excerpt from this selection is available.)

Reading Check. You might want to use the following questions as a check for literal comprehension. Have the students complete the statements with words or phrases that express the sense of the answers below.

1. The climate near Rainy Mountain is <u>hard; severe; blizzards in winter, tornadoes in spring, extreme heat in summer</u>.
2. Before they migrated to the plains, the Kiowa were <u>hunters in the mountains of the Yellowstone region of Montana</u>.
3. According to Kiowa legend, the seven stars of the Big Dipper originated as <u>seven sisters</u>.

356 Modern Nonfiction

4. The sacred Kiowa dance was called the Sun Dance.
5. The Kiowa ruled the southern plains in alliance with another tribe, the Comanche.

Reteaching Alternatives. If some students still find it hard to understand Momaday's flowing, imagistic narrative, you might break the selection up into short passages and have a small group of students write a simple paraphrase of each passage, and then have the whole class share the paraphrases.

Responding to the Essay   Text page 1025
Analyzing the Essay
Identifying Facts

1. Explain why the narrator returns to Rainy Mountain. What "pilgrimage" does he make, and why? His grandmother has died in the spring, and he wants to go back to the sacred landmark of the Kiowa Indians in order to commemorate her.

2. Momaday takes pain to describe the land the Kiowas traveled through on their journey, mentioning not only the large features of the landscape—plains and mountains—but also creatures, crops, and trees that flourish there. List some of these details that help you feel as if you know what the Great Plains are like. Student answers will vary, but may include the following: the groves of hickory and pecan, willow and witch hazel; the green and yellow grasshoppers and the tortoises; the cornfields.

3. What did you learn from this essay about the Kiowa religion and the role of the sun in their rituals? Student answers will vary. Students should mention that the sun was a divinity in the Kiowa religion, and that the Kiowa believed that they participated in this divinity through their possession of Tai-me, the sacred Sun Dance doll.

4. What was the origin of the Big Dipper, according to Kiowa legend? Kiowa legend told of seven sisters who were terrified of their brother when he was magically transformed into a bear. The sisters climbed into a tree and were lifted into the sky, where they became the stars of the Big Dipper.

How does this myth also explain the peculiar formation called Devil's Tower? (This rock outcropping, by the way, played a key role in the movie *Close Encounters of the Third Kind*.) The rock is "upthrust" against the sky like the tree that bore the seven sisters into the sky.

5. What eventually happened to the Kiowa? They were dispersed, and their religion died out.

Interpreting Meanings

6. Momaday says about the Kiowa's long migration to the south and east, "It was a journey toward the dawn . . ." (page 1022). How would you interpret this statement? Momaday seems to imply that the migration was a "journey toward the dawn" because it led to a "golden age" for the Kiowa before their eventual dispersal toward the end of the nineteenth century.

7. What does Momaday mean on page 1024 when he says his grandmother "bore a vision of deicide"? Momaday uses this phrase as a figure of speech for the fact that Aho witnessed the death of the Sun Dance religion in 1890, when the Kiowas were dispersed.

Do you think the Kiowa religious feeling survived in Aho? In her grandson? Students will probably agree that the Kiowa religious feeling survived in both Aho and her grandson.

8. Toward the end of this essay, Momaday tells of seeing a cricket in such a way that "the creature filled the moon like a fossil." It is an important *image*, one that his father chose to illustrate with a picture. Momaday comments: "It had gone there, I thought, to live and die, for there, of all places, was its small definition made whole and eternal." How do you interpret this comment? Do you think the cricket has any value as a *symbol*? Student answers will vary. But from the references connecting the Kiowas with celestial kinsmen in the night sky, the cricket might be interpreted as symbolic of the Indians themselves—or of the scattered descendants of a dispersed tribe, who might be said to resemble a cricket in their fragility, and also a fossil in the age of their heritage.

9. List the *images* that Momaday uses to convey strong contrasting feelings of light and life, darkness and death. Which set of images seem to you to be dominant? Some of the images Momaday uses to convey strong feelings of light and life are the bright sun of the plains, the Sun Dance, and dawn. Image of darkness and death include the dark mist over the Black Hills, the darkness of night, and the dark stones of the cemetery. In general, most students will probably agree that the images of darkness predominate in the essay.

In your opinion, is the overall *mood* of this essay light or dark? Explain your answer. The tone of the essay is meditative and elegiac—dark, although not despairing.

10. The book *The Way to Rainy Mountain* is in part an *elegy*. Strictly speaking, an elegy is a funeral song or a poem praising a dead person. What does Momaday praise about the Kiowa? What does he mourn? Momaday praises the Kiowas' ability to survive their migration, their fine horsemanship in warfare, their piety in their religion, and their sense of freedom. He mourns their defeat by the U.S. Cavalry, the forced disintegration of their religion, and the passing of customs and traditions, such as the feasts and the nocturnal prayer meetings that he remembers as a child.

11. Do you think Momaday and the Kiowa, like the earlier Puritan and Romantic writers, "read lessons" in nature? Explain. Most students will probably agree that the Kiowa resemble the earlier Puritans and the Romantic writers in that they "read lessons" in nature. Ask the students to defend their opinions.

Writing About the Essay
A Creative Response

1. Writing a Description. To evoke a nostalgic response similar to Momaday's, continue the list of suggestions—the first place the student remembers living, a special park, a favorite relative's house, a friend's back yard, the zoo—until it is evident that students have a starting place. Recall Momaday's images (response questions 8–9) to help students focus on mental pictures, sound, smells or sights associated with their special place.

Criteria for Evaluating the Assignment. The essay uses both direct description and images to evoke what a remembered place looked like and what it meant to the student.

A Critical Response

2. Analyzing Atmosphere. List major elements of setting (the mountain itself, weather, isolation) and recall also response question 9 on the dominant images of the essay. Encourage students to list as many additional words as they can find, related to setting and imagery about that setting, before they generalize about the mood the words and images suggest.

Criteria for Evaluating the Assignment. The essay cites many details from the essay to support a concluding sentence which states that the overall atmosphere is dark, elegiac, or meditative, but not despairing.

3. Responding to a Statement. You may wish to elicit one or two initial responses from your more outgoing students to suggest a starting point, but make it clear that the assignment requests the ideas or feelings the statement evokes for each student personally.

Criteria for Evaluating the Assignment. The response consists of a few sentences or a paragraph explaining the student's personal response to the quotation from Momaday's essay.

Analyzing Language and Style
Poetic Prose

1. a. "stairway to the plain"
   b. The meadows must descend in step-like levels.
2. a. The expansion of something small to something large
   b. Pieces of land extending farther and farther like a large sheet of paper opening into new sections
3. a. "clouds . . . are shadows"
   b. "shadows that move . . . like water"
   c. The shadows create dark patches between lighted areas.
4. a. It is "at home" like a person.
   b. To emphasize the words "character of a god"
5. a. "caldron of the land," "wean their blood," "hold the mountains in view"
   b. Answers will vary, but any revision is flat and dull compared with the original.

Extending the Essay

The complete book, *The Way to Rainy Mountain*, is only eighty-nine pages long, including illustrations. Interested students may want to read it and report to the class on its individualistic format. Other students may want to read and report on other notable works about American Indians, several of which are mentioned in the introduction to the essay, text page 1020.

James Baldwin
Text page 1027

"Autobiographical Notes"
Text page 1028

Objectives

1. To evaluate tone
2. To analyze the essay
3. To write an essay responding to the writer

Introducing the Essay

This brief essay displays the sense of narrative movement, the ability to dip in and out of various portions of the writer's memory and intellect and establish connections among them, that your students will have seen previously in this unit in essays by White, Thomas, Wright, and Momaday. Baldwin begins with the most straightforward kind of autobiographical statement—"I was born in Harlem thirty-one years ago"—and after a short, impressionistic description of his upbringing, goes on to examine his literary influences and then his views on the situation of the black writer in America, and the role of the writer, and citizen, in general. You might discuss with your students the possibility that the special gift of a good essayist is to proceed inductively from the facts of a specific phenomenon to broader truths.

Background on the Essay. "Autobiographical Notes" appeared as a preface to Baldwin's first collection of essays, *Notes of a Native Son*. At that time the young writer, though not yet the preeminent spokesman he would become, was known in literary circles through a series of book reviews he had written for magazines such as *Commentary* and *The Partisan Review*. Though Baldwin's childhood had been quite miserable, he had the benefit of supportive teachers in the New York City public schools he attended, including the poet Countee Cullen (included in Unit Eight) at Frederick Douglass Junior High School. Baldwin went on to edit the school magazine, *The Magpie*, at De Witt Clinton High School in the Bronx. A few years later, in 1944, he met his idol, Richard Wright, who encouraged him and helped him get a grant to work on his first novel.

Summary. Baldwin grew up in Harlem in a troubled family situation, but was sustained by reading and writing. He expresses his ambivalence about the problems of being a black writer, asserts that one writes only out of one's own experiences, and says that his love for America causes him to insist on the right to criticize it.

Teaching Strategies

Providing for Cultural Differences. This essay was written before the civil rights struggle of the 1960's, and therefore some of its statements—such as that neither blacks nor whites are willing to face the past—may seem somewhat anachronistic. Black and white students' reactions to the essay may be conditioned by the intervening history: Baldwin was a powerful spokesman for integration, but during the late 1960's and 1970's, some black writers, such as Eldridge Cleaver, assailed him for this. The further passage of time, and Baldwin's death in 1987, will no doubt have led to further reassessment and an appreciation of what is enduring in his views. If there are black students in your class, you might ask them whether they remember hearing of Baldwin's death, and how his memory is viewed in their families and communities.

Providing for Different Levels of Ability. The elegance of Baldwin's style may make the selection a challenge for some students, but the more factual, autobiographical passages should pose fewer difficulties. Some of Baldwin's key concepts will probably require detailed discussion, such as his view of the problems of being a black writer (text page 1029, paragraphs 2 and 3), his alienation from Western civilization (page 1029, paragraph 4), and his suspiciousness of theories (page 1030, paragraph 2).

Introducing Vocabulary Study. Knowing the meanings of the following words will help students understand the selection. (Starred words are listed in the Glossary.)

fellowship	1028	interloper	1029
effect (v.)	1029	dilemma*	1030
articulate	1029	pulverized*	1030

Reading the Essay. This short piece has a good deal of intellectual meat in it, so you might want to assign it as homework, along with the above vocabulary study, and then have it read aloud before discussing it in class.

Reading Check. You might want to use the following questions as a check for literal comprehension. Have students respond *True* or *False*.

1. James Baldwin was the youngest in a family of many children.   False
2. His parents encouraged him to read the Bible.   True
3. As a young man, Baldwin lived for a while in Mexico.   False
4. Baldwin accuses both blacks and whites of dwelling too much on their past conflicts.   False
5. Baldwin says that he loves above all the bohemian life.   False

Reteaching Alternatives. You might want to use the board to list Baldwin's major assertions about racial issues, about being a writer, about his attitude toward Western civilization, and about life.

Responding to the Essay   Text page 1030
Analyzing the Essay
Identifying Facts

1. **What was "the most crucial time" in Baldwin's own development? What did he learn about himself then?**
Baldwin says that the most crucial time in his development was when he realized that he was a "kind of bastard of the West": he approached the masterpieces of Western culture with an African perspective. He says that he hated and feared the world.

James Baldwin   359

2. How does Baldwin describe "the business of the writer," and what does this have to do with what he calls "the Negro problem"? Baldwin says that the business of the writer is going beneath surfaces and examining attitudes. He writes that the "Negro problem" is inaccessible, because, although it is written about widely, it is analyzed badly. Although it may be painful for both blacks and whites, it is vital to assess the past honestly.

3. What does Baldwin say is his greatest responsibility? He says that his ambition is to last and to get his work done. He wants to be an honest man and a good writer.

Interpreting Meanings

4. Baldwin says that Ralph Ellison was the first black novelist to express brilliantly "some of the ambiguity and irony of Negro life." What do you think he means? Student answers will vary. Ask the students if they are acquainted with any of Ellison's works, especially his landmark novel, *The Invisible Man*.

5. How would you describe Baldwin's *tone*? The tone of the essay could be described in various ways: some possibilities include "serious," "retrospective," and "personal."

6. Could any of Baldwin's points be challenged today? Student answers will vary. Ask the students to support and defend their opinions.

Writing About the Essay
A Creative Response

Writing a Response. Have students work in small groups to state in their own words Baldwin's major points about the dilemma faced by a black writer, before they begin to respond to his points.

Criteria for Evaluating the Assignment. The essay correctly identifies several points made by Baldwin and offers a reasonable response to those points from the perspective of more than thirty years later.

Extending the Essay

If time permits, you might want to have your students write their own "Autobiographical Notes," in which they briefly describe their upbringing and how they feel it has affected their personalities, their goals, and their views of life.

Maxine Hong Kingston
"The Girl Who Wouldn't Talk"

Text page 1031

Text page 1032

Objectives

1. To write a paragraph analyzing a character
2. To analyze descriptive images

Introducing the Memoir

In outline form, for your reference, here are the major elements of the memoir:

- **Characters:** Maxine Hong Kingston as a schoolgirl; "the quiet girl"
- **Conflicts:** silence vs. speech; individual personality vs. peer pressure; assimilation vs. ethnic identity
- **Themes:** the cruelty of children toward each other; the insecurities that underlie that cruelty
- **Point of view:** first-person memoir
- **Significant techniques:** ambiguity, imagery
- **Setting:** Stockton, California, early 1950's

Background on the Memoir. In addition to being a powerful voice of the Chinese-American experience, Maxine Hong Kingston writes specifically and forcefully as a voice for women. She emphasizes the emotional fortitude of Chinese women who endured lives of subordinacy through the ages. Her second book, *China Men*, begins with a fable about a man who crossed an ocean and came upon a Land of Women. He was captured by women who proceeded to inflict upon him the same pains that were routinely inflicted on women in traditional Chinese society: foot binding, ear piercing, and humiliation. The fable makes clear that forms of treatment which were scarcely given a second thought were in fact forms of torture.

Summary. As a schoolgirl, Maxine Hong Kingston had a classmate who never spoke a word except to read out loud.

360 Modern Nonfiction

The girl was protected by an older sister, but one day Maxine caught the girl alone in the school lavatory and tried to force her to speak through physical and psychological means. The girl cried piteously but didn't speak. Soon afterward, Kingston says, she herself developed a mysterious illness that kept her bedridden for eighteen months.

Teaching Strategies

Providing for Cultural Differences. This selection will have special meaning for Chinese-American students, but the basic story line, one of taunting and shyness and cruelty among children, will be recognizable to students from all cultures.

Non-Asian teachers should be cautious about generalizing the Chinese-American experience to other Asian immigrant groups—Japanese-American, Korean-American, Vietnamese-American, and so on—for each is a separate culture, just as are the British, French, and German.

Providing for Different Levels of Ability. This is a very readable narrative written in relatively simple, though evocative, contemporary prose, and the subject matter will be a relatively easy one for students to handle. More advanced readers might want to delve into the question of whether every incident in the narrative is literally true, or whether some incidents might be a kind of poetic invention. You might want to discuss the strengths and weaknesses of this approach to memoir. Less advanced students may find the selection a trifle long and thick.

Introducing Vocabulary Study. Knowing the meanings of the following words will help students understand the selection.

self-assertion	1032	spigots	1033
faltering	1032	recluses	1037

Three of these four words are tied to the central emotional issues behind the "quiet girl's" behavior, and to the way she is protected by her family. The issue of self-assertion and its relationship both to the socialization of females and to the differences between Chinese and American customs are important undercurrents in this memoir. Spending some time with these vocabulary words might be a good way to introduce a discussion of these issues.

Reading the Memoir. You might want to assign the selection as homework and have some representative passages read out loud: perhaps the first two paragraphs (text page 1032); the two paragraphs beginning from, "I joined in at lunchtime," (page 1033); the passage beginning, "I ran back into the girls' yard," and ending with, "'Talk!' I shouted into the side of her head," (page 1035); the passage beginning, "I looked right at her," and ending, "'Say, "Stop it."'" (page 1036); the long paragraph beginning, "'Why won't you talk?'" on page 1037; and the passage from "Suddenly I heard footsteps," on page 1037, to the end of the piece.

Reading Check. You might want to use the following as a check for literal comprehension. Have students complete the statements with words or phrases that express the sense of the answers below.

1. The girl who wouldn't talk did use her voice when she read aloud.
2. The quiet girl and Maxine were similar in sports.
3. One day Maxine caught the quiet girl in the school lavatory.
4. Maxine tormented the quiet girl by mocking her; trying to make her talk; telling her she would never attract boys; pinching her.
5. Soon after the incident with the quiet girl, Maxine became ill with a mysterious paralysis.

Reteaching Alternatives. The core of the story line is a very dramatic confrontation between two schoolgirls, so you might want to have two female students act out the parts in front of the class for reteaching purposes. You might even want to have two male students act it out afterward, too, to show that with some very minor adjustments and reversals of pronoun, the same incident can be envisioned between boys. And since the dialogue in the essay is in student vernacular, it probably wouldn't hurt to allow for some improvisation by your youthful actors.

Responding to the Memoir   Text page 1038
Analyzing the Memoir
Identifying Facts

1. What are the reasons the narrator hates the younger sister, despite the fact that the girls were alike in so many ways? The narrator hates the younger sister because she regards her as passive, weak, soft, fragile, delicate, neat, privileged, and too "Chinese."

2. How does the narrator try to make the silent girl talk? (Note the psychological and physical torments she applies.) Maxine uses a variety of physical and psychological torments. She pushes, pinches, and shakes her, and she pulls her hair. She taunts her by calling her a sissy; she shouts at her and orders her to stop crying; she calls her stupid, and mockingly orders her to call her sister for help; she calls her disgusting, and she tells her that she will never be married because she is a "plant" with no personality.

What is the girl's response? She is puzzled and alarmed, but she endures the narrator's torments without ever speaking.

3. What happens to the narrator after this incident that makes her say that "the world is sometimes just"? The narrator falls ill and is forced to spend a year and a half at home in bed.

Interpreting Meanings

4. Why do you think that the narrator cares so intensely about making the silent girl talk? Students will have various opinions. For the narrator, the girl seems to represent the delicate, traditional Chinese image of femininity and submission—an image that the narrator, at this stage of her life, has firmly rejected. She thus hates the girl as representative of the aspects of her own heritage that she would prefer to suppress.

Do her feelings strike you as credible—have you experienced feelings like this yourself, or observed them in others? Student answers will vary.

5. Underlying this passage is a deep undercurrent of anger, which at first seems directed simply at the silent girl. What else could the narrator be angry about? Student answers will vary. The narrator seems angry at her own family, at the "ghosts" of American society, at herself, and at the conflicts posed by loyalty to her own family and community on the one hand, and the pressures to become assimilated to the "ghost" society on the other.

6. The silent girl was obviously able to speak. Why do you think she did *not* speak? Student answers will vary. Obviously, the girl is characterized as habitually silent. In these circumstances, she may have been so shocked and petrified with fear that she could not possibly have uttered a word, even if she had wanted to speak.

7. What implication do you draw from the fact that Kingston says that her time in bed "was the best year and a half of my life"? Kingston herself provides a cryptic explanation in the next line when she says that during this period "nothing happened." Perhaps she means that her seclusion at home temporarily spared her the tension and conflicts of growing up "between two cultures."

Do you think the illness really had anything to do with her treatment of the silent girl? Student answers will vary. Some students may suggest that the illness was a psychosomatic reflex of the narrator's sense of guilt for having treated the younger sister so cruelly.

8. This episode comes from a chapter called "A Song for a Barbarian Reed Pipe." What could be the significance of the title, and how is this story of the silent girl related to it? Student answers will vary. Note that the narrator refers to the "weak little toots" that the silent girl makes on her flute. Perhaps part of the narrator's motivation in writing the essay is as a belated atonement for her cruelty to the silent girl.

Writing About the Memoir
A Critical Response

Analyzing a Character. Write across the chalkboard the headings "Appearance," "Speech," "Actions," "Private thoughts and feelings," and "Responses of others." Elicit from the class—in any order—details from the essay that fit any category. Stop when responses slow down, and suggest that students copy those already listed, skim the essay for additional details, and decide whether Kingston omits any of the categories.

Criteria for Evaluating the Assignment. The essay uses details from the essay to discuss the character of the narrator as actually portrayed by Kingston (not as the student thinks it should have been done). The essay ends with the student's opinion of this self-characterization.

Analyzing Language and Style
Imagery and Feelings

1. Responses will vary. In general *ghosts* suggests beings which are not only pale in color, but perhaps also powerful, mysterious, or scary.

2. The images appear on page 1036. Feelings revealed about the girl may be interpreted differently—perhaps the narrator's feeling of superiority and strength in comparison with the other girl's weakness. The student may feel indignant or angry at the actions of the narrator.

Extending the Essay

As a creative exercise, you might ask your students to write short stories about incidents of cruelty between students. (Since this is a rather personal subject, you might emphasize that the students don't have to write autobiographically or in the first-person, and that the stories are to be written as fiction.)

Susan Allen Toth

"Out East"

Objectives

1. To analyze character
2. To evaluate stereotypes
3. To write a passage imitating the writer's technique
4. To rewrite an incident using a different point of view
5. To write an essay developing a statement
6. To write an essay evaluating the writer's objectivity

Introducing the Memoir

In outline form, for your reference, here are the major elements of the essay:

- **Character:** Sue Allen
- **Conflicts:** heartland vs. Ivy League; naiveté vs. sophistication; desire to belong vs. insecurity
- **Theme:** a wide-eyed college freshman's gradual adjustment to her new environment
- **Point of view:** first-person reminiscence
- **Significant technique:** well-chosen detail
- **Setting:** Smith College, Northhampton, Massachusetts, the late 1950's

Background on the Memoir. It's important to make certain that students understand the prestige attached to a Seven Sisters school such as Smith College; the achievement that admission to such a school represented, then and now, for a small-town girl; and the mystique that surrounded the Ivy League style of life. Sue Allen, in short, is experiencing a transition not only from one place to another, and from high school to college, but also from one ethos, one social grouping, to another.

Summary. Sue Allen goes through the ordeal of taking "Posture Pictures" and of choosing her wardrobe.

Teaching Strategies

Providing for Cultural Differences. College-bound students may be more immediately seized by this selection than non-college-bound, upper middle-class students more than students from other backgrounds, New England students more than students from other areas of the country, and female students more than male students. The essential underlying experience, however, is the rite of passage between the high school years and the beginning of adulthood, and all students will share this to some degree despite external differences.

Providing for Different Levels of Ability. The essay is about being a very advanced student, so your less advanced students may not recognize many of the references to the styles and mores of the university elite. Your more advanced students, in contrast, may be positively eager to read about the kind of college experiences that—except for the differences between generations—may lie ahead of them. A discussion of such differences in their attitudes might be a good way to get your less advanced students involved in the selection.

Introducing Vocabulary Study. Knowing the meanings of the following words will help students understand the selection. (The starred word is listed in the Glossary.)

mesmerizing*	1040	disparate	1042
diagnostic	1040	determinedly	1043
fabrications	1040	studied (adj.)	1044
swathed	1041		

Reading the Memoir. You might assign the selection as homework and have a female student read a passage from it aloud as an introduction to discussion—not the passage about "Posture Pictures" at the beginning of the piece, but one of the passages about the "Eastern look" and clothes shopping, which can be found from the middle of page 1042 to the end of the selection.

Reading Check. You might want to use the following questions as a check for literal compehension. Have students respond *True* or *False*.

1. The selection takes place during the late 1950's.
   True
2. Each Smith girl's body received a grade before she was allowed to graduate.
   True
3. Sue's literary idol at the time was Emily Dickinson.
   False
4. Before going to Smith, Sue had never been to a cocktail party.
   True
5. Sue solved her wardrobe problem by buying a rumpled trenchcoat on sale.
   True

Reteaching Alternatives. If some students have trouble understanding the nature of Sue's anxieties, you might turn the discussion toward their own feelings about the prospect of college, or about leaving home. You might guide them toward understanding that the specific details of Sue's experience—Posture Pictures, choices of wardrobe—however charming, are not presented for themselves alone, but for what they reveal about the state of mind of a teenage girl eagerly but nervously facing imminent adulthood.

Responding to the Memoir   Text page 1044
Analyzing the Memoir
Identifying Details

1. Before she came to Massachusetts, where had Sue Allen gotten her ideas about the East? She says that she drew her ideas about the East from "many disparate images": Currier & Ives calendar pictures, New England writers she had read in high school literature class (including Melville, Whittier, Longfellow, Edna St. Vincent Millay, and Hawthorne), and issues of *Mademoiselle*.

2. What did she think was the "Eastern look"? She thought that the "Eastern look" consisted of sports and party clothes: blazers, tennis skirts, ski sweaters, riding costumes, and cocktail dresses.

3. The writer says she finally achieved a "dirty, rumpled look" that she felt was her only alternative to "Green Street." What details describe these two alternatives? The dirty, rumpled look is described as involving a trenchcoat that Sue bought on sale—worn with jeans, a sweatshirt, and gray, soiled "tennies," or tennis sneakers. The "Green Street" look was traditional and affluent: skirts, blazers, sweaters, and chintz knitting bags.

Interpreting Meanings

4. Why does this section (the first chapter in the book) begin with a description of Posture Pictures? What is the emotional effect of the opening paragraph? Student answers will vary. Considering that the whole piece focuses so much on clothes, it is ironic that the first image we have of the college freshmen is in gym class, stripped for "posture pictures." The emotional effect perhaps conveys some of the nervousness and anxiety of a freshman in her first days away from home at college.

5. Although the writer talks about clothes, she is trying to convey some of her feelings about her first days at college. What were these feelings? Sue Allen lacked confidence and was eager to fit in with those around her.

Do you think they are fairly universal? Students will probably agree that these feelings are universal.

6. Why was it so important to Sue Allen that she look like the "Eastern girls"? What does this reveal about her *character* at this stage of her life? She was self-conscious and wanted to fit in with the other girls who were strangers to her. Her attitude reveals that she was relatively insecure and nervous about other people's acceptance at the time.

7. Groups have different ways of identifying who belongs, who is "in" and who is "out." What are some of the different groups you see in your school, and how are they identified? Student answers will vary. Encourage them to identify as many different groups as they can, and to be as specific as possible about details of clothing, posture, language, and so on.

8. This passage also talks about *stereotypes*—fixed ideas about people and events that allow for no individuality. Stereotypes are often based on racial or religious prejudice. What are these stereotypes? The essay refers to stereotypes of fashion and maturity, of self-assurance, attractiveness, and sophistication.

What pictures do you have about areas of the United States you have never seen—the East, West, North, or South? For example, what do you see in your mind's eye when someone talks about Nashville? New York? San Francisco? New Orleans? Gary, Indiana? Where do you think such stereotypes come from? Student answers will vary. Encourage students to offer specific responses and to defend their opinions.

9. Do you think the memoir is about something important, or do you think clothing is essentially a trivial subject? (Is clothing the real topic of the memoir?) Whatever their opinions about the importance of clothing, most students will agree that clothing is only the superficial subject of the memoir. The memoir is really about the narrator's feelings as she confronts a new, adult world.

Writing About the Memoir
A Creative Response

1. Imitating Toth's Technique. If students find it too painful or embarrassing to deal with a recent experience, suggest that they go back to early childhood—a time when they wanted to be included in an older sibling's games with friends, to be in the first-grade play, and so on.

Criteria for Evaluating the Assignment. The description clearly presents the "something" the student wanted to belong to and why he or she could not, and evokes the desperation of the student's feelings.

2. Changing the Point of View. Have students suggest some incidents that could be explored from another point of view, such as the one where the narrator receives her award.

Remind students to think about the tone they wish to convey before they begin to write.

Criteria for Evaluating the Assignment. The narration consistently remains in the new point of view, and conveys a tone suitable for that speaker.

A Critical Response

3. Developing a Statement. As background for this assignment, you might remind students that whole books exist on how to "dress for success." Response question 7—how groups identify those who are "in" and "out"—will also have prepared students to think of clothing as a language.

Criteria for Evaluating the Assignment. The essay is at least one paragraph long. It explains that clothes are a "language" in that they are often used to make statements about the wearer's personality, attitudes, and so on. Most students will conclude that people in general agree with this idea.

4. Evaluating Objectivity. The assignment in general focuses not on Toth's feelings, but on the *facts* she uses in her essay. Reading "Primary Sources: 'The Importance of Being Remembered'" should help students make this distinction. The last question of the writing prompt does veer into feelings in that no matter how objectively facts are reported, one's personal feelings still dictate *which* facts to report.

Criteria for Evaluating the Assignment. The essay cites several facts Toth uses in her essay, such as the "Posture Pictures" of Orientation Week, and comments on the writer's apparent bias or lack of bias. The essay offers an opinion as to whether another person might report the same events differently, and explains this opinion by use of examples.

Extending the Essay

You might ask your students to discuss, or write a short essay about, what they anticipate their post-high-school experiences will be like. How similar to Sue Allen's will they be? How different?

Sandra Cisneros

Text page 1046

"Straw into Gold: The Metamorphosis of the Everyday"

Text page 1047

Objectives

1. To identify images and figures of speech
2. To evaluate the use of metaphor
3. To write an essay imitating the writer's technique
4. To write a paragraph identifying purpose and main idea

Introducing the Essay

In outline form, for your reference, here are the major elements of the essay:

- **Character:** Sandra Cisneros
- **Conflicts:** "rule-oriented," mechanistic production vs. intuitive creativity; Mexican-American culture vs. stereotypes of the culture
- **Theme:** transformation, through imagination, of everyday experiences into art

- **Point of view:** first-person
- **Significant techniques:** images and figures of speech

Background on the Essay. As indicated in the autobiographical introduction (text page 1046), Sandra Cisneros is the youngest writer represented in this book. By her early thirties, she had had the many experiences described in this essay and was already a recognized writer.

Summary. In a speech at Texas Lutheran College, Sandra Cisneros describes family experiences and other influences that shaped her as a writer. To make the point that everyday experiences, through imagination, can be shaped into fiction, poetry, and other forms of art, she uses the metaphor of the *Rumplestiltskin* fairy tale, where straw is transformed into gold.

Teaching Strategies

Providing for Cultural Differences. Students who live in large cities with Mexican-American populations or who themselves are Mexican-American may already understand some of Cisneros's references to customs of that culture, such as expectations for the daughter in a family of males. An important point to be made with this essay is the cultural stereotypes that are revealed: Cisneros's hosts expected her to be able to cook Mexican food because she was Mexican.

Providing for Different Levels of Ability. Less advanced students may have some difficulty with the Spanish phrases used in the essay. You might point out to students that most of the phrases are defined within the context of the essay. *Provinciales*, for example, is identified in the next phrase as "country"; the meaning of *chilango* becomes clear when Cisneros writes that her father is from a large city.

Introducing Vocabulary Study. Knowing the meanings of the following words is important to understanding the essay. (The starred word apears in the Glossary.)

| metamorphosis | 1047 | nomadic* | 1048 |
| vagabonding | 1048 | nostalgia | 1048 |

The key word in this list is, of course, *metamorphosis*. As a concept-formation exercise, you might discuss with students the fact that stories of metamorphosis, such as the Rumplestiltskin story and the "ugly duckling into swan" story, may be as old as humanity itself. Have students brainstorm other examples of metamorphosis stories, including more contemporary ones, and discuss with them the fact that the stories have such universal and timeless appeal. What do they say about the enduring belief in the ability of humans to attain higher and nobler goals?

Reading the Essay. Since this essay was originally a speech, you might prefer to have it read aloud, perhaps with a little dramatic flair.

Reading Check. You might want to use the following responses as a check for literal comprehension. Have students respond *True* or *False*.

1. While living in Mexico, the writer was asked to make tortillas. ___False___
2. Cisneros's most satisfying accomplishment was writing a critical essay for her MFA degree. ___False___
3. Cisneros was an only daughter in a family of six men. ___True___
4. Cisneros was not an especially bright student and did not like school. ___True___
5. As an adult, Cisneros did many things that she didn't think she could do. ___True___

Reteaching Alternatives. You might want to divide discussion of the essay into four chronological parts: (a) childhood experiences and influences on Cisneros as a writer, (b) making tortillas in the south of France and the relationship of that experience to writing the essay for her MFA degree, (c) Cisneros's experiences as an adult writer, (d) Cisneros's "metamorphosis" theory.

366 Modern Nonfiction

Responding to the Essay   Text page 1049
Analyzing the Essay
Identifying Facts

1. How do the writer's feelings about making the tortillas connect to her feelings about writing the MFA essay? To the writer, making tortillas is a step-by-step process that must be followed. Unlike creative writing, which Cisneros says that she does intuitively, the critical essay for the MFA exam also is a step-by-step process, and Cisneros feels that both the tortillas and the critical essay are impossible tasks. When finished, both Cisneros's tortillas and her MFA exam seem to her poorly shaped, but they have both been finished.

2. Exactly how did her family help shape her into a writer? Cisneros feels that she has inherited certain qualities from her family that have shaped her career as a writer. From her father, she inherited a love for traveling and for storytelling and, evidently, a certain amount of sentimentality. From her mother, Cisneros inherited a "street smart" voice that is reflected in her writing. Her brothers and the boys that they brought home also helped to shape her as a writer, especially the second oldest brother, Henry.

3. Why does she think nostalgia for a home is a theme that obsesses her? As a child, Cisneros was taken so often to her grandparents' home in Mexico City that it seemed like home to her. The nostalgia was for this home in Mexico that was perhaps the only home she ever had.

Interpreting Meanings

4. How would you interpret the subtitle "The Metamorphosis of the Everyday"? Although responses will vary somewhat, answers should be consistent with the meaning of the word *metamorphosis* ("change of form or substance") and with Cisneros's allusion to the Rumpelstiltskin story, in which straw is miraculously transformed into gold. The subtitle emphasizes the writer's ability to transform everyday occurrences into the universal themes of poetry, fiction, and other forms of writing.

5. What do you think Cisneros means when she says she documented the women "who sat their sadness on an elbow and stared out a window"? Literally, Cisneros probably refers to women in certain neighborhoods who propped themselves on their elbows in open windows to watch goings-on. For many of these women, daily life was filled with the sadness of unfulfilled dreams, and it was this sadness that was propped on an elbow to stare out the window.

6. What *images* and *figures of speech* in this essay reveal that the writer is also a poet? The images and figures of speech Cisneros uses in her descriptions of places that she has traveled reveal her poetic ability, as do the descriptions of herself as an eleven-year-old schoolgirl and of the women who stare out the window.

7. How does Cisneros use the fairy tale of Rumplestiltskin as a *metaphor* for her writing? Cisneros uses the Rumplestiltskin tale in two ways. The feelings of the woman facing the overwhelming task of spinning straw into gold are a metaphor to describe Cisneros's feelings when she was faced with making tortillas and when she had to write a critical essay for her MFA degree. The actual transformation of the straw into gold is used as a metaphor to describe the writer's belief that the experiences of life can be the raw material for art, which is a representation of humanity's nobler instincts.

What do you think of the metaphor? Student answers will vary.

Writing About the Essay
A Creative Response

1. Imitating the Writer's Technique. Note that the assignment asks students not so much to imitate the writer's technique as to use the writer's theme and title. However, you might want to review with students Cisneros's use of metaphor and imagery in this essay and require that student essays imitate this aspect of Cisneros's technique.

Criteria for Evaluating the Assignment. The essay, titled "The Metamorphosis of the Everyday," relates in detail experiences that can become the basis for poetry, fiction, or some other form of art.

A Critical Response

2. Identifying the Main Idea. Before students begin work on this assignment, you might review with them the meanings of the terms *purpose* and *main idea*. To help students imagine how the speech might have affected them as members of Cisneros's audience, you might want to have the essay read aloud by a talented student, perhaps one who contemplates being a writer.

Criteria for Evaluating the Assignment. The paragraph states convincingly that the writer's purpose is to inform and/or to persuade her audience of the possibilities of transforming everyday experiences into art and that the writer's main idea is the transformation, through imagination, of everyday occurrences into fiction, poetry, or another form of art.

John Hersey
Text page 1050

"A Noiseless Flash"
Text page 1051

Objectives

1. To examine imagery
2. To analyze attitude
3. To write an essay analyzing the use of suspense
4. To write an essay classifying the history
5. To evaluate the writer's objectivity or subjectivity
6. To define Japanese terms through context clues

Introducing the History

In outline form, for your reference, here are the major elements of the selection:

- **Characters:** Toshiko Sasaki, a clerk; Dr. Masakazu Fujii, owner of a private hospital; Hatsuyo Nakamura, a tailor's widow; Father Wilhelm Kleinsorge, a Jesuit missionary; Dr. Terufumi Sasaki, a Red Cross doctor; the Rev. Tanimoto, a Methodist minister

- **Themes:** the horror of atomic warfare; the arbitrariness of catastrophe
- **Point of view:** third-person, omniscient
- **Significant techniques:** reportorial journalism; simple imagery; factual detail
- **Setting:** Hiroshima, Japan, August 6, 1945

Background on the History. Before having your students read "A Noiseless Flash," you'll probably want to make sure they're familiar with the basic facts of the dropping of the atomic bomb on Hiroshima, in the context of World War II. You might ask them whether they've discussed that event in their history classes, or have read about it elsewhere. Students who are familiar with the history of the event can transmit their knowledge to their classmates during the course of discussion. If your students' knowledge on the subject seems thin, you might ask a volunteer to prepare a brief report and present it to the class.

Summary. Hersey presents the experiences of six survivors of the Hiroshima bombing, immediately before and after the blast.

Teaching Strategies

Providing for Cultural Differences. The selection may have particular meaning for Japanese-American students, but in a larger sense it's appropriate for any person of any culture to find this selection moving and thought-provoking. Hersey himself, who had been his characters' enemy very shortly before writing *Hiroshima,* provided a lasting example by writing about atomic warfare objectively and without regard for nationality. You might want to discuss how Hersey's presentation of Japanese culture makes your students feel about the characters in the essay, in conjunction with question 7, text page 1059.

Providing for Different Levels of Ability. More advanced readers will probably be intrigued by the way Hersey achieves his intended tone despite a completely factual reportial surface. (This is developed further in question 3 under "Writing About the History," text page 1059.) Less advanced readers may find it hard to keep up with the wealth of detail, particularly the Japanese names and customs. You might make a list of the characters' names on the board, and elicit from students a thumbnail description of each character. In addition, Hersey gives the distance and direction of each character from the blast center, and you might want to make a simple diagram showing this information on the board.

Introducing Vocabulary Study. Knowing the meanings of the following words will help students understand the selection. (Starred words are listed in the Glossary.)

deltaic*	1052	hedonistic*	1055
volition*	1052	convivial*	1056
abstinence	1052	repugnant*	1057
intermittent*	1055	actuality	1057
incendiary	1055		

This is a substantial list in terms of difficulty, so you might want to assign the words as homework the night before discussing the selection. One strategy might be to divide the class into three groups, have each group look up three of the words, and have the students share their definitions in class as a warm-up to discussing the essay.

Reading the History. The selection is too long to be read aloud in its entirety, so after having the students read it at home, you might want to have them read aloud one passage for each of the six characters: Mr. Tanimoto, the three paragraphs beginning, "Then a tremendous flash of light," bottom of page 1053; Mrs. Nakamura, the five paragraphs beginning, "As soon as the planes had passed," on page 1055; Dr. Fujii, the three paragraphs beginning, "Dr. Fujii had been relatively idle," on page 1056; Father Kleinsorge, the two paragraphs beginning, "After an alarm," on page 1057; Dr. Sasaki, the passage beginning, "He arrived at the hospital" and ending, "for a long, long time," on page 1058; Miss Sasaki, from "Miss Sasaki went back to her office," on page 1058, to the end of the selection.

Reading Check. You might use the following questions as a check for literal comprehension. Have the students respond *True* or *False.*

1. The two characters names Sasaki were brother and sister. False
2. Hiroshima had been left relatively unharmed before the atomic blast. True
3. Mrs. Nakamura heard only one of her three children after the blast. True
4. The Japanese called B-29's "the big guys." False
5. Dr. Sasaki was the only doctor in his hospital who was unhurt. True

Reteaching Alternatives. Some students may find the narrative too "busy," in the sense that they have to keep track of the experiences of six characters in different parts of the city at the same moment. You might ask them to divide a sheet of paper into six horizontal columns, and briefly summarize the occupation, actions, and experiences of each of the six characters.

Responding to the History Text page 1059

Analyzing the History

Identifying Facts

1. Who are the six survivors presented in this section, and what do they have in common? They are all fairly ordinary people: a clerk, a private doctor, a priest, a widow, a young surgeon, and a minister. According to Hersey, each still wonders why he or she survived the bombing, which killed a hundred thousand people. Each of them attributes his or her survival to "small items of chance or volition."

2. What simple *images* does Hersey use to make us imagine the actual physical impact of the bomb? For example, how does he describe the flash as seen by each character? Mr. Tanimoto remembers the flash as a "sheet of sun" that traveled from east to west across the sky. Mrs. Nakamura recalls the flash as "whiter than any white she had ever seen." Dr. Fujii, looking away from the sky at his newspaper, remembered a brilliant yellow. Father Kleinsorge thought of something he had read as a boy about a large meteor colliding with the earth. Dr. Sasaki saw the light of the bomb reflected, like a gigantic photographic flash, in the hospital corridor. Finally, the office of Miss Sasaki was filled with a "blinding light."

3. What small, commonplace *human interest* details does Hersey give about his *characters* so that they come alive and seem like people we might know? Students may

368   Modern Nonfiction

choose among many such details. For example, the first paragraph refers to Miss Sasaki turning her head to speak to the girl at the next desk in her office; Dr. Fujii is sitting cross-legged on the porch of his hospital to read the morning newspaper; Mrs. Nakamura is standing at the kitchen window, watching a neighbor tear down his own house for defense purposes; Father Kleinsorge is in his underwear reading a magazine; Dr. Sasaki is carrying a blood specimen in one of his hospital's corridors; and Mr. Tanimoto is helping a friend move. The details help provide a vivid, authentic picture of everyday life in Japan at the time the bomb was dropped.

4. How does Hersey explain the *ironic* fact that an all-clear signal sounded just before the bomb was dropped? The Japanese radio operators, who detected only three planes, thought that the fatal mission was simply a reconnaissance.

5. Does Hersey give any details in this section to suggest the reasons the bomb was dropped? Explain. Hersey does not offer any reasons for the dropping of the bomb in this section. He focuses instead on the reactions of ordinary, everyday people.

Interpreting Meanings

6. What *ironies* can you find in each character's story—including the irony of the last image? Irony is inherent in each character's story, in that the daily routines of each character are sharply reversed by the horrible, violent reality of the bomb's being dropped. In the last image, it is especially ironic that books, which might be regarded as symbols of humane civilization, fall over and seriously injure Miss Sasaki when the bomb is dropped.

7. In this selection, Hersey refrains from moralizing. Nevertheless, he does communicate an *attitude* toward war. How does he accomplish that? Student answers will vary. Certainly the grim, almost unimaginable power of the bomb, is rendered vividly in this selection. Perhaps the destruction is the more terrifying for being objectively reported.

How would you describe his attitude toward the Japanese? Toward the Americans? Hersey seems humane and sympathetic toward both nationalities.

8. During World War II, most Americans felt that the Japanese, like the Germans, were enemies and aggressors to be destroyed no matter what the cost. How do you respond to Hersey's treatment of the Japanese in this piece? Most students will be free of preconceptions, even though they know that the Japanese were the enemy in World War II. They may agree that Hersey treats the Japanese in this selection as ordinary people, affected by war just as Americans might be affected by it. Some will say that the piece evokes their sympathy for the victims of the bomb. Try to encourage the students to discuss this question within the bounds of Hersey's piece; urge them to note that Hersey deliberately downplays political and military matters, confining his attention to an objective description of what typical citizens of Hiroshima were doing at the moment of the bombing.

How do you think readers in 1946—one year after the war ended—would have responded? Students may readily imagine that the reception of *Hiroshima* was more controversial in 1946, the year after the atomic bomb was dropped. You may want to encourage them to discuss the role of time's passage in our perspectives on history. How, for example, do they regard the Vietnam War today? How would their views contrast with those of students ten years ago?

9. What other methods might a historian or journalist have used to tell this story? Historians or journalists might have given, for example, a drily objective description of the bare facts of the incident, together with a few quotations from some of the eyewitnesses who survived.

What do you think of Hersey's method? Student answers will vary. Encourage the students to support and defend their opinions.

10. From what you have read here, and from what you know of history, can you explain why in human and political terms, the explosion at Hiroshima was a central event in the twentieth century? Student answers will vary. Certainly, students should be able to single out the atomic bomb as a weapon of unparalleled force and violence in the course of human history.

Writing About the History
A Critical Response

1. Analyzing Suspense. In discussion, most students will suggest that suspense is set up because the reader knows something is coming that the people described do *not* know about, and this knowledge raises questions about what is going to happen to each of these people.

Criteria for Evaluating the Assignment. The essay lists some questions Hersey plants in the reader's mind and cites the specific places where those questions are answered.

2. Classifying a Literary Work. Elicit from the students the criteria they associate with the word "literature"—perhaps "enduring value," "permanent interest," "universal themes," and so on. Guide them to a definition broad enough to include more than what we traditionally call "classics." They might also wish to consult a dictionary.

Criteria for Evaluating the Assignment. The essay offers a reasonable definition of the word *literature* and makes a good case for or against Hersey's *Hiroshima* fulfilling the criteria associated with the definition.

3. Evaluating the Report. Discuss carefully the distinction between objectivity and subjectivity made in the writing prompt. Most students will see that Hersey's report is objective, if only because even an extensive search fails to turn up passages stating his feelings.

Criteria for Evaluating the Assignment. The essay identifies Hersey's overall approach as objective, and cites several passages to support that opinion.

Analyzing Language and Style
Foreign Terms

(a) *tonarigumi*, Neighborhood Association; (b) *tansu*, a large Japanese cabinet; (c) *Chugoku*, clearly the name of a newspaper from the context, "sat down to read that morning's Hiroshima *Chugoku*"; (d) *Sankoku*, brand name for a sewing machine; (e) *Suntory*, a Japanese brand of whiskey; (f) *Murata-san*, Mr. or Mrs. Murata by analogy with *B-san* or Mr. B for the B-29 bomber; (g) *Shu Jesusu, awaremi tamia*, Our Lord Jesus, have pity on us; (h) *gambare*, beware.

Extending the History

1. Interested students may want to read the entire book, *Hiroshima*, and report on it to the class.
2. As a creative exercise, you might have each student write a brief first-person account in the voice of any of the six characters, showing what the character was doing, thinking, feeling, and experiencing just before the blast and just afterward.

Michael Herr
Text page 1060

From *Dispatches*
Text page 1061

Objectives

1. To interpret imagery
2. To write an essay assessing the selection's impact
3. To compare and contrast two reports
4. To write a paper analyzing the author's personality
5. To write an essay on the role of women in war

Introducing the Reports

In outline form, for your reference, these are the major subsections of the selection:

- **"The Highlands":** a physical description of the "spooky" highlands of Vietnam and the Montagnard villagers
- **"'Tell My Folks...'":** An anecdote about an American Indian Green Beret who, having a presentiment of death, asked Herr to give a message to his folks, then survived
- **"The Wounded":** A description of seriously wounded Vietnamese civilians and an Army surgeon working in harrowing conditions
- **"The Correspondents":** A satire on an old-fashioned war correspondent
- **"Back Home":** A description of Herr's troubling dreams and memories after he returned to the States
- **"Remembering the Dead":** A description of the unnerving experience of mistaking a living soldier for another who has died
- **"The War Ends":** Herr's reactions to seeing scenes of evacuation and photographs of the war

Background on the Reports. While you will probably want to avoid getting bogged down in a debate on the rightness or wrongness of the Vietnam War, you'll probably want to make sure that your students know something of the basic historical facts before they read this selection. You might ask your students what they already know about the war from other sources. Since this knowledge is likely to be fragmentary, you might recommend that they read about the Vietnam War in their history textbooks; or you might assign a student volunteer to present an oral report on the subject.

Summary. Herr, a correspondent in Vietnam during the height of the war, presents a series of brief, sometimes enigmatic vignettes intended to depict the surreal, confusing quality of that war and of the Vietnamese landscape.

370 Modern Nonfiction

Teaching Strategies

Providing for Cultural Differences. Student reactions are likely to vary depending on whether or not they know people who served in Vietnam, and this in turn will be correlated to some extent with students' social backgrounds. Herr himself, while not a supporter of the war, portrays individual American soldiers as sympathetic human beings, and impresses us with the overwhelming nature of the ordeal that soldiers and civilians alike went through in this war, and go through in any war. Any reader is likely to emerge from this selection feeling that healing wounds is preferable to opening them.

Providing for Different Levels of Ability. The collage-like nature of the piece, and the interweaving of fantasy and reality, are likely to excite more advanced students and confuse less advanced ones. For instance, "The Correspondents" is a satirical caricature rather than a portrait of one real correspondent; the image of the "chopper" flying out of Herr's chest, text page 1065, may need some explication; and the description of the Battle for Hill 875, on text pages 1062–1063, is presented in the tones of a tall tale even though the facts are apparently accurate. You might want to point out that this shifting sense of unreality was an important part of the psychological experience of fighting in Vietnam, and that Herr is deliberately trying to convey this.

Introducing Vocabulary Study. Knowing the meanings of the following words will help students understand the selection. (Starred words appear in the Glossary.)

erratic*	1062	nomadic*	1062
demi-enlightened	1062	recalcitrance	1062
aborigine	1062	benign*	1062
enmity*	1062	dispersion	1065

Reading the Reports. For purposes of reading aloud, you might divide the first section, "The Highlands," into two parts: the long opening paragraph, and the rest of the section. Each section after that is a good length to be read aloud by one student.

Reading Check. You might use the following items as a check for literal comprehension. Have students complete the statements with words or phrases that express the sense of the answers below.

1. Most Vietnamese and Montagnards considered each other inferior.
2. The Green Beret in "Tell My Folks" wanted Herr to tell his folks that he had looked for a chaplain.
3. The Army surgeon in "The Wounded" couldn't hold his own beer can because his hands were slippery with blood.
4. Herr writes, "They were always telling you that you mustn't forget the dead, and they were always telling you that you shouldn't let yourself think about them too much."
5. Herr watched helicopters drop into the sea as their Vietnamese pilots jumped clear.

Reteaching Alternatives. You might divide your class into seven small groups, one for each section of the reports, and have each group prepare a short synopsis, including the facts of the report and an interpretation of the effect they feel Michael Herr is trying to achieve. Be sure they support their interpretations with examples from the text.

Responding to the Reports   Text page 1065
Analyzing the Reports
Identifying Facts

1. Herr says that the Vietnam Highlands are "spooky," and that the "Puritan belief that Satan dwelt in nature could have been born here." What details support his characterization? Among the details that students may mention are the following: the gnarled valleys and jungled ravines, the description of the mysterious Montagnards, the sudden mists, the extremes of heat by day and cold at night, and the smell of the jungle.

2. Why does the ex-medic say "Don't bet on it, man," to the blind man's sign on 57th Street? The ex-medic rejects the notion that his own nights are "dark"; in fact, nightmares about the war disturb his sleep and he never turns the lights off when he goes to bed.

3. How does Herr remember the dead? Herr cannot shake the memories of those who have been killed, even though he knows that it is a mistake to become too morbid.

Interpreting Meanings

4. What visual *images* from these excerpts make you feel the horror of the war most acutely? Student answers will vary. Ask the students to cite specific images from the extract.

5. Herr tells us that in the Battle of Dak To, the American command announced that they had killed four thousand. "But when the top of the hill was reached, the number of NVA found was four." What does Herr imply here? Why doesn't he solve the puzzle for us? He doesn't solve the puzzle because he wants to leave the hanging implication that there was something deceptive about "official" tallies of war casualties.

6. What is the effect of the anecdote about the soldier who is sure he will be killed on a suicide mission? The effect is both poignant and ironic.

Michael Herr   371

Why do you think the soldier wouldn't look at Herr after he came back from the mission unharmed? The soldier was probably ashamed of the premonitions he had about his own death. Perhaps he thought that he had revealed his own vulnerability to Herr.

7. Does Herr's picture of "The Correspondent" conform to the stereotyped picture most people have of war correspondents? How does Herr want you to feel about this correspondent? Student answers will vary. Ask the students to support their opinions.

8. Herr writes, "You were there in a place where you didn't belong, where things were glimpsed for which you would have to pay and where things went unglimpsed for which you would also have to pay, a place where they didn't play with the mystery but killed you straight off for trespassing." What do you think this passage means? Student interpretations of the passage will vary. In general, Herr seems to be saying that the Americans in Vietnam had the deck stacked against them; they were completely out of their element, in a mysterious land where no conventional rules of warfare were relevant to their situation.

Writing About the Reports
A Creative Response

1. Assessing the Impact of the Essay. Response to this assignment will vary according to the student's view of war before reading the essay.

Criteria for Evaluating the Assignment. In order to explain why Herr's essay did or did not affect the student's feelings and attitudes about war, the student explains what his or her feelings and attitudes were before reading the report, and how Herr either justified or challenged those feelings and attitudes.

A Critical Response

2. Comparing and Contrasting Two Writers. Note that the assignment calls for students to seek both similarities and differences between the reports by Hersey and Herr. You may wish to suggest that they make a chart, using the four-point list as column one; notes on Hersey in relation to each point, column two; and notes on Herr, column three.

Criteria for Evaluating the Assignment. The essay follows a coherent pattern of comparison/contrast, such as dealing first with similarities and then with differences, or going through the topics one by one and stating whether Hersey and Herr are alike or different on each item. Details from both Hersey and Herr support each of the student's conclusions.

3. Analyzing a Writer's Personality. First ask students for their impressions of Herr, and then send them back to the text to find passages documenting those impressions.

Criteria for Evaluating the Assignment. The paper is at least one paragraph long. It cites evidence from the report to support what the student thinks he or she knows about Herr.

4. Analyzing Women's Roles. Ask the students for names or phrases identifying the women in the two reports. List these on the chalkboard or overhead projector. From what students recall about each woman or group, what conclusions can they immediately begin to draw about the role of women in war, according to these two reports?

Criteria for Evaluating the Assignment. Conclusions offered are documented by a balanced use of supporting details from the two reports.

Extending the Reports

1. Interested students may want to read the rest of the book *Dispatches*, or other books on Vietnam, several of which are listed in the introduction to this selection, text page 1060. The class may want to compare and contrast the approaches of several different writers on the subject.

2. If you or your students have relatives, friends, or neighbors who fought in Vietnam, you might ask them to speak to the class about their experiences—bearing in mind that if they are reluctant to do so, their feelings should be respected.

William Least Heat Moon

Text page 1066

From *Blue Highways*

Text page 1067

Objectives

1. To find images, expressions, proverbs, and uncommon grammar used for characterization
2. To write an essay about colorful place-names
3. To write a description of the writer's character
4. To compare and contrast two literary journeys
5. To analyze metaphors

Introducing the Journal

In outline form, for your reference, here are the major elements of the journal selection:

- **Characters:** William Least Heat Moon; a waitress; Madison Wheeler; Thurmond, Virginia, and Hilda Watts
- **Themes:** the enduring value of rural life; the search for the true America
- **Point of view:** first-person
- **Significant techniques:** regional speech patterns; metaphor; concrete detail
- **Setting:** Nameless, Tennessee, and environs, 1977

Background on the Journal. William Least Heat Moon's other name is William Trogdon. That family name originated in this country with an Englishman who emigrated to North Carolina and was killed by Tories for giving food to rebel Colonists during the American Revolution. The first leg of Least Heat Moon's journey, from Missouri to North Carolina, retraced in reverse the journey his forebears had made. He was thirty-eight at the time—you might want to emphasize to your students that this is a notoriously unsettled age for men, when the onset of middle age often leads to self-doubts and a desire for change: a kind of second adolescence. His book about his journey was not published until five years after the fact, but when it finally was, it topped the best-seller lists for a considerable period, partly, no doubt, because it struck a responsive chord in readers going through emotional changes of their own.

Summary. Least Heat Moon, reading an atlas, sees the name Nameless, Tennessee, and decides it will be the next stop in his odyssey. During his search he eats at a "three-calendar" cafe, asks directions of a man loading tools into a pickup truck, and then, finally finding Nameless, talks with the Watts family, owners of a very old-fashioned general store, who make him welcome with good food and conversation.

Teaching Strategies

Providing for Cultural Differences. Both rural and urban students will probably enjoy this selection, but the enjoyment may come in different flavors. Rural students may see themselves to some extent, although the overwhelming majority of them will have far more contact with modern conveniences, and may not want their increasingly suburban way of life confused with that of the Watts. (Rural America today does not by any means avoid the main highways.) Urban students may appreciate the citizens of Nameless, Tennessee, for their unfamiliarity and quaintness, and you'll doubtless want to draw a line between appreciation and condescension—a line, it must be said, that Least Heat Moon, despite his efforts, does not always strictly observe.

Providing for Different Levels of Ability. More advanced readers will enjoy Least Heat Moon's uncanny ability to record the various shadings of regional speech, and individual speech patterns as well. Less advanced readers may find the twists and turns of his journey a bit too complicated, and may wonder why so much time is spent asking directions. The answer, of course, is that the characters discovered, rather than the directions themselves, are the important things for us as readers. It's not important to remember where Shepardsville Road and Steam Mill Holler are, but Madison Wheeler, who gives the directions, is a memorable character.

Introducing Vocabulary Study. Knowing the meanings of the following words will help students understand the selection.

saturated	1067	effete	1069
infallible	1067	meditative	1070
translucent	1068		

Reading the Journal. The selection can be broken down into sections fairly readily for the purpose of oral reading: from the beginning to "there were also mothers and children," page 1068; then to "You carry a dog?" page 1069;

William Least Heat Moon   373

then to, "the ones to ask you to dinner," page 1070; then to "how long he'd been in the store," page 1071; then to, "It is for this I have come," page 1071; then to the end of the selection. Most of the dialogue is in a regional accent, and if your students don't share that accent, and aren't unusually gifted actors, it might be best for them to read the lines in their natural voices.

Reading Check. You might use the following items as a check for literal comprehension. Have students identify the correct response.

1. The author says that the way to find the best cafes is to (a) count the trucks in the parking lot (b) count the calendars on the wall (c) see if the cook is fat or skinny ____(b)____
2. What town is the author trying to find? (a) Nameless, Tennessee (b) Nameless, Kentucky (c) Nameless, North Carolina ____(a)____
3. The author feels that those most likely to invite a traveler to supper are (a) those who have plenty to spare (b) those who are superstitious (c) those who have little ____(c)____
4. Thurmond Watts (a) has just bought his store (b) is trying to sell his store (c) has just sold his store ____(b)____
5. Ginny Watts keeps a (a) birth book (b) death book (c) wish book ____(b)____

Reteaching Alternatives. You might have the students each divide a sheet of paper into three columns and list the places the author stops in the left-hand column. Next to that, they can list the people he meets at each stop, and in the right-hand column—the most important one—they can briefly state what he learns from each person. If you prefer, you can do this at the board, eliciting answers in discussion.

Responding to the Journal   Text page 1073
Analyzing the Journal
Identifying Facts

1. What system does Least Heat Moon use to judge the food at small cafes in blue-highway America? He counts the wall calendars.

2. According to what he tells the waitress in the cafe, what is Moon searching for? He says he is searching for something that can be called harmony.

What is the waitress's response? The waitress says that she started out in life not liking anything, but that "then it grew on me."

3. Explain how Nameless, Tennessee, got its name. The Post Office insisted that the community have a name so that mail could be delivered. When the inhabitants met to name the town, they couldn't agree, so the place went by the name of "Nameless."

Interpreting Meanings

4. The notion that the honesty of the food and the justice of the prices in a cafe can be "infallibly" judged by the number of calendars on the wall is nonsense (a clear indication that "nonfiction" does not always deal in statistical fact). What sort of truth does the idea nevertheless suggest? A common bit of American travel lore has it that the eight-wheelers will be parked outside the best cafe—the logic being that truckers travel enough to discover where the good food is. What sort of logic would lead you to choose wall calendars as a guide? Student answers will vary. Ask the students to support their opinions.

5. Least Heat Moon knows that food—what it is, how it is served, who shares it—tells a lot about the people who eat it. Where in this excerpt does food tell us about character? The generosity of the Wattses in sharing their food with Least Heat Moon shows that they are good people.

6. What *concrete detail* helps paint a vivid picture of the Watts's home? Students should point to the paragraph beginning, "The old store, lighted only by three fifty-watt bulbs . . ." (page 1071).

Of the economic deterioration of the area? Numerous passages indicate that the area is poor.

What details keep the Watts's story from being a depressing one? The Watts's cheerfulness and generosity, despite their poverty, keep their story from being depressing.

7. The writer lets Madison Wheeler and the Watts family speak for themselves, and though it is highly unlikely that Least Heat Moon has total recall of their words, he captures the flavor of the country in recreating their dialogue. Find examples of *images*, *expressions*, *proverbs*, and uncommon *grammar* that tell us who and what these people are. Students should point to a variety of examples from the dialogue.

8. Least Heat Moon eats buttermilk pie while an old man plays music on a hand-cranked phonograph, and he says, "It is for this I have come." What does he mean? He feels that he has found the "harmony" that he was searching for.

9. Why does Least Heat Moon want to go to Nameless? He is whimsically curious.

What do you think of his reasons? Student answers will vary.

10. The waitress of the City Cafe insists that she would travel with a dog for company. But Least Heat Moon takes his journey "accompanied" (as he says elsewhere) "only by a small gray spider crawling the dashboard."

374   Modern Nonfiction

What evidence supports Moon's contention that "You get sociable traveling alone"? What do you think of this idea? Student answers will vary. Ask the students to support their opinions.

Do you hear echoes of Thoreau here? (See page 204.) Most students will agree that Least Heat Moon's idea parallels, or echoes, Thoreau's satisfaction in living alone in very simple surroundings.

Writing About the Journal
A Creative Response

1. Writing an Essay. Bring to class an atlas containing detailed maps of English-speaking countries, or ask students to bring travel maps from home. Discuss some usual sources of place names—words of translations from languages of the early inhabitants of an area, names of explorers, and names derived from geographical features, historical events, or immigrants' origins. Give students time to browse through the maps and share discoveries before they select a specific area to write about.

Criteria for Evaluating the Assignment. The essay identifes the state, county, or area under discussion, lists several names that appeal to the student, and offers reasonable explanations for the origins of those names.

A Critical Response

2. Describing the Writer's Character. Briefly discuss which scenes stand out in the students' minds, and what those scenes reveal about Least Heat Moon.

Criteria for Evaluating the Assignment. The essay cites evidence from the journal to support its description of several aspects of Least Heat Moon's character.

3. Comparing and Contrasting Literary Journeys. Students might again construct a comparative chart, listing in the first column "purpose," "effect," and "other" (for elements that interest the student), and adding columns for Momaday and for Least Heat Moon.

Criteria for Evaluating the Assignment. The essay follows a coherent pattern of comparison/contrast, such as dealing first with similarities and then with differences, or going through the topics one by one and stating whether Momaday and Least Heat Moon are alike or different on each item. Details from both accounts support conclusions drawn.

Analyzing Language and Style
Metaphors

1. He's been wandering since the mid 1960's.
2. a. Ready to enter "yonder," the next life
   b. A creature is comfortable in its own environment.
   c. Supplies for the future

Extending the Journal

1. Interested students may want to read at least parts of the rest of *Blue Highways*. Since the book is episodic, you might have several students read a chapter apiece and report to the class.
2. As a creative exercise, you might ask students to imagine that William Least Heat Moon is stopping in their community during his journey. Have them write down his imaginary encounters with local residents.

The American Language

Text page 1078

1. Students should tell which technology each of the following terms comes from. They should then identify what each term has come to mean in standard usage and explain how the term acquired that meaning. Answers will vary. Sample answers are provided.

A jerkwater town: trains; an insignificant town off the main line, only important because steam locomotives would be supplied with water there by "jerking" or pumping the water into the boiler.

To sidetrack: trains; to distract someone or digress, by analogy with moving a train from the main track to a siding.

A stopover: trains; a brief stop on a journey to rest, visit friends, and so on; from the original meaning of being able to stop at one place and then proceed to one's destination using the original ticket.

The wrong side of the tracks: trains; a socially undesirable neighborhood in a community; from the idea of getting off a train on the side next to another track rather than on the platform side.

A back-seat driver: cars; an annoying meddler; from the idea of a person in the back seat confusing the driver with unnecessary comments or instructions.

A tailspin: cars; a sudden confusion; from the idea of a car going out of control.

To bail out: airplanes; to rescue; from the idea of jumping out of a plane with a parachute if the plane is going to crash.

A nosedive: airplanes; a sudden plunge; from the physical movement of a plan that is going to crash.

2. Students are to identify the clinical meaning of the italicized words. They should then tell what each word means metaphorically in the sentence.
- a. **Stuart is *allergic* to hard work.** hypersensitive to an allergen; averse
- b. **Brooklyn was *obsessed* with baseball that season.** abnormally dominated by one persistent idea or image; preoccupied
- c. **Economists predict an *anemic* recovery.** deficient in hemoglobin; weak
- d. **Julia is not *sanguine* about the prospect of a job.** having blood as the predominating humor and thus ruddy-faced; optimistic
- e. **There has been an *epidemic* of burglaries on Sixteenth Street.** a disease affecting many persons at the same time in a community and spreading from person to person; large number

3. Students are to use newspapers and magazines to find five acronyms in current usage. They should then comment on whether the acronym is pronounced as a word or as separate letters. Answers will vary.

4. Students are to list five computer words or phrases that are in standard usage and then tell how each term is used. Students should then list five more computer terms that they think might enter standard usage in the future; they should tell what these terms mean. Answers will vary.

Exercises in Critical Thinking and Writing

Text page 1079

Evaluating Nonfiction: Fact and Opinion

This assignment asks students to evaluate any one of the selections from Unit Twelve. Key terms are *fact* and *opinion*.

Students often accept as a truism, "One opinion's as good as another." Stress that like many truisms, this one isn't accurate: as stated in the first paragraph of the section "Background," *without support, an opinion does not have much substance.* To explore the difference between fact and opinion, have students do the exercise included in the background section—stating three facts, deciding how each could be verified, and discussing this information with the class. (You may wish to use small groups so that everyone has a chance to speak.) After students have completed this activity, read and discuss with them the newspaper review (page 1080) evaluating a biography of James Madison. Students should then be ready to read and follow the section "Evaluating Nonfiction," the guidelines it contains, and the suggestions for prewriting and writing.

Criteria for Evaluating the Assignment. The opening paragraph of the essay cites the author and title of the piece being evaluated and contains the thesis statement. Subsequent paragraphs cite evidence from the selection to support the student's opinions on how the writer has used opinion, fact, and evidence in his or her work; and to support any comments made on the writer's style and how well the selection held the student's interest. The concluding paragraph of the essay summarizes the student's evaluation of the selection.

376 Modern Nonfiction

Unit Thirteen: *Poetry in a Time of Diversity* Text page 1081

Teaching the Poetry Unit

This unit presents a wide sampling of postwar American poetry, ranging in time from Theodore Roethke to Julia Alvarez, and in setting from a rural pasture to the Detroit ghetto, from a bomber over Europe in World War II to a televised Vietnam in a living room. It will give your students a taste of what American poetry is like today: a far cry from the traditional rhythms and rhymes of William Cullen Bryant and Ralph Waldo Emerson, though some of the underlying stances, the emotional concerns, remain similar.

As the title of this unit implies, diversity has been the keynote in American poetry written after World War II. A number of schools have flourished, and many individual poets have flourished without belonging to any stylistic school. No single poet has loomed so large as to provide an intimidating example, in contrast to the modernist era, when Pound and Eliot dominated the scene. Instead, more recognition has been given to poetry from outside the traditional mainstream, poetry written by Americans of diverse ethnic and racial origins, and by women. In addition, "mainstream" poetry has become decentralized in that it is written and published in places throughout the nation, and there is no single center of bohemianism—no Paris of the 1920's—to which poets feel they must flock. (The closest thing to it, today, is Iowa City, home of the Iowa Writers' Workshop.)

As the student introduction points out, the formalism, the view of poems as purely external esthetic objects, which dominated critical thought in the age of Eliot, has now largely been replaced by subjectivism. The poet Donald Hall, in his anthology, *Contemporary American Poetry*, makes a distinction among several different kinds of subjective poetry currently being written. Probably most familiar is confessional poetry, a direct, colloquial style in which the poet speaks of the most intimate emotional problems, usually in free verse. Sylvia Plath's *Ariel* is probably the most popular book of the confessional school, while Robert Lowell's *Life Studies* was the early monument that provided inspiration for many others. Confessionalism was at its height in the 1950's and 1960's; later in that turbulent decade a new style of subjective writing that Hall calls "expressionism" or "neo-surrealism" became current. It is a poetry of wild imagery, where what is most important is not the technical, prosodic skill of the poet or, on the other hand, the harrowingness of the poet's private life, but the originality of the poet's imagination. Alongside these two movements, black poetry and the poetry of other ethnic Americans has developed in a manner marked by forcefulness, linguistic vigor, and above all, a sense of reality—sharply perceived external reality, in contrast to the painstakingly analyzed internal reality of the confessionalists.

While no poetic tradition that contained Emily Dickinson and Marianne Moore could have been said to lack for a female voice, women poets in recent decades have come to the fore in a new way, making conscious statements about their identities as women and lending strength both to the confessionalist school and to the reality-oriented school. Adrienne Rich is perhaps the outstanding example of a poet who has at times worked in both styles. In contrast, Elizabeth Bishop deliberately steered her work away from identification with the concerns of women in any partisan sense. She was, however, an inspiration to female poets—and male ones as well—through the sheer quality of her work.

The biographical introductions to individual poets in this unit often emphasize stylistic developments during the course of the poets' careers. For the most part, this has been a development from a more formal verse early on to a less restrictive verse form later on. (Robert Lowell is the most obvious and perhaps most impressive such case.) This repeated pattern is as good evidence as any of the overall development of American poetry in this period: an opening-up, a loosening of formal bonds, and a willingness to take on any subject and reveal any emotion, no matter how "unliterary" or "shocking" it may once have been considered. At the same time, however, it should be remembered that standards of craftsmanship have not declined. Quite the opposite: The average American poem published today, with its subtle uses of internal rhyme, assonance, syllabic stresses, and varying line lengths, is undoubtedly more sophisticated, more well-crafted, than the rather mechanical rhymed and metered average American poem of a century ago.

*O*bjectives of the Poetry Unit

1. To improve reading proficiency and expand vocabulary
2. To gain exposure to notable modern poets and their works
3. To define and identify elements of poetry: figures of speech (simile, metaphor, personification), symbol, imagery, sound effects (rhythm, rhyme, assonance, alliteration), tone, diction, paradox, and anthropomorphism
4. To respond to poetry, orally and in writing, through analysis of its elements
5. To write original poems

6. To analyze the language and style of notable modern poets
7. To practice the following critical thinking and writing skills:
   a. Comparing and contrasting poems
   b. Analyzing a poem
   c. Interpreting a poem
   d. Using another point of view
   e. Imitating a poet's technique
   f. Comparing and contrasting poetry and prose
   g. Analyzing an image
   h. Evaluating a poem

Introducing the Poetry Unit

You might briefly review with students poems they have read in previous units, and ask them to summarize what they did and didn't like about that older kind of poetry. You may find that the things they liked—instances of powerful emotional expression—are the things most strongly present in this unit, while the things they didn't like—singsongy rhyme and meter, an old-fashioned quality—are for the most part not found here.

In introducing the various poetic "schools" of this period, you might point out that such labels are convenient for providing an overview of the poets of the period, but that they don't do justice to the diversity and scope of any individual poet's work. Theodore Roethke, for example, wrote traditional formal verse, free verse, confessional verse, and "deep image" poems (a type of poetry influenced by Pound's imagist ideas). Allen Ginsberg, who started out as an outrageous Beat, is now a "grand old man" of American poetry. Stylistic labels are good teaching tools, but each poet, and each poem, must be considered individually.

Theodore Roethke

Text page 1084

"Elegy for Jane"

Text page 1085

Objectives

1. To analyze the poem
2. To compare the treatment of death in two poems

Introducing the Poem

"Elegy for Jane" is filled with nature imagery, used by the speaker to develop Jane's personality and to come to an understanding of his relationship to Jane. You might have students pay particular attention to Roethke's use of metaphor in describing Jane, watching for variation or progressions of images.

Background on the Poem. In introducing the poem, you might first give a short history of the elegy as a literary form. An elegy is traditionally a meditation on the death of a person of particular importance to the poet or world. In the elegy, the poet seeks to invoke or bring to life the image of the dead person, usually to praise him or her. Point out to students that the speaker in the poem addresses the dead girl, a convention in the tradition of the elegy.

The Literal Meaning. In the first stanza, the speaker remembers his student's hair, her smile, her speech. He compares her speech and body language to a wren. In stanza 2, he describes her being lost in melancholy. She is compared to a sparrow and fern in stanza 3, and the speaker reveals his sadness over her death. In the final stanza, Jane is compared to a pigeon. The speaker stands over her grave, expresses his love for her, and qualifies that love.

Teaching Strategies

Providing for Cultural Differences. The poem is accessible to students from all backgrounds.

Providing for Different Levels of Ability. Less advanced students are likely to have difficulty with the central metaphors of this poem—the wren, the sparrow, and the pigeon. Discuss with these students the qualities of each of these birds and how the poet imparts those qualities to Jane.

Reading the Poem. As students read, they should be mindful of the speaker's voice and the fact that each stanza reveals or describes his mood. What mood shifts does he undergo? How does the poem reveal these shifts? Have students consider why the poem begins with the lively description and closes with the declaration and qualification of the speaker's love. How would the poem read if the stanza order were reversed?

378   Poetry in a Time of Diversity

Reteaching Alternatives. The last two lines of this poem have received much attention. Ask students to observe their reactions to the lines when the poem is read aloud. Why do they think Roethke put in the lines? Perhaps he feels he has to qualify his feelings for his student, lest the poem is misinterpreted. An argument that contradicts such an interpretation is that the poet would be more likely to state his relationship at the beginning, rather than the close, of the poem. Or are the lines very much a natural part of the poem? They certainly convey the strength of Jane's character through her effect on a person not close to her. Perhaps the most acceptable and natural explanation is that the speaker discovers both his feelings for Jane and his role in her life through the poem. The poem is this discovery.

Responding to the Poem   Text page 1085
Analyzing the Poem
Identifying Details

1. Count the number of times in the poem when the dead girl, or something about her, is compared to a plant or animal. Such references include: the comparison of Jane's hair to "tendrils" (line 1); the metaphor linking her look to that of a pickerel, or small fish (line 2); the comparison of Jane to a wren (lines 5–6); the implication that she is an animal "scraping her cheek against straw" (line 12); the apostrophe to "my sparrow" (line 14); the comparison to a fern (line 15); the metaphor of a "skittery pigeon" (line 19).

Interpreting Meanings

2. What do the comparisons to plants and animals tell us about the speaker's personality? Student answers will vary. In general, the references reveal the speaker as a tender, observant type of person who has great sympathy for nature and its creatures.

3. What, in your opinion, is the effect of the speaker's saying he has "no rights in this matter" (line 21)? Most students will probably agree that the statement intensifies the poem's expression of grief. The parenthetical expression emphasizes the speaker's sense of propriety, even as it enforces his feeling of loss. The implication of the statement is, perhaps, that if one "with no rights" can feel so deeply about Jane's death, how much more will her family and friends feel the tragedy.

Writing About the Poem
A Critical Response

Comparing Poems. Briefly review Ransom's poem, checking for students' awareness of the affectionate tone, before they compare Ransom's poem with Roethke's "Elegy for Jane." Response questions 2 and 3, page 693, and question 1, page 1085, call attention to figures of speech in the poems.

Criteria for Evaluating the Assignment. The essay cites phrases from both poems to identify similarity in warm, affectionate tone and use of figures of speech involving nature.

Extending the Poem

The critical response question asks students to compare the poem to another elegy. You might also have students compare Roethke's use of nature imagery with that of other poets in the unit. Ask them to look for the speaker's or poet's relationship with nature. In Plath they will find an antipathy, in Sexton a kind of otherworldly pact. In contrast, they will see that Roethke's relationship is intimate and basically one of joy.

Robert Hayden   Text page 1086

"'Summertime and the Living...'"   Text page 1087

Objectives

1. To identify images
2. To analyze irony and tone
3. To give an oral reading of the poem
4. To write an essay analyzing the poem

Introducing the Poem

Although the poem is written in free verse, Hayden does apply some formal restrictions, one of which is a consistency in stanza length. You can ask students to consider why the poet set the last line of stanza 3 apart, leading them to understand that the line is a causal transition from one stanza to the next. The line leads the reader from one time period or consciousness into another.

Background on the Poem. As the headnote points out, the title is taken from *Porgy and Bess*. A very brief summary of that story would be helpful to a fuller understanding of Hayden's poem. You might simply tell students that the two characters lived in a ghetto and were in love, and that Porgy was crippled. Despite their circumstances they did not give up hope.

The Literal Meaning. In stanza 1, the speaker recalls sunflowers, tough as the children growing up on the streets. He remembers a circus poster of horses and his fantasy as a boy of riding them. In stanzas 2 and 3, he recalls that roses were bought only for the dead, that no one had vacations, and that life was hard and people were angry. He recalls people sitting on steps in the summer. He feels the "Mosaic eyes" of those people bearing down on him in the present. In the last stanza, he recalls street preachers, Elks parades, and Jack Johnson, the boxer, bringing hope to the people of the ghetto.

Teaching Strategies

Providing for Cultural Differences. You will want to make vivid the stark contrast between ghetto life and that acquired by Jack Johnson.

Providing for Different Levels of Ability. With less advanced students, you may want to emphasize the literal meaning of the poem, pointing out to them that the poem is a recollection and consideration of the speaker's past. The present enters the poem in the third stanza, when the speaker feels the "Mosaic eyes" of the past upon him.

Reading the Poem. Before the class reads the poem, you might direct them to the multiple use of flower imagery in the poem. As they read, they should note the purpose and meaning of each flower image, for the poem is, in the end, about the attempt to come to flower of a neighborhood, or, if extended, an entire people.

Reteaching Alternatives. You might give extra consideration to question 9, "Responding to the Poem," for these sections (stanza 1, stanza 5) tie together the major themes of the real versus the imagination. A more intensive study of the final lines also gives students further time to reflect on the magnificent last lines of the poem, which echo the fantasy of the boy in stanza 1.

Responding to the Poem   Text page 1088
Analyzing the Poem
Identifying Details

1. What *images* does the poet use in the first three stanzas to describe the ghetto of his youth? The speaker mentions sunflowers, children, shattered glass, hard-working adults who often quarrel and can never afford to take vacations, and people sitting and gossiping in summer on the broken steps of urban houses and apartment buildings.

2. Roses are mentioned three times in the poem. Identify these contexts, and explain what the speaker connects with roses in each instance. Roses are first mentioned in line 1: the speaker says that "nobody planted" them in the ghetto. In lines 9 and 10, roses are mentioned in the context of funerals: people of the ghetto could only afford to buy such expensive flowers when someone died. This reference is echoed when the speaker mentions the "florist roses" that "only sorrow could afford" in lines 21–22. Throughout the poem, roses seem to be connected with luxury and death.

3. What does the speaker remember in the last stanza? The speaker remembers the grim street preachers, the Elks parades, and Jack Johnson in his "diamond limousine."

Interpreting Meanings

4. What is the implied contrast between the "grim street preachers" (line 25) and Jack Johnson? The contrast is between the austerity of the preachers and the extravagant, indulgent luxury of Jack Johnson.

5. In the first stanza, what do the "sunflowers" (line 2) and the "vivid children" (line 4) have in common? Both the flowers and the children have "tough stalks" and are "bold."

6. How did the boy react to the circus poster (line 5)? The circus posters delighted him; he imagined that he was the bareback rider of the horses on them.

How does the *image* of the circus poster contrast with the boy's all-too-real setting? The circus poster suggests the exotic realm of the imagination, which contrasts with the boy's drab surroundings in the ghetto.

7. "Burgeoning" (line 30) means "suddenly growing or developing." What does the use of this word in this context suggest? The word suggests the fertile power of the "fantasies" that the speaker mentions. Although the ghetto of the speaker's youth was vastly different from ancient

380   Poetry in a Time of Diversity

Ethiopia, dreams of power, pomp, and dignity still had the power to inspire the people of the ghetto.

8. In what way is the poem's title *ironic*? By omitting the last words ("is easy") of the well-known Gershwin song line, the poet calls attention to the ironic gap between dreams and reality for the residents of the ghetto of his youth.

9. How does the *tone* of the last five lines echo the tone of the first stanza? The first stanza underscores toughness, resilience, and optimism in the face of hardship. The last five lines of the poem revert again to an optimistic tone, this time inspired by a proud, luxuriant vision of ancient African roots.

Writing About the Poem
A Creative Response

1. Giving an Oral Reading. If you cannot easily locate a recording of "Summertime," ask a colleague who teaches music for help. You may wish to assign this activity to a small number of students or to make it optional, because of the time it would take for all students to present the reading.

Criteria for Evaluating the Assignment. The reading captures the mood and interprets the meaning of " 'Summertime and the Living...' " and works well with its background of "Summertime."

A Critical Response

2. Analyzing the Poem. To prepare students to deal with the ambiguity, mixed feelings, and mixed values of the poem, thoroughly discuss all nine response questions, and then elicit comments on specific lines that point to values—for example, "diamond limousine" (material values) and "Mosaic eyes" (spiritual values).

Criteria for Evaluating the Assignment. The paper cites lines of the poem that reveal a mixture of fond and painful memories and of material and spiritual values. The paper may or may not comment on the irony of the poem's title.

Elizabeth Bishop
Text page 1089

"First Death in Nova Scotia"
Text page 1090

Objectives

1. To identify and evaluate images
2. To analyze tone

Introducing the Poem

A way into this poem is to discuss with students how people often approach particularly painful and sad events by focusing on the objects around them. Bishop, through the voice of the child-speaker, does exactly that in the poem—each stanza takes the speaker closer and closer actually to comprehending Arthur's death. The first stanza deals with the chromographs and the loon. The second stanza focuses on the loon, which becomes a metaphor for death, and therefore for Authur. The third stanza physically moves the speaker toward her dead cousin in the coffin, but the speaker focuses on the strange beauty of the coffin and the loon who is able to look at it. The fourth stanza describes Arthur as a doll—unreal. It is not until the fifth stanza that the speaker, after imagining the warmth of the figures in the chromographs and imagining Arthur's place with them, realizes that her cousin must actually leave, and that in fact he has already gone into the cold and foreign place called death. It may also be helpful to explore the use of repetition (line 1, lines 8–9, line 10, lines 21–22, lines 26–27, lines 34–35, and so on) in the poem, which often reflects a play on the meanings of the words repeated, while adding a musical element to the language.

Background on the Poem. Elizabeth Bishop is often considered an unemotional writer. While this might appear so in a dramatic comparison with Plath and Sexton, it is far from correct. As is evident in both poems included here, Bishop's poems certainly do contain deep feelings and a powerful understanding of human nature. Bishop's poems can be read and loved for their storyline and their brilliant use of language, or they can be explored as prisms—the reader can search for the irony, humor, sorrow, and wisdom that is almost always there, but almost always revealed beneath the surface.

Elizabeth Bishop   381

The Literal Meaning. The speaker's cousin Arthur is laid out in his coffin beneath chromographs of the Royal Family. Beneath the chromographs is a stuffed loon on a table. The child speaker observes the room, the objects in the room, and her cousin in his coffin. She speculates on Arthur's future as the "smallest page at court," and then expresses her fear of her cousin having truly died.

Teaching Strategies

Providing for Cultural Differences. As the introduction to the poem mentions, the practice of being "laid out" in a coffin at home was common during the time of Bishop's childhood in Nova Scotia, and is continued in some cultures today. Students from other cultures might benefit from a discussion of these customs. Pictures of chromographs and loons may also be helpful for students. The photography department of your local library will likely have books with such photographs.

Providing for Different Levels of Ability. Less advanced students may have difficulty realizing why the speaker does not refer directly to death, but, rather, to the objects around her. An approach to this aspect of the poem is suggested under "Extending the Poem." More advanced students might do some research on the loon and consider why it is an appropriate symbol in this poem.

Reading the Poem. Although the poem is narrative and the language is direct, the poem may be difficult for some students to fully comprehend after just one reading. It is the kind of poem that should be read several times, so that the many important and evocative details are not overlooked. Suggest that students read the poem two or three times to themselves and then have it read aloud in class.

Reteaching Alternatives. "First Death in Nova Scotia" is a narrative poem in which a child-speaker relates her first experience with death. Have students assume the voice of that child-speaker and write a letter to a friend in which they describe the experience of seeing Arthur in his coffin.

Responding to the Poem   Text page 1091
Analyzing the Poem
Identifying Details

1. Describe the situation in the poem. The speaker remembers the appearance of her little cousin Arthur, who died when the speaker was a small child.

2. What *images* help you picture the parlor? Among the images students may mention are the stuffed loon and the marble-topped table.

3. What does the speaker imagine the royal family has invited Arthur to be? The speaker imagines that the royal family has invited Arthur to be the smallest page at the court.

Interpreting Meanings

4. How can you tell that this poem is written from the perspective of a child? Evidence that hints at the perspective of the poem is the statement that "I was lifted up" in line 24 and the childish reference to Jack Frost "painting" Arthur.

5. What do you think the stuffed loon contributes to the meaning of this poem? The loon, a beautiful white sea bird, is compared to Arthur in death: white, silent, and cold. Shot by Uncle Arthur, the father of the dead boy, the loon almost becomes an emblem for the dead child. Perhaps the poet indirectly suggests that the violence of the bird's death was as unnecessary as the premature death of her young cousin.

6. Find all the *images* in the poem that have to do with cold or snow. Why are they appropriate? Among the images are the following: the white, frozen lake (line 15), the "cold and caressable" breast of the child (line 18), the mention of Jack Frost (line 34), and the reference to the roads deep in snow (line 50). The images are appropriate because they suggest the ice-like shock of the child at the fact of death.

7. The poem ends with a *rhetorical question*—one that does not call for an answer. How does this question affect the emotional content of the poem? The question, which poignantly underlines the impossibility of Arthur's becoming a "page at court," reminds us that destiny has forever foreclosed Arthur's possibilities in life.

8. Suppose the speaker in the poem were Arthur's mother. How would that change the *tone* of the poem? Are the sentiments in the poem appropriate to the person who is expressing them? Explain. Student answers will vary. Encourage the students to support their opinions with reasons.

Extending the Poem

You might have students relate an emotional event they have experienced by describing the physical surroundings within which the event took place. Suggest that they focus on details that mirror their emotional states and that they use a variety of similes and metaphors.

"Little Exercise"

Text page 1092

Objectives

1. To identify similes and personification
2. To write a series of notes or a poem imitating the writer's technique
3. To write an essay comparing and contrasting two poems
4. To define words with multiple meanings

Introducing the Poem

This narrative poem is divided into seven three-line stanzas. The language and images are clear and direct and include the use of similes and personification. The music of the poem comes mainly from the meter, end rhymes (lines 4, 6, 10, 16), alliteration (lines 2, 3, 17), and repetition of the imperative form. Because the poem sounds as though someone were simply daydreaming aloud, it may at first appear simple, but the order of events is precise. You might discuss with students the effect on the poem if the order of events were reversed.

Background on the Poem. This is an early poem by Elizabeth Bishop, included in her first book, *North and South*. Within the poem are elements found in other Bishop poems: a description with qualities of the familiar and the unfamiliar, a slightly sardonic tone, clear and precise language, and a matter-of-fact voice. Many of the images are commonplace, yet described in a distinct and unusual manner that makes the observations memorable and haunting.

The Literal Meaning. The speaker asks the reader to imagine a storm. She asks the reader to picture what the mangrove keys will look like, and the boulevard lined with palm trees. She describes the boulevard and the rain, and then describes the storm's departure. In the last stanza she asks the reader to imagine an uninjured and "barely disturbed" person asleep in the bottom of a rowboat.

Teaching Strategies

Providing for Cultural Differences. Students who are unfamiliar with the scenery of warm climates may find this poem slightly confusing—you may want to show them pictures of mangrove keys, palm trees, a mangrove root, and so on. Having a few particular images in their minds will make the poem more immediate.

Providing for Different Levels of Ability. Less advanced students may have difficulty understanding that this is a poem about the mind wandering, about seeing things and imagining. You might suggest to these students that the poem is like a daydream and that perhaps each of them—the reader—is the person asleep in the bottom of the rowboat. For these students the activity suggested under "Reteaching Alternatives" might also prove helpful.

Reading the Poem. You may want to have four students read this poem aloud, with each of the four reading a "Think . . ." passage. The first student would then read the first stanza; the second, the second and third stanzas; the third student, the fourth, fifth, and sixth stanzas, and the fourth student, the final stanza. To emphasize the variety of images in the poem, you might suggest that each of the students vary his or her pitch, tone, and voice quality.

Reteaching Alternatives. The movement of this poem traces the way the mind can work—skipping from one image to another. To reinforce this concept, you might have students write as a class activity a description of a scene, perhaps a sidewalk fair or a baseball or soccer game. Have one student suggest an image that is a part of the scene, and then, without giving them time to think or to make logical connections between the images, have other students suggest additional images.

Responding to the Poem

Text page 1092

Analyzing the Poem

Identifying Details

1. Geographically, where does the poem occur? Name the clues that support your sense of its locale. Most students will agree that the poem occurs in a tropical locale, perhaps in Florida or on one of the islands of the Caribbean. Clues include the mangrove keys, the heron, and the palm trees. The mention of "keys" would suggest southern Florida.

2. The movement of the poem has much in common with that of a documentary movie. A series of quick shots, one after the other, tell a story in pictures. Describe the "shots" you see. In the first stanza, a tropical storm gathers force. In the second, the poet conjures up the scene of the mangrove keys, waiting "unresponsive" for the storm to break; in the third stanza, a heron shakes his feathers. The fourth stanza shifts the scene from the country to the town, where the little palm trees on the boulevard shake their leaves in the wind. This picture is amplified in

Elizabeth Bishop 383

the fifth stanza, with the description of the rain on the cracked sidewalks. In the sixth stanza, the storm abates, perhaps with intermittent lightning flashes. Finally, the poet gives us a picture of a person riding out the storm, uninjured, in the bottom of a rowboat.

3. In a poem full of comparisons of one thing with another, two are full-fledged *similes*. Which are they? The storm is "like a dog looking for a place to sleep in" (line 2); the palm trees are revealed "as fistfuls of limp fish-skeletons" (line 12).

4. What uses of *personification* can you identify in the poem? Examples include: the mangrove keys in "families" (line 6), the heron making "an uncertain comment" (line 8), the relief of the boulevard and the sea (lines 13–15).

Interpreting Meanings

5. The only human being in the poem is "someone" who does not make an appearance until the very end. Who might this person be? Student answers will vary. Perhaps it is the speaker herself, who has witnessed the storm.

What might the poet want to suggest by telling us to think of this person as "uninjured, barely disturbed"? Again, answers may vary. Most students will agree that the reassurance of the last line underscores the speaker's pleasure in nature. For the speaker, the storm in neither ominous nor menacing; it is simply a natural event.

6. By calling her poem "Little Exercise," Elizabeth Bishop seems to make light of her verse, as though it were no more than a skillful assemblage of observations about a storm. But perhaps her light-hearted approach disguises deeper meanings. What might at least one of these meanings be? Student answers will vary. Some will suggest that the storm described in the poem is a "little exercise" of nature: transient, and ultimately insignificant. Others may argue that it is the poem that is the "little exercise": a whimsical comment on one of nature's dramatic scenes. Encourage students to present and defend their own interpretations.

Writing About the Poems
A Creative Response

1. Imitating the Writer's Technique. Ask students to list some scenes of action or some settings that would lend themselves to a "Little Exercise"—for example, a ball game, shoppers in a mall, a concert, a busy skiing slope.

Criteria for Evaluating the Assignment. The student's paragraph or poem is titled "Little Exercise," begins with "Think of," and lists five or more vivid images which form part of an easily identifiable setting or scene of action.

A Critical Response

2. Comparing Poems. You might suggest that students turn to the Moore poem first (page 743) and list the details that strike them, and that they then choose the Bishop poem which seems to use details in a similar way.

Criteria for Evaluating the Assignment. The essay is at least one paragraph long. It names the Bishop poem being compared with Moore's "The Steeplejack" and, by citing specifics from both poems, shows how both poets use detail upon detail to bring a scene to life.

Analyzing Language and Style
Multiple Meanings

1. *Manners:* rules of behavior, types or sorts, customs, styles. The word could apply to behavior at a funeral or to funeral customs.
2. *Frosted:* covered with ice crystals, iced as a cake is iced, touched with silvery coloring, killed (especially in the case of a young plant) by freezing. Several of these apply to "First Death in Nova Scotia."
3. *Exercise:* physical exertion, discharging a duty, practicing a drill, performance that demonstrates a skill. "Little Exericise" could be a performance or practice drill.
4. *Disturbed:* deranged, alarmed, inconvenienced, interrupted. "Inconvenienced" is good for the last line of "Little Exercise."

Randall Jarrell

Text page 1094

"The Death of the Ball Turret Gunner"

Text page 1095

Objectives

1. To interpret the meaning
2. To write a paragraph or poem from an imagined point of view

Introducing the Poem

In five powerful lines, the speaker of this poem describes his grisly death in a ball turret. The poem is filled with womb and unborn child images that reinforce the innocence of the speaker—"my mother's sleep," "hunched in its belly," "my wet fur." In contrast, the gruesome images of the speaker's death emphasize the destruction of that innocence. Students should note how the repetition of the contrasting *s* sounds in line 1 and *k* sounds in line 5 reinforces the meanings of those lines. In oral reading, students might also note the regular meter of the first four lines that moves the speaker, without pause for contemplation, from birth to death, and the varying meter of the fifth line that suggests the speaker's separation from birth and life.

Background on the Poem. The headnote tells students that the poem is perhaps the most famous World War II poem. You might also tell them that Jarrell's war poems taken together are considered to be some of the greatest war, or antiwar, poems ever written. James Dickey describes the effect of Jarrell's poems most eloquently:

> The poems . . . put on your face, nearer than any of your own looks, more irrevocably than your skin, the uncomprehending stare of the individual caught in the State's machinery: in an impersonal, invisible, man-made, and uncontrollable Force. They show in front of you a child's slow, horrified, magnificently un-understanding and growing loss of innocence in which we all share and can't help: which we can neither understand nor help in ourselves in the hands of the State any more than can the children in *our* hands.

The Literal Meaning. There is contention over the literal meaning of this poem. Taking into consideration Jarrell's other work, the most accepted interpretation is that the speaker is taken into the army before he is fully conscious of himself, while metaphorically still a child. The State, or army, and literally the ball turret, becomes his new mother in the sense that the formation of his self continues in it. Hunched in the freezing turret, six miles from the earth, he wakes, or becomes conscious, under fire. This is his nightmare. He is killed in the air, his body literally torn apart. Nothing is left of him—the pieces of his remains have to be washed out of the turret.

Teaching Strategies

Providing for Cultural Differences. Students with relatives who served in Vietnam may have heard firsthand about some of the horrors of war; for other students, the death in this poem may seem unnecessarily gruesome. At this point, you may want to review with students Walt Whitman's description of the "real war," text page 351, or Stephen Crane's imagery in "War Is Kind," text page 508. Both works illustrate the universal, timeless horrors of war.

Providing for Different Levels of Ability. Less advanced students might have difficulty with the layers of literal and metaphorical meaning in this poem. For these students, you might discuss the fact that the "State" in this poem is sometimes seen to represent the faceless, nameless forces that seem to drive us.

Reteaching Alternatives. If students have not already done so, have them read "Primary Sources: The Ball Turret," text page 1095. With this information, have students describe, on a literal level, how the ball turret gunner dies.

Responding to the Poem

Text page 1095

Analyzing the Poem

Identifying Details

1. What is the temperature like in the ball turret? It is very cold.

2. How far from earth does the bomber ascend? It ascends six miles from earth.

   What happens at that altitude? The gunner's "wet fur" (namely, his skin) freezes.

3. What happens to the gunner? The gunner meets his death in a combat airplane, six miles above the earth. He is fatally wounded by flak from enemy aircraft. The mutilated remains of his body are washed out of the gunner's turret with a hose.

Interpreting Meanings

4. "Belly" here can be read on two levels. What two bellies could the speaker be talking about? How is the ball turret like a womb? The "belly" could refer either to a section of the plane or to a mother's womb. The ball turret could be said to be like a mother's womb because it is dark and because it completely surrounds the gunner.

5. How do you know that the speaker didn't enter the army as a result of a rational decision? He says that he "fell into the State" (line 1), implying that he was drafted or that he blundered in an involuntary way into military service.

6. What is the speaker's "wet fur"? Why do you think he compares himself to an animal? The "wet fur" is the speaker's skin. He probably compares himself to an animal to indicate obliquely his fear, powerlessness, and dependence on instinct.

7. How does the grisly process described in the final line fit in with the rest of the poem? Student answers will vary. In general, the grotesque realism of the final line, demeaning the gunner's final remains, accords with the bleak pessimism of the rest of the poem.

8. While the speaker is not around to receive a medal, he *is* a hero. Why do you think he shows no awareness of that fact? Again, student answers will vary. Urge students to present and defend their own opinions.

9. What, in the long run, is this poem about? Is it about political dissent? It is a statement about the way things in the world are regimented and mechanized? Is it about the destruction of the innocent? Student answers will vary. Encourage the students to support their interpretations with reasons.

Writing About the Poem
A Creative Response

Writing from Another Point of View. The assignment demands a thorough understanding of the poem, to be gained from completion of the nine response questions. Bring several newspaper articles about people who have died—celebrity notices are especially good—for students who are unable to locate one.

***C**riteria for Evaluating the Assignment.* The poem or paragraph is as brief as Jarrell's, is written from the point of view of the person who died, and packs its message into metaphors in Jarrell's style.

Extending the Poem

Have interested students locate one of the collections of Jarrell mentioned on text page 1094, *Little Friend, Little Friend* (1945) or *Losses* (1948). Students can then compare and contrast the war poems in this collection with "The Death of the Ball Turret Gunner." In particular, students might look for themes of fantasy vs. fact and life vs. myths about life.

Gwendolyn Brooks

Text page 1096

"Of De Witt Williams on His Way to Lincoln Cemetery"

Text page 1097

Objectives

1. To interpret the poem
2. To describe the tone
3. To perform a choral reading

Introducing the Poem

The clear imagery and direct language should make this an easily understood poem. You may want to emphasize the rhyme, meter, and repetition—all of which contribute to the poem's songlike quality.

***B**ackground on the Poem.* This poem is a section of a longer poem titled "A Street in Bronzeville," the title poem of Gwendolyn Brooks's first book. The entire poem consists of twenty sections, each of which focuses on different people and circumstances in a neighborhood.

***T**he Literal Meaning.* Addressing the driver of the hearse in which the casket has been placed, the speaker requests that the body of De Witt Williams be driven by the landmarks of his life. The place of his birth, Alabama, and

386 Poetry in a Time of Diversity

where he was raised, Illinois, are repeated in the poem, along with the refraining line, "Swing low swing low sweet sweet chariot...."

Teaching Strategies

Providing for Cultural Differences. This poem assumes a knowledge of the history of blacks in America. You may want to make certain that students understand the symbolic importance of the song "Swing Low, Sweet Chariot" to this history. It has long symbolized a place of refuge in troubled times.

Providing for Different Levels of Ability. Less advanced students may have difficulty understanding the effect of the line repetitions. The choral reading, suggested under "Reading the Poem," should help these students. More advanced students might benefit from writing an elegy of their own, imitating the song-like rhythm of the poem.

Reading the Poem. You may want to have students prepare the choral reading suggested for "A Creative Response," text page 1097.

Reteaching Alternatives. Focusing on question 3, text page 1097, you might ask students what they think the line, "Nothing but a plain black boy," means. (The repetition indicates that it is an important line to the poem.) Have students discuss whether they believe there is any such thing as a "plain" person.

Responding to the Poem   Text page 1097
Analyzing the Poem
Interpreting Meanings

1. On the basis of the details given about the route of his funeral procession, how would you characterize De Witt Williams? Certain details suggest that De Witt Williams led less than a model life: the pool hall (line 7), the "Show" (line 8), the dance halls (lines 15–16), and the references to picking his women and drinking "liquid joy" (lines 17–18). No references are made to Williams's job or family life. The subject of the poem was evidently fond of entertainment and pleasure.

2. What is the effect of the word "maybe" in line 10? Student answers may vary. The word "maybe" introduces a note of doubt about Williams's ability, once he is dead, to recognize his favorite haunts on the route of the funeral procession. The speaker seems to acknowledge the possibility of an afterlife, but she does not present any conviction in a hereafter as a matter of faith.

3. With a background so humble, why do you think De Witt Williams is important enough to be the inspiration for a poem? Student answers will vary. The poet appears to have selected De Witt Williams as a pathetic instance of a phenomenon all too common: a life wasted and prematurely ended in the urban ghetto.

4. "De Witt" and "Lincoln" are both prominent names in American history. Do you think the poet wants us to accept them as merely incidental facts? Or do you think she intends a touch of *irony* here? Students will have various opinions. Abraham Lincoln, of course, was the sixteenth president of the United States. In 1863, he issued the Emancipation Proclamation, freeing America's blacks from the evil of slavery. De Witt Clinton of New York was a Republican presidential candidate who was defeated by James Madison in the election of 1812. Students may argue that the names "De Witt" and "Lincoln" in the title of the poem are intended to be both realistic and ironic: distinguished names from America's past are juxtaposed with the fate of a "plain black boy" who made his way from the South to Chicago's urban ghetto, only to waste away his life there.

5. How would you describe the *tone* of this elegy? The tone could be described as a mixture of irony and pathos.

Writing About the Poem
A Creative Response

Preparing a Choral Reading. The poem is brief enough for as many as six or seven groups (of three to five students each) to present during a single class period. To get students started, you might ask whether the refrain (the variations on "Nothing but a plain black boy") calls for single or multiple voices. Allow groups to compare interpretations before they formalize their own decisions, and, if they wish, to use "Swing Low, Sweet Chariot" or other music as background.

Criteria for Evaluating the Assignment. The reading conveys an interpretation of the poem in keeping with points discussed in response to the five "Interpreting Meanings" questions.

Gwendolyn Brooks   387

Robert Lowell

Text page 1098

"For the Union Dead"

Text page 1100

Objectives

1. To identify and interpret images and metaphor
2. To describe the tone
3. To write a paragraph or a poem describing a building
4. To write an essay comparing and contrasting two poems

Introducing the Poem

The varying perspectives, or time points, in the poem are complex—the speaker seems to be everywhere at once. He is at the aquarium, then the Boston Common, then on Boylston Street, and, finally, in front of a television set. To simplify the shifts between both personal and historical time, you might tell students that it is likely the speaker is at the aquarium for the entire poem. The aquarium of his youth becomes the inspiration for the poem.

The tone in this poem shifts throughout from nostalgic to bitter and ironic, and figures of speech play a central role in establishing that tone. Students should note, for example, the effect on the poem's tone of such figures of speech as "my nose crawled like a snail on the glass," "yellow dinosaur steam shovels," and the monument that "sticks like a fishbone / in the city's throat." Alliteration also affects the tone, as students will especially note in the last three lines of the poem where the string of *s*'s mimics the silent flow of fish and grease. The somewhat bitter, ironic implication is that nothing sticks, nothing holds, not the speaker's treasured childhood aquarium nor the monument to black war heroes. Both are forgotten and spiritually destroyed by the action of progress or history.

Background on the Poem. Judging from this poem, some students may question why Lowell is considered a confessional poet. You might tell students that this poem and the book in which it was first published were considered by critics as a move away from the loose lines and purely personal qualities of *Life Studies*. Critic Karl Malkoff responds to this question: "Although Lowell himself has described the poem as more 'public' than the poems of *Life Studies*, it is possible that by plunging deep beneath the singleness of ego he has reached a public world that is nonetheless completely defined in terms of the self."

The Literal Meaning. The comment at the end of the poem, text page 1102, provides a detailed paraphrase.

Reading the Poem. An audiocassette recording accompanies this poem. If possible, have students listen to the recording first, paying particular attention to the varying tones and emotions expressed by the performer. (An alternative might be for you or a talented student to prepare a reading.) Afterwards, have students read "A Comment on the Poem," text page 1102, so they will approach the poem itself with confidence. You might also suggest to students that the entire poem takes place in the speaker's imagination. In fact, his contemplation of the statue of Colonel Shaw becomes a kind of revery. In line 37, the colonel actually seems to come alive.

Reteaching Alternatives. Because the poem does have such shifting tones and emotions, you might have students look at word connotations. In line 9, for example, the poet uses the word "sigh," a word that connotes nostalgia. In the same stanza, steam shovels are "dinosaur," the inference being that their work is thoughtless. archaic, and destructive. Students might also investigate the many ironies in the poem. The bulldozers, for example, work for "progress," but, in reality, are digging an underworld and undermining the Statehouse and statue, symbols of the city's heritage.

Responding to the Poem

Text page 1103

Analyzing the Poem
Identifying Details

1. What *images* describe the old South Boston Aquarium? The aquarium is said to be standing in a Sahara of snow; it has broken and boarded windows; the airy tanks are dry.

2. What *images* describe what the speaker saw on Boston Common? The speaker says that he pressed against a barbed and galvanized fence on the Boston Common, where he saw yellow steam shovels that looked like dinosaurs, gouging up earth to construct an underground parking garage.

What *metaphor* describes the steam shovels? The steam shovels are compared to yellow dinosaurs.

3. What *images* describe the St. Gaudens monument? The monument is described as "shaking"; it is made of bronze figures.

388 Poetry in a Time of Diversity

How many things is the colonel compared with? The colonel is compared with an angry wren (line 33) and a taut greyhound (line 34).

4. What do the frayed flags in the graveyards remind the speaker of? They remind the speaker of quilts.

5. What details tell you what happened to Colonel Shaw and his men? Half the regiment was dead two months after marching through Boston (lines 25–26); the body of the colonel and the bodies of his troops were thrown into the ditch (lines 50–52).

6. What *image* in the last stanza reminds us of the scene described in the second stanza? The luxury automobiles that "glide by" are compared to "fish" (line 66), reminding us of the fish in the old aquarium.

Interpreting Meanings

7. What does the poet mean by saying Colonel Shaw "rejoices in man's lovely, / peculiar power to choose life and die" (lines 37–38)? Lowell seems to mean that only in man is found the reasoning power that can choose either life or death.

8. What historical events in Boston and other American cities might the poet be referring to with the mention of the "drained faces" of black children on television (line 60)? This reference probably refers to the lengthy crisis sparked by the desegregation of the Boston city schools in the 1950's and 1960's. Similar crises occurred in other American cities.

9. What do you think is the "savage servility" mentioned in the last stanza? Student answers will vary. The phrase might imply a materialism (symbolized by the luxurious, showy cars) which the speaker regards as savage, or barbaric. "Servility" would thus be a reference to the modern world's worship of money. The word "grease" is appropriate in the context of cars and machines—it also may connote flattery and dishonesty as means to achieve wealth in a materialistic society.

10. Explain how the title of the poem could have at least two meanings. Students may point out that "union" could be used as an adjective—the meaning of the title would thus be "the dead who served the Union." But if "union" is used as a noun, and "dead" as an adjective, the meaning changes; read this way, the title implies that our nation, preserved at such price by the likes of Colonel Shaw and his men, has died a spiritual death in the modern world.

11. How does the speaker feel about what he sees in his city? How would you describe the poem's *tone*: Is it ironic, nostalgic, or sarcastic? Explain. Student answers will vary. Many students will agree that Lowell's tone is mixed, in that he seems to feel ironic, nostalgic, *and* sarcastic about life in his city.

Writing About the Poem
A Creative Response

1. Writing a Description. Discuss some local buildings the students could use—perhaps a restored "Old Town" area where banks have become boutiques, or a gas station that has become a convenience store because of gas wars.

Criteria for Evaluating the Assignment. The paragraph or short poem describes a building as it is now and as it once was, and states whether the change reflects town events or wider changes in society.

2. Comparing and Contrasting Poems. Discuss "Comment on the Poem" (Lowell's poem), page 1102, and Timrod's poem (page 1103), before having students work in pairs to chart the similarities and differences between the poems. The first column of the chart should read (a) theme or message, (b) tone, (c) diction, and (d) form. The second and third columns should list appropriate comments for Timrod's and Lowell's poems.

Criteria for Evaluating the Assignment. The essay cites specific details from both poems to demonstrate that they are similar only in commemorating war dead, and contrast in every other way listed: word choice (Timrod's poetic language and Lowell's diction of daily life), message and tone (Timrod glorifies the dead, Lowell takes a grimmer stance), and form (Timrod uses four-line stanzas rhymed abab; Lowell uses free verse).

Extending the Poem

You might have interested students read a few poems from Lowell's earlier rhymed work and then a few lines from Part Four of *Life Studies*. After comparing these two aspects of Lowell, students may acquire a greater appreciation for Lowell's progression into the more refined free verse of "For the Union Dead."

Robert Lowell

Richard Wilbur

Text page 1104

"The Beautiful Changes"

Text page 1105

"Year's End"

Text page 1106

Objectives

1. To interpret images
2. To paraphrase the statement of a stanza
3. To identify the speaker's problem
4. To write an essay analyzing the poems
5. To analyze sound effects

Introducing the Poems

You will want to have your students think about the poetic uses of ambiguity as they study Wilbur's poems. In composition, students are often told to avoid constructions that can be understood in two or more ways. Poets, however, rely on ambiguity. Wilbur, for example, wants his readers to see multiple meanings in both the title and content of "The Beautiful Changes." He wants readers to realize that *downs* in line 1 of "Year's End" can have more than one meaning.

Background on the Poet. If any of your students are familiar with the comic operetta *Candide*, based on Voltaire's classic satire, they may be interested to know that Richard Wilbur wrote the witty and memorable lyrics for Leonard Bernstein's music. *Candide* opened in New York at the Martin Beck Theatre on December 1, 1956, and has been revived many times since then.

The Literal Meaning. *"The Beautiful Changes"*: In the first stanza, the speaker walks through a meadow in autumn. Seeing the beautiful weed called Queen Anne's Lace (wild carrot), he compares it to lilies and the meadow to a lake. Its effect on him is somewhat the same as when the woman he loves makes him think of a lovely Swiss lake. In the second stanza, the speaker notes the changes in a forest and a leaf wrought by a chameleon (changing color to match the forest) and a mantis (appearing to be part of the leaf). In the third stanza, the woman, first mentioned in stanza 1, is said to hold roses in such a way that they are not hers alone. Other rose/beauty associations perhaps come to the speaker's mind. For a moment, he believes, beauty transforms everything it touches into beauty.

"Year's End": In winter, the speaker notes the snow and the thinly frozen lake. He remembers seeing leaves partially frozen into the ice, fluttering all winter. The speaker then mentions ferns that became fossils, mammoths that froze in Arctic ice, and the little dog preserved in the volcanic ash of Pompeii. In the last stanza, the speaker ponders these "sudden ends of time," implying that our journey into the future is always uncertain. New Year's bells contend with the immediate but also timeless snow.

Teaching Strategies

Providing for Cultural Differences. Standards of beauty vary from culture to culture and from generation to generation. Since Wilbur's first poem concerns beauty, you may want to explore with students the nature of beauty. Why does beauty vary from one era to another? (You might mention the "beautiful" women in Rubens's paintings, who, by today's standards, are grossly overweight.) Is beauty relative, or are there absolute standards? Such a discussion is especially relevant to the poem "The Beautiful Changes," because it suggests still another meaning for the poem's title—one outside the poem—that also makes sense.

Providing for Different Levels of Ability. With less advanced students, you will want to read both of these poems aloud in class and to paraphrase as necessary. The poems are lyrically beautiful, and all students should be able to appreciate their rhythm and euphony.

Reading the Poems. By now your students probably realize that beauty, love, and death are common themes in poetry. Point out that these themes recur because of their universality. The poet's challenge is to say something new about them, or else to say something familiar in a striking or different way. The two poems should be read aloud in all classes, at some point, either before or after the "Responding" questions have been assigned. (An audiocassette recording of "The Beautiful Changes" accompanies the text.)

Reteaching Alternatives. As students discuss their responses to the poems, make clear that poetry often *is* ambiguous, often *is* susceptible to more than one "right" reading or "correct" interpretation, but that an interpretation must be grounded in the poem itself. In class discussion have student volunteers summarize their interpretations to

390   Poetry in a Time of Diversity

the poems, and then have the class attempt to agree on which of the interpretations, within the framework of the poem, seem most logical.

"The Beautiful Changes"

Responding to the Poem   Text page 1105
Analyzing the Poem
Identifying Details

1. What does the Queen Anne's Lace do to the dry grass? The Queen Anne's Lace turns the dry grass into a lake.

What does the thought of "you" do to the speaker? The thought creates images of fabulous, blue lakes, like Lake Lucerne in Switzerland.

2. What do the chameleon and the mantis in stanza 2 have in common? Both the chameleon and the mantis can be absorbed into their environment because of their color.

3. What does the beautiful do in the last stanza? It changes in kind ways.

Interpreting Meanings

4. With great delicacy, the final stanza makes a strong statement. *Paraphrase* that statement. In general, the central thought of the last stanza is that beautiful things can always be appreciated anew; beauty always offers "a second finding" for its beholder, as fresh and wonderful as the first.

5. In your own words explain the two meanings expressed by the title. Does the poem as a whole support one meaning or the other, or both? The title could mean that "the beautiful" (as an abstract concept) is always in flux; or it could be a reference to "changes" that are beautiful. Most students will agree that the title may be deliberately ambiguous, and that the poem may support both interpretations.

6. Is this a love poem? Pick out the lines that support your answer. Students who argue that this is a love poem may cite the references to "the slightest shade of you" in line 5 and the reference to "your hands" in lines 13 and 14. Some students may argue, however, that the speaker, even as he pays tribute to his love, intends the application of the poem more generally—as a universal comment on the nature of "the beautiful."

"Year's End"

Responding to the Poem   Text page 1107
Analyzing the Poem
Identifying Details

1. At what time of year is the speaker expressing his thoughts? The setting is the street of a snow-covered town, late on the night of New Year's Eve.

2. In line 1, what two different meanings of the word *down* are suggested? The word, as a verb, could mean to "defeat" or "lay prostrate"; it could also mean "to line with down, or soft feathers."

3. What examples does the poet use in the third and fourth stanzas to illustrate the "sudden ends of time"? In the third stanza, the poet uses the examples of the traces of ferns on ancient rocks and of the "mammoths," or huge extinct elephants, whose remains have been found in the Arctic regions. In the fourth stanza, he uses the example of the remains of a pet dog at Pompeii, the ancient Roman city near Naples which was buried by lava and ash in the eruption of Mount Vesuvius in 79 A.D. The dog was found remarkably preserved after being covered up for centuries.

4. What does the poet compare people to in lines 26 and 27? The metaphor implicitly compares our lives to threads of yarn or cloth. Just as we usually live without thought for the future, we may be said to "fray." The cloth of which we are made is only "wrought"—that is, finely worked into an artistic creation such as a tapestry—in "afterthoughts."

Interpreting Meanings

5. Why does the speaker ask for "more time" (line 28)? The speaker asks for more time because he wants to have the assurance of living longer.

6. Why do you think the radio is "buried" (line 29)? The radio may be under a blanket, or buried in the snow. Or perhaps the sounds of the radio are muffled because the radio is some distance away.

7. What is the *problem*, or tension, that the speaker presents in this poem? The tension is between past, present, and future—between human beings' aspirations for perfection and their actual accomplishment.

How does the *image* in the last line concisely express that tension? The last line juxtaposes hope for the future,

Richard Wilbur 391

symbolized by the "New-year bells," and the certainty of time's passage, symbolized by the fallen snow. The disharmony between the two elements, or ideas, is suggested by the word "wrangling" in the final line.

8. Do you agree that we "fray into the future"? Explain. Student answers will vary. Ask the students to explain and defend their opinions.

Writing About the Poems
A Critical Response

Analyzing the Poems. Completion of the response questions on both poems prepares students for this assignment. You may wish specifically to elicit from students what they think the poems say about beauty, love, and death, and whether any of these ideas seems to contradict the usual way people look at the subject.

Criteria for Evaluating the Assignment. The essay cites details from the poems to demonstrate Wilbur's attempt to show us that beauty, love, and death blend into simple daily images which we often fail to notice as we "fray into the future." The essay contrasts Wilbur's views with more usual ways of addressing these topics.

Analyzing Language and Style
Sound Effects

1. abbacc
2. A slant rhyme occurs internally in "*winter* long *into*" (line 10).
3. Iambic pentameter
4. In stanza 1, the third line begins with an accented syllable; in stanza 2, the fourth and fifth lines do so; and so on.
5. Examples of alliteration include "*d*owns and *d*ying" (line 1), "the *l*ate *l*eaves down" (line 8), "*f*ray into the *f*uture" (line 26). Instances of assonance include "fr*o*zen-*o*ver" (line 5), "b*a*nks to sh*a*ke" (line 7), "sh*a*pely thing th*ey*" (line 24).
6. Answers will vary. The sounds of "down(s)," "curled," "fray," and "wrangling" are especially evocative.

Extending the Poem

In "Year's End," Richard Wilbur makes a poetic statement about time. Ask students to write an original paragraph in which they, too, make a point about the nature of time. In their paragraphs, have students use appropriately at least one of the following quotations.

the "corridors of time"—Henry Wadsworth Longfellow

the "sands of time"—Henry Wadsworth Longfellow

the "scythe of time"—Napoleon Bonaparte

the "tooth of time"—Edward Young

the "whirligig of time"—William Shakespeare

"Time, the wisest counsellor"—Plutarch

"Time, the subtle thief of youth"—John Milton

the "inaudible and noiseless foot of time"—William Shakespeare

"Time, a maniac scattering dust"—Alfred, Lord Tennyson

James Dickey
Text page 1108

"Sled Burial, Dream Ceremony"
Text page 1109

Objectives

1. To analyze the poem
2. To interpret metaphor and simile

Introducing the Poem

This poem is an excellent example of a lucidly written, easy-to-read poem that nevertheless requires interpretation. As the headnote on text page 1109 indicates, the poem is exactly like a dream. The details are sharp and unmistakable, yet their meaning, like the meaning of a dream, is not obvious.

Background on the Poem. There is a tradition in the English language of poetry about dreams and dreaming. In fact, one of the most famous poems in English—actually a fragment of a poem—was written not *about* a dream but *in* a dream. Samuel Taylor Coleridge's "Kubla Khan" was composed, according to Coleridge, while he was sound asleep. When he awoke, he started writing frantically, only to be interrupted after fifty-four lines by "a person on business from Porlock." When the visitor left more than an hour later, Coleridge could not remember the rest of the poem. It was lost forever.

The Literal Meaning. A dead Southerner is taken north by train in an open casket for burial. In a small, snowy village, warmly bundled men unload his body and put him on an old-fashioned, horse-drawn sled. They take him out of town, past barns, through woods, and between houses of ice-fishers on a lake. They go to the center of the lake, where they cut a coffin-sized rectangle in the ice. After lifiting out the slab of ice, they take his body, holding the coffin by ropes, and lower him into the water.

Teaching Strategies

Providing for Cultural Differences. Dreams would seem to be cross-cultural. The only likely cultural dilemma with this poem, as with many others, is perhaps a linguistic one. Students who lack fluency in English may need some extra help, although Dickey's poem, on a literal level, is fairly simple.

Providing for Different Levels of Ability. Students at all levels should be able to understand the events in this poem. With more advanced students, you will want to look into possible interpretations of the poem—that is, into interpretations of the dream. With less advanced students, you may wish to limit the discussion to what happens in the dream—the literal events.

Reading the Poem. To vary the presentation of the poem, you may want to consider appointing eight students to read it aloud in class, one student for each stanza. Give them some time to read their stanzas silently and, if necessary, to ask questions. Advise them to read aloud according to the way the poem is punctuated, not according to line breaks. (Line breaks should, of course, be acknowledged with a very slight pause, since they are there for a reason.) Tell students to allow a brief pause after the preceding stanza before beginning to read the next one. They should not need, or expect, a cue from you. If you choose good readers, and if they do their parts conscientiously, the poem can be handled very effectively in this manner.

Reteaching Alternatives. If you did not use the eight-reader technique suggested under "Reading the Poem," you may want to use it now. If you did use it, you can expand it when reteaching by having the same student who reads each stanza follow the reading with an interpretation of it in his or her own words. Then ask the class to discuss the stanza.

Responding to the Poem Text page 1110
Analyzing the Poem
Identifying Details

1. Briefly summarize what happens to the southerner. The body is borne by train to a village in the far North, where it is loaded onto a sled and taken to an icy lake. A hole is dug in the ice and the body is buried in the water.

2. What is the dead person compared to in lines 39–40? The corpse is compared to a sailboat.

Interpreting Meanings

3. The phrase "gunny-sacked bushes" appears twice. What is compared to the wrapped-up bushes in each *metaphor*? In the first instance (line 16), the gunny-sacked bushcs are compared to the people who watch the corpse depart; in the second (line 35), the bushes are compared to the people who stand by while the body is buried.

4. What new *simile* is introduced in the last stanza? The new simile introduced in the last stanza is the body of the southerner, swaying as it is let down into the grave, is compared to a rocking boat.

Do you think this could suggest that one kind of journey may lead to the beginning of another? If so, what could that other journey be? The image of the sailboat suggests that the dead person may be embarking on a journey to a land of "utter foreignness." Perhaps this is a journey to a different sort of life after death.

5. This is a dream meditation on death. Why do you think the poet chose to make the dead man from the South and to situate the burial spot in the North? Students may venture various opinions. If the dream meditation ends by suggesting that, despite our typical dread of death, it is no more than an altered state—or a journey to a foreign land—the geographical details of South and North, evoking the Civil War, might furnish a parallel. At one period in our history, South and North were as estranged and apparently separate from one another as life and death. The North and South were divided by a border, as death is divided from life. By dramatizing the events of the southerner's funeral as a journey from the South to the far North, the poet may indirectly be suggesting some type of continuity, from life into death and beyond.

James Dickey

6. What lines in the poem seem appropriate to the perception of events in a dream? Such lines include: "an army of gunny-sacked bushes" (line 16), "Not fooled that the snow is cotton" (line 22), "The woods fall / Slowly off all of them" (lines 22–23), "Summoned from village sleep into someone else's dream" (line 36).

7. Do you think this poem has anything in common with Williams's poem, "Tract" (page 738)? Explain. Student answers will vary. Have the students present specific similarities and differences.

Extending the Poem

Although "Sled Burial, Dream Ceremony" is a poetic account of a dream, have students suppose that it really happened. Ask them to write a brief local news article about the strange "burial beneath the ice" that a man from the South has just received on a snowy day, with resident pallbearers, in the middle of a nearby lake. Have your students invent details that will make the event plausible, or else have them report it without change in a deadpan-humorous way.

James Merrill

Text page 1111

"Kite Poem"

Text page 1112

Objectives

1. To identify internal rhymes, approximate rhymes, and alliteration
2. To analyze symbols
3. To write a response from another point of view

Introducing the Poem

This poem makes good use of both internal rhyme and approximate rhyme. Students will already be familiar with internal rhyme within the same line:

The Northern Lights have seen queer sights (*Lights/sights*)

They should be reminded that internal rhyme can also occur from line to line, as it does in "Kite Poem" (*port* in line 3 and *sport* in line 4). Merrill makes use of approximate rhyme, too; *person/parson, chair/chore,* and *kite/coat* are examples.

Background on the Poem. As the headnote to the poem indicates, this poem apparently is set in the nineteenth century. Today the man in the parson's story could emulate the "sport of birds" by hang-gliding, which is the nearest approach to using a kite for manned flight. Hang-gliding can be almost as dangerous, however, as the doomed kite adventure of the man in the parson's "improbable" tale.

The Literal Meaning. A parson tells his daughters a cautionary tale about a man who tried to fly by climbing on a kite. The man was never seen again, although his coat was found two counties away. The parson's daughters are amused by this half-hour tale, which was meant to teach them a serious lesson. When the wind blows out the candles, and the moon entices the daughters, they flee to their boyfriends. They kiss repeatedly, "as though to escape on a kite."

Teaching Strategies

Providing for Cultural Differences. There is nothing stated in this poem to show that it is not set in the twentieth century, yet students will almost certainly feel in reading it that neither the parson nor his daughters act in a modern manner. Most teenagers will see some kind of cultural difference between the people in the poem and the people they know. The headnote, text page 1112, places the events of the poem properly in time.

Providing for Different Levels of Ability. With less advanced students you may want to go over some of the vocabulary before reading the poem in class. Make sure that students know the meanings of *parson* (l. 2), *port* (l. 3), *tittered* (l. 7), *improbable* (l. 12), and *wrought* (l. 14). Encourage more advanced students, or ones especially interested in poetry, to read more of James Merrill's poems.

Reading the Poem. Since much of the comic effect of this poem depends on its sound, you will want to read it aloud or have a student read it aloud. As the poem is read, have students listen especially for the internal rhymes, approximate rhymes, and alliteration. (An audiocassette recording accompanies this selection.)

Reteaching Alternatives. Ask students to write a one-paragraph prose summary, or paraphrase, of the poem. Remind them to concentrate on main points and not to try to include everything. You may want to check students' paragraphs against the five-sentence summary under "The Literal Meaning."

Responding to the Poem Text page 1112
Analyzing the Poem
Identifying Details

1. What story does the parson tell his daughters? The parson tells his daughters a story about a person who climbed up on a kite, and who then disappeared. People found this person's coat two counties away.

Why does he tell it? The parson tells the story because he means it as a lesson to the daughters: They should keep their feet on the ground and not get romantically involved with their young sweethearts.

2. How do the daughters react to his instructive tale? They titter.

3. What do the daughters do later? They sneak out of the house by the light of the moon to meet their sweethearts near the raspberry bed.

4. How many *internal rhymes*, approximate rhymes, and examples of *alliteration* can you find in the poem? Among the internal rhymes are the following: "person" (line 1) and "parson" (line 2); "port" (line 3) and "sport" (line 4); "kite" and "coat" (line 5); "missing" (line 6) and "kissing" (line 9); "crescent" (line 9) and "pheasant" (line 10); "dangers" (line 13) and "changes" (line 14); "night" (line 17) and "kite" (line 18). Some of these are slant rhymes. Examples of alliteration include: "person" and "parson" (lines 1–2), "climbing up on a kite" (line 5), "the man himself was missing" (line 6), "His daughters tittered" (line 7), "finishing his pheasant, their father began" (line 10), "And kissed and kissed, as though to escape on a kite" (line 18).

Interpreting Meanings

5. The poem begins with a little story containing a moral. When it ends, that moral has been forgotten and replaced by another. What is the moral we are left with? The moral we are left with is that young people seldom listen to sermons; they live for pleasure and freedom.

6. The parson stands for one thing; the moon for another. How would you state the difference? The parson stands for prudence and restraint; the moon, which is "crescent" (that is, slender, but increasing) may stand for the forces of nature or desire.

7. Why does the poet call this "Kite Poem"? Students may suggest that the kite symbolizes freedom and escape. Ask students to defend their suggestions in class.

Writing About the Poem
A Creative Response

Taking Another Point of View. Response questions 5 through 7 prepare students for this writing response.

Criteria for Evaluating the Assignment. The paragraph or poem is from the daughters' point of view and points out the moral of grasping the joy of escape when one can.

Extending the Poem

Ask students to find a poem in this text or in any standard collection of British or American poetry that expresses the viewpoint of the daughters in the poem. (Possibilities include Robert Herrick's "To the Virgins to Make Much of Time"; Edmund Waller's "Go, Lovely Rose"; and Ralph Waldo Emerson's "Give All to Love.") Have students share their poems, with the class as a whole deciding which poem makes the strongest case for the daughters.

Adrienne Rich

Text page 1113

"Power"

Text page 1114

Objectives

1. To identify ironies
2. To write an essay analyzing the poem

Introducing the Poem

Metaphor is extremely important in this poem. In fact, the movement of the poem depends on one metaphor (the uncovered bottle) leading into another (Marie Curie, uncovered from the obliterating dimness of history). In the final stanza Marie Curie becomes a metaphor for all famous women, famous women a metaphor for all women. The narrative poem is written in free verse with very little punctuation. The spacing of the words on the lines and the line breaks create the rhythmical quality and the music of the poem. Seeming somewhat unstructured, the poem is, on a closer reading, carefully organized and constructed, culminating in the last stanza which ties in the title and Marie Curie.

Background on the Poem. According to some critics, this is a poem about women as the disregarded faction of society. Adrienne Rich herself, writing in the essay "Blood, Bread, and Poetry," acknowledges the need to treat women's issues as a serious theme in her poetry:

> Breaking the mental barrier that separated private from public life felt in itself like an enormous surge toward liberation.... To write directly and overtly as a woman, out of a woman's body and experience, to take women's existence seriously as theme and source for art, was something I had been hungering to do, needing to do, all my writing life.... It placed me nakedly face to face with my anger; it did indeed imply the breakdown of the world as I had always known it, the end of safety... I felt for the first time the closing of the gap between poet and woman.

The Literal Meaning. The speaker describes a backhoe's uncovering of a 100-year-old amber bottle that might have contained a medicine. She then says that she was reading that day about Marie Curie, who suffered from and died from radiation poisoning—a sickness derived from her own crucial discovery used in treating illness, radium. The poem relates Curie's denial of the source of her illness and the irony of her death from "the same source of her power."

Teaching Strategies

Providing for Cultural Differences. Depending on their cultural backgrounds, students may have varying degrees of familiarity with women's issues that have been raised in this country since the 1960's. It is important for students to understand the concern among many people in our society—both men and women—that women have historically lacked power.

Providing for Different Levels of Ability. With less advanced students, you might want to read the poem aloud, review the literal meaning, and then read the poem aloud a second time. If students are confused by the spacing of words in the poem, read the poem aloud a third time, emphasizing with pauses the many spaces between words. Students might also discuss reasons, such as emphasis or anger, that they might pause between words in their own speech.

Reading the Poem. For oral reading, have a different student read each of the first three stanzas and all three students read the last stanza together. Before reading, ask students to notice how the shift in voices parallels the shifts of meaning within the poem. Ask students to describe the effect of joining voices in the final stanza.

Reteaching Alternatives. Focusing on "Responding" question 4, you might ask students what makes a poem—or any creative expression—political. In the late sixties, the philosophy "the personal is political" was introduced. You may want to discuss the different levels in which the phrase can be applied to "Power." Ask students to discuss an element in their own lives that exemplifies that phrase.

Responding to the Poem

Text page 1114

Analyzing the Poem
Identifying Details

1. **What accidental discovery, described in the first stanza, is the occasion for the poem?** A backhoe uncovers a hundred-year-old medicine bottle, perfectly preserved.

396 Poetry in a Time of Diversity

Interpreting Meanings

2. How would you state directly the grim *ironies* of this poem? The last line sums up the poem's irony: Marie Curie's "wounds" (that is, the wasting away of her body) "came from the same source as her power."

3. Can you think of other situations in which "wounds" might come from the same source as "power"? Student answers will vary. To some, the "wounds" of Marie Curie may suggest the wounds of Christ, who suffered and died for humanity. Christ's submission to suffering, students may say, was intimately linked with His power. Other students may suggest that no religious metaphor is involved, but rather a connection between self-sacrifice and "power," or greatness.

4. Do you think this is a political poem? If so, give your reasons. Again, students will have various opinions. Urge them to defend their views with reasoned arguments and with references to the text of the poem.

Writing About the Poem
A Critical Response

Analyzing the Poem. Ask students to identify the discoveries (a hundred-year-old bottle; radium) and to give one major similarity (from the earth) and one major difference (helpful/dangerous) before they begin to write.

***Criteria* for Evaluating the Assignment.** The paper may be as brief as one paragraph, but correctly identifies the two discoveries, states one similarity, and explains an essential difference.

Extending the Poem

You might suggest that students read several other poems from Rich's collections and/or an essay from one of her other books. You may also want to suggest that students read more about the life of Marie Curie.

Sylvia Plath
Text page 1115

"Spinster"
Text page 1116

Objectives

1. To analyze the poem
2. To explain symbolism and metaphors
3. To analyze the use of words with multiple meanings

Introducing the Poem

The orderliness of the poem's structure is important in that it mirrors the content of the poem. The poem is made up of five six-line stanzas, and the line lengths are consistent between stanzas (short, long, short, long, short, shorter). Plath's use of nature as metaphor is particularly distinct. Unlike many poems in which nature is a vision of comfort, the nature imagery here is disturbing and accosting. This feeling is evoked in adjectives and verbs as well as in the harshness of specific sounds. The resulting tone is one of anger, panic, and fear.

***Background* on the Poem.** Plath has been dismissed by some poets, critics, and readers for being too emotional and too self-absorbed in her writing. Her direct language and exposure of the unpleasant, and her focus on mothering, her role as a wife, and her place as a woman in society, have been regarded by some as inappropriate poetic material. Her poems are extremely important, however, for just those reasons—they have helped to extend the realm of "acceptable" subject matter.

***The* Literal Meaning.** The poem describes a girl who, while walking with her suitor, is overwhelmed with love—but not love as a comfort or a source of excitement—love as a disordering and disturbing influence. The descriptions of nature in spring mirror the girl's distressed psychological state. She retreats to her home, protected from the intruding elements, alone.

Teaching Strategies

***Providing* for Cultural Differences.** Some language may seem dated and therefore unfamiliar to the students, and

Sylvia Plath 397

you may need to clarify the meanings of "spinster," "suitor," and "lover." Discuss with students that even though the word "spinster" is rarely used today, the feelings expressed are both universal and timeless. Most people have, at one time or another, felt the frightening power of emotion and the urge to retreat to a more logical existence.

Providing for Different Levels of Ability. The events in this poem are fairly straightforward, and students should have little trouble understanding that a girl goes for a walk, becomes disturbed, and retreats to her home. Less advanced students may have trouble interpreting the metaphors of winter and spring, although they have probably read many poems in which winter represented death or sterility, and spring, rebirth and fertility. You might tell these students that the symbolic meanings are essentially the same in this poem, but that it is winter that the girl finds desirable, rather than spring. Discussion can then focus on why the girl yearns for winter.

Reading the Poem. Because Plath's language is so powerful and unusual, with such enormous attention paid to the sound and placement of words, this poem should be read aloud. As it is read, have students look for the nature imagery that reveals the girl's fright.

Reteaching Alternatives. In class discussion, have students paraphrase the poem twice, changing the point of view first to that of the girl and then to that of the suitor. Students can "fill in" details of thought and feeling that can be supplied by the new speaker.

Responding to the Poem   Text page 1117
Analyzing the Poem
Identifying Details

1. Describe the situation in the first stanza. The girl is taking a walk with her suitor in springtime.

What sounds and sights so upset the girl? The girl is upset by the sound of the birds' chirping ("irregular babel") and by the sight of the leaves ("litter").

2. What increases the girl's sense of affliction in the second stanza? She continues to be upset by the young man's gait and his gestures.

3. What aspects of winter in the third stanza contrast with the aspects of April that the girl observes on her walk? The poet says that the girl "longed for winter"; that season is "scrupulously austere," and well defined in white and black, as opposed to the sloven "disarray" of spring.

4. What does the girl do in the fourth and fifth stanzas? She withdraws, and then sets a barbed barricade around her house.

What is she trying to "keep out" in the fifth stanza? According to the speaker, the girl is trying to keep out mutinous weather, and also the curses, fists, threats, and love of "insurgent man."

Interpreting Meanings

5. *Bedlam* **in stanza 4, is the archaic word for an insane asylum. It is drawn from the name** *Bethlehem***, the name of the famous "madhouse" in the city of London. How can "spring" be regarded as a kind of "bedlam" or "chaos"? Why would anyone "fear" spring?** The disorder of spring, at least to this particular girl, threatens to send her wits over the brink into insanity. The girl's imagination seizes upon a dangerous correspondence between nature's "unruly burgeoning" in spring and the disorder she fears within her own mind.

6. The fifth stanza is about defenses put up by "this particular girl" once she has withdrawn from April, her suitor, and the normal expectations of society. What are these defenses? She erects a barricade of "barb and check" around her house.

Do you think they are actual defenses, or are they more *symbolic***? Explain.** The poet probably intends the defenses to be both literal and symbolic. The "barricade" the girl erects can keep stormy weather out of the house; it can also prevent any "insurgent man" from offering her love. The girl is evidently fearful of growth and fertility (symbolized by spring) and of offering her love and trust to a suitor.

7. How might the poem be read not only as a comment on a particular kind of female psychology, but also as a series of *metaphors* **that illuminate a kind of temperament that is not necessarily female?** Student answers will vary. Most will agree that it is possible to read the poem as a commentary on a certain type of person, male or female. Suffering acutely from anxiety and insecurity, and perhaps from a fear that they may be going insane, such people seal themselves off from the rest of the world.

Analyzing Language and Vocabulary
Multiple Meanings

1. *Burgeoning* refers both to the spinster's unruly feelings and the new spring growth around her.
2. Her "queenly," mentally disciplined senses are being overwhelmed with "vulgar," common emotions.

Extending the Poem

Have interested students read some of Plath's poems in the collection *Ariel*. (Some particularly powerful poems are "Lady Lazarus," "Daddy," "Plaster," and "Poppies in July.") Students can then compare and contrast these later poems with the earlier "Spinster." How, for instance, does the language differ? What similarities do they find in the ideas expressed in the poems?

Anne Sexton

Text page 1118

"Her Kind"

Text page 1119

Objectives

1. To interpret metaphor
2. To analyze paradox

Introducing the Poem

Sexton uses metaphor, simile, rhyme, repetition, assonance, and alliteration in this poem. In terms of meaning, the metaphor of the witch, line 1, is most important. Other metaphors serve to support and expand upon that primary metaphor to create the full image of "her kind." The end rhyme (ababcbc) and the repetition in the first, sixth, and seventh lines of each stanza create a songlike quality and dramatic power and coherence in the poem. The use of assonance (line 3) and alliteration (line 2) also contribute to the poem's musicality—which is lyrical without being soft or gentle.

Background on the Poem. Sexton's interest in the images of women is clearly evident in this early poem, published in her first collection, *To Bedlam and Part Way Back*. Traditionally, the label *witch* has been given to a woman who lives and behaves differently than other "normal" women, but does, however, have a certain power. Because of her different lifestyle, she threatens the more traditional (patriarchal) society in which she lives.

The Literal Meaning. In the first stanza, the speaker, in a metaphorical sense, describes herself as "a possessed witch"—a creature of night dreaming of evil. The speaker then describes her harbor in the woods—what she keeps there and who she cooks for. She says that this type of woman is often misunderstood. In the last stanza, the speaker addresses the driver of a cart who takes witches to be burned. She calls herself a survivor and says that this type of woman is not afraid to die.

Teaching Strategies

Providing for Cultural Differences. Students from all cultures will be familiar with the idea of "the witch." Ask students to describe—through stories (especially folktales)—the character and appearance of a witch. Then tell students that Sexton is basing "her kind" of woman on the stereotypes of the witch that are prevalent in virtually all cultures.

Providing for Different Levels of Ability. The use of metaphor in this poem may confuse some students. (This is not a poem that is intended to be understood literally.) You might help these students by brainstorming with them all the possible qualities that are associated with witches, such as magical powers. Then discuss why a poet might want to be identified with those qualities.

Reading the Poem. For oral reading, you may want to divide the class into two groups with the majority of the students in the first group and two or three female students in the second group. Ask the first group to read the first five lines of each stanza and the second group to read the last two lines of each stanza. Then you can reverse the order and have the second group read the first five lines and the first group read the last two lines. What tone does this create? What does the reading emphasize?

Reteaching Alternatives. You might suggest that students analyze the use of metaphor in stanza 2. If witch suggests the creative and powerful woman, what do the caves, woods, skillets, carvings, shelves, closets, and silks represent? Who do the worms and the elves stand for? You might suggest that these images combine the stereotypes of the housewife and nurturer with the idea of woman as nature or creator—of having access to hidden worlds.

Responding to the Poem   Text page 1119
Analyzing the Poem
Identifying Details

1. What line is repeated in each stanza? The last line of each stanza is repeated without variation.

In each stanza, what comment about "a woman like that" is stated? In line 6 in the first stanza, "a woman like that" is not quite a woman. In line 13 in the second stanza, "a woman like that" is misunderstood. In line 20 in the third stanza, "a woman like that" is not ashamed to die.

2. In line 5, what might be the significance of the adjective "twelve-fingered"? Traditionally, a witch could be recognized by an extra finger on each hand.

3. What future event is conjured up in the third stanza? The speaker conjures up her own public torture and execution.

Interpreting Meanings

4. The whole first stanza might serve as a metaphor for a state of mind or emotion. What could the "witch" here stand for? The stanza might metaphorically describe a despairing, violent state of mind—perhaps even the emotions of a mad person.

5. What is *paradoxical*, in context, about the phrase, "rearranging the disaligned" (line 12)? What do you think the phrase means? The context is full of alienation, violence, and disorder; the phrase, which implies "putting things back in order" is thus unexpected and apparently contradictory.

6. Who is the driver addressed in the third stanza? He is the driver of the cart that bears the witch to her death.

Who is *you* in "your flames" and "your wheels"? The word *you* refers to the survivors (see line 17) who live on after the suffering and death of the woman.

7. Do you think that the speaker is meant to be merely an ordinary soul driven to extremes? Or is she really someone extraordinary who is misunderstood? In either case, support your answer with references to the poem. Student answers will vary. Urge students to support and defend their own opinions.

John Berryman   Text page 1120
"Winter Landscape"   Text page 1121

Objectives

1. To determine implications of words
2. To write a description using the poet's technique

Introducing the Poem

As the text introduction to the poem indicates, "Winter Landscape" has strict iambic rhythm. It is written in five five-line stanzas, all contained in a single sentence. The effect of the single sentence is one of tension that is further enhanced by the juxtapositions of stillness depicted in the actual painting, the movement of the characters in the first two stanzas, and the philosophy expressed in the final three stanzas. This is a poem about ideas as much as it is a poem about the images and the characters that act as the subject.

Background on the Poem. This is an early Berryman poem, written in a somewhat traditional form. Berryman's later work illustrates a departure from this traditional mode—vernacular language and provocative style. You may enjoy reading some of the powerful *Dream Songs* to students to help them develop a fuller comprehension of Berryman as a poet.

The Literal Meaning. The speaker describes men returning from a day of hunting. He describes the surroundings—the trees, the burning straw, the snow drifts, the skating rink, the children. He describes men by the church and the appearance of the street. The speaker remarks on the idea of these men being captured alone through history. He comments on how the men will be known and interpreted through time because of the position in which they were captured by the painter. Berryman remarks on how—

unknown to these characters—the scene and the purpose of their excursion becomes motive for projection in the future.

Teaching Strategies

Providing for Cultural Differences. Because this poem does not directly speak about contemporary issues, it may seem slightly inaccessible to some students. You may want to emphasize that although the figures in the poem are greatly removed, the feelings conveyed are timeless. Students might relate the poem to their own experience viewing family photo albums or watching old newsreels that happen to capture people in the midst of activities and freeze them in time unknowingly.

Providing for Different Levels of Ability. The last three stanzas may be confusing to some students. It may be helpful for you to stress that the painting described in the first two stanzas is used by the poet in the final three stanzas to express his philosophical views on history and our place within it.

Reading the Poem. The steady iambic rhythm of this poem will make the poem pleasant to read aloud—for you or a student. Before reading, however, review the punctuation of the poem, pointing out that there is only one period and that the pause at the end of a line is only very slight, with a comma getting a slightly more pronounced pause.

Reteaching Alternatives. It may be helpful for students to list details that depict a sense of movement in the poem. The scene is frozen in time, yet Berryman's description of the scene through stanzas 1 and 2 is active. From reading these stanzas, the reader does not know that the characters are not participating in an actual event seen by the poet. Ask students how the sense of "reality" affects their reading of the poem. By taking us into the scene, the poet makes the later emphasis on frozen time seem particularly accosting.

Responding to the Poem Text page 1122
Analyzing the Poem
Identifying Details

1. Describe the scene in the painting that Berryman uses as the basis for the poem. The painting shows three men dressed in brown, who are presumably hunters. They descend a hill, carrying tall poles and accompanied by a pack of hounds. On their way back to town through the snow, they pass five figures gathered around burning straw. The town contains red houses, a church, children who cluster around a rink, and men with ladders. The time is twilight (line 10).

2. What details emphasize that the scene has been frozen in time? Students may mention the following: "cold and silent" (line 5), "the long companions they can never reach" (line 8), "irrevocably lost" (line 15).

Interpreting Meanings

3. In stanza 1, what does the word *arrangement* suggest? The word "arrangement" suggests the deliberate, conscious effort of the painter to compose and balance the elements of his picture.

What are the implications of this word for both a poet and a painter? Student answers will vary. Many may propose that the word suggests that both the poet and the painter, as creative artists, may exercise an almost supernatural control over both nature and the human imagination.

4. In the second stanza, the statement about the "older men" in lines 6 and 7 has to do with both life and with art. In terms of life, what does this statement suggest? Students will have various opinions. On the surface, the reference seems to evoke a company of elders who are less vigorous than the three hunters. The older men are forced to stay at home in the town to perform mundane jobs. The poet may be commenting on a common plight of the old, who are relegated to a "second childhood" by many societies.

What does it say about art? Student answers will differ.

5. What are the implications of the word *sandy* in line 11? In this context, the word connotes a treacherous, shifting surface—a surface that offers no sure footing or grounding.

In what ways might history be considered an "evil waste"? Student answers will differ. Given the fact that time itself is called "sandy," the poet may be implying that history is an "evil waste" because humans fail to learn from it: the same errors and cruelties are repeated throughout the centuries.

6. In the fourth stanza, what word echoes *arrangement* in line 3? The word echoing *arrangement* is *configuration* (line 18).

How does this word remind us that art does not merely record life, but manipulates it? The word *configuration*, like the word *arrangement*, implies that the artist—whether painter or poet—consciously shapes reality to conform to an imaginative vision.

Writing About the Poem
A Creative Response

Imitating the Poet's Technique. Give students the choice of looking for another painting that especially interests them or of continuing with Breughel's winter landscape. Note that the assignment has two parts—what the student believes the original scene was like, and what will "never happen" in the painting.

Criteria for Evaluating the Assignment. The poem or essay is clearly based on a specific painting, describes what the student believes the original scene was like, and describes what will "never happen" in the painting.

James Wright

Text page 1124

"A Blessing"

Text page 1125

Objectives

1. To identify the uses of anthropomorphism
2. To identify a metamorphosis
3. To write an essay comparing two works

Introducing the Poem

This narrative poem is written in clear and direct language. Various literary techniques create the gentleness, or softness, of the poem: assonance (highway, twilight, eyes; munching, young, tufts); alliteration (body, break, blossom); and rhymes. Similes (lines 11 and 21) enhance the mood.

Background on the Poem. "A Blessing" is one of Wright's most anthologized poems, and justly so, for the poem is representative of Wright on a profound level. Many of James Wright's poems carry a deep sense of human tragedy and vulnerability, yet these poems are never ugly. Instead, they exude enormous beauty and pathos, and there is often a sense of transcendence similar to the transcendence at the end of this poem.

The Literal Meaning. The speaker describes stopping off the highway to visit with two Indian ponies. The speaker and his friend step into the pasture, where the ponies are pleased to have company. The ponies begin to feed, and the speaker relates his desire to hold one when she walks over to him. The speaker describes the appearance of the ponies and realizes suddenly that he is so moved by the experience that if he could step out of his body, he "would break / Into blossom."

Teaching Strategies

Providing for Cultural Differences. Urban students unfamiliar with the rural areas may not immediately relate to the scene that Wright carefully describes. You may want to describe to these students how the highways in areas such as Minnesota can be empty for mile upon mile. Students who are familiar with such sparsely populated countryside can describe its appearance at twilight during the spring.

Providing for Different Levels of Ability. Ask students who might have trouble visualizing the scene to describe exactly what they see in Wright's description. What is the twilight like? Describe the ponies—their eyes, their markings, their movements. How do the ponies behave together? Where is the speaker standing? What does he do?

Reading the Poem. Students who might otherwise be put off by the depth of emotion in the poem will probably best respond to an almost matter-of-fact reading of the narrative. The sound effects and images in the poem will convey the speaker's emotion.

Reteaching Alternatives. Have students assume the viewpoint of the speaker and write a journal entry about the encounter with the horses. The entry should describe the scene as well as the thoughts and feelings of the speaker.

Responding to the Poem

Text page 1125

Analyzing the Poem

Identifying Details

1. In one sense, the poem is a progression from a road in Minnesota to a "place" that exists only in the realm of feeling. Trace the steps by which the speaker is led

402 Poetry in a Time of Diversity

from a spot on the map to a "place" with no physical location. At twilight, the speaker stops with a friend at a point off the highway. He sees two Indian ponies who come from the willows to meet him. The speaker and his companion step over the barbed wire and walk into the pasture. They observe the sweetness and companionship of the ponies, and watch them munching "young tufts" of spring grass. The speaker reflects that he would like to hold one of the ponies in his arms when the pony comes to nuzzle his hand. His intense pleasure in the scene is suddenly objectified, when he thinks that his happiness is like the burgeoning energy of a flower, ready to burst into blossom.

2. *Anthropomorphism* is a term used to describe the tendency of human beings to read their own feelings into nonhuman objects. In how many places in this poem does the author ascribe human feelings to the ponies? References that students may mention include the following: the ponies' eyes "darken with kindness" (line 4); they come "gladly" to "welcome" the speaker and his friend (lines 5–6); they can "hardly contain their happiness" (line 9); they "bow shyly" (line 11); they "love each other" (line 11); they share a "loneliness" (line 12); they are "at home" (line 13); one pony's ear is as delicate as the skin of a girl's wrist (lines 21–22).

Interpreting Meanings

3. What is the significance of the poem's title? The title, "A Blessing," refers to the speaker's sense of gratitude for the beauty of the scene he has witnessed and for the feelings of love which the scene has inspired in him. He implies that he has been blessed.

4. What do you think the author means by the phrase, "There is no loneliness like theirs" (line 12)? Student answers may vary. The phrase is somewhat paradoxical, in that it immediately follows the observation that the ponies "love each other" (line 11). The speaker compresses two thoughts: whereas the ponies are devoted to each other in perfect love (thereby implying a certain "loneliness" with respect to other creatures), they are still overjoyed to be greeted by human beings.

5. In Greek mythology, human beings often undergo marvelous transformations called *metamorphoses*. What metamorphosis ends this poem? Do you think it is a good one to describe a particular feeling? The speaker feels as if his body is breaking into blossom, like a flower. Students' responses to the metamorphosis will differ. Ask the students to defend their opinions.

Writing About the Poem

Comparing Two Writers. Have students jot down brief notes on the major points of the extract from Emerson's *Nature* (page 191) and Wright's "A Blessing" before they begin to write.

Criteria for Evaluating the Assignment. The essay cites details from Emerson's essay and Wright's poem that make the two works similar: for example, exhilaration, loss of egotism, and perfect harmony with nature.

Extending the Poem

Leslie Marmon Silko, a Native American poet and prose writer, corresponded with James Wright from 1978 until his death in 1980. In 1986, a book of their letters, *The Delicacy and Strength of Lace* was published (Graywolf Press). In it, the two tell each other stories; discuss writing, language, and human nature; and talk about their own experiences. You may want to suggest that students read several of these letters. They are extremely beautiful—filled with wisdom, humor, and sensitivity—and are written in direct and unpretentious language that will be accessible and inspiring to students.

Julia Alvarez

Text page 1126

"How I Learned to Sweep"

Text page 1127

Objectives

1. To analyze the use of rhyme
2. To describe the meter
3. To write an essay analyzing an image
4. To write an essay comparing and contrasting the imagery in two poems

Introducing the Poem

As is mentioned in the text introduction to the poem, the language of the poem is relaxed, like everyday speech, but the meter and rhyme are carefully structured. You may want to have students look carefully at the structure and the seemingly contrasting content—the chaos and disorder of war. What purpose does this contrast serve?

Background on the Poem. The poem describes the speaker's first experience sweeping and her introduction to the realities of war. The poem is more than an antiwar poem, however, it is a poem about maturation—about growing up through increasing awareness of life and death. You might ask students how the speaker takes responsibility in the poem. Because this poem incorporates television, home life, and the world—in fact, the terrible world—outside the home, you should get an interesting response.

The Literal Meaning. The speaker's mother asks her to sweep the floor. She begins, and as she sweeps the speaker watches the President talk about the Vietnam War ("the war") on TV news. She sees news clips of helicopters being shot down and men falling from the helicopters through the sky, at which point she sweeps again. She sees a dozen men die and sweeps the floor harder, more thoroughly, as if by cleaning she can remove death from the room. The mother returns, turns the TV dial, inspects the room, and admires the cleanliness. The mother doesn't see a sign of death.

Teaching Strategies

Providing for Cultural Differences. The most obvious cultural difference that may be difficult for students in this poem is Alvarez's reference to the Vietnam War. The reference (lined 16–29) to the TV broadcasts of the Vietnam War should be explained to students so that they have a clear understanding of the time frame.

Providing for Different Levels of Ability. Most students will have little difficulty understanding the literal events of the poem through line 20. Less advanced students, however, might have some difficulty with the interweaving of literal and metaphorical meaning that begins in line 21. With these students, you might lift lines 18–25 from the context of the poem and discuss how helicopters are being fired on as they attempt to land in the jungle. Discuss, also, the qualities of a dragonfly that make it an appropriate metaphor for a helicopter.

Reading the Poem. If you have students who are interested in dramatics, you might stage a somewhat theatrical reading of this poem. Have the student reader stand before the class with a prop designated as a broom, going through sweeping motions. Another prop can represent the television set by which the speaker is distracted.

Reteaching Alternatives. Have students paraphrase the poem, substituting the Vietnam War metaphor with a more timely one, such as a horrible automobile accident or a terrorist kidnapping. Students can discuss how the substitution affects the poem.

Responding to the Poem

Text page 1127

Analyzing the Poem
Identifying Details

1. **What was on TV the afternoon the speaker learned to sweep?** The news was on TV.

2. **According to the speaker, why was her mother impressed with her work?** Her mother was impressed because the entire room was thoroughly swept and dusted.

3. **Where does this poet use *rhymes*?** The poet uses full rhymes and half rhymes in some couplets; she also uses rhymes in groups of four lines.

   How would you describe the poem's *meter*? Give reasons for your answers. The meter is a mixture of iambic tetrameter and trochaic tetrameter.

Interpreting Meanings

4. **What are the dragonflies in line 24? Why do you**

404 Poetry in a Time of Diversity

think the speaker sweeps all the harder as they fall out of the sky? The dragonflies are the helicopters. The speaker sweeps all the harder because she is shocked by the deaths of a dozen men who are landed by the helicopters in the jungle.

5. What do you think she is trying to clean, in addition to her mother's dusty floor? Student answers will vary. Some students will suggest that she is trying to "wipe away" the deaths of the soldiers.

6. What is the significance of the last line, in light of what the speaker has seen on TV? Explain. The last line has an ironic significance, in light of what the speaker has seen on TV.

7. Is the poem about sweeping, or is it really about something else? Explain your opinion. Most students will probably agree that the poem is not really about sweeping, but about the child speaker's shock at seeking the grim realities of war (perhaps in Vietnam) broadcast graphically on television.

Writing About the Poem
A Critical Response

1. Analyzing an Image. Response questions 4 through 7 should help students interpret the metaphoric meaning of the word "dust," but opinions will vary as to why Alvarez chose *dust* rather than *dirt* or *grit*.

Criteria for Evaluating the Assignment. The paragraph or brief essay identifies both the literal dust swept by the girl and the metaphoric dust of death she tries to scrub from her home. The writer offers a reasonable explanation for Alvarez's choice of *dust* rather than *dirt* or *grit*.

2. Comparing Poems. Lead students to recognize the imagery of *cleansing*. They should have no difficulty recognizing that Ginsberg's imagery comes from industry and technology while Alvarez's comes from war.

Criteria for Evaluating the Assignment. The essay compares the Ginsberg and Alvarez poems, citing their similar use of images of cleansing; and contrasts them, citing the different aspects of modern life they tackle.

Allen Ginsberg
Text page 1128

"Homework"
Text page 1129

Objectives

1. To analyze the poem for its underlying metaphor
2. To characterize the tone of the poem
3. To interpret the title
4. To state the main idea
5. To write a poem imitating the writer's technique
6. To write an essay evaluating the poem

Introducing the Poem

Although your students are well-acquainted with metaphor by now, you may want to emphasize it again with this poem. Extended metaphors that comprise a whole poem are not uncommon, especially in short poems such as Emily Dickinson's or Edgar Lee Masters's. Even so, the one in Ginsberg's poem is striking enough to warrant students' attention. Nearly every laundry term imaginable appears in it.

Background on the Poem. To appreciate this poem fully, students need at least a passing acquaintance with environmental issues and international politics. Most students should have some knowledge of these matters, since many of the poet's specifics are the continuing background items mentioned in the daily news. Among the lesser-known ones, perhaps, are Rock Flats and Los Alamos—nuclear waste sites in the Southwest; Cesium-Love Canal—industrial pollution near Buffalo, New York; Neckar—polluted river in Germany.

The Literal Meaning. The speaker says that if he were doing his laundry, he would wash Iran and the United States, clean up Africa, the Amazon River, the Caribbean, and the Gulf of Mexico. He would get the smog off the North Pole, the oil off the Alaskan pipelines, the chemicals out of Love Canal. He would clean the acid rain off the

Parthenon and the Sphinx, drain the sludge from the Mediterranean, put the blue back in the sky over the Rhine, and whiten the clouds. He would clean various rivers and get the pollutants out of Lake Erie. He would wash the blood and Agent Orange out of Asia, put Russia and China in the wringer, and squeeze out the "tattletail Gray" of some Central American nations. Finally, he would put the planet in the drier and let it sit for twenty minutes, or indefinitely, until it comes out clean.

Teaching Strategies

Providing for Cultural Differences. While most students will favor environmental protection in theory, and will agree that nations ought to act honorably in international relations, some are almost sure to feel that Ginsberg's indictment of the current situation is overdrawn. It is probably best not to argue the point one way or the other, but simply to deal with the poem as a personal statement of what the poet thinks needs "cleaning."

Providing for Different Levels of Ability. This is a poem that will be most effective for students with the greatest general knowledge. More advanced students should need little help with most of the references. Less advanced students, on the other hand, will probably see far fewer familiar names and ideas. Although it may take something away from the poem, you will probably want to go over the geographical and environmental references one by one with less advanced students.

Reading the Poem. The headnote to the poem suggests that students think of the poem as a series of exaggerated cartoons. As they read, ask students to think how they might sketch such cartoons, possibly having them do so after reading.

Reteaching Alternatives. The "Responding" questions do not ask specifically for students to identify all the words and phrases that connote laundry. Try having students conduct a laundry-word search, going through the poem word by word in class, identifying (and putting on the chalkboard) every word and phrase commonly associated with laundry. This exercise will not only demand a slow, thoughtful rereading of the poem, but it will also show students graphically how well the poet has sustained his washday metaphor.

Responding to the Poem Text page 1129
Analyzing the Poem
Identifying Details

1. This poem refers to a number of social and environmental ills in the modern world. Identify as many of these situations as you can. Students may mention the following categories: (1) violent revolution (Iran and the taking of American hostages in 1979: see line 1); (2) political oppression (the references to Russia and China and the U.S. Central American police state); (3) environmental damage (the references to the jungle in line 2, to the Amazon River and the "oily Carib and Gulf of Mexico" in line 3, to the smog on the North Pole and the Alaskan oil pipelines in line 4, to the toxic waste at Love Canal, New York, in line 5, and so on); (4) air pollution (the reference to acid rain in line 6, the reference to the sky over the Rhine River in Germany in line 7); (5) chemical warfare (the reference in line 9 to the use of the defoliant Agent Orange during the Vietnam War).

2. In the last line, how long does the speaker say he will wait for the wash to come "out clean"? He says, humorously, that he will wait either twenty minutes or an "Aeon"—an immensely long span of time.

3. List the verbs in the poem that give it a sense of action. Do all the verbs have to do with doing a laundry? Among the verbs that students may list are the following: "wash" (line 1), "throw" (line 2), "pour" (line 2), "soap" (line 2), "scrub up" (line 2), "clean" (line 3), "rub" (line 4), "wipe" (line 4), "rinse" (line 6), "drain" (line 6), "bleach" (line 7), "cleanse" (line 7), "dump" (line 10), "squeeze" (line 10). Most students will agree that the majority of the verbs have to do with doing a laundry.

Interpreting Meanings

4. What underlying *metaphor* pervades the poem? The underlying metaphor is that of the speaker purifying the world, just as one might stuff one's dirty laundry into a washing machine, clean it with detergent, and then put it in the drier.

5. Characterize the *tone* of the poem. How does Ginsberg mingle amusing and serious elements? The whimsy of the underlying metaphor provides the humor. Ginsberg's incidental references to well-known world problems (war, revolution, environmental pollution, political tyranny) provide the serious elements. Students will have various opinions of the poem's tone. On the whole, the whimsical metaphor creates a light tone for the poem.

6. What significances can you identify in the poem's *title*? Students will have different opinions. The title "Homework" ironically suggests that the speaker may be a young student, trying to solve a few problems for the next day's class. This interpretation would deliberately clash with the serious, apparently intractable problems of world affairs referred to in the poem. But perhaps Ginsberg's intention is to suggest that the problems are not really intractable: with good will and serious effort, they may be resolved as quickly and as easily as a child does his or her homework, or as an urban apartment dweller runs his or her laundry through a washing machine. The open-ended conclusion, where the speaker says he will put the planet in the drier and wait for "20 minutes or an Aeon" till it comes out clean, seems to underscore the view that solving world crises may be simply a matter of possessing the necessary determination. The title "Homework" could also be read as more generally prescriptive: perhaps Ginsberg means to imply that working to solve what he sees as evil in the world should be a "homework" assignment—or a daily obligation—for all concerned citizens of the planet.

7. What is Ginsberg's *main idea*? What do you think of his specific choices for the wash? One statement of Ginsberg's main idea is that the world needs to be cleaned up, both physically and morally. Students will have differing opinions about the poet's specific choices for the wash. Ask the students to defend their opinions with reasons in class.

Writing About the Poem
A Creative Response

1. Imitating the Writer's Technique. Elicit from the students additional things needing "washing" not listed by Ginsberg—perhaps local eyesores or issues in current headlines. Call attention to key elements of Ginsberg's technique—use of long lines, proper names, strong verbs, ampersands (&) for the word "and," and inclusion of the effects of many of the washings.

Criteria for Evaluating the Assignment. The poem begins with the line "If I were doing my laundry, I'd wash . . ."; lists several "things" the student would wash; uses strong verbs, proper names, and ampersands; and states the effect of at least some of the washings.

A Critical Response

2. Evaluating the Poem. Ginsberg's repetition of verbs and occasional rhymes ("Rub a dub dub") are easy to spot, but you may wish to suggest that students also review "The Elements of Literature: Free Verse," page 333, which deals with imagery and such types of repetition as alliteration and assonance.

Criteria for Evaluating the Assignment. The essay cites examples of Ginsberg's repeated verbs, alliteration ("*c*lean the oily *C*arib") and assonance (dr*a*in/Mediterr*a*nean/b*a*sin/m*a*ke in line 6), figurative language ("Flush that . . . Cesium out"), and rhythmic cadence (use of two washings per line, as in lines 5 and 8).

Extending the Poem

You might have a number of volunteers do library research on the poets of the "Beat" generation, beginning with Allen Ginsberg, Lawrence Ferlinghetti, and Kenneth Rexroth. Students should determine the approximate dates of the movement, the main ideas underlying it, the principal poets involved (in addition to the three named), and the reasons for its decline and relative insignificance.

Exercises in Critical Thinking and Writing Text page 1131

Evaluating a Poem

This assignment asks students to evaluate John Malcolm Brinnin's "That Gull" or Simon Ortiz's "Washyuma Motor Hotel." The key term *evaluate* is explained under "Background." Read the poems with the class (the French phrase *n'est-ce pas?* in "The Gull" means "Not so?" or "Isn't it?"). Consider also the model of another writer's notes, based on Ginsberg's "Homework," given under the heading "Prewriting." Stress the fact that the guide questions demand *judgments* about the poem, and that each judgment must be backed up by citations from the poem. Another set of guidelines offers directions for setting up the final essay. You may wish to let students work either as individuals or in groups once they have chosen the poem to evaluate.

Criteria for Evaluating the Assignment. The essay contains a thesis statement which expresses the student's overall evaluation of the poem. The rest of the essay supports that thesis statement strongly, presenting the most important point either first or last. All judgments made are supported by citations of word choice, images, figures of speech, or sound effects, with the line number for each citation included. The essay correctly observes the conventions (grammar, spelling, punctuation, capitalization) of written English.

Bibliography

Works listed are suitable for both students and teachers, unless the annotation ends with the note [Teachers].

General References

The following general works are helpful for more than one unit.

Contemporary Authors and its companion series, *Contemporary Literary Criticism* (Gale Research Company)

Multi-volume, frequently updated source of information on current writers.

Dictionary of American Biography (Scribner's, 1927-1977)

Ten volumes plus index and supplemental volumes added periodically. [Teachers]

Gottesman, Ronald, et al., *The Norton Anthology of American Literature*, First ed. (W. W. Norton, 1979)

Two-volume, compendious anthology with good introductions on authors' lives.

Hart, James D., ed., *The Oxford Companion to American Literature*, Fifth ed. (Oxford University Press, 1983)

Entries arranged alphabetically by author, title, or (sometimes) major characters.

Mainiero, Lina, and Langdon Lynne Faust, eds., *American Women Writers* (Frederick Ungar, 1981)

Readable, informative two- to three-page articles on women writers from Colonial times through the 1970's.

Parrington, Vernon L., *Main Currents in American Thought: An Interpretation of American Literature from the Beginnings to 1920* (Harcourt Brace Jovanovich, 1927-1930, 1955)

Still a valuable resource on earlier American literature. [Teachers]

Spiller, Robert, et al., *Literary History of the United States*, Fourth ed. (Macmillan, 1974)

Substantial historical and critical reviews. [Teachers]

Urdang, Laurence, ed., *The Timetables of American History* (Simon & Shuster, 1981)

Chronological, columnar entries from the year 1000 to 1980, paralleling events in literature and the arts in America and elsewhere with events in politics, technology, etc.

The following general works are helpful for the units named.

Unit One. The Colonial Period: The Age of Faith

Dillon, Francis, *The Pilgrims* (Doubleday, 1975)

A lively social history of the Pilgrims. [Teachers]

Heaton, Vernon, *The Mayflower* (Mayflower Books, 1980)

A clearly organized, well-illustrated book on the European background of Puritanism, the Atlantic crossing, and life in the New World.

Miller, John C., *The First Frontier: Life in Colonial America* (Dell, 1966)

An excellent source of information on all aspects of Colonial life from recreation through health, housing, and education. [Teachers]

Rowse, A. L., "Pilgrims and Puritans," *American Heritage*, October 1959

British perspective on the story of American Puritanism and Puritan writing.

Wright, L. B., ed., *The American Heritage History of the Thirteen Colonies* (American Heritage, 1967)

Beautifully illustrated, concise overview of the Colonial period.

Bibliography   409

Unit Two. The Revolutionary Period: The Age of Reason

Commager, Henry Steele, *The Empire of Reason* (Anchor Press/Doubleday, 1977)

Excellent overview of the Enlightenment in America from both European and American perspectives.

Crèvecoeur, J. Hector St. John de, *Eighteenth Century America*, ed. Albert E. Stone (Penguin, 1981)

Continues Crèvecoeur's descriptive commentary on the American landscape and people begun in *Letters from an American Farmer*.

Tyler, Moses Coit, *The Literary History of the American Revolution*, two volumes (Frederick Ungar, 1957)

Considered an outstanding critical history despite subsequent revival of authors not available to Tyler. [Teachers]

Unit Three. American Romanticism

Brooks, Van Wyck, *The Flowering of New England: 1815–1865* (Houghton Mifflin, 1981)

A noted history containing chapters on Longfellow, Lowell, Holmes, and others. [Teachers]

Parrington, Vernon L., *The Romantic Revolution in America, 1800–1860*, Volume II of *Main Currents in American Thought* (Harcourt Brace Jovanovich, 1955)

Definitive account of the Romantic Period, with chapters on Irving, Bryant, Holmes, and others in this unit. [Teachers]

Sullivan, Wilson, *New England Men of Letters* (Macmillan, 1972)

Chapters devoted to ten writers: Emerson, Thoreau, Hawthorne, Dana, Melville, Prescott, Parkman, Longfellow, Lowell, and Holmes.

Unit Four. The American Renaissance: Five Major Writers

Barbour, Brian, ed., *American Transcendentalism* (University of Notre Dame Press, 1973)

A collection of studies. [Teachers]

Crawley, Thomas Edward, *Four Masters of the American Mind: Emerson, Thoreau, Whitman, and Melville* (Duke University Press, 1976)

Good analysis of the authors listed. [Teachers]

Gura, Philip F., and Joel Myerson, eds., *Critical Essays on American Transcendentalism* (G. K. Vesel, 1982)

A collection of critical essays. [Teachers]

Lewis, R. W. B. *The American Adam: Innocence, Tragedy, and Tradition in the Nineteenth Century* (University of Chicago Press, 1955)

A classic study. [Teachers]

Matthiessen, F. O., *American Renaissance: Art and Expression in the Age of Emerson and Whitman* (Oxford University Press, 1968)

A highly recognized study. [Teachers]

Parrington, Vernon L., *The Romantic Revolution in America, 1800–1860*, Volume II of *Main Currents in American Thought* (Harcourt Brace Jovanovich, 1955)

Definitive account of the Romantic Period, with chapters on writers from this unit. [Teachers]

Unit Five. A New American Poetry: Whitman and Dickinson

Allen, Gay Wilson, *A Reader's Guide to Walt Whitman* (Farrar, Straus & Giroux, 1970)

A guide to Whitman bibliography, scholarship, and criticism. [Teachers]

Dickinson, Emily, *The Complete Poems of Emily Dickinson*, ed. Thomas H. Johnson (Little, Brown, 1960)

The first one-volume edition containing all of Dickinson's poems.

Pearce, Roy Harvey, ed., *Whitman: A Collection of Critical Essays* (Prentice-Hall, 1962)

Scholarly essays by fourteen writers including Ezra Pound. [Teachers]

White, Hilda, *Truth Is My Country: Portraits of Eight New England Authors* (Doubleday, 1971)

Informative, readable biographical essays on Dickinson, Hawthorne, Emerson, Thoreau, Stone, Robinson, Millay, and Frost.

Whitman, Walt, *Leaves of Grass*, ed. Emory Holloway (Doubleday, 1926; Book League of America, 1942); or *Leaves of Grass*, ed. Harold W. Blodgett and Sculley Bradley (Norton, 1973)

Comprehensive editions of Whitman's poems.

Unit Six. The Rise of Realism: The Civil War and Post-War Period

Brooks, Van Wyck, *The Confident Years* (Dutton, 1952)

Good studies of Bierce, Norris, London, Wharton, Howells, Dreiser, James, Crane, and Mencken.

Delblanco, Nicolas, *Group Portrait* (William Morrow, 1982)

Biographical study of the interacting of Crane, James, Conrad, Ford, and H. G. Wells when they were living in England.

Dickens, Charles, *American Notes* (St. Martin's Press, 1985)

Classic, razor-sharp satirical report of Dickens's impressions during a lecture tour of the United Sates.

Hazard, Lucy Lockwood, *The Frontier in American Literature* (Frederick Ungar, 1961)

Reissue of a penetrating study first published in 1927. Sections on Twain, Harte, Norris, Garland, Dreiser, Cather, and earlier American writers.

Kazin, Alfred, *An American Procession* (Knopf, 1984)

A major study of American literary history with chapters on Twain, James, and Crane.

Parrington, Vernon L., *The Beginnings of Critical Realism in America*, Volume III of *Main Currents in American Thought* (Harcourt, Brace & World, 1930)

Still a standard, readable, interesting work.

Wilson, Edmund, *Patriotic Gore* (Oxford University Press, 1962)

Wilson's crowning achievement; excellent study of the relationship of the literature and history of the Civil War era. Treats both political and literary figures.

Unit Seven. The Moderns: The American Voice in Fiction

Allen, Frederick Lewis. *Only Yesterday* (Harper & Row Perennial Library, 1964)

A reissue of the classic social history of the 1920's first published in 1930.

Bryer, Jackson R., ed., *Fifteen Modern American Authors: A Survey of Research and Criticism* (Duke University Press, 1969)

An excellent resource. [Teachers]

Hoffman, Frederick J., *The Twenties: American Writing and the Postwar Decade* (Viking Press, 1955)

A specialized book focusing on the 1920's.

Kazin, Alfred, *On Native Grounds* (Harcourt Brace & Company, 1942)

A noted critic's tracing of the development of American prose from the time of William Dean Howells. [Teachers]

Unit Eight. Poetry: Voices of American Character

Gregory, Horace, and Marya Zaturenska, *A History of American Poetry 1900–1940* (Harcourt Brace Jovanovich, 1946)

A historical survey of American poetry. [Teachers]

A Pocket Book of Robert Frost's Poems with an introduction and commentary by Louis Untermeyer (Washington Square Press, 1967)

More than one hundred poems by Robert Frost.

White, Hilda, *Truth Is My Country: Portraits of Eight New England Authors* (Doubleday, 1971)

Informative, readable biographical essays on Dickinson, Hawthorne, Emerson, Thoreau, Stone, Robinson, Millay, and Frost.

Williams, Oscar, and Edwin Honig, *The Mentor Book of Major American Poetry* (New American Library, 1962)

A compact anthology of poems by twenty American poets: Taylor, Emerson, Longfellow, Poe, Whitman, Dickinson, Robinson, Stephen Crane, Frost, Lindsay, Stevens, Williams, Pound, Moore, Ransom, Millay, MacLeish, Cummings, Harte Crane, and Auden.

Unit Nine. Imagism and Symbolism

Allen, Gay Wilson, et al., *American Poetry* (Harper & Row, 1965)

An excellent anthology which includes many peoms by Pound, Williams, Moore, Sandburg, Cummings, Eliot, and Stevens.

Coffman, Stanley K., Jr., *Imagism: A Chapter for the History of Modern Poetry* (University of Oklahoma Press, 1951)

A study of modern poetic forms which begins with a chronology of the Imagist movement and then presents an account of the movement's history, values, and deficiencies.

Goodwin, K. L., *The Influence of Ezra Pound* (Oxford University Press, 1966)

Pound's influence on T. S. Eliot, William Carlos Williams, E. E. Cummings, and others.

Gregory, Horace, and Marya Zaturenska, *A History of American Poetry 1900–1940* (Harcourt Brace Jovanovich, 1946)

A systematic record of poetic developments during the first four decades of the twentieth century. [Teachers]

Mathiessen, F. O., *The Oxford Book of American Verse* (Oxford University Press, 1950)

A standard anthology which includes many peoms by Pound, Williams, Moore, Sandburg, Cummings, Eliot, and Stevens.

Unit Ten. American Drama

Esslin, Martin, *The Theatre of the Absurd*, rev. ed. (Overlook Press, 1973)

The authority on Absurdist drama. [Teachers]

Gassner, John, *Masters of the Drama*, Third ed. (Dover Publications, 1954; reprint of Random House, 1940)

A comprehensive history of world drama. [Teachers]

Gassner, John, and Morris Sweetkind, eds., *The Reader's Encyclopedia of World Drama* (Crowell, 1969)

Alphabetically arranged entries on playwrights, plays, and dramatic movements, through the mid 1960's. [Teachers]

Gilman, Richard, *The Making of Modern Drama* (1974)

An influential work by a noted critic. [Teachers]

Nicoll, Allardyce, *World Drama from Aeschylus to Anouilh*, Second ed. (London: Harrap, 1976)

An overview of world drama. [Teachers]

Unit Eleven. Fiction: 1945 to the Present

Balakian, Nona, and Charles Simmons, eds., *The Creative Present: Notes on Contemporary American Fiction* (Doubleday, 1963)

Essays on Baldwin, Welty, Malamud, Updike, and others.

Gass, William H., *Fiction and the Figures of Life* (Knopf, 1970)

A leading fiction writer and philosophy professor discusses Barthelme, Updike, and others. [Teachers]

Hoffman, Daniel, ed., *Harvard Guide to Contemporary American Writing* (Belknap Press, 1979)

Sections on various aspects of fiction, poetry, and drama, by ten distinguished critics. [Teachers]

Karl, Frederick R., *American Fictions: 1940–1980* (Harper & Row, 1983)

A comprehensive history and critical evaluation of four decades of American fiction. [Teachers]

Kiernan, Robert F., *American Writing Since 1945* (Frederick Ungar, 1983)

A brief survey with chapters on Realism, Southern Fiction, Jewish Fiction, Black Fiction, and Metafiction. [Teachers]

Weaver, Gordon, ed., *The American Short Story 1945–1980* (Twayne Publishers, 1983)

A critical survey of high quality, covering both traditional and experimental writers. [Teachers]

Unit Twelve. Modern Nonfiction

Hollowell, John, *Fact and Fiction* (University of North Carolina Press, 1977)

Knowledgable, readable study on the history and techniques of the "new journalism." [Teachers]

Howard, Maureen, ed., *The Penguin Book of Contemporary American Essays* (Viking Press, 1984)

More than two dozen fine essays—by Baldwin, Baker, Thomas, and others—introduced by a noted memoirist.

Margolies, Edward, *Native Sons* (Lippincott, 1968)

Critical survey of twentieth-century black male writers, with chapters on Wright and Baldwin. [Teachers]

Sims, Norman, *The Literary Journalists* (Ballantine, 1984)

An excellent introduction on the "new journalism," with examples by Tom Wolfe, Joan Didion, and others.

White, E. B., *The Second Tree from the Corner* Harper and Brothers, 1954)

White's classic collection of essays, including several on the writer's craft.

Wolfe, Tom, and E. W. Johnson, eds., *The New Journalism* (Harper & Row, 1973)

Excellent anthology with an introduciton by an influential nonfiction writer of the 1970's.

Wright, Ellen, and Michael Fabre, eds., *Richard Wright Reader* (Harper & Row, 1978)

Contains several of Wright's nonfiction pieces, as well as poetry and fiction.

Unit Thirteen. Poetry in a Time of Diversity

Carruth, Hayden, ed., *The Voice That Is Great Within Us* (Bantam, 1970)

An excellent anthology of modern and contemporary American poetry.

Cook, Bruce, *The Beat Generation* (Scribner's, 1971)

An examination of the era of the "beat" poets. [Teachers]

Dickey, James, *Babel to Byzantium, Poets & Poetry Now* (Farrar, Straus & Giroux, 1968)

Dickey's impressions and analyses of contemporary poets.

Ellman, Richard, and Robert O'Clair, eds., *The Norton Anthology of Modern Poetry* (W. W. Norton, 1973)

An anthology of British and American poetry of the twentieth century.

Kramer, Jane, *Allen Ginsberg in America* (Random House, 1969)

An intensive look into the "beat poets" era. [Teachers]

Malkoff, Karl, *Crowell's Handbook of Contemporary American Poetry* (Thomas Y. Crowell, 1973)

An overview and analysis of the poetic schools, theories and poets since World War II. [Teachers]

Specific References

The following works focus on specific authors, works, or genres of American literature.

Albee, Edward, *The American Dream and The Zoo Story* (New American Library, 1961)

Two examples of absurdist drama.

Allen, Gay Wilson, "Plain Talk from Ralph Waldo Emerson," *American Heritage*, July 1986

Allen suggests that Emerson was not the "solemn prig" that Hemingway and others thought him to be.

Allen, Harvey, *Israfel: The Life and Times of Edgar Allan Poe*, 2 volumes (Doran, 1926)

A thorough study. [Teachers]

Allentuck, Marcia, ed., *The Achievement of Isaac Bashevis Singer* (Southern Illinois University Press, 1969)

A collection of previously unpublished essays dealing with specific aspects of Singer's writings, and with individual works. A good general introduction.

"Andrea Lee," *Contemporary Literary Criticism* 36 (Gale Research Company, 1986)

A brief, illustrated biography of Andrea Lee followed by the critical comments of twelve reviewers.

Arvin, Newton, *Herman Melville* (Greenwood, 1973)

A biography of Melville.

Bloom, Harold, ed., several anthologies of contemporary criticism on the authors' lives and works, published by Chelsea House:
Modern Critical Views: Bernard Malamud (1986)
Modern Critical Views: Edgar Allan Poe (1985)
Modern Critical Views: Henry David Thoreau (1986)
Modern Critical Views: Nathaniel Hawthorne (1986)
Modern Critical Views: Ralph Waldo Emerson (1985)

Bowen, Catherine Drinker, *Yankee from Olympus* (Houghton Mifflin, 1962)

A detailed biography of Justice Oliver Wendell Holmes, Jr., which brings in many other figures of the period.

Brown, Martha C., "Henry David Thoreau and the Best Pencils in America," *American History Illustrated,* May 1980

Fascinating article on the family pencil business and its influence on Thoreau's life and writing. Excellent photographs.

Callahan, North, *Carl Sandburg: Lincoln of Our Literature* (New York University Press, 1970)

Brief, readable biography, a good introduction to the life and works of Carl Sandburg.

Carlson, Eric W., ed., *The Recognition of Edgar Allan Poe* (University of Michigan Press, 1966)

A collection of Poe criticism. [Teachers]

Chopin, Kate, *The Awakening* (Holt, Rinehart & Winston, 1970)

Consciousness-raising novel written by a contemporary of the writers in Unit Six, enjoying a strong revival today.

Cortage, Andy, "Self-Reliance in Today's World," *Ideas Plus: Book II* (National Council of Teachers of English, 1985)

Activities encouraging close reading of Emerson and application of his philosophy to today's problems. [Teachers]

Courturier, Maurice, and Regis Durand, *Donald Barthelme* (Methuen, 1982)

An 80-page introduction to Barthelme's writing, discussing his use of language, sense of comedy and parody, and his vision of the fragmented modern self. [Teachers]

Davis, William T., ed., *Bradford's History of Plymouth Plantation, 1606–1646* (Barnes & Noble, 1946)

Complete text from which excerpts in the student text are drawn. Spellings are from Bradford's original manuscript.

Doyal, Charles, *William Carlos Williams and the American Poem* (St. Martin's Press, 1982)

The development of Williams's poetry from *Poems* (1909) through his Imagist and Objectivist phases to his culminating work, *Paterson*.

Duberman, Martin, *James Russell Lowell* (Houghton Mifflin, 1966)

A biography presenting Lowell not only as a poet but also as intellectual leader, reformer, and diplomat.

Famous American Plays of the 1940s, selected and introduced by Henry Hewes (Laurel Drama Series [Dell], 1967)

For extension of the American Drama unit. Includes Thornton Wilder's *The Skin of Our Teeth*, Arthur Laurents's *Home of the Brave*, Arthur Miller's *All My Sons*, Maxwell Anderson's *Lost in the Stars*, and Carson McCullers's *The Member of the Wedding*.

Fishwick, Marshall, "The Pepys of the Old Dominion," *American Heritage*, December 1959

A fascinating look at William Byrd through his private diaries.

Friedman, Norman, *E. E. Cummings: The Growth of a Writer* (Southern Illinois University Press, 1964)

Literary biography of Cummings guiding the reader through Cummings's literary development and individual works.

Gardner, John, *On Moral Fiction* (Basic Books, 1978)

A distinguished teacher's discussion of the need for moral vision in fiction.

Gordon, Lois, *Donald Barthelme* (Twayne, 1981)

A helpful discussion of specific stories which also contains a list of references.

Gunn, Sidney, "Knight, Sarah Kemble," *Dictionary of American Biography*, Vol. 5 (Scribner's, 1933)

A good general introduction to Knight's life.

Haley, Alex, *Roots* (Doubleday, 1976)

A well-known saga of a black American family, of interest in connection with the works of Lorraine Hansberry, James Baldwin, and Richard Wright.

Hall, Donald, *Marianne Moore: The Cage and the Animal* (Pegasus, 1970)

A noted poet's study of the life, character, and art of Marianne Moore, based in part on personal interviews. Appealing, opinionated, and informative.

Hansberry, Lorraine, *The Sign in Sidney Brustein's Window* (1964)

A play in which a middle-class Jewish protagonist renews his sense of integrity after serious disillusionment.

Hansberry, Lorraine, *To Be Young, Gifted, and Black* (New American Library, 1969)

A montage of letters, journal entries, speeches, and play excerpts. Introduction by James Baldwin.

Harding, Walter, ed., *Thoreau: A Century of Criticism* (Southern Methodist University Press, 1954)

A collection of critical essays. [Teachers]

Helprin, Mark, *A Dove of the East and Other Stories* (Random House, 1975)

A collection of twenty stories by Mark Helprin.

Hershinow, Sheldon J., *Bernard Malamud* (Frederick Ungar, 1980)

Straightforward analysis of six of Malamud's novels, followed by a discussion of some of his short stories.

Holberg, Ruth Langland, *John Greenleaf Whittier* (Thomas Y. Crowell, 1958)

A small volume containing the facts, geared toward the younger reader (short chapters, large print, appealing drawings by Aldren A. Watson).

Howard, Leon, *Herman Melville: A Biography* (University of California Press, 1981)

A critical biography of Melville.

Howarth, William, *The Book of Concord: Thoreau's Life as a Writer* (Penguin, 1983)

Perceptive account of how Thoreau's inner thought and experiences motivated his writing.

Howarth, William, "Following the Tracks of a Different Man—Thoreau," *National Geographic*, March 1981

Informative article illustrated with photographs by Farrell Grehan that would make excellent slides to accompany the study of *Walden*.

James, Henry, *Hawthorne* (Cornell University Press, 1956)

A major study. [Teachers]

Jimenez, Francisco, ed., *The Identification and Analysis of Chicano Literature* (Bilingual Press, 1979)

An anthology of readings about Chicano literature, some in English, others in Spanish. Suarez and his story "Senor Garza" are discussed in a Spanish-language article. [Spanish-speaking students/teachers]

Kaplan, Justin, *Mr. Clemens and Mark Twain* (Simon & Shuster, 1966)

The standard biography of Mark Twain, emphasizing the dual nature of his identity.

Kidder, Rushworth M., *E. E. Cummings: An Introduction to the Poetry* (Columbia University Press, 1979)

A poem-by-poem analysis of each of Cummings's twelve collections of poetry. A good one-volume source for help with a specific poem.

Kinnamon, Kenneth, ed., *James Baldwin* (Prentice-Hall, 1974)

A collection of critical essays in the Twentieth Century Views series. [Teachers]

Krutch, Joseph Wood, *Henry David Thoreau* (Greenwood, 1973)

A biography.

Lawrence, Jerome, and Robert E. Lee, *The Night Thoreau Spent in Jail* (Bantam, 1972)

An excellent drama, parts of which could be acted in class.

Leach, Douglas Edward, *Flintlock and Tomahawk: New England in King Philip's War* (Macmillan, 1958)

Full, readable history of the two-year war in which Mary Rowlandson was taken captive, mentioning her from time to time.

Lee, Andrea, "A Funeral at New African," Chapter 12 in her novel *Sarah Phillips* (Random House, 1984)

The final chapter of the novel concerns the death and funeral of Sarah's father. [Teachers]

Levin, David, ed., *Jonathan Edwards: A Profile* (Hill and Wang, 1969)

An excellent collection of biographical and critical readings, including a brief biography by Samuel Hopkins first published in 1765, essays by noted critics, and two relevant poems by Robert Lowell.

Malone, Dumas, *Jefferson and His Times*, five volumes (Little, Brown, 1948–1974)

The most complete biography of Jefferson.

Matthiessen, F. O., *The Achievement of T. S. Eliot: An Essay on the Nature of Poetry*, Third ed. (Oxford University Press, 1958)

A classic first published in 1935, assessing Eliot's poetic method. One chapter deals with the objective correlative. [Teachers]

Matthews, T. S., *Great Tom: Notes Toward the Definition of T. S. Eliot* (Harper & Row, 1974)

Biography offering a good introduction to Eliot's life, with brief comments on some of his poems. Students may appreciate a number of parodies of Eliot in the appendix (one is by James Joyce).

McPherson, James Alan, *Elbow Room* (Atlantic-Little, Brown, 1975)

A collection of twelve stories, beginning with "Why I Like Country Music," exploring the borderline between black and white America. Warm, humorous stories.

Miller, Perry, *Jonathan Edwards* (Greenwood Press, 1973)

Originally published in 1949, a skillful interspersing of the "external biography" of Edwards with his "life of the mind." The Great Awakening in New England is well described. [Teachers]

Morgan, Edmund S., *The Puritan Dilemma: The Story of John Winthrop* (Little, Brown, 1958)

Biography of the Puritan leader, John Winthrop, and also a brief, clear explanation of Puritan beliefs.

Morrow, Lance, "The Bishop of Our Possibilities," *Time*, 10 May 1982, 124

Stimulating essay on the relevance of Emerson to the twentieth century.

Mumford, Lewis, *Herman Melville* (Harcourt, Brace, 1929)

A work by the noted American social philosopher, writer, and teacher. [Teachers]

Nitchie, George W., *Marianne Moore: An Introduction to the Poetry* (Columbia University Press, 1969)

A straightforward introduction to Moore's poetry, concentrating on her themes of adaptation and endurance.

O'Brien, Tim, *Going After Cacciato* (Delacorte, 1975)

A novel about an American soldier in Vietnam, combining reality and fantasy. Characters include Paul Berlin and Stink Harris. [Teachers]

O'Connor, Frank, *The Lonely Voice: A Study of the Short Story* (World, 1963)

Discussion of the fundamental nature of the genre by the Irish short story writer.

Paul, Sherman, ed., *Thoreau: A Collection of Critical Essays* (Prentice-Hall, 1962)

A varied selection. [Teachers]

Poe, Edgar Allan, "A Chapter on Autography," *American Heritage*, February 1975

Autographs of famous writers of Poe's period and his comments on each author.

Preston, Richard M., "William Byrd II," *Dictionary of Literary Biography*, Vol. 24 (Gale Research Company, 1984)

A seven-page article listing all of William Byrd's writings plus references.

Rasky, Harry, *Tennessee Williams: A Portrait in Laughter and Lamentation* (Dodd, Mead, 1986)

Perceptive account of Williams's life and works, built upon the Canadian filmmaker's interviews and ten years' acquaintance with Williams.

Regan, Robert, ed., *Poe: A Collection of Critical Essays* (Prentice-Hall, 1967)

Poe criticism through the mid 1960's. [Teachers]

Sandburg, Carl, *Always the Young Stranger* (Harcourt Brace & World, 1953)

Autobiography of Sandburg's childhood and youth in Galesburg, Illinois, revealing much about small-town Midwestern life of the nineteenth century.

Singer, Isaac Bashevis, *Love and Exile: A Memoir* (Doubleday, 1984)

A combination of three autobiographical memoirs telling of Singer's youth in Poland and his emigration to the United States.

Spoto, Donald, *The Kindness of Strangers: The Life of Tennessee Williams* (Ballentine, 1985)

A thorough, well documented, balanced biography.

Stallman, R. W., *Stephen Crane* (George Braziller, 1968)

A good solid biography, though Crane scholarship has since been updated by discovery of new letters.

Stanford, Ann, *Images of Women in Early American Literature* (New York University Press, 1977)

Perceptive discussion of Knight and her *Journal*, and interesting commentary on Mary Rowlandson, Anne Bradstreet, and other Colonial women writers.

Tatum, Charles M., *Chicano Literature* (Twayne, 1982)

Excellent introduction containing one chapter on the contemporary short story, in which Suarez is identified as a writer who emphasizes the folklore aspect of Chicano writing.

Thorburn, David, and Howard Elland, *John Updike: A Collection of Critical Essays* (Prentice-Hall, 1979)

A varied collection of Updike's novels and short stories, with emphasis on the Rabbit novels, though the short story collections are also discussed. [Teachers]

Turner, Arlin, *Nathaniel Hawthorne: An Introduction and Interpretation* (Barnes and Noble, 1961)

The literary work and style of Nathaniel Hawthorne.

Tyler, Anne, *Searching for Caleb* (Alfred A. Knopf, 1976)

A lively and tender depiction of four generations of a family, described by one critic as the "sunniest" of Tyler's novels.

Uphaus, Suzanne Henning, *John Updike* (Frederick Ungar, 1980)

Straightforward summaries of Updike's major novels and brief explications of his most frequently anthologized stories. [Teachers]

VanDerBeets, Richard, ed., *Held Captive by Indians: Selected Narratives, 1642–1836* (University of Tennessee Press, 1973)

An outstanding collection of ten captivity narratives, including an informative preface and map for Mary Rowlandson's narrative. [Teachers]

Van Doren, Mark, *Nathaniel Hawthorne: A Critical Biography* (William Sloane Associates, 1949)

Hawthorne's life and works.

Wagenknecht, Edward C., Biographies for the general reader published by Oxford University Press:
Edgar Allan Poe—The Man Behind the Legend (1963)
Henry Wadsworth Longfellow: Portrait of an American Humanist (1966)
Nathaniel Hawthorne, Man and Writer (1961)
Ralph Waldo Emerson: Portrait of a Balanced Soul (1974)

Wagner, Linda Welshimer, *The Poems of William Carlos Williams: A Critical Study* (Wesleyan University Press, 1964)

A clear, readable account of Williams's poetic interests and development.

Westbrook, Perry D., *William Bradford* (Twayne, 1978)

Discussion of Bradford as a man of letters; a good introduction to Bradford, the writer and historian. [Teachers]

Williams, Harold, ed., "Whaling Life," *American Heritage*, June 1964

A journal kept by Eliza Williams during a three-year voyage on a New Bedford whaler; interesting for use with selections from Melville's *Moby-Dick*

Williams, Tennessee, *Memoirs* (Doubleday, 1975)

Disorganized impressions of family and friends; source of Primary Sources on text page 829. [Teachers]

Woodson, Thomas, ed., *Twentieth Century Interpretations of "The Fall of the House of Usher"* (Prentice-Hall, 1969)

Excellent background for the text excerpt. [Teachers]

Writing About Literature

Relating composition to the study of literature produces numerous benefits for both students and teachers. In order to write about a literary work, students must read it closely and must formulate their thoughts about it clearly: They gain a deeper understanding of what they have read and of how it applies to their own lives and values. At the same time, they practice essential critical thinking and composition skills as they use the basic forms of discourse: narration, description, persuasion, and, primarily, exposition, the form they will use most frequently throughout their lives.

Having students write about their reading provides advantages for you as well. When students write on the same topic, you can evaluate their essays more equitably, and when they write on different topics, their common knowledge of the literary work makes collaborative writing, evaluating, and revising especially fruitful. Students' written work can also alert you to individual problems in reading comprehension or to a general need for reteaching: If many essays evidence a similar difficulty, you will know where to clarify the analysis of a selection.

Draw students' attention to the "Writing About Literature" section early in the term, explaining that it provides strategies for answering the text's essay questions and for choosing and writing about their own topics for essays on literary works. Throughout the year, remind students to refer to this section when they are writing or preparing for an essay test.

If you want to teach the section in one or two lessons, some suggestions for presentation follow. This is also a good time to explain whether you will regularly set aside class time for writing, how often you will give timed essay tests, and how you will grade students' papers.

Writing Answers to Essay Questions

You probably cannot overemphasize to students the importance of understanding exactly what an essay question is asking. What are the mental tasks required? What specifics of the literary work are to be dealt with? What kind of support, and how much, is stipulated? Suggest that students read a question more than once as they work, to make sure they are following all of the directions.

In discussing the key verbs that are listed in the text, whenever possible use examples from selections the class has already read. As a further illustration of *analyze*, for example, you could ask students how they would proceed to analyze Poe's creation of suspense in "The Masque of the Red Death." As they answer, emphasize that they are *isolating* elements (foreshadowing, details that create ambiguity or doubt, vivid descriptions of physical and emotional states): They are "taking apart" the suspense in order to understand it.

When you discuss *compare* and *contrast*, remind students of the two methods for organizing this type of paragraph or essay. Using block organization, students write about one work (or element) and then the other; using point-by-point organization, they alternate between two works or elements as they cover each point of comparison or contrast. Be sure to emphasize that a direction to compare may mean to look for both similarities and differences. Suggest that students check with you when they are not sure whether *compare* has this comprehensive meaning in a particular question.

Few students are likely to misinterpret a direction to *describe*; however, you might spend a few minutes reviewing spatial order as a method for organizing details of physical description. Also emphasize the importance of using precise words and of including a variety of sensory details.

Students may have more difficulty with a question that requires them to *discuss*. Explain that this direction allows a broader response than do some other key verbs, but that it does not permit superficiality or vagueness. If the generality of *discuss* confuses your students, stress the alternate verb *examine*, and also point out that, in order to discuss, one must almost always first analyze.

Another way for students to think of *evaluate* is as a judgment of how well a literary element or technique "works"—how effectively it creates a desired effect. Emphasize that evaluation is not merely an expression of personal preference: It is a test against certain criteria, or standards. For evaluation questions, suggest that students refer to the lists of criteria on text pages 163, 339, and 444. They can then specify how the work fulfills or falls short of those standards, providing the required "proof" for their positions.

For the next verb, *illustrate* (similar verbs are *demonstrate* and *show*), stress that students must always provide examples from the work (details, dialogue, figurative language, etc.) to support their ideas; otherwise, even good ideas appear as mere opinions, lacking force.

Students should see that such support is especially important when a question asks them to *interpret* meaning or significance. Explain that *interpret* implies that no single, or absolute, statement of meaning exists; students must therefore carefully explain what has led them to their interpretation.

Finally, point out that a direction to *explain your response* does allow students a purely personal reaction to a work but that, again, support is required, this time in the form of reasons. Offer an example: The statement, "Robert Frost's 'Mending Wall' is the best poem in the book" is acceptable—but not by itself. The student must tell why he or she thinks so.

Be sure students see that a question may contain or imply more than one key verb. For example, in *discussing* the use of irony in Stephen Crane's "War Is Kind" (text page 508), a student might use *illustration* and *description* to develop the essay's thesis. In every case, however, the question will provide a clear purpose on which to focus.

The next step, item 3, is crucial for students and should be stressed: Write a brief, direct, and specific thesis statement. You could ask students to rephrase actual essay questions from the text as thesis statements, following the example. Then note that in gathering supporting ideas and evidence, students usually can draw from class discussion of a selection. In fact, class work on the "Analyzing the [Selection]" questions can be thought of as prewriting: Explain that active participation and note-taking will yield ideas and data for later writing.

In discussing items 4 and 5, be sure students see that an essay's main ideas will come from the information gathered to support the thesis statement. Emphasize that each paragraph should contain a single idea, buttressed with evidence, and suggest that students draft a thesis statement and a topic sentence for each paragraph before writing the complete answer.

Make clear that all of this thinking, note-taking, and organizing is essential no matter what form the rough outline takes. It is not time wasted, *especially* when time is restricted. If students begin writing without planning, their essays will be incomplete or unorganized no matter how correct the grammar and mechanics. Emphasize that, in timed writing, students must set a schedule for themselves, allowing time for all major stages of the writing process: prewriting, writing, evaluating and revising, and proofreading. (On occasions that seem to warrant it, you may want to consider allowing students who run out of time to turn in their prewriting notes along with their papers. The notes may demonstrate that a student understood the question and had planned a sound answer but simply did not have time to execute it.)

Writing and Revising an Essay About a Literary Work

Students should recognize the significance of choosing a limited topic, one narrow enough to cover in detail in a fairly brief essay. If they are afraid they won't find enough to say about a narrow topic, assure them that developing a specific idea is actually easier than thoroughly supporting a broad generalization. Suggest that they find limited topics by asking further questions about information discussed in class. They might look at *why* a character changed in attitude, *which* conflict or conflicts revealed a major theme, or *how* word choice set a particular tone. Students should skim a selection they want to write about and review their reading and class notes. Encourage them to take more notes as they reread, even if they haven't yet settled on a topic; the notes can help them define their thesis and gather supporting evidence.

Go over each of the remaining prewriting steps with the students, illustrating how formulation of the thesis statement will control, or direct, the subsequent steps. Remind students to write a plan or outline, even if informal; you might refer them to the discussion of outlines in their composition and grammar text.

The text's outline of essay form is a good general reference. Emphasize that students should write their first drafts by working steadily through to the end, referring as needed to their outlines and notes. You may want to take this opportunity to warn against overusing direct quotations to pad the body of an essay. Tell students to ask themselves whether the precise wording of the quotation is important to their point or whether a shorter reference or paraphrase will suffice.

When you discuss revision, note that this final step presupposes evaluation: Students must first read a draft to evaluate its strengths and weaknesses; then they can make the changes—adding, deleting, replacing, or reordering words and phrases—that will improve the draft. Suggest that students go through their drafts once for content and organization, a second time for style (wordiness, monotonous sentence structure, etc.), and a third time for mechanical errors (spelling, punctuation, etc.). Explain that learning the proofreader's symbols can streamline this part of the process. Also encourage the use of peer evaluation, illustrating appropriate constructive criticism if your students do not regularly exchange work.

You might guide the class through the model essay twice, to focus attention on different aspects. First have students concentrate on content and organization, using the sidenotes that highlight development of the thesis. The second time, they can focus on the writer's revisions. Ask students why they think the changes were made and how each one improves the essay.

Documenting Sources

Specify for students the style you prefer for documenting sources, and be sure to make available a reference containing several examples of citations, whether a published style book, your own information sheet, or the students' composition and grammar text. Students could also use good essays from your previous classes as models of correct documentation.

Model Student Essays

The following papers were written by eleventh-grade students in response to three "Writing About the [Selection]" assignments and to one of the "Exercises in Critical Thinking and Writing" sections in *Elements of Literature: Fifth Course*. They are included here as samples of the writing you can expect from eleventh-graders using the text.

On "Self-Reliance"

Often I find the ideas in nineteenth-century literary works to be outdated: they no longer seem to pertain to the world as we know it today. The ideas of one writer, however—Ralph Waldo Emerson—do not fit into this category. In spite of having been born almost two hundred years ago, Emerson wrote pieces that can help us guide our lives in today's rapidly changing society. "Self-Reliance" is one such piece.

Emerson's main ideas in "Self-Reliance" revolve around individualism, the principle of independent thought or action, or as Emerson wrote, "whoso would be a man must be a nonconformist." This is valuable advice that can be applied in many contemporary situations. When dealing with school cliques, for example, these words are especially meaningful, since cliques are essentially made up of people who seem to feel a need to conform. In an effort to be accepted, members act, talk, and dress like others in the group. If a certain designer's blue jeans are the order of the day, then every member of the clique wears those jeans. If studying is "out," members would rather fail classes than be found with a book. Emerson felt that people are the best that they can be if they are themselves, and most teenagers who are "clique-concerned" would, in moments of honest reflection, admit that he is correct.

Another basic idea Emerson expressed in "Self-Reliance" that is still relevant today is that the way to succeed is for people to try their very best at whatever they do: "A man is relieved and gay when he has put his heart into his work and done his best; but what he has said or done otherwise shall give him no peace." This statement still stands true today, as the student who has put in hours of work to pass a difficult subject or an athlete, who after years of rigorous training stands to hear the "Star-Spangled Banner" and receive an Olympic medal, can attest.

In writing "Self-Reliance," Emerson did not, of course, have in mind school cliques or Olympic medals. His advice, however, still fits easily into today's society, and may, indeed, be a hook on which to hang our future hopes.

—Lyn Rutledge
Mrs. Barbara Freiberg, Teacher
University Laboratory School
Baton Rouge, LA

Magic and Mystery

"An Occurrence at Owl Creek Bridge" is a captivating story written by Ambrose Bierce, a genius of unique, haunting fiction and a man deeply influenced by his own war experiences. In the story Bierce makes use of many literary tools, including evocative imagery and dramatic irony, but the one tool that Bierce uses most effectively is point of view.

"An Occurrence at Owl Creek Bridge" begins and ends with third-person, limited omniscient narration. With such narration, the narrator, who is not in the story, enters the mind of one character and focuses on his or her actions and thoughts. Thus, we are taken, in a limited way, into Peyton's Farquhar's mind as he stands on the bridge about to be hanged and as the hanging takes place. Closer to Farquhar at this point, through first-person narration, or further away, through objective narration, and the dream vs. reality motif would have been destroyed. Only in the second section, when background information on Farquhar becomes important, does narration appropriately shift to third-person objective.

A crucial aspect of third-person narration is, of course, the withholding of certain information, with the result that the reader must constantly make inferences. Some important inferences in "Occurrence" deal with the war that is being fought and what Farquhar has done or tried to do to be dealt such a fate. For example, the narrator never states directly that the story takes place during the Civil War. Clues, such as the fact that Peyton Farquhar owns a plantation and that a Federal scout pretends to be a Southern soldier, enable the reader to make the inference. Another inference that the reader must make is what Farquhar did to get himself into such a predicament. From the text we draw the conclusion that Farquhar followed up on the scout's information and tried to burn down the bridge. Unfortunately, it was a trap and Farquhar was caught.

All of these inferences lead to the climax of the story. Here, once again, the narrator withholds information, this time until the very last moment. In a scene painted with vivid and realistic details, we see the exhausted Farquhar stagger toward his wife, his arms outstretched, reached to embrace her. It is with a jolt that we realize, for the last time, the effectiveness of our third-person, limited narrator. What we have not known until this moment is that Farquhar has died. His body swings from the railroad bridge.

—Rob Armstrong
Barbara Freiberg, Teacher
University Laboratory School
Baton Rouge, LA

Countee Cullen's "Only the Polished Skeleton"

What is the one idea that plagues a human being's deceitful life? This question is answered in Countee Cullen's "Only the Polished Skeleton," through the poet's description of three parts of the human body.

The first description is of the flesh, which is a machine fueled by deceit. The second part of the body described is the brain: the brain is trying to deceive itself into thinking it is immortal. The mind tries to "beat off the onslaughts of the dust." The final part of the human focused on is a quiet, polished skelton. The skelton is contemplating from the grave the life it once had.

In this manner, Cullen concludes that only the dead realize how humans waste their lives hating others. Alive, humans do not understand because their minds deceive them into thinking they are immortal and thus have time to waste in hating others. The first stanza, however, rationalizes this behavior, explaining that human lives are fueled by this deceit and hatefulness toward others. It therefore suggests that humans would not be happy knowing of impending death.

Even with this rationalization, the final attitude presented to the reader is one of almost helpless disgust for the human race. Humans live under the shadow of hypocrisy, deceiving themselves and wasting their lives with anger and hatred. The only one who realizes this ironic situation is the quiet, "polished" skeleton in the grave.

—Holly Bartels
Mr. Steve Delacroix, Teacher
University Laboratory School
Baton Rouge, LA

Leon Pugh: Someone I Have Known

Leon Pugh, the protagonist in James Alan McPherson's "Why I Like Country Music," is a character that everyone has met at one time or another. He is the brash, outspoken-leader type who everyone else resents but tries to imitate. Possessing the poise and social grace that others only dream about, Leon gets what he wants. As he waits on the school bus in the afternoon, he loudly exclaims "Move off! Get away! This here seat is reserved for the girl from Brooklyn, New York." Of course, the other boys just sit, watching as their goddess, Gweneth Lawson, is taken in by Leon's charm. Everything about Leon, indeed, reflects his considerable flair. He is a "dancing fool," strutting proudly while the other males are awkwardly tumbling "over their own feet." When the big dance day comes, Leon's sharp outfit captures "the attention of all eyes." He proudly exclaims, "My daddy says it pays to look good no matter what you put on."

Leon is the classic romantic adversary. He is everything that everyone else wants to be. The catch, of course, is that he loses Gweneth (for one dance, anyway) to the narrator in the end. Presumably, Leon will wake up the morning after the dance and attack the new day just as vigorously as always, and in the end he will truly win Gweneth. When one reads the story, he or she may find it hard not to substitute some peer's name for Leon's. Leon is a very believable character. I know. I've met him before.

—Matthew Tomlinson
Mr. Frank Militano, Teacher
Jefferson Township High School
Oak Ridge, NJ

Assessing Students' Mastery of Subject Matter and Concepts

Students' writing is an excellent measure of their understanding of literary works and concepts. Whether writing compositions or answers to essay questions, students must organize and apply the knowledge they have acquired through reading, note-taking, and class discussion. They must demonstrate their understanding of particular selections as well as their understanding of literary genres and techniques.

With the aids in this manual, you can plan your evaluation strategies carefully and reduce the time needed for grading or reviewing papers. For example, for each writing assignment in the text, the manual provides "Criteria for Evaluating the Assignment," two or three major points to guide your assessment of students' work. In addition, the model responses that follow the criteria for some of the assignments and the sample essays that appear in "Writing About Literature" can serve as assessment aids. Finally, you can make use of the following evaluation methods, which include checklists, written comments, self-evaluation, and peer evaluation.

Holistic Scoring

For some writing assignments, you may want to use holistic scoring, a method in which you read each paper quickly and respond to it as a whole, making no comments or corrections. With a carefully prepared scoring guide, holistic evaluation is an efficient and consistent means of judging students' work. Even though it does not provide students with your personal comments, it is not superficial or vague: Students receive an evaluation of key features of their papers. Two types of holistic scales you may find useful are the analytic and the general impression.

Analytic Scales

Using an analytic scale, you rank each of several features of a piece of writing from high to low. Here is one scale that lists features common to all writing and uses a numerical ranking.

Analytic Scale				
	Low	**Middle**	**High**	
Ideas	2	4 6 8	10	
Organization	2	4 6 8	10	
Word choice	1	2 3 4	5	
Tone	1	2 3 4	5	_____
Usage, grammar	1	2 3 4	5	
Punctuation, capitalization	1	2 3 4	5	
Spelling	1	2 3 4	5	
Legibility	1	2 3 4	5	_____
			Total	_____

Adapted from Paul B. Diederich, *Measuring Growth in Writing* (Urbana, IL: NCTE, 1974).

In other analytic scales, the features are specific to a form of writing (description, narration, etc.). Such scales can be adapted for many different assignments; in fact, the revision checklists in the text's critical thinking and writing exercises are excellent for this purpose: For example, you can use the revision checklist on text page 988 to develop an analytic scale for evaluating a poem, and you can adapt that scale for evaluation papers in other genres.

The scales that follow cover four common writing tasks, each applied to a different genre. These examples use the dichotomous, or yes–no, scale.

Fiction: Summarizing a Plot Analytic Scale	Yes	No
The story's title and author are cited.		
The summary includes the story's most important events.		
The events are summarized in the order in which they occur.		
The summary explains how one event causes or leads to another.		
The setting is briefly described.		
Extraneous details are omitted.		
The student primarily uses his or her own words.		
Word choice is precise and appropriate.		
Sentence structure is varied.		
Grammar, usage, and mechanics errors do not interfere with reading.		

Poetry: Responding to a Poem Analytic Scale	Yes	No
The poem's title, author, and subject are stated.		
The student describes his or her general response to the poem.		
At least two details about the poem's content are used to explain the response.		
At least two details about the poem's construction are used to explain the response.		
Quotations from the poem are exact and are cited correctly.		
A concluding or summary statement ends the composition.		
Word choice is precise and appropriate.		
Sentence structure is varied.		
Grammar, usage, and mechanics errors do not interfere with reading.		

Assessing Students' Mastery

Nonfiction: Analyzing a Report Analytic Scale	Yes	No
The report's title and author are cited.		
The main idea of the report is stated.		
A sufficient number of the strongest facts supporting the main idea are cited.		
The facts in the report are distinguished from the author's opinions.		
Any appeals to emotion are identified and discussed.		
Significant narrative techniques are identified and discussed.		
Organization is clear and coherent.		
The conclusion summarizes main points of the analysis.		
Word choice is precise and appropriate.		
Sentence structure is varied.		
Grammar, usage, and mechanics errors do not interfere with reading.		

Drama: Analyzing and Evaluating a Theme Analytic Scale	Yes	No
The play's title and author are cited.		
A clear theme statement is presented.		
The theme statement is supported with at least three examples of action and dialogue.		
The student expresses an evaluation of the theme.		
The student presents at least two reasons for the evaluation, supported by evidence from the play.		
Quotations are exact and are cited correctly.		
The conclusion summarizes or restates the statement of theme and the student's evaluation.		
Word choice is precise and appropriate.		
Sentence structure is varied.		
Grammar, usage, and mechanics errors do not interfere with reading.		

General Impression Scales

A general impression scale is also keyed to the form of writing, but the individual features of the paper are not ranked separately. Instead, the paper as a whole is judged high, average, or low. In this case, developing a scoring guide entails outlining the general characteristics of high, average, and low papers for the assignment. For example, you could use the following general impression scale to evaluate a descriptive paragraph:

There is no one prescribed format for writing the general characteristics for this type of scale. What is important—whether you use complete sentences, a series of phrases, or even a list of items—is that you cover the key features of the writing assignment and that you address the same features in each ranking. Here is a second example of a general impression scale, one for use in evaluating an essay comparing and contrasting elements in two poems.

Descriptive Paragraph General Impression Scale

Assignment: To write a subjective description of a person, place, or object

4   The topic sentence expresses a main impression of the topic; many concrete and sensory details create a vivid picture; each sentence supports the main idea in the topic sentence; organization is clear; ideas flow smoothly, with effective transitions; sentences are varied and diction fresh; grammatical and mechanical errors are minimal.

3   The topic sentence expresses a main impression of the topic; concrete and sensory details are used, but the description could be fuller and more vivid; organization is clear; some transitions could be added or improved; sentences are varied and diction accurate but unoriginal; occasional grammatical and mechanical errors appear.

2   The topic sentence is vague or inexact; details are not specific or are insufficient; organization is flawed but can be followed; few transitions are provided between ideas; sentences are correct but often awkward or monotonous, with some inexact wording; occasional grammatical and mechanical errors interfere with reading.

1   The topic sentence is missing or does not clearly identify the topic; details are not specific and are insufficient to develop the description; organization is unclear; ideas are missing or irrelevant; word choice is often inaccurate; frequent syntax and mechanical errors interfere with reading.

0   The paragraph does not develop a description.

Comparison and Contrast Essay General Impression Scale

Assignment: To compare and contrast the messages and tones of two poems

4   The essay addresses both similarities and differences, insightfully interprets the poems' messages and tones, supports main ideas with appropriate details, is well organized (with a clear thesis statement in the first paragraph, a main supporting idea in each body paragraph, and a concluding paragraph), flows smoothly, and contains few errors in grammar and mechanics.

3   The essay addresses both similarities and differences, interprets the messages and tones thoughtfully, and is well organized, but it provides less support for main ideas, displays occasional awkwardness or monotony, and contains occasional errors in grammar and mechanics.

2   The essay does not address (or address equally) both similarities and differences, interprets the messages and tones sketchily, omits some needed supporting detail, is difficult to follow in places, and contains errors in grammar and mechanics that occasionally interfere with reading.

1   The essay does not address both similarities and differences, lacks insight into or misinterprets the messages and tones, does not support main ideas with sufficient evidence, is disorganized, lacks clarity of expression, and contains errors in grammar and mechanics that frequently interfere with reading.

0   The essay does not follow the assignment or does not develop its thesis.

Assessing Students' Mastery

When you use a general impression scale, be sure to provide students with your scoring guide so that they know the specific criteria that determined their score. If possible, provide each student with a copy; students with lower scores should use the guide to identify the errors and weaknesses in their papers, and all students can use the guide when developing similar papers in the future.

Remember that holistic scoring, while allowing you to evaluate many papers rapidly, does not preclude your giving more personal attention to students who need help. For example, you can invite students to consult with you individually when they cannot pinpoint the errors in their papers. You can also ask students to submit their revised papers; the revisions will show you exactly where they need further instruction.

Comments and Corrections

Some papers you will want to mark thoroughly, commenting on students' ideas and writing style and indicating where errors lie. You cannot afford to do this for all assignments, but you should do it for some: Students respond remarkably well to such personal attention and specific guidance.

Only with written comments can you react to a student's individual thoughts and use of language. Whether you are agreeing or disagreeing, praising or finding fault, your comments show that you are paying attention to students' ideas and that you care about students' skills. Always include some praise or encouragement. Even when a student has written poorly, you can often offer encouragement by referring to real strengths: "You used some fresh, original words in last week's character sketch. I *know* you have the vocabulary to go beyond the trite expressions I've marked in this essay. I'll be looking for your vivid wording in the next assignment."

Keep in mind that a heavy marking of a paper is not a rewriting. Even if you suggest some specific content revisions, students must decide how to make the changes. Even though you isolate errors in grammar, usage, and mechanics, students must correct them. (Don't hesitate occasionally, however, to show students how to rework or correct a passage; students need models when they are acquiring skills.)

Using correction symbols will speed your marking of papers. You may want to distribute a list such as the following one with students' first marked papers. After students have worked with the list, you can ask for questions about particular symbols and writing problems.

Correction Symbols

Symbol	Meaning	What to Do
	Content	
concl	conclusion missing, weak, or unrelated to main idea	Add or rephrase summarizing statement or paragraph.
irr	irrelevant detail	Delete or replace phrase or sentence.
spec	needs to be more specific	Clarify a detail, or add supporting details.
ts	thesis statement or topic sentence missing or not clear	Add or revise main idea.

Symbol	Meaning	What to Do
Organization		
org	organization not clear	Rearrange ideas in a more logical order.
tr	transition between ideas missing or confusing	Add or replace connecting words or phrases.
¶, no ¶	paragraphing problem	Begin new paragraph (¶), or join paragraphs (no ¶).
Style		
agr	agreement error	Make a subject and verb or an antecedent and pronoun agree in number.
awk	awkward sentence or passage	Rephrase sentence or section.
cap	capitalization error	Add capital, or lower-case capital.
frag	sentence fragment	Add subject or verb, or attach fragment to nearby sentence.
gr	grammatical error	Determine type of error, and correct it.
p	punctuation error	Add, replace, or delete punctuation.
pv	unnecessary shift in point of view	Eliminate shift in person.
ref	pronoun reference error	Clarify reference of a pronoun to its antecedent.
ro	run-on sentence	Correct with needed punctuation and capitals.
sp	misspelled word	Correct spelling.
t	tense error	Correct verb tense.
var	sentences lack variety	Vary structure and length of sentences.
wc	word choice problem	Replace with correct, more exact, or livelier word.

Grading

In grading students' writing about literature, you will want to focus on the quality of their ideas. Without diminishing the importance of mechanics and style, let students know that *what* they have to say is of first importance in their grades: An error-free paper that is either shallow or incomplete should not receive an *A*.

Some teachers use a double grade on papers, for example *B+/C*, to distinguish between content and mechanics. Whatever system you use, explain clearly to students how your marking relates to their grades. Sample papers are especially helpful for this purpose. From previous classes, accumulate a file of marked and graded papers that students may examine, and review in class *A*, *B*, *C*, *D*, and *F* papers for a typical assignment. These papers will illustrate for students exactly what you expect.

Self-Evaluation

Students help both themselves and you by evaluating their own papers. Good writers evaluate automatically, although usually not in writing; most students, however, skip this essential step altogether. By assigning even brief and informal evaluations, you can show students the importance of this writing stage and instill a habit of lasting benefit. What you gain is not only improved papers but also insight into the students' ideas about writing. You may uncover misconceptions (a student is more concerned with correct spelling than with organization) and problems in composing (a student is a perfectionist and writes and rewrites an opening sentence). You can then help individual students or plan class sessions on particular aspects of the writing process.

One self-evaluation assignment is to have students rank the papers they are submitting as either high, average, or low and to explain their criteria for the ranking. Stress that you are not grading the evaluations and simply want honest, thoughtful responses to this question: What do you think of your paper and *why*? It will be most helpful if you combine this self-evaluation with your own evaluation, of whatever method; when you return the papers, students will see how their judgments compare to yours and can use the discrepancies to improve their evaluation skills. You can also use a simple form, such as the following one, for a self-evaluation of this type.

Self-Evaluation Comments

Name _____ Date _____

Assignment or Title of Paper _____

1. I think one strength of this paper, or one thing that works well, is _____
_____.

2. The weakest aspect of this paper is _____
_____.

3. One problem I faced and was not sure how best to solve was _____
_____.

Students should evaluate and revise the first draft of every paper: No first draft is ever perfect. If students evaluate and revise for themselves—rather than submitting first drafts—they will take a great step toward improved writing and better grades. Students can use the following general checklist to evaluate and then revise their writing about literature. (If you use holistic scoring guides, also alert students that the guides may be reused as evaluation checklists for particular assignments.)

Self-Evaluation Checklist for Writing About Literature	Yes	No
1. Have I followed all of the directions for the assignment?		
2. Have I understood the literary terms and used them correctly?		
3. Have I clearly expressed a main idea in a strong topic sentence or thesis statement?		
4. Have I included enough details from the literary work to support my ideas?		
5. Are all the details accurate and directly related to the main idea?		
6. Does my paper have a clear beginning, middle, and end?		
7. Have I used precise words and avoided clichés and repetitious phrases?		
8. Have I correctly punctuated quotations and dialogue?		
9. Have I checked other punctuation, spelling, and use of capitals?		
10. Have I read the paper aloud to listen for missing words and awkward phrasing?		

Peer Evaluation

When properly prepared for, peer evaluation can be highly rewarding and enjoyable for both writers and evaluators, producing new insights about the literary work and about the writing process. Unguided, though, peer evaluation can be ineffective or unpleasant; irrelevant comments merely confuse, and heavy-handed criticisms wound. What is required is sensitivity, objectivity, and a common understanding of the evaluation criteria.

For successful peer evaluation, provide students with evaluation forms, and demonstrate constructive criticism. First conduct a class evaluation of a paper from a previous class. Explain the writer's assignment, read the paper aloud, and offer samples of the comments you would make. As students enter the discussion, point out off-target comments or negative comments that serve no purpose; help students redirect or rephrase these criticisms, and remind them always to point out a paper's good features: Evaluation identifies both strengths and weaknesses. You may want to go through two or three papers in this way before students work on their own.

At least for initial peer evaluations in small groups, use some type of prepared form. After students hear or read a paper, they can complete the form and then base group discussion on their written responses. Using a form need not limit discussion; always encourage students to react to each other's comments and to brainstorm solutions for writing problems. After the discussion, the writer can use the completed forms for revising.

Depending on your students' abilities and maturity, you can use a highly structured checklist or a form that elicits a more general impression. For example, you could adapt the preceding self-evaluation checklist for peer evaluation, providing room for the evaluator to explain every No response. A sample of a less-structured evaluation form follows.

Peer Evaluation Comments

Reader _____ Writer _____

Assignment or Title of Paper _____ Date _____

1. What I liked best in this paper was _____
   _____.

2. The most effective sentence was _____
   _____.

3. Good word choices were _____
   _____.

4. Ideas that I felt needed clarification or further support were _____
   _____.

5. Other positive comments are _____
   _____.

6. Other suggestions for revision are _____
   _____.

Reading Development in the *Elements of Literature* Program: *The Student as Reader/The Teacher as Facilitator*

Nancy E. Wiseman Seminoff

Elements of Literature is a comprehensive program of literature study for grades 7–12. Each anthology includes a wide range of significant literary works, as well as supporting instruction that helps students become more proficient readers and writers as they learn to analyze, interpret, and evaluate literature. The first six units of the eleventh-grade anthology are organized chronologically; units seven through thirteen—the modern period—are divided by genre (fiction, poetry, drama, nonfiction). Often, selections are grouped to facilitate comparison and contrast of theme, structure, or style and technique. The list of the selections organized by themes (text page 970) allows teachers the flexibility of using a thematic approach.

The instructional materials include background information for understanding the genres, the selections, and the writers' lives; factual and interpretive discussion questions; and creative and critical writing assignments. The questions and assignments, designed to stimulate critical thinking, emphasize reading and writing strategies in which students use their own experience and knowledge to comprehend and appreciate literature. For twenty selections in the anthology, the *Connections Between Reading and Writing* worksheets provide further intensive reading and writing practice.

Additionally, exercises throughout the text use specific linguistic features of the selections as springboards to language and vocabulary instruction in some sixty skills. The exercises cover literary terms and techniques, such as allusions and figures of speech, as well as word-study skills important in all reading, such as context clues, dictionary use, and word roots. For a listing of all skills taught in the program, see the index on text pages 964–968 and the scope and sequence chart in the front of this manual.

Elements of Literature provides you with excellent materials and tools with which to help your students become better readers. Naturally, your role in the classroom is pivotal to students' success; by understanding the reading process and basing your teaching strategies on it, you can draw out the anthology's full potential for reading development.

Understanding the Reading Process

Educators in the past viewed reading as a series of discrete skills, sequential and hierarchical in nature. They increasingly found, however, that students who learned these skills in the elementary grades did not necessarily develop into proficient readers in the higher grades. Something was missing in the traditional view of the reading process: the interaction between the reader and the author.

According to recent research, reading is a dynamic process that involves the reader, the author's text, and the situation in which the reading takes place. The assumption behind previous reading theory was that the author bore sole responsibility for conveying meaning; educators now recognize that readers must actively expect and seek meaning as they read and must be able to modify their approach to a text if the approach doesn't yield meaning. The reader's characteristics and background (linguistic, social, cultural, and psychological) and the author's characteristics (as evidenced in the text) necessarily influence the reader's understanding.

Students actually *construct* meaning as they read; they do not simply absorb it. They bring prior experience and knowledge (which includes expectations about the type of literature) to the work, drawing tentative conclusions as they begin to read and modifying those conclusions as they continue; the reading process is thus one of accumulating meaning.

The development of schema theory by cognitive psychologists during the past decade has helped illuminate this process, showing how people approach new information by setting it against a known framework. In reading, schemata (frameworks) enable a student to recall relevant facts and experiences, to anticipate what will happen next, to fill in missing information, and to know when an author's meaning is not clear. Important to a student's schemata, therefore, is experience not only with the topic of a reading selection but also with the genre (sometimes called the story grammar or text structure). In reading about spring, for example, a student's comprehension may be aided by prior knowledge of how plants form and grow, no matter what the genre of the writing. But a student cannot approach the reading of William Carlos Williams's "Spring and All" and the reading of a scientific discussion of the season in the same way. To obtain (construct) full meaning from "Spring and All," the student must be familiar with poetic conventions and techniques, as well as with stylistic variations within genres; the student must have appropriate expectations against which to gauge understanding.

Teachers, in turn, must be alert to gaps in students' experience and knowledge that will prevent them from being "active" readers, supplying (or guiding students in finding) necessary background in the many ways suggested in this manual and in the text. If students face a literary work that seems thoroughly unfamiliar, the reading will seem a difficult chore; students will not read, or continue to read, with interest—and interest is another fundamental element in the dynamics of reading.

The purpose for reading a selection, either self- or teacher-imposed, is an additional variable in the reading situation. A student uses quite different reading skills to gain an initial impression of an essayist's position and to read a dramatic soliloquy; for the first task, the student reads in "chunks," with wide eye sweeps, while for the second, the student reads closely, ideally aloud, with attention to specific phrasing and detail. ("Teaching Students to Vary Reading Rates" in this manual provides a discussion of different reading strategies as well as genre-specific guidelines for close reading.)

Reading involves adapting to each reading situation as it is encountered. The selection (topic, genre, structure, and author's style), the purpose for reading, and the student's interest (conditioned by prior experience) all affect comprehension. The successful reader is able to "shift gears," to approach differently each encounter with a literary selection. It is important that your students recognize the need for this variation and know appropriate strategies to apply in different situations.

The conscious awareness and control of cognitive processes is termed *metacognition*; in reading, metacognition is the adjustment of reading strategies to control comprehension. You should encourage students to monitor their own comprehension: to pause and raise questions when they

The Reading Development Program 435

do not understand, to reread a section to seek clarity, to use context clues to determine meaning, and so on. You should help students see, in short, that the response to difficult reading is not to stop reading. Students can learn techniques to become flexible, strategic readers—a necessity if they are to understand and enjoy literature.

Using the Instructional Materials

The instructional materials that accompany the selections in the anthology provide a framework for your classroom activities, which can be considered in three phases: preparation for reading the selection, an encounter with the selection, and extension beyond the selection. Before deciding on the specific activities you will use in these phases, you have two key tasks: establishing content and deciding on approach.

The "content" of your instruction is both your own analysis and interpretation of the literary work and the aspects of the work you choose to highlight. Arriving at a personal understanding of the work's meaning in no sense means that you will prescribe a single interpretation to the students, but that your own thoughts about the work are organized and focused; in this way you will better lead students to their own understandings. When you clarify for yourself a selection's possible meanings, you can then choose, or create, questions and assignments that will move students toward meaning, not simply test their recall.

Another part of your planning is deciding on your teaching emphasis: historical background, symbolic interpretation, analysis and evaluation of theme, language exercises, and so on. The objectives in this manual show at a glance the text's instructional emphases; they can guide you in choosing those "Responding" items that meet your specific teaching goals.

Finally, all your initial judgments of what and how to teach involve your students' particular needs. In preparing to teach a selection, you not only master content; you also consider how best for your class to bring about the interaction at the heart of the reading process. This manual provides many suggestions for accommodating different ability levels and cultural backgrounds.

An overview of using *Elements of Literature* in the three phases of teaching a selection follows.

Before Reading—Moving into the Selection

Students' preparation for reading a selection often determines the success of their reading and therefore cannot be left to chance. In the students' text, unit and section introductions and selection headnotes supply background information and help students anticipate topics and themes. (At times you may also wish to use the "Elements of Literature," "Primary Sources," and "A Comment on the [Selection]" sections before, rather than after, students read a selection.) This manual offers additional information and ideas for introducing the selections.

Also important are activities to bridge the gap between students' prior knowledge and an unfamiliar literary work, activities that will motivate them to want to begin reading. The teaching guides in this manual present many hints for stimulating interest in individual selections. Remember, however, that students do not need exhaustive introductions to begin reading, understanding, and appreciating a selection. Reading preparation should be stimulating and revealing, not oppressive. When students must learn many new facts, concepts, and terms, the introduction should be a separate lesson.

During Reading—Moving Through the Selection

The questions in "Analyzing the [Selection]" are intended to assist students in understanding the literary work. They are instruction, not testing, and students should refer freely to the selection when answering them. (You may on occasion select some questions for closed-book reading checks or essay tests.)

Good reading questions help students organize information by leading them to identify facts and an author's salient points, to draw inferences, to combine the facts and inferences with their prior knowledge, and to consider the author's suggested meaning in light of the broader context of life and other literature. Questions should lead readers to *accumulate* understandings of the selection while encouraging them to think on their own. The "Identifying Facts" and "Interpreting Meanings" questions are therefore not linear and hierarchical. As students answer the questions, they are continually gathering information, interpreting, and raising their own questions in a process that causes them to refine their understandings and to confirm or reject initial predictions. Cognitively, they move between and among the questions as they build comprehension and understanding.

Consequently, you should encourage students to answer questions as fully as possible but to be open to revising their responses in light of new evidence. In this process of deepening comprehension, other students' responses also play an important role. It is particularly effective to have students discuss questions, or compare their written answers, in small groups. In this way, students can refine, reconsider, reject, revise, or confirm their understandings as a consequence of others' ideas.

Keep in mind that while all reading questions should guide students to find meaning and contribute their own ideas, the amount and type of guidance can vary. Debate exists among reading experts about how structured the guidance should be, but your students' needs should be the determining factor. For some students and in some situations, a highly structured question may be best. In other cases, you may be able to use open-ended questions and provide minimal guidance. For further discussion of questioning strategies, particularly to provoke critical thinking, see "Using Literature to Teach Higher-Level Thinking Skills."

After Reading—Moving Beyond the Selection

Activities after reading serve two purposes: assessing students' understanding of a selection and helping students apply what they have learned to a new situation or selection. Culminating small-group discussions—following your instruction and guided class discussion—are one simple but effective way for you to determine students' comprehension. As students express and explain their final thoughts about the work, you should move among the groups, listening for problem areas. You can determine how many students still have not read successfully and how best to help them.

Exercises in "Writing About the [Selection]" and "Analyzing Language and Style" require students both to demonstrate comprehension and to go beyond the selections. Many of the writing assignments encourage students to use their insights about a work to explore a literary element more deeply, to compare and contrast another selection, or to relate the work to other life situations. The language and vocabulary exercises, while assessing students' mastery of selection-related skills and terms, usually extend and apply the language study to other areas. Thus the students' schemata, the frameworks available to them, increase as they complete each exercise.

Discussing one or more selections in relation to each other also broadens students' schemata. You may ask students to consider theme, style, genre, historical period, or another element or combination of elements. You may ask them to apply what they have learned through study of a selection to the creation of an original work. (This manual provides many "Extending the Selection" suggestions.) In these activities, students are synthesizing; they analyze the selections, but they arrive at understandings (comparisons, contrasts, original works) that are external to the selections. In applying elsewhere what they learn from a literary work, students learn how to use past reading to approach new reading. They extend the schemata that make them proficient, strategic readers.

In summary, the study of literature can be a means for students to become proficient readers, capable of varying their reading strategies to meet the demands of the task, but the teacher must be the facilitator of this accomplishment. The decisions you make for moving students into, through, and beyond a literary work are important in helping them both appreciate literature and monitor their own reading methods. *Elements of Literature* provides excellent materials to assist you in this important process.

Further Reading

Alvermann, D. E. "Metacognition." *Research Within Reach: Secondary School Reading*. Eds. D. E. Alvermann, D. W. Moore, and M. W. Conley. Newark, DE: International Reading Association, 1987. 153–168.

Anderson, R. C., et al. "Frameworks for Comprehending Discourse." *American Educational Research Journal* 14 (1977): 367–381.

Armbruster, B. "The Problem of 'Inconsiderate Text.'" *Comprehension Instruction: Perspectives and Suggestions*. Eds. G. Duffy, L. Roehler, and J. Mason. New York: Longman, 1984. 202–217.

Baker, L., and A. L. Brown. "Cognitive Monitoring in Reading." *Understanding Reading Comprehension*. Ed. J. Flood. Newark, DE: International Reading Association, 1984. 21–44.

Langer, J. A. "Examining Background Knowledge and Text Comprehension." *Reading Research Quarterly* 19 (1984): 468–481.

Meyer, B. J. F. "Organizational Aspects of Text: Effects on Reading Comprehension and Applications for the Classroom." *Promoting Reading Comprehension*. Ed. J. Flood. Newark, DE: International Reading Association, 1984. 113–138.

Mosenthal, P. "Reading Comprehension Research from a Classroom Perspective." *Promoting Reading Comprehension*. Ed. J. Flood. Newark, DE: International Reading Association, 1984. 16–29.

Paris, S. G., M. Lipson, and K. K. Wilson. "Becoming a Strategic Reader." *Contemporary Educational Psychology* 8 (1982): 293–316.

Pearson, P. D., ed. *Handbook of Reading Research*. New York: Longman, 1984.

Pearson, P. D., and R. J. Spiro. "Toward a Theory of Reading Comprehension Instruction." *Topics in Language Disorders* 1 (1980): 71–88.

Rosenblatt, L. M. *The Reader, the Text, the Poem*. Carbondale, IL: Southern Illinois University Press, 1978.

Rumelhart, D. E. "Toward an Interactive Model of Reading." *Attention and Performance*. Ed. S. Dornie. Hillsdale, NJ: Erlbaum, 1977. 573–603.

Using Literature to Teach Higher-Level Thinking Skills

Because human life is its subject, imagination its method, and words its medium, literature is rich and subtle in both meaning and form. Critical thinking is inherent in its study. In order to discuss and write about literature, students must use the very skills that define critical thinking, including analysis, inference, interpretation, comparison and contrast, hypothesis testing, argumentation, evaluation, and synthesis. Moreover, they must use these skills on a subject matter that requires them, as few other subjects do, to confront ambiguity and relativity; to comprehend irony; to arrive at moral and aesthetic judgments; and to make connections on many levels—the concrete and the abstract, the personal and the impersonal, the literal and the figurative. These are the sophisticated, but essential, mental processes that are increasingly recognized as the realm of higher-order thinking.

Critical Thinking in the *Elements of Literature* Program

The *Elements of Literature* program not only thoroughly exercises students' critical thinking skills in the interpretive questions and composition assignments following each selection, it also uses literature to teach thinking skills. At the end of each unit or division of a unit, a critical thinking and writing exercise isolates an important cognitive skill to be applied to a writing assignment. (For a complete listing of these exercises, see the "Index of Skills" on text page 964.) The "Background" material defines and explains the skill; then the student is given detailed instruction—prewriting, writing, and revision—on using the skill in writing.

The importance of this feature for students' intellectual development is great. Students are not simply being put through the paces of an exercise; they are being shown how to think, how to approach problems, how to transfer cognitive skills from one setting to another, how to make critical thinking a habit of mind.

As you use the *Elements of Literature* program to develop students' critical thinking, the following teaching strategies, derived from educational theory and cognitive psychology, will assist you.

Three Basic Teaching Strategies

First, continually lead students to relate literature to their own lives. This approach has several connected benefits: It makes unfamiliar material less threatening or alien; it helps students find ways to discover writing and project topics of particular interest; and it enables students to make connections between an external reality and their personal experience—an important criterion of higher-level thinking. The text and manual demonstrate many ways to elicit these personal relations.

Second, take every opportunity to help students perceive the ambiguities, ironies, multiple meanings, and contrasting points of view that abound in literature. Emphasize exploration of a number of positions and supporting arguments, rather than the search for a single right answer. This attempt to see several sides of an issue is what philosopher Richard Paul calls dialogical, or dialectical, thinking; a related concept is Jean Piaget's ideal reciprocity, the ability to empathize with other people, ideas, and values.

Collaborative activities foster dialogical thinking, as do questions that require students to choose a position and assignments that concentrate on point of view. Especially important is the atmosphere you create in your classroom: When you communicate your willingness to entertain alternatives, to consider differing interpretations, students will respond in kind. They will learn to listen more open-mindedly to their classmates' conclusions, as well as to examine their own more carefully.

Students' assessment of their own reasoning is related to the third basic teaching strategy: Make students *conscious* of their critical thinking; make them think about their thinking. (The term for this awareness is *metacognition*.) The text establishes this method in the critical thinking and writing exercises. You can extend it to daily classroom work in several ways: by calling students' attention to their cognitive processes during discussion; by asking them how they arrived at an idea or opinion; by insisting that they justify interpretations with textual evidence; by requiring them, when they disagree with a classmate's conclusion, to explain how the argument is flawed. When you build students' awareness of how they think, students' thinking improves.

These three teaching strategies—guiding students to relate literature to their own lives, to think dialectically, and to consider their own thought processes—underlie the questions and exercises in the text and manual, and additional teaching ideas follow. Using them, you can make critical thinking a central focus in your students' study of literature.

Questioning Strategies

To make students think, you must ask questions; to make students think in particular ways, you must ask the right questions. These pedagogical truths bear reexamination as you use literature to teach critical thinking. By planning the questions you ask and when you ask them, you will be rewarded not only with more enthusiasm for literature but also with keener thinking about it.

Initial Questions

First, simply question frequently: Use questions to stimulate discussion, not just to check comprehension. For example, begin the discussion of a selection with a question: Is "The Battle with Mr. Covey" (text page 386) a short story, or some other genre of literature? How does the speaker in Emily Dickinson's "A Bird came down the walk" (text page 358) feel about birds? Rather than presenting your ideas about a work, let students offer theirs first. An initial question immediately creates an atmosphere of inquiry, frees students to form their own hypotheses (or to voice feelings) without reference to your ideas, and provides focal issues around which they can organize new information (Meyers 59–60). (See "Teaching Students to Vary Reading Rates" for a discussion of using predictive prereading questions to provoke critical thought.)

Dialogue Questions

Remember, too, that you can respond to students with questions, not statements. Meet a question with a question; turn a statement into a question; throw a problem back to the student who raised it or to the rest of the class. Whenever possible, do not "give" answers; help students find them.

A student may offer, for example, that Donald Barthelme's "Game" isn't very realistic. Rather than disagreeing (or agreeing) and offering your own examples, draw out the student's thoughts: Why do you say that? Compelled to go beyond the vague statement, the student may reply, "The government has all kinds of safeguards. Two guys would never be left alone that long with missiles they could launch." You can of course press the student further (What safeguards are you thinking of?), but even at this point, the class has a specific judgment to explore (the government wouldn't let the situation continue), and other students may want to jump in.

As the discussion unfolds, continue probing with questions (What information from real life supports your opinion? What could cause the breakdown of those government or military safeguards? Could Barthelme have intended to create an absurd situation?), so that students define their criteria for judgments, offer examples and evidence, generate hypotheses to explain inconsistencies, and so on. Such questions create group dialogue and also put students in dialogue with themselves: Pushed to elaborate, reflect, or defend, students will learn more about both the content of their thought (what they "really mean") and its quality (how they arrived at a position).

Structured Questions

When choosing or creating discussion questions, you can structure them to call forth particular types of critical thinking, but another approach is to focus on three areas: the literary work, the student's personal experience, and the external world (Christenbury and Kelly 12–15; Swope and Thompson).

About *A Raisin in the Sun*, for example, you could ask: Why doesn't the Younger family want to accept Mr. Lindner's offer? (The question elicits facts and inferences solely about the story.) What do people need, even more than money, to feel right about their lives? (The question calls for the student's personal opinion.) What social biases common to mid-twentieth century American life were hidden within the apparently generous offer? (The question seeks information external to the literary work.)

Each type of question can provoke critical thinking, but questions that combine two or three of the areas will lead students to more complex reasoning. A question that simultaneously elicits textual facts, opinion or personal experience, and outside information—what Christenbury and Kelly call a "dense question"—can be the focus of a class discussion, presented to the students in advance. (For example: If you were Walter Lee Younger, couldn't you have used the money to solve all the family's problems in another way?) The single- and two-area questions that you ask during the discussion will help students approach the complex question, clarifying its issues and guiding students to a more fully thought-out response. (For example, is there any way in which Walter could have both accepted the money and retained his self-esteem? Could making successful investments and seeing Beneatha attend medical school balance out any blows to self-esteem involved in accepting the money?)

Classroom Activities
Collaborative Interpretation

Collaborative activities are especially conducive to critical thinking because they necessarily involve dialogue and exchange. Many teachers find, in fact, that lively whole-class discussions are greatly aided by initial small-group work. Dragga suggests the following collaborative-learning method for discussing interpretive questions.

Assign each group the same question, one that will generate different answers and require reference to the

Using Literature to Teach Thinking Skills 439

selection. Give each group about fifteen minutes to devise a collective answer, with textual justification, to be reported by a group spokesperson. (Change speakers during the term so that each student serves in this role.) Because each group must arrive at a single answer, every group member is drawn into the discussion. Each student must offer, if not an original idea, at least a reasoned judgment of any suggested answer and evidence. As the groups work, you can move among them, monitoring the content and process of the discussions and aiding students through impasses.

When the time limit is reached, have each spokesperson report the group's answer, explaining reasons for main ideas and citing support from the text. (For early collaborations, speakers may report from notes; later, you may want groups to write collective essays, which the speakers will read.) In the ensuing discussion, students will challenge each other's interpretations, defend their own arguments, build on another group's position by offering overlooked evidence, and attempt an evaluation of the differing interpretations.

The critical thinking benefits of this collaboration and discussion are manifold: Students model their thinking processes for one another; examine literary works closely to find logical supporting evidence; synthesize their thoughts into a coherent spoken or written answer; and evaluate divergent interpretations of literature.

Courtroom Trials

A more structured collaborative activity is a courtroom trial about a compelling conflict in a literary work (Segedy). The trial format captivates students' imaginations as it challenges their reasoning power; it keeps students' interest high not only because of its inherent drama but also because of the variety of activities required: close reading, research, debating, role-playing, and composition.

For this project, choose a narrative containing a conflict appropriate to courtroom investigation, plan how you will delineate the actual "case" (who is bringing suit against whom for what), and decide the roles students will play. Stories, novels, and plays that focus on crimes are of course excellent choices, but any work that raises questions of social, ethical, or moral injustice may yield issues for prosecution and defense.

Generally, you will appoint a team of three or four lawyers for each side of the case and will choose students to play characters who must appear at the trial. (For some cases, you might need to involve some students as expert witnesses, such as psychologists or scientists.) The attorneys must work together to develop the best possible cases to represent their clients, without contradicting the literary work in any way. They must prepare strong logical arguments, support their arguments with compelling evidence, plan their questioning of witnesses, create persuasive rhetoric, and practice their public speaking. The students playing characters must do in-depth character analyses, gleaning from the text all facts about the characters and making inferences about feelings, motives, and experiences not explicitly described. The expert witnesses must research their areas sufficiently to be able to offer sound and relevant testimony. Any students not playing roles are paired with either a lawyer or a character as research aides; they actively participate in case preparation or in character analysis and can thus substitute for their partners during the trial if necessary.

After both sides have presented their cases, every student prepares a written summation to the jury. Students should be preparing for this persuasive composition during all pretrial work; they must also attend keenly during the trial itself, for the proceedings may yield new ideas or arguments. For the essay, all students assume the persona of an attorney, address themselves to an imagined jury, and argue for conviction or acquittal as persuasively as possible.

Thus a courtroom trial project uses a variety of methods to improve students' critical thinking. Working in small groups and pairs to prepare for their trial roles, students analyze, interpret, and synthesize many elements of a literary work. Participating in the trial, students think on their feet to present and defend logical arguments in dynamic, unrehearsed exchanges. Listening to the trial, students observe and evaluate others' thought processes and refine their own positions accordingly. Writing the summations, students work individually to synthesize all of their experience into strong persuasive compositions.

Expert Groups

In addition to having groups of students research and report on particular aspects of a literary work (see "Varying Teaching Techniques" in this manual), you can have them take complete responsibility for presenting—teaching—one of the text selections (Bonfiglio). This more sophisticated collaborative activity should be reserved for later in the term, after students have worked through many selections with you, and assigned only to students capable of independent work: The expert groups must devise an entire project plan, not simply follow directions, and must accomplish their plans without supervision.

Assign an appropriate text selection, and explain that the group's charge is to serve as teacher: They must decide how to present the work (classroom methods and teaching focus), conduct necessary research, and delineate divisions of labor. Stipulating the use, or creation, of visual aids enriches the activity, and you can also require a written outline of the presentation. Encourage students to use their imaginations, to think of innovative ways to engage their classmates' interest while presenting sound insights into the literary work.

This activity requires critical thinking on two levels: Students analyze, interpret, and evaluate the literary work, and they propose, prepare, and execute a teaching plan. Throughout the project, they must make judgments both about the selection and about their presentation; they must solve problems of interpretation and of group interaction, compare and contrast teaching methods, organize their presentation into a coherent sequence, and so on. The task is challenging but extremely beneficial, and satisfying, particularly for advanced students: They use higher-level reasoning not only to investigate literature but also to communicate their findings to others.

Oral Composition

Oral composition is a collaborative activity that specifically develops metacognition. Again, students need some preparation for this technique; you should attempt it only after students have completed several of the text's critical thinking and writing exercises or after you have accustomed students—through comments and questions during discussion—to reflecting on their own and their classmates' reasoning processes. Vinz describes an effective paired-student approach to oral composition.

Give each student in the pair a different interpretive essay question about a selection. Select or create questions that do not have clear right and wrong answers, such as those requiring decision making or problem solving. (Which character in *The Glass Menagerie*—Amanda, Tom, or Laura—do you think is the protagonist, and why? How could you change the ending of *The Glass Menagerie* to preserve the story's drama and theme, and yet provide a more hopeful future for Laura?). You may use the same two questions for all pairs in the class.

For this open-book activity, students take turns as speaker-writers and listeners. The speaking-writing student is to compose *aloud* an answer to the question. The listening student is to take notes on the speaker's composition process. Explain that the composers are simply to say aloud exactly what they are thinking as they plan and draft their essays. Remind them of what they do normally during prewriting: brainstorm, consider and reject ideas, articulate a possible thesis, look for supporting evidence, contemplate how best to arrange their main points. Students should now verbalize these processes, writing down important prewriting notes and then beginning to draft their essays.

The listeners are to observe, interpret, and record the composers' thought processes; they do not comment aloud. They might note how much time their partners spend on different processes (free-associating ideas, searching for supporting facts, evaluating their own thoughts, rereading and revising a draft paragraph); how often good ideas come from chance associations; what seems most often to stop the flow of the composer's ideas; whether the composer is methodical, completing each line of thought before starting another, or more unstructured, willing to leave a difficulty unresolved and move on to something else.

You may want to set aside portions of two class periods for each composer to generate a first draft (students can work alone to write final versions of their essays). Then have the pairs exchange and discuss their listener-notes. As a summarizing activity, both students should write, perhaps as a journal assignment, what they learned about their own thinking processes. The oral composition process itself, as well as the listener's written observations, should lead to some insight for all students. They may ask themselves: Exactly how, and how well, do I think my way through problems? What could I change, improve? What did I learn from my partner's reasoning and composing process that I could adopt?

References and Further Reading

Bonfiglio, Joseph F. "Collection, Connection, Projection: Using Written and Oral Presentation to Encourage Thinking Skills." NCTE 93–96.

Christenbury, Leila, and Patricia P. Kelly. *Questioning: A Path to Critical Thinking*. Urbana, IL: ERIC Clearinghouse on Reading and Communication Skills and National Council of Teachers of English, 1983.

Dragga, Sam. "Collaborative Interpretation." NCTE 84–87.

Educational Leadership 42 (1984).

Lazere, Donald. "Critical Thinking in College English Studies." Urbana, IL: ERIC Clearinghouse on Reading and Communication Skills and National Council of Teachers of English, 1987.

Meyers, Chet. *Teaching Students to Think Critically*. San Francisco: Jossey-Bass, 1986.

NCTE (National Council of Teachers of English) Committee on Classroom Practices. Chair Jeff Golub. *Activities to Promote Critical Thinking*. Urbana, IL: NCTE, 1986.

Parker, Walter C. "Teaching Thinking: The Pervasive Approach." *Journal of Teacher Education* 38.3 (1987): 50–56.

Segedy, Michael. "Adapting the Courtroom Trial Format to Literature." NCTE 88–92.

Swope, John W., and Edgar H. Thompson. "Three *R*'s for Critical Thinking About Literature: Reading, 'Riting, and Responding." NCTE 75–79.

Vinz, Ruth. "Thinking Through Dilemmas." NCTE 107–111.

Teaching Students to Vary Reading Rates

The ability to read flexibly, that is, at different rates according to purpose and subject matter, is a valuable skill for students of literature. If students learn to adjust their reading habits, they are likely both to improve their comprehension and to increase their enjoyment of literature.

To introduce the concept of flexibility, draw on students' experience with recreational reading. Suppose they have just acquired a new novel by a favorite author. Ask what they read first, how many times they read all or part of the novel, and what they look for as they read. Responses might run along these lines: They first read the title and any other information on the cover and may glance at any illustrations or chapter titles, all to get an idea of the subject and the plot. They may also read a few pages quickly to see whether the setting, characters, tone, and style are familiar. Then they probably settle on a comfortable pace to read the whole story, perhaps stopping occasionally to think about what a character says or does. Later they may come back to the story, rereading certain pages quickly to locate a character's exact words or more slowly to recapture the feeling of a favorite scene; they may even reread the whole story to see more clearly how early events led to the climax. Use the example to show students that (1) they usually read something more than once to get the most out of it, (2) they do sometimes vary the speed at which they read, and (3) they choose a pace based on their purpose for reading.

Setting a Purpose

Students often mistakenly believe that studying literature and enjoying literature are two mutually exclusive purposes. Some may argue that their main purpose in reading the anthology's excellent selections should be pleasure—having to "appreciate" each selection through study spoils the fun. These students don't realize that enjoyment is built on understanding. They cannot take pleasure in the irony of a story if they do not recognize it; they cannot articulate a personal response to a work if they do not possess the tools of evaluation—the literary concepts and reading skills that lead to understanding. Full enjoyment, then, requires study, or, more specifically, reading for several purposes: to get an overview, to analyze and evaluate ideas and literary techniques, to locate details, to refresh the memory, or to generate new ideas.

Naming one of these purposes for a particular reading is just the first step; an active reader takes another: formulating intitial questions to be answered while reading. For example, to get an overview, a reader might ask: What type of work is it? What is the topic? When was it written, and by whom? To locate particular details, a reader might ask: What key words or phrases will help me find the details? Am I likely to find them near the beginning, the middle, or the end of the work? Such questions not only further define the purpose but also provide an active reading plan.

With a definite purpose in mind, students should more easily identify a suitable reading rate. In general, they should use an average, or "most comfortable," rate when reading for pleasure; faster rates when reading to get an overview, locate details, refresh the memory, or generate ideas; a slower rate when reading to analyze and evaluate the writer's ideas and language. Students can apply this approach to literature by using the following reading techniques.

Skimming

Skimming is reading quickly for main ideas—just how quickly, in terms of words per minute, will vary from person to person. A rule of thumb is that the skimming speed should be twice as fast as the individual's average reading rate (Fry). To achieve the higher speed, the reader skips some sentences, or details, concentrating instead on reading just enough of each paragraph to get its main idea. Since the reader does not consider every detail, the level of comprehension necessarily decreases somewhat. Some teachers like to describe skimming as a "prereading" or "rereading" activity; this distinction often helps students decide when to use the technique.

As a rereading activity, for example, skimming is an efficient way to review main ideas of a work and mentally summarize a personal response to it. A student might quickly go over a selection with questions such as these in mind: What did the writer say about life or about people? What literary devices did the writer use? Did the piece end as I expected it to? How did it make me feel, and why? If skimming reveals a point of confusion, the student can slow down for a more careful rereading. Note that students may also use skimming to review their class discussion notes.

Skimming is useful, too, for generating writing topics. To questions like those above, a student searching for a topic might add these: Why was I drawn to a particular character, passage, or scene? Which literary element of the work seemed most effective? Does this work have something in common with another I have read? How does the theme of the work relate to my own life?

Perhaps most important is the use of skimming as a prereading activity. Explain to students that the common habit of simply opening the book to the right page and reading straight through once at an average rate is not the most efficient—or rewarding—reading approach. When they open the book to read a selection, they should first skim the title, the headnote, background information about the writer and the work, chapter or section titles, the questions and assignments that follow the selection, and their own notes from preliminary class instruction. The intent is to obtain an overview of the work; this skimming is an exercise in orientation that will help students prepare specific questions to be explored in a close reading.

Close Reading

A close reading is a slow and careful reading for the purpose of analyzing and evaluating a literary work. For class discussion and many assignments, mature readers may need to read at this "thoughtful" pace only once: others, more than once. When reading a difficult or lengthy work and when writing comprehensive essays, almost all students should do two or more close readings, at least of portions of the work. All of your twelfth-graders should begin to realize that in reading literature closely, they are seeking three levels of understanding: literal, inferential, and critical. Put another way, they must read the lines, read between the lines, and read beyond the lines (Poindexter and Prescott). You no doubt have found students to be most comfortable, and most practiced, at the literal level—understanding directly stated details. They usually need more help at the inferential level—understanding implied ideas—and at the critical level—understanding a writer's purposes and making value judgments about a piece of literature. As "coach" for a close reading, you can guide students toward full comprehension in several ways.

Posing Questions

Before students begin a close reading, have them list a few questions about the selection to guide their initial reading. Use the text's headnotes and the teaching suggestions in this manual to prompt appropriate and specific questions. The headnote introducing each selection directs attention to a particular aspect of the work, often by raising issues that will require higher-level comprehension. Several sections in this manual, in particular "Introducing the [Selection]" and "Reading the [Selection]," will give you additional ideas for elements that students can look for and consider as they read. Posing initial questions sets a precise purpose for close reading, activates students' prior knowledge of both literature and cultural values, and arouses personal interest in a literary work.

Predicting Outcomes

For several selections, the text and this manual suggest a stopping place in the reading, a point at which students are asked to predict what will happen and to give reasons for their opinions. Take full advantage of this strategy, and use it for other selections whenever practicable. Many teachers have found that predicting outcomes encourages not only a rich exchange of ideas in the classroom but also multilevel comprehension, more so than would a traditional review of what has been read so far (Nessel). In order to predict the resolution of events, students must recall essential literal details, draw inferences about the situation created, and evaluate the writer's intent; thus, the class gains a review as well as practice in critical thinking. Evaluate the predictions not on how close students come to the writer's conclusion but rather on how logically they form and support their hypotheses.

Responding Personally

Suggest to students that their ultimate goal in reading closely is to understand their own intellectual and emotional responses to a literary work—what they liked or disliked and why. They should think about their reactions as they read and when they discuss the work in class. Alert them to the design of the "Responding" sections in the text: The questions and assignments will help guide them, during a close reading, through the three levels of comprehension and will lead them, after the reading, to an organized expression of their personal responses through creative and critical writing.

Following Guidelines

Certain close-reading techniques apply generally to literature; others are important to particular types of literary works. You may want to duplicate and hand out the following guidelines, which are addressed to students.

Guidelines for Reading Literature Closely

1. Write down a few questions you would like to answer as you read the selection. The skimming you did to get an overview of the work will help you pose questions, as will your teacher's introduction.

2. Take brief notes as you read. Jot down answers you find to your initial questions as well as any further questions that come to mind. Note your impression of the characters in the selection. Note passages that seem to hint at the writer's purpose or theme, passages that are particularly vivid to you, and passages that seem confusing. Identify the emotions you feel when reading different parts of the work.

3. Stop occasionally to think about what you have read. Ask yourself these questions: What main ideas or events have been presented so far? What do I think will happen next?

4. Look up unfamiliar words and allusions. First check for a special note on the page that explains the word or phrase; then see whether the context gives you clues to its meaning. Refer to any vocabulary list your teacher has provided, and check for a definition in the textbook's Glossary. Remember that you can also use "A Handbook of Literary Terms" at the back of the text. Keep your dictionary handy for words not defined in the text. Add the word or phrase to your reading notes so that you can come back to it later and confirm or review its meaning.

5. Keep in mind the type of literature you are reading. The questions you ask and the understanding and pleasure you gain from a work often relate to the writer's chosen form. Here are some specific hints:

Fiction. Look for the elements of narration: What is the point of view? The narrator's tone? What conflict or conflicts does the writer create? What complicates the problem? What are the main events of the plot? How does the setting affect the story? What passage marks the climax of the tale? How is the main conflict resolved? What is the theme of the story? Be careful not to identify the central conflict solely on the basis of which character you feel closest to or like best. Decide which character sets out to do something (the protagonist) and who or what works against the attempt (the antagonist).

Poetry. Read a poem several times, at least once out loud. (If the poetry is in an epic or a play, read each section or scene several times.) Pay particular attention to the punctuation; it will help you follow the writer's ideas and help you "hear" the emphasized words. Paraphrase any lines or passages that are not immediately clear to you. Make a note of figures of speech and sound effects, and look for the writer's main idea. Is a central thought or emotion expressed? Or is a theme presented by telling a story? Try to state the main idea in one or two sentences. When the poetry tells a story, apply what you know about plot and character development.

Nonfiction. Be alert for the writer's attitudes toward the topic and toward the people described. Is the writer's tone humorous, serious, sympathetic, hostile, or some combination of these feelings? Is the work objective, or is it written from a subjective, or personal, point of view? Does the writer use narrative techniques, such as foreshadowing or suspense, to hold your interest? Decide what the writer's main purpose is: to tell a story, to explain or inform, to describe, or to persuade. Notice how the writer organizes information, and make an informal outline of the main points. Then determine the main idea of the work. Is it directly stated? Implied?

Drama. Identify the mood of the play (Serious and sad? Light and humorous?). What do you see and hear happening on the stage? Remember that you are "overhearing" conversations: What tones of voice and facial gestures would actors use in saying their lines? Think about the personalities of the main characters, and predict how they will react to each other's comments and actions. Decide how each scene moves the plot along and reveals character. Determine when the action of the play "turns" and begins moving toward resolution (the crisis), as well as the most intense or emotional moment (the climax). Be sure to read the stage directions as carefully as you read the dialogue. They will give you clues to the setting and the action and to the appearances and emotions of the characters.

Scanning

Scanning is reading very rapidly to locate details. Students unfamiliar with the term are likely to recognize the technique when it is explained: They use it to find a name and number in the telephone book, a listing in the television program guide, or a definition in the dictionary. Scanning is faster than skimming, because the reader is searching for key words rather than reading sentences or phrases to isolate ideas. The reader focuses the mind and eye by moving a finger rapidly across and down the page, not stopping until the key word or phrase is found.

In the study of literature, scanning is most useful as a rereading activity. When students have already read a work and know its organization, they can use scanning to answer certain kinds of follow-up questions, usually ones of literal comprehension (Who? What? Where? When?). For example, you may ask a student to identify Homeric similes that help describe a certain episode in an epic. The student would first locate the episode and then find the similes by scanning for key words such as *like* and *as*.

Essential to the process are having a sense of a work's organization (Should I look first in the beginning, middle, or end? Didn't that scene close an early chapter?) and choosing key words or phrases appropriate to the search (Which words in the question are keys? What key words are implied by the question?). When students think they have located the detail, they should stop to read the sentences around it to make sure they are correct. If they discover that they are frequently inaccurate when scanning, they should slow their pace for a while and check their choice of key words. Remind students to take notes when they scan.

You can give the class a timed practice in scanning during your vocabulary exercises. List on the board ten vocabulary words, out of alphabetical order, that are defined in the Glossary. Tell students to write down for each one the word that follows it in the Glossary. Explain that you will start the stopwatch when they begin scanning and after one minute will begin putting the time on the board in ten-second intervals. When each student has finished the last item, he or she can then write down the last time given on the board. Check the answers and response times in class, and suggest further practice at home to increase speed or improve accuracy.

References

Fry, Edward B. *Skimming and Scanning, Middle Level.* Providence, RI: Jamestown, 1982.

Nessel, Denise. "Reading Comprehension: Asking the Right Questions." *Phi Delta Kappan* 68 (1987): 442–444.

Poindexter, Candace A., and Susan Prescott. "A Technique for Teaching Students to Draw Inferences from Text." *The Reading Teacher* 39 (1986): 908–911.

Promoting the Growth of Students' Vocabulary

Many teachers have found that a concentrated effort on vocabulary during literature study results in great gains in students' active vocabularies. Often in such efforts you first must convince students of the value of a larger vocabulary. Besides continually sharing your own enthusiasm for words, you can easily demonstrate the necessity and power of language. Tell students to close their eyes for a few moments and to think thoughts for which there are no words. After a minute or so, the class will probably protest that it can't be done. This response is the point of the exercise: Words are essential to thought. Point out that the more words students know, the better able they will be to understand and communicate ideas.

In guiding students through vocabulary for the selections, you will probably find that a multifaceted approach is most effective—a combination of dictionary use, context study, and structural analysis.

Dictionary Use

Here are a few ideas for encouraging the dictionary habit.

- Have students turn to the Glossary during your general introduction to the anthology. Go over the pronunciation key to review common symbols for sounds, and point out the abbreviations for parts of speech. Remind students that many words have multiple meanings, and note that the Glossary defines words according to their use in the selections.

- Use a short, timed exercise to check students' basic dictionary skills. Provide dictionaries, and give the class five minutes to look up and write down the pronunciation and first definition of three words from a selection. Check responses for the third word, asking about problems in following guide words, alphabetization, or pronunciation symbols.

- Show students how to use dictionaries quickly and effectively when reading literature. Tell them to keep handy a supply of blank index cards. As they encounter unfamiliar words, they can jot down each one on a card, with the page number for reference, and later look up several words at once. Direct them to write the pronunciation under the word, say the word aloud, and, on the back of the card, write the part of speech and meaning that fit the context. Have students bring in their cards every week or two and compare their collections.

- Pay special attention to words with interesting histories. Help students discover that a word is borrowed from another language, for example, or that it derives from an old custom. Show students how to use special dictionaries of word and phrase origins.

- Review usage labels in the dictionary when the class studies Americanisms, jargon, colloquialisms, and so on.

- Be sure students understand that a dictionary's method of numbering definitions is significant. Some dictionaries begin with the oldest sense of a word, others with the most frequent usage. Have the class look up words such as *dashboard*, *temperance*, and *wardrobe* to see how the use of certain words has changed over time.

- Emphasize pronunciation in your dictionary drills to help students "sound out" new words.

Context Study

The following activities will help students learn *and use* new words through recognizing context clues, making connections between words, and creating new contexts through original writing. The first six items offer ways to reinforce students' use of context clues when they are reading or listening.

- Before class begins, write on the board a sentence about the day's literary topic that uses two or three new vocabulary words, with some clue to their meanings. Underline the vocabulary words. When students arrive, ask them to write a paraphrase of the sentence, without using the underlined words, while you call the roll. Discuss their responses, asking what context clues they used. Use the exercise as a springboard to your reading or discussion of the selection.

- If you are reading a selection aloud, stop occasionally when you come to a vocabulary word, and ask students for context clues to its meaning.

- Use the vocabulary words in your own comments to let students hear them in context.

- When the vocabulary list for a selection is long, assign different words to different students. Ask them to find for each word a context clue, a synonym, and an antonym, to be shared in a class discussion.

- Have students look for abstract vocabulary words in contexts other than the text selection. For example, ask them to locate and paraphrase famous quotations in which the words appear.

- For quick reviews, write on the chalkboard the sentences from the selection that contain the vocabulary words, but replace the words with blanks. Ask students to fill in the blanks with the correct word from an alphabetized list, and discuss how they made their choices.

The next two activities emphasize word relationships.

- Review synonyms or antonyms for vocabulary words by devising short matching quizzes. You might have students create them: Assign a small group to select ten words and put together a scrambled list of synonyms (or antonyms). Check the group's work, and have them write the two lists on the chalkboard, one list numbered, the other lettered. Ask the rest of the class to match the words.

- Review any group of related words with a simple crossword puzzle using the words' definitions as clues. You may create the puzzle yourself or have students volunteer to do it. Give the puzzle a title that classifies the group of words, such as "Vivid Adverbs" or "Words That Describe [a character's name]." Some teachers also find such puzzles effective as a review of literary terms: "The Elements of Drama," "Sound Effects in Poetry," and so on.

The following activities require students to create new contexts for the words they are studying; they put new words to use through writing. Several suggestions also take advantage of the strategy of centering word study on a concept.

- Have students create their own direct context clues for new words. Ask them to write sentences for vocabulary words, giving a clue to meaning by definition, example, restatement, comparison, or contrast.

- To explore connotative meaning, have students use five vocabulary words in original sentences and then substitute a synonym for each vocabulary word. How well does the synonym work in the same context? Ask students what difference in meaning or feeling is created.

- Choose two or three vocabulary words that have distinctive multiple meanings, and ask students to write a sentence using each meaning.

- If the vocabulary words for a selection number fewer than ten, offer students the challenge of writing one sentence using as many of the words as possible. However fanciful, the sentence must be intelligible.

- When the vocabulary list for a selection is long, group the words by part of speech. Have students write a sentence using one word from each group and compare their sentences.

- For a group of adjectives, ask students to create comparisons.

- Promote students' personal use of active verbs by having them write sentences in which they apply new verbs to a school situation.

- When several vocabulary words for a selection relate to a particular geographical or cultural setting, introduce the words as a group. For example, *adobe*, *arroyo*, *mesa*, *mission* (church), and *tumbleweed* are words of the West or Southwest. Have students identify the common element through definitions and etymologies and then write sentences or a paragraph using the words.

- If students are learning descriptive words that apply to a character in a selection, ask them to write sentences applying the words to other characters they have studied.

- Assign different students, one or two at a time, to use vocabulary words in writing three or four quiz questions about a selection's plot, characters, or setting. At the beginning of class, the students can call on classmates to answer the questions, orally correcting the answers and clarifying the meanings of the vocabulary words when necessary.

- For a review of words from several selections, group them according to an emotion or idea. Have students write new sentences using each word.

- Encourage regular attention to new words by offering bonus points for the appropriate use of vocabulary words in the text writing assignments and in class discussions.

- On Fridays, have students vote on their favorite new word from the week's vocabulary. Ask them to explain their choices.

Structural Analysis

Students can often learn and remember new words by breaking them into recognizable parts. Try these activities for a morphemic approach focused on roots and affixes. A selected list of common Greek and Latin word parts follows the activities.

- Have students build a personal set of flashcards of roots and affixes. Introduce a few roots, prefixes, and suffixes at a time, having students write each one on an index card. On the other side of the card, students should write the meaning of the root or affix, along with an illustrative word that you provide (preferably a vocabulary word or literary term already assigned). Then direct students to be alert throughout the term to vocabulary words (as well as words from other sources) that contain these roots and affixes and to add the words to their cards. Remind them that some words, such as *infallible*, will be recorded on more than one card.

Every week or two, ask students to bring in their collections. Divide the class into small groups for peer quizzing with the cards. Spot-check the cards and quizzing to evaluate students' progress and to decide on review strategies. (After you have introduced several groups of word parts, you may want the students themselves to begin presenting new roots and affixes obtained from their assigned vocabulary or from other reading.)

- Present in one lesson prefixes that show position. Guide students in identifying and defining words with these prefixes. The examples might be vocabulary words from the selections, literary terms, or more familiar words encountered in the text.
- Encourage students to recognize prefixes that create a negative or opposite meaning. Ask students to complete a list of "not" definitions with words they have studied.

- To help students recognize the grammatical function of an unfamiliar word in context, show them how suffixes often—*not always*—signal a particular part of speech. Students can make a note on their suffix flashcards or list the groups in a vocabulary notebook, but remind them to watch for exceptions. In some words the ending looks like a suffix but actually is part of a root or base word.
- After you define a common Greek or Latin root in a new word, divide students into small groups, and, setting a time limit, have them list familiar words built on the same root. The group with the longest list could receive bonus points.
- Occasionally review small groups of prefix, suffix, and root definitions with oral and written quizzes. For variety in the quizzes, you could create crossword puzzles or conduct a group competition on the pattern of a spelldown.

There are hundreds of roots and affixes, and the following lists contain only a selection of those that students may learn through their vocabulary study in literature. As you introduce the study of word parts, point out that the spellings of roots and affixes sometimes vary, that affixes almost always alter the root's meaning in some way, and that the meanings of some Latin and Greek roots have undergone slight changes over time.

Roots

Greek

-bio-	life (*biography*)
-chron-	time (*chronological*)
-cris-, -crit-	separate, judge (*crisis, critical*)
-cycl-	circle (*Cyclops*)
-glos-, -glot-	tongue (*glossary, polyglot*)
-graph-	write, record (*biography, photograph*)
-log-, -logy-	speaking, study (*dialogue, chronology*)
-ops-, -opt-	eye (*Cyclops, optical*)
-phon-	sound (*phonetic*)
-stereo-	firm, solid (*stereotype*)

Latin

-aud-	hear (*audible*)
-cred-	believe (*incredulous*)
-dict-	tell, say (*prediction*)
-duc-, -duct-	lead, draw (*deduction, produce*)
-fac-, -fic-	make, do (*benefactor, fiction*)
-flect-	bend (*reflection*)
-ject-	throw (*projectile, reject*)
-leg-, lect-	read (*lecture, legend*)
-loqu-	speak (*eloquent, soliloquy*)
-mis-, -mit-	send (*commission, noncommittal*)
-mort-	die (*immortality*)
-quer-, -quest-, -quir-	seek, ask (*inquiry, quest*)
-sci-	know (*omniscient*)
-scrib-, -script-	write (*describe, manuscript*)
-spec-, -spic-, -spect-	look at, examine (*circumspect, speculate*)

-tens-, -tent-	hold (*contention, tension*)
-vers-, -vert-	turn (*averse, invert, versatile*)
-vid-, -vis-	see (*videotape, visage, visual*)
-viv-	live (*vivacious*)

Prefixes

Greek

a-	not, without (*atheist, atypical*)
ant-	against (*antagonist*)
auto-	self (*autobiography*)
dia-	through, across, between (*dialogue*)
exo-	out of, outside (*exodus*)
mono-	one (*monologue*)
poly-	many (*polytheism*)
syn-	with, together (*synthesis*)

Latin

a-, ab-, abs-	away, from (*abominable, abscond, averse*)
ad-	to, toward (*adversary, advocate*)
ante-	before (*antecedent*)
bene-	well (*benediction, benefactor*)
circum-	around, on all sides (*circumstance*)
com-, con-	with, together (*complicity, connotation*)
contra-	against (*contrary*)
de-	from, down (*denotation, denouement, depress*)
dis-	apart, away (*dispel, disrepute*)
e-, ex-	out (*evade, exorbitant*)
extra-	outside of, beyond (*extravagant, extraordinary*)
il-, im-, in-, ir-	not (*incredulous, irresolute*) or in, into, on (*impetus, inversion*)
inter-	between (*intermediary*)
non-	not (*nonentity*)
omni-	all, everywhere (*omniscient*)
per-	through (*perpetual*)
post-	after, behind (*postpone, postscript*)
pre-	before (*prewriting*)
pro-	forward (*projectile*)
re-	again, back (*redress, reference, resolution*)
soli-	alone, only (*soliloquy, solitude*)
sub-, sup-	under, beneath, below (*subversive, support*)
super-	above, over, outside (*superficial*)
trans-	across (*translucent*)

Suffixes

-able, -ible	able to (*formidable, infallible*)
-age, -ance, -ence, -ity, -ment, -ness, -ship, -tion	a state or condition (*carnage, vigilance, indulgence, calamity, atonement, happiness, gyration, kingship*)
-al, -ic, -ly	similar to (*acutely, cynical, heroic*)
-an, -ee, -eer, -er, -ian, -ist, -ite, -or	a person, one who (*barbarian, mountaineer, strategist, writer, actor*)
-ate	to act or do (*evaluate, perpetrate*)
-er, -est	degree (*shadier, shadiest*)
-ful, -ous	full of (*fearful, ominous*)
-less	without (*aimless, ruthless*)

Varying Teaching Techniques

Using a variety of teaching techniques keeps students' interest high, fosters personal involvement with literature, and takes advantage of individual learning styles. With the following teaching suggestions, you can make the study of literature a thoroughly active, multifaceted experience for your class.

Collaborative Learning

To foster regular collaborative learning, you may want to assign students to groups (no more than five or six members) and to matched pairs early in the year, using a random-selection method such as counting-off. Then you will waste no time forming groups for each new activity. You may change the groups and pairs at some point, but do not change them too frequently. Students benefit from working with the same classmates for an extended period: They begin to appreciate different learning styles and abilities, and they develop a team spirit. The two group methods that follow have many applications in a literature course.

Expert Groups. In this technique, members of a small group become highly knowledgeable about one aspect of a topic or literary work and serve as experts for the other students. When you are reading *The Red Badge of Courage*, for example, one group might become experts on military methods of the Civil War era and another on the literary techniques of realism and impressionism. The expert groups report to the class and stand for questions. The benefit of this strategy is twofold: Group members gain experience in intensive research, and all students gain more information about a topic or a work.

Jigsawing. Jigsawing, which uses two levels of groups, is another method by which students become each other's teachers. The method is particularly effective for covering lengthy or complex material when class time is limited. For example, suppose you want your class to paraphrase five paragraphs of difficult prose. Divide the students into five groups, assign one paragraph to each group, and set a time limit for the paraphrase. (Whenever possible, use any standing groups for this first jigsaw level.) When the students have finished, make a second-level group assignment: Within each group, have students count off (or designate themselves by letters, colors, etc.) and then move into their second groups—all 1's (A's, reds) together, 2's (B's, blues) together, and so on. Each student now becomes the "expert" for the paragraph paraphrased in his or her original group, presenting the information to members of the new group. Jigsawing also works well with lengthy vocabulary lists or an exercise containing many items. In those cases, divide the words or items equally among the first-level groups and then proceed as before to the second-level groups.

Into, Through, and Beyond Techniques

Many teachers think of three distinct stages in teaching a selection: preparing students for it, guiding them through it, and offering them bridges from it to other works, ideas, and activities. What follows is a summary of types of activities appropriate to each stage. (Detailed descriptions of concept formation, imaging, debating moral dilemmas, journal writing, sensory recall, and readers' theater follow the summary.)

To lead students *into* a work:

- Use filmstrips, films, or recordings to arouse students' interest.
- Invite lecturers to provide special background on a selection. The speakers may be knowledgeable about a particular work, author, or literary topic or may have experience that relates to a selection (someone who has visited or lived in Iran, for example, could provide background for "Your Place Is Empty").
- Introduce the work with a variety of background information (history, the author's biography, technical explanations), using the text's introductions and the supplementary information in this manual.
- Distribute plot summaries, study guides, or character lists for difficult or lengthy works.
- Have students master vocabulary words before they begin to read, using a variety of strategies (see "Promoting the Growth of Students' Vocabulary").
- Encourage skimming as a prereading step, and guide students in posing questions for a close reading (see "Teaching Students to Vary Reading Rates").
- Use the techniques of concept formation, imaging, and journal quick-writes.
- Read portions of the selection orally.

To guide students *through* a work:

- Assign the questions following the text selections for discussion or writing. Assign the creative and critical writing exercises for individual or collaborative work.
- Pause during in-class readings to allow students to predict narrative outcomes.
- Assign groups of students to dramatize and perform brief scenes from a story or novel.

- Organize debates on issues and moral dilemmas raised by a work.
- Have students keep dialectical journals.
- Schedule readers' theater presentations.
- Lead imaging and sensory recall exercises.
- Assign reports and projects for class presentation, encouraging forms of expression other than writing (creating maps, illustrations, charts, timelines; performing; composing original music; etc.).

To lead students *beyond* a work:

- Encourage students to make connections between the work and other works in the same genre, as well as between works in different genres. Possible connections include subject, theme, major symbols, imagery, allusions, historical setting, and so on. Students may present their comparisons and contrasts in compositions, reports, and projects.
- Suggest further reading of works by the same author, of books and articles related to the selection's background, and of works in the same genre.
- Have a group of students write and produce an original video play inspired by some aspect of the selection (a moral dilemma, a character, a striking element such as horror).
- Have students create games based on literary selections.
- Have a group of students assume the personae of characters from different works and engage in a panel discussion on a specific topic. Instruct students to prepare carefully for their roles so that they can respond in character, correctly reflecting their different fictional settings.

Concept Formation

When students use concept formation to approach a new work, they practice both classifying and predicting. To use this technique, present students—without any preliminary explanation—with a list of words, objects, names, or ideas taken from or related to the selection. (You may restrict the list to one category of information or mix the categories.) Ask the students to group items that seem related and then to formulate predictions about the selection based on the items and their common elements. For example, from the vocabulary list for the selections from *Moby-Dick*, students might isolate *metaphysical*, *presentment*, *preternatural*, *presaging*, and *maledictions*, predicting—even without knowing the story's title—that something supernatural or out of the ordinary is involved in the story. From a list of poem titles drawn from Units One, Three, and Four, students might predict that early American writers often used nature as a metaphor of human experience.

Concept formation, in addition to sharpening critical thinking, involves students actively in a work even before they begin reading. An unexplained list can be an intriguing puzzle, and once students have made predictions from it, they may read a selection with more eagerness and more purpose.

Imaging

Imaging taps students' imaginations, leading them into a literary work through sensory awareness. Acting as guide, you ask students to close their eyes and then "talk" them into a specific time, place, or mental state. Play mood-setting or period music if possible, and tell students to draw on their sensory memories to participate vicariously in the experience you evoke.

Imaging is effective with image-rich poetry as well as with narratives; you may use it to introduce a selection as well as to focus on individual passages and sections. For example, you may want to set the stage for E. B. White's "The Decline of Sport" by guiding students in imagining the sights, sounds, and smells of a football stadium. Imaging not only helps remove barriers of culture, time, and place but also shows students their own considerable power to invoke sensory experiences from words.

Moral Dilemmas

Moral dilemmas arising from conflicts within literary works are excellent ways to engage students' feelings and stimulate their critical thinking. You may use an actual situation from a work (the moral dilemma about the source of his wound faced by Henry Fleming in *The Red Badge of Courage*) or an extrapolation from it (a situation similarly involving the dilemma of heroism vs. cowardice, in the case of a conscientious objector). Whichever you choose, describe the situation in such a way that students are forced to take sides. (Some other provocative conflicts are those pitting individual conscience against law and those forcing a choice between loyalties to two friends or two family members.)

Have students articulate the opposing positions, write each as a statement on the board, and ask students to take sides by a show of hands. Divide students on each side into smaller groups for developing supporting arguments. Allow sufficient time, and then, taking one side at a time, have each group's spokesperson present one supporting argument. Go from group to group until supporting arguments are exhausted, and then allow a free exchange of rebuttals, guiding the discussion as necessary. Be sure each student comes to some formal closure about the moral dilemma, perhaps through a journal entry or a brief essay.

Journals

Journals are excellent tools for literature study: They encourage personal responses to literary works; allow freer, less formal writing; build a repository of writing ideas; and offer students a full year's record of their changing perspectives and thoughts. A loose-leaf notebook will allow students to make both private entries and assigned entries for your review. When you make journal assignments, specify those that must be turned in.

Two specialized uses of journals follow.

Dialectical Journals

Sometimes called dialogue journals, dialectical journals are double-entry records in which students take notes about a literary work and then add their own reflections about the notes. Each page is divided into two columns labeled "Note-taking" and "Note-making." Notes about the work may include facts, passages, quoted dialogue, significant plot developments, and so on. The students' recorded musings about these notes will be personal, but occasionally you may want to direct a response (for example, you could direct students to "take" notes about a poem's imagery and then to "make" notes about their emotional responses to the images).

A dialectical journal is valuable because students are forced to go beyond facts to reflection; they must think about what they read. Encourage students also to review all their entries for a selection, synthesize the thoughts, and write a summary, or distillation, of their personal response.

Quick-Writes

The aim of a quick-write journal entry is an immediate, spontaneous, unedited response to a stimulus. Possible stimuli are many: a passage from a selection, an idea you supply, music, guided imaging and sensory recall, and so on. Quick-writes can be used in all three stages of teaching a selection (into, through, and beyond).

Sensory Recall

Literature presents all readers with emotions and situations far removed from their own experience; sensory recall, a technique by which professionals prepare for acting roles, is one means of making these foreign experiences more understandable. An actress playing a character who, after extreme provocation, physically attacks someone may have no experience with such violence, for example. The director may ask her to remember being driven crazy by mosquitoes and to act out the resulting scene. Under the director's coaching, the actress begins to understand her character's response to the provocation and can then build a believable series of emotions for her role.

An adaptation of this theatrical approach can help students identify with unfamiliar characters and understand emotions otherwise out of their reach. As an introduction, students may enjoy watching a classmate with acting experience demonstrate the technique, but all students can participate in sensory recall through writing. First isolate an experience in a selection, build an appropriate parallel situation (or brainstorm situations with students), and then direct students to put themselves in the situation and to write their thoughts and feelings. You might use sensory recall, for example, to make accessible the bizarre events in "The Pit and the Pendulum," beginning with the narrator's awakening in the pitch-black dungeon. If you ask students to recall awakening in the middle of the night in a strange room, eliciting from them memories of the common feelings of disorientation and momentary panic, they will begin to feel more acutely the narrator's horror.

Initially, you will have to lead students in using sensory recall, but after practice, they will be able to create their own parallel situations and record their responses in their journals.

Readers' Theater

Readers' theater is simply a group oral reading of a selection, whether the work is a play, story, poem, or essay. Effective readers' theater is not impromptu, however. Students are assigned roles, or passages, and practice their reading outside of class. Readers' theater hones students' skills in oral interpretation and makes a work come alive for the whole class; it is a dramatic presentation with a minimum of production worries (you need only stools or chairs) and stage-fright problems (most students are less frightened of sitting and reading than of acting).

Students may read whole plays or single acts or scenes; they may create their own scripts from short stories, novels, and epics; they may present poems and essays by alternating the reading of stanzas and paragraphs. One way to accomplish the latter is to count off the stanzas or paragraphs according to the number of readers: The first reader reads all the stanzas or paragraphs numbered one, the second reads those numbered two, and so on. Remember also that, for scripts, one reader should be assigned the scene setting, necessary stage directions, and any prologue or explanatory narrative.

You may want to assign roles for certain dramatic readings, but at other times students may form their own groups and choose roles. If students in a particular small group want to read a script in which the number of roles exceeds the number of members, some students can read more than one role, indicating their character changes with simple props (hats, glasses, shawls, etc.) or with name signs.

Obtaining Audio-Visual Aids

Guides and Indexes

The following sourcebooks contain information about the wealth of educational audio-visual materials available.

AV Instruction: Technology, Media, and Methods. Ed. James W. Brown, Richard B. Lewis, and Fred F. Harcleroad. 6th ed. 1983. McGraw-Hill Book Co., 1221 Avenue of the Americas, New York, NY 10020.

Educational Film/Video Locator. 3rd ed. 2 vols. 1986. R. R. Bowker Co., 205 E. Forty-second St., New York, NY 10017. (This reference includes 194,000 titles held by members of the Consortium of University Film Centers.)

Educational Media and Technology Yearbook. Ed. Elwood E. Miller. 13th vol. 1987. Libraries Unlimited, Inc., P.O. Box 263, Littleton, CO 80160. (The yearbook is published in cooperation with the Association for Educational Communications and Technology.)

Educators Guide to Free Audio and Video Materials. Ed. James L. Berger. *Educators Guide to Free Films* and *Educators Guide to Free Filmstrips and Slides.* Ed. John C. Diffor and Elaine N. Diffor. Annual eds. Educators Progress Service, Inc., 214 Center St., Randolph, WI 53956.

NICEM Index Series. 1984, 1985 eds. in hardcover, monthly bulletins (separate multivolume sets for tapes, films, videotapes, slides, and transparencies). National Information Center for Educational Media, Access Innovations, Inc., P.O. Box 40130. Albuquerque, NM 87196. (The center works closely with the Library of Congress to update indexed titles.)

Suppliers

The following producers and distributors publish catalogs of their offerings.

Agency for Instructional Technology (formerly AITelevision), Box A, Bloomington, IN 47402.

AIMS Media, 6901 Woodley Ave., Van Nuys, CA 91406.

Allyn and Bacon, Inc., 470 Atlantic Ave., Boston, MA 02210.

Association Films, Inc., 866 Third Ave., New York, NY 10022.

Barr Films, P.O. Box 5667, Pasadena, CA 91107.

Blackhawk Films, Eastin-Phelan Corp., 1235 W. Fifth St., Davenport, IA 52808.

Bowmar Records, 622 Rodier Dr., Glendale, CA 91201.

Cassette Information Services, P.O. Box 9559, Glendale, CA 91206.

Center for Humanities, Inc., Communications Park, Box 1000, Mount Kisco, NY 10549.

Churchill Films, 662 N. Robertson Blvd., Los Angeles, CA 90069.

Classroom Film Distributors, Inc., 5610 Hollywood Blvd., Los Angeles, CA 90028.

CRM/McGraw-Hill Films, 110 Fifteenth St., Del Mar, CA 92014.

Encyclopaedia Britannica Educational Corp., 425 N. Michigan Ave., Chicago, IL 60611.

Epcot Educational Media (Walt Disney Co.), 500 S. Buena Vista St., Burbank, CA 91521.

Films for the Humanities, Inc., P.O. Box 2053, Princeton, NJ 08540.

Films, Inc. (also distributes Audio Brandon, Macmillan, and Texture Films), 1144 Wilmette Ave., Wilmette, IL 60091.

Folkways Records, 43 W. Sixty-first St., New York, NY 10023.

Great Plains Instructional TV Library, University of Nebraska, P.O. Box 80669, Lincoln, NE 68501.

Grover Film Productions, P.O. Box 12, Helotes, TX 78023.

Guidance Associates, Communications Park, Box 3000, Mount Kisco, NY 10549.

HBJ Video (Harcourt Brace Jovanovich, Inc.), 6825 Academic Dr., Orlando, FL 32821.

Holt, Rinehart, and Winston, School Division, 1627 Woodland Ave., Austin, TX 78741.

Indiana University Audio-Visual Center, Indiana University, Bloomington, IN 47405.

International Film Bureau, 332 S. Michigan Ave., Chicago, IL 60604.

Listening Library, Inc., 1 Park Ave., Old Greenwich, CT 06870.

Lucerne Films, Inc., 37 Ground Pine Rd., Morris Plains, NJ 07950.

National Audio-Visual Center, National Archives and Records Service, General Services Administration, Washington, DC 20409.

National Council of Teachers of English, 1111 Kenyon Rd., Urbana, IL 61801.

National Education Association, Audio-Visual Instruction, 1201 Sixteenth St. N.W., Washington, DC 20036.

National Film Board of Canada, 1251 Avenue of the Americas, New York, NY 10020.

National Public Radio, Educational Cassettes, 2025 M St. N.W., Washington, DC 20036.

National Video Clearinghouse, Inc., 100 Lafayette Dr., Syosset, NY 11791.

Phoenix/BFA Films and Video, Inc., 470 Park Ave. S., New York, NY 10016.

Public Television Library (Public Broadcasting System), 475 L'Enfant Plaza S.W., Washington, DC 20024.

Pyramid Film and Video, P.O. Box 1048, Santa Monica, CA 90406

Silver Burdett Co., 250 James St., Morristown, NJ 07960.

Simon and Schuster Communications (also distributes Centron, Coronet, LCA, and Perspective Films and MTI Teleprograms), 108 Wilmot Rd., Deerfield, IL 60015.

Smithsonian Recordings, P.O. Box 23345, Washington, DC 20026.

Society for Visual Education, Inc., 1345 Diversey Pkwy., Chicago, IL 60614.

Time-Life Films and Video, 100 Eisenhower Dr., Paramus, NJ 07652.

Vineyard Video Productions, Elias Lane, West Tisbury, MA 02575.

Index of Authors and Titles

Adventures of Huckleberry Finn, The, Selections from 161
Alvarez, Julia 404
America 255
American Drama, Unit Introduction 291–292
American Renaissance, The: Five Major Writers, Unit Introduction 67–68
American Romanticism, Unit Introduction 41–42
Anderson, Sherwood 178
Anecdote of the Jar 287
Annabel Lee 93
Apparently with no surprise 46
Art 113
Autobiographical Notes 358
Autobiography, The (Franklin), Selections from 24
Autobiography, The (Jefferson), Selection from 36

Babbitt, Selection from 181
Baker, Russell 349
Baldwin, James 358
Barthelme, Donald 322
Battle with Mr. Covey, The 150
Beautiful Changes, The 390
Because I could not stop for Death 142
Bells for John Whiteside's Daughter 247
Berryman, John 400
Bierce, Ambrose 163
Birches 238
Bird came down the Walk, A 138
Bishop, Elizabeth 381
Black Boy, Selection from 353
Blessing, A 402
Blue Highways, Selection from 373
Book of Negro Poetry, The, Selection from 253
Bradford, William 2
Bradstreet, Anne 12
Brooks, Gwendolyn 386
Bryant, William Cullen 45
"Butch" Weldy 227
Byrd, William 18

Cather, Willa 184
CETI 347
Chambered Nautilus, The 60
Chicago, Selection from 276
Cisneros, Sandra 365
Colonial Period, The: The Age of Faith, Unit Introduction 1
Concord Hymn 73
Crane, Stephen 166

Crisis, The, No. 1 34
Cross of Snow, The 50
Cullen, Countee 261
Cummings, E. E. 279

Death of a Pig 343
Death of a Soldier, The 287
Death of the Ball Turret Gunner, The 385
Death of the Hired Man, The 242
Declaration of Independence, The 38
Design 234
Dickey, James 385, 392
Dickinson, Emily 133
Dirge Without Music 232
Dispatches, Selection from 370
Douglass, Frederick 150
Dunbar, Paul Laurence 228

Edwards, Jonathan 10
Egg, The 178
Eldorado 91
Elegy for Jane 378
Eliot, T. S. 77, 282
Emerson, Ralph Waldo 68
Emerson's Aphorisms 78
End of Something, The 196

Fable for Critics, A, Selection from 64
Fall of the House of Usher, The 88
Faulkner, William 208
Fiction 1945 to the Present, Unit Introduction 311–312
First Death in Nova Scotia 381
Fitzgerald, F. Scott 189
Fog 277
Follow the Drinking Gourd 152
For the Union Dead 388
Franklin, Benjamin 24
Frost, Robert 234

Game 322
Garden, The 266
Gatsby's Party 189
Ginsberg, Allen 405
Girl Who Wouldn't Talk, The 360
Glass Menagerie, The 292
Go Down Death 253
Go Down, Moses 152
God's Determinations Touching His Elect, Selection from 17
God's Trombones (Selection from, Primary Sources) 255

454 Index of Authors and Titles

Grapes of Wrath, The, Selections from 201
Grave, The 206
Great Figure, The 269
Great Gatsby, The, Selection from (*Gatsby's Party*) 189

Hansberry, Lorraine 301
Harlem 257
Harte, Bret 154
Haunted Oak, The 229
Hawthorne, Nathaniel 98
Hayden, Robert 379
Heart! We will forget him! 134
Helprin, Mark 325
Hemingway, Ernest 192
Henry, Patrick 31
Her Kind 399
Here Follow Some Verses upon the Burning of Our House, July 10, 1666 12
Herr, Michael 370
Hersey, John 367
Higginson, Thomas Wentworth 148
Hiroshima, Selection from (*A Noiseless Flash*) 367
History of the Dividing Line, The, Selection from 18
Holmes, Oliver Wendell 57
Homage to Mistress Bradstreet 14
Homework 405
How I Learned to Sweep 404
Hughes, Langston 257
I died for Beauty—but was scarce 139
I Hear America Singing 119
I heard a Fly buzz—when I died— 140
I never saw a Moor— 144
I, Too 258
If you were coming in the Fall 141
Imagism and Symbolism, Unit Introduction 265–266
In Another Country 193
Incident 262
Irving, Washington 42
Ivy Days, Selection from (*Out East*) 363

Jarrell, Randall 385
Jeffers, Robinson 250
Jefferson, Thomas 36
Johnson, James Weldon 253
Journal of Madam Knight, The, Selection from 8

Key, The 310
Kingston, Maxine Hong 360
Kite Poem 394
Knight, Sarah Kemble 8

Leader of the People, The 198
Least Heat Moon, William 373
Lee, Andrea 338
Lewis, Sinclair 181
Life on the Mississippi, Selection from 157

Life You Save May Be Your Own, The 212
Limited 276
Little Exercise 383
Little Red Riding Hood Revisited 349
Longfellow, Henry Wadsworth 50
Look Homeward, Angel, Selection from 187
Love Song of J. Alfred Prufrock, The 282
Love the Wild Swan 252
Lowell, James Russell 62
Lowell, Robert 388
Lucinda Matlock 225

Maestria 320
Magic Barrel, The 314
Malamud, Bernard 314
Masque of the Red Death, The 85
Masters, Edgar Lee 224
McKay, Claude 255
McPherson, James Alan 331
Melville, Herman 106
Mending Wall 239
Merrill, James 394
Migrant Way to the West, The 201
Millay, Edna St. Vincent 230
Minister's Black Veil, The 98
Miniver Cheevy 220
Moby-Dick, Selections from 106
Modern Nonfiction, Unit Introduction 343–344
Moderns, The: The American Voice in Fiction, Unit Introduction 177
Momaday, N. Scott 356
Moore, Marianne 273

Narrative of Her Captivity, A (Rowlandson) 5
Narrative of the Life of Frederick Douglass, Selection from (*The Battle with Mr. Covey*) 150
Nature, Selection from 68
Negro Speaks of Rivers, The 260
Neither Out Far Nor in Deep 236
New African 338
New American Poetry, A: Whitman and Dickinson, Unit Introduction 117
Nobel Prize Acceptance Speech, 1950 (Faulkner, Primary Sources) 211
Nobel Prize Acceptance Speech, 1954 (Hemingway, Primary Sources) 198
Nobel Prize Acceptance Speech, 1962 (Steinbeck, Primary Sources) 203
Nobel Prize Acceptance Speech, 1978 (Singer, Primary Sources) 313
nobody loses all the time 279
Noiseless Flash, A, Selection from *Hiroshima* 367
Nothing Gold Can Stay 245

O'Brien, Tim 329
O'Connor, Flannery 212

Index of Authors and Titles 455

Occurrence at Owl Creek Bridge, An 163
Of De Witt Williams On His Way to Lincoln Cemetery 386
Of Plymouth Plantation, Selection from 2
Old Ironsides 57
On the Beach at Night 127
On the Beach at Night Alone 128
Once by the Pacific 241
Out East, Selection from *Ivy Days* 363
Outcastes of Poker Flats, The 154

Pact, A 269
Paine, Thomas 34
Parting, Without a Sequel 248
Plath, Sylvia 397
Poe, Edgar Allan 85
Poetry in a Time of Diversity, Unit Introduction 377–378
Poetry: Voices of American Character, Unit Introduction 219–220
Poor Richard's Almanack, Selection from 29
Porter, Katherine Anne 206
Pound, Ezra 266
Power 396
Preludes, Selection from 77

Raisin in the Sun, A 301
Ransom, John Crowe 246
Rappaccini's Daughter 102
Raven, The 96
Recuerdo 231
Red Badge of Courage, The 166
Red Wheelbarrow, The 269
Remarks Concerning the Savages of North America 27
Resistance to Civil Government, Selection from 82
Revolutionary Period, The: The Age of Reason, Unit Introduction 23–24
Rhodora, The 74
Rich, Adrienne 396
Richard Bone 224
Richard Cory 222
Rip Van Winkle, Selection from 42
Rise of Realism, The: The Civil War Period and Post-War Period, Unit Introduction 149
River-Merchant's Wife: A Letter, The 266
Robinson, Edwin Arlington 222
Roethke, Theodore 378
Ropewalk, The 52
Rowlandson, Mary 5

Sacramental Meditations, XXXVIII 18
Sandburg, Carl 276
Sayings of Poor Richard 29
School Vs. Education 351
Secret Life of Walter Mitty, The 203
Self-Reliance, Selection from 70
Sexton, Anne 399

She Came and Went 62
Shiloh 113
Shine, Perishing Republic 250
Sight in Camp in the Daybreak Gray and Dim, A 131
Singer, Isaac Bashevis 310
Sinners in the Hands of an Angry God 10
Sled Burial, Dream Ceremony 392
Snow Bound: A Winter Idyll, Selection from 55
Snow-Storm, The 76
Son 317
Song of Myself, #1 120; *#10* 121; *#26* 123; *#33,* Selection from 124: *#52* 126
Soul selects her own Society, The 135
Speaking of Courage 329
Speech to the Virginia Convention 31
Spinster 397
Spirituals and "Code" Songs 152
Spotted Horses 208
Spring and All 269
Steeple-Jack, The 273
Steinbeck, John 198
Stevens, Wallace 287
Stowe, Harriet Beecher 12
Straw into Gold: The Metamorphosis of the Everyday 365
Suarez, Mario 320
Success is counted sweetest 135
"Summertime and the Living..." 379

Tableau 261
Tamar 325
Taylor, Edward 14, 18
Tell all the Truth 145
Thanatopsis 47
Thomas, Lewis 347
Thoreau, Henry David 78
Thurber, James 203
Tide Rises, the Tide Falls, The 53
To a Waterfowl 45
To Helen 94
To make a prairie it takes a clover and one bee 147
Toth, Susan Allen 363
Tract 269
Trollope, Frances 45
Twain, Mark 157
Tyler, Anne 334

Updike, John 317
Upon a Spider Catching a Fly 16

Wagner Matinée, A 184
Walden, or Life in the Woods, Selections from 78
Way to Rainy Mountain, The, Selection from 356
Weary Blues, The 259
Welty, Eudora 215
what if a much of a which of a wind 279
When I Heard the Learned Astronomer 130

456   Index of Authors and Titles

White, E. B. 344
Whitman, Walt 118
Whittier, John Greenleaf 55
Why I Like Country Music 331
Wilbur, Richard 390
Williams, Tennessee 292
Williams, William Carlos 269
Winslow, Edward 4

Winter Landscape 400
Wolfe, Thomas 189
Worn Path, A 215
Wright, James 402
Wright, Richard 353

Year's End 390
Your Place Is Empty 334